In the Know

Emotional intelligence is an important trait for success at work. IQ tests are biased against minorities. Every child is gifted. Preschool makes children smarter. Western understandings of intelligence are inappropriate for other cultures. These are some of the statements about intelligence that are common in the media and in popular culture. But none of them are true. *In the Know* is a tour of the most common incorrect beliefs about intelligence and IQ. Written in a fantastically engaging way, each chapter is dedicated to correcting a misconception and explains the real science behind intelligence. Controversies related to IQ will wither away in the face of the facts, leaving readers with a clear understanding of the truth about intelligence.

Russell T. Warne is an associate professor of psychology at Utah Valley University, USA, and an educational psychologist. He is the author of the widely successful textbook for undergraduates: *Statistics for the Social Sciences* (Cambridge, 2018).

D1260499

In the Know

Debunking 35 Myths about Human Intelligence

RUSSELL T. WARNE

Utah Valley University

CAMBRIDGE
UNIVERSITY PRESS

CAMBRIDGE
UNIVERSITY PRESS

University Printing House, Cambridge CB2 8BS, United Kingdom

One Liberty Plaza, 20th Floor, New York, NY 10006, USA

477 Williamstown Road, Port Melbourne, VIC 3207, Australia

314–321, 3rd Floor, Plot 3, Splendor Forum, Jasola District Centre,
New Delhi – 110025, India

79 Anson Road, #06–04/06, Singapore 079906

Cambridge University Press is part of the University of Cambridge.

It furthers the University's mission by disseminating knowledge in the pursuit of
education, learning, and research at the highest international levels of excellence.

www.cambridge.org
Information on this title: www.cambridge.org/9781108493345
DOI: 10.1017/9781108593298

First published 2020

Printed in the United Kingdom by TJ International Ltd, Padstow Cornwall

A catalogue record for this publication is available from the British Library.

Library of Congress Cataloging-in-Publication Data
Name: Warne, Russell T., 1983– author.
Title: In the know : debunking 35 myths about human intelligence / Russell T. Warne, Utah
Valley University.
Description: Cambridge, United Kingdom ; New York, NY : Cambridge University Press,
2020. | Includes bibliographical references and index.
Identifiers: LCCN 2020014739 (print) | LCCN 2020014740 (ebook) | ISBN 9781108493345
(hardback) | ISBN 9781108593298 (ebook)
Subjects: LCSH: Intellect. | Intellect – Research – History.
Classification: LCC BF431 .W33185 2020 (print) | LCC BF431 (ebook) | DDC 153.9–dc23
LC record available at https://lccn.loc.gov/2020014739
LC ebook record available at https://lccn.loc.gov/2020014740

ISBN 978-1-108-49334-5 Hardback
ISBN 978-1-108-71781-6 Paperback

For Dallin

Thank you for serving without complaint as "backup dad" so that
I could have more time to write this book.

Contents

Contents   ix

Figures

Tables

Acknowledgments

I am pleased to have finished writing this, my second book. What started out as a vague idea has blossomed into a full-fledged book. It is hard to believe that it happened so quickly – until I think of the people who aided me along the way.

A legion of other people has been very supportive of this book from its earliest days. I have to first thank David Repetto and the folks at Cambridge University Press for accepting my book proposal. David is an academic writer's dream: endlessly supportive, open to ideas, and friendly. He is an advocate for his authors and has a passion for watching them succeed. José Abarca worked hard to give me a favorable writing contract. James J. Lee and other proposal reviewers provided a lot of encouragement for this book and set high expectations that I have worked hard to meet. My co-workers at Utah Valley University, especially my department chair (Cameron John) and my fellow psychologists, picked up my slack on campus when I spent a disproportionate amount of time writing this book.

Two of my students, Hannah Bruce and Daniel A. Melendez, read every chapter and gave me feedback that helped me clarify confusing passages, strengthen my arguments, and eliminate flawed ideas. I was thrilled when these two stellar students volunteered to help me with my book. Whatever they choose to do in life, they will go far. They are both ambitious, industrious, and – yes – intelligent people who will succeed in whatever goals they set for themselves. Keep an eye on them.

I am also indebted to my Utah Valley University student co-authors that I cite in this book. In alphabetical order, they are Victor "Rafa" Angeles, Mayson Astle, Cassidy Burningham, Jared Z. Burton, Aisa Gibbons, Lindsey Godwin, Anne Marie Malbica, Daniel A. Melendez, Chanel Nagaishi, Chris J. Price, Michael K. Slade, and Kyle V. Smith. I have been extremely blessed by the caliber of students at Utah Valley University, and each of them has improved my research, teaching, and writing.

I am also indebted to the intelligence research community, especially the members of the International Society for Intelligence Research. I have never encountered a more welcoming group of scientists. Members often disagree, but are never disagreeable. This group embraced me and has given me more support than I deserve as I have tried to contribute to the field of intelligence research. I am afraid for three reasons to create a list of specific people whom I appreciate. First, the list would be too long. Second, I am deathly afraid of forgetting a name and slighting a colleague unintentionally. Third, these people already know who they are, and because of their humility, they don't need to be acknowledged by name. The intelligence research community is full of remarkably wonderful people who would be justified in having bigger egos than they do.

It is also important to mention that certain members in the intelligence community have also influenced me, even when I disagree with them vigorously. I am thankful for people who dissent from orthodox theories of intelligence because they expose blind spots in my thinking. Encountering their ideas has helped me write a better book because they forced me to craft arguments against them. Although some of these people are not cited favorably in the book, they still wielded an influence that I appreciate.

I also thank my former professor and graduate school mentor, Joyce Juntune, for exposing me to intelligence research. For years, she has been a lone voice in the wilderness discussing the importance of intelligence in gifted education. She started me down this path when she assigned course readings on human intelligence and then encouraged me to incorporate that work into my theorizing as an educational psychologist. It is because of her that I got sucked into human intelligence research.

From a personal perspective, I am thankful for my wife, Katie, for her unwavering love and support. Being the wife of a workaholic is a lonely existence, and writing the first draft of this book in less than a year meant a lot of solitary evenings for her. My brother, Dallin, was a godsend in his service as "backup dad," helping to care for my children while I worked or traveled. My children are lucky to have him as an uncle.

Preface

This book is the culmination of more than a decade of study and research related to human intelligence. I have learned a lot over the years, sometimes about areas far outside my professional training (which was in educational psychology). As I learned more about intelligence, I discovered that the scholarly knowledge about the topic was out of sync with popular opinion – sometimes alarmingly so. I wrote this book to try to reduce some of the distance between the beliefs of laymen and experts.

This book is aimed at anyone who is not a psychologist specializing in human intelligence. Students, non-psychologists, K-12 teachers, interested laymen, and scientists from outside the field can gain from reading this book. I have tried to make the book as nontechnical as possible. My goal is not to make readers into experts, but rather to give them the tools to recognize common incorrect arguments and beliefs about intelligence.

I am not naïve enough to think that this book will fix every incorrect idea about intelligence. But if this book corrects some of the mistaken beliefs that readers have, it will be worth it. Intelligence is one of the most important topics of study in the social sciences. But erroneous ideas about intelligence are surprisingly common, and this leads people to dismiss, ignore, or marginalize research on intelligence far too often.

ORGANIZATION OF THE BOOK

This book is organized into 7 sections that contain a total of 35 chapters:
- Section 1 is comprised of Chapters 1–6 and discusses the nature of intelligence.
- Section 2 discusses intelligence testing and covers Chapters 7–10.
- Section 3 is organized around the theme of the genetic and environmental influences on intelligence levels. Chapters 11–17 are in this section.

- Section 4 discusses the relationship between intelligence and the education system and comprises Chapters 18–21.
- Section 5 is about the life consequences of different intelligence levels and is made up of Chapters 22–26.
- Section 6 is comprised of Chapters 27–30 and discusses demographic differences in intelligence.
- Section 7 explores societal and ethical issues related to intelligence and includes Chapters 31–35.

Additionally, the book begins with an introduction that provides background about the nature of intelligence, tests and procedures used to measure intelligence, some important statistical concepts, and the history of research in the field. This information provides useful context for the 35 chapters in the book, and the main chapters refer frequently to the concepts that the introduction explains. After Section 7, there is a conclusion with some thoughts about the overall state of intelligence research and some unanswered questions.

BOOK VIEWPOINT

Throughout the book I have tried to voice opinions that are widely held among intelligence researchers. Unanimity is rare, though, and some experts may disagree with some chapters. I know it is impossible to please everyone all the time, but my goal is to have any mainstream expert in intelligence agree with the vast majority of what I say in the book, with the disagreements being on the level of typical differences of professional opinion. I am sure that some of my colleagues will think I am overconfident on some topics and not firm enough with my opinions in others. I hope this does not detract from the "big picture" of the book about the reality of intelligence, the importance of intelligence differences, and the mismatch between popular belief and expert opinion.

Despite my efforts to describe consensus positions about scientific topics, this book should not be taken as an authoritative position for any scholarly organization or group of scientists. Inevitably, the content is filtered through a single scientist, and my personal viewpoints and perspectives may color the discussion somewhat. I have tried to minimize my individual influence by leaning heavily on the scholarly literature and adopting the perspectives of senior leaders in the field. The court of professional opinion will determine whether I have been successful in this goal.

Some chapters in this book – especially towards the end – touch upon social and political issues. I have tried to be politically neutral in these sections, mostly because I am not a very political person. I find the tribalism of modern American politics distasteful, mostly because I find the idea that "the other side" is completely wrong or evil to be highly unlikely. I think that most politicians and advocates are motivated by a genuine goal to improve society, though I do disagree with the goals and methods of actors on both sides of the political aisle. I believe that political views should accommodate the reality of human nature, including facts about intelligence. For many people, these accommodations will be minor because intelligence research is compatible with many political positions.

But people at the extremes in political belief will undoubtedly find the chapters in the book that discuss political and social issues to be distasteful, perhaps even incendiary. That says more about their beliefs than about intelligence research or my book. Facts are value-neutral, and only reality deniers will find anything in this book that is so threatening that they must fight against it.

INFORMATION ABOUT CITATIONS

This book contains more citations than many scientific books aimed at a non-expert audience. This is especially apparent because of the in-text citation format I have chosen, which can disrupt the flow of the text. However, I prefer this style because (1) it clearly shows which statements are supported by the scholarly literature – and which are not, and (2) it is easier to identify the source of a statement than other citation formats.

The research on intelligence started over 100 years ago and encompasses tens of thousands of articles, books, dissertations, and technical reports. It is impossible for anyone to read every scholarly publication about intelligence. As a result, I do not cite every study ever published to support my claims. I have preferred to select either (a) particularly strong studies or (b) studies that are representative of the wider literature on a topic. I encourage readers to explore this research to verify for themselves whether the scholarly literature supports my positions.

WHAT IS NOT IN THIS BOOK

This book is not a comprehensive overview of intelligence research. Instead, it is meant as a guide to correct common false beliefs that the public has about intelligence. As a result, it provides little or no discussion about some topics, especially in neuroscience, cognitive psychology, and mental aging. These topics are important, but I do not discuss them much because non-experts rarely have strong incorrect opinions about them. Readers who are interested in neuroscience should read Haier's (2017a) book *The Neuroscience of Intelligence*. People interested in cognitive aging would benefit from the books summarizing the two most important studies on the topic, written by Schaie (2013) and edited by Deary, Whalley, and Starr (2009). Books by Hunt (2011) and Mackintosh (2011) are more comprehensive than my book, and both have thorough discussions of how intelligence relates to research in cognitive psychology, neuroscience, and other areas. Jensen's (1998) book

The g Factor: The Science of Mental Ability is an indispensable classic on the topic and holds up extremely well more than two decades after its publication.

LAST WORDS . . . BEFORE THE FIRST WORDS

This book may be read cover to cover, or – after reading the introduction – it is possible to skip around the chapters and read them in any order. The chapters are designed to be self-contained. However, often content from one chapter will be relevant to one or more other chapter(s), especially chapters contained within the same section. When this occurs, I reference the other chapter(s) so that readers can explore a specific topic more comprehensively. Regardless of how readers choose to tackle this book, I hope they find it as enjoyable to read as I have found to write. If you wish to give me any feedback, please visit my professional website (www.russellwarne.com), my public Facebook page (www .facebook.com/russwarnephd) or follow me on Twitter at @Russwarne.

Introduction

Theory about intelligence is more fully developed and more mathematically sophisticated than for almost any other psychological construct. More is known about the underlying cognitive, genetic, and brain processes for intelligence than for any other complex psychological construct.

(Detterman, 2014, p. 148)

Intelligence testing may be psychology's greatest single achievement . . .

(Gottfredson, 2009, p. 11)

As these quotes show, the scientific study of intelligence is probably the greatest success story in psychology – possibly in all the social sciences. For over 100 years scientists – first psychologists, but later education researchers, sociologists, geneticists, and more – have studied human intelligence. Now, two decades into the twenty-first century, the results are impressive. The evidence of the importance of intelligence has accumulated to such an extent that informed scientists now cannot deny that intelligence is one of the most important psychological traits in humans (Detterman, 2014; Gottfredson, 1997a).

But many people – even psychologists – are not aware of this fact. Unfortunately, inaccurate information and mistruths abound. In media reports the public is told that, "IQ tests are meaningless and too simplistic" (McDermott, 2012). Textbook authors state that, "the question [exists] of whether our tests truly measure intelligence, or whether they merely measure what is *called* intelligence in our culture" (Gleitman, Gross, & Reisberg, 2011, p. 440). Colleges do not teach about the concept (Burton & Warne, 2020), and the scholarly literature contains claims that the concept of intelligence and/or intelligence testing has been debunked (e.g., K. Richardson, 2002).

I wrote this book as an attempt to correct the mismatch between what experts believe about intelligence and what the public often hears – a mismatch that scholars have commented on many times (e.g., Detterman, 2014;

Gottfredson, 1994; Lubinski, 2004; Rindermann, Becker, & Coyle, 2020; Snyderman & Rothman, 1987, 1988; Wainer & Robinson, 2009). Having studied the topic for over 10 years, it is apparent to me that intelligence is underappreciated and neglected among both psychologists and laypeople. Misunderstandings and inaccuracies – sometimes propagated with the best of intentions – have inhibited scientific and social progress. These erroneous beliefs are so common that when I compiled a list, I found that there were enough to fill a book. This is that book.

WHAT IS INTELLIGENCE?

While there is not unanimous agreement about a definition of intelligence (there never is for any concept in the social sciences), the definition that seems to have a great deal of consensus states:

Intelligence is a very general mental capability that, among other things, involves the ability to reason, plan, solve problems, think abstractly, comprehend complex ideas, learn quickly and learn from experience. It is not merely book learning, a narrow academic skill, or test-taking smarts. Rather, it reflects a broader and deeper capability for comprehending our surroundings – "catching on," "making sense" of things, or "figuring out" what to do. (Gottfredson, 1997a, p. 13)

Although it may not seem like a bold statement at first glance, Gottfredson's (1997a) definition is audacious in its claim that the same mental ability that causes people to think abstractly also causes people to learn quickly, comprehend the environment, and plan. In the early days of psychology, many people thought that these different tasks would require different mental abilities (e.g., Joseph Peterson, 1926/1969; Terman, 1932; Thurstone, 1936). However, in the twenty-first century the consensus is that there is one general ability – often called intelligence – that helps people perform all the mental tasks in the definition.

Intelligence Test Items. The best way to measure intelligence is through a professionally designed test that requires examinees to reason, solve problems, think abstractly, or demonstrate their knowledge. Questions on intelligence tests, often called *items*, can take many forms. Some will look familiar, perhaps because you remember similar questions on academic tests or because you have taken an intelligence test. Others may appear very strange. One of the oldest types of items on an intelligence test is vocabulary items, which require an examinee to define words in their native language. Easier items tend to ask examinees to define basic words (e.g., "moon," "hand," or "mother"), while more difficult items ask about abstract or unusual word (e.g., "conflate," "perturb," or "esoteric").

There are other types of *vocabulary items* that do not ask the examinee to generate a definition for a word. For some tests (especially written tests), the examinee must know the definition of a word in order to answer a question about vocabulary correctly. For example, in a series of four words, the examinee may need to identify which does not belong with the others (e.g.,

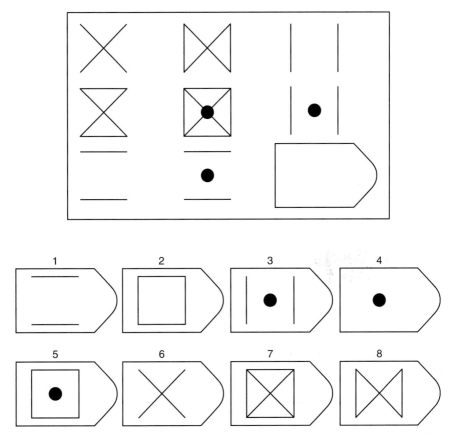

FIGURE I.I Example of a matrix item. The series of geometric shapes at the top of the image forms a pattern which is missing the bottom right portion. One of the eight options below correctly completes the pattern. The correct response is 4.
Source: Fox & Mitchum, 2013, p. 982.

"photograph, painting, calculator, sculpture"). Verbal analogies (such as "old is to young as white is to _____") are items asking about the relationship among words, and sentence completion questions often measure vocabulary knowledge and word usage.

Another common type of intelligence test item is called a *matrix item*, an example of which is shown in Figure I.1. The large box in the upper portion of the image contains a series of geometric shapes that form a pattern. The bottom right portion of the pattern (indicated by the outline that looks like a price tag) is missing. The examinee then must decide which of the eight options below completes the pattern.

A common type of intelligence test item is the *digit span* procedure. In this technique, the examiner reads a series of one-digit numbers to the examinee, who

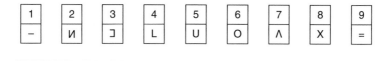

FIGURE I.2 Example of a coding item. The upper portion of the image is a key indicating which symbols should be matched with each number. In the lower portion, the examinee is supposed to draw below each number the symbol that it corresponds to.
Source: Yerkes, 1921, p. 254.

then must repeat the digits in the same order back to the examiner. Other forms of digit span include backward digit span (requiring the examinee to repeat the sequence in reverse order), picture span (which uses pictures that must be reproduced in the correct order, instead of a verbal presentation of numbers), letter–number sequencing (where a combination of letters and numbers is in the sequence, instead of just numbers), and block span (where the examiner taps a sequence of blocks, which the examinee must also touch in the same order).

More straightforward are *information items*, which ask an examinee to recall information that is important in their native culture. For example, one now-obsolete information item asked American children, "Who wrote *Romeo and Juliet?*" Many information items appear similar to trivia questions and are seemingly random in their content.

Another type of intelligence test question is *coding items*; an example from a long-obsolete test (Yerkes, 1921, p. 254) is shown in Figure I.2. The top portion of the figure is a key that shows which symbols correspond to each number. The examinee must draw the correct symbol below each number in the lower portion of the image. Often coding items have short time limits that make the test more difficult.

Other types include *arithmetic* items, *cancellation* (where a person is given a page full of random letters or numbers and told to cross out all of the same symbols – like *a*'s or *3*'s – on the paper), *block design* (which requires an examinee to assemble a set of colored blocks to produce a design that they are shown), and *picture completion* (a type of item where examinees must explain what essential component of an object is missing from a picture they are shown). Another item type is the *sequence completion* items, which give a series of symbols – usually numbers – that form a pattern that the examinee must complete (for example, "5, 2, 9, 6, 13, _____").

There are also picture items that have a visual stimulus. For example, a *picture absurdity* item might show an image of a hose spraying water while disconnected from a water source. The examinee would then have to explain what is absurd about the image. Pattern completion items and memory sequences can also be administered with pictures. Many items that measure *spatial reasoning*, which is the ability to reason and think about objects in two or three dimensions, also have a pictorial format, such as the ones shown in Figure I.3.

These are just some of the most common types of intelligence test questions. Jensen (1980a, pp. 148–166) describes many more – all with examples. It is important to recognize, though, that no intelligence test has every type of item on it. In fact, some have only one.

Other Characteristics of Intelligence Tests. Beyond item format, intelligence tests vary in many other ways. Some are administered to one examinee at a time by a professional with a master's or doctorate degree, while others require no special training for the examiner and can be administered to groups. Some require examinees to respond verbally, while others accept written responses or non-verbal responses (e.g., pointing, pressing a button, or clicking a mouse). Some intelligence test questions require the examinee to perform a task – like assemble a puzzle or draw a picture – while others merely require answering questions. Some use culturally relevant knowledge like information about the history of the examinee's native country, while the creators of other tests try to minimize cultural content by using geometric figures or culturally universal concepts (e.g., up and down, the sun and moon) in the test materials.

Despite the diversity in test administration, format, and content, all these tests measure intelligence because *it is not the surface content of a test that determines whether it measures intelligence. Rather, it is what the test items require examinees to do that determines whether a test measures intelligence.* As long as a test requires some sort of mental effort, judgment, reasoning, or decision making, it measures intelligence (Cucina & Howardson, 2017; Jensen, 1980a; Spearman, 1927). As a result, many tests function as intelligence tests, even if the test creators do not label them as "intelligence tests." These include college admissions tests (Frey & Detterman, 2004; Koenig, Frey, & Detterman, 2008), literacy tests (Gottfredson, 1997b, 2004), primary and secondary school academic achievement tests (W. M. Williams & Ceci, 1997), many job application tests (P. L. Roth, Bevier, Bobko, Switzer, & Tyler, 2001), and even everyday life tasks (Gottfredson, 1997b). Chapter 7 discusses this point further.

This is not to say that all of these tests are equally good at measuring intelligence. They're not. Backward digit span, for example, is a better measure of intelligence than digit span, but matrix items are better than both. In general, test items that are more complex are better measures of intelligence than basic tasks. But it is true that any task that requires cognitive work from a person will measure intelligence – at least partially.

Intelligence Test Scores. Often, the results of a professionally developed intelligence test produce an overall score of the person's performance on the test, called an *IQ score*. In the early days of intelligence testing, "IQ" was an abbreviation for "intelligence quotient," and the score was calculated using the

Three Dimensional Spatial Visualization

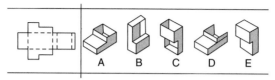

Two Dimensional Spatial Visualization

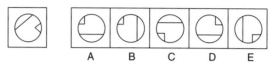

Mechanical Reasoning

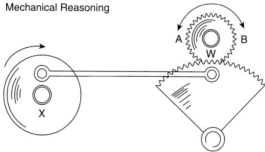

While wheel X turns round and round
in the direction shown, wheel W turns
A. in direction A.
B. in direction B.
C. first in one direction and then in the other.

Abstract Reasoning

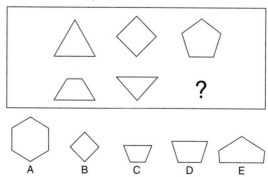

FIGURE 1.3 Examples of items that measure spatial reasoning in two or three
dimensions.
Source: Wai, Lubinski, & Benbow, 2009, p. 822.

following formula, introduced (according to Fancher, 1985) by German psychologist William Stern:

$$\frac{mental\ age}{chronological\ age} \times 100 = IQ$$

The fraction is the "quotient" part of the equation and is calculated by dividing the mental age by the chronological age. The examinee's "mental age" was found by identifying the age group that – on average – performed as well as the examinee. The "chronological age" was the examinee's actual age. For example, if a 5-year-old obtained a score that was typical for a 6-year-old, then her "mental age" would be 6, and her chronological age would be 5. Therefore, her IQ score would be calculated as:

$$\frac{6}{5} \times 100 = 120$$

Multiplying by 100 eliminates the decimal and sets 100 as the standard for average performance on an intelligence test in all age groups. Under this system, IQ scores greater than 100 indicate that the examinee scored above average for their age, while scores less than 100 indicate that the examinee performed more poorly than average for their age group.

This method of calculating IQ scores is now obsolete. Even when it was first developed and popularized during the 1910s, psychologists realized it had problems. First, scores were not comparable across age groups. For example, if our smart examinee with an IQ score of 120 at age 5 is still one year advanced compared to her peers when she is 10, her IQ would drop to:

$$\frac{11}{10} \times 100 = 110$$

Therefore, the interpretation of an IQ score varied from age group to age group. Indeed, 100 was the only score that was comparable across ages. It indicated that the examinee was average compared to their peers, no matter what age those peers were. A related problem is that the variability of scores changes from age to age, with children at younger ages usually having more variable IQ scores than older groups, which created additional difficulties when comparing scores across age groups.

Another problem was that this method of calculating IQ scores is completely inadequate for adults. While in children it makes sense to measure intelligence in terms of development, for most adults, intellectual development does not match age. It does not make sense, for example, to be concerned that a 40-year-old is as smart as a 20-year-old (which the quotient IQ formula would indicate means that the 40-year-old has an IQ of 50) because there is no reason to believe that normal adults would keep getting smarter as they age, the way children do.

To remedy these problems, psychologists now use a different method of calculating scores from intelligence tests. Called the *deviation score method*,

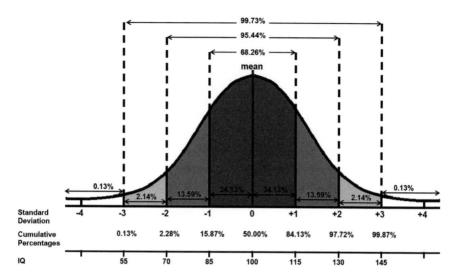

FIGURE I.4 A normal distribution of intelligence test scores. The average intelligence test score is 100 points, and the standard deviation is equal to 15 points. This means that 68.26% of individuals have an IQ score between 85 and 115, while 99.73% have an IQ score between 55 and 145.

Image created by Rosalma Arcelay, copyright Russell T. Warne, 2009.

it takes advantage of the fact that scores on intelligence tests often create a symmetrical bell-shaped distribution called a normal distribution (W. Johnson, Carothers, & Deary, 2008; Warne, Godwin, & Smith, 2013), which is pictured in Figure I.4. In this method, the examinee's test performance is compared to scores from a comparison group of the examinee's age peers (called a *norm group*). The degree of difference between the person's score and average is measured in a unit called the *standard deviation*. Figure I.4 shows that individuals who score at the average for a test are 0 standard deviations away from the mean score. Slightly more than two-thirds of people – 68.26% – score between -1 and +1 standard deviations from average, and almost everyone – 99.73% – scores between -3 and +3 standard deviations from the mean.

Once it is known how far above or below a person's score is compared to the average, this value is converted into an IQ score with the following equation:

$$IQ = z(15) + 100$$

In this equation, z is the number of standard deviations the person's score is away from average.

Although the deviation score method is more complicated, it is far better than the quotient method of calculating intelligence test scores. Scores are comparable across groups, have the same variability across age groups, and can be used for adults. Moreover, the deviation score method preserves all the advantages of the quotient method: average performance is still assigned a score of 100, and scores above 100 indicate better than average performance, while scores below 100 indicate poorer performance than average.

Modern professionally designed tests that are labeled as intelligence tests use the deviation score method to produce intelligence test scores that have an average of 100 points and a standard deviation of 15 points. However, academic tests, aptitude tests, employment tests, and other measures of intelligence often use other scales. These scores can be mathematically converted into the intelligence test score scale – and this is standard practice in intelligence research (e.g., Frey & Detterman, 2004; Koenig, Frey, & Detterman, 2008). In this book, I will always use this IQ metric, even if the original studies that I cite originally reported scores in another scale.

RELATIONSHIP WITH OTHER MENTAL ABILITIES

Intelligence is not the only mental ability, and everyone doing scholarly work in this field acknowledges that other mental abilities matter. For much of the twentieth century, there was active disagreement about how intelligence related to abilities like short-term memory, spatial reasoning, and verbal ability. Although there is still dissent within the scientific community, the most common model that psychologists use to understand the relationships among mental abilities is the *Cattell–Horn–Carroll (CHC) model* (Warne, 2016a), which is shown in Figure I.5.

The CHC model is organized in a hierarchy, with more general abilities at the top of the hierarchy, and narrower abilities at the bottom. The layers of abilities are labeled, from most specific to most general, as Stratum I (the bottom row), Stratum II (the middle row), and Stratum III (the top row). The only ability in Stratum III is general intelligence (labeled *g*), and it is the only ability that is theorized to be useful in performing all cognitive tasks. Beneath *g* is Stratum II, which consists of broad abilities that are not applicable in every situation. Examples include verbal ability, spatial reasoning, and processing speed. Finally, at the bottom of the CHC model is Stratum I, which consists of very specific abilities, including vocabulary knowledge, memory for digit span, arithmetic performance, reaction time, and many others.

The CHC model has a few important implications. First, it shows why so many tasks measure intelligence: only intelligence is applicable across every cognitive task, and every narrow task (shown in Stratum I) is subsumed beneath general intelligence. Second, it also shows how intelligence exerts its influence when people perform specific mental tasks: general intelligence is filtered through Stratum II abilities to be used to perform narrow, specific tasks.

Although the CHC model is the most popular theory of intelligence today (Hunt, 2011), there are other theories that have their adherents. One of these is

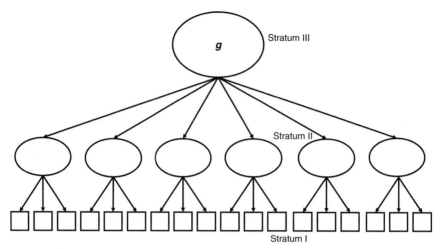

FIGURE 1.5 Schematic of the Cattell–Horn–Carroll model of mental abilities. The bottom row of squares represents Stratum I, which consists of very narrow, specific abilities (e.g., vocabulary knowledge, memory for digit span, arithmetic performance). The middle row – called Stratum II – consists of ovals that represent broad abilities that are applicable in many situations (e.g., verbal ability, spatial reasoning, processing speed). At the top of the hierarchy is Stratum III, which consists only of general intelligence, abbreviated as *g*.

termed the *bifactor model* and is shown in Figure I.6. The bifactor model and the CHC both organize narrow abilities, broad abilities, and intelligence into Strata I, II, and III, respectively. The difference is that in the bifactor model, narrow abilities are subjected to the direct influences of a Stratum II ability *and* intelligence (Jensen, 1998). In the CHC model, *g* transmits its impact on a narrow Stratum I ability *through* a Stratum II ability, not directly.

For most purposes, whether one prefers the bifactor or CHC model does not matter. In most situations they produce very similar data and have similar practical implications. There are some minor exceptions (for example, in what to expect from efforts to raise IQ scores), but readers should assume – unless I state otherwise – that I am basing my discussion on the CHC model. Also, readers should be aware that I describe these models in terms of a mathematical procedure called factor analysis (described later in this introduction). However, the theories are not dependent upon any particular data analysis method. The three-strata structure emerged from other analysis procedures (Corno et al., 2002).

Finally, it should be noted that I will discuss two alternate theories about intelligence in this book: multiple intelligences theory (Chapter 5), and the triarchic theory of intelligence (Chapter 6). Although these theories have their

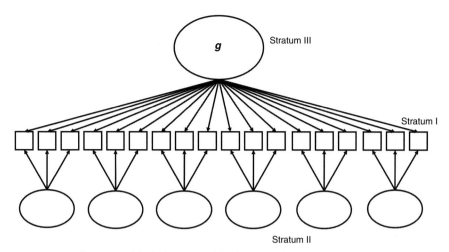

FIGURE I.6 Schematic of the bifactor model of mental abilities. In this model, Strata I, II, and III are still narrow, broad, and fully general abilities, respectively. The difference is that in the bifactor model, performance on a narrow ability is the product of the independent influences of general intelligence (labeled *g*) and a Stratum II ability.

proponents, they have found little support among psychologists, mostly because fundamental tenets of these theories are regularly unsupported by data.

FOUR RELATED CONCEPTS: COGNITIVE ABILITIES, INTELLIGENCE, *g*, AND IQ

Already in this introduction I have used four technical terms: cognitive abilities, intelligence, *g*, and IQ. These four concepts are closely related, but there is value in distinguishing among them because sometimes the differences become important.

The term *cognitive abilities* is a comprehensive term that includes every ability or capacity that requires any level of thinking or reasoning. In terms of the CHC and bifactor models, every Stratum I, II, and III ability is a cognitive ability. In this book, I will sometimes need to discuss them collectively because of the interrelationships or the similarities that they share.

Intelligence (also called *general intelligence*) is the broadest, most applicable, and most important of all cognitive abilities. As defined at the beginning of this introduction, it is the general capacity to reason, learn, and understand complex ideas (Gottfredson, 1997a). It is largely similar to non-psychologists' general understanding of intelligence (at least in Western cultures). But this definition, and the Gottfredson (1997a) definition, lack the degree of precision often needed for scientific investigation (Warne, 2016a). For this purpose, many researchers use the

concept of *g*. Charles Spearman (1904) discovered *g* when he observed
that, on a series of academic tests and a test of tone discrimination (which
is the ability to determine whether two similar sounds were the same pitch
or different pitches), children who did well on one test tended to perform
well on all the others. Likewise, children who did poorly on one test tended
to score poorly on all the others. Spearman claimed that the same mental
ability caused people to perform similarly on all these tests. He invented
factor analysis (explained later in this introduction) to support this belief
and found that all the scores could combine into one group, which he
called a *factor*. Because this factor was important in performance on all
tests, he called it a *general factor*, abbreviated it as *g*, and claimed that it
was equivalent to general intelligence.

Although Spearman saw *g* as being equivalent to intelligence or general
intelligence, there is no strong agreement on this issue today. Some leaders
in the field agree with Spearman and see *g* as being equal to general
intelligence (e.g., Carroll, 1993, pp. 591–599). Others have argued that
intelligence is a concept that is not exact enough to be useful and that
carries a great deal of cultural baggage with it that may not apply to the
findings related to *g* (e.g., Jensen, 1998, Chapter 3). Others state that
intelligence can include abilities beyond *g* (e.g., Haier, 2017a). Some of
these other abilities may include creativity, implicit learning, or other traits
that are not measured on intelligence tests. What experts do mostly agree
on is that *g* is a general mental ability that is related to every other mental
ability; that it helps individuals create and execute plans, engage in
reasoning, and learn; and that it has real-life implications. To me, that
sounds a great deal like intelligence, and so for the purposes of this book,
I will treat the terms *g*, general intelligence, and intelligence as being
interchangeable. After all, if it looks like a duck, walks like a duck, and
quacks like a duck, then it's probably a duck.

IQ, or an IQ score, is not the same as intelligence or *g*. Instead, IQ is
a measure of general intelligence. To use an analogy, just as kilograms and
pounds are measures of weight, IQ is a measure of intelligence. IQ is not
intelligence itself any more than the number on a scale is a person's weight.
In both cases, the number is a measurement and not the real topic of
interest.

It is also important to realize that IQ is an imperfect measure of intelligence.
Because intelligence cannot be isolated from other abilities in the CHC model,
IQ scores are the product of a mix *g* (in Stratum III) and non-*g* sources (in
Strata I and II). Well designed, professionally developed tests that are
culturally and developmentally appropriate for the examinee will minimize
those non-*g* sources. But these non-*g* influences on IQ are impossible to
eliminate completely because measuring *g* will inevitably require
administering tasks that have content that draws upon abilities in Stratum
I or Stratum II.

STATISTICS CRASH COURSE

While I have done my best to make this book as non-technical as possible, it is impossible to discuss intelligence for long without mentioning a few important statistical methods. While being a statistics whiz is not necessary, a brief discussion of four statistical concepts is crucial for a complete understanding of this book. Those concepts are (1) descriptive statistics, (2) correlation, (3) the effects size Cohen's *d*, and (4) factor analysis.

Descriptive Statistics. Some of the most basic statistics are *descriptive statistics*. As the name implies, these are statistics that describe data. The most common descriptive statistics in intelligence research are the *mean* (also called the *average*), the standard deviation, and the variance. Some readers may remember learning about the average in school, and averages are frequently used to convey the "typical" score in a set. Mathematically, the average is calculated by adding all the scores together and dividing by the number of scores.

The *standard deviation* is a little more complicated mathematically, but it is not important to discuss the formula here (see Warne, 2018, pp. 86–88, for the formula and discussion of the mathematics of the standard deviation). What matters is that the standard deviation is a measure of how much scores differ from another – a property called *variability*. In intelligence research, the scores are converted to the IQ scale, which automatically has a standard deviation of 15.

The *variance* is another measure of variability. Mathematically, it is the square of the standard deviation (see Warne, 2018, pp. 88–89). Variance is useful because when comparing multiple variables (for example, income and IQ scores), each variable has a variance value. If these two variables are related, then they will share some of their variance. The more related they are, the more variance they will share. Usually this value of shared variance is expressed on a scale of 0% (where the two variables share no variance and are therefore unrelated) to 100% (where the variables share so much variance with one another that one variable is redundant).

Correlation. One of the most common statistical methods in the social sciences is the *correlation coefficient* (Skidmore & Thompson, 2010; Warne, Lazo, Ramos, & Ritter, 2012), which was invented by Pearson (1896) and is often abbreviated as *r*. This statistic, ranging between -1 and +1, describes the strength of the relationship between two variables. When the correlation between two variables is positive, it indicates that people with high scores on one variable tend to have high scores on another variable. An example of a positive correlation is height and weight: taller people tend to weigh more. Conversely, when a correlation coefficient is negative, it indicates that people that have higher scores on one variable tend to have lower scores on the other variable. For example, individuals who brush their teeth tend more to have a lower number of cavities.

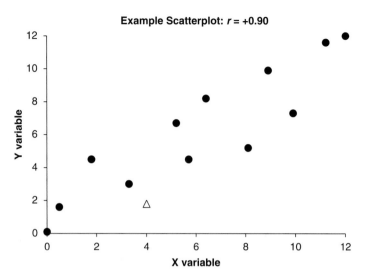

FIGURE I.7 A scatterplot demonstrating a correlation of *r* = +.90. This is a very strong, consistent, and positive correlation with few exceptions to the general relationship between variables. The triangle at the coordinates (4, 2) represents a sample member with a score 4 on the *x* variable and a score of 2 on the *y* variable.
Image modified from Warne (2018, p. 340).

Correlation coefficients also describe the consistency of a relationship between variables. A value of zero indicates that there is no relationship between the two variables (such as eye color and fitness for being a parent). Numbers further from zero (and therefore closer to –1 or +1) indicate stronger, more consistent relationships that have fewer exceptions. This is shown in Figures I.7 through I.11. These images are called *scatterplots*, and in each of them a dot represents a sample member. The dot for a sample member is located at the coordinates (*x*, *y*) that correspond to a person's *x* and *y* variable scores. For example, the point in Figure I.7 that is marked with a white triangle represents a person who has a score on the *x* variable of 4 and a score on the *y* variable of 2. This is why their point on the scatterplot is located at the point (4, 2).

Generally, weak correlations require larger sample sizes to discern patterns in the data, while very strong correlations are noticeable to non-experts in their day-to-day life. As an example, in one large study, IQ scores for the same individuals at age 11 and age 77 were correlated *r* = +.63 (Deary, Whalley, Lemmon, Crawford, & Starr, 2000). A correlation this strong is noticeable in everyday life and is why most people would recognize that smart children grow up to be smart adults. (This strong correlation is also why not-so-smart children tend to grow up to be less intelligent adults.) On the other hand, the correlation between ADHD and IQ is *r* = –.13 (Bridgett & Walker, 2006),

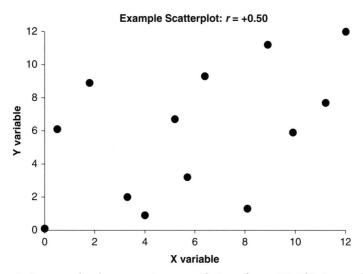

FIGURE 1.8 A scatterplot demonstrating a correlation of r = +.50. This is a moderately strong correlation that has some exceptions to the general relationship between variables.
Source: Warne (2018, p. 340).

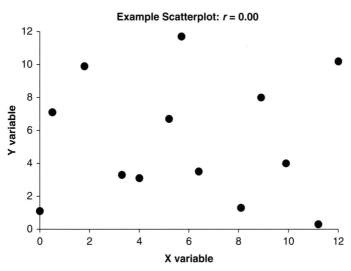

FIGURE 1.9 A scatterplot demonstrating a correlation of r = 0. This shows a complete lack of correlation or relationship between variables.
Source: Warne (2018, p. 341).

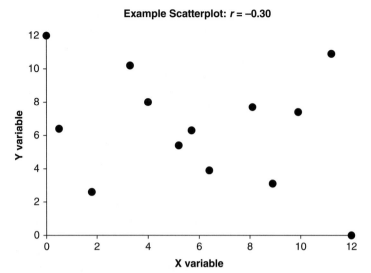

FIGURE I.IO A scatterplot demonstrating a correlation of *r* = -.30. This is a modest negative correlation with many exceptions to the general relationship between variables. Notice now that because the correlation is negative, individuals who score high on variable *x* tend to score low on variable *y* (and vice versa).
Source: Warne (2018, p. 341).

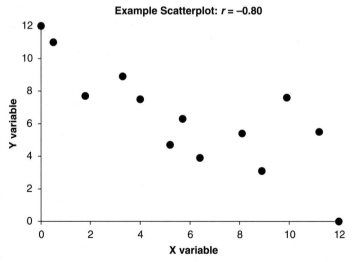

FIGURE I.II A scatterplot demonstrating a correlation of *r* = -.80. This is a strong negative correlation with few exceptions to the general relationship between variables. Notice that because the correlation is negative, individuals who score high on variable *x* tend to score low on variable *y* (and vice versa).
Source: Warne (2018, p. 342).

a correlation that takes a sample size of nearly 500 people to observe because it is far too weak to notice in daily life. To learn more about the mathematics behind correlation coefficients and how to interpret this important statistic, see Chapter 12 of Warne (2018).

Correlation and shared variance both describe how strongly variables are related to each other. In fact, correlation can be converted to shared variance by squaring the correlation. For example, the r = +.63 in the Deary et al. (2000) study means that .63 × .63 = .3969, or 39.69% of the variance in age 77 IQ is shared with the variance in age 11 IQ. That means that nearly 40% of the reasons why some people were smarter than others at age 77 are the same reasons why some people are smarter than others at age 11.

One shortcoming with the correlation statistic is that it is sensitive to a phenomenon called *restriction of range*. This occurs when the scores used to calculate the correlation do not span the entire range of variability. This distorts the correlation, usually by making it weaker (i.e., driving the correlation closer to zero). A good example of this occurs in college admissions tests. Most universities have only a slice of the range of test scores in their student body; students who score too low are usually not admitted, while students who score too high often enroll in a more elite university. Because of this restriction of range, the correlation between SAT scores and freshman grade point average is $r \approx .35$. But test researchers estimate that if a university had the full range of SAT scores the correlation would rise to $r \approx .55$ (Sackett, Borneman, & Connelly, 2008; Zwick, 2007, pp. 18–20).

Cohen's *d*. The statistic *Cohen's d* is used to describe the average difference between two groups. The value of Cohen's *d* indicates the number of standard deviations between the two groups' average scores. Cohen's *d* can – theoretically – range from 0 to +∞. However, in the social sciences, most Cohen's *d* values are between 0 and +1, and almost all are between 0 and +2.[1]

A Cohen's *d* value of zero indicates that the averages for the two groups are precisely equal. Figures I.12 through I.14 show what Cohen's *d* values greater than 0 look like. In all three images, the two curves represent the distribution of scores for two different groups. One group is represented as a black line, while the other is represented as a grey line. Notice that in all three figures there is a great deal of overlap between the two groups. Even when the Cohen's *d* value is 1.00 (very large in most areas of psychology), there are still a lot of people

---

[1] Cohen's *d* values are sometimes expressed as negative numbers. This is because the first step in calculating Cohen's *d* is to subtract one group's mean from another. If the larger mean is subtracted from the smaller mean, the number will be negative. If the smaller mean is subtracted from the larger mean, the number will be positive. It is arbitrary which group's mean is subtracted from the other group's mean. It still produces the same Cohen's *d* value – only the sign of the value (negative or positive) changes. In this book, I have only used positive Cohen's *d* values.

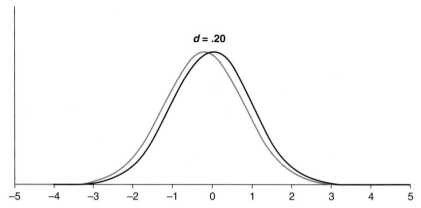

FIGURE I.12 Two normal distributions with averages that differ by $d = .20$. There is so much overlap between these two groups that 42.1% of people from the lower-scoring group (in grey) exceed the average for the higher-scoring group (in black).

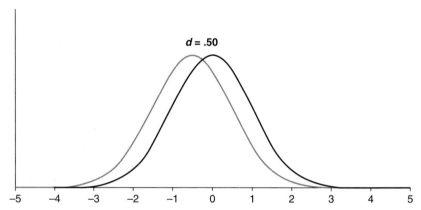

FIGURE I.13 Two normal distributions with averages that differ by $d = .50$. Although there is not as much overlap as in Figure I.12 (where $d = .20$), a total of 30.9% of people from the lower-scoring group (in grey) exceed the average for the higher-scoring group (in black).

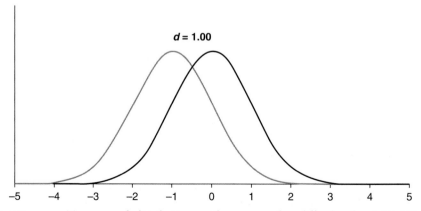

FIGURE I.14 Two normal distributions with averages that differ by $d = 1.00$. With a relatively low amount of overlap between the two groups, only 15.9% of people from the lower-scoring group (in grey) exceed the average for the higher-scoring group (in black).

from the grey group who have a higher score than people in the black group. Nevertheless, as Cohen's *d* increases, the two groups become more dissimilar.

Cohen's *d* is a standardized method of measuring average group differences in the social sciences. But when discussing intelligence, it is often useful to convert a Cohen's *d* value into the IQ score metric by multiplying *d* by 15 (because the standard deviation for IQ scores is 15). Therefore, the Cohen's *d* values in Figures I.12 through I.14 are equivalent to:

$(0.20)(15) = 3.0$ IQ points
$(0.50)(15) = 7.5$ IQ points
$(1.00)(15) = 15.0$ IQ points

Throughout the book I will often make these conversions for you. But readers should be aware that differences between group averages can be measured in Cohen's *d* values or in IQ score points. Understanding how to move from one metric to the other can be useful.

Factor Analysis. A much more complex statistical procedure is *factor analysis*. As stated above, Spearman (1904) invented the original version of factor analysis. Since then it has been one of the most important statistical methods for learning about intelligence and intelligence tests, though no one today conducts a factor analysis in the way that Spearman did originally. (Generations of statisticians and other scientists have improved the technique, and more improvements are likely in the future.) The mathematics of factor analysis is too complex to discuss here, but it is essential to understand conceptually what the procedure does.

As applied to intelligence research, the purpose of factor analysis is to identify groups of variables that correlate with one another more strongly than they correlate with other variables. These groups of variables are called *factors*. In one version of factor analysis (called *exploratory factor analysis*), the factors are formed without any regard to theory. In another version (called *confirmatory factor analysis*), a scientist specifies beforehand how they believe the variables group together into factors and how the factors relate to one another. Then, the scientist uses confirmatory factor analysis to determine whether the data fits with their pre-specified belief. For example, if a researcher collects data from a series of tests, they can use exploratory factor analysis to see if the data forms a general factor from the intercorrelating variables (e.g., Burningham & Warne, 2019; Carroll, 1993). On the other hand, if a researcher wants to test whether the CHC theory or the bifactor model are better representations of their data, then they would use confirmatory factor analysis. Both methods have their strengths and weaknesses, and readers interested in learning more can examine books on the topic (e.g., B. Thompson, 2004).

Factor analysis is a highly useful tool, but it does have limitations. One is that there are subjective choices required to perform factor analysis, and there is not always consensus regarding the "correct" decisions (Larsen & Warne, 2010).

Another problem is that the results of a factor analysis often depend on what variables were in the dataset. Although cognitive tests almost always produce one general factor (*g*) in their data, the makeup of that general factor or of Stratum II factors can vary greatly. For example, if some of my variables in a dataset are scores from subtests that require a lot of verbal skills and several other subtests that measure a variety of other mental abilities (e.g., arithmetic knowledge, visual memory, reaction time), then the verbal tests scores will produce a strong verbal factor, and the other variables may produce a weak factor that consists of scores that do not measure the same ability. Those non-verbal scores may merely form a factor because they do not belong in the verbal factor.

Another shortcoming of factor analysis is that the factors are merely groups of variables, which means that there is no guarantee that they correspond to a psychological trait, process, or phenomenon (Kane, 2013). It can be tempting sometimes to see a series of scores on memory tests that form a factor and say, "This memory factor must arise from a memory trait that is in people's minds." Well, maybe … and maybe not. To show that factors correspond to something inside people's minds, it is necessary to gather evidence that scores derived from the factor correspond to biological variables or observable mental processes (Kane, 2006, 2013). This is a shortcoming in factor analysis that has been recognized for decades, and Chapter 3 focuses largely on how psychologists know that the *g* factor is the product of brain biology and functioning.

PERIODS IN THE HISTORY OF INTELLIGENCE RESEARCH

Finally, it is important to learn some basic historic background of intelligence research. I divide this history into four periods: (a) pre-history, (b) early advances, (c) twentieth-century controversies, and (d) the modern consensus period. I will briefly explain each of these in turn and discuss important individuals, events, and issues within each period.

Pre-history: Antiquity to 1903. The early period of intelligence research is marked mostly by philosophy and theory. Ancient Greek had a word for intelligence (*dianoia*), which the Romans incorporated by translating it literally into *intelligentia*; the word had the meaning of a mental faculty for understanding. According to the *Oxford English Dictionary*, this word was imported into Middle English in the late fourteenth century, later becoming the modern word "intelligence." This linguistic evidence shows that the idea that people have an ability to understand the world around them is an old cultural concept in Western civilization.

In addition to this linguistic evidence, there is literary evidence that Westerners understood that people could differ in their intelligence. Many incidents in Homer's epic *The Odyssey* show how Odysseus uses his cleverness to survive, whereas other men succumb to danger because they lack this trait. Several Shakespeare plays have characters who are fools who are clearly less intelligent than other characters. Some of these fools are easily confused or tricked by characters who are smarter than they are (e.g., the young shepherd in *The Winter's Tale* whom Autolycus tricks, or Launce and Speed in *The Two Gentlemen of Verona*). As another example, the fourth-century Christian writer Eusebius in his history of Christianity wrote that the second-century author Papias of Hierapolis "was a man of very limited intelligence, as is clear from his books" (trans. 2007, 3.39.113).

The first theorist to consider intelligence from a scientific perspective was Sir Francis Galton in the late nineteenth century, who was greatly influenced by reading *On the Origin of Species* by Charles Darwin.[2] Galton applied new evolutionary principles to humans and believed that intelligence was an important trait that separated humans from animals. As a result, he saw intelligence as a key to humans' evolutionary success (Gillham, 2001). To test his theories, Galton attempted to measure intelligence by gathering data about people's visual acuity, head circumference, grip strength, lung capacity, tone discrimination, height, reaction time, and more. He hoped to find correlations between these variables and education level and socioeconomic status. Galton chose these measures because he believed that more intelligent people would be healthier, have better-functioning nervous systems, and would belong to better-educated groups and higher social classes. Despite his best efforts, Galton was unable to find any correlations between these variables and education level or social class. Others following his line of reasoning had similar results. It is now known that some of these variables do not correlate with intelligence, but that for others (e.g., reaction time, head circumference) the statistical and measurement methods at the time were not sensitive enough to detect the correlations (R. C. Johnson et al., 1985). Despite – what seemed at the time – Galton's failure, he is still credited as the first person to attempt to measure intelligence scientifically.

Early Advances: 1904 to 1930s. After the failures of Galton and others, the work of creating an intelligence scale languished for several years. The early twentieth century is marked by a series of breakthroughs in intelligence testing, the consequences of which are still apparent today. I have already explained Spearman's discovery of *g* and creation of factor analysis in 1904, and it is hard to overstate the importance of this dual breakthrough.

Nearly simultaneously, a Frenchman named Alfred Binet, who was trained in law but preferred to conduct research in the nascent science of psychology, was hired by the Parisian school system to create a method of identifying children who were struggling in school and not receiving any benefits from instruction in typical classrooms. These children were to be taught in their own classrooms

---

[2] Darwin and Galton were half-cousins; they shared a grandfather in Erasmus Darwin, but Charles Darwin was descended from his first wife, while Francis Galton was descended from Erasmus Darwin's second marriage.

with specially trained teachers in an early form of special education (Fancher, 1985). Binet had been conducting research on cognitive development in children since the early 1890s (Wolf, 1973), and he used what he had learned over the previous decade and a half to create a series of tasks for a child to perform (Gibbons & Warne, 2019). Binet compared an examinee's performance to the typical performance of children of various ages and determined that children who performed at a level typical of younger children would be likely to benefit from special classes. Binet published his first scale in 1905, with revisions in 1908 and 1911 (Binet & Simon, 1905/1916, 1908/1916; Binet, 1911/1916) before his untimely death in 1911 at the age of 54.

Binet's scale attracted a lot of attention, and within a few years it had been translated into several languages, including multiple times into English. In the United States, a Stanford University psychologist named Lewis Terman translated the test and added many items so that it was suitable for identifying the intelligence level of children across the entire range of ability – not just students struggling in school. This expanded test was named the Stanford–Binet; it was published in 1916 (Terman, 1916) and has been updated several times, with a modern version in use today. Like Binet's original tests, Terman's was hugely popular with at least 3.3 million tests administered one-on-one to children from 1916 to 1937 (Thorndike, 1975).

Shortly after the original Stanford–Binet was published, the United States entered World War I, and the president of the American Psychological Association, Robert Yerkes, formed a committee of psychologists to create two intelligence tests that could be used to sort the millions of men being drafted into the American army (Carson, 1993). The tests were called the Army Alpha – intended for men who could sufficiently read and write English – and the Army Beta – which was intended for men who read and/or wrote little to no English (Yerkes, 1921; Yoakum & Yerkes, 1920). Though the tests did nothing to change the course of the war, the experience taught psychologists much about how to create tests that were suitable to administer to large groups of people. The Army Alpha and Army Beta served as the basis for many tests developed for educational, clinical, and employment settings that were popular in the twentieth century (Chapman, 1988).

One influential test that grew out of the army tests was called the Wechsler–Bellevue Intelligence Scales (Wechsler, 1939). Its creator, David Wechsler, had been a soldier in the army administering Army Alpha and Army Beta tests in Texas (Matarazzo, 1981), and used these tests – and others – as inspirations for the Wechsler–Bellevue (Boake, 2002). The Wechsler–Bellevue was highly popular because it was designed for adults, whereas the Stanford–Binet was designed for children and adolescents. Moreover, Wechsler, as a clinical psychologist, recognized that subscale scores (which would today correspond to Stratum II abilities in the CHC and bifactors models) would be useful for diagnosis and other purposes. The Stanford–Binet at the time could only yield an overall IQ score.

Twentieth-Century Controversies: 1930s to 1990s. With a firm foundation in how to measure intelligence, the field moved into theory building and understanding the real-world impacts of intelligence. Unlike the previous period, which had a remarkable degree of agreement about the definition of intelligence, how to measure it, and the theoretical value of intelligence (see, for example, Freeman, 1923), the mid-twentieth century is marked by dissent, disagreement, and controversy. As the middle of the twentieth century edged into view, the consensus among scientists shattered.

One of the most prominent disagreements in intelligence research was the question of the very existence of g. L. L. Thurstone was an American psychologist who questioned whether intelligence was a single g-like entity after his factor analyses produced seven cognitive abilities – not just one (e.g., Thurstone, 1936, 1948). Thurstone argued that g did not exist and was a mere statistical artifact of Spearman's procedures for conducting factor analysis. He favored a view that "intelligence" was a collection of seven broad abilities that he called "primary mental abilities." These were "verbal comprehension, word fluency, number facility, spatial visualization, associative memory, perceptual speed, and reasoning" (Beaujean & Benson, 2019, p. 201). Later J. P. Guilford proposed a separate theory of mental abilities that at first had 40 factors (Guilford, 1956) and then later 180 factors (Guilford, 1988). Both Thurstone and Guilford served a term as president of the American Psychological Association, and their prominence within the scientific community gave credence to their criticisms of g.[3]

There are various reasons for this move away from g and to views of intelligence that emphasized multiple abilities. One is that advances in factor analysis made it easier to detect more than one factor. Psychologists and statisticians understand today that Spearman's original factor analysis method made it extremely difficult for him to ever find more than one factor (Carroll, 1993, pp. 40, 53; Jensen, 1998, p. 28). This was clear by the mid-twentieth century, but it was not in 1904 when Spearman first invented the method. The move towards recognizing non-g abilities was also fueled by the fact that g was clearly not the totality of all mental abilities – something recognized today in the CHC and bifactor models by including Strata I and II.

Another reason for the movement away from general intelligence is that the social context changed and made the concept much less fashionable to many scientists. For example, many leading psychologists in the UK and US at the beginning of the twentieth century were involved with *eugenics*. This was a social movement – started by Sir Francis Galton – that aimed to improve the human gene pool in the hopes of bettering the health and quality of life of future generations. Eugenics took many forms in different nations, including

---

[3] By the 1940s Thurstone had recognized that his primary abilities were correlated and could produce a general factor (Corno et al., 2002, p. 66). Spearman also came to recognize the existence and importance of non-g cognitive abilities.

encouraging people with "more favorable" genes to reproduce at greater numbers, genetic counseling to discourage people with genetic conditions from having children, forcibly preventing individuals with "unfavorable" conditions from reproducing (often through social isolation or forced sterilization), legalization of and education on the use of birth control, and legalization of abortion (Broberg & Roll-Hansen, 2005; Kevles, 1995). The most notorious manifestation of eugenics was the German Nazi regime's forced sterilization laws, euthanasia, and genocide. Like numerous other prominent individuals at the time, many leading psychologists – including those involved with intelligence testing – were part of this movement. Though most changed their minds about eugenics, the perspective of many postwar scientists was that intelligence research and intelligence testing were tainted by their association with Galton and eugenics (e.g., Gould, 1981). Chapter 32 will discuss this issue further.

Even without this tainted history, it is likely that intelligence research and testing would have decreased in popularity anyway. The changing attitudes towards greater political equality in Western nations – especially the United States – in the mid-twentieth century made intelligence testing unpopular because these tests showed the presence of major individual differences and implied an elitism that was difficult to reconcile with the move towards increased democracy and legal equality. The sex group and racial group differences in average scores (the topic of Chapters 27–30) and the correlation between IQ and social class (discussed in Chapter 11) also did not fit in well with the political mood of the time.[4] As a result, the research on intelligence and the use of intelligence tests came to be seen as controversial, socially regressive, factually or morally wrong, and sometimes even dangerous (e.g., Gould, 1981, 1996; Greenberg, 1955; Lewontin, 1970; Mercer, 1979; Sorokin, 1956).

Fueling the controversy around intelligence research at the time was a 123-page article written by Arthur Jensen and published in 1969 in the *Harvard Educational Review*. The article opened with the sentence, "Compensatory education has been tried and it apparently has failed" (Jensen, 1969, p. 2). Supporting his argument were data showing that – contrary to popular belief at the time and now – differences among individuals in school performance were mostly due to intelligence differences and not differences in family background, neighborhood, or school characteristics. In turn, Jensen said that these differences were probably mostly genetic in origin and that educational programs would be unlikely to boost IQ scores. Based on these views, Jensen concluded that educational programs of all types would be ineffective at equalizing differences in academic performance among students, though they had other benefits. Adding to the controversy surrounding the article, Jensen also argued that socioeconomic class differences in intelligence and racial

---

[4] To a degree, they still don't. This book probably would not be needed if the political and social climate were hospitable to the existence of individual and average group differences in intelligence.

differences could also be partially genetic in origin and that educational programs would not be able to equalize group differences either.

It would be extremely difficult to write something that would be more unwelcomed in the political and social milieu of 1969 than Jensen's article (Cronbach, 1975; Nyborg, 2003; Snyderman & Rothman, 1987, 1988). The opposition was so fierce that Jensen needed police protection at his job on the campus of the University of California (Fancher, 1985), and a bomb squad had to X-ray and open his mail (D. H. Robinson & Wainer, 2006). Credible threats against Jensen forced him and his family to temporarily move from their house (Nyborg, 2003). Others who wrote about intelligence – even if they did not touch on racial controversies – also faced protests, physical danger, or threats to their employment (Carl & Woodley of Menie, 2019; see Gottfredson, 2010, and Herrnstein, 1973, for examples).

Social controversies aside, as the twentieth century marched on, other theories emerged that demonstrated how there was little consensus about theories regarding intelligence. Most notably, Howard Gardner in 1983 published his theory of multiple intelligences, arguing that there is no one global intelligence, but rather that there were seven separate intelligences – a number later expanded to eight or nine. Shortly thereafter, Robert Sternberg (1985) published his triarchic theory of intelligence, arguing that g was a limited ability and that practical intelligence (an ability to function well in one's environment) and creative intelligence (i.e., creativity) were equally important – and sometimes more important – than g. For the purposes of this brief history, the details of these theories are not important. (Chapters 5 and 6 are devoted to them.) What matters is that they are part of a mid-twentieth-century tradition of dissent among experts about the existence and/or importance of general intelligence.

Consensus Period: 1990s to Present. When the 1990s dawned, it was not clear at all that general intelligence/g would ever be mainstream again. However, all that changed in 1993 with the publication of *Human Cognitive Abilities: A Survey of Factor-Analytic Studies* by John Carroll (1993). This behemoth of a book showed the results of a then-modern method of factor analysis on over 450 datasets from 19 countries. The vast majority of datasets produced a hierarchy of factors with g at the top. This soon led to the development of the CHC model (McGill & Dombrowski, 2019), which resolved a great number of controversies that had plagued intelligence research for decades. The CHC model showed, for example, that Spearman was correct that g existed, but also that Thurstone was correct that broad, non-g abilities existed and were important. Just five years later, Arthur Jensen (1998) published a landmark book, *The g Factor: The Science of Mental Ability*. This now-classic compiled all of the evidence available at the time on the existence of g, how to measure it, its practical importance, and genetic and environmental influences on people's intelligence. Jensen also addressed many alternative interpretations of intelligence research and convincingly demonstrated that *g* theory was the best theory to explain the totality of the data on intelligence. These two books effectively ended many debates about intelligence among experts and got the field to focus on *g*. One prominent psychologist (Meehl, 2006, p. 435) explained the impact of these books by stating:

Verbal definitions of the intelligence concept have never been adequate or commanded consensus. Carroll's (1993) *Human Cognitive Abilities* and Jensen's (1998) *The g Factor* ... essentially solve the problem. Development of more sophisticated factor analytic methods than Spearman and Thurstone had makes it clear that there is a *g* factor, that it is manifested in either omnibus IQ tests or elementary cognitive tasks, that it is strongly hereditary, and that its influence permeates all areas of competence in human life. What remains is to find out what microanatomic or biochemical features of the brain are involved in the heritable component of *g*. A century of research ... has resulted in a triumph of scientific psychology, the footdraggers being either uninformed, deficient in quantitative reasoning, or impaired by political correctness.

By the dawn of the twenty-first century, critics of the existence of *g* were "on the semi-popular fringes of scientific psychology" (Deary, 2001, p. 15).

Though not the intention of Carroll or any of the CHC model's creators, the CHC model also ordered the strata by the degree of genetic influence. Higher strata were more genetically influenced and lower strata were generally more environmentally influenced (Bouchard, 1997; Mollon et al., 2019; Plomin & Petrill, 1997). The CHC model also arranged abilities by how sensitive they are to training, with higher-strata abilities being less trainable and lower-strata ones being relatively easy to improve. Psychologists rallied around the model remarkably quickly, though there are holdouts.

The 1990s and 2000s also was an era where a massive amount of data emerged showing that intelligence was even more important for many life outcomes than earlier theorists had imagined (Chapters 22–26 discuss much of this research). For much of the twentieth century, most of the data regarding intelligence was about its correlation with educational outcomes and job performance. In the 1990s, strong data emerged showing that intelligence correlated with economic outcomes, health outcomes, and more (e.g., Gordon, 1997; Gottfredson, 1997b; Hunter & Schmidt, 1996; Lubinski & Humphreys, 1997). Most famous in this avenue of research was *The Bell Curve: Intelligence and Class Structure in American Life*, published in 1994 by Richard Herrnstein and Charles Murray. In this book, the authors argued that many disparities in social outcomes were better explained by differences in IQ than by socioeconomic differences. This conclusion – despite the firestorm of controversy the book stirred up at the time – is in line with the consensus position of intelligence experts today.

By the late 1990s a consensus had also emerged regarding the genetics of intelligence. While studies of the influence of genetics on intelligence date back to the 1920s (e.g., Burks, 1928/1973; Wingfield, 1928), this line of research also found itself at odds with the social and political climate of the mid-twentieth century. Additionally, the leading researcher on the topic, Sir Cyril Burt, was posthumously accused of fraud in the 1970s (see Fletcher, 1991, for an account of the accusations and the evidence behind them). By the 1990s, though, the research literature had strengthened to the point where the influence of genes was impossible to deny (Bouchard, 1997; Bouchard, Lykken, Tellegen, & McGue, 1996; Plomin & Petrill, 1997). The 1990s also saw the first studies in the hunt for specific "intelligence genes," and the 2010s would see the first studies published in which specific segments of DNA associated with IQ scores had been identified (Plomin & von Stumm, 2018). At the time of writing, hundreds of such portions of DNA have been identified in humans (Savage et al., 2018), and this number increases frequently.

Although disagreements still exist within the intelligence research community (see the book's concluding section), and there are non-mainstream voices that disagree with many points in this introduction, the field is currently in a state of consensus that is stronger than at any stage since the early 1930s. Indeed, writing a book like this would probably have been impossible until recently because for a long time there was not enough agreement among experts to state authoritatively what was true about human intelligence and what was not (Mackintosh, 2014). Now, though, the research is strong enough that I can confidently tell readers about the science of intelligence without worrying that important parts of the book would be overturned by new discoveries within a few years.

CONCLUSION

Intelligence is one of the most important topics in the social sciences. And after more than a century of research, psychologists understand more about intelligence than ever before. I hope you enjoy this fascinating topic and that it encourages you to take intelligence seriously as a scholarly topic and an influence in daily life.

THE NATURE OF INTELLIGENCE

Although the Introduction presents a useful working definition of intelligence, it does not fully explain what intelligence is. As you will see in the next six chapters, people have several important misconceptions about the nature of intelligence that I will explore and debunk. In the process, I hope you will be able to answer the following questions:

- What is *g*?
- Does intelligence have many parts, or is it a single entity?
- Where is *g* in the brain?
- Is there one type of intelligence, or are there other intelligences?

These chapters will demonstrate that intelligence is something real in the human mind, that it is a single entity (although it is related to other abilities in a way described by the Cattell–Horn–Carroll or bifactor models), and that it is a universal human trait. These concepts are fundamental to understanding the nature of intelligence and lay the foundation for much of the rest of the book.

I

Intelligence Is Whatever Collection of Tasks a Psychologist Puts on a Test

> . . . many psychologists simply accept an operational definition of intelligence by spelling out the procedures they use to measure it . . . Thus, by selecting items for an intelligence test, a psychologist is saying in a direct way, "This is what *I* mean by intelligence." A test that measures memory, reasoning, and verbal fluency offers a very different definition of intelligence than one that measures strength of grip, shoe size, hunting skills, or the person's best *Candy Crush* mobile game score.
>
> (Coon & Mitterer, 2016, p. 290)

I found that quotation in a general psychology textbook written for college students. Setting aside the question of why anyone today would use grip strength or shoe size to measure intelligence, almost everything that the authors state in this quotation is incorrect. But it is a common belief, even among psychologists, that intelligence is nothing more than an arbitrary collection of abilities (Warne, Astle, & Hill, 2018).[1]

Gottfredson (2009, p. 30) stated that people who believed this idea are arguing that, "Intelligence is a marble collection." They see intelligence as being like a bag of marbles, where each marble represents a different mental ability. In this view, the only reason why "intelligence" seems to exist is because a psychologist put all these abilities together and forced them to produce one overall IQ score. Under this incorrect reasoning, intelligence is the sum of a collection of tasks a psychologist arbitrarily chooses to put on an intelligence test. Scientists who think that memory is important will create a test that emphasizes that ability; others who believe that logical reasoning or language abilities are important will emphasize those abilities. If this idea were

---

[1] Though not related to the main topic of this chapter, it is interesting to note that Sir Francis Galton did use hand-grip strength as a measure of intelligence (R. C. Johnson et al., 1985). Also, video game scores *do* correlate positively with intelligence test scores (Ángeles Quiroga et al., 2015; Foroughi, Serraino, Parasuraman, & Boehm-Davis, 2016). Although the textbook authors probably didn't realize it, *Candy Crush* scores in a group of players with equal levels of experience playing the game probably measure intelligence – at least partially.

correct, there would be no way to know which abilities are the "right" or "wrong" components of intelligence, and it would be theoretically possible to have two people each create their own intelligence tests that measure completely different abilities. The resulting scores from these intelligence tests would be – theoretically – unrelated.

The first reason why this reasoning is wrong is that g itself is not a simple sum of a set of mental abilities (Jensen, 1998). Rather, factor analysis (a statistical procedure explained in the Introduction) finds the *overlap* of the variances of scores from different tasks and eliminates the unique component of each of these scores. This overlapping portion across all scores is the general ability factor, or g. Because g is made up of the ability that is measured across all tasks on an intelligence test, the measure of g (in other words, an IQ score) has little to do with specific tasks. Anything unique to any specific task is pulled out of g during the course of factor analysis (B. Thompson, 2004). One way of explaining this distinction is as follows:

It is also important to understand what g is not. It is not a mixture or average of a number of diverse tests representing many different abilities. Rather, it is a distillate, representing the single factor that all different manifestations of cognition have in common . . . It does not reflect the tests' contents per se, or any particular kind of performance. (Arthur Jensen, quoted in D. H. Robinson & Wainer, 2006, p. 331)

It is because all these tasks have a common characteristic – g – that measuring a global mental ability like intelligence is even possible. Additionally, because factor analysis distills g and removes the unique portions from a score, the collection of tasks on a test really does not matter much, as long as there are several types of tasks on a test and they are all cognitive in nature. All cognitive tasks measure g to some degree.

This last point was discovered by Charles Spearman (1927, pp. 197–198), and he named this principle the *indifference of the indicator*. For Spearman, the indicator was the surface content of a test. For example, in the Introduction, I discussed vocabulary, matrix, digit span, information, spatial reasoning, and coding items. Each of these types of items would be what Spearman called an indicator. When using the word "indifference," Spearman wasn't saying that psychologists didn't care about test content. Instead, the phrase "indifference of the indicator" means that the surface content of the test does not matter; all cognitive items measure intelligence, and g is indifferent to the format of a test item. Spearman's claim was radical in 1927, but it has since been strongly supported by research (Carroll, 1993; Cucina & Howardson, 2017; Gottfredson, 1997b).

However, this does not mean that every cognitive task on an intelligence test is an equally good measure of g (Jensen, 1980b). Some tasks are better than others at measuring intelligence. How well a task measures intelligence is called its g *loading*, a value ranging from 0 to 1 that is produced by factor analysis. Vocabulary and matrix reasoning items tend to have very high g loadings (up to

.80 on many professionally developed tests), while measures of short-term recall and reaction time tasks tend to have low *g* loadings (Carroll, 1993). Generally, more complex tasks have higher *g* loadings, while simpler tasks have lower *g* loadings (Gottfredson, 1997b). Test creators don't have to choose tasks with high *g* loadings when they create their tests, but a test that consists of tasks with high *g* loadings can be shorter and produces a better estimate of a person's intelligence than a test that is made up of tasks with low *g* loadings. Tasks that have *g* loadings of 0 (and therefore do not measure *g*) are tasks that are clearly not cognitive in nature – like running speed. Thus, because every cognitive task measures *g* – at least to some extent – it does not matter much what tasks are on an intelligence test, though there is a strong preference among psychologists for tasks that have high *g* loadings.

Apart from test construction, there is another source of evidence showing that the claim that intelligence is merely the sum of an arbitrary set of test items is not correct. This evidence is found in studies that administer multiple intelligence tests to a sample of people in order to determine how strongly the two *g* factors from the tests are correlated. If there is a strong correlation between the two tests, it would indicate that the *g* factor in each test is the same – even if the tasks on the tests are different. A correlation near zero would indicate that (a) what each test labels as *g* is different, (b) the combination of tasks on each test produces two very different measures of intelligence that are not interchangeable, and (c) what each test measures is just a unique combination of the tasks that a test creator chose to put on the test.

The authors of one of the earliest studies of this type (Stauffer, Ree, & Carretta, 1996) gave 10 common pencil-and-paper intelligence subtests and a series of 25 computerized tasks called the Cognitive Abilities Measurement (CAM) battery. The CAM battery was intended to measure processing speed, working memory, declarative knowledge (i.e., information that the person can state that they know), and procedural knowledge (which is the knowledge of how to complete tasks). The intelligence subtests and the CAM battery each produced a *g* factor that correlated almost perfectly ($r = .950$ to $.994$).

In a more recent study (Keith, Kranzler, & Flanagan, 2001), a team of psychologists administered two intelligence tests, the Woodcock–Johnson III (WJ-III) and Cognitive Assessment System (CAS), to a sample of 155 children. Keith et al. (2001) used factor analysis to identify each test's *g* factor and found that the correlation between the two was $r = 0.98$ (p. 108). What makes this result more remarkable is that the CAS was created by psychologists who did not intend to create a test that measured *g*. As a result, most of the tasks on the CAS do not resemble tasks on the WJ-III at all. Nevertheless, the CAS still produced a *g* factor, and the CAS's *g* factor is identical to the *g* on the WJ-III test.

Floyd, Reynolds, Farmer, and Kranzler (2013) conducted a more elaborate follow-up with six samples of children or adolescents that took two intelligence tests out of a group of five tests: the Differential Ability Scales (DAS), DAS II, Wechsler Intelligence Scale for Children (WISC) IV, WISC-III, WJ-III, and

Kaufman Assessment Battery for Children II.[2] The sample sizes ranged from 83 to 200, and the correlations between these tests' g factors ranged from $r = .89$ to $r = 1.00$ and averaged $r = .95$. Again, this shows that the g factors produced by different tests are largely identical. Additionally, Floyd et al. (2013) found that the similar Stratum II factors that each test produced were largely the same (e.g., the processing speed factor on one test was highly correlated with another test's processing speed factor). This means that Stratum II abilities in the Cattell–Horn–Carroll model can also have a high degree of similarity across tests.

A team headed by psychologist Wendy Johnson found similar results with even larger samples. In a group of 436 adults who took three test batteries (the Comprehensive Ability Battery, the Hawaii Battery supplemented with some additional tests, and the Weschler Adult Intelligence Scale), the different g factors from these test batteries all correlated $r = .99$ or $r = 1.00$ (W. Johnson, Bouchard, Krueger, McGue, & Gottesman, 2004). The researchers summed up their findings by saying that across these three tests there was, "Just one g" (p. 95). Johnson and her colleagues followed up this work with another study of 500 Dutch seamen. With four different tests (a test battery for the Royal Dutch Navy, a battery of 12 subtests from the Twente Institute of Business Psychology, the General Aptitude Test Battery, and the Groninger Intelligence Test), the correlations of their g factors were all between $r = .95$ and $r = 1.00$ (W. Johnson, te Nijenhuis, & Bouchard, 2008, p. 88).[3]

The idea that intelligence is just a set of arbitrarily chosen tasks that are thrown together on an intelligence test is simply not true. Regardless of the content that psychologists choose to put on a test, any cognitive task measures intelligence to some extent. When the scores from these tasks are combined via factor analysis, the unique aspects of each test are stripped away, and only a score based on the common variance among the tasks – the g factor – remains. Scores from these g factors correlate so highly that they can be considered equal. As a result, the idea that intelligence is an arbitrary collection of test items is completely false. Instead, intelligence, as measured by the g factor, is a unitary ability, regardless of what tasks are used to measure it.

---

[2] The Roman numerals after the name of a test refer to the edition of the test. For example, the WISC-IV, was the fourth edition of the WISC.

[3] A fifth test, the Cattell Culture Fair Test, had a g factor that had a much weaker correlation with the other g factors: $r = .77$ to $r = .96$. This is almost certainly because this test consists of four extremely similar tasks, instead of – as on the other tests – a diverse set of tasks. A narrow variety of tasks on a test means that factor analysis cannot fully remove the unique aspects of each task when identifying a g factor. This lowers the correlation of the Cattell Culture Fair Test's g factor with the g factors derived from other tests. W. Johnson et al.'s (2008) example shows a limitation of factor analysis: without a broad range of tasks on a test, the g factor identified in a test will not represent the entire breadth of intelligence. This is a well-known shortcoming of factor analysis (Jensen, 1998) and why the best intelligence tests include several different types of tasks for examinees to do.

2

Intelligence Is Too Complex to Summarize with One Number

> ... the study of intelligence within the human species has followed two traditions: the scientific and the pseudoscientific. The scientific tradition recognizes the complexity of the behavioral repertoires called "intelligence" ... It further recognizes that intelligence cannot be reduced to a simple metric or number such as IQ. The pseudoscientific tradition, on the other hand, is typified by a simple-minded attempt to reduce intelligence to a single rank ordering ...
>
> (Graves & Johnson, 1995, p. 280)[1]

> However, except to a small band of dedicated psychometricians, it seems obvious that to try to capture the many forms of socially expressed intelligent behavior in a single coefficient – and to rank an entire population in a linear mode, like soldiers on parade lined up by height – excludes most richly intelligent human activities. Social intelligence, emotional intelligence, the intelligent hands of the craftsman or the intelligent intuition of the scientist all elude the 'g' straightjacket.
>
> (Rose, 2009, p. 787)

From the time Spearman discovered g in 1904, people have been skeptical about the idea that intelligence was one entity in the mind that could be summarized by a single number. In the Introduction, I showed how psychologists in the twentieth century used factor analysis to argue about whether intelligence was one entity (as Spearman believed) or consisted of multiple mental abilities (as Thurstone claimed). For decades, psychologists repeatedly gathered data, performed factor analyses, and modified their tests, statistical methods, and theories in an effort to better understand intelligence. Though it was a slow process that lasted over half a century, it was productive in shedding light on the debate over the nature of intelligence.

---

[1] The ellipses in the quote indicate citations omitted from the original passage.

This work paved the way to the general consensus that dominates psychology today: that intelligence is a general ability (like Spearman's *g*) that is related to other mental abilities. The Cattell–Horn–Carroll model and the bifactor model are leading theories of intelligence that represent this compromise position. (The models are diagrammed as Figures I.5 and I.6 in the Introduction.) In a way, both the Spearman camp of psychologists – who believed that intelligence was one ability – and the Thurstone camp of psychologists – who believed in a collection of abilities – were correct. But both camps failed to recognize the entirety of human cognitive abilities and how these were all related to one another.

What is important to note about this discussion is that it was data driven. As scientists, these psychologists built, tested, and modified theories on the basis of the data they collected. Though it may have taken a while, the history of intelligence research shows that the scientific method of using data to modify beliefs does indeed help scientists get closer to the truth.

On the other hand, some people just claim – usually without any attempts to test whether their beliefs are true – that intelligence is too complex a psychological entity to summarize in a single number, like an IQ score. As can be seen in the quote above, Graves and Johnson (1995) go so far as to call the idea that intelligence can be summed up by a single number as "pseudoscience." As I will demonstrate in the rest of this chapter, not only is intelligence a single entity which can be summarized into one score, it is also impossible for intelligence to be as multidimensional as anti-*g* theorists argue.

WHY *g* EXISTS: THE POSITIVE MANIFOLD

If *g* were a mere personal preference or an untested theory, then the opponents of *g* would be on strong ground in criticizing its existence. However, *g* is an empirical fact that emerges from the *positive manifold*, which occurs when almost all scores on cognitive tasks are positively correlated with one another. Spearman first noticed this in his 1904 article, where the exam grades in five school subjects (classics, French, English, mathematics, and music), and a tone discrimination test all correlated positively with one another (r = .40 to .83). Modern samples also demonstrate the positive manifold. For example, the Stanford–Binet Intelligence Scales, Fifth Edition has ten subtests that all intercorrelate (r = .46 to .69) in the norm sample (Roid, 2003, p. 165). The Wechsler tests show the same positive manifold. The subtests on the Wechsler Preschool and Primary Scale of Intelligence IV intercorrelate (r = .30 to .67 in children under age 4 and r = .25 to .67 in children ages 4 to 7; Wechsler, 2012, pp. 70–71), as do the subtests on the WISC-V (r = .09 to .71; Wechsler, 2014) and the WAIS-IV (r = 21 to .74; Wechsler, 2008, p. 62).

The positive manifold matters because this is where *g* comes from. Spearman's brilliant insight in 1904 was that test scores were correlated because they were all caused by the same ability: *g*. He created factor analysis to demonstrate that one ability was all that was needed to explain all these positive correlations among all these abilities. In fact, it is impossible to pull a g factor out of a set of data unless the variables all intercorrelate with one another. Thus, the existence of g is dependent on the positive manifold. If there is no positive manifold, there is no g, and intelligence is not a unitary entity.

Conversely, all it takes to demolish g is to find a cognitive variable – any cognitive variable – that does not correlate with other cognitive variables. Another way to disprove the existence of g would be to find independent, non-correlating clusters of abilities because such a dataset would produce multiple factors that are unrelated to each other. Either of these scenarios would be sufficient to disprove the theory that one general ability dominates human cognition and problem solving. Despite searching for over 100 years, no one has *ever* found a cognitive variable that was uncorrelated with other cognitive variables or a test that consistently produces multiple factors. This is extremely strong evidence that intelligence is one entity.

Once g has been shown to exist, it is a simple matter to sum up a person's level of g with a single score. Because g is a general problem-solving ability, creating a score is a matter of rank ordering people according to how well they solve problems. Well-designed intelligence tests require problem solving on a variety of tasks, some of which were explained in the Introduction. By tallying up how many problems of varying difficulty people can solve, it is possible to ascertain who are the most successful (and least successful) individuals in a group at problem solving. This score will be a close approximation of the relative rankings of individuals in their level of g.

BUT g ISN'T EVERYTHING

That being said, the skeptics of g are partially correct about the complexity of human cognition. Spearman and other early theorists of intelligence severely underestimated the breadth of human cognitive abilities, and no expert in the past 60 years has argued that g is the only important cognitive ability. Anyone who attacks intelligence research by arguing that "IQ isn't everything" is attacking a straw man. Modern viewpoints take into account the complexity of human cognition while still finding a place for g. Both the Cattell–Horn–Carroll theory and the bifactor model of mental abilities recognize that g is not the entirety of mental abilities. There are other abilities in Stratum I and Stratum II that are part of both theories. These abilities are important, even if they are not as general as g.

As a result, the best-designed intelligence tests produce more than just a global IQ score. For example, the WISC-V produces a full-scale IQ score but also scores for verbal comprehension, visual-spatial ability, fluid reasoning, working memory, and processing speed. Even if two people have the same full-scale IQ score, their scores on the Stratum II abilities may be very different. These Stratum II scores often produce important information about a person's relative cognitive strengths and weaknesses. These strengths and weaknesses matter, especially for making choices about careers or college majors. Research has shown that – in countries where students have a great deal of freedom to choose their occupations or college majors – most people gravitate towards fields that allow them to use their strengths (Makel, Kell, Lubinski, Putallaz, & Benbow, 2016; Wai et al., 2009). Even if a person has an ability above average in a particular area, if it is not their highest Stratum II ability, they are unlikely to choose a job or college major where that ability is essential. For example, a person with above-average spatial reasoning and even higher verbal ability would be more likely to become a patent lawyer (an occupation which uses both abilities, but relies more on verbal ability) than to become an engineer (which requires very little verbal ability).

This discussion of differences in Stratum II abilities is important because most people have at least one distinct Stratum II ability that they score higher on than others. For example, in one sample of over 100,000 children, 60.2% of examinees had at least one subscore on the Cognitive Abilities Test that was higher than at least one other subscore, and 3.3% of people had one Stratum II score differ by 22 IQ points or more(!) from at least one other score (Lohman, Gambrell, & Lakin, 2008). Thus, for the majority of people, planning occupational or educational goals on the sole basis of an IQ score is probably going to be ineffective; taking into consideration a person's relative strengths and weaknesses in other abilities is important. Of course, non-cognitive variables matter, too. If a person lacks the motivation, interest, or values needed to succeed in a particular career, then it is irrelevant if intelligence tests results show that the person could do that job.

ARGUMENTS AGAINST *g* THAT CONSIDER THE POSITIVE MANIFOLD

Although not in the mainstream, there are some scientists who argue that the positive manifold is not necessarily proof of *g*'s existence – and, therefore, an IQ score does not represent a person's intelligence level. These theories take various forms, but generally, they are based on the claim that the brain has many modules or processes for performing different tasks and that tasks on intelligence tests require examinees to use multiple modules or cognitive processes to solve problems (e.g., Conway & Kovacs, 2018; Hampshire, Highfield, Parkin, & Owen, 2012). In this view, the positive correlations among scores on mental tasks are a result of overlapping cognitive processes or modules that are required to complete different tasks.

There are two problems with this line of argumentation. The first is that such a model requires nearly every task to draw on nearly every psychological cognitive process or module because scores on all cognitive tasks are positively correlated with one another. The result is a theory that becomes so complex that it becomes implausible (Ashton, Lee, & Visser, 2014). For example, such a theory would require reaction time tasks to draw on a person's language-processing module – even though these tasks are so simple and performed so rapidly that language is not necessary to perform them (Jensen, 1998).

Another problem with this line of argumentation is that it does not reflect the degree to which cognitive tasks correlate with one another. If the theory were true, then similar tasks would correlate more strongly with one another than tasks that do not resemble each other. (Likewise, dissimilar tasks would be weakly correlated because they would draw on different mental processes.) But task similarity is a poor guide for how strongly tasks correlate with each other. For example, if *g* were an artifact of different tasks requiring the same processes or mental modules, then the digit span and backward digit span tasks should be more correlated with one another than any other pair of tasks. However, this is not what happens in real datasets. In most samples, correlations between the two digit span tasks are $r \approx .30$ to 50 (e.g., Wechsler, 2008, 2014), but other dissimilar tasks (such as the similarities task and the arithmetic subtest on the WISC-V) have stronger correlations.

CONCLUSION

Modern theories of intelligence are based on the belief that *g* is related to every mental ability, either directly (in the bifactor model) or indirectly (in the Cattell–Horn–Carroll model). While the view that general intelligence is the only important mental ability was discarded long ago, *g* inevitably arises from the positive correlations among scores on different mental tasks. Because intelligence is one global ability, it is not hard to create one score – often called IQ – that summarizes how well a person can solve problems. While IQ is not the only important score for understanding a person's cognitive abilities, it is a useful score for understanding general problem-solving ability.

3

IQ Does Not Correspond to Brain Anatomy
or Functioning

> The reification of IQ as a biological entity has depended upon the conviction that Spearman's g measures a single, scalable, fundamental "thing" residing in the human brain ... no set of factors has any claim to exclusive concordance with the real world [or in the brain].
>
> (Gould, 1996, pp. 295, 299)

The biologist Stephen Jay Gould's most popular work was *The Mismeasure of Man*, a book arguing that intelligence testing and intelligence research were part of a lengthy history of social scientists fudging or misinterpreting their data to support their incorrect preconceived (and often racist) beliefs (Gould, 1981, 1996). One of the main arguments in Gould's book is that intelligence is a *reification*, which is the term for an abstract idea that is treated as if it were real. The quote above encapsulates one of Gould's reasons why he believes that intelligence or g is not a real entity: it has no apparent connection with the physical or functional properties of the brain. While this belief was not completely unreasonable when Gould wrote the first edition of his book in 1981, neuroscientists have since amassed findings that suggest that g has real connections to the anatomy and functioning of human brains.

Contributions to intelligence research from neuroscience only date back a few decades. There are two reasons for this: one obvious and another that is not so clear. First, the obvious reason: the tools of neuroscience for most of the twentieth century were too inexact to make important contributions to intelligence research. The pioneers of neuroscience were limited to studying the behavior of individuals who had a brain injury (such as a stroke or other brain damage), experimenting on individuals during neurosurgery, or conducting postmortem autopsies to learn about brain functioning. While there are a few success stories – most famously the discoveries by Broca and

Wernicke in localizing important centers of language in the brain[1] – progress was limited for many decades. All this changed with the invention of technologies that could examine the structure or functioning of brains of living individuals. The first of these technologies was electroencephalography (EEG), which measures brain waves via electrodes placed on the scalp. In the 1970s the invention of the computed tomography (CT) scan and magnetic resonance imaging (MRI) both allowed scientists to view living brains without subjecting people to neurosurgery. Later, the invention of positron emission tomography (PET) and functional MRI (fMRI) allowed scientists to determine the location of brain functioning with a much higher degree of precision than EEG technology (though not as quickly or directly). Today, neuroscientists have a wealth of technologies available to them to understand many aspects of brain functioning – including intelligence (Hunt, 2011).

The second reason why neuroscience has until recently made few contributions to the study of intelligence is that most neuroscientists are usually interested in the general principles of brain functioning. As a result, they usually focus on the commonalities of how different people's brains function or are structured. Intelligence research, though, is built upon a focus on individual differences in task performance (i.e., who is smarter – or not) and pays much less attention to common characteristics across humans. This split in psychology between scientists interested in general principles and those interested in individual differences is an old one and not unique to neuroscience and intelligence research (Cronbach, 1957). But since the 1980s some neuroscientists have worked to bridge the gap between these two fields, and in the twenty-first century their evidence and theories support the belief that *g* does indeed have connections to brain anatomy and functioning (Haier, 2017a).

CORRELATIONS BETWEEN IQ AND BRAIN CHARACTERISTICS

If I Only Had a (Large) Brain. Contrary to Gould's (1981, 1996) claims, there are brain characteristics that do correlate with IQ scores. One of the best known is the correlation between brain size and intelligence, which when measured via brain-imaging techniques in living individuals is between $r = .20$ and .40. Other measures of brain size (e.g., data from autopsies, or measures of head circumference) have weaker, though positive, correlations (Cox, Ritchie, Fawns-Ritchie, Tucker-Drob, & Deary, 2019; Gignac & Bates, 2017; J. Lee, McGue, Iacono, Michael, & Chabris, 2019; Pietschnig, Penke, Wicherts,

---

[1] The areas of the brain associated with language that these men discovered are now called Broca's area and Wernicke's area in their honor. Individuals with damage to Broca's area in the left frontal lobe of the brain lose the ability to speak, but have no loss of comprehension of language. Conversely, people with damage to Wernicke's area in the left hemisphere lose the ability to comprehend language, but their speech is fluent, though meaningless.

Zeiler, & Voracek, 2015; Rushton & Ankney, 2009). Conversely, better measures of *g* produce stronger correlations with brain size (Gignac & Bates, 2017), and measures of the size of the whole brain are more strongly correlated than measures of specific brain regions. It is important, though, to note that the size of the frontal lobes seems more strongly correlated with IQ than other regions of the brain (Cox et al., 2019; Flashman, Andreasen, Flaum, & Swayze, 1997). Regardless of the details, Gould dismissed a lot of research that showed a relationship between IQ and brain size (see especially Chapter 3 of Gould, 1996). This viewpoint in Gould's book must have been deliberate because, as Rushton (1997, p. 170) stated,

I know Gould is aware of them [the studies on the brain size–IQ relationship] because my colleagues and I routinely sent him copies as they appeared and asked him what he thought! For the record, let it be known that Gould did not reply to the missives regarding the published scientific data that destroyed the central thesis of his first edition [of *The Mismeasure of Man*].

Brain size is the variable that has the most research regarding its correlation with IQ scores. However, it is certainly not the only (or most important) biological variable that is correlated with IQ, nor does brain size fully explain why some people are smarter than others. For example, males and females have equal average intelligence test scores (see Chapter 27), but males have larger brains, even when controlling for their larger body size (Jensen & Johnson, 1994). Moreover, based on estimates from skull size, modern human brains are smaller than the brains of humans who lived about 100,000 years ago (Hennenberg, 1988). Today, human brains are about the same size as the typical Neanderthal brain (Hare, 2017). All of this information makes it hard to argue that "big brains are smart brains" is the entire story about the brain and IQ. As one expert explained, "[Brain] Size dominates the literature not simply because it is important in its own right, but because it is easy to measure . . ." (Bouchard, 2014, p. 557). Despite this lukewarm view towards brain size, the research does show that there can be important correlations between IQ and neurological variables.

Other Brain Characteristics. Since the 1990s, neuroscientists have discovered more variables correlated with IQ. For example, research has shown the importance of the white matter in the brain, which is the tissue that connects brain regions to one another. Volume of white matter is correlated with speed of problem solving (Penke et al., 2012) and with IQ, thus showing that connectivity of brain regions is likely to be an important determinant of intelligence levels (Haier, 2017a; Kievit et al., 2016). Likewise, grey matter (where the neuron cell bodies are found) is important; loss of neurons due to disease is associated with decreases in IQ (van Veluw et al., 2012). Additionally, smarter people have more neurons in their brains, and those neurons are more densely packed together (Genç et al., 2018). Another intriguing recent finding is that neurons are better organized in high-IQ individuals' brains than in the

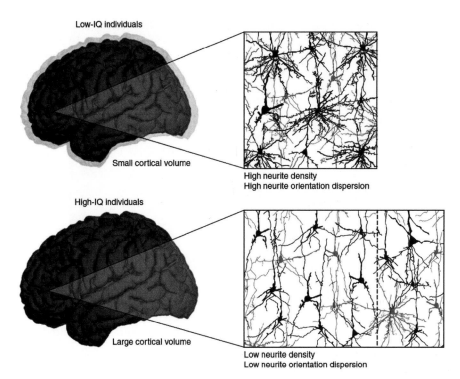

FIGURE 3.1 Depiction of the differences in brain cortex volume and neuron organization in low- and high-IQ individuals. High-IQ individuals have more neurons because of their larger grey matter volume. The neurons in a high-IQ individual tend to be better organized and with fewer, less chaotic branches (called neurites) off the cell body.
Source: Genç et al., 2018, p. 7.

brains of people who score poorly on intelligence tests. This is shown in Figure 3.1, where high-IQ individuals have fewer neurites (the branches off the main body of a neuron) than low-IQ individuals.

THEORIES OF *g* AND THE BRAIN

These correlations are informative because they demolish any claim that *g* is a statistical artifact, a reification, or a social construct (Jensen, 1998; Jung & Haier, 2007). If *g* were not real, then IQ scores would not correlate with any properties of the brain. But these correlations do not explain what *g* is, biologically. Once enough data had been amassed, though, some neuroscientists who study intelligence could create theories about how *g* arises from the brain. The leading theory today is called the Parieto-Frontal Integration Theory (P-FIT).

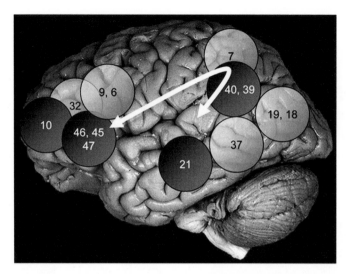

FIGURE 3.2 A schematic showing the P-FIT model. The circles correspond to brain regions that are often functionally important for solving tasks related to *g* and abstract reasoning. Dark circles are areas that are usually in the left hemisphere of the brain, while light circles are usually in the right hemisphere. The numbers correspond to Brodmann areas, which is a standardized system of mapping regions of the brain. The double-headed arrow corresponds to the arcuate fasciculus, a white matter structure that connects many of these brain regions.
Source: Jung & Haier, 2007, p. 138.

A visual representation of P-FIT is depicted in Figure 3.2. In this model, there are several brain regions, mostly located in the frontal lobe (towards the front of the brain) and the parietal lobe (on the top part of the brain, somewhat towards the rear), that are connected with a white matter tract called the arcuate fasciculus. According to the P-FIT model's creators, *g* arises from both how well these areas function and how well they are connected to one another in the brain (Jung & Haier, 2007). This explains two initial hurdles to understanding how *g* relates to the brain. The first is why there is no one area in the brain that is activated when a person engages in reasoning tasks. The second hurdle is why several previous studies had suggested that the size and use of multiple areas in the parietal and frontal lobes were correlated with IQ.

Euler (2018) has recently proposed another theory of how the brain generates *g*. Rather than focusing on specific brain regions, Euler has built on the *predictive processing theory* of brain functioning, which posits that the brain is a "prediction machine" that is adapted to help an organism form expectations about the environment and to give attention to events that violate those expectations (e.g., the presence of a danger in a location that the person thought was safe). Euler believes that intelligence may be the manifestation of the brain's ability to handle unexpected situations and that more intelligent people are better able to manage unexpected events than people with less intelligence.

This theory would explain why intelligence differences are more apparent in more complex tasks (see Chapters 24 and 28). Other characteristics of intelligence that predictive processing theory could explain are the positive manifold (see Chapter 2), why cognitive abilities may form a hierarchy (like in the Cattell–Horn–Carroll model; see the Introduction), and why so many different tasks can measure *g* (see Chapter 7). This is just a hint at the non-neurological data that support predictive processing theory, and it has the potential to serve as a bridge between the neurology of brain functioning and manifestations of intelligence in people's behavior.

Readers should recognize that predictive processing and P-FIT are not necessarily contradictory. Predictive processing is based mostly on research about brain functioning, while P-FIT is based mostly on brain-imaging data about the size and performance of larger brain regions. It is possible that both theories are correct and that predictive processing explains how the brain generates intelligent behavior while using the regions highlighted in the P-FIT model.

CONCLUSION

Research into the neurological basis of *g* is still in an early stage. It takes time for evidence to accumulate, theories to be tested, and for new data to either support or undermine a theory. Both P-FIT and predictive processing theory are too new for this process to be complete, and it is possible that these theories will need major modifications in order to accommodate the results of future studies. Indeed, both theories may be completely wrong and may one day be replaced. One of the creators of P-FIT recognized this when he told me that, "It's a framework for testing hypotheses. Results will refine what we know and drive progress, even if P-FIT turns out to be mostly incorrect" (Haier, 2017b, punctuation altered slightly).

Regardless of what the future holds for the neurology of *g*, enough correlational evidence has accumulated that it is indisputable that some characteristics of brain functioning and anatomy correlate with *g*. The claim that some people (e.g., Gould, 1996) make that intelligence does not relate to the biology of the brain is completely at odds with decades of neuroscience research. What is most astonishing about these correlations is that they exist at all. Intelligence tests are not designed with the goal to produce scores that correlate with brain size or neuron density – but they do anyway. This is extremely strong evidence that *g* is real and that it is a product of the biology of the brain (Jensen, 1998).

4

Intelligence Is a Western Concept that Does Not Apply to Non-Western Cultures

> The group of skills which we refer to as intelligence is a European and American middle-class invention ... It is a kind of intelligence which is especially well adapted for scientific analysis, for control and exploitation of the physical world, for large-scale and long-term planning and carrying out of materialistic objectives. It has also led to the growth of complex social institutions such as nations, armies, industrial firms, school systems, and universities ... Other cultures have evolved intelligences which are better adapted than ours for coping with problems of agricultural and tribal living.
>
> (Vernon, 1965, p. 727)

> Ultimately, intelligence will not mean quite the same thing across the cultures, so that one will be in the proverbial position of the person who believes he or she can compare apples and oranges because they are both fruits.
>
> (Sternberg, 1985, p. 53)

The leading figures in intelligence research – both past and present – are individuals who come from Western cultures.[1] Because intelligence research and testing originate in Western cultures, it would be naïve to believe that Western culture does not influence the development of intelligence theories, research, and tests. As a result, many people argue that the perspectives of psychologists who study intelligence – and develop intelligence tests – are ethnocentric (e.g., Berry, 1974; Gardner, 2004; K. Richardson, 2002; Sternberg, 1985). In this viewpoint, intelligence, as understood by Western scientists, is at best too narrow. At worst, the concept is so foreign that it doesn't even make sense to study or measure intelligence in non-Western individuals. Critics like Vernon (1965, 1969) say that Western views of intelligence are incompatible with views originating in other cultures and that

---

[1] Intelligence research is an international endeavor, but researchers in the UK and US dominate this work. From a historical perspective, it is valuable to remember that Binet was French. Wechsler was born in Romania but immigrated to the United States as a child.

one must consider these groups' views of intelligence when studying mental abilities. In this chapter, I will explain why this idea is incorrect and why there is strong evidence to believe that intelligence – as defined by g – is a trait that exists in most (probably all) human cultures.

Like many of the incorrect beliefs about intelligence, the idea that intelligence is a culturally bound concept that only applies to Western cultures is not unreasonable. The reality is that different cultures have different ideas about what intelligence is and what intelligent behavior looks like. It is not realistic to expect the word "intelligence" to translate equivalently into all other human languages – or to even exist in every language. Inevitably, there will be differences in meaning, some of which will be major.

The diversity of abilities that different cultures see as being intelligent is impressive. For example, in Chinese cultures, intelligence seems to include knowing how to use one's knowledge ethically, an idea perhaps akin to "wisdom" (Yang & Sternberg, 1997a, 1997b). In some cultures originating in East Africa, India, and elsewhere, the ability to keep working on a task is a valued cognitive capacity (Berry & Bennett, 1992; B. D. Jones, Rakes, & Landon, 2013; Srivastava & Misra, 2001). In Zimbabwe, many competencies that are "non-cognitive" (in Western perspectives) are seen as vital components of intelligence, especially social competence. Mpofu (2004) reported that caring for one's family before helping friends or strangers is an important part of intelligence, while Ngara and Porath (2004) claimed that witchcraft and lovemaking were important domains in which Zimbabweans could manifest intelligence within their culture.[2] Meanwhile, the Cree (a First Nations people in Canada) value deliberation, persistence, and patience as part of intelligence (Berry & Bennett, 1992). This brief survey clearly shows that Western definitions of intelligence do not include some abilities and skills that some non-Western cultures value. This is why some psychologists believe that Western definitions of intelligence are too limited, especially when examining the abilities of non-Western individuals (e.g., Sternberg, 2003a, 2004; Yang & Sternberg, 1997a).

However, these contending cultural definitions of intelligence do not prove that Western definitions are limited. A cultural belief that a specific skill is part of intelligence does not make it so. As I have written elsewhere,

The same logic that researchers use to argue that a folk belief regarding intelligence provides evidence of the nature of intelligence could also be used to argue that widespread cultural beliefs in elves, goblins, or angels provide evidence of the existence of supernatural beings. (Warne & Burningham, 2019, p. 238)

This fact applies to Western perspectives as well as non-Western perspectives.

---

[2] Unfortunately, Ngara and Porath (2004) did not explain what sort of test would measure these abilities. A test of lovemaking skills would probably be more fun to take than most intelligence tests.

There will never be any worldwide agreement about what the "correct" definition of intelligence is. (Indeed, there isn't even complete agreement among Western scholars about the best definition of intelligence.) This is one of the weaknesses of verbal definitions of psychological concepts. Language is – by its nature – inexact; ambiguity and disagreement are inevitable.

Instead of asking whether "intelligence" means the same thing in different cultures, it is much more valuable to examine whether g exists in different cultures (Warne & Burningham, 2019). This is because g is derived statistically – not verbally – through factor analysis and therefore is largely independent of what any particular definition of what skills constitute intelligent behavior.[3] Thus, whether intelligence is a cross-cultural concept is not reliant on similarities in verbal definitions, but rather on whether g exists in different cultures.

My student and I conducted the most rigorous test of whether g exists in non-Western cultures in a recent article (Warne & Burningham, 2019). We searched for archival cognitive test data from groups of examinees in non-Western, non-industrialized countries. We selected these countries because we thought that if g were an artifact of Western culture and philosophy, then these individuals would be the least likely to display g.

We found 97 analyzable datasets from 31 countries in every non-Western region of the world, including Latin America (e.g., Guatemala, Bolivia), Sub-Sahara Africa (e.g., Zambia, Ghana, Ethiopia), and Asia (e.g., Pakistan, Bangladesh, Cambodia). In total, there were 50,103 individuals in the dataset, ranging in age from 2 to the elderly. After identifying the datasets, we then performed exploratory factor analysis on all the datasets to determine whether g emerged from the data.

The results were striking. Of the 97 samples, 71 (73.2%) produced g unambiguously. The remaining 26 datasets produced more than one factor, but when these factors were factor analyzed, 23 of the datasets (88.5%) produced g.[4] Of the remaining three datasets, one produced g under one

---

[3] Factor analysis results are not completely independent of scientists' theories and beliefs, though. The decision of what test scores to collect is largely based on what a psychologist believes should be on an intelligence test. However, with a broad array of cognitive tasks, factor analysis will still produce a g factor that is largely the same from test to test (see Chapter 2).

[4] It is not unusual for psychologists to conduct a second factor analysis on factors produced from the first factor analysis (e.g. Carroll, 1993). When only one factor emerges from an initial factor analysis – as it did in almost three-quarters of datasets in our study – then the variables produce g unambiguously. When an initial factor analysis produces more than one factor, these factors may be correlated. When this happens, a second factor analysis of the factors can determine whether the correlations among factors is due to the presence of a higher-level g. The presence of a single factor (g) in this second factor analysis is evidence that the different cognitive abilities have the hierarchical structure shown in the Cattell–Horn–Carroll model (see the Introduction). If more than one factor emerges from the second factor analysis, then it is evidence that mental abilities are not all due to g and that the Cattell–Horn–Carroll model does not capture the nature of the relationships among cognitive abilities.

method of exploratory factor analysis but not another, while it was not possible to do the second-stage factor analysis for two samples. Therefore, 94 of the 97 (96.9%) samples produced *g* either immediately or after a second factor analysis. Moreover, the *g* factor is about as strong in the non-Western samples as it is in typical Western samples. All of these findings show that *g* is not a culturally specific phenomenon confined to Western populations.

In fact, the results were more consistent than even Burningham and I had expected. Our original intention was to examine all the datasets that did not produce *g* and look for common characteristics that distinguished them from *g*-producing samples. But this kind of analysis was not possible with only three datasets that failed to produce *g*. This consistency is remarkable when one considers the diversity of samples in terms of age, education level, lifestyle, and degree of contact with Western cultures.

There was also remarkable diversity in the types of tasks that non-Western examinees performed in these datasets. While some of them resembled Western intelligence tests (often translated into examinees' native language and/or adapted to their culture), some did not. Other datasets included data from scholastic tests, neurological tests, and even intelligence tests developed by non-Western scholars. Regardless of the collection of tasks administered to examinees, almost all of these datasets still produced *g*. Moreover, some of these datasets were collected without any intention of producing a *g* factor, and some of the original data collectors are opponents of theories of intelligence based on *g*. These people would have been best suited to create datasets that disproved the theory that *g* is real, and yet they could not (Warne & Burningham, 2019).

Another interesting fact that emerged from this study was how common Western (or Western-style) intelligence and cognitive tests are used in non-Western countries. Despite theorists arguing that Western theories and intelligence tests are too narrow (e.g., Ogbu, 1994; K. Richardson, 2002), non-Western psychologists have adopted these and use them frequently in their countries (though often in translated or culturally adapted versions). These indigenous psychologists rarely see the need to add tasks or subtests that measure the components of intelligence that are important to their culture but which are missing from Western theories. If Western definitions of intelligence are deficient and lack vital components of intelligence, few non-Western test creators and users seem to have noticed.

Skeptics could still argue that *g* is not synonymous with intelligence and that the presence of *g* across cultures does not mean that intelligence also exists across cultures. Again, this takes the discussion back to a verbal argument about the meaning of the word "intelligence." As my co-author and I stated,

Whether "intelligence" exists across cultures or whether the term has the same meaning across cultures is unknowable and probably irrelevant. The term is culturally loaded and will often have a somewhat altered meaning when translated into other languages.

However, the statistical abstraction of Spearman's *g* is apparent across cultural groups in 31 non-Western, non-industrialized nations. (Warne & Burningham, 2019, p. 266)

There is good reason to explore cross-cultural definitions of the term "intelligence," and what different human groups think about the skills and mental processes that they find important. But these cultural disagreements say little – if anything – about the nature of intelligence. Rather, what matters is whether *g* is present in non-Western groups. The research shows that it probably is.

If *g* is universal, the question then arises of why cultural differences do not seem to obliterate, mask, or change *g*. My theory is that *g* originated early in humans' evolution and that it is a fundamental property of human brain functioning. This theory is supported by research that has shown that other species have a *g* factor, including dogs (Arden & Adams, 2016), rats and mice (B. Anderson, 1993; Galsworthy, Paya-Cano, Monleón, & Plomin, 2002; Matzel & Sauce, 2017), donkeys (Navas González, Jordana Vidal, León Jurado, McLean, & Delgado Bermejo, 2019), and non-human primates (Fernandes, Woodley, & te Nijenhuis, 2014; Herndon, Moss, Rosene, & Killiany, 1997; Hopkins, Russell, & Schaeffer, 2014; Matzel & Sauce, 2017). All of these are mammal species with a common evolutionary ancestor. It is possible that *g* originated in the early evolutionary history of mammals and that all of these modern descendent species have *g* as part of their psychology. If this theory is true, then it would indicate that *g* *cannot* be culturally specific because if *g* can persist across different mammal species, then it is unlikely that the comparatively subtle differences among humans would be sufficient to eliminate *g* in any group. Even if this evolutionary theory is wrong (which is possible), it does not change the fact that *g* appeared in over 95% of samples from 31 countries where it would be least likely to be present if *g* were a culturally specific concept.

If *g* is universal among humans, it would not mean, though, that one can take an intelligence test developed in a Western nation and give it to people from any culture. (Chapter 10 explains this matter further.) Regardless of who the examinees are, it is still necessary for tests to be culturally appropriate and understandable to test takers. When examinees – from any culture – take an intelligence test, there should be no vocabulary, stimuli, or tasks that are culturally alien.[5] Otherwise, a psychologist is collecting meaningless and

---

[5] It would be inappropriate (and even unethical), for example, to ask a child information items that contain knowledge that is not part of their cultural tradition. In the Introduction, I gave an example of an outdated information item for children: "Who wrote *Romeo and Juliet*?" This is an appropriate item for native English speakers in industrialized countries, but it would be inappropriate for a child whose culture does not tell the story of *Romeo and Juliet*, or does not value Shakespeare and his writings. Few – if any – psychologists are giving such obviously inappropriate test items to non-Western examinees because an examinee's inability to answer such a question provides no information about the examinee's cognitive abilities.

uninterpretable data because the *manifestations* of intelligence – the skills, knowledge, and abilities that are a product of g – may be culturally specific, even though all humans have intelligence. This variability in how intelligence appears across cultures is a product of the cultural environment, such as language, the values of the culture, child-rearing practices, the climate and physical environment, and other characteristics (Ogbu, 1994). Measuring intelligence requires culturally appropriate methods of getting people to demonstrate their abilities, and these tasks may vary greatly from group to group. But the different tasks can (and do) measure intelligence. Chapter 7 discusses this at length.

5

There Are Multiple Intelligences in the Human Mind

> ... I argue that there is persuasive evidence for the existence of several relatively autonomous human intellectual competencies, abbreviated hereafter as "human intelligences." ... the conviction that there exist at least some intelligences, that these are relatively independent of one another, and that they can be fashioned and combined in a multiplicity of adaptive ways by individuals and cultures, seems to me to be increasingly difficult to deny.
>
> (Gardner, 2011, pp. 8–9)

Howard Gardner's *Frames of Mind: The Theory of Multiple Intelligences*, published originally in 1983,[1] is one of those works, like Sigmund Freud's *The Interpretation of Dreams* or B. F. Skinner's *Walden Two*, that has seeped into the wider culture and pop psychology. Even people who have never read *Frames of Mind* know of the theory of multiple intelligences and may identify themselves as having, for example, high logical-mathematical intelligence, low intrapersonal intelligence, or high bodily-kinesthetic intelligence. In almost all introductory psychology textbooks Gardner's theory of multiple intelligences is summarized (Warne et al., 2018), and *Frames of Mind* is one of the most commonly cited works in those textbooks (Griggs, Proctor, & Cook, 2004).

Despite the popularity of Gardner's theory, it is not a viable theory of human cognitive abilities because of two major types of problems. The first problem is empirical, where Gardner's theory does not find support in the data from psychological research on cognitive abilities. The second is that the theory has fundamental flaws in its logic and construction that prevent it from being a useful scientific theory. I will explore these issues in this chapter.

---

[1] In this chapter, I will be quoting and citing the current version, published in 2011. The two editions are largely the same; the 2011 version contains a new 18-page foreword and a 19-page foreword that originally appeared in the 1993 edition.

DESCRIPTION OF THE THEORY OF MULTIPLE INTELLIGENCES

Before discussing criticisms of Gardner's work, it is important to summarize the theory of multiple intelligences. Originally, Gardner posited that there were seven intelligences, which were:

1. Linguistic intelligence: the ability to show dexterity in oral and/or written language.
2. Musical intelligence: the capacity to learn, perform, create, and/or interpret music.
3. Logical–mathematical intelligence: the skill of dealing with logical systems.
4. Spatial intelligence: the ability to handle stimuli in two or three dimensions.
5. Bodily-kinesthetic intelligence: the capability of using one's body in culturally useful ways (e.g., in athletics or artistic expression).
6. Interpersonal intelligence: the skill in dealing with others' behavior, such as in a leadership situation.
7. Intrapersonal intelligence: the capacity to engage in self-reflection to better understand one's self.

In 1999, Gardner combined the interpersonal and intrapersonal intelligences and added the naturalistic intelligence, which is the ability to understand and have empathy for objects in nature. From time to time, Gardner has suggested possible additional intelligences, such as an existential intelligence (Gardner, 1999). Some adherents of multiple intelligences theory only count the original seven, while others include the naturalistic and/or existential intelligences. Depending on which iteration of Gardner's theory proponents prefer, they may say that there are as few as seven or as many as nine intelligences. Gardner also recognizes that there may be other, heretofore undiscovered intelligences (von Károlyi, Ramos-Ford, & Gardner, 2003).

The changing number of intelligences in the theory is not necessarily a bad thing; good scientists change their opinions and alter their theories as new information comes to light. Some people (e.g., Ritchie, 2015) argue that Gardner invents intelligences arbitrarily, but actually he has specific criteria for when an ability warrants being called an "intelligence." These criteria for the existence of an intelligence are (1) brain damage that impacts the intelligence but no other abilities; (2) the existence of savants, prodigies, and eminent individuals in an area; (3) central operations that must be executed to work in that intelligence; (4) a developmental trajectory starting in childhood with a possible endpoint of expertise; (5) a plausible evolutionary theory of how the intelligence formed in humans; (6) support from experimental psychology; (7) evidence from psychological testing; and (8) a symbol system in which a person can demonstrate their accomplishment in the intelligence.

As described in *Frames of Mind*, the theory of multiple intelligences posits that there are a number "relatively independent" mental abilities that have separate biological foundations and manifestations. Gardner (2011, pp. xxxix, 337) explicitly rejects the concept of *g* and argues that it is an illusion resulting from how intelligence tests are created. Instead, Gardner believes that these intelligences can – and often do – work at the same time (von Károlyi et al., 2003). For example, when writing a song, one may draw upon musical intelligence for composing the music and linguistic intelligence for writing the lyrics. But Gardner argues that this is merely different modules in the brain operating simultaneously, and not evidence of the existence of a global intelligence.

EMPIRICAL PROBLEMS WITH GARDNER'S THEORY

If the theory of multiple intelligences is correct, then it should be supported by empirical data. To an extent, it is. Gardner cites hundreds of sources in *Frames of Mind* from research in education, psychology, anthropology, and other areas as supporting evidence of the existence of his intelligences. The problem is that Gardner habitually cherry picks evidence in his favor and ignores evidence that contradicts his theory (Bouchard, 1984; Messick, 1992; Scarr, 1985; Snow, 1985). Indeed, much of the evidence that Gardner cites is ambiguous and can support a variety of theories. For example, Gardner (2011, Chapter 5) has an excellent description of how language develops in childhood and becomes more complex as individuals age. This developmental trajectory can fit into many theories and does not prove the theory of multiple intelligences true, nor does it disprove any other theory.

When Gardner does confront the evidence that undermines his theory, he dismisses it, a tendency best shown in the following passage:

Several critics have reminded me that there are generally positive correlations (the so-called positive manifold) among tests for different faculties (for example, space and language). More generally, within psychology, almost every test of abilities correlates at least a little bit with other tests of ability. This state of affairs gives comfort to those who would posit the existence of "general intelligence." I cannot accept these correlations at face value. Nearly all current tests are so devised as to call principally on linguistic and logical faculties. Often the very wording of the question can tip off the test takers. (Gardner, 2011, p. xxxix, paragraph break eliminated; see also von Káolyi et al., 2003, p. 100)

Whether Gardner can "accept these correlations" or not does not change the fact that the correlations exist, regardless of the culture, tasks, and examinee population (see Chapters 1, 2, and 4).

Moreover, neither of Gardner's statements about intelligence tests is true. How a test of block span (where an examinee must touch a sequence of blocks in the same order that the examiner touched them) or reaction time would tap into linguistic and logical faculties is not clear. Additionally, the wording of items does not "tip off the test takers" in regards to the correct response. Indeed, for most item formats (e.g., vocabulary, matrix reasoning, digit span), it is not clear how the wording of the items can give hints that advantage some examinees over others.

Despite Gardner's beliefs, the reality is that even when researchers attempt to measure the multiple intelligences, the result is a series of correlated variables that produce a general factor (e.g., Castejon, Perez, & Gilar, 2010; Pyryt, 2000). A *g* factor emerges from these scores, even though that is exactly what should never occur, according to the theory of multiple intelligences. Yet it does anyway.

Frames of Mind also has the drawback of relying heavily on anecdotal data. Case studies of people with brain injuries, ethnographies of non-Western cultures, and quotes from biographies of famous scientists and artists are common in *Frames of Mind*. What Gardner does not have is large, representative samples of individuals performing tasks grounded in his intelligences (Lubinski & Benbow, 1995). While many of the stories in *Frames of Mind* are vivid, case studies are inherently limited in their ability to provide scientific data. Loftus and Guyer (2002) explained the limited nature of case studies well:

> Case studies therefore illuminate, but can also obscure, the truth. In many cases, they are inherently limited by what their reporter sees, and what their reporter leaves out. This is especially true if the writer is untrained in the scientific method, and thus unaware of the confirmation bias, the importance of considering competing explanations before making a diagnosis and so forth. To the scientist, therefore, most case studies are useful largely to generate hypotheses to be tested, not as answers to questions. (p. 26)

Most of Gardner's examples of individuals with a high level of a particular intelligence come from non-scientific sources, such as biographies. There is also no evidence that Gardner sought case studies or examples of individuals who excel in more than one intelligence – the sorts of individuals who would provide evidence undermining his theory. Gardner discusses T. S. Eliot (linguistic intelligence) and Igor Stravinsky (musical intelligence). But he does not discuss Hedy Lamarr, who is best known as an actress (interpersonal intelligence), but was also an inventor (spatial and/or logical–mathematical intelligences). As another example, there is also no mention of Winston Churchill, one of the greatest leaders of the twentieth century (requiring high interpersonal intelligence), but whose Nobel Prize was in literature (an undeniable display of high linguistic intelligence). If Gardner's theory were true, then people who are eminent in multiple areas should be as rare as a Leonardo da Vinci because these intelligences would be uncorrelated, making multiple high abilities in the same person exponentially more unusual than high abilities in just one area. But people with high abilities in multiple areas are not as rare as Gardner claims; many eminent people in history had high achievement in multiple areas (White, 1931), and most science Nobelists are more accomplished in non-scientific fields than the general public (Root-Bernstein et al., 2008). With some knowledge of history and biography, one could create a lengthy list of eminent individuals who have achieved prominence in more than one intelligence (e.g., William Blake, Julius Caesar, Sir Francis Galton, Florence Nightingale, Lewis Carroll, Stephen Sondheim, Galileo Galilei).

Another problem with Gardner's examples is that they are all people who have high general ability – a minimum IQ of 120 by his own estimate (Jensen, 1998, p. 128). Thus, to be highly eminent in one of Gardner's intelligences requires high general intelligence. This is not surprising; for nearly a century, psychologists have known that scores on tests are correlated less strongly among high-IQ samples than among low-IQ samples (Spearman, 1927, pp. 217–221; see te Nijenhuis & Hartmann, 2006, and Tommasi et al., 2015, for examples of this phenomenon from the twenty-first century). If they do exist, the multiple intelligences seem to be the playground of high-g people.

Another problem with Gardner's anecdotes is his emphasis on eminent individuals, which makes the intelligences appear distinct and uncorrelated with each other. But when studying the entire population, these abilities are clearly correlated. If one considers – as Gardner (2011) does – these individuals in isolation, then the vast differences between composing a symphony and writing a clever poem become clear, and it does appear that Igor Stravinsky and T. S. Eliot have very different abilities. But when one considers the entire population, then it is apparent that musical ability and verbal accomplishment are positively correlated and not as independent as Gardner believes. (Indeed, in Spearman's 1904 study, the two abilities were correlated $r = .51$.)

It is well known that studying outliers and other eminent individuals exaggerates differences. This is apparent when imagining space aliens who abduct an Olympic gymnast, weight lifter, and basketball player. The aliens would see huge differences in these people's training regimens, body types, physical capabilities, and diets. These differences might be so large that the aliens would find it difficult to classify all of them as athletes. But in a more general population of athletes – ranging from weekend warriors and kiddie league participants to elite professionals – the similarities in abilities would be more apparent (Lubinski, 2004). Thus, Gardner erred when considering only outliers because this masked the similarities among individuals.

Eminent individuals are not the only outliers Gardner builds his theory on. He also uses savants (i.e., individuals with low IQ scores but who have extreme abilities in one area, such as artistic production, piano playing, or mathematical computation) as evidence that an intelligence can be independent of other cognitive abilities. However, Gardner oversimplifies this evidence; while savants can sometimes have amazing abilities, they do not display all facets of any of Gardner's intelligences. For example, a musical savant may be able to play a piano piece after hearing it a single time, but a musical savant cannot compose, improvise, transpose, arrange, orchestrate, or engage in other high-level displays of musical ability (Klein, 1997). Savants seem to have a prodigious memory, which is scientifically interesting, but not evidence for Gardner's theory.

THEORETICAL PROBLEMS WITH GARDNER'S THEORY

The empirical problems with Gardner's theory are enough to disprove it, but the theoretical problems associated with his theory of multiple intelligences are also a serious threat to the theory. These problems show that the theory lacks important characteristics of useful scientific theories, especially because of the theory's (a) vagueness, (b) incoherence, and (c) inability to make new predictions. I will address each of these ideas in turn.

One of the essential characteristics of a scientific theory is that it has to be specific enough to test. Unfortunately, Gardner's theory of multiple intelligences is too vague for any scientific purpose (Jensen, 1998). How uncorrelated do abilities have to be in order for them to be "relatively independent of one another"? Is it $r = .40$? .25? .10? 0? Gardner never says. Additionally, Gardner (2011) recognizes that intelligences can be used in tandem and that few human activities require just one intelligence. But he never specifies how to distinguish between multiple intelligences operating simultaneously and a general ability that functions in different domains. Gardner also never explains how the intelligences can work together if they are "relatively independent" and do not overlap neurologically (Klein, 1997).

What is most staggering is that Gardner acknowledges that his theory cannot be tested like a real scientific theory. For example, he stated, "I've never felt that MI theory was one that could be subjected to an 'up and down' kind of test, or even series of tests. Rather, it is and has always been fundamentally a work of synthesis" (Gardner, 2011, p. xix). And elsewhere: "I do not believe that educational programs created under the aegis of MI theory lend themselves to the kinds of randomized control studies that the US government is now calling for in education" (Gardner, 2011, p. xxi). How convenient.[2]

A second – and related – problem is that the theory is not coherent. One way the theory is incoherent is in its circular reasoning of how to identify intelligences. As an example, Gardner (2011, p. xxxiv) stated:

There is no "pure" spatial intelligence: instead, there is spatial intelligence as expressed in a child's puzzle solutions, route finding, block building, or basketball passing. By the same token, adults do not exhibit their spatial intelligence directly but are more or less proficient

---

[2] Strangely, in the main text of *Frames of Mind* (written in 1983), Gardner recognized the importance of testing a theory: "But science can never proceed completely inductively ... It is necessary to advance a hypothesis, or a theory, and then to test it. Only as the theory's strengths – and limitations – become known will the plausibility of the original postulation become evident" (Gardner, 2011, p. 63). It is not clear what changed his mind in the intervening 28 years.

chess players or artists or geometricians. Thus, we are advised to assess intelligences by watching people who already are familiar with and have some skills in these pursuits.

In other words, it is only possible to identify an intelligence once it has been developed (von Károlyi et al., 2003). Consequentially, identifying an intelligence becomes a circular process that goes something like this:

> "Why does Anne perform well in chess?"
> "Because she has high spatial intelligence."
> "How do we know Anne has high spatial intelligence?"
> "Look at how good she is at chess!"

This circular definition is an "explanation" for Anne's competence in chess that explains nothing and is too incoherent to function as a meaningful scientific theory. It is also untestable, to boot.

Another incoherence in Gardner's theory is why the abilities he emphasizes must be "intelligences" at all. He recognized this ambiguity and explained that he chose the term because he wanted "to replace the current, largely discredited notion of intelligence as a single inherited trait" (Gardner, 2011, p. 300). However, by including physical abilities (in bodily-kinesthetic intelligence), personality traits (in interpersonal intelligence) and other non-cognitive traits, Gardner has stretched the word "intelligence" so much that it ceases to have any real meaning (Hunt, 2011; Jensen, 1998; Scarr, 1985). Gardner sees g as being a narrow concept that encourages "a limited view of intelligence" (von Károlyi et al., 2003), but believing in the existence of g does not preclude the existence of other abilities. In fact, both the CHC and bifactor models explicitly recognize the existence of non-g cognitive abilities (as this book's Introduction makes clear).

Finally, any useful scientific theory must be able to make predictions about phenomena or – in the case of the social sciences – individuals. Multiple intelligences theory is unable to do this (Hunt, 2011). One reason is that Gardner never creates a feasible plan for assessing the intelligences in his theory; indeed, he has stated that he does not endorse any psychological test to measure the multiple intelligences (von Károlyi et al., 2003). In *Frames of Mind* he spends only a few pages (2011, pp. 404–406) explaining how to measure the intelligences. These tips are extremely impractical to implement on a large scale. For example, Gardner suggests giving children a wide variety of materials from different intelligence domains (e.g., puzzles, a computer, musical instruments) and then examining which areas a child excels in. Gardner estimates that this endeavor will take 5–10 hours per child over the course of a month. Multiply that assessment time by the number of children in an elementary school and the result is a time commitment that is too impractical for real-world implementation.[3] Without a practical method of assessing the

---

[3] As if that weren't overwhelming enough, in 2003, Gardner and two of his co-authors stated that assessing children's multiple intelligences needs to occur regularly, because a child's relative strengths and weaknesses can change over time (von Károlyi et al., 2003).

intelligences accurately, there is no way to predict who will be successful in a drama program, a basketball team, the math Olympiad, or a pottery class.

In later works Gardner developed more sophisticated ideas – such as using portfolios of rating scales – about how to measure the intelligences (e.g., von Károlyi et al., 2003), but these methods have profound deficiencies. Lubinski and Benbow (1995) explained that these new procedures were susceptible to producing inconsistent data (i.e., "low reliability," in the technical jargon; see Chapter 7) and that there was no evidence that these scores had any educational utility. Klein (1997) argued that these sorts of assessment have the same problems as traditional intelligence tests – except now the problems exist for a series of tests for the intelligences, instead of a single test that measures *g*. Again, without meaningful data, the ability to make predictions based on multiple intelligences theory is nonexistent.

Gardner dismisses these concerns:

> In speaking of measurement, I touch on the issue about which psychologists interested in intelligence have spilled the most liquid or electronic ink. Having put forth the theory, they maintain, I should be required to test it and, on the basis of the results of those tests, either revise or scuttle the theory. In their view the fact that I've elected not to become a psychometrician is no defense! (Gardner, 2011, p. xix)

But it *is* no defense. Without a coherent method of measuring a trait, it is impossible to study the trait thoroughly, make predictions based on the trait, and test the theory (Hunt, 2001; Waterhouse, 2006). The fact that a theorist does not want to define how a trait is measured does not excuse them from that duty because other scientists will never completely know whether they are truly measuring the theorized trait. Moreover, because the intelligences cannot be measured until they are already developed, the theory is utterly useless at predicting which children will profit from music lessons, need additional instruction in math, or have difficulty reading. This is the sort of information that teachers and parents want that Gardner's theory will never be able to provide.

OTHER PROBLEMS

There are other problems with Gardner's *Frames of Mind* that bear mentioning, but which do not impugn the central issues of his theory. One is that the main text of *Frames of Mind* has never been updated since 1983, which makes much of the research that Gardner bases his theory on is woefully out of date. Reading *Frames of Mind* in the twenty-first century is like visiting a museum of antiquated knowledge about the brain. There is little discussion of modern cognitive psychology theories, and – aside from a single mention of CT scans (Gardner, 2011, p. 53) – there is no hint in the book that neuroscientists have brain-imaging technology available to them. To his credit, Gardner recognizes this and recently wrote:

I readily admit that the theory is no longer current. Several fields of knowledge have advanced significantly since the early 1980s. Any reinvigoration of the theory would require a survey similar to the one that colleagues and I carried out thirty-five years ago. (Gardner, 2016, pp. 169–170)

Why anyone would want to work with a theory that its own creator recognizes as outdated is not clear.

Gardner's theory of multiple intelligences has seen its warmest reception in education (Gardner, 2011, 2016; Hunt, 2011), where many teachers and educators see the theory as validating their folk theories of learning (Klein, 1997). In one survey of educational professionals, a majority endorsed each of Gardner's intelligences as useful traits for identifying gifted children (Schroth & Helfer, 2009). I agree that Gardner has many positive ideas for school reform, and he argues convincingly that schools should educate all areas of talent, instead of focusing on the "core" areas of math and language arts. However, none of Gardner's suggestions for school improvement requires his theory in order to be implemented. And if these ideas are successful, they do not prove his theory true (Hunt, 2001; Klein, 1997; Waterhouse, 2006). One can support, for example, stronger musical education programs in schools without referring to the existence of a musical intelligence.

The educational establishment's embrace of the theory of multiple intelligences is not without cost, though. Interventions based on incorrect ideas are more likely to cause harm than programs based on correct theories. For example, Gardner's (2011) recommendation to identify a child's strongest intelligence(s) in order to foster and build that intelligence may close off educational and career opportunities from children at an early age (Klein, 1997). Gardner (2011) also states that schools and society should value all intelligences equally. This sounds good, but business, science, and technology are major drivers of economic growth and human progress; giving equal school time and funding to manifestations of neglected intelligences – like dance, self-reflection, music theory, or leadership – may stunt economic growth and slow medical, technological, and scientific breakthroughs.

CONCLUSION

Despite its popularity in the education establishment, Howard Gardner's theory of multiple intelligences has fundamental theoretical problems that make it incoherent, untestable, and unable to generate predictions. Moreover, empirical evidence is overwhelming that different cognitive abilities are not independent of one another and that a general mental ability – g – exists. I agree with Hunt (2011, p. 119), who stated that "there is virtually no objective evidence for the theory" of multiple intelligences.

Perhaps because the theory of multiple intelligences and its creator are so identified with one another, it has become impossible to avoid criticizing

Howard Gardner's behavior regarding the theory. I disapprove of Gardner's resistance to testing his theory and his blasé dismissal of unfavorable evidence, both of which are not how scientists should behave with regard to their theories. One final quote encapsulates his attitude well:

And even if at the end of the day, the bad guys [who advocate for a general intelligence] turn out to be more correct scientifically than I am, life is short. And we have to make choices about how we spend our time, and that's where I think the multiple intelligences way of thinking about things will continue to be useful, even if the scientific evidence isn't supportive. (Gardner, 2009, 0:45:11–0:45:32)[4]

I suppose that if a person wants to make studying multiple intelligences theory their pastime, then there is no harm in that. (Most hobbies don't have a scientific basis.) But the theory of multiple intelligences lacks empirical support and a coherent theoretical foundation. Therefore, in situations where it could impact people's lives – like in education and in scientific research – it should be completely abandoned.

---

[4] The reference to the "bad guys" who oppose Gardner's theory is a rhetorical touch, implying malevolence in people who do not support his theory (see Cofnas, 2016, for a discussion of this issue).

6

Practical Intelligence Is a Real Ability, Separate from General Intelligence

> ... practical intelligence is a construct that is distinct from general intelligence and that general intelligence is not even general but rather applies largely, although not exclusively, to academic kinds of tasks. Moreover, practical intelligence is at least as good a predictor of future success as is the academic form of intelligence that is commonly assessed by tests of so-called general intelligence.
>
> (Sternberg et al., 2000, p. xi)

Everybody knows someone who is smart in the traditional, academic sense – and would presumably have a high IQ score – but who functions poorly in everyday life. The "absentminded professor" stereotype is a good example. People like this are memorable because their foolish behavior is so surprising, given their "book smarts." From a scientific perspective, these people undermine the claim that intelligence is general and that it helps in all aspects of life. After all, if intelligence really is general, then people who are good at navigating one aspect of their environment (e.g., school) should be good at navigating all of them. If there are people who function poorly in everyday life but function well in school, then it seems plausible that there could be more than one broad cognitive ability.

Because academic intelligence and everyday functioning seem like separate abilities, some people have suggested that g is not a general ability at all. They argue that intelligence may be helpful in school, but that succeeding in the workplace or in a non-academic environment requires a different ability. Foremost among these theorists is a psychologist, Robert J. Sternberg, who has proposed a theory of practical intelligence as an ability that is required to succeed in daily life. According to Sternberg, the separate nature of practical intelligence and academic intelligence is why some smart people seem to perform poorly on non-academic tasks, especially outside the school environment (Sternberg et al., 2000; Wagner & Sternberg, 1985).

WHAT IS PRACTICAL INTELLIGENCE?

In Sternberg's view, practical intelligence is the ability to learn, organize, and use *tacit knowledge* – the untaught information that is important for a person to flourish in their environment – in order to accomplish their goals (Sternberg, 2003b; Sternberg et al., 2000; Wagner & Sternberg, 1985). People with high practical intelligence are theorized to be able to better learn the unwritten knowledge regarding their workplace, neighborhood, family, or culture. If they can master this information, then a person with high practical intelligence would be able to succeed in their environment better than someone with a similar (or higher) level of *g* who does not have high practical intelligence.

An informal way of understanding practical intelligence is that it is similar to "street smarts," a term used in everyday language to refer to the knowledge that people need to succeed in their environment (Sternberg & Hedlund, 2002). Like street smarts, practical intelligence is separate from academic knowledge that people learn in school or from books, but is important for functioning in the real world. One of the reasons that Sternberg and his colleagues theorize the existence of practical intelligence is the same reason that some laymen infer the existence of street smarts: some people who are smart have difficulty dealing with the everyday world (Sternberg et al., 2000; Wagner & Sternberg, 1985).

Sternberg first proposed the existence of a practical intelligence ability in the mid-1980s (Sternberg, 1985; Wagner & Stenberg, 1985) in the context of his triarchic theory of intelligence. This is Sternberg's attempt to create a theory of intelligence that encompasses more than the cognitive abilities in traditional models of intelligence. The triarchic theory consists of three subtheories, which are (a) the contextual subtheory, (b) experiential subtheory, and (c) componential subtheory. Each of these subtheories emphasizes a different aspect of the behavior that differences in intelligence produce. The contextual subtheory focuses on how people react to, change, or leave an environment in order to accomplish their goals. The experiential subtheory is a proposed explanation of how people adapt to novel tasks (e.g., new job duties) and automize learned actions (such as learning to drive without feeling overwhelmed). Finally, the componential subtheory is based in cognitive psychology and is a proposed explanation of how the mind solves problems (Sternberg, 1985).

According to Sternberg (1985, 2003b), practical intelligence is part of the contextual subtheory of his triarchic theory of intelligence. If the triarchic theory is correct, then practical intelligence is an important mental ability that helps a person understand and behave in an adaptive way in their environment. In addition to practical intelligence, *g* (which Sternberg calls *analytical intelligence*) and creativity are two other important abilities for helping people cope with, change, or leave their environment in order to achieve their goals (Sternberg, 2003b). The triarchic theory is too broad to critique here (see

Hunt, 2008, Kline, 1991, and Messick, 1992, for brief critiques). Instead, what I focus on in this chapter is the evidence for the existence and/or importance of practical intelligence.

CLAIMS ABOUT PRACTICAL INTELLIGENCE

Sternberg and his colleagues make two important claims about practical intelligence. The first is that it exists separately from traditional intelligence, which Sternberg sees as a narrow academic ability (Sternberg et al., 2000; Wagner & Sternberg, 1985). This separation between the academic intelligence that is important for succeeding in the schoolhouse and the practical intelligence needed to succeed in the real world is an essential distinction in Sternberg's theory (Sternberg, 2004). If these two abilities are not separate and independent, then there is no need for practical intelligence because it would be redundant.

The second claim that Sternberg makes is that practical intelligence is as important as – or more important than – academic intelligence for job and life success (Sternberg et al., 2000). According to the triarchic theory, practical intelligence helps someone succeed in their environment because it causes them to learn the tacit knowledge that g does not help people learn. Much of Sternberg's evidence supporting his belief in the importance of practical intelligence is based on tests of tacit knowledge that his team has created for specific jobs, such as salespeople and military leaders.

Is Practical Intelligence Separate from g? Sternberg has published several studies that seem to support the existence of a practical intelligence that is separate from g or academic intelligence. An early article (Wagner & Sternberg, 1985) reported that, in three samples of individuals working in academic psychology or business, measures of tacit knowledge were correlated with various measures of career success. However, the authors' attempt to establish the separate nature of practical intelligence and g was feeble and consisted of giving two subsamples of elite college students a measure of verbal intelligence, which was uncorrelated with the measures of tacit knowledge. However, these sample members were not actually working in their career fields, and the restriction of range in intelligence among sample members almost surely reduced the strength of these correlations. (See the Introduction for an explanation of restriction of range.) Additionally, the average scores on the verbal intelligence test (45.3 and 46.2) were close to the maximum possible score of 50, which also restricted the range and weakened the correlation further. All in all, this was an unimpressive attempt to show that practical and academic intelligences were separate.

In later research projects on practical intelligence, Sternberg merely took it for granted that his practical intelligence was separate from g. However, my factor analyses of his data show that his measures of practical intelligence and other abilities (e.g., creativity, academic intelligence) often produce a general factor: g (e.g., Jukes et al., 2006; Stemler et al., 2009; Stemler, Grigorenko, Jarvin, & Sternberg, 2006; Sternberg et al., 2002; see also N. Brody, 2003). In other words, even though Sternberg denies the general nature of g, his own data often produces the traditional g factor anyway – and no separate factor for practical intelligence. Not only does this support the existence of g, but it also undermines any claim that practical intelligence is separate from g.

Others' efforts to identify a separate ability to cope with problems in the environment have been unsuccessful. One famous organization that has an incentive to identify a separate practical intelligence is the National Football League (NFL). As part of their screening process, the NFL administers a brief written intelligence test called the Wonderlic Personnel Test (WPT) to potential players. The items on the WPT are a mix of applied math, verbal reasoning, and other questions that often resemble school achievement tests. Wonderlic scores do correlate modestly with NFL performance, especially for experienced players who play in more complex positions (Lyons, Hoffman, & Michel, 2009). However, there seems to be no separate practical intelligence that the NFL has found to be valuable in identifying successful players.[1] As a result,

IQ testing [in the NFL] is more widely accepted now. The idea that a guy can be dumb off the field but a genius once he puts on pads and cleats that he can have "football smarts" as opposed to real smarts, is pretty well discredited. (P. Zimmerman, 1984, p. 291)

Does Practical Intelligence Function Better than g in the Real World? The question of whether practical intelligence is more important for real-world functioning is an empirical question that can be answered through scientific inquiry. To his credit, Sternberg has attempted to gather data to support his theory. His studies show that scores on tests of tacit knowledge often correlate positively with job performance (see Sternberg et al., 2000, for a thorough review). However, this is rather weak evidence in support of the theory because in every step of the tests' creation, they are designed to be customized for the job, and every attempt is made to maximize the correlation between test scores and job performance. If they do correlate better with job success than an IQ score, then that is an artificial consequence of test construction and not because of any predictive power of practical intelligence.

On the other hand, it is impressive that IQ correlates with many non-academic variables because intelligence tests are not explicitly designed to correlate these measures. There is an abundance of evidence (spanning over a century of psychological research) that general intelligence or g – as measured

---

[1] This fact has profound theoretical importance because the NFL is the ideal environment to identify a practical intelligence. The job environment of NFL players bears no resemblance to academic environments, and most or all of the training and knowledge about how to successfully play football is picked up through experience and practical training. The NFL has a very strong incentive to identify any non-g abilities that help players succeed on the field because the league's teams are in intense competition with one another and any slight edge in selecting high performing players can result in major financial advantages.

by IQ scores – does help a person function in many environments and in many jobs (see Chapters 22 and 24). Sternberg ignores all this information and instead clings to a small handful of idiosyncratic studies (many of which are unpublished and not peer reviewed) demonstrating that job performance correlates more strongly with scores on extremely context-specific practical intelligence tests than with IQ scores (Gottfredson, 2001). None of these studies favoring practical intelligence has been replicated, whereas studies showing how *g* can predict job performance and other life outcomes have decades of replications.

THEORETICAL PROBLEMS WITH PRACTICAL INTELLIGENCE

To find evidence supporting this claim that practical intelligence is important for helping a person learn the tacit knowledge needed to succeed in their environment, Sternberg and his colleagues often study the context of a group of people to determine what knowledge is important in their environment and then create a test of practical intelligence based on this information. Often, this new test of tacit knowledge will correlate with success in the environment (e.g., job success), and Sternberg sees this as supporting his theory (e.g., Grigorenko et al., 2001; Sternberg et al., 2001; Wagner & Sternberg, 1985). Sternberg then argues (e.g., Wagner & Sternberg, 1985) that the non-academic learning ability needed to become successful in one environment (as a bank manager, for example) is the same as the skills needed to be successful in another environment (e.g., as an academic psychologist). However, there is no reason why *g* cannot help people succeed in both environments, and Sternberg has not shown that a person moved from one environment/job to another will use the same non-*g* ability to learn the tacit knowledge needed to succeed in both environments.

The claim that practical intelligence is the same across contexts is often taken to absurd levels when comparing different measures of practical intelligence. For example, in one early study, a test of practical intelligence for managers at large corporations asked examinees to rate 11 different incentives for pursuing a career in management, including "I think my abilities are a good match to this career choice," "I enjoy working with people," and "I want to lead others but not be led by others" (Wagner & Sternberg, 1985, p. 458). However, for a test of practical intelligence for children in rural Kenya one question was:

Your younger mother (i.e., the co-wife of the mother) visited your mother's house and sat for some time, while your mother fed your baby brother. Now they have gone and you are alone with him; he is crying a lot and has stomachache.

(1) What do you think he is suffering from?
    i. Mosquitoes have bitten him.
    ii. He has eaten rotten food.
    iii. He has worms in the stomach.

iv. He is affected by the evil eye (*sihoho*).
v. He has eaten food restricted by food taboos (*ichiema mokwero*).
(Sternberg et al., 2001, p. 408)

Astonishingly, Sternberg and his team stated that any answer is correct, except the first option. Thus, believing in superstitions (e.g., that a child can be sickened by the evil eye or breaking a food taboo) is a sign of practical intelligence in this population, according to Sternberg and his colleagues. While the last two options might be considered correct in this rural African culture, using this tacit knowledge (gathered via practical intelligence) to apply a remedy is unlikely to cure a sick baby. It might even harm the child. Yet this behavior would supposedly be an exercise of practical intelligence that helps a person succeed in their environment. Somehow, this is the same practical intelligence that would help a person become a successful manager in an American company!

These examples demonstrate an inherent problem with practical intelligence: it is context-specific, but must also apply across contexts (Gottfredson, 2003a, 2003b). In her withering critique of practical intelligence theory, Gottfredson (2003a) called this a "heads-I-win-tails-you-lose" strategy because if results showed that practical intelligence applied to multiple contexts, then it supports the theory; if results showed that practical intelligence was context-specific, then it supports the theory, too. This makes the theory unfalsifiable – and therefore unscientific (Gottfredson, 2003a).[2] In practice, Sternberg and his colleagues (2000, Chapter 10) explicitly stated that it is necessary to create tests that measure the fruits of practical intelligence for each individual job. This shows the context-specific nature of practical intelligence and precludes it from being a general ability the way g is (assuming practical intelligence exists at all).

Another theoretical problem with practical intelligence is that Sternberg's description of what practical intelligence does is extremely similar to the mainstream view of g's function, and it is not clear how the two really differ. Recall from the Introduction that many scholars believe that intelligence "is not merely book learning, a narrow academic skill, or test-taking smarts. Rather, it reflects a broader and deeper capability for comprehending our surroundings – 'catching on,' 'making sense' of things, or 'figuring out' what to do" (Gottfredson, 1997a, p. 13). Compare that with Sternberg's definition that "Practical intelligence is what most people call common sense. It is the ability to adapt to, shape, and select everyday environments" (Sternberg et al., 2000, p. xi), and that "Practical ability involves implementing ideas; it is the ability involved when intelligence is applied to real world contexts" (Sternberg et al., 2000, p. 31). These similar definitions do not prove that the mainstream view of general intelligence and Sternberg's practical intelligence are the same ability.

---

[2] For the importance of falsifiability as a characteristic of a scientific theory, see Chapter 5.

However, they do put the burden of proof on Sternberg to explain why the functions of practical intelligence are not (or cannot be) performed by g.[3] If practical intelligence really is a separate ability, then it is necessary to describe why g cannot or does not also solve real-life problems or help people function in their environment outside school (Gottfredson, 2003a). So far, the results have been unconvincing (Hunt, 2011, pp. 215–216).

If practical intelligence and g are truly separate, then Sternberg must also solve a basic evolutionary problem: it is not clear how a separate academic intelligence that is only useful in school environments would evolve. Traits can only evolve in an environment in which they are useful for surviving. However, academic environments did not exist for the vast majority of humans' evolutionary history. So, any intelligence that is unique to academic environments must have evolved after much of humanity started attending school, but that is not enough time for a new psychological ability to have developed.[4] Sternberg has failed to reconcile his theory with this basic tenet of evolutionary theory.

CONCLUSION

Ironically, every attribute Sternberg has claimed for practical intelligence actually is an attribute of g. Unlike practical intelligence, g is real (see Chapters 1 and 3), important for functioning in everyday life (see Chapters 22 and 24), and applicable across contexts (see Chapter 4). Conversely, the claims that Sternberg makes about g – that it is a narrow ability, solely useful in academic settings, or a trivial ability – are only believable if one ignores (or is not aware of) over a hundred years of research on intelligence (Gottfredson, 2003a; Ree & Earles, 1993). In claiming that practical intelligence exists and is at least as important as g, Sternberg has advanced an argument that is at odds with a century of data about the importance of g outside academic settings.[5]

Where does this leave people with high intelligence but poor skills on the job or in everyday life? Most psychologists just chalk this up to the fact that IQ does not correlate perfectly with other traits (e.g., $r \neq 1.0$) and that other,

---

[3] Sternberg – and not proponents of g – has this burden of proof because of the scientific principle of parsimony, which is that if two competing explanations for a phenomenon both have equally good explanatory power, then the simpler explanation is to be preferred (see Chapter 29). Because g theory requires only one ability, and the triarchic theory requires both academic intelligence and practical intelligence, g theory is favored by default unless Sternberg can show that practical intelligence is required to improve the explanatory power over g theory.

[4] The alternative is to argue that evolution knew in advance that humans would one day need an academic ability to succeed in school. However, this is impossible because (a) evolution has no conscious mind and cannot know anything, and (b) evolution cannot prepare a species for an environment that does not exist yet.

[5] See also Gottfredson (2003a, pp. 379–392; 2003b) and Hunt (2008) for examples of Sternberg's penchant for cherry picking data that supports his claims.

non-cognitive traits are important for success in everyday life (such as motivation or personality). As a result, exceptions to the general trend are inevitable. It is not necessary to claim that there is another intelligence at work in the human mind. Indeed, the evidence is very scarce that there is any general cognitive ability besides g, though there are many other abilities in Stratum I and Stratum II in both the CHC and bifactor models (see the Introduction).

MEASURING INTELLIGENCE

Most non-experts know little about the research on human intelligence – but many have heard of intelligence tests and IQ scores. The tests appear in TV shows, movies, and books, and the scores are included in educational records. And almost everyone knows that to have a "low IQ" is an insult.[1]

Despite this general awareness of intelligence tests, there are several myths about them. Perhaps these myths exist because intelligence tests are often shrouded in secrecy to keep test content confidential and prevent cheating. And some incorrect ideas of intelligence tests arise because some of the misunderstandings treated elsewhere in the book (e.g., Chapters 11, 21, 22, 28–30) are connected to test scores and their interpretations.

The four chapters in this section are not a comprehensive explanation of intelligence tests. Rather, they touch upon four incorrect claims that are often made about intelligence tests:

- Intelligence is difficult to measure (Chapter 7).
- The questions on intelligence tests are trivial and therefore cannot measure something as important as intelligence (Chapter 8).
- Because intelligence tests are imperfect, research based on IQ scores cannot be trusted (Chapter 9).
- Intelligence tests are biased against racially diverse populations (Chapter 10).

All four of these ideas have been around for decades. While it is a little depressing that people still have incorrect beliefs after all these years, there is a benefit: there has been a lot of research investigating – and debunking – these ideas. In this section, I will explain why these widely held beliefs are incorrect.

---

[1] Some people prefer the term "IQ tests," but I do not. As Geisinger (2019) stated, the tests do not measure IQ. Rather, they measure intelligence and produce a score called the IQ. A test should be named after the trait it is designed to measure – not the score it produces.

Hopefully, you will see why one prominent psychologist of the twentieth century wrote:

The measurement of intelligence is psychology's most telling accomplishment to date. Without intending to belittle other psychological ventures, it may be fairly said that nowhere else – not in psychotherapy, educational reform, or consumer research – has there arisen so potent an instrument as the objective measure of intelligence. (Herrnstein, 1971, p. 45)

7

Measuring Intelligence Is Difficult

> Equally challenging [as defining intelligence] has been finding ways of measuring intelligence.
>
> (Pastorino & Doyle-Portillo, 2016, p. 328)

> Given the variety of approaches to the components of intelligence, it is not surprising that measuring intelligence has proved challenging.
>
> (R. S. Feldman, 2015, p. 270)

The two quotes above come from introductory psychology textbooks, and the authors clearly believe that intelligence is difficult to measure. If this belief is true, then the intelligence testing enterprise is fraught with uncertainty, and any interpretations of IQ scores are tentative at best (and misleading at worst). As a result, people who believe that intelligence is difficult to measure also often believe that intelligence research is not trustworthy.

In reality, these textbook authors are completely wrong. Intelligence is extremely easy to measure because – as stated in the Introduction – *any* task that requires some degree of cognitive work or judgment measures intelligence (Jensen, 1998). All of these tasks correlate positively with one another and measure *g* (see Chapter 1). As a result, all it takes to measure intelligence is to administer at least one task (preferably more) that requires cognitive work; the resulting score is an estimate of the examinee's intelligence level.

(ACCIDENTALLY) MEASURING INTELLIGENCE

Intelligence is so easy to measure that some people have created tests with the intention of measuring another trait or ability and accidentally created a test to measure intelligence instead. Chapter 1 already gave two examples of this occurring: the Cognitive Assessment System (CAS) and the Cognitive Abilities Measurement (CAM) battery. Both the CAS and CAM were designed to measure cognitive processes – not *g*. But they still measure *g* anyway (Keith et al., 2001; Stauffer et al., 1996).

It should not be completely surprising if tests of "cognitive processes" measure *g* because intelligence is the ability to solve problems, which is clearly a cognitive process. But other psychological tests measure *g*, even though that was not their creators' intention. For example, a popular test of moral reasoning, called the Defining Issues Test (DIT), is designed to measure moral development and reasoning in examinees. Yet the test correlates with measures of verbal intelligence (Sanders, Lubinski, & Benbow, 1995). The best evidence indicates that examinees reason about the questions on the DIT, even though the test's content does not relate to academic topics. Even studies designed to demonstrate the integrity of the DIT as a measure of moral development show that DIT scores are moderately good measures of verbal intelligence (e.g., Derryberry, Jones, Grieve, & Barger, 2007), though DIT scores are not completely interchangeable with IQ scores.[2]

The accidental creation of intelligence tests does not just happen in psychology. Gottfredson (2004) described how the National Adult Literacy Survey (NALS) functions as a test of intelligence. The NALS is designed to measure reading comprehension, but NALS scores have the same pattern of correlations with life outcomes that intelligence test scores have.[3] Moreover, factor analysis of NALS data shows that the items produce just one general factor,[4] which is exactly what happens when intelligence tests are subjected to factor analysis. When the staff and researchers at the US Department of Education created the NALS as a measure of adult literacy, they did not intend for NALS scores to mimic intelligence test scores so closely. But they do nonetheless, and NALS scores can function as proxies for IQ scores (e.g., Gottfredson, 1997b). As a result, the interpretation of low NALS scores as being a product of low literacy is insufficient. In reality, the deficits of people with low NALS scores extend beyond low literacy because the scores are a manifestation of low general intelligence (Humphreys, 1988).

Even more specific than a literacy test like the NALS is the Test of Functional Health Literacy of Adults (TOFHLA), a short test that measures examinees' ability to comprehend health-related texts, such as doctor's orders and

[2] The traditional interpretation of the correlation between DIT scores and IQ scores is that some level of cognitive development is necessary for moral development and that it is therefore natural for smarter people to be more moral. However, the DIT asks people to reason about moral issues; it does not require examinees to actually act morally. It is possible that high scorers on the DIT are smart, immoral reprobates. The simpler interpretation of DIT scores is that smarter people are better able to solve the moral dilemmas presented in the DIT. Whether that reasoning translates into moral behavior is not something that the DIT, by itself, can reveal.

[3] See Chapter 22 for the life outcome variables that are correlated with intelligence test scores.

[4] The NALS produces a single factor, despite the intention of the developers to create a test with three factors. Scores from the three NALS subscales all correlate between .89 and .92, a clear indication that all three subscales measure the same trait (Reder, 1998).

prescription instructions. Just like the NALS, the TOFHLA functions in exactly the same way that an intelligence scale does. TOFHLA scores correlate with traditional intelligence test scores ($r = .53$ to $.74$) and measure a general ability, even after controlling for a person's years of education, quality of education, occupational prestige, age, race, and gender (Apolinario, Mansur, Carthery-Goulart, Brucki, & Nitrini, 2014; Gottfredson, 2004). Moreover, the pattern of TOFHLA correlations with health outcomes mimics the correlations between IQ scores and health outcomes (Gottfredson, 2004). In fact, these results have led some researchers to suggest that "health literacy" is nothing more than *g* manifested in a health-care setting (Reeve & Basalik, 2014). The fact that the TOFHLA material is strictly related to health-care information and intelligence tests are more general in content is irrelevant.

These facts are surprising to many people. A test question that requires examinees to read a prescription label (like the TOFHLA) or a bus schedule (like the NALS) appears to have little in common with the tasks on traditional intelligence tests, which often require little – if any – reading. The reason why these other tests can function like intelligence tests is that the surface content of a test is *not* what determines the trait that a test measures. Rather, the mental abilities or functions that a test requires examinees to use are what determines what the test measures (Gottfredson & Saklofske, 2009; Warne, Yoon, & Price, 2014). Because intelligence is such a general ability, many different tasks require examinees to use their intelligence. As a result, a wide variety of test question formats can measure intelligence – even if these tests do not resemble each other at all. Lubinski and Humphreys recognized that these tests can take many different forms and have different labels when they wrote, "Many psychological measures with different names and distinct items (such as academic ability, aptitude, scholastic ability, scholastic achievement) can, and often do, measure essentially the same thing" (Lubinski & Humphreys, 1997, p. 163).

THE INDIFFERENCE OF THE INDICATOR

The fact that the CAS, CAM, DIT, NALS, TOFHLA, and many more tests all measure intelligence is more evidence for the indifference of the indicator. This was a concept that Charles Spearman (1927, pp. 197–198) proposed (see Chapter 1). Today, the evidence is overwhelming that he was right that any task that requires cognitive effort or work measures *g*, regardless of the task appearance (Cucina & Howardson, 2017; Jensen, 1998). It is because of the indifference of the indicator that scores on different tests are positively correlated – they all measure intelligence. In fact, tasks don't even have to appear on an intelligence test for people to use their intelligence to respond (Gordon, 1997; Gottfredson, 1997b; Lubinski & Humphreys, 1997).

Although the indifference of the indicator is widely accepted as fact among intelligence researchers, it is a concept that is poorly understood outside the field. Many individuals who try to analyze tests by the surface content produce incomplete or incorrect interpretations of intelligence test data. For example, some individuals (e.g., Helms, 1992; K. Richardson, 2002) have claimed that intelligence tests do not measure reasoning ability at all, but instead measure culturally specific knowledge that is acquired through formal schooling or exposure to certain cultural experiences. While this interpretation could be viable for information items and vocabulary items, it cannot explain why these tasks correlate with test formats that have no apparent cultural content (e.g., matrix reasoning tests) and reaction time tasks. This interpretation also does not explain why items with cultural content correlate with biological variables (see Chapter 3).

Another consequence of a poor understanding of the indifference of the indicator is that it leads to misinterpretations of test scores. For example, most law schools try to select students with the highest scores on the Law School Admission Test (LSAT). After finishing their education, law school graduates must pass a bar exam to practice law. Both tests are designed to measure reasoning ability, though bar exams' content is drawn from legal principles and information (Bonner, 2006; Bonner & D'Agostino, 2012) and LSAT content is more general and abstract. Both tests correlate with one another (Kuncel & Hezlett, 2007) and are measures – at least partially – of g. Law schools often publish their students' passing rates on the bar exam as evidence of the quality of education they provide. But they are largely ignoring the fact that bar exam passing rates are, to an extent, the consequence of the intelligence level of students that the law school enrolled. (That is, schools that select smarter students, as judged by LSAT scores, have higher bar passing rates.) Therefore, ranking law schools on the basis of bar exam passing rates is largely an exercise in ranking schools by the intelligence level of their students. A similar misinterpretation happens when K-12 schools are ranked by the average test score on the end-of-year academic achievement tests. A higher score does not indicate a better school (or better teachers) because these tests are mostly measuring students' g levels. It is likely that some schools with lackluster test scores have dedicated teachers, good funding, and superb educational programs; likewise, high test scores at some schools are likely to be just a product of the high levels of intelligence that the student body would exhibit in almost any typical educational environment. Thus, interpretations of test scores that are widespread in the accountability movement or in college rankings probably do not reflect educational quality to the extent that policy makers, legislators, or educators believe because these groups do not realize that the tests are measuring g.

The indifference of the indicator has an important implication about g. Because test item content and appearance do not matter when measuring g, the nature of g is independent of any test item. In other words, g is not a product of test design. Instead, test questions elicit g by encouraging people to demonstrate the behaviors that are caused by g, such as abstract problem solving and engaging in complex cognitive work (Jensen, 1980a). There is no known test that measures cognitive abilities without also measuring *g*, and even test creators who attempt to minimize the influence of *g* and emphasize broad Stratum II abilities fail in their attempts and end up creating tests that mostly measure *g* (Canivez & Youngstrom, 2019).

LENGTHY TESTING NOT NEEDED

Traditional intelligence tests, such as a Stanford–Binet or a Wechsler test, take approximately 90-120 minutes to administer. Many group battery tests of intelligence, such as the SAT, take a few hours. As a result, there is the impression that measuring intelligence is a long, drawn-out testing process. There is value in using a lengthy test to measure intelligence, but often it is not needed. This is because one of the reasons intelligence is easy to measure is that it produces highly stable scores very quickly.

The technical term for the stability of scores is called *reliability*. High reliability is vital for any score that supposedly measures a stable trait like intelligence. If scores have poor reliability, then it means that either (1) the trait is not stable, or (2) the scores fluctuate too much to provide a useful measure of the trait. Poor reliability also depresses correlations and makes them artificially closer to zero. That means it is harder to identify a correlation for a score with low reliability (R. M. Kaplan & Saccuzzo, 2018).

Reliability is usually measured on a scale from 0 (corresponding to purely random scores) and 1 (for scores with perfect stability, which is not possible). The desired level of reliability depends on how scores will be used. If scores are not to be used to impact examinees' lives, or if the decisions are temporary and/or easily reversible, then lower reliability is acceptable. For high-stakes situations, though, reliability should be much higher. A common rule of thumb is that reliability should be at least .70 for scores that will only be used for research purposes. Reliability of .85 or .90 might be necessary for diagnostic purposes. And when scores are to be used for a decision that is extremely important and/or irrevocable – like whether someone is mentally competent to be stand trial – then reliability should be at least .97.

By itself, a single intelligence test item produces a score that is not reliable: only about .25 (Lubinski, 2004; Lubinski & Humphreys, 1997). This means that a score on a 1-item test is too unstable to be useful. However, when items are combined, the total reliability based on those items increases.[5] With 7 items, score reliability increases to .70 – good enough for research purposes. An intelligence test with 12 items has an estimated reliability of .80. And it only takes 27 items (about the length of a single-subject academic test for children) to

---

[5] This is because the randomness from each individual item is not cumulative. Instead, the randomness cancels out as items are combined to form a single test score (Allen & Yen, 1979; R. M. Kaplan & Saccuzzo, 2018).

reach reliability of .90. Thus, it does not take many questions on an intelligence test to produce reliable scores – another way that intelligence is not a difficult trait to measure.

These numbers show that – generally – longer tests produce more reliable scores.[6] But this relationship is not regular. At higher levels of reliability, it takes more items to produce small increases in reliability. To raise reliability from .90 to .95 requires a test to expand from 27 items to 57 items. Reliability of .97 requires 97 items, while reliability values of .98 and .99 require 147 and 297 items, respectively. This is why tests of g that are used to make very important decisions (e.g., college admissions, diagnosing a disability) tend to be very long. Still, a 297-item test is not unreasonable. Examinees would need to take breaks, and perhaps the test would be spread across multiple testing sessions, but a 297-item test is still shorter than some other tests in psychology.

CAVEATS

There is one important caveat to this discussion: while any cognitive task measures g to some extent, different tasks are often not equally good at measuring intelligence. In other words, some are better measures of g than others (Jensen, 1980b, 1985). Matrix reasoning and vocabulary knowledge tasks are extremely good measures of intelligence, which is why they appear on many intelligence tests. Other tasks are not as good, such as maze tests (e.g., Porteus, 1915), which require examinees to complete a two-dimensional maze without errors. These maze tests used to appear on some intelligence tests, but they were a much poorer measure of g compared to other question formats that are widely available. As a result, maze tasks have been eliminated from most tests and are no longer in widespread use.

Another caveat to remember is that professional test development consists of more than just writing and administering items (Schmeiser & Welch, 2006). Although writing items that measure g is not difficult (especially when a test creator uses formats that have been shown to measure g well), it takes a lot of training and work to create an intelligence test that is good enough for professional use. The professional standards of test creation – established by the American Educational Research Association (AERA), American Psychological Association, and the National Council on Measurement in Education (2014) – are complex and must be met for ethical testing practices to occur.

---

[6] There are modern test creation and score calculation methods that can produce highly reliable scores with fewer items (see Embretson, 1996; Embretson & Reise, 2000). The calculations here are based on the Spearman–Brown formula (Brown, 1910; Spearman, 1910) and the assumption that a score based on a single item has reliability of .25.

CONCLUSION

Nonetheless, because of the indifference of the indicator and the fact that high reliability does not take many test items, it is not true that intelligence is difficult to measure. In fact, intelligence is incredibly easy to measure. K-12 school accountability tests, licensing tests for jobs, college admissions tests, spelling bees, driver's license tests, and many other tests are all measures of g – though many measure other abilities also (e.g., job knowledge, memorization). And they are not equally good measures of g.

Ranking examinees on these tests from highest score to lowest score will produce a rank order that is similar to a rank order based on the IQ scores or level of g of the same examinees. Thus, compared to other psychological traits, measuring intelligence is relatively easy. It is likely that most readers have taken a test that measures intelligence without realizing it.

8

The Content of Intelligence Tests Is Trivial and Cannot Measure Intelligence

> The first subtest the child encounters [on the WISC-III] is picture completion . . . For example, an item might depict a lamp, and the child would be required to glean that the light bulb is missing. As items progress in difficulty, so too do the missing details increase in irrelevant minutiae . . . Why should the ability to notice these missing details be considered intelligent behavior?
>
> (Kwate, 2001, p. 229)

> . . . the tasks featured in the IQ test are decidedly microscopic, are often unrelated to one another, and seemingly represent a "shotgun" approach to the assessment of human intellect. The tasks are remote, in many cases, from everyday life.
>
> (Gardner, 2011, p. 19)

Imagine that you are a parent whose child is being evaluated by a school psychologist to determine if the child should be placed in special education classes. You sit in the corner of the room behind your child as the school psychologist sits at a table with your child. After a few minutes of chatting with your child, the school psychologist engages them in a series of simple tasks and questions:

> "I want you to count backwards for me from 20 to 1."
> "What's the thing for you to do when you have broken something which belongs to someone else?"
> "I am going to name two things which are alike in some way, and I want you to tell me how they are alike. Wood and coal: in what way are they alike? An apple and a peach?"
> "What is a soldier?"
> "What does 'scorch' mean?"

After more than an hour of this, the testing ends. A few days later, you get the results from the psychologist. They believe that your child's intelligence is substantially below average and that the child belongs in special education classes. You are not sure you agree with the school psychologist. Although they appeared competent, you are skeptical because the questions and tasks seemed more like games and trivia questions than any serious evaluation of your child. The testing seemed superficial and unrelated to much of what happens in school.

In reality, the example items were part of the 1916 version of the Stanford–Binet intelligence test (Terman, 1916) and were designed for typical 8-year-olds at the time. While these test items are no longer in use, many modern intelligence tests have similar questions and tasks. Skeptics like Kwate (2001) and Gardner (2011) do not believe that such trivial tasks can measure something as important and complex as intelligence. Indeed, the impression that some of the items resemble games is accurate: some early intelligence test creators were inspired by children's games and activities when they created some subtests (Gibbons & Warne, 2019).

In a way, the skeptics are correct. When they administer a test, psychologists are not really interested in whether an examinee can define words, count backwards, explain how two objects are similar, perform on a digit span task, or solve a matrix problem. The reason these tasks appear on intelligence tests is that they are manifestations of intelligence – not intelligence itself. In other words,

> most psychologists are no more interested in digit span than a physician is intrinsically interested in oral temperature. What these scientific practitioners are interested in are the correlates and the causes of individual differences assessed by these measures, because this network enables them to generate many more valid inferences than if they were ignorant of their client's status on these dimensions. (Lubinski & Benbow, 1995, p. 936)

To elaborate on Lubinski and Benbow's analogy, a person's performance on an intelligence subtest is a symptom of a person's intelligence level. By systematically examining the collection of these symptoms, a psychologist can infer how intelligent an examinee is. Thus, it is not the tasks themselves – trivial as they appear – that matter. Instead, these tasks are part of intelligence tests because they give clues into an examinee's broader abstract reasoning and intelligence.

EVIDENCE THAT COGNITIVE TASKS MEASURE INTELLIGENCE

The evidence is strong that Lubinski and Benbow (1995) are correct that intelligence test tasks provide insight into *g*. The evidence comes from multiple sources, but I will focus on two in this chapter. The first is the results of factor analysis, while the second is how the subtests on intelligence test scores correlate with other variables.

Earlier chapters and the Introduction have discussed factor analysis extensively, and the results from factor analysis often indicate that the items on intelligence tests indeed measure a global mental ability.

Chapter 1 explained that any assortment of cognitive tasks will form a general intelligence factor. As a result, any task that engages thought or cognitive effort will relate to *g* in some way.[1] Yes, some of these tasks will appear trivial, but they all relate to *g*. No one has *ever* found a cognitive task that has a correlation of zero with *g*.

But factor analysis alone is not enough to demonstrate that an item, subtest, or test measures intelligence. After all, factors are nothing more than groups of variables that correlate with one another. To establish that a test really measures intelligence, there must be evidence that test scores correlate with variables outside the test that are theorized to also be manifestations of intelligence (Kane, 2006, 2013). In technical language, these manifestations are called *criteria* (singular: *criterion*). From the earliest days of the field, test creators knew that a test score is useless if it does not correlate with or predict the criteria of real-life behavior. This requirement is an important part of *validity*, which is the degree to which a test score can be interpreted as measuring a psychological trait. The need for validity is why Sir Francis Galton examined whether there was a relationship between his measures of intelligence (e.g., head size, visual acuity, reaction time) and the criteria of education level and social class. Galton believed that smarter people would also be better educated and belong to a higher social class. When Galton did not find a correlation between his measures of intelligence and these criteria, he abandoned his measures of intelligence.

The next generation of intelligence test creators followed the same strategy of verifying that their tests measured intelligence. Alfred Binet's criterion for his test score was whether the examinee was struggling in school (Binet & Simon, 1905/1916). When there was a correlation between Binet's test score and the criterion, he understood this (correctly) as evidence that his test measured intelligence. Some of the tasks on Binet's test indeed appeared trivial. For example, he tested whether children recognized that a piece of chocolate was food and a similarly sized wooden block was not. Another task on Binet's original test required a child to determine which of two boxes of identical size and shape was heavier. Binet also asked children to generate words that rhymed with a word he gave them. The superficial appearance of these tasks did not matter. What mattered was how well the score they produced correlated with Binet's criterion. In fact, a few tasks from Binet's original test correlate so well with relevant criteria that similar items are still on intelligence tests today (Gibbons & Warne, 2019).

Later test creators followed Galton's and Binet's lead in investigating whether intelligence test scores correlated with criteria. Because intelligence tests are most often used in schools, many of these criteria are educational in nature. IQ scores correlate positively with grade-point averages (Coyle, 2015),

---

[1] This is Spearman's (1927) principle of the "indifference of the indicator," a topic discussed in Chapters 1 and 7.

performance on standardized educational tests (Deary, Strand, Smith, & Fernandes, 2007), the number of years of education in adulthood (Damian, Su, Shanahan, Trautwein, & Roberts, 2015), adult socioeconomic status (Deary, Taylor, et al., 2005), and being labeled as gifted (Wechsler, 2014). For a bunch of items that seem trivial, this is impressive.[2] To argue that items on intelligence tests are too superficial to measure intelligence, one also has to argue that these educational criteria are also unrelated to intelligence, despite the fact that they are correlated with IQ scores – a hard argument to make. Even prominent modern critics of *g* concede that educational success requires the skills needed to perform well on an intelligence test.

Apart from the importance for showing that intelligence tests measure *g*, the correlations between IQ scores and educational outcomes are important in their own right because they can be used for making predictions. Even if one does not believe in the existence of *g*, it is still possible to make predictions about a child's educational future based on an intelligence test score,[3] despite the fact that much of the material on many intelligence tests is not explicitly taught in school. These scores can still help teachers and other school personnel know which children will need extra help or which are prepared for advanced course work.

CONCLUSION

The belief that intelligence test items are too trivial to measure a complex ability like intelligence implies that a person can ascertain what a test measures just by reading the test questions. In discussing this implication, one intelligence expert wrote:

Like reading tea leaves, critics list various superficialities of test content and format to assert, variously, that IQ tests measure only an aptness with paper-and-pencil tasks, a narrow academic ability, familiarity with the tester's culture, facility with well-defined tasks with unambiguous answers, and so on. Not only are these inferences unwarranted, but their premises about content and format are often wrong. In actuality, most items on individually administered batteries require neither paper nor pencil, most are not timed, many do not use numbers or words or other academic-seeming content, and many require knowledge only of the most elementary concepts (up-down, large-small, etc.). (Gottfredson, 2009, p. 29)

Ascertaining what a test really measures requires more than just reading the items and making a subjective judgment. Indeed, this strategy for understanding test functioning is practically useless, and has been recognized as such for over 100 years. As Terman and his colleagues (1917, p. 135) stated, "The

---

[2] Chapters 22–24 will discuss non-educational criteria that correlate with intelligence test scores.
[3] Indeed, any time a correlation exists between two variables, it is possible to predict one from the other. The stronger the correlation is (i.e., the closer to -1.0 or +1.0), the more accurate those predictions will generally be (see Warne, 2018, Chapter 13).

classification and criticism of tests by mere inspection may form an interesting pastime, but it can hardly be taken seriously as a contribution to science" (see also Clarizio, 1979; Reschly, 1980).

Instead of armchair judgments, critics must use data from factor analysis and correlations with criteria to understand what a test measures. The evidence is overwhelming that these tests measure intelligence – and measure it well. While test items may seem unimportant, they are the "yardstick" that scientists use to measure intelligence. The "yardstick" of intelligence tests does not reflect the ability that they measure (Gottfredson, 2009). To say otherwise is like claiming that a thermometer does not measure temperature because a thermometer only appears to display the expansion of mercury in a glass tube.

Items that appear superficial can (and do) measure a complex cognitive ability. Indeed, because of Spearman's (1927) indifference of the indicator (see Chapters 1 and 7), the fact that items may appear trivial is irrelevant. What matters is the cognitive processes that people engage in to answer test items, and every cognitive task encourages examinees to demonstrate g to some extent.

9

Intelligence Tests Are Imperfect and Cannot Be Used or Trusted

> Standardized tests . . . are too limited, too imprecise, and too easily misunderstood to form the basis of crucial decisions about students.
>
> (D. W. Miller, 2001, p. A14)

> . . . talent is great, but *tests* of talent stink. There's certainly an argument to be made that tests of talent – and tests of anything else psychologists study . . . are highly imperfect.
>
> (Duckworth, 2016, p. 34, emphasis in original)

Nothing in this world is perfect, and that includes intelligence tests. Though they are a useful tool for a variety of purposes, intelligence tests – and other tests that measure *g* – sometimes produce inaccurate scores for individual examinees. And inaccurate scores can lead to incorrect decisions. Sometimes the consequences of using an inaccurate test score can have a lasting impact on an examinee, such as in college admissions testing, diagnosing a disability, or employee selection or promotion. Under extreme circumstances, test score accuracy can be a matter of life and death. After the US Supreme Court ruled that executing someone with an intellectual disability was unconstitutional in 2002 (*Atkins v. Virginia*), accurately estimating the IQ score of an inmate with an intellectual disability can save that person's life.

The question is not whether intelligence tests are perfect – everyone agrees that they have flaws. Rather, the misconception I address in this chapter is that intelligence tests (and other measures of *g*) are so flawed that they cannot be used for research or practical decision making. In this chapter, I show that intelligence tests are good enough for these purposes.

MEASURING SCORE IMPERFECTIONS

Professional test creators – called *psychometricians* – have long been aware that no test is a perfect tool for measuring the trait that it is designed to measure. This awareness is summed up in the fundamental equation of the scientific field of testing:

$$X = T + E$$

In this equation, X is the score that a person obtains on a test. T is the examinee's actual level of the trait being measured, which is called *true score*. Finally, E stands for *error*, which is anything that influences a test score that is different from the trait that the examiner wants to measure (Allen & Yen, 1979; R. P. McDonald, 1999). While the equation appears simple, it has the profound implication that any observed score on a test is the result of a mix of the trait being measured and other, irrelevant influences (i.e., error). Test creators are very aware that their tests are imperfect and that score inaccuracies happen.[1] The goal of every psychometrician is to reduce error and maximize a test's ability to measure the true score of a person's trait.

Error can be positive (and boost a person's observed score) or negative (which would decrease a person's observed score). Positive error might arise from a lenient test scorer, a lucky guess on a test question, or other favorable circumstances. Negative error may result from a hungry examinee, a stressful event on the way to the testing location, or a distracting environment. Across test items, test versions, administration times, settings, etc., error is theorized to be random.[2] As such, it cancels out across test items because the positive error and the negative error counteract each other. When a test is designed to minimize error, this cancelling out can happen very quickly and consistently.

This cancelling out was apparent in the section in Chapter 7 about reliability. Error is the source of score instability, which means that high consistency requires low error in a test score. Chapter 7 also showed that reliability increases (and, therefore, error decreases) as test length increases. A reliability value of 1 is an unobtainable ideal because it would unrealistically indicate that error somehow does not influence the observed score on a test.

Most intelligence tests tend to produce scores with high reliability. As an example, the ACT produces scores that have a reliability value of 0.94 (ACT, Inc., 2017, Table 10.1). The overall SAT score has similar reliability value of .96 (College Board, 2017, Table A-6.2). Because many colleges and universities use this score to decide who is admitted (a hugely important decision for applicants), this high reliability value is important. On the other hand, in one study I did on how adolescents solve difficult cognitive test items, the reliability values ranged from .681 to .886 (Warne et al., 2016), but because the test scores were only used in a research setting, this lower reliability was acceptable.

---

[1] This concept is so fundamental that in my undergraduate class on psychological testing, I teach this as part of the very first lesson on test theory.

[2] Non-random error does occur, and is a serious concern among testing experts. Test bias, a topic of discussion in Chapter 10, is an example of non-random error.

TABLE 9.1 *Standard error of measurement (SEM) of IQ scores, given reliability values*

Reliability value	SEM
0.00	± 15.0 points
0.50	± 10.6 points
0.70	± 8.2 points
0.80	± 6.7 points
0.85	± 5.8 points
0.90	± 4.7 points
0.95	± 3.4 points
0.98	± 2.1 points
0.99	± 1.5 points
1.00	± 0.0 points

Note. SEM values are calculated using the formula $SEM = \sigma\sqrt{1 - r_{xx'}}$, where σ is the 15-point standard deviation of IQ scores and $r_{xx'}$ is the reliability value.

Because error is random, reliability is a measurement of how consistent observed scores are across time points, test versions, test questions, etc. Reliability statistics can be used to estimate the range of scores we can expect if an examinee retakes a test, which is called the standard error of measurement (SEM). In IQ points, where the average is 100 and the standard deviation (see the Introduction) is 15, Table 9.1 shows the SEM values for different reliability values.

In the table, notice how high reliability values are paired with low SEM values, which confirms that high reliability indicates high consistency (and therefore low error) in scores. But there is always some degree of error in scores, as long as reliability is not 1. Additionally, it is important to note that for reliability values that are typical for tests used to make decisions (about .85 or higher), test scores are fairly consistent.

DECISION ACCURACY

Thus, the critics of tests are correct that the tests are not perfect. But tests used for practical purposes tend to produce highly consistent data. As a result, the question is whether the tests are good enough to use as part of making decisions. The evidence is overwhelming that they are.

Academic tests produce highly consistent results. As an example, the psychometricians who create the ACT use their test scores to estimate whether or not examinees are "college ready" (defined as having at least a 50% chance of earning a B and a 75% chance of earning a C in a freshman-level college general education course). Across four subjects – English, mathematics, reading, and science – the accuracy of these classifications ranged from 85% to 89% (ACT, Inc., 2017, Table 10.4), an impressive level of correctness. It is unlikely that most humans (especially if they have not met a student) would be able to classify students' college readiness accurately 85–89% of the time.

The college admissions research also shows that to predict college grades, admissions test scores are about as accurate as high school grades (Zwick, 2007).[3] This does not mean that college admissions test scores are redundant, though. Combining both grades and test scores to make a prediction is better than using either alone. Therefore, high school grades and college admissions test scores provide information that the other does not. In addition to measuring knowledge, grades measure students' long-term behaviors and non-cognitive traits that lead to academic success (e.g., ability to meet deadlines, attention to assignment requirements). College admissions test scores measure g and also provide a common score that can be compared across high schools or state lines, which compensates for inconsistencies in grading systems (e.g., Warne, Nagaishi, Slade, Hermesmeyer, & Peck, 2014). Results are similarly impressive in hiring job applicants (see Chapter 23).

THE PERFECT AS THE ENEMY OF THE GOOD

These accuracy classification studies are impressive, but none reach 100% accuracy. Errors still occur, and they can have unfortunate consequences for examinees (Lubinski & Humphreys, 1996). However, this is not a reason to eliminate tests. The standard for usefulness is not whether the tests have perfect accuracy; rather, tests should be judged by whether they are more accurate than alternative decision-making strategies. Decades ago, when discussing using tests for selecting job applicants, Paterson (1938, pp. 44, 45) criticized the proposal to judge tests by the standard of perfect accuracy:

Strangely enough, those who demand perfect tests are the very ones who are complacent in the face of the far larger errors being committed daily in school and shop through sole reliance upon traditional methods … Our perfectionists however show another strange symptom. They survey with hypercritical eyes existing tests and measurements and find them wanting when tested by the severe standard of perfect validity … I refer to those who reject tests and measurements but parade before the public an array of guidance techniques that are far less reliable and valid. What is the reliability and validity of a guidance interview? Of an occupational pamphlet? Of a lad's earnest but misguided desire to study medicine?

Paterson (1938) also applied this logic to medicine and showed the absurdity of demanding perfection before intervening in people's lives. If medical tests and interventions must be perfect before replacing existing treatments, then no

---

[3] Given this fact, it is odd that critics of standardized tests do not also criticize grades for being too imperfect to use. Where are the proposals to eliminate the use of high school grades in the college admissions process?

medical advances would be possible at all. People demanding perfection from scientific tests and treatments are proposing unrealistic standards of perfection that would prevent any possible scientific progress or improvement in people's lives.

CONCLUSION

Thus, even though every intelligence test produces an imperfect score, the tests are still highly useful in making decisions. Indeed, demanding that the tests be perfect before they can be used is such an unrealistic standard that it would prevent any intelligence test from ever being used (Gottfredson, 2009). Holding any tool used for decision making to this standard would be the equivalent of banning the tool completely. For some critics of intelligence tests, that is probably the point.

Whether intelligence tests can be used to make decisions does not depend on whether the tests are perfect. Rather, whether to use a test for decision making depends on whether the test is better than alternative methods of decision making. The need to select individuals (for jobs, college admission, promotions, or gifted programs) does not magically disappear if tests are banned. Any time that the number of applicants exceeds the number of positions available, selection has to occur. If intelligence tests can make more accurate judgments than other tools – as is often the case – then the tests should be used whenever possible (especially in combination with other variables). Doing so will result in fewer errors, more fair selection, and more successful experiences in educational programs and jobs.

10

Intelligence Tests Are Biased against Diverse Populations

> It has already been established that standardized tests are biased and unfair to
> persons from [non-dominant] cultural and socio-cultural groups since most psy-
> chometric tests reflect largely white, middle class values and they do not reflect the
> experiences of and the linguistic, cognitive and cultural styles and values of
> minority or foreign groups.
>
> (Zindi, 2013, p. 164)

> The literature presents an abundance of data and criticism indicating that such
> [traditional intelligence] tests, standardized as they are on White middle-class
> norms, show bias in favor of Whites . . .
>
> (Harris & Ford, 1991, p. 6; see also Ford, 1995, p. 56)

Of the 35 misconceptions in this book, one of the most common is the belief that
intelligence tests are biased against African Americans, Hispanics, and Native
Americans. In one study of introductory psychology textbooks, this was the
most common inaccuracy that authors perpetuated (Warne et al., 2018).
Indeed, this belief often extends to academic tests and tests used for hiring
and promotion (Reeve & Charles, 2008). Because these tests also measure
g (see Chapter 7), it is unsurprising that people often believe that these tests,
too, are biased against diverse groups.

Like many incorrect beliefs discussed in this book, the idea that intelligence
tests are biased against diverse examinees is not completely unrealistic. Most of
these groups score – on average – lower on intelligence tests than examinees of
European descent (Gottfredson, 1997a; Neisser et al., 1996). Generally, within
the United States, European Americans have an average IQ of approximately
100, followed by Hispanic Americans and Native Americans (average IQ ≈ 90),
and African Americans scoring lowest (average IQ ≈ 85). Conversely, Asian
Americans tend to score higher than all other large racial groups (average
IQ ≈ 105). Given these differences, it is natural for some people to suspect

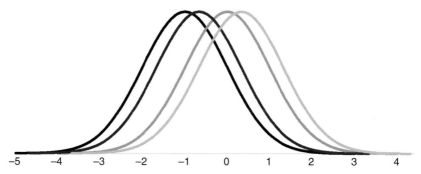

FIGURE 10.1 Distribution of IQ scores for the major American racial groups. Left to right, these are African Americans, Hispanics and Native Americans, European Americans, and Asian Americans. Note that there is a lot of overlap among the distributions and that people from all groups can be found at all IQ score levels.

that something is wrong with how the tests measure intelligence in examinees with Hispanic, Native American, or African ancestry.

It is important to note, though, that these are merely averages, and these numbers do not apply to every member of these groups. As Figure 10.1 shows, there is tremendous overlap among these groups, and it is possible to find people from every group at every intelligence level (Frisby, 2013; Gottfredson, 1997a). In other words, there are some people with low IQ scores who belong to groups with a higher average, and there are some people with high IQ scores who belong to a group with a lower average score. These group averages, therefore, often do not apply to particular individuals.

No one disputes that average IQ scores differ across racial groups, and this rank order of groups' averages is remarkably consistent across tests of *g* (Humphreys, 1988). The real dispute is over what causes these different mean scores. One proposed explanation for these average differences is that intelligence tests are not functioning correctly, and that the tests are biased against low-scoring examinees, thereby penalizing them and underestimating their true level of intelligence. (Chapters 28–30 will discuss other proposed causes of these mean group differences.) This belief that a fundamental problem with the test is the cause of these different average scores is at the core of the arguments that intelligence tests are biased against diverse examinees.

A PROFESSIONAL VIEW OF TEST BIAS

What Is Test Bias? In contrast to the widespread belief that intelligence tests are biased, the mainstream viewpoint among psychometricians and psychologists who use tests is that "the issue of test bias is scientifically dead" (Hunter & Schmidt, 2000, p. 151) and that professionally developed intelligence and academic tests are not biased against native English speakers who are born in the United States – regardless of their racial heritage (Reeve & Charles, 2008; Reynolds, 2000). Outside the United States, it is standard practice to design tests to be administered without bias in other multicultural societies, as long as examinees are born in that country and speak the test language as a native.

The reason that professional test creators and the public have opposite beliefs may stem from the different ways in which the two groups use the word "bias" (Kuncel & Hezlett, 2010; Reynolds & Lowe, 2009; Warne, Yoon, & Price, 2014). In everyday usage, "bias" is a synonym for "unfairness," and when one group scores higher than another, that can easily seem biased in the sense that it is unfair. But the statistical definition of bias is more complex. In the testing world, *bias occurs when two people with equal levels of a trait consistently obtain different scores solely because they belong to different groups.* For example, if men and women with the same intelligence level take an intelligence test, but women consistently receive scores 5 points higher solely because they are female, then test bias would be present. This is a much more nuanced definition of bias than the everyday definition.[1]

What Test Bias Is Not. The everyday definition of bias – though intuitive – is not adequate for scientific purposes for two reasons. The first is that what is fair or unfair is a value judgment. People with different ethical or moral values may have different opinions about what is fair (or unfair), and there is no scientific way to decide which values are best.

A second problem is that the existence of differences in average scores is not enough to prove that bias is present on a test because the score differences might reflect real differences in what the test measures (Clarizio, 1979; Frisby, 2013; Jensen, 1980a). In an example I have used before, imagine that a psychologist gives a test of job satisfaction to two groups: medical interns and tenured college professors. When the tests are scored, the medical interns received job satisfaction scores that were – on average – lower than the scores of tenured college professors.

A typical intern's schedule includes 80 hours of work per week, nights on call, and very stressful working conditions, while tenured university faculty have a great deal of work flexibility, high job security, and tend to enjoy their jobs. Under these circumstances, the professors *should* outscore the medical interns on a test of job satisfaction. Any other results would lead a reasonable observer to strongly question the validity of the test results. The lesson from this thought experiment is that mean score gaps are not evidence of test bias because there may be other explanations of score gaps. In fact, score gaps may indicate that the test is operating exactly as it should and measures real differences among groups ... (Warne, Yoon, & Price, 2014, p. 572, emphasis in original)

---

[1] Usually, the definition of test bias is applied to demographic groups (e.g., racial groups, sex groups, age groups). But it does not have to be limited to these groups. It is also possible to examine whether bias exists when comparing tall people and short people, or people with diabetes and people without a chronic health condition, or Catholic nuns and Hell's Angels. In practice, though, examinations of test bias are limited to demographic groups.

This is not to say that differences in average scores are irrelevant. Often these differences are an indication that the possibility of bias should be investigated. But the average differences are not – by themselves – sufficient evidence of test bias (Dyck, 1996; Frisby & Henry, 2016; Jensen, 1980a; Linn & Drasgow, 1987; Sackett et al., 2008; Scarr, 1994).

Professional Reactions to Test Bias. The statistical procedures used to identify test bias are too complex to explain in detail. In short, all of these methods attempt to match examinees from different groups on their actual ability level and then ascertain whether test scores or test items are functioning the same way for both groups.[2] The ethical standards of the testing profession require professional test creators to screen tests for the presence of bias (AERA et al., 2014). To comply with this mandate, test creators routinely perform examinations for bias, and biased tests are revised to remove the bias long before test creators release them to the public. As a result, professionally developed tests are unbiased against all major racial and ethnic groups that make up the examinee population in the countries that the tests are designed for.

Individual items – not just entire tests – can also show bias. When professional test creators find individual items that are biased, they can take one of two courses of action. One option is to eliminate the item from the test. (This is often viable because test creators usually write many more items than they intend to put on the final version of a test.) Another response is to balance biased items so that there is the same number of items favoring one group as there are items disadvantaging that group. Thus, the individual bias in different items cancels out (Warne, Yoon, & Price, 2014).

Because procedures to identify and eliminate test bias are so routine – and mandated as part of the profession's ethical code – it is nearly impossible to sell a test that hasn't been subjected to carefully scrutiny for bias. If anyone tried, there are two likely consequences. First, the test would not be commercially successful, because consumers would be so concerned about the potential for bias that they would not purchase and use the test. Any company selling a biased test would have to contend with competitors touting their unbiased test as being superior to the biased test. Second, any customers who use the test for decision making – especially in education or employment – would be vulnerable to a lawsuit because using a biased test to make decisions about people in the group whose scores are underestimated would be discriminatory.[3] Thus, there

---

[2] For an accessible introduction to these methods, see R. M. Kaplan & Saccuzzo, 2018, Chapter 19, or Warne, Yoon, and Price, 2014. Readers with some exposure to psychometric theory can benefit from Camili, 2006, pp. 228–243, or Jensen, 1980a.

[3] Such lawsuits were common in the 1970s and 1980s (see Elliott, 1987; Jensen, 1980a, Chapter 2; Phillips & Camara, 2006). These lawsuits do still occasionally happen, but they are rare now (Buckendahl & Hunt, 2005; Mehrens, 2000). If the critics are right and intelligence tests (and similar tests) are obviously biased, then surely it would be illegal to use them in employment and educational settings. So, where is the avalanche of lawsuits? The only explanations are that (a) the

are very strong ethical, legal, and economic incentives for test developers to create and sell unbiased tests. As a result, it is incorrect to make blanket claims that intelligence tests are biased.

Caveat. It is important to note that this discussion about test bias – and its absence from professionally designed tests – only applies to groups that speak the test language as a native and who were born in the country the test was designed for. In the United States, this means that tests of *g* are unbiased for native English speakers born in that country. Everyone in the debate about test bias agrees that it is inappropriate to administer a test to a person who does not speak the language of the test and then interpret the low score as evidence of low intelligence. Indeed, this is a gross violation of the ethical standards of the field (AERA et al., 2014), and professional test creators are very specific about the language proficiency that is needed to take a test. Research shows that it takes about three years of residency in the United States for foreign-born children to be able to take a test in English without having their educational achievement test scores penalized for poor language proficiency. Native-born bilingual children whose parents speak a non-English language are not disadvantaged by taking an intelligence test in English (Akresh & Akresh, 2011).

Another common point of agreement is that the test content must be culturally appropriate to the examinee for a test to produce an interpretable score. When tests are used in a new culture, often they must be adapted to ensure that culturally loaded test content is understandable to examinees in the new culture (AERA et al., 2014). Professional test creators have known this for over 100 years. For example, when Binet's test was translated into English for use in the United States, it was obvious to American psychologists that an arithmetic task that required knowledge of French money needed to be changed because there were no ½-cent or 2-cent coins in the United States, and using French money would be baffling to American children (Terman, 1916). When comparing scores of examinees from different backgrounds, it is generally recognized that the test content must be culturally appropriate for all examinees. It is standard practice when translating or adapting a test to another culture, language, or country to ensure that all test items are culturally accessible to examinees.

EXPLORING CRITICS' CLAIMS OF TEST BIAS

Criticism of Test Content. Some critics of intelligence tests (and similar tests) have arguments about test bias that are more sophisticated than merely claiming that

tests are not biased, (b) civil rights advocates have lost interest in remedying the injustice of using biased tests, or (c) lawyers are not self-interested enough to pursue a high-profile case against a wealthy defendant – like a state or large company. Of these three options, only (a) seems plausible.

different average scores are proof of test bias. One common claim – exemplified by the quotes at the beginning of this chapter – is that test content is decided by people who are generally middle-class individuals of European descent in a Western culture, which means that intelligence tests merely measure one's conformity or exposure to this culture. As a result, racially diverse individuals or people from other cultures are disadvantaged by the tests because their culturally specific ways of thinking are not rewarded on intelligence tests (e.g., Kwate, 2001; Moore, Ford, & Milner, 2005; Ogbu, 2002).

This argument has been thoroughly disproved. One problem with the claim that intelligence tests merely measure knowledge or conformity to Western middle-class culture is the fact that the racial group with the highest average on these tests is not Europeans, but East Asians (Gottfredson, 1997a); this has been true since the 1920s (e.g., Goodenough, 1926). Another piece of contradictory evidence comes from testing indigenous people in other nations. If intelligence tests measure acculturation to Western culture, then indigenous communities who have had more contact with Europeans should score higher than people in communities in the same nation who have had less contact. However, this is not the case (Porteus, 1965). Finally, the content of many test formats (e.g., matrix tests, digit span) contains very little information that is unique to Western culture. It is not clear how numbers or geometric patterns are special to Western middle-class individuals.

Many claims of biased test content are based on examinations of item content, with critics of intelligence testing claiming that a particular item is so culturally loaded that it cannot measure intelligence in diverse populations. Critics sometimes cherry pick a few items to argue that intelligence tests are biased, but rarely mention that items that appear biased are a small fraction of intelligence test items. Testing opponents seldom have much to say about nonverbal items, for example (Elliott, 1987; Jensen, 1980a). A classic example of this cherry-picking tendency is the "fight item," which appeared on a now-obsolete version of the WISC: "What is the thing to do if a fellow much smaller than yourself starts a fight with you?"[4] Based on little more than reading the item, people have attacked the WISC as being entirely biased because, in their view, it might be appropriate in some cultures – such as African American culture – for a child to fight back if someone acts aggressively towards them (Reschly, 1980).[5] However, this item functions nearly identically for African American and European American children (Miele, 1979), which indicates that there is no unique influence (e.g., a cultural bias) that makes the item easier or harder for one group or another.

---

[4] The correct answer was to not fight back. Any response that a child gave, such as telling an adult or running away, that involved not retaliating was marked as correct.

[5] Zindi (2013), a black Zimbabwean psychologist, included this item on his Zimbabwe Psychological Evaluation intelligence test for Zimbabwean children. Apparently, the "fight item" is not culturally inappropriate for his black examinees.

This example shows that it is not possible to judge by merely reading an item whether cultural differences influence responses. An illustration of this fact occurred in a court case (*PASE v. Hannon*, 1980) in which the Chicago school system was sued for using intelligence tests to identify minority children for special education. Of the hundreds of items on three intelligence tests (the 1960 version of the Stanford–Binet, the WISC, and the first revised version of the WISC), the judge identified just nine (including the "fight item") that he believed were culturally biased against minority students. Seven of these items were on two subtests on the WISC; when a team of psychologists (Koh, Abbatiello, & McLoughlin, 1984) examined the WISC items for bias, they found that *none* of them was biased (in the statistical sense of the term) against African Americans. Moreover, for three of the seven items, the response that the judge believed that African American children would be culturally disposed to give was actually given more frequently given by European American children (Koh et al., 1984). Therefore, merely reading test items provides no clues about whether a test question really is biased against a cultural group (Jensen, 1980a).

In a more constructive vein, some people have made suggestions to try to change test content to reduce or eliminate average score gaps between racial groups while maintaining the ability of a test to measure intelligence. Unfortunately, these efforts have been unsuccessful. One suggested technique is to eliminate the test questions that show the largest differences in passing rates for different racial groups. The problem with this method is that it eliminates the items that tend to be the best at measuring intelligence while retaining test questions that are poorer measures of intelligence (Linn & Drasgow, 1987; Phillips, 2000). The result is a test that correlates poorly with important criteria, such as success in school.

Another proposal has been to design tests that have content that is culturally relevant to non-European American examinees. The most famous example is the Black Intelligence Test of Cultural Homogeneity (BITCH). Originally announced in 1972 by psychologist Robert L. Williams, the BITCH is a culturally specific test designed to measure knowledge of concepts and language that are unique to African Americans. The test items were all multiple-choice questions in which the examinee had to select the correct definition of a word or phrase taken from African American dialects or culture at the time (R. L. Williams, 1972). For example, Question 22 requires examinees to select whether "Deuce-and-a-Quarter" refers to (a) money, (b) a car, (c) a house, or (d) dice[6] (Long & Anthony, 1974, p. 311).

Just as Williams expected, his test was difficult for European American examinees, whereas African Americans excelled (Matarazzo & Wiens, 1977; R. L. Williams, 1972, 1975). He interpreted this as evidence that a test designed for one culture could not be used on a population from a different culture

[6] The correct answer is (b).

(R. L. Williams, 1972). But evidence that the BITCH measures intelligence is non-existent. BITCH scores for African American examinees correlate weakly ($r = .04$ to $.39$) with traditional intelligence and academic tests (Long & Anthony, 1974; Matarazzo & Wiens, 1977; R. L. Williams, 1972), though this is exactly what would occur if traditional tests are grossly inappropriate for African Americans (R. L. Williams, 1975). However, there is no evidence that BITCH performance correlates with successful functioning in an African American culture or context, which is necessary for a culturally specific test to be a better measure of African Americans' intelligence than traditional intelligence tests (R. L. Williams, 1972, 1975). The same is true for similar tests (Jensen, 1980a). The BITCH most likely measures knowledge of 1970s African American slang and idioms, but there is no evidence that it measures anything else.[7]

A modern – and more promising – approach is to ensure that the format of a test is culturally appropriate for examinees. An example of a culturally sensitive test that does this is the Panga Munthu test, developed in Zambia as a way of measuring African children's intelligence (Kathura & Serpell, 1998). Whereas R. L. Williams (1970) and others (e.g., Ford, 1995; Harris & Ford, 1991) argue that thinking and learning styles in disparate cultures are so different that the each group must have its own tests that are developed, scored, and interpreted in culturally specific ways, the Panga Munthu's creators believe that intelligence is universal, but that traditional tests need to be modified if examinees are not familiar with the demands of the test. Instead of responding to questions verbally or using a pencil and paper (often unavailable in rural Zambia), the Panga Munthu requires children to sculpt a human figure in clay or wire – a common activity for children in Zambia. The examiner then scores the figure, with more complex figures indicating higher intelligence. Thus, the creators of the Panga Munthu believe that intelligence is part of Zambian psychology (as it is for Westerners), but that the tasks on a test must be understandable and appropriate for examinees' culture for an intelligence test to produce meaningful results.

Unlike the BITCH, research supports the claim that the Panga Munthu measures intelligence in its African examinee population. For example, scores correlate positively ($r = .19$ to $.44$) with the highest grade that examinees

---

[7] Some people treat the BITCH as a parody of or commentary on "real" intelligence tests. While Williams did state that the test was originally a protest, he later developed the test in earnest, and the work by European American psychologists (Long & Anthony, 1974; Matarazzo & Wiens, 1977) to search for evidence supporting Williams's beliefs shows that the psychological community in the 1970s saw the BITCH as a serious contribution to intelligence testing. Moreover, Williams received a $153,000 grant (worth over $900,000 in 2019 dollars) from the National Institute of Mental Health to develop the BITCH (Delaney, 1975). Perhaps people do not give the BITCH the attention it warrants because of its acronym. The original name "Black Intelligence Test Counterbalanced for Honkies" does not help, nor does the name of the version Williams created for children, the S.O.B. Test (R. L. Williams, 1970). On the other hand, the term BITCH probably made the test much more memorable than an innocuous name would have, so I cannot criticize Williams for the name he chose for his test. He is a master of marketing.

complete and their literacy scores in English and their native language ($r = .29$ to .43; Serpell & Jere-Folotiya, 2008). The Panga Munthu is not the only test that is adapted to the practices of a specific culture. I believe that cross-cultural testing would benefit from more customization of tests to examinees' cultures (Warne & Burningham, 2019), especially in light of evidence that g likely exists in all human groups (see Chapter 4).

Tests as Tools of Oppression. A more serious claim is that intelligence tests are designed with the explicit goal of oppressing non-European populations (e.g., Carter & Goodwin, 1994; Helms, 1992; Mercer, 1979; Moss, 2008). This is basically a conspiracy theory that would require decades of complicity from thousands of individuals who work in the testing industry and even more people in education, employment, and law who decide when and how tests are used. In reality, "No reputable standardized ability test was ever devised expressly for the purpose of discriminating [against] racial, ethnic, or social-class groups" (Jensen, 1980a, p. 42). And some tests of g were developed explicitly to tear down social barriers to education or jobs (see Chapter 21).

One common example of how intelligence tests were supposedly designed to discriminate is in the immigration process in the United States in the early twentieth century (e.g., Gould, 1981, 1996). It is true that in the 1910s, American immigration inspectors started using intelligence tests to help in identifying "feeble-minded" individuals (who could not legally immigrate to the United States). But these tests were not designed to discriminate against any nationality of immigrants. In reality, the government physicians at Ellis Island developed some of the earliest non-verbal intelligence tests to create a fair method of measuring intelligence that did not disadvantage people who were unfamiliar with the English language or American culture (J. T. E. Richardson, 2011; Mullan, 1917).

It would not have been feasible to give every immigrant at the time an intelligence test. Instead, the American government instituted a screening process to identify immigrants who were ineligible for entry into the country. The process for identifying people at Ellis Island (the most common point of entry for potential immigrants) with low intelligence is shown in Figures 10.2 through 10.5. First, immigrants were medically and psychologically screened while in processing lines. As part of the examination, two physicians individually asked each immigrant in their native language basic questions, such as their name, their nationality, their occupation, or simple addition problems (Mullan, 1917). About 9% of immigrants failed this screening procedure, and these individuals received another brief examination in a separate room to screen for low intelligence and psychological conditions like delusions, hallucinations, dementia, or (in modern terminology) bipolar disorder, and schizophrenia.

Those who failed (about 11–22% of those who failed the original screening procedure and about 1–2% of all prospective immigrants) were tested again after 1–7 days of rest. On that later date, a physician screened the immigrants again with basic questions, and those that passed were released. Those who did

FIGURE 10.2 Initial medical screening of potential immigrants at Ellis Island in the early twentieth century. As part of this screening, physicians (shown in this photograph standing with their backs turned towards the camera) would ask immigrants in their native language basic questions. Immigrants who struggled with these questions or who acted erratically or otherwise abnormally were led to a large room for a brief mental examination, shown in Figure 10.3.
Source: National Institute of Health, https://bit.ly/2W1IMXv

not received an individual 20–60 minute examination from a different physician later that same day. Non-passers received a third examination on a later date; failing this resulted in some immigrants being labeled "feeble-minded" and barred from entering the United States. Others received a fourth or fifth examination at another time and those who passed this latest examination were allowed to enter the country.

Immigrants could not be diagnosed as "feeble-minded" unless they failed the original screening procedure, a brief examination the same day, and at least three later individual examinations[8] (Mullan, 1917). But to be labeled as

---

[8] This is in addition to any inspections they had to pass in their home countries. Passenger ship companies could be fined up to $200 (the equivalent of $3,400 in 2019 dollars) if they transported an immigrant to the United States who should have been identified as being unable to pass the

FIGURE 10.3 Potential immigrants at Ellis Island awaiting a brief psychological exam – including an intelligence test – after failing an initial screening procedure. The seated uniformed men wearing hats are government employees, possibly physicians and/or interpreters.
Source: Mullan, 1917, Figure 3.

"normal" and allowed to enter the United States, an examinee only had to pass once. The onus was on the inspecting physicians to show that the immigrant indeed had low intelligence. According to the inspection manual, "The immigrant should be given the benefit of any doubt which may arise as to his mental status and therefore regarded as normal until it has been clearly shown that he is not" (United States Public Health Service, 1918, p. 35).

The individual examinations were conducted in the immigrant's native language, and were a mix of verbal questions and tasks that had few or no language demands. Some of the questions were derived from Binet's tests, and others were designed for the immigrants specifically (United States Public

American physical or mental health inspections before leaving the home country's port. The companies also had to refund the ticket of any immigrants who were rejected for entry into the country (United States Public Health Service, 1918). Thus, passenger ship personnel had an economic incentive to screen immigrants for any conditions that would prevent entry into the United States, which probably included low intelligence.

FIGURE 10.4 Two government employees (the seated men in the foreground), at least one of whom is a physician, test a potential immigrant at Ellis Island after she had failed the original screening procedure and the brief follow-up examination on a previous day. The seated individuals in the rear of the photograph are other potential immigrants awaiting their examinations. They had also failed the screening procedure and brief follow-up examination.
Source: Mullan, 1917, Figure 4.

Health Service, 1918). The tasks included watching an examiner tap a set of blocks in a specific order and then repeating the sequence (J. T. E. Richardson, 2011) and putting together simple wooden puzzles, such as the one pictured in Figure 10.6.

Based on official government statistics, only a tiny proportion of prospective immigrants were turned away due to low intelligence. Between 1892 and 1931 – when 21,862,790 immigrants arrived in the United States – a total of 4,303 prospective immigrants were turned away for being (in the language of the time) "idiots," "imbeciles," or "feeble-minded." Therefore, a total of 0.02% of immigrants were rejected for low intelligence. The annual percentage of immigrants who were rejected for low intelligence reached its peak in 1915, when 0.103% of immigrants were turned away for this reason (data from Unrau, 1984, Vol. 1, pp. 185, 200–202). If intelligence tests really were designed to discriminate against some groups of immigrants, they were

UNITED STATES PUBLIC HEALTH SERVICE

FIGURE 10.5 Two government employees (the seated men), at least one of whom is a physician, test a potential immigrant at Ellis Island who seems to be the same examinee as shown in Figure 10.4. This woman has already failed the screening procedure and follow-up examination on the day she arrived at Ellis Island. She failed two individual examinations on a later day and in this picture is taking her third or fourth individual examination (on yet another day). According to the photograph's original caption, she failed this examination too and was designated "feeble-minded."
Source: Mullan, 1917, Figure 5.

remarkably ineffective. Far more potential immigrants were turned away for carrying contagious diseases, having a physical disability, or being stowaways (Unrau, 1984, Vol. 1, pp. 200–202).

UNBIASED ≠ FAIR

While the common assertion that intelligence tests are biased is not supported by data, that does not mean that society has a blank check to use intelligence tests. This is because using the test may still be unfair – even if the test is unbiased in the technical sense of the word. Whereas bias is a scientific issue, fairness is an ethical or moral issue, and the two ideas are not interchangeable (Jensen, 1980a). People will inevitably have different moral or ethical values; when these values clash, there may be disagreements about whether and how to use tests. Some people may have good reasons to

FIGURE 10.6 Wooden puzzle that served as a non-verbal intelligence test for immigrants at Ellis Island whom physicians suspected were "feeble-minded." The physician would assemble the puzzle two or three times as the immigrant watched and then ask the immigrant to assemble it.
Source: National Park Service (https://bit.ly/2WyEmrw).

not use intelligence tests – even if they are unbiased (e.g., to foster a more diverse workforce). Unlike bias, fairness cannot be settled scientifically because science is morally neutral; its tools can be used for a variety of beneficial or harmful purposes. Ethical and moral arguments are best resolved by public decision making through the mechanisms of a free society – such as open debate, legislatures, and the court system. Chapters 33 and 34 will discuss the issue of fairness in more detail.

CONCLUSION

Among people without training in psychological testing, there is a widespread belief that intelligence tests (and many academic or employment tests) are biased against racially diverse examinees – especially people of African, Hispanic, and Native American descent. Sometimes these arguments are based on the mere fact that the average score on these tests varies across racial groups; sometimes the arguments are more sophisticated and are based on test content or the appropriateness of testing diverse examinees. But the evidence is overwhelming that professionally designed tests are not statistically biased against native speakers of the test language who are born in the country that the test is designed for. Professional developers go to great lengths to ensure that bias is minimized and that the content of professionally designed tests is appropriate for diverse individuals. Nevertheless, it may not be fair to use an unbiased test for some examinees, and values and ethics are important in determining fairness of test use.

SECTION 3

INFLUENCES ON INTELLIGENCE

With a firm understanding of the nature of intelligence (from the Introduction and Section 1) and how *g* is measured (from Section 2), a few questions inevitably arise: Where does intelligence come from? Why are some people smarter than others? Can I raise my intelligence (or my child's)? This section is designed to address these questions by debunking common misconceptions about the influences on intelligence.

With seven chapters, this section is the longest in the book. Chapter 11 addresses the frequently seen claim that intelligence tests (and related tests, like college admissions tests) are merely measures of an examinee's wealth. Chapter 12 addresses the genetic influences on intelligence and what that means for interventions to raise IQ. In Chapter 13, I discuss how relatively subtle genetic differences in genes can result in important differences in intelligence.

The last four chapters of this section are all concerned with how intelligence can be improved. In Chapter 14, I investigate whether fluctuations in IQ scores mean that intelligence is malleable through interventions to raise *g*. Chapter 15 discusses interventions with more detail, as I consider the results of common attempts to raise intelligence, such as preschool programs. Chapter 16 is an examination of "brain-training" games that have become popular in the early twenty-first century. Finally, Chapter 17 discusses whether interventions to improve IQ can result in equal IQs among individuals.

The source of individual differences – and whether *g* can be changed or improved – has been part of the scholarly research on intelligence since Sir Francis Galton coined the term "nature versus nurture" in the late nineteenth century. Since Galton's day, psychologists have learned that both nature (in the form of genetics) and nurture (i.e., the environment) are important in determining a person's intelligence level. That is an uncontroversial statement;

the misconceptions that this section addresses are more nuanced than asking whether nature or nurture determines intelligence. The conversation about the causes of intelligence has moved beyond a simple either/or question about genes and environment. That makes this section one of the most illuminating in the book.

11

IQ Only Reflects a Person's Socioeconomic Status

The SAT is supposed to measure aptitude, but what it actually measures is parental income, which it tracks quite closely.

(Deresiewicz, 2014, paragraph 33)

Social scientists have long known that the best predictor of test scores is family income ... Standardized tests are best at measuring family income.

(Ravitch, 2016, p. SR8)

CORRELATIONAL EVIDENCE

The evidence is clear: wealthier individuals tend to score higher on intelligence and academic tests. This is true, both in adulthood (Herrnstein & Murray, 1994) and childhood (Zwick, 2002). As a result, some people – like those quoted above – have argued that the tests of *g* are actually little more than tests of someone's socioeconomic status.[1] Others have argued that differences in wealth or socioeconomic status *cause* differences in performance on tests of *g*. In other words, they believe that money makes people smarter, or that it can buy higher scores through test preparation classes, better schools, or home life advantages (e.g., L. Brody, 2018; Zwick, 2002). As a result, some skeptics of intelligence testing believe that these tests reflect economic advantages more than any cognitive abilities.

---

[1] *Socioeconomic status* is a term in the social sciences for an individual's economic and social position in society. There are different ways to measure socioeconomic status; the most common methods do so by considering income, accumulated wealth, educational attainment or degrees, occupational prestige, and/or neighborhood exclusivity. (For children, these variables are usually calculated using information from their parents.) There is no single way to measure socioeconomic status, but most measures produce similar results.

Like many ideas debunked in this book, the idea that IQ scores (and other test scores) are determined by socioeconomic status is based on a grain of truth: the correlation between the two is positive. However, it is a weak relationship. In a study of nearly 1.3 million college-bound teenagers, the correlation between SAT scores and parental income was just $r = .10$; in a sample of almost 35,000 college students, the correlation between SAT scores and parental income was $r = .23$ (Camara, 2009). Slightly stronger is the correlation of $r = .30$ between parental income and IQ at ages 14–22 in a representative sample of young Americans (Rindermann & Ceci, 2018, supplemental file p. 3). If tests of g really were proxies for socioeconomic status, the correlations would be much stronger. Discussing the same evidence, Mackintosh (2011, p. 29) stated that the correlations are so weak that the idea that intelligence tests measure socioeconomic status "is a singularly foolish assertion." I agree.

Controlling for confounding variables (e.g., school quality, number of books in the home, technological access) only makes the relationship between family income and intelligence weaken. This was most apparent in a recent study with data from 19 samples in 7 countries on 4 continents in which the correlation between the two variables went from $r \approx .25$ to $r \approx .12$ after controlling for confounding variables (Rindermann & Ceci, 2018). This means that the relationship between income and intelligence test scores can be partially explained by other variables, though controlling for these other influences does not make the correlation between IQ and socioeconomic status disappear completely.

Another piece of statistical evidence indicating that intelligence tests are not proxies for socioeconomic status comes from educational testing. Scores on tests of g – like college admissions tests – are the best predictors of academic performance (see Chapters 18–20). Statistically controlling for socioeconomic status has almost no impact on the ability of test scores to predict grades (Sackett et al., 2008), and even after controlling for childhood socioeconomic status, IQ has a moderately strong positive correlation with later income and educational success (Kuncel & Hezlett, 2010; Murray, 1998, 2002). This indicates that the correlation between IQ and academic performance is mostly independent of socioeconomic status – even though all three variables are positively correlated with one another.

Even if intelligence test scores are not total reflections of socioeconomic status, there exists the possibility that socioeconomic status could cause a boost in intelligence test scores. The best evidence for this comes from adoption studies, which generally show that children in adopted families (which tend to be middle or upper class) often score at or above average on intelligence tests (e.g., Spinks et al., 2007). The best study, from Sweden, showed that adopted children had IQ scores that were an average of 4.41 points higher than the scores of their biological sibling who had been raised by their biological parents (Kendler, Turkheimer, Ohlsson, Sundquist, & Sundquist, 2015). Even this evidence, though, does not indicate that income causes increases in intelligence test scores because low, middle, and high socioeconomic status families vary in many ways besides income (Protzko, Aronson, & Blair, 2013). For example, in middle-class homes, mothers talk to their children more, and children watch less television (Elardo & Bradley, 1981). Likewise, children in poor households are less healthy and less likely to live in a two-parent home (Brooks-Gunn & Duncan, 1997). Indeed, children in homes with positive social characteristics that are unrelated to income tend to have higher IQ scores (Cleveland, Jacobson, Lipinski, & Rowe, 2000). Thus, it is very possible that the correlation between test scores and socioeconomic status may not be entirely due to the impact of family income on intelligence.

GENETICS: SETTING LIMITS ON THE INFLUENCE OF ENVIRONMENT

In addition to the many ways that homes from different socioeconomic statuses vary, it is important to consider one factor which limits the causal impact that income can have on intelligence test scores: genetic influences on intelligence. An interdisciplinary science called *behavioral genetics* studies the influence of genes on psychological traits and behaviors. One technique of behavioral genetics is to use correlations between family members' scores on a trait to determine the trait's *heritability*, which is the degree to which trait differences among people are due to genetic differences. The exact methods are too complex to explain here (see Plomin, DeFries, Knopik, & Neiderhiser, 2012, for a detailed explanation), but if the correlation between family members' traits is stronger for close relatives than for more distant relatives, it is an indication that the trait is genetically influenced. For example, Bouchard and McGue (1981, p. 1056) reported that IQ scores are correlated $r = .15$ for cousins and $r = .47$ for siblings. Because siblings share – on average – 50% of their genes and cousins share only 12.5% of their genes, the stronger correlation among siblings indicates that intelligence is genetically influenced.

Heritability is abbreviated as h^2 and ranges from 0 (indicating that differences in a trait are solely due to environmental differences) to 1 (indicating that genetic differences are the only influence determining differences in a trait). When h^2 is low, environmental variables are more important than genetics in determining trait variability; when heritability is close to 1, then genes are a powerful influence on a trait, and the environment has very little impact in determining differences on the trait. In reality, h^2 values of 0 or 1 are very rare; for almost every trait, heritability is between these two extremes (Plomin, DeFries, Knopik, & Neiderhiser, 2016).

Correlations in IQ scores among relatives show evidence of a genetic influence on intelligence. For identical twins (who share 100% of their genes), the correlation between their IQ scores is $r = .86$; the fact that this value is not $r = 1.00$ indicates that genes are not the only factor determining IQ scores. Likewise, adoptees and their non-biological relatives (who share 0% of their DNA) have IQ scores that are correlated $r = .19$ to .24 (Bouchard & McGue,

1981, pp. 1057–1058). This positive correlation indicates that the environment these family members share has an influence on IQ scores,[2] though the environmental influence is not as strong as the genetic influence on IQ scores.

Heritability for intelligence tends to be around .50 (i.e., about 50% of IQ score differences are due to genetic differences), though there are differences from study to study. Generally, studies of children tend to produce lower heritability (and therefore higher environmental/non-genetic influence), often as low as .20. Studies of adults produce higher heritability – sometimes above .80 (Bouchard, 2004, 2014; Deary, 2012; Hunt, 2011). This indicates that the importance of genes increases as people age (Plomin & Deary, 2015). In other words, intelligence differences among adults are more genetic in origin, whereas in young children, environmental variables matter more.

What does genetics have to do with understanding the impact of socioeconomic status on intelligence? Heritability sets limits on the influence that non-genetic variables can have on intelligence in typical environments (Hunt, 2011). If the differences in IQ scores are 50% caused by genetic differences (as indicated by a h^2 value of .50), then *all environmental variables combined* must account for no more than 50% of people's differences in intelligence. While this does not exactly tell scientists the strength of the impact of income on intelligence, it does limit the magnitude of that impact. Because genetics is as important for determining intelligence as all other environmental variables combined, it is not possible for differences in IQ scores – or scores on other tests that measure g – to be determined solely (or mostly) by income or socioeconomic status differences.

ADDED COMPLEXITY: GENETICALLY INFLUENCED ENVIRONMENTS

There is another finding from behavioral genetics that makes it difficult to argue that intelligence test scores are solely caused by socioeconomic differences: many "environmental" variables are also heritable. In other words, genes can influence the environment that people find themselves in. This idea was postulated long ago (e.g., Pearson, 1903, pp. 179–180), but in the past generation the evidence has mounted that it is correct (Vinkhuzen, Van Der Sluis, De Geus, Boomsma, & Posthuma, 2010). As far as socioeconomic status is concerned, heritability is high enough that genes are a major influence on income differences: .42 in one highly cited study (Rowe, Vesterdal, & Rodgers, 1998), which is typical in developed countries (Plomin, 2018, p. 100). Moreover, some of the genes that influence socioeconomic status also influence intelligence (Marioni et al., 2014; Trzaskowski et al., 2014). Therefore, some of the impact that socioeconomic status has on intelligence is ultimately genetic in origin – even

---

[2] This correlation cannot be because of a genetic influence because these people share no genes. The only thing they share is some of the environment.

though many people consider socioeconomic status and related variables (e.g., income, poverty) to be environmental variables.

It is not always clear what causes this genetic influence on environmental variables. One leading theory is that people's genetic proclivities lead them to choose environments they feel comfortable in. For example, a child who has a genetic propensity to enjoy reading may choose to spend more time in their school's library. This may explain why heritability is higher for adults (who have more freedom to choose their environments) than for children (Plomin & Deary, 2015). Another possibility is that people in the surrounding environment, such as parents, teachers, or employers, may respond to a person's behavior and foster development in areas where the person has a (genetically influenced) interest or talent. This might be what occurs when a parent buys a trumpet or violin for a child who shows interest in music; the access to an instrument will then amplify the child's genetic propensity for musical talent. In all likelihood, both theories have some truth to them.

Most children are raised by one or both biological parents, which means that a child shares 50% of their genes with at least one caregiver. As a result, genes have multiple ways of influencing the development of both individual traits – like intelligence – and "environmental" variables – like socioeconomic status. An important implication of these shared genes is that a correlation between parental behavior and child outcomes may be genetically caused. For example, it is known that the number of books in a home is correlated with a child's school performance and that more educated parents tend to buy more books (e.g., Rindermann & Ceci, 2018). This does not prove, though, that buying more books causes children to do well in school. Instead, the same genes that may make a parent succeed in school may also influence them to buy more books; half of those genes from each parent are then passed on to the child. These genes that the child receives may then cause the child to read at home and also do well in school. What is apparently an environmental influence (of the number of books on a child's school success) may be an entirely genetic phenomenon.[3]

SHORTCOMINGS OF HERITABILITY ESTIMATES

Although h^2 values provide extremely strong evidence that a person's intelligence level is partially influenced by their genetic heritage, there are a few limitations

---

[3] This means that *all* correlations between parent behavior and outcomes in their biological children that they raise are confounded by shared genes. Therefore, most research studies on parenting practices, like the effects of reading to a child (e.g., Barnes & Puccioni, 2017) or spanking (Strassberg, Dodge, Pettit, & Bates, 1994), are confounded by shared genes. Without controlling for these shared genes, it is impossible to state whether parental actions cause child life outcomes. The easiest way to control for shared genes is to only study parents who have adopted children they are not biologically related to. Most researchers do not do this, though, and the result is an overestimate of the effects of parental behavior on child outcomes. Remember that the next time you receive parenting advice.

that anyone dealing with heritability should know. The first is that h^2 estimates can only apply to the population and environments under investigation. Most studies of heritability occur in wealthy, industrialized countries, and these results may not apply to other nations. This is well illustrated in heritability studies conducted in impoverished countries. In one study in Sudan, the h^2 for intelligence in a sample of 10-year-old children was between .13 and .17 (Toto et al., 2019), which is about half of the h^2 value seen in wealthy nations for that age group. This indicates that genes are a less influential cause of differences in intelligence than environmental variables in Sudan. On the other hand, the h^2 for IQ in a sample of Nigerian adolescents aged 11–18 was .50 (Hur & Bates, 2019), which is consistent with the h^2 values for adolescents in Western countries. Thus, heritability values do not apply to environments that were not part of the study. Moreover, h^2 values say nothing about biological immutability of a trait (Cronbach, 1975).

To a lesser extent, a problem with heritability study samples is that they tend to consist of more middle- and upper-class individuals than a representative sample would have. This is especially true of adoption studies because the poorest families in industrialized nations are usually not allowed to adopt children, nor are parents who have a history of violence, drug problems, or other dysfunctional behaviors. Therefore, the range of environments in these studies is reduced (Mackintosh, 2011), which makes the influence of genetics appear inflated (Nisbett et al., 2012). Adoption studies also cannot investigate the impact of abuse, neglect, and threats to physical safety because governments and adoption agencies try to prevent children from being placed into these extremely negative environments.[4] Therefore, when behavioral geneticists produce a study that genes are a powerful influence on intelligence, it is important to consider the population and the environment that the study was conducted on. Often, the results of behavioral genetics studies will indicate that genes are important – *if a person already lives in an industrialized nation in a home where basic needs are met.* It is not clear how well these results apply to individuals in severe poverty or in highly unfavorable environments.

Another shortcoming of heritability statistics is that they do not state what portion of a person's IQ originates from their genes and what portion originates from their environment (Tal, 2009). That is because *heritability is a group-level statistic of variance* that refers to the genetic influences on the variability of a trait among a group of individuals (Hunt, 2011). Therefore, if h^2 is .50 (i.e., 50%), and someone has an IQ of 100, it does *not* make sense to say that 50 points of their score come from genetics and 50 points come from environmental influences. Despite this apparent drawback, h^2 values do provide important information about groups as a whole.

---

[4] That is a good thing. The primary concern for adopted children should always be that they are placed in a safe, nurturing home. Scientific considerations are much less important.

CONCLUSION

It is abundantly clear that IQ scores do not merely reflect an examinee's socioeconomic status. Indeed, the correlations between the two variables were never strong enough for that to be a plausible interpretation of the data. A more important influence for determining intelligence is a person's genetic makeup. Among individuals living in middle- or upper-class homes in wealthy, industrialized nations, heritability is approximately .50. Among people outside this group, heritability may or may not be the same (though it is probably not zero). At least some of the correlation between socioeconomic status and IQ scores is probably due to genetic factors. Adoption studies do show that children adopted into middle- and upper-class families have a boost to their intelligence, but it is not clear how much of this is due to wealth and how much is due to the other characteristics of these homes. The research on this topic is complex, and new discoveries are certain to unfold.

12

High Heritability for Intelligence Means that Raising IQ Is Impossible

> If we assume intelligence is primarily the result of innate (hereditary) factors, we will likely conclude it is fixed and unchangeable.
>
> (Zimbardo, Johnson, & McCann, 2017, p. 221)

Chapter 11 stated that heritability of intelligence for adults in positive environments in industrialized countries is about .80. A high h^2 value like .80 indicates that differences among adults' IQ scores are strongly related to the differences in their genes. This fact can lead some people – like the textbook authors that I quote above – to feel fatalistic about the likelihood of raising intelligence. The logic goes something like this:

1. Genes are fixed before a person's birth.
2. Those genes are very important in determining a person's intelligence level.
3. Therefore, environment is unimportant.
4. Because people cannot change their genes, intelligence cannot be changed.

This chapter is about how this logic has flaws in it. That being said, I am a realistic optimist. My description of heritability and its meaning showed that heritability does place limits on the influence of environment. However, high heritability does not rule out the possibility of environmental changes that can increase intelligence – sometimes substantially.

EXAMPLES

High Heritability and Effective Interventions. There are two classic examples of traits in humans that have high heritability, but which also have effective environmental interventions that can improve the lives of people. The first is *myopia* (i.e., nearsightedness), which has very high heritability – .75 to .88 in one typical study (Dirani et al., 2006). But there are simple interventions that correct this highly heritable trait: eyeglasses and contact lenses. Thus, it is possible to change the environment to improve people's functioning, even if a trait is highly heritable.

The second example is a disorder called phenylketonuria (PKU). People with PKU are unable to metabolize an amino acid called phenylalanine, which is found in chicken, egg whites, nuts, some seafood, potatoes, and many other common foods. PKU is caused when a person inherits two copies of a defective version of a gene on Chromosome 12; everyone who has both copies of the defective gene is born with PKU, which means h^2 for the trait is 1. As children develop, untreated PKU causes intellectual disability and other neurological problems. However, by eating a special diet of foods with little or no phenylalanine, people with PKU develop completely normally. This is more proof that high heritability does not mean that people are condemned to live the life dictated by their genes.

Successful Interventions to Raise IQ. The examples of nearsightedness and PKU demonstrate that high heritability of a trait is compatible with effective treatments. That does not automatically mean, though, that the same principle applies to intelligence. Nearsightedness has a simple cause – usually an eyeball that is too long – and the treatment is so simple that eyeglasses were invented in the Middle Ages. PKU is caused by a single gene, and the biochemistry of how the metabolic system of people with PKU malfunctions was discovered in the twentieth century, which led to an effective treatment (Kevles, 1995). In contrast, intelligence seems to be far more genetically and biologically complex than either of these examples. Within the range of normal development, there are likely to be thousands of genes that could potentially lower intelligence, and how these genes act in brain development and functioning is often not clear.

Nevertheless, there has been progress with finding ways to increase intelligence in people. One of the most successful started in the 1970s when scientists noticed that children with high levels of lead had lower IQ scores (about 4–5 points) than children with low lead levels. This was true even if the children with high lead levels appeared to be in good health and showed no outward symptoms of lead poisoning. These differences could not be explained by family or parental variables, such as socioeconomic status, parental attitudes towards school, and many other potentially confounding variables (de la Burdé & Choate, 1975; Landrigan et al., 1975; Needleman et al., 1979). Because of these results and other potentially negative consequences of lead poisoning, the United States government took steps to reduce lead exposure in children and adults. Lead was banned as an ingredient in paint, dishes and cookware, toys, and products marketed towards children in 1978, and lead was banned from new plumbing systems in 1986.[1] Leaded gasoline was phased out gradually until it was banned in 1996. Industrial sites are now required to emit less lead into the atmosphere, and contaminated sites are being cleaned up. Other countries are following this trend, which is reducing lead levels in the atmosphere worldwide.

As a result, Americans have lower concentrations of lead in their bodies; in the 1970s studies, a low level of lead in a child's blood was 20 µg/dL, which is the standard unit for measuring lead levels in blood[2] (Landrigan et al., 1975; Needleman et al., 1979). In 2016, only 0.50% of American children had blood lead levels of 10 µg/dL or higher, and 3.5% had blood levels of 5 µg/dL or higher[3] (Centers for Disease Control, 2018, p. 8). These decreases in blood levels are encouraging, and during that time, intelligence test scores have risen in the United States by about 9–12 points, though this increase in IQ is probably not due solely to reductions in lead exposure. (Chapter 14 will discuss this increase in IQ scores in more detail.) It is likely that reducing lead levels in children's bodies increases IQ. However, there is no known safe level of lead in the body, and even low concentrations of lead are associated with lower IQ (Huang et al., 2012).

Another successful intervention to raise intelligence is to cure a child's iodine deficiency. People with low iodine suffer from thyroid and neurological problems. Giving iodine supplements to people with an iodine deficiency cures this health problem, and – in children – raises IQ by about 8 points (Protzko, 2017a). Two billion people worldwide suffer from iodine deficiency, mostly in southern Asia and Sub-Sahara Africa, and these people are at risk for lower IQ and intellectual disabilities. In fact, iodine deficiency is the most common cause of preventable intellectual disability in the world. The good news is that iodine deficiency is inexpensive to cure, costing about 2 to 5 cents per person per year, which makes treating iodine deficiency the most cost-effective way of raising intelligence. The most common method of increasing a person's iodine intake is

---

[1] Today, as houses are renovated or city water systems are repaired, it is common practice to update plumbing systems to remove pipes containing lead.

[2] µg/dL is the abbreviation for micrograms of lead per deciliter of blood. A microgram is one-millionth of a gram, and deciliter is one-tenth of a liter. If you prefer non-metric measurements, 20 µg/dL is equal to 0.00000070548 ounces of lead per 6.76 tablespoons per blood.

[3] In late 2015, a scandal broke in the United States when it was discovered that the water in Flint, Michigan, was contaminated with high levels of lead. It is not clear what impact this had on blood lead levels in children. In 2013, before the water contamination started, 2.2% of children in Flint had blood level levels above 5 µg/dL. This percentage rose slightly in 2014 (the year the contamination started) and 2015, but declined in 2016 and 2017 (the latter being the year in which the city-wide contamination ended, though some buildings still had high levels of lead in the water). It is possible that these fluctuations are random, and even at the peak of the crisis (in 2015, when 3.7% of children had blood lead levels above 5 µg/dL), the percentage of children in Flint with high levels of lead in their blood was lower than in every year between 2006 and 2012. During the contamination, children's blood lead levels were consistent with levels found elsewhere in Michigan and the United States (Gómez et al., 2018).

by adding iodine to salt to create iodized salt. Nutrient supplements to provide iodine are also available (M. B. Zimmerman, Jooste, & Pandav, 2008).

In the United States and other industrialized nations, severe iodine deficiency is very rare because of the widespread use of iodized salt. There is no evidence that providing iodine to people who already have enough of the nutrient will raise intelligence. Indeed, too much iodine in a person's diet can cause health problems, though these are less severe than the problems arising from an iodine deficiency (M. B. Zimmerman et al., 2008).

RECONCILING HERITABILITY AND ENVIRONMENTAL INTERVENTIONS

The examples above prove that high heritability does not exclude the possibility of an effective intervention that changes a trait. But, from a theoretical perspective, the paradox remains: heritability demonstrates the strength and importance of genes, but large changes in IQ are possible. How to reconcile these two facts?

The answer comes from the statistical basis for h^2 and intervention changes. Heritability is based on variance, whereas the effectiveness of interventions is based on the averages. The Introduction explained that the average is a measure of the score of a typical person in a sample, whereas the variance is a measure of how much people's scores differ from one another (Warne, 2018). Because these statistics measure two different characteristics of a sample, it is possible for genes to act on the variability of IQ scores (via heritability), while an environmental treatment, like improving blood lead levels, can impact the average. The two influences on IQ scores can act independently of one another.

Figures 12.1 and 12.2 show how this is possible. The first graph is a set of imaginary data showing the relationship between blood lead levels and IQ scores in a sample that has high exposure to lead. The second graph shows the same two variables in a sample from the same community after blood lead levels have been reduced by 9 µg/dL. The group with the lower lead exposure has an average IQ that is 4 points higher than the group with the high lead exposure. Within each sample, the correlation between the two variables is the same ($r = -.34$). The two groups also have the same standard deviation (2.53 for lead levels and 15 for IQ scores) and variances (6.40 for lead levels and 225 for IQ scores).

The 4-point average IQ difference between the two groups shows that lowering blood levels in this community has a beneficial impact on intelligence test scores. However, the variability in IQ scores (as shown by the equal standard deviations and variances in the two samples) within each group is the same because the lower lead levels impacted all community members equally, which did not change how much scores within each group differ from one another.

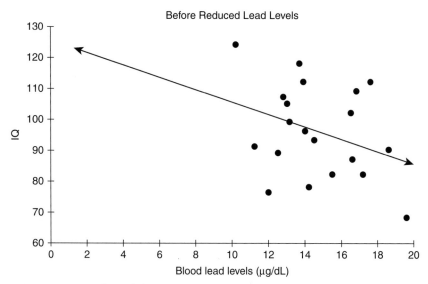

FIGURE 12.1 Hypothetical data showing the relationship between blood lead levels and IQ scores in a group of 20 individuals with high lead exposure. The average blood lead level is 14.68 µg/dL (standard deviation = 2.53, variance = 6.40). The average IQ score is 96 (standard deviation = 15, variance = 225). The correlation between the two variables is $r = -.34$.

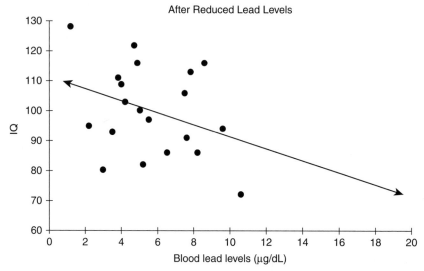

FIGURE 12.2 Hypothetical data showing the relationship between blood lead levels and IQ scores in a group of 20 individuals with low lead exposure. The average blood lead level is 5.68 µg/dL (standard deviation = 2.53, variance = 6.40). The average IQ score is 100 (standard deviation = 15, variance = 225). The correlation between the two variables is $r = -.34$.

One of the causes of the IQ variability within each group is genetic variability, and the percentage of IQ variance that is due to genetic variance is measured by h^2 values. Both groups can have high heritability,[4] but that would only reflect the impact of genes *within* each group. Because the h^2 values cannot give information about environmental characteristics outside the sample, the potential impact of much lower (or much higher) lead levels than what group members experienced cannot be measured by h^2. On the other hand, the difference *between* the groups – where the higher average IQ is seen in the group with low lead exposure – is a purely environmental impact on the groups' averages, and it acts independently of the genetic impact that operates within each group. This example is a good reminder that heritability measures the influence of genetics *under current environmental conditions*; change that environment radically enough, and the trait may change.

The example here is idealized, but it is not completely unrealistic. Height is highly heritable (h^2 values between .87 and .93 for men, and between .68 and .84 for women in one typical study; Silventoinen et al., 2003), and yet, in many countries, adults are taller today than in the past (Komlos, Hau, & Bourguinat, 2003; Komlos & Lauderdale, 2007). The gains in nutrition and health care that have caused people to be taller today have not reduced the importance of genetic differences in determining height differences within modern populations.

A similar situation really does occur with intelligence. IQ scores are much higher today than in the earliest days of intelligence testing (Flynn, 1984, 1987; Pietschnig & Voracek, 2015). Chapter 14 will discuss this increase and its potential causes in more depth. But the important message is that IQ scores are influenced by genes (as seen by the high heritability values) but also that environmental changes – like reduced exposure to lead or a proper diet for people with PKU – can also increase IQ.

CONCLUSION

Untreated PKU, lead poisoning, and iodine deficiency all have one thing in common: they all have large detrimental effects on intelligence (Hunt, 2011). This is in spite of the strong influence of genes, where h^2 in many studies is approximately .50. The examples in this chapter show that environmental variables can have a strong influence on heritable traits – including intelligence. By making important changes to the environment, individuals can see remarkable boosts in their IQ scores. However, this does not mean that every treatment will be as effective or as inexpensive as the treatments in this chapter. Chapters 14–16 will discuss the limits of other interventions that are often proposed to increase IQ scores in healthy populations.

---

[4] The exact h^2 value does not matter for the purposes of this example. The principles are the same, regardless of the actual h^2 value.

13

Genes Are Not Important for Determining Intelligence

... the psychologist's typical strategy of partitioning the determinants of behavioral characteristics into separate genetic versus environmental causes is no more sensible than asking which areas of a rectangle are mostly due to length and which to width.

(Mischel, 2005, paragraph 17)

Despite the high heritability values for intelligence, there are people who still make a variety of arguments to nullify or deny the genetic influence of intelligence. These people use mental gymnastics to argue that even though heritability can be high, environment still matters far more than genetics in determining someone's intelligence. While no scientist argues that environment is irrelevant, the evidence has mounted that genes are a far more important influence on intelligence than many psychologists believed in the twentieth century.

The quote at the beginning of the chapter is from Walter Mischel, one of the most influential psychologists of the twentieth century (E. Diener, Oishi, & Park, 2014; Haggbloom et al., 2002). Mischel studied how environments influence people's behavior and found that people's actions were consistent – as long as the environment stayed somewhat consistent. Changing environments, though, often led to changes in behavior. Given this perspective, it makes sense why he would see the value of considering the impact of the environment on people's behavior. However, Mischel (2005) was mistaken to minimize genetic influences so quickly. High heritability does indicate that genes matter – not just for intelligence, but for many other human traits.

TWO TO TANGO: GENETICS AND ENVIRONMENT

First, it is important to explain what Mischel gets right: it is true that genes and environment do both contribute to a person's intelligence level.[1] If a person does not have enough of the versions of genes that boost IQ, then no environment – no matter how favorable – will make a person earn a high IQ on an intelligence test. Conversely, even the luckiest win in the genetic lottery is irrelevant if an environment is extremely negative, such as a childhood marred by long-term iodine deficiency, lead poisoning, famine, neglect, or severe brain injuries. Both genes and environment make their contributions to a person's intelligence level.

The generally accepted theory is that genes set limits on the possible intelligence levels a person can have. These limits are called the *reaction range*. Within the reaction range, environmental variables determine the exact intelligence level of a person (Hunt, 2011). Scarr and Weinberg summed up the idea well when they stated, "Genes do not fix behavior; rather, they establish a range of possible reactions to the range of possible experiences that the environment provides" (1978, p. 29). Where within the reaction range a person's IQ develops is a consequence of the environment. Thus, it does take both genes and environment to produce a trait, and both are important.

Where Mischel (2005) erred was in claiming that these contributions to a trait make it impossible or nonsensical to separate genetic and environmental influence. Yes, it is true that all rectangles get their area from their width and their length, just as it is true that intelligence is always a product of both genetic and environmental influences. But heritability is a measure of the influence of genetic differences on trait differences (i.e., variance, as explained in Chapter 12). Thus, heritability explains relative differences among individuals within a sample. To apply this to Mischel's (2005) analogy, if genes are similar to a rectangle's width and environmental influences are like a rectangle's length, then heritability would be a measure of how differences in width correspond to differences in rectangle area. The fact that every rectangle has length and that this also influences rectangle area does not negate the influence of width.

One leading intelligence scientist used another analogy that makes the same point when she wrote:

The irrelevant truth is that an organism's development requires genes and environments to act in concert. The two forces are inextricable, mutually dependent and constantly interacting. Development is their mutual product, like the dance of two partners. The irrelevant conclusion is that it is therefore impossible to apportion credit for the pair's joint product to each partner separately – say, 40% of the pair's steps to the man and 60% to the woman. The inappropriate generalization is that behavior geneticists cannot possibly do what they claim – namely to decompose [trait] *variation* among individuals ... This is analogous to saying that it would be impossible to estimate whether *differences* in quality of tango performances among American couples is owing more to skill variation among the male partners than to skill variation among

---

[1] This discussion does not just apply to intelligence. The concepts of how genes and environment create a trait are valid for any trait.

the female partners (i.e., genetic vs. nongenetic variation) ... (Gottfredson, 2009, p. 38, emphasis added)

Yes, it takes genetics and environment to create a trait – just as it takes two partners to dance a tango. But that does not change the fact that some couples are better dancers than others and that it is possible to identify whether couples vary in their quality more because of the variability in how well the man dances compared to the woman (or vice versa). Thus, everyone agrees that genes and environment matter. Where Mischel (2005) and people in his camp disagree with Gottfredson (2009) and people in her camp (including me) is whether it is possible to talk about the influence of genes separately from environment. Decades of behavioral genetics research – especially in producing data about heritability – show that this it is possible to talk about the differences in genes and the differences in environment and how each impacts *differences* among individuals in a trait.

SEND IN THE CLONES: HIGH GENETIC SIMILARITY AMONG HUMANS

Another tactic people sometimes use to dismiss the importance of genes on intelligence differences (e.g., Grison, Heatherton, & Gazzaniga, 2017, pp. 301, 302) is to state that high genetic similarity among humans means that genetic differences are trivial in their impact. This belief is based on the fact that humans are about 99% genetically identical. With so much genetic similarity, it can seem like that last 1% can be trivial. If this genetic similarity is high, then it may seem implausible that high heritability can have much influence on the development of a trait.

This viewpoint oversimplifies the relationship between genetic similarity and physical and/or psychological differences. First, the 99% of genes that are identical in all humans are what makes people all belong to the same species and be able to interbreed with one another. Without a high degree of genetic similarity, individuals would belong to separate species. This is apparent when comparing humans with their closest relatives: chimpanzees. The two species are "only" about 96% genetically identical (The Chimpanzee Sequencing and Analysis Consortium, 2005).

The 99% of DNA that is identical in all humans is what creates the similarities among every member of the species. The reason why everyone has a head, two lungs, fingernails, two eyes, a brain, etc., is because the DNA that is identical in all humans encodes for the characteristics that all humans share. Therefore, these traits are genetically transmitted, but they are not considered in discussions of heritability because heritability focuses on differences – not similarities. Heritability values do not apply to traits that are identical in all humans; those traits are genetically inherited, but h^2 does not describe anything about these traits because there are no trait differences to quantify.

Second, the genes that are identical in all humans cannot contribute to heritability because h^2 is a measure of the influence of genetic *differences*. Therefore, all of the influence in heritability lies in that 1% of genes that differ from person to person (Bouchard, 2014). While this does not seem like much, that 1% corresponds to millions of subtle differences in each person's DNA (Hunt, 2011). Some of these will have an impact on individual differences in intelligence.

Third, subtle genetic differences can sometimes correspond to big differences in a trait. An obvious example of this is when a person is born with a genetic condition because they inherited two defective recessive versions of a gene. Examples of this type of genetic condition include PKU (discussed in Chapter 12), sickle cell anemia, cystic fibrosis, Tay-Sachs disease, and xeroderma pigmentosum. For all these conditions (and others), possessing two defective copies of a single gene can lead to a major medical condition that drastically affects the person's life, even if all other genes in the person's DNA are completely normal. When a defective version of a gene is on an X chromosome, then males are particularly susceptible to genetic disorders because they do not have a second, normal copy of the gene on their Y chromosome. Common disorders of this type include red–green color blindness, muscular dystrophy, and hemophilia.

Even within the normal range of development, subtle genetic differences can result in major differences in traits (Cochran & Harpending, 2009). For example, the 1% of genetic differences among humans is at least partially responsible for the major differences in height, which in adult men range from an average of 143 cm in Pygmies to 184 cm in Dutchmen[2] (McEvoy & Visscher, 2009). The 1% of genes which vary in humans also entirely accounts for the genetic influence on other heritable traits like heart disease, weight, aggressive behavior, and intelligence (Warne et al., 2018).

An example from another species makes it clear that small genetic differences can result in major changes in traits. Domesticated dog breeds differ from one another in approximately 0.15% of their genes, which means humans are over six times more genetically diverse than dogs. Yet, the differences between toy poodles and huskies are very obvious and drastic. In fact, genetic diversity among dogs and related species is so low that many of them (e.g., dogs, coyotes, wolves, foxes, dingoes, and jackals) can interbreed (Wayne & Ostrander, 1999).

To recap, humans do exhibit a high degree of similarity among one another. This does not nullify the impact of genes on intelligence (or any other heritable trait, for that matter). High genetic similarity among humans is necessary for

---

[2] In non-metric measurements, this corresponds to the average Pygmy man being 4 feet, 8.3 inches tall, and the average Dutchman being 6 feet, 0.4 inches tall. These are extremes in group averages. The differences among all individuals (i.e., the absolute tallest person in the world compared to the shortest adult in the world) are even more extreme.

people to all belong to the same species. The comparatively few remaining genetic differences (about 1% of the entire human genome) are the source of all genetic influence on the differences (i.e., heritability) found in any trait. Additionally, that 1% of the genome corresponds to millions of potential genetic differences between any two randomly selected people. It is within these varying portions of people's DNA that heritability lies. Finally, even subtle differences in genetic makeup can result in major differences in traits. All of these facts combine to show that high genetic similarity among humans does not negate the importance of genetic influences on any trait – including intelligence.

CONCLUSION

While no one dismisses the importance of environmental influences, genes do have an impact on people's intelligence. Some individuals who want to ignore the research on the heritability of intelligence have made arguments that dismiss genetic influences. These arguments, though they sound enticing to the uninformed listener, fall apart under scrutiny. Yes, both genes and environment are necessary to create a trait in a person; but heritability is concerned with the influence of genetic differences on trait differences. This emphasis on differences does not negate the importance of environment, nor does investigating the influence of environmental differences negate the influence of genetics. While humans are extremely similar genetically to one another, this says little more than that they belong to the same species. The genetic differences that do exist are important influences on differences in intelligence – and any other heritable trait.

14

Environmentally Driven Changes in IQ Mean that Intelligence Is Malleable

> Being raised by different parents changes not only a child's family environment, but also all factors contributed by the neighborhood, peer, and school environments. These often-drastic environmental changes make adoption studies a particularly powerful method to assess the malleability of intelligence.
>
> (Sauce & Matzel, 2018, p. 34)

Chapter 12 shows that high heritability and strong environmentally driven change are both possible in the same trait. By providing an appropriate diet to people with PKU, reducing lead exposure to children, and treating iodine deficiency, it is possible to either increase intelligence or prevent large drops in intelligence. These environmental interventions are major successes that are probably responsible for millions of people being smarter today than they would have been otherwise. Adoption studies also show that being raised in a middle- or upper-class family home probably raises IQ scores by as much as 4–5 points, an increase that would have major positive impacts on people's lives (see Chapter 11).

Because of the success of these environmental interventions, some people believe that intelligence is highly malleable and that it is possible to increase IQ through other common interventions. An example of this is at the opening of the chapter, where Sauce and Matzel (2018) argue that a handful of large, environmentally induced changes in IQ must lead to the conclusion that intelligence is a trait that is changeable and that – with available interventions – many people can become smarter. Unfortunately, studies that investigate the effectiveness of treatments to increase intelligence do not support this high level of optimism. This chapter will discuss some other large changes in IQ scores and why they do not necessarily mean intelligence is malleable. In Chapters 15 and 16, I will discuss the results of specific interventions to raise IQ.

ADOPTION STUDIES

The impacts of adoption on IQ are unquestioned, and even scholars who are very skeptical of the effectiveness of interventions to raise IQ agree that adoption causes an increase in IQ by about 5 points (e.g., Jensen, 1998). However, it is not clear what it is about adoptive families that causes their adoptive children to be smarter than if they had stayed with their birth parents. As stated in Chapter 11, in industrialized nations, adoptive families are usually middle- and upper-class, but that does not mean that income is the cause of higher IQ for adopted children. These families differ from low-income families in many ways that are not economic, and it is impossible to isolate these differences and to examine them individually to determine why adopted children experience an IQ increase. Perhaps having access to high-quality services (e.g., health care, preschool, K-12 education) increases IQ. Maybe it is the nicer, safer neighborhoods that these families live in. Perhaps the greater stability of the homes – with less divorce and greater likelihood of having two parents in the family – makes adopted children smarter. Maybe parental behavior (for example, more parent–child interactions, parents involved in the child's education) increases IQ. Perhaps they each make their own little contributions that then combine to increase IQ by approximately 5 points.

Or maybe it is none of these characteristics that have a causal impact on higher IQ at all. There is no way to know for sure with the current evidence. Scientists can't force adoptive parents to eliminate a potentially beneficial piece of their home environment just to see if it reduces the impact of adoption on IQ scores. That would not be ethical, and few parents would agree to be part of a study like that.[1]

Because the characteristics of adoptive homes are not possible to isolate, it is not clear what, exactly, other parents should do to increase their child's IQ. The best possible answer based on adoption data is, "Try to make your home environment good enough that you would be eligible to adopt a child." This is not an effective foundation for a targeted intervention to raise IQ.

UP, UP, AND AWAY: THE FLYNN EFFECT

Environmental impacts on IQ scores are not limited to individual people who have been adopted, or escaped the ravages of PKU or lead poisoning. Worldwide, IQ scores drifted higher over the course of the twentieth century. This means that people today perform better on intelligence tests than their grandparents did. This phenomenon was publicized by philosopher James Flynn, who knew that when intelligence tests were created, the average IQ score was set to be 100. Yet, as time passed, that average gradually increased

---

[1] Imagine a psychologist saying to you, "Congratulations on adopting a baby! Will you cancel your family's health insurance for the next 18 years so that we can learn if that has an impact on your new child's IQ?" Of course, you would answer no.

at a rate of 3 points per decade in the United States (Flynn, 1984). Later, Flynn found this increase in IQ scores was a regular phenomenon that occurred in many other countries (Flynn, 1987), and later research has confirmed his work (Pietschnig & Voracek, 2015).

IQ score increases of 3 points per decade is a lot. This would indicate that a person with an average IQ of 100 from 1970 who had traveled through time to 2020 would only score 85 compared to a twenty-first-century population. A person of average intelligence from 1920 if transported through time to today would score 70, which is about the average IQ for people with Down's Syndrome and the approximate cutoff for being diagnosed with an intellectual disability.[2] Projecting this trend further back in time produces results that simply don't match reality if these IQ score increases were the result of a real rise in intelligence. For example, someone from the era of the American Revolution (almost 250 years ago) would score approximately 25 on a modern intelligence test. This score is so low that the average person would not be expected to master language or feed themselves. But it is simply not possible that the *average* person from the 1770s would have a disability this severe. After all, this is the generation that produced George Washington, Benjamin Franklin, and the other Founding Fathers. If their fellow Americans were really so disabled, someone would have probably mentioned it in surviving documents.

So, IQ scores were increasing, but clearly actual intelligence was not – or at least, not as quickly. Because Flynn was a philosopher, he was willing to consider implications of rising IQ scores that were almost unthinkable to psychologists. Flynn rocked psychology by suggesting that this was evidence that intelligence tests really did not measure intelligence. He also argued that group comparisons of intelligence scores were meaningless and that studies on intelligence and the aging process were invalid (Flynn, 1984, 1987).

Flynn brought so much attention to the increasing IQ scores that Herrnstein and Murray (1994) called it the *Flynn effect*, a name that has since stuck. Ironically, Flynn was not the first to notice the increasing IQ scores,[3] and he never claimed to have discovered the phenomenon. What Flynn did was discover how universal and regular the increases in IQ scores were. He also asked some tough questions about intelligence tests that psychologists were not always prepared to answer. Before Flynn, psychologists just took the idea that intelligence tests measure intelligence for granted. When they did discuss the increasing IQ scores, it was with the belief that it was a quirk of test construction (e.g., Garfinkle & Thorndike, 1976), and not with the understanding of how far-reaching the increases were (e.g., Thorndike, 1975; Tuddenham, 1948).

---

[2] An IQ of 85 is lower than 84.1% of the population. An IQ of 70 is lower than 97.7% of the population.

[3] According to Lynn (2013), that honor goes to Runquist (1936).

TABLE 14.1 *Percentage of Americans, ages 25 and over, with a high school diploma or bachelor's degree, 1940–2017*

	1940	1960	1980	2000	2017
High school diploma	24.5%	41.1%	68.6%	84.1%	89.6%
Bachelor's degree	4.6%	7.7%	17.0%	25.6%	34.2%

Source: National Center for Educational Statistics, 2017, Table 104.10.

The Flynn effect is relevant to the debate about the malleability of intelligence because these IQ increases cannot possibly be genetic in origin. Human gene pools just do not change quickly enough for IQ scores to increase 3 points every decade (Ceci, 1991). The Flynn effect provides incontrovertible evidence that IQ scores can increase dramatically due to changes in the environment. After Flynn's articles in the mid-1980s, the race was on to discover the cause of the Flynn effect because discovering it could hold the key to creating interventions that make people smarter.

After more than three decades of research, it is clear that there is no single cause of the Flynn effect (Mackintosh, 2011). Instead, several causes seem to act at the same time to increase IQ scores in a country. One highly likely cause is increased education (Hunt, 2011). Compared to previous generations, people who live in industrialized nations in the twenty-first century are much more educated. This is apparent in Table 14.1, which shows that a far greater percentage of Americans graduate from high school and college in the twenty-first century than did in 1940. An additional year of education causes IQ to increase 1–5 points (Ritchie & Tucker-Drob, 2018), and disruptions in school attendance seem to lower IQ in children (Ceci, 1991). However, the degree to which this effect is cumulative is not clear. In other words, there is no guarantee that each additional year of school keeps adding 1–5 IQ points until people stop going to school. Still, it would be very surprising if school – where people are taught knowledge and how to think – did not contribute to the Flynn effect.

Other suggested causes of the Flynn effect include improved physical health. Blood lead levels are lower in industrialized nations (see Chapter 12). Additionally, brain size in the UK and Germany is larger today than it was a generation ago (Woodley of Menie, Peñaherrera, Fernandes, Becker, & Flynn, 2016), which may be important because brain size is positively correlated with intelligence (see Chapter 3). Birth weight – a measure of prenatal health – has increased (e.g., Surkan, Hsieh, Johansson, Duckman, & Cnattingius, 2004), probably due to better medical care and healthier behavior from pregnant women, such as lower smoking rates during pregnancy. Because the time before birth is very critical in brain development, this may result in the Flynn effect being apparent even in very young children (e.g., Bassok & Latham, 2017).

One intriguing theory about the Flynn effect is that environments have become more cognitively complex – that is, they require more thinking to navigate in. As the industrial revolution and then the computer revolution took hold, navigating life required more brain power. As people went to school for longer periods of time and learned how to reason and think better, they were better able to think abstractly. The more complex environment ensured that they would have to use these skills in daily life. The unintended side effect of all this abstract thinking is higher performance on intelligence tests compared to previous generations. James Flynn summarized this theory well:

> The ultimate cause is the trend to modernity, caught but only partially so by the industrial revolution ... The intermediate causes are the spinoffs of modernity, such as better nutrition, smaller family size, hothouse "education" of preschoolers, new parenting, more formal education, far more creative work and leisure, the new visual culture, and urbanization. (Flynn, 2013, p. 856, emphasis removed)

Flynn sees all these consequences of industrialization and modernization as creating this increase in IQ. This would explain why the twentieth century saw such large gains in IQ in many countries as they adopted these innovations. It is because of the dramatic gains in IQ scores (which, it must be remembered, can *only* have an environmental cause) that many people see the Flynn effect as evidence that treatments can increase intelligence.

However, this optimism is misplaced. While the Flynn effect shows that improvements in the environment can increase IQ in populations, it doesn't say much about what to do to help boost IQ in *individuals*. Sure, the Flynn effect suggests that to raise IQ people need to go to school, be healthy, and live in the modern world. But in wealthy countries, almost everyone experiences these conditions to some degree. Based on the Flynn effect, it is not clear what more anyone can do to raise IQ in a country like the United States or in other wealthy nations. On the other hand, developing nations that implement reforms to improve public health, education levels, and modernize the economy are seeing larger IQ gains than anything seen in industrialized nations in the twentieth century (e.g., Daley, Whaley, Sigman, Espinosa, & Neumann, 2003; Liu & Lynn, 2013; Wang & Lynn, 2018). Many nations are already implementing these changes to their societies for reasons that often have little do with an explicit attempt to raise IQ, such as a desire to increase economic growth or to develop the local education system.

Since the early 2000s, there has been a new development in research on the Flynn effect. The increase in IQ has stopped in some countries: Denmark (Teasdale & Owen, 2000), Norway (Sundet, Barlaug, & Torjussen, 2004; Bratsberg & Rogeberg, 2017), Finland (Dutton & Lynn, 2013), the Netherlands (Woodley & Meisenberg, 2013), and France (Dutton & Lynn, 2015). Additionally, the Flynn effect has slowed down and may stop soon in Germany, Austria, the United States, Australia, and the United Kingdom (Pietschnig & Gittler, 2015; Russell, 2007). These countries are all industrialized and wealthy, with access to all the technological, societal, and cultural changes that modern society brings to a nation. The countries also have widespread access to a quality education, and some provide universal health care to their citizens. These countries may have reached (or may soon reach) a saturation point where environmental improvements provide no additional boost in IQ. If this is true – as some experts believe (Rindermann, Becker, & Coyle, 2017) – then there is little more that Flynn effect-driven improvements in the environment can do to raise IQ for most people living in these countries.

STEPPING INTO THE RIVER TWICE: INDIVIDUAL GROWTH AND FLUCTUATIONS

At the individual level, IQ scores seem to stabilize between the ages of (approximately) 7 and 10. Thereafter, "Small changes are common, large changes are rare" (Jensen, 1980b, p. 283). However, large changes in IQ do occasionally happen, even in people who are experiencing typical development. About 10–15% of children experience a 15-point change or more during their childhood after their peers' scores have stabilized (Baldwin & Stetcher, 1922; Burks, Jensen, & Terman, 1930; Jensen, 1980b, 1998; Moffitt, Caspi, Harkness, & Silva, 1993). Some people see these exceptions as evidence that IQ can be changed.

Moffitt et al. (1993) published the best study on IQ fluctuations in childhood. The researchers administered an intelligence test to almost 800 children at ages 7, 9, 11, and 13. A total of 13% of children had a large IQ fluctuation from one test administration to another, but a change was "variable in its timing, idiosyncratic in its source and transient in its course" (Moffitt et al., 1993, p. 455). In other words, the fluctuations were random, and after a large change the child's IQ score would then rebound to about its previous level at the following testing. Additionally, there seemed to be no triggering event for these changes. "For every child who had a life event linked with IQ change, we found at least five children who had experienced that same event, but with no measurable effect on IQ" (Moffitt et al., 1993, p. 491). So, while IQ changes do happen after age 7, they only occur in a minority of children, the changes usually are temporary, and there does not seem to be any apparent environmental cause. Earlier research on IQ fluctuations showed similar results (Baldwin & Stetcher, 1922, pp. 36–39; Burks et al., 1930, pp. 41–61).[4] As a result, no intervention to improve IQ has come out of the study of children with large IQ fluctuations, and that fact seems unlikely to change.

But the stabilization of IQ seems confusing because children *do* get smarter over time. Children's mental ability increases as they go to school, learn new knowledge, and have new experiences. This is why a typically developing

---

[4] This led one leading expert to write, "'late bloomers' are quite rare as far as IQ is concerned" (Jensen, 1980b, p. 285).

10-year-old will be smarter than a typically developing 5-year-old, and it seems to contradict the stability of IQ in childhood. (If IQ is so stable, it seems odd that any learning would be possible.) As a result, some people believe that the change that is apparent from age to age can lead to clues on how to change IQ.

However, this thinking mixes up two concepts: (1) IQ as a measure of someone's performance on a test of *g* compared to their peers and (2) individual absolute changes in knowledge or ability. An IQ score is the relative standing compared to one's peers, and that does not change much after middle childhood. In other words, a child with an IQ of 85 at age 10 is going to have a similar IQ at age 20 because their rank order compared to members of that person's peer group does not change drastically. Age-to-age development (where someone's knowledge or abilities grow) is where the real change happens. But as everyone in the same age group experiences that change, the relative standing of individuals – i.e., their IQ score – changes little (Rindermann, 2018, p. 57). Thus, there are two kinds of change, and because they are different, age-to-age change does not impact IQ and is irrelevant for creating an intervention to raise IQ compared to a person's peers (Gottfredson, 2009).

CONCLUSION

All four of these changes in ability – adoption studies, the Flynn effect, individual fluctuations in IQ, and absolute growth in knowledge and intelligence – appear to offer hope for creating interventions that would increase intelligence. However, all four are dead-ends for providing information that could result in interventions that make people smarter. Adoption studies show that growing up in a middle- or upper-class home is beneficial for a person's IQ, but it is not clear how this IQ boost occurs or what specific elements of these homes cause adopted children to have IQ score increases. The Flynn effect is a population-level phenomenon (not an occurrence for individuals), and wealthy nations are already reaping the IQ-related benefits of industrialization. The Flynn effect also provides little guidance about what other environmental changes or treatments citizens of wealthy nations should experience in order to raise their IQ. The fluctuations in IQ that are sometimes seen in individuals seem to be random and temporary – two characteristics that do not form a useful foundation for interventions. Finally, while the absolute change in knowledge and intelligence across the lifespan is a real phenomenon, it does not provide information about raising IQ because IQ is not a measure of absolute intelligence. Rather, it is a measurement of an examinee's intelligence compared to that person's age mates – who are also experiencing the same development changes. The absolute changes arising from development and the relative changes required to raise IQ are not interchangeable.

Other chapters in this book show that environmental influences are important for determining intelligence. The Flynn effect and the interventions discussed in Chapter 12 (i.e., treating PKU, eliminating iodine deficiency, and preventing lead exposure in children) show that massive improvements in IQ are possible. However, these examples are very specific, and for people already in positive environments – as many people in industrialized nations are – current knowledge about the environmental causes of high IQ provides few clues about how to raise IQ.

15

Social Interventions Can Drastically Raise IQ

> The good news is, raising a smarter child is easier than you think. It doesn't require making an investment in expensive equipment of high-priced tutors. Nor do you have to devote every waking minute to demanding academic drills. There are easy (and I do mean easy) yet highly effective strategies that can vastly improve your child's brain power. It's as simple as playing the right games with your child, putting the right food on your child's plate, maintaining a brain-enhancing environment in your home, and last but not least, giving your child lots of love.
>
> (Perlmutter & Colman, 2006, p. 3)

Authors of self-help books, like the book I quoted above, have no shortage of suggestions for how to increase intelligence. Blogs, parenting websites, and social media also have tips for raising IQ, usually in children. Scientists who have studied the issue, though, are usually more cautious, and the promises of raising a child's IQ by 30 points (as in the book by Perlmutter & Colman, 2006) are not realistic. In this chapter, I'll discuss the scientific evidence about social interventions to raise intelligence.

SOCIAL INTERVENTIONS

A social intervention is a treatment or program to raise intelligence that is not medical or biological in its basis. Unlike social interventions, the methods of raising IQ that I discussed in Chapter 12 are all biologically based. They raise intelligence by improving brain health (i.e., treating iodine deficiency) or preventing brain damage (i.e., treating PKU or preventing lead poisoning). Social interventions, however, improve intelligence by helping a person's psychological functioning or learning. They do not create major changes in the biology of the brain, but they do change how people think and reason.

In this book, I have already discussed one social intervention: education. Strong evidence indicates that keeping people in school longer results in higher IQ (Ceci, 1991; Ritchie & Tucker-Drob, 2018). Education has been a wildly successful social intervention to raise IQ, and it is likely to be the cause for some of the IQ gains seen in the Flynn effect (see Chapter 14). Another social intervention is adoption, which raises IQ by approximately 4–5 points (Jensen, 1998; Kendler et al., 2015). Therefore, it is reasonable to expect other social interventions to also increase IQ.

I'M JUST A POOR BOY. NOBODY LOVES ME: CONSEQUENCES OF SEVERE NEGLECT

It is known that severe deprivation lowers IQ in humans. An early study of this topic was conducted in Iowa on children who lived in cramped conditions in a state orphanage with highly regimented and socially isolated lives. The focus of the few adults operating the orphanage was on meeting the children's basic needs of food, shelter, and clothing. One-on-one interaction and care were rare, and there were few toys available. While these conditions are deplorable, they were typical of orphanages of the 1930s in the United States (Skeels, 1966). Regardless of initial IQ when they were admitted to the orphanage, prolonged time in the orphanage tended to result in an IQ score below 80 (Skeels, Updegraff, Wellman, & Williams, 1938, p. 42).

Yet, when children in this institution were transferred to a different environment with more social interaction, their IQ scores increased – often by a large amount. In one group of 13 children, IQ increased an average of 27.5 points in 18.9 months after transfer to a different state facility with more social interactions. Twelve similar children who stayed in the unfavorable conditions for an average of 26.5 months had IQ score declines averaging 26.2 points (Skeels, 1966, pp. 10, 13).[1] In later follow-ups, 11 of the 13 children placed in a more favorable institution were adopted into homes, and 2½ years later had an average IQ of 101.4, and the average of all 13 was 95.9 points – which is in the range of normal intelligence. The 12 children who stayed in the unfavorable institution had an average IQ of 66 at an average age of 6.9 years, and only three had an IQ score above 80 (Skeels, 1966, pp. 21–23).

---

[1] These IQ scores are not directly comparable to modern scores because they were based on the old quotient IQ equation, and not the modern method of calculating IQ, which is based on standard deviations (see the Introduction). Additionally, the children in this study were 7–30 months old when it began, and their original IQ scores were mostly based on reaching physical developmental milestones, like rolling over, sitting up, and walking. These developmental milestones are generally poor predictors of later intelligence (Månsson, Stjernqvist, Serenius, Ådén, & Källén, 2019). Therefore, the IQ score gains and losses in the study are inflated. But even if the gain of 27.5 points and the loss of 26.2 points are four or five times larger than the "real" gains and losses based solely on reasoning ability, this study is still a testament to the powerful benefits of removing children from a neglectful environment.

Two decades later, Skeels tracked down the 25 children, and though he did not administer any intelligence tests, the differences between the two groups were apparent. All 13 of the children who spent time in the more favorable institution were able to live normal lives as adults, while 5 of the 12 people who stayed in the worse environment remained institutionalized. Only 1 of the 7 who lived outside an institution had a job that was not menial (Skeels, 1966, p. 33). The educational differences were stark, with the group that lived in more favorable conditions completing over seven more years of education, on average (Skeels, 1966, p. 37). Clearly, the early environmental differences had a long-lasting impact on these individuals.

While this study has a small sample size of 25, similar research has replicated these results many times. Across 42 studies totaling 3,888 individuals in 19 countries, the average IQ of children growing up in an orphanage was 84, while the average IQ of similar children living in foster homes was 104 (van IJzendoorn, Luijk, & Juffer, 2008). These studies show that prolonged exposure to an unfavorable environment in childhood probably has a long-term detrimental impact on a person's intelligence.

These studies do not apply to children in the United States or other industrialized countries any more. Wealthy countries have eliminated overcrowding in orphanages and modern facilities, and an increased use of foster homes means that children whose birth parent(s) cannot care for them have a much more positive environment than what was common two or three generations ago for such children.

It is not entirely clear what aspect(s) of orphanages depressed IQ scores. Skeels (1966) suggested that it might be the lack of "nurturance and cognitive stimulation . . . love and affection and normal life experiences" (p. 56). Physical health conditions and a lack of a family structure may also be important. Because no one knows why orphanage living depresses IQ, it is unclear how these studies apply to children who are subjected to long-term abuse and neglect while living with family members. This latter group is much larger in industrialized countries than the orphanage population, but they are hard to study. (Most people who are abusing a child do not volunteer for scientific studies about the effects of that abuse – for obvious reasons.) Based on the information from adoption studies and orphanage studies, it seems likely that putting children who are abused or mildly neglected by their parents into a more favorable environment could boost IQ, but it is not clear by how much.

PRESCHOOL

It is even less clear what more typical levels of poverty do to individuals' IQ scores. Many children live in poverty, but not in environments that are neglectful or disadvantaging enough for the authorities to remove them from the care of their family. However, many of these children experience one intervention that is designed to increase their cognitive abilities: preschool.

Preschool is hugely popular, with 65.9% of 4-year-olds and 41.6% of 3-year-olds in the United States attending some form of preschool in 2016 (National Center for Educational Statistics, 2017, Table 202.10).[2] Enrollment, though, is uneven, with children from wealthier families more likely to attend preschool (Tucker-Drob, 2012). Because education is known to increase IQ, it seems reasonable that preschool can be a social intervention that could raise intelligence. Early studies on the topic were promising. The most famous were the Perry Preschool Project, the Carolina Abecedarian Project, and the Milwaukee Project.

The Milwaukee Project. Started in 1966, the Milwaukee Project had a sample size of 48 African Americans. A total of 20 infants in an experimental group and 20 infants in a control group were considered "at risk" for an intellectual disability because of household poverty and having a mother with an IQ below 75. The remaining 8 were "low risk" because their mothers had IQ scores of 100 or above. The 20 children in the experimental group experienced one of the most intensive social science intervention programs ever devised. The mothers received home visits for 3–5 hours per week for the first 18 months in order to be trained in child care, hygiene, nutrition, financial management, and other parenting and household skills. Every day until the age of 6 (when the 20 children in the experimental group entered the first grade), the children spent time in a high-quality preschool. The child-to-caregiver ratio at this preschool started at 1:1 and gradually increased to 3:1 as the children aged. The experiences the children had in the preschool were numerous:

They [the experiences] include more ways that might conceivably promote cognitive development than a team of child psychologists could think up given a month with nothing else to do. Just about every form of didactic stimulation ever suggested by child development experts . . . seems to have been scheduled. (Jensen, 1989, p. 244)

None of the children in the other two groups received any intervention, though they were given various tests at the same ages as the children in the experimental group.

At age 6, children in the experimental group outscored children in the control group by 21–32 IQ points (Jensen, 1989, p. 248). The children in the experimental group also outscored their siblings by 22.5 points (Jensen, 1989, p. 247), which indicates that the preschool intervention was probably an effective component of the Milwaukee Project because siblings would have also experienced the benefits from the home visits and any changes in parental behavior. By age 10, the experimental group IQ advantage had declined to 18 points. At age 14, there was "only" a 10-point difference between groups.

---

[2] In comparison, only 27.8% of 4-year-olds and 12.9% of 3-year-olds were enrolled in preschool in the United States in 1970.

Academic performance also showed a similar decline for the experimental group. At the end of first grade, the children scored at the 49th percentile (compared to the 30th percentile for children in the control group) for reading, which is almost exactly equal to the average of the 50th percentile.[3] However, by the end of the fourth grade, the experimental group scored at the 19th percentile (compared to the 9th percentile for the control group) in reading. Similar declines were observed in math (from the 34th to 10th percentile for the experimental group in the same grades, compared to a decline from the 18th to 9th percentile for the control group at the same ages).

The score declines and the mismatch between IQ scores and academic performance for the experimental group suggest two conclusions. First, the benefits of the Milwaukee Project's preschool program were not permanent. After they ended, children in the experimental group gradually lost the academic benefits they received in their early childhood. Second, the Milwaukee Project probably raised the IQs of the experimental group children, but did not raise their levels of *g*, as indicated by the severe underachievement in school (Jensen, 1989, 1991, 1998). Thus, the gains in the Milwaukee Project are likely because the staff at the preschool taught the children how to answer intelligence test problems – but not how to improve their general reasoning ability to situations outside the testing setting.

The Carolina Abecedarian Project. The Carolina Abecedarian Project started in 1972 when children were an average of 4.4 months old and continued until age 5. During this time the 57 children in the experimental group attended an academically focused day care for "8 hours a day, 5 days a week, 50 weeks a year" (Spitz, 1997, p. 72). The experimental group also received home visits, and parents were taught how to help their children in school (Protzko, 2017a). Almost all of the 111 participants in the study were African American, though their mothers' IQ scores were higher than in the Milwaukee Project, with an average of 84 (Jensen, 1998, p. 342). At age 5, the experimental group had IQ scores that were 7.5 points higher (on average) than the average IQ score of the 54 members of the control group. This difference declined to 5 points by age 8, where it stayed through adolescence.

Like the Milwaukee Project, the Carolina Abecedarian Project has IQ gains that favor the group that experienced preschool, but some of these IQ score gains were lost over time. Unlike the Milwaukee Project, though, the Carolina Abecedarian Project's IQ score gains also were accompanied by improved performance in school (Jensen, 1998; Neisser et al., 1996). This might indicate that these are real gains in *g*, though some people (e.g., N. Brody, 2008; Spitz, 1997) are still skeptical.

---

[3] A percentile is the percentage of individuals on a test who score below a given score. Therefore, the 49th percentile indicates that children in the experimental group performed better on a reading test than 49% of children in the general school population. A person who is exactly average (in a normal distribution of scores) will outscore 50% of other children.

The Perry Preschool Project. Of the three early studies in the effectiveness of preschool, the Perry Preschool Project is the one that most resembles typical preschool programs. The Perry Preschool Project started in 1962 in Ypsilanti, Michigan, and has followed a total of 123 subjects through age 40. Beginning at age 3, and continuing until age 5, the 58 children in the experimental group spent 2½ hours per weekday in a preschool for 30 weeks per year. The preschool had a student-to-teacher ratio of 6:1 and a curriculum focused on cognitive growth and social skills (Nisbett, 2009). Additionally, once per week, teachers visited the children's home. All children had IQ scores between 70 and 85 and lived in families with low socioeconomic status.

At age 5, when the children entered kindergarten at their regular schools, the experimental group had an IQ of 95, and the 65 children in the control group had an IQ of 83. By the end of grade school, both groups had an IQ of 85 (Nisbett, 2009). However, the school performance of the experimental group was much higher than the school performance of the control group, which did not occur in the Milwaukee Project.

Discussion of the Early Preschool Studies. Advocates of preschool point to these early studies as evidence that they raise intelligence (e.g., Nisbett, 2009), but my summaries of them show that such an interpretation is incomplete. In all three studies, IQ gains diminished greatly after children left the preschool program and entered the regular school environment. This tendency for IQ gains to diminish over time after an intervention ends is called *fadeout,* and it is extremely common in interventions to raise intelligence (Protzko, 2015). Apparently, the only way to eliminate fadeout completely is for a treatment to continue indefinitely. This may explain why adoption and removing children from severely neglectful environments (like an overcrowded orphanage) are effective at producing a permanent increase in IQ: these interventions almost always last until adulthood when the children leave their adoptive parents' home and begin their own independent lives. However, even in adoption studies, the impact of the beneficial home environment is stronger for young children than for older adolescents (e.g., compare Scarr & Weinberg, 1976, and Weinberg, Scarr, & Waldman, 1992), indicating that a form of fadeout still occurs for the long-lasting, pervasive "treatment" of adoption.

It is also important to note that these early studies are much more intensive – and therefore expensive – than most preschool programs. A representative example of this is in teacher-to-student ratios. In the United States in 2016, there were 4.701 million preschoolers (National Center for Educational Statistics, 2017, Table 202.10) and 478,500 preschool teachers (Bureau of Labor Statistics, 2018). This means that the average student-to-teacher ratio is 9.8:1 – higher than the ratios in these early studies.[4] Additionally, the

---

[4] To bring the ratio down to 6:1 (to match the ratio in the Perry Preschool Project) for all 3- and 4-year-olds, the United States would have to hire 850,000 more preschool teachers, which would

educational curriculum of these preschool programs would most likely require much more teacher training than the typical preschool teacher currently has. As a result, these studies provide little evidence that typical preschools increase IQ. For that, it is necessary to turn to modern studies.

Modern Studies of Preschool. The best modern studies of the effects of preschool use a design called the randomized control trial (RCT), which randomly assigns subjects to experimental or control groups. Randomization balances out the groups in every way so that any remaining differences can only be due to the treatment that one group received and the other group did not.

RCTs of preschool are promising. Protzko and his colleagues (2013) found that the average impact of preschool across 16 RCT studies was 4 IQ points for typical preschools and 7 IQ points for preschools that include a language component. Unfortunately, these studies – and many other interventions – suffer from fadeout, and over time the gains are lost as children age (Protzko, 2015).

Moreover, recent studies indicate that preschool interventions produce smaller differences between preschoolers and non-preschoolers in the twenty-first century than they did in the early research on the topic (Duncan & Magnuson, 2013). While this may be surprising to readers, it may merely indicate that the home environment of non-preschoolers has improved, which means that there is less that modern preschool can do to improve a child's outcomes. This is another reason why the findings of the Perry Preschool Project or the Carolina Abecedarian Project may be misleading for a typical, modern setting.

Two recent RCTs are worth discussing in detail. The first was an RCT commissioned by the US Congress to investigate the Head Start program (US Department of Health and Human Services, 2012). With a sample size of 4,667 children who were randomly admitted to or rejected from Head Start, this is the largest RCT ever conducted on preschool. The second was an RCT study of 2,990 children whose parents or guardians applied for them to attend the preschool program created by the state of Tennessee (Lipsey, Farran, & Durkin, 2018). Although neither study includes data from intelligence tests, both studies report scores from academic tests, which are reasonably good measures of *g*.

The findings of both studies are remarkably consistent. At the start of kindergarten, children who participated in preschool had higher scores on a variety of academic measures. However, most of these advantages were gone by the end of first grade. By the end of third grade, children who did *not* attend preschool were performing as well or better on almost every academic measure. Both of these studies showed that fadeout is not a phenomenon unique

cost $24.6 billion annually in payroll costs alone, based on typical salaries for preschool teachers (Bureau of Labor Statistics, 2018). Where the money and bodies to staff preschools at this level would come from is unclear.

to IQ scores. Indeed, the Head Start study reported a variety of health, home, and social/emotional variables, and these all showed fadeout, too (US Department of Health and Human Services, 2012).

Does this mean that preschool is a waste of time and money? Not necessarily. The short-term gains in cognitive and academic variables are undeniable. Whether those gains are worth the expense is a value judgment that will depend on the social goals of parents, government personnel, and others. And there may be non-academic benefits to preschool. For example, if a child's caregiver would prefer to join the workforce, then sending a child to preschool may improve caregiver happiness, contribute to the economy, and improve the family's financial situation. Additionally, many preschool programs (especially those funded by government entities) also encourage immunization of children and provide vision and hearing screenings. Some preschool programs also provide regular nutritious meals for children. These are unequivocal benefits for a child, especially for children whose parents cannot afford these services. Preschool does not have to raise IQ to be a beneficial experience for children.

Additionally, it is possible that some long-term benefits of preschool do not manifest themselves until adolescence or adulthood. Follow-up studies of the Perry Preschool Project participants[5] indicate that children who participated in preschool had higher rates of high school graduation, less criminal behavior, higher incomes in adulthood, higher rates of college attendance and home ownership, and lower rates of smoking (Conti, Heckman, & Pinto, 2016; Nisbett, 2009; Schweinhart & Weikart, 1993). Proponents of preschool call these positive impacts *sleeper effects*, because they are dormant for a long time and do not show themselves until many years after the intervention ends. Both the Carolina Abecedarian Project and the Perry Preschool Project provide evidence of sleeper effects in the children in their experimental groups. If these sleeper effects are real, then investing in high-quality preschool could provide society with major economic benefits as these preschoolers reach maturity.

Sleeper effects are plausible, and nobody has produced a study that disproves their existence. However, it is not clear how sleeper effects develop. (A young adult isn't going to say to himself, "My friends want me to, but I won't steal a car today because I went to preschool when I was 4 years old.") Clearly, sleeper effects cannot be a direct consequence of improved school performance or intelligence because these fade out during the first few years after preschool ends. Theories based on improved social skills or emotional regulation are not promising because these improvements also fade out after preschool ends (Lipsey et al., 2018; US Department of Health and Human Services, 2012). Verifying the existence of sleeper effects and explaining their exact cause is a major challenge to preschool research in the coming decades (Duncan & Magnuson, 2013).

---

[5] Try saying that five times fast.

It is not promising that sleeper effects are based on early studies that do not resemble modern preschool programs. It might not be reasonable to expect sleeper effects to emerge from typical preschool programs. Moreover, all the preschool programs I have discussed in this chapter have been designed for children from low-income families. Expecting sleeper effects and long-term benefits of preschool for children from middle-class and wealthy families may not be justified (Woodhead, 1985). Indeed, it is possible that middle-class and wealthy children experience none of the cognitive benefits of preschool – even the short-term academic benefits.

An additional challenge is that any educational program – no matter how well designed – will appear ineffective when implemented poorly. Carefully controlled pilot studies of educational programs often show strong benefits. But when these are scaled up to encompass many classrooms and communities, there is less control on how staff members operate the program, and the effective component(s) may not be implemented well. This often causes programs to appear ineffective when implemented on a large scale (e.g., Cook et al., 2018) and may be why the Perry Preschool Project and other local, carefully supervised studies produce different results than the nationwide Head Start RCT or the statewide Tennessee RCT.

OTHER SOCIAL INTERVENTIONS TO RAISE INTELLIGENCE

While there have been other social interventions to raise intelligence, most have been too sporadically studied to produce any firm conclusions. Evidence regarding social interventions to raise IQ has been slow to develop for a variety of reasons. One is that – apart from education – there is little consensus about what other interventions would produce a large, noticeable change in problem-solving abilities. As a result, it is not clear what sort of interventions might be worth implementing as an attempt to raise IQ. Additionally, social interventions often have many components, which can make it difficult to isolate the aspects of an intervention that might have a positive impact on intelligence. This is certainly true for preschool programs, adoption studies, and the negative aspects of orphanages.

However, one social intervention that has been studied quite a bit is the famous *Mozart effect*, which originated in a study in which college students who listened to a Mozart sonata performed better on a spatial reasoning task immediately afterwards (Rauscher, Shaw, & Ky, 1993). This study usually does not replicate (e.g., Pietschnig, Voracek, & Formann, 2010; Stough, Kerkin, Bates, & Mangan, 1994), and psychologists believe that the effect is not real. There is no evidence that Mozart's music is special in any way or that playing it – or any genre of music – increases listeners' intelligence. Unfortunately, one recent study showed that 59% of the general public and 55% of teachers believe that classical music increases children's reasoning ability (Macdonald, Germine, Anderson, Christodoulou, & McGrath, 2017).

CONCLUSION

The evidence is unequivocal that children who spend a long period of time in a neglectful, deprived environment experience a lowered IQ and long-term negative effects. Removing children from an environment like this – whether through adoption or improving their living conditions – is a boon for their intelligence (and their quality of life, in general).

For children who live in poverty, preschool is, by far, the most studied social intervention to raise intelligence, and early studies were promising. Initial results of preschool are always strong, but as soon as the intervention ends, fadeout starts, and any gains are usually gone within a few years. Although benefits of preschool may accrue in adolescence or adulthood, it is unclear how this happens and whether these benefits occur in typical preschool programs.

Raising intelligence permanently is hard, and it seems that nothing short of an intensive, years-long intervention that includes academic, social, and health improvements throughout childhood and adolescence will permanently raise IQ.[6] Psychologists do not know, at this time, how to use social interventions to improve the intelligence of children who live in middle- or upper-class homes in industrialized countries.

---

[6] Hey, that sounds like adoption!

16

Brain-Training Programs Can Raise IQ

> LearningRx clients see an average 15-point increase in IQ and an average age equivalence increase of 3.4 years in as little as 12 weeks.
>
> (LearningRx, 2018, p. 139)

> . . . significant increases in general intelligence, of 28 points on average, can be produced by undertaking online . . . skills training.
>
> (Roche, 2016)

Attempts to increase intelligence are not limited to social interventions. Since the early 2000s, there has been a desire among psychologists, educators, and the public to improve intelligence by training people how to think better and solve problems. These programs take many different forms, but with interactive technology becoming cheaper and more available (especially through mobile devices) several user-directed "brain-training" programs have become popular. The theory behind these programs is that training people to use the cognitive skills that intelligence test items require will result in improved problem solving and, therefore, intelligence (e.g., Cassidy, Roche, Colbert, Stewart, & Grey, 2016).

BRAIN TRAINING: THE WHAT AND THE WHY

The theory behind these brain-training programs is plausible because everyone uses these thinking skills as they answer intelligence test items – and smarter people are better at using those skills. If the mastery of thinking skills causes people to earn higher scores on intelligence tests, then training these skills may raise intelligence.

One important skill for solving intelligence test items is working memory, which is a temporary mental store of information. By storing information temporarily, a person can easily recall it and use it for conscious problem solving (Baddeley, 1992). A simple math problem can show how most people use their working memory:

$$\frac{20 - 4}{2}$$

Most people approach this problem by solving the portion in the numerator first: 20 − 4 = 16. They then divide 16 by 2 to produce a final answer: 16 ÷ 2 = 8. Completing this process requires that a person remember the number 16 (the solution from the first step) in order to begin the second step. That number 16 is held in working memory for conscious use. Many multi-step mental tasks require some use of working memory, including backwards digit span, analogies, and matrix reasoning problems.

Although everyone has a working memory, some people are able to hold more information in their working memory or are able to use their working memory more efficiently (Baddeley, 1992; G. A. Miller, 1956). So, it should be unsurprising that people with a larger or better-functioning working memory score higher on intelligence tests (Brydges, Reid, Fox, & Anderson, 2012; Kyllonen & Cristal, 1990). As a result, some people have hypothesized that improving people's working memory will produce higher intelligence (Melby-Lervåg, Redick, & Hulme, 2016).

Additionally, it is reasonable to expect programs that train people's thinking to increase intelligence because of the most successful known method of raising intelligence: education. It is known that requiring someone to stay in school longer raises IQ (Ritchie & Tucker-Drob, 2018), and this is most likely because schooling teaches students how to think, solve problems, and use information (Ceci, 1991). Thus, a targeted intervention designed to teach these very skills could raise intelligence without requiring extensive time in school.[1]

EVALUATING BRAIN TRAINING

Unquestionably, brain-training games improve scores on the tasks that users engage in (Protzko, 2017b; Simons et al., 2016; Stojanoski, Lyons, Pearce, & Owen, 2018). This should be unsurprising because it means that training people on a task makes them better at that task. It is also clear that brain-training programs produce improvements in similar tasks – a phenomenon called *near transfer* (Melby-Lervåg et al., 2016; Sala & Gobet, 2017). Again, this is not

[1] The websites for brain-training programs use other rationales for why their programs should work. For example, LearningRx's website states that because the brain – especially early in life – is able to modify its functioning in response to injury or environmental changes (a property called *neuroplasticity*), brain training can improve intelligence. The evidence supporting these other justifications is slim, and the connection between pure neurology and human learning is often unclear. I prefer to keep my discussion related to the research about environmental impacts of intelligence/IQ research because this research is most likely to produce an intervention that actually raises intelligence.

surprising because near transfer happens frequently in life: teaching a person how to dance the tango will give them skills that help them learn how to dance the foxtrot better.

Brain-training programs, though, rely on one of two processes to raise intelligence: the first is called *far transfer*, which occurs when the training on a task improves skills on dissimilar tasks. An example of far transfer would be if teaching someone how to dance a tango made them better at computer programming. The second process by which brain training could work is if it develops general skills or traits (like intelligence) that apply to many tasks.

The evidence is clear that brain-training interventions do *not* result in either far transfer or general training (Protzko, 2017b; Redick, 2019; Sala & Gobet, 2017, 2019; Simons et al., 2016; Stojanoski et al., 2018). For example, the authors of a thorough review of 87 studies on working memory training found that, "there is no good evidence that working memory training improves intelligence test scores or other measures of 'real-world' cognitive skills" (Melby-Lervåg et al., 2016, p. 512). Studies that show large gains in IQ from brain-training programs are generally poorly designed; the better designed the study is, the less likely it is to show any far transfer or general skill training (Redick, 2019; Sala & Gobet, 2017, 2019).

An example of low-quality research suggesting that far transfer or general training can occur is in an article by Cassidy et al. (2016) on the Strengthening Mental Abilities with Relational Training (SMART) brain-training program[2] in which children completed 55 modules to teach them how to identify the relationships between pairs of items in order to understand the relationship between items that were not paired. For example:

RIH is the opposite of MOJ
 MOJ is the same as WIK

The child would then be taught how to discern that RIH is the opposite of WIK. More difficult items like this can be created by increasing the number of components and adding superfluous information. Cassidy et al. (2016) found that children who used the SMART program for 8.6 weeks had IQ scores that were an average of 23.3 points higher on the British version of the WISC-IV. Another study in the same article showed that 6.2 weeks of training on the same program raised children's scores on an educational aptitude test by approximately 30 points. However, these studies were extremely poorly designed. They had small sample sizes (15 in the first study and 30 in the second study), no control group, no follow-up to determine if fadeout occurred, and no attempt to discern whether the gains in IQ were related to

---

[2] Available at http://raiseyouriq.com. When I wrote this chapter in 2019, the front page of the website promised to "Raise IQ by 20–30 points – Increase intelligence – Make learning easier." That claim has since been removed from the main page, but is still present on some of the other pages.

improvements in thinking outside the testing situation (e.g., in the form of school performance).

Moreover, the authors' own data provides evidence against their claims. In both studies, there was a *negative* correlation between improvement on the SMART program task and the improvement of IQ scores. This indicates that the children who improved the most on the relationship task had the smallest gains in IQ – and vice versa – which is the exact opposite result that one would expect if the SMART program really did raise IQ. So why did IQ scores increase? It is not entirely clear, but one possibility is that the rules that the relationship task taught are also the same rules that are used to solve some intelligence test questions. As a result, the children were well trained to look for patterns in carefully constructed test questions, which caused inflated IQ scores. This shows that it is possible to have gains in IQ without gains in *g*.

Gains in IQ without gains in *g* are not unique to the SMART brain-training program. The same result probably occurred in the Milwaukee Project (Jensen, 1989, 1998; see Chapter 15 of this book). It is also probably why matrix tests saw some of the strongest Flynn effect gains (see Chapter 14) of any intelligence test formats: solving matrix items requires mastering a limited number of rules. Once a population learns how to identify the patterns in these rules, scores on matrix items increase greatly (Armstrong & Woodley, 2014). Indeed, the Flynn effect may mostly be a result of improvements of narrow cognitive abilities (in Stratum I and Stratum II of the Cattell–Horn–Carroll model, described in the Introduction) that lead to higher IQ scores without contributing to increases in *g*.

An extreme example of increasing IQ without increasing *g* or intelligence occurs with cheating. If an examinee memorizes the answer to intelligence test questions, then their IQ score will increase greatly – but that doesn't make the examinee smarter. Goode (2002) reported a high-profile example of cheating where a child's mother gained access to the test's manual (which included the answer key) and trained her 6-year-old child to give correct answers to the questions. The child obtained an IQ of 298![3] But there is no evidence that he actually became smarter or better at problem solving by memorizing the test answers.

---

[3] The cheating was not the only reason this IQ score was inflated. The psychologist, Linda Silverman, administered the 1972 version of the Stanford–Binet. At the time of testing (April 2000), the test was 28 years old, and the Flynn effect would have increased the child's scores by about 8–10 points. Also, that version of the Stanford–Binet used quotient IQ scores, which tend to produce inflated scores for bright young children compared to the modern deviation IQ score (see the Introduction for the differences between these two scores). I estimate that a quotient IQ of 298 is equal to a modern deviation IQ between 256 and 272. The likelihood of a person having an IQ score this high is less than 1 in 1 quadrillion (i.e., 1 in 1,000,000,000,000,000). An IQ score of 298 is so absurdly high that Silverman should have realized that the results were not realistic.

I FOUGHT THE LAW AND THE LAW WON: LUMOSITY'S LEGAL TROUBLES

The evidence that far transfer occurs or that brain training produces real-world benefits is so thin that one company even got into legal trouble in the United States because of unsubstantiated claims about their brain-training program. Lumos Labs, creator of the Lumosity program, claimed that engaging in their brain-training games could improve school or work performance, improve the symptoms of mental health diagnoses (e.g., attention deficit/hyperactivity disorder, post-traumatic stress disorder), and reverse mental decline in elderly people (Fair, 2016; Simons et al., 2016). Some of their advertising claims promised to increase intelligence.[4] The company's unproven claims about the effectiveness of brain training resulted in a $2 million fine and over 13,000 customers receiving refunds. The evaluation from the Federal Trade Commission (FTC) about the effectiveness of Lumosity was not flattering for the company:

> Let's set the record straight. Playing Lumosity's games might make you better at those games, the FTC says, but that doesn't necessarily mean it will sharpen your memory or brain power in the real-world ... If you remember nothing else, remember this: You can be skeptical of any app, product, or service that says it can improve your memory or brain power quickly and easily. (Jhaveri, 2016, paragraphs 7, 9)

I endorse the FTC's evaluation about the effectiveness of brain-training games in raising intelligence. Healthy skepticism about other claims of large benefits from brain-training programs is also probably warranted (Sala & Gobet, 2019). These companies' main goal is to make money, and they are happy to let the press tout studies that show that their product raises IQ or cognitive functioning, but disconfirming research rarely gets the same level of attention (Detterman, 2014).

SO CLOSE, BUT YET SO FAR: WHY FAR TRANSFER DOES NOT OCCUR

The failure of brain-training programs to raise intelligence is disappointing, but it is a consequence of the way that cognitive abilities are related to each other. As stated in the Introduction, the leading theories of cognitive abilities are the Cattell–Horn–Carroll model and the bifactor model. Both of these models assume that *g* is a cause of people's performance on specific tasks in Stratum I – not vice versa. This is shown in Figures I.5 and I.6 with the arrows that point from *g* to Stratum II abilities and from Stratum II to Stratum I (in the Cattell–Horn–Carroll model) or from *g* to Stratum I abilities (in the bifactor model). If either of these models is correct and *g* really does influence people's

---

[4] The Federal Trade Commission's complaint against Lumos Labs at www.ftc.gov/system/files/documents/cases/160105lumoslabscmpt.pdf quotes three advertisements claiming that using Lumosity could improve intelligence.

performance in specific tasks, then training people on those tasks will not improve *g* because those tasks have no causal influence on people's levels of *g* (Protzko, 2017b). Although it was not the intent of people who are trying to increase IQ, the failure of brain-training programs to increase *g* has provided evidence that (a) *g* is largely independent of explicit training and (b) theories of the relationship between *g* and performance on specific tasks in the bifactor or Cattell–Horn–Carroll models are correct (Protzko, 2017b; Sala & Gobet, 2019).

BUT DON'T LOSE HOPE

This is the third chapter in a row where I wrote that many popular interventions to raise intelligence have disappointing results. These can be depressing chapters to read (and write!). Yes, large gains in IQ are possible, but these are generally only for people in extremely disadvantageous environments and a level of deprivation that is not common in wealthy countries. Interventions designed for people who already live in positive environments – preschool, brain-training programs, etc. – consistently show minuscule or temporary results. To substantially raise intelligence permanently apparently requires major, long-term life changes, such as adoption, requiring additional schooling, or a change from an extremely deprived environment to a better one.

It is not my intention to make readers feel fatalistic about interventions. These results make it tempting to say that it is impossible to raise IQ for people who already live in positive environments. But there is reason to hope: the fact that most interventions have failed to produce intelligence gains does not mean that such improvements are impossible. It merely indicates that, *on the basis of current knowledge and technology*, nobody knows how to raise intelligence for people who already live in beneficial environments (Lee, 2010). Some scholars who study intelligence are optimistic about the possibility of increasing intelligence (e.g., Haier, 2017a), and no one can say that every possible intervention has been tried. Psychologists, neuroscientists, or educators may one day propose a targeted intervention that does successfully raise intelligence.

However, it is valuable to be realistic about what to expect from interventions. The public should be highly skeptical of claims that a temporary training program based on current technology and science can permanently raise intelligence by 5 points or more. Such claims are not plausible, given the realities of fadeout, the results of brain-training programs, and the massive changes in environment that are needed to produce a 5-point IQ gain (e.g., from adoption). Fads like the Mozart effect (discussed in Chapter 15) can be discarded and ignored. Given the disappointing history of efforts to raise intelligence, the default assumption for the effects of any new intervention should be that it does not work until proven otherwise in well-designed, replicated studies.

17

Improvability of IQ Means Intelligence Can Be Equalized

> The so-called Flynn effect is leveling off in the West, but Kenya is still on an upward trend, notching 25 points since testing began in the '80s. Many impoverished countries have yet to turn this corner [of the Flynn effect stopping]. When they do, we should expect to see a great IQ equalizing.
>
> (Chodosh, 2018, p. 9)

Although Chapter 16 encourages us to hold our enthusiasm in check, it is clear from the evidence that I have presented in this book that IQ can improve through environmental interventions. Indeed, the Flynn effect (see Chapter 14) shows that the twentieth century was one big demonstration that improved environments can lead to higher IQ scores. As a result, some people – as demonstrated by the quote at the beginning of the chapter – believe that the changeability of IQ means that IQ can be equalized. While improvability of IQ scores – and intelligence – is possible, it is quite a different matter to make everyone's intelligence equal.

DOES EQUALIZING ENVIRONMENTS RESULT IN EQUAL IQS?

An extreme example of an attempt to equalize environments occurred after World War II when the Soviet-supported regime in Poland rebuilt the city of Warsaw, almost three-quarters of which had been destroyed. To implement communist ideals, the government built neighborhoods that were as uniform as possible, with homes, apartment buildings, and commercial buildings being similar throughout the city. Social and cultural services were distributed approximately evenly throughout Warsaw, and families were assigned homes so that every neighborhood contained a mixture of people who worked in low-, mid-, and high-prestige occupations. After three decades of this intensive, egalitarian urban planning, a team of scientists administered a non-verbal intelligence test to a large, representative sample of children in the city. The results indicated that the process to equalize the neighborhood environment did nothing to neutralize the positive correlation that IQ had with parental occupational prestige and parental education. As the authors stated, "Despite this social policy of equalization, the association [between parental characteristics and child IQ] persists in a form characteristic of more traditional societies" (Firkowska et al., 1978, p. 1362).

In the Polish study, the similar living conditions and uniform education system were (a) not only unable to eliminate IQ differences, but also (b) incapable of eliminating the correlation between parental socioeconomic status and child IQ. In fact, the correlation between these two values was similar to what is found in capitalist countries (see Chapter 11), and the authors recognized this. The implication is that a massive effort to remake the social and socioeconomic environment of an entire city did little to equalize intelligence. The authorities in post-World War II Poland had far more power to change the environment than any democratic government does, which should make anyone skeptical about the ability of social programs in democratic nations to equalize intelligence.

ANOTHER ATTEMPT: IMPROVING THE ENVIRONMENT

Perhaps equalizing intelligence is too ambitious. Instead, some people who create environmental interventions have the more modest goal of reducing individual differences in IQ by improving environments. There is some evidence that obtaining this goal is reasonable. For example, Tucker-Drob (2012) found that preschool reduced differences in math and reading skills (though there was no follow-up to determine whether fadeout occurred later). Likewise, educational policies that focus on struggling students lead to greater improvements in these students' academic performance and reduce overall variability (Lee, 2002). Statistically controlling for important environmental variables like socioeconomic status also reduces IQ differences among individuals (though in the real world the unadjusted differences still exist), which might indicate that reducing socioeconomic differences could reduce IQ differences.

The evidence is clear that providing a more positive environment to people in an unfavorable environment does reduce inequality of intelligence among the population as a whole. On the other hand, giving an intervention or an environmental improvement to the entire population usually does *not* eliminate intelligence differences because people in both the top and bottom IQ groups experience improvements (Jensen, 1991). In other words, even if environmental changes help people with lower intelligence, the inequality of IQ persists because these changes also help people with higher intelligence. Thus, the best way to reduce individual differences in intelligence or related abilities (e.g., academic skills or cognitive skills) is to provide a beneficial treatment to low-performing individuals and withhold it from high-performing individuals.

GENETICS: WHY INTERVENTIONS DO NOT EQUALIZE ABILITIES

Inequality of intelligence stubbornly persists because of one simple fact: IQ scores are partially influenced by genes, as indicated by h^2 values greater than zero (see Chapter 11). As a result, environmental interventions do not equalize intelligence in people because the genetic influences still remain. Changing educational programs, improving a family's socioeconomic status, or making neighborhoods as similar as possible will not equalize people's intelligence because *none of these environmental changes alter the fact that people vary genetically and that those variations cause some of the differences in intelligence.* As long as genetic variation exists in humans, so will IQ differences. This is why Chodosh's (2018, p. 9) prediction of "a great IQ equalizing" is unrealistic. Even if all countries eventually become wealthy, educated, and industrialized (which itself is not guaranteed; see Rindermann, 2018), this would not equalize IQ scores worldwide because genetic differences among humans would still exist.[1]

Table 17.1 shows the estimated variability in IQ that would be observed if all environments were equalized. The variability is measured with the standard deviation (SD), and currently, intelligence tests have a standard deviation of 15 points (as stated in the Introduction). If all environmental influences were eliminated or equalized, then variability would be reduced and intelligence differences would decrease. However, Table 17.1 also shows that this drop in variability is small when h^2 is high. For example, in a population with heritability of .80 (as is common in studies of adults in wealthy countries), eliminating environmental differences in IQ would only decrease the SD of IQ scores by 10.6%, from 15 points to 13.4 points. If h^2 is .50, then equalized environments would decrease the SD of IQ scores by 29.3% to 10.6 points. Only for traits with low heritability (for which environments already exert a powerful influence on intelligence differences) do individual differences get substantially reduced if environments are equalized.

It is important to recognize that improving environments for everyone is different from removing environmental differences. Improving environments in general can increase the average IQ score without impacting the importance of genetic and environmental differences in producing relative differences in IQ scores. Chapter 12 had an example of how this could happen if lead levels are

---

[1] This reality is not unique to IQ. Equalizing environments will reduce differences – but not eliminate them – for any variable that does not have zero heritability. See Murray (1998, 2002) for an example analysis showing that ideal environments for a sample reduce, but do not eliminate, income inequality.

TABLE 17.1 *Change in standard deviation (SD) of IQ scores if environments were equalized*

Heritability (h^2)	SD with environmental influences eliminated	% Reduction in SD
.00	0.0 IQ points	100.0%
.10	4.7 IQ points	68.4%
.20	6.7 IQ points	55.3%
.30	8.2 IQ points	45.2%
.40	9.5 IQ points	36.8%
.50	10.6 IQ points	29.3%
.60	11.6 IQ points	22.5%
.70	12.5 IQ points	16.3%
.80	13.4 IQ points	10.6%
.90	14.2 IQ points	5.1%
1.00	15.0 IQ points	0.0%

Note. SD for IQ = 15 points (see the Introduction for an explanation of the SD).
Note. New SDs calculated as $SD_{new} = \sqrt{15^2 \times h^2}$

improved for a population in order to increase mean IQ without changing the differences in IQ among a population. On the other hand, to remove the influence of environmental differences is the equivalent of giving everyone the same environment. If this occurs, then heritability *must* increase because the influence of heritability and the influence of environmental differences must add up to 100%. Therefore, if one influence decreases (e.g., environmental differences), then the other gets bigger to compensate. As a result, equalizing environments will not remove the impact of genetic influences at all; it will *increase* the relative power of genetic influences.

A similar phenomenon seems to happen when environments are improved. Preschoolers in Tucker-Drob's (2012) study had higher heritability for reading and math scores than similar children who did not attend preschool.[2] Apparently, sending children to the more intellectually stimulating preschool environment allowed their genes to express themselves in ways that increased the genetic influences on math and reading scores. Positive environments seem to allow genetic influences to be most pronounced. Therefore, any efforts to improve the environment for the entire population will probably increase the influence of genetics, because heritability will increase. Ironically, an improved environment may increase the importance of genetic differences among people, which is the exact opposite of the goal of some people who are trying to improve environments.

---

[2] At age 5, heritability for math scores was .185 for non-preschool attenders and .344 for preschool attenders. Heritability at age 5 for reading scores was .207 for non-preschool attenders and .426 for preschool attenders.

EQUALIZING DIFFERENCES: WHAT IT WOULD TAKE

Three facts suggest that real-world attempts to equalize intelligence in people will not be successful: (a) the meager results of the Polish attempt to equalize environments, (b) the important influence of genes in creating IQ differences, and (c) the higher heritability in more positive environments. This raises the question of what it would take to equalize intelligence in a population. Reducing all individual differences in any trait (including intelligence) requires eradicating the causes of those differences. I believe there are three ways that this could theoretically happen.

One way to equalize intelligence differences would require equalizing everybody genetically and also equalizing environments. Current technology does not permit that level of genetic engineering. Even if it were possible, the result would probably not be sustainable. The temptation to break any pact of genetic equality in order for one's offspring or one's country to gain an advantage over others would be too great. The technology that could make people genetically equal would be just as easily used to engineer new genetic inequalities by anyone willing to ignore any agreement to equalize people genetically.

The second option to equalize intelligence would be to change environments so that people who have a genetic predisposition to be smarter would be placed in negative environments and people with genetic disadvantages would receive more beneficial environments (Gottfredson, 2011). In this way environmental advantages would cancel out the genetic disadvantages that predispose some people to a lower IQ, and vice versa – at least in theory. There are two problems with this proposal. First, environmental influences on IQ are strongest in childhood, but as people age, h^2 increases, indicating that environmental influences fade in importance (Bouchard, 2014). As a result, a scheme to have environmental and genetic advantages and disadvantages cancel each other out might only be effective in childhood. As people grow older and gain freedom to select their environments, this social engineering would be less effective – perhaps completely ineffective.

And that makes the second problem clear: a plan to place genetically disadvantaged individuals in a positive environment (and genetically advantaged individuals in a negative environment) would require a total loss of freedom that only a massively oppressive regime could carry it out. Most (maybe all) children would be taken away from their parents and placed with new families. Precocious individuals would be denied an education or any access to libraries and books. If these measures were ineffective, then more drastic actions might be required: maybe individuals whose intelligence was too high would be given brain injuries to reduce their IQ. This option for eliminating intelligence differences is a horribly dystopian scenario, and it would inflict huge levels of suffering on people. Proposing (let alone implementing) such a program is not feasible.

The final option would be to give everyone such uniformly deprived environments that genes do not have the opportunity to express themselves enough for intelligence differences to develop. This would require denying *all* people in the population any known positive environmental influences: schooling, access to healthy environments and medical care, sufficient food and nutrition, physical safety, a nurturing caregiver in childhood, etc. This option is unspeakably cruel and would inflict great misery on a population that experienced it. The costs would not only be huge, but the benefits would be meager: even if IQ scores were equalized, they would be equally low, and no industrialized society could function with a population mired in ignorance, disease, and starvation.

No one advocates any of these three methods for equalizing IQ. However, the drastic measures that would probably be required to equalize IQ should show why more modest interventions to eliminate individual differences in intelligence have failed.[3]

IMPROVING LIVES, NOT EQUALIZING THEM

While improvability of intelligence does not imply equalizability, it is also false that the non-equalizability of intelligence means non-improvability (Gottfredson, 2009). Because feasible options for equalizing IQ are likely to be ineffective, I believe that it is fruitless to worry about eradicating individual differences. A better goal is to improve people's lives. Sometimes this will result in higher IQ scores (e.g., treating iodine deficiency, discouraging women from drinking alcohol during pregnancy), and sometimes it will not (e.g., providing nutritious meals for children who live in poverty). There are many ways to improve people's lives, and the best way to do so will depend on a society's resources, goals, and ethics.

Just as with any intervention, though, it is important to have a realistic understanding of what probably is (or is not) possible, given current knowledge. Two leading scholars from the past, Scarr and Weinberg (1978, p. 36), described the issue well:

Three decades of naive environmentalism have locked most Westerners into wrong-headed assumptions about the limitless malleability of mankind, and programs based on this premise can lead a country into a thicket of unrealistic promises and hopes. The fallacy is the belief that equality of opportunity produces sameness of outcome. Equality of opportunity is a laudable goal for any society. Sameness of outcome is a biological impossibility.

---

[3] I recognize that the urban planning of post-World War II Warsaw doesn't seem modest by Western standards. But compared to the three methods of equalizing IQ that I suggest, it certainly is.

Despite the best efforts of a society, inequality of IQ will happen. Some children will get "left behind," and some people will not be able to attend college or reap the benefits of high reasoning ability. (Chapter 33 discusses how industrialized societies can adapt to this fact.) On the other hand, lying about intelligence differences and their malleability or equalizability only sets people up for disappointment.

INTELLIGENCE AND EDUCATION

The previous sections discussed the nature of intelligence, how to measure it, and where it comes from. Section 4 and 5 focus instead on intelligence in the real world. In this section, I discuss intelligence and its place in the education system. This section is based on a long research tradition that dates back over a century. In the Introduction I told the story of how Alfred Binet designed the first successful intelligence test to identify children who were struggling in typical classes. Thanks to Binet's test, school personnel could identify children who needed their own classes with specially trained teachers and using instructional methods designed to accommodate their needs. Binet's test was quickly translated, and just five years after his death, Lewis Terman expanded it into the Stanford–Binet test, which could identify both academically struggling children and very bright children. All research about intelligence's place in the education system can be traced to the works of these scientific pioneers. Today, this is one of the strongest bodies of research in all of psychology, and it all points to one conclusion: "individual differences in general cognitive ability is the single most important variable for understanding how well students ... learn academic material" (Frisby, 2013, p. 201). No other variable is a better predictor of academic outcomes.

In a perfect world, this would be a well-known fact, and school personnel would consider IQ and intelligence differences when making educational decisions about individual children. Unfortunately, the educational establishment in the United States (and many other countries) has ignored g – much to the field's detriment. This section addresses some of the fallacies that educators believe which prevent them from recognizing the true impact of intelligence on student educational outcomes.

This section is comprised of four chapters. The first, Chapter 18, is concerned with giftedness and how intelligence differences among students necessitate the creation of separate academic programs and educational interventions for high-IQ children. Chapter 19 examines whether the education system is capable of eliminating differences in children's mental abilities or academic performance (which makes it an education-specific discussion of some of the ideas in Chapter 17). In Chapter 20, I investigate whether non-cognitive traits that are not part of the Cattell–Horn–Carroll model have an influence on educational achievement that is as powerful as g. (Spoiler alert: they don't.) Finally, Chapter 21 examines a popular myth that states that college admissions tests are designed to keep certain student groups out of college.

Although this section is only four chapters long, it shows that intelligence has important consequences for the education system. Yet teachers, educational administrators, and others who work in the education industry often ignore intelligence (Burton & Warne, 2020; Warne, 2016a). These chapters show that there are real consequences when educators implement policies that ignore g. Because schools are where most people spend much of their formative years, these policies impact children more than anyone else.

18

Every Child Is Gifted

> Every child is gifted and talented. Each is unique. Every child needs, wants, and deserves opportunities for continuing learning, healthy development, and success in school.
>
> (Lawson, 2002, p. ix)

> All children are gifted ... I think it not at all implausible that a broadened view of giftedness would reveal that every child is gifted in some socially valued way.
>
> (D. Feldman, 1979, pp. 662, 663)

One common misconception about individual differences in the educational realm is the belief that every child is gifted. This belief can take a variety of forms, as shown in the quotes above. Lawson's (2002) perspective was that the uniqueness of each child and their need for a nurturing education is the root of their giftedness. David Feldman's (1979) viewpoint was that if "giftedness" were just defined broadly enough, then it would be apparent that every child is gifted.

A common modern sentiment is the statement that "Every child is gifted. They just unwrap their packages at different times." This treacly claim is on T-shirts, wall decorations, hats, tote bags, and other merchandise. Taken literally, this viewpoint means that if a child seems behind their peers, then they are just a late bloomer who will "unwrap their gifts" and catch up with their classmates at a later time. While later bursts of intellectual development do happen, it becomes increasingly rare as children age. By approximately age 10, a child who – in a favorable environment – does not display high intelligence is very unlikely to do so in the future (see Chapter 12).

What's puzzling about the belief that every child is gifted is that no one would ever say this about adults. No one would claim that every adult is gifted or brilliant and has areas in which they exceed other people's performance. Nobody believes that if people just look hard enough, they will find an area of exceptional ability in every adult. For some reason, total mediocrity is only permitted in adults – never children. I wonder where the non-gifted adults come from.

WHAT IS GIFTEDNESS?

Just as there is no definition of intelligence that has 100% agreement, a definition of giftedness that appeals to all scholars (or even a majority) is elusive. In the early part of the twentieth century, many scholars defined "gifted" as being synonymous with having a high IQ score. That changed in the 1970s when the US government issued a report on gifted education in the United States. In this report (Marland, 1971), there were six possible areas where students could be gifted:

1. General intellectual aptitude
2. Specific academic aptitude
3. Creative or productive thinking
4. Leadership
5. Visual and performing arts
6. Psychomotor ability (i.e., athletic or physical skill)

Of these six areas of giftedness, an intelligence test would be most useful for identifying gifted students in the general intellectual aptitude group. Therefore, this report expanded the definition of giftedness to include a much larger group of abilities and developed skills than merely high general intelligence. Later definitions of giftedness have included some of these abilities, though legal definitions vary from state to state and from country to country. Among scholars in gifted education, there is even more diversity in definitions, with some people seeing giftedness as advanced development compared to one's age peers (e.g., Morelock, 1992) or including motivation and other non-cognitive traits (e.g., Renzulli, 1978).

YES, VIRGINIA, THERE ARE GIFTED CHILDREN

Without doubt, a broader definition of giftedness will mean that more people are defined as "gifted," especially if a person only needs to excel on one trait, ability, or talent in order to be gifted (Lakin, 2018; McBee, Peters, & Waterman, 2014). But this does not mean that every child is gifted. Regardless of one's preferred definition, the term "gifted" implies an exceptionality and a difference in ability compared to the regular population. Stretching the term "gifted" until it encompasses everyone makes the term lose any meaning. If everyone is gifted, then nobody really is. The claim that every child is gifted is really a denial of giftedness and/or individual differences – and it is a preposterous claim. People *do* vary from one another in their intelligence, specific aptitudes, leadership ability, skill in visual or performing arts, psychomotor ability, or any other ability or skill that one prefers to include in their definition of giftedness. Anyone who has attended a high school football game or a school choir concert can attest to that.

More commonly, the claim that every child is gifted is a denial that some people are smarter than others. I believe that people usually have good motivations for denying individual differences in intelligence. They may not want to discourage a child, or they may believe in the power of interventions to improve or equalize intellectual differences. But individual differences in intelligence *do* exist, even if some people wish they did not. Every person has different genetic and environmental influences that have resulted in their intelligence level, with some people getting dealt a lucky hand from nature and nurture to make them smarter, and others not being so fortunate.

Apart from denial, some people seem to believe that every child is gifted based on an emotional response:

if we were willing to invest more of our national income in education, we could pay teachers better, educate them better, and provide them with the results of better educational research and with much better teaching aids. We could reduce class size ... We would discover what in our hearts we already know – every child is gifted. (Gruber, 1963, p. 166)

Though over 50 years old, Gruber's quote is typical of a belief that is guided by emotion and not by rational evidence. It's a comforting thought, but it is a fiction. Many people (with the best of intentions) allow what they wish were true to stand in for reality. And although it may feel good to believe that every child has the potential to be an Einstein or a Picasso if only they had just the right environmental conditions, it is not true. Any educational policy – such as the one Gruber (1963) proposed – based on an incorrect understanding of human psychology is unlikely to achieve its creators' goals, despite what the creators believe in their hearts.

The Rise and Fall of the Pygmalion in the Classroom. To be fair, sometimes the belief that every child is gifted is based on more than wishful thinking. One famous study that bolsters this belief is called the Pygmalion in the Classroom, which was originally reported in a brief journal article (Rosenthal & Jacobson, 1966) and later a book (Rosenthal & Jacobson, 1968). In this study, all the children in Grades 1 to 6 in a California elementary school took a group-administered intelligence test. The researchers selected a random 20% of the children (65 across Grades 1–6) and told the teachers that these children were expected to experience unusually strong academic growth in the coming year. But there were no real differences between these children and the other 80% of the children in the school, who totaled 255 children in Grades 1–6. (The teachers did not know that their students had taken an intelligence test.) At the end of the school year, the children were retested, and those that were labeled as due for strong academic growth had IQ scores that increased by an average of 12.2 points. Because of these strong IQ gains, some people have argued that the label of "gifted" is a self-fulfilling prophecy and that if teachers merely believed that all their students were gifted, then all children would perform at a high level (e.g., Weiler, 1978).

The original Pygmalion in the Classroom study has been highly contentious, and people have interpreted it many ways. However, it is incorrect to argue that the study means that (1) all children are gifted, (2) the "gifted" label is meaningless, or (3) gifted programs create self-fulfilling prophecies for children. Several aspects of the Pygmalion in the Classroom study are questionable and prevent any straightforward, simple interpretation (Jussim & Harber, 2005). One curious characteristic was that all the IQ gains were concentrated in first- and second-grade students; no other grades showed any difference in end-of-year IQ between groups of children (Rosenthal & Jacobson, 1966). Therefore, if teacher expectations have any impact on IQ, it is only for young children. Moreover, IQ scores for the "regular" children also increased – by 8.4 points (Rosenthal & Jacobson, 1966, p. 116).[1] This means that any effects of labeling were not damaging for children in either group (Jussim & Harber, 2005). Regardless of this increase in the control group, the IQ scores for the group of children that the teachers were told would have academic growth still increased by 3.8 IQ points more, on average, than the control groups' IQs.

One prominent critic (Snow, 1995) also noted that the entire difference between the two groups of students was driven by five children who had IQ gains of 69 points or more. These gains are so unrealistic that it seems more likely that there was a problem with the intelligence test than that teacher expectations raised intelligence so much. Two of these children had IQs below 20 (so low that a child would have difficulty speaking or feeding themselves) and were above average by the end of the school year. The other three were above average at the first testing and scored above 200 at the end of the year![2] Another problem with the data that Snow (1995) identified was that the test was only designed to produce meaningful IQ scores between 60 and 160, yet 35% of children scored below 60. Not only were these scores not useful, but it would indicate that over one-third of children in this school had mild to severe intellectual disabilities and would have great difficulty learning in a typical classroom. Unless the school caters to children with disabilities, this percentage is unrealistically high.

---

[1] The IQ increases for the control group could indicate that the mere act of taking the test twice increased scores – a phenomenon called *practice effects*. This does not invalidate the claim that positive teacher beliefs could cause students to benefit academically, but it does show that the IQ gains for the group that teachers were told would have IQ score increases were not entirely due to the beliefs of the teachers.

[2] The IQ scores in the Pygmalion in the Classroom study were calculated using the quotient score formula (see the Introduction for an explanation). Modern IQ scores would be less extreme, but would not greatly change the overall pattern of IQ score differences (between groups or from one time point to another).

The Pygmalion in the Classroom study has problems that extend beyond questionable test scores. The following year, Rosenthal and Jacobson administered the intelligence test to the children again, and any differences between the two groups had disappeared (Rosenthal & Jacobson, 1968; Spitz, 1999). Later studies trying to replicate the original work have been disappointing, with most failing to find any relationship between teacher expectations and children's IQ scores (Jensen, 1980b; Jussim & Harber, 2005; Raudenbush, 1984; Spitz, 1999). Even Rosenthal's own attempts[3] to replicate his results failed to show any difference in IQ for children that teachers were told should experience sudden cognitive growth and children that teachers were told were developing normally (e.g., Conn, Edwards, Rosenthal, & Crowne, 1968; J. T. Evans & Rosenthal, 1969).

A likely reason why the Pygmalion in the Classroom study usually fails to replicate is that the manipulation to change teachers' beliefs about their students' abilities was – in the words of one prominent psychologist – "unbelievably casual" (Cronbach, 1975, p. 7). The researchers (one of whom was the principal at the school) gave the teachers a list of the students who were supposedly due for an increase in academic performance. There is no indication that the teachers actually treated the children on this list differently in their classrooms than the other children that were not expected to have strong academic growth. Indeed, Rosenthal and his co-authors reported that teachers usually did not remember which students were expected to have a sudden increase in academic performance (J. T. Evans & Rosenthal, 1969; Rosenthal & Jacobson, 1968).

This illustrates what I call Warne's First Law of Behavioral Interventions: "Brief, subtle, or weak interventions will produce brief, subtle, or weak changes in human behavior."[4] Earlier chapters of this book show that long-term IQ increases require massive, prolonged interventions, such as reducing lead exposure (no easy task in an industrialized society), long-term schooling, and adoption. Less drastic interventions, like Head Start, listening to Mozart's music, or "brain-training" games, produce small or negligible impacts on IQ that fade out after the intervention stops (see Chapters 12, 14–17). Given this pattern of attempts to raise intelligence, it is difficult to believe that merely giving a teacher a list of names is enough to make those people smarter. Taking the same viewpoint, Jensen (1980a, p. 608) wrote:

It should not seem surprising that the teacher expectancy effect has failed to materialize with respect to [increasing] IQ. After all, even much more direct instruction on the test, tutoring, and compensatory education programs have failed to yield appreciable gains in IQ. Why should as subtle a condition as the teacher's

---

[3] Spitz (1999, pp. 209–211) described Rosenthal's four unsuccessful attempts to replicate his own work.

[4] There is no second law – right now. I use the term "First Law" in case I formulate another later. Check on me at the end of my career in 35 years to see if I have had any more insights on this topic.

expectation about the child's intelligence have a greater effect? Teacher expectations may in fact be quite realistic.

Jussim and Harber (2005) agreed on this point and reported research showing that teacher impressions of children's abilities are generally reflecting – not causing – a child's academic performance. Even a supporter of the Pygmalion in the Classroom's work found that the effect was smaller than in the original study and only had an impact in the first two weeks of the school year (Raudenbush, 1984). This is when teachers generally do not know their students well, and so any new information may influence the teacher's opinions and behavior towards a child. Giving false information about a child to a teacher does not impact that child's academic performance if the teacher already knows how the child performs scholastically (Jussim & Harber, 2005).

While the Pygmalion in the Classroom has not been shown to be a consistent phenomenon, it is possible that teacher beliefs about what their students can – and can't – do could have an impact on classroom learning (Jussim & Harber, 2005; Snow, 1995; Spitz, 1999). A teacher who sets high academic goals for their students and pushes them to work hard to achieve those goals may genuinely cause their students to learn more. Additionally, teacher expectations may be more important for the academic performance of some groups of students – such as low-income students, children from minority backgrounds, and younger children – than others (Jussim & Harber, 2005). What is highly implausible is that teacher beliefs impact *intelligence*. And because children's intelligence levels are resistant to their teachers' beliefs, the Pygmalion in the Classroom does not prove that all children are gifted – or that all would be if adults just treated them like they were.

ARE GIFTED CLASSES APPROPRIATE?

The belief that all children are gifted (or a total denial of academic giftedness) leads some people to propose that special classes for "gifted" children should be available to most or all children. While this idea sounds good, there are unintended consequences to opening gifted classes to all children. As these classes become less academically selective, one of two scenarios inevitably arises: either (a) academically unprepared students in these courses experience high rates of failure, or (b) the classes must become watered down to accommodate the new students. Both of these consequences occur because typical children have difficulty handling advanced coursework that their academically gifted peers find manageable.

The best evidence regarding the drawbacks of admitting many non-gifted students into academically intensive classes comes from Advanced Placement (AP) tests. AP is a program owned by the College Board that allows high school teachers to teach an introductory college-level course. At the end of the school year, students take a standardized test created by the College Board, and students who earn a high enough score (usually a 3, on a scale of 1 to 5) receive college credit from the university that they later attend. The AP program is very popular; a majority of American high schools offer at least one AP course (Warne, Sonnert, & Sadler, 2019), and between 2006 and 2018, the number of students who took at least one AP test grew from 1.3 million to 2.8 million.

However, as more students have participated in AP, the average test score in the most popular classes has dropped. For example, the average score for the AP English Literature & Composition test was 3.05 in 1998 when there were 163,520 examinees. Twenty years later, in 2018, the average score was 2.56 for 396,350 examinees. For the AP US History exam, the average score was 3.02 in 1998 when there were 160,674 examinees. In 2018, the average score was 2.66 for 497,290 examinees. Additionally, the correlation between the number of examinees and the average test score was $r = -.51$ across all 38 AP exams in 2018. This indicates that the most popular tests tend to have the lowest AP scores, which is consistent with my claim that letting less academically gifted students participate in AP has lowered scores and increased the failure rate on AP exams.

The effects are even more drastic when school personnel implement a policy to eliminate non-AP courses in certain subjects so that all students enroll in AP. When this occurred in Philadelphia, only 4 of the 41 high schools in the city had passing rates of 50% or higher, and these were schools that had selective admissions and test scores at or above the national average. Among the other 37 schools, none of them had passing rates above 33%, and 30 of them had passing rates less than 10%. A few high schools did not have a single student pass *any* AP exams (Lichten, 2010). Similar results have happened elsewhere when schools have opened AP classes to less prepared students (e.g., Blagaich, 1999; Bowie, 2013). In New York City, Mayor Bill de Blasio started an initiative in 2017 called "AP for All" that is designed to implement AP in more New York City schools (Finn & Scanlan, 2019). While there has been an increase in the number of students taking AP exams and earning passing scores, the passing rate has dropped. In 2018 (the most recent year with available data), only 51.9% of AP examinees citywide passed at least one AP exam – the lowest percentage on record. The same year, in "AP for All" schools, the percentage was the lowest since 2007: only 21.8% (New York City Department of Education, 2019).[5] Pushing all students into AP courses does

---

[5] Note that the New York City and Philadelphia percentages are two different measures that are not interchangeable. The Philadelphia percentages are passing rates – i.e., the percentage of AP exams passed. The New York City numbers are the percentage of students who passed at least one AP test. If every AP student took exactly one test, these numbers would be equal. However, because many AP students take more than one test, the New York City percentages are higher than the passing rates. This is because a student raises the percentage if they pass a single AP test, no matter how many other tests they fail. For example, if 20 students each take 2 tests, and all of them pass 1, then the passing rate is 50%, but the percentage who pass at least one exam is 100%. Passing rates for New York City are not available.

not result in large-scale academic success; instead, it results in an increase in failing grades on AP exams. Increased failure is apparent in AP because the College Board sets their standard for passing scores and local schools have no control over this measure of academic success.

A more common outcome in opening up advanced classes to the general student population is that the rigor and curriculum get relaxed to accommodate less gifted students. Firm evidence of this consequence is harder to find because most gifted programs do not have objective measures of advanced student learning (like an AP test) that can be used to evaluate them.[6] However, the characteristics of high-IQ learners make it inevitable that a class that includes a significant portion of average students will serve bright children more poorly. One succinct comparison is that:

> low-*g* learners require highly structured, detailed, concrete, and "contextualize" instruction that omits no intermediate steps, but that such "complete" instruction is actually dysfunctional for high-*g* individuals. The latter easily fill gaps in instruction on their own and benefit most from abstract, self-directed, incomplete instruction that allows them to assemble new knowledge and reassemble old knowledge in idiosyncratic ways. (Gottfredson, 1997b, p. 124)

Therefore, lessons tailored for students with high intelligence will be effective by starting from general, abstract principles and then using specific examples to illustrate. These lessons will be loosely structured and include connections to different topics and school subjects. If a substantial proportion of average students are in the class, then an effective lesson will inevitably need to be less abstract, more concrete, and more carefully structured.

High-IQ individuals also generally learn faster and need less repetition and practice than average and low-IQ people to master a new concept (N. M. Robinson, Ziegler, & Gallagher, 2000). Many gifted children can master the K-12 curriculum in less than 13 years and are excellent candidates for grade skipping, especially if the curriculum prepares them to advance through grades more rapidly than one per year (Assouline, Colangelo, VanTassel-Baska, & Lupkoswki-Shoplik, 2015; Assouline, Colangelo, VanTassel-Baska, & Sharp, 2015). Courses set at their pace will inevitably be a place where average students struggle to keep up. If there are enough students who are only modestly above average in intelligence, then the teacher must steer the class towards their needs by slowing down and reducing the complexity of the lessons.

Therefore, educational decisions based on the idea that every child is gifted result in unfavorable consequences: either widespread failure ensues when

---

[6] Gifted students usually take the state-mandated end-of-year exam test that almost all students take. However, these tests almost always measure basic skills, and academically gifted children pass these tests with ease. Many of them can even pass the exams for a higher grade without having been taught the curriculum (Peters, Rambo-Hernandez, Makel, Matthews, & Plucker, 2017; Warne, 2014).

average children take advanced classes, or the teacher of a "gifted" class is forced to slow down or reduce the complexity of lessons in order to accommodate the typical learner. Exposing average children to lessons they are not ready to master, or setting them up for likely failure in advanced classes is cruel. Watering down the curriculum or slowing down a gifted class to accommodate less academically elite students is failing to deliver on a promise to gifted students that the class would help them learn at their pace and cognitive complexity. Instead, a *g*-aware policy would recognize the differences in intelligence among students by creating advanced classes and identifying children who can skip grades or experience other forms of academic acceleration (Assouline, Colangelo, VanTassel-Baska, & Lupkoswki-Shoplik, 2015; Assouline, Colangelo, VanTassel-Baska, & Sharp, 2015).

A RIGOROUS EDUCATION FOR ALL, NOT GIFTED EDUCATION FOR ALL

I hope readers do not misunderstand me. While the evidence indicates that gifted children can benefit from their own classes and from academic acceleration, this does *not* mean that only gifted children should receive a rigorous education. All children should to be challenged by a curriculum and learn something new every day in school. Ideally, all children would also experience the best teaching methods and a rich, engaging curriculum that prepares them for their post-high school life path, whether that is in the workforce, the military, college, or technical training. But giving the same curriculum and educational experience to all children leads to undesirable consequences. Some children will inevitably fall behind, and some will go months or years without learning much because the curriculum is not challenging. Ironically, treating students in the same way in school is profoundly unfair (Benbow & Stanley, 1996).

The reason gifted education programs need to exist is that the curriculum that works for the typical students will not provide high-IQ children with regular opportunities to learn. The further a child's IQ is from average, the worse the typical curriculum and teaching methods will be for the child (Gottfredson, 2003c). As children's abilities are further from average, more drastic changes are needed to provide a challenging, appropriate education (Ruf, 2005). This is true for people who are significantly above the average IQ or below the average IQ (N. M. Robinson et al., 2000). While people recognize the importance of adjusting the educational experience for children with abilities that are below average, few recognize that the need can be equally strong for children with above average abilities. For example, only about 0.25% of children per year skip a grade (Warren, Hoffman, & Andrew, 2014, p. 435), and only about 2–3% will do so during the course of their K-12 experience (Warne, 2017). However, by Grade 11, nearly 25% of students are college-ready in every core subject and could attend college immediately (Dannenberg & Hyslop, 2019).

Creating a rigorous education should not be a zero-sum game. In the elementary grades, these programs do not cost any more than the regular education program.[7] And when an experience does not require high ability to provide a benefit, it should be open to all students. For example, participating in a school play, career day, or field trip is probably beneficial for everyone, so all students should get to participate in these activities. Allowing gifted children to flourish does not mean that other students are neglected; it merely means that their educational needs are met – just as any child deserves. But it does not happen on its own; serving the needs of high-g students requires administrative flexibility and support from school personnel, including the staff and teachers serving the regular student body (Benbow & Stanley, 1996).

CONCLUSION

In conclusion, some children are gifted, and some are not. Stating this is not elitist. Rather, it is a recognition that individual differences exist and that adapting to these differences will shape the education that children have. Educational programs that reflect this reality will inevitably give different educational experiences to gifted and non-gifted students. Ignoring these differences, though, will produce negative consequences. Gifted children shoulder the brunt of the negative consequences of a curriculum designed for the child with an average or below average IQ. They sit through lessons covering topics that they already know and go weeks or months without learning anything new. They spend longer than they need to in the K-12 education system and miss out on an early start in their postsecondary education or careers, which can have negative economic consequences for them (Warne, 2017; Warne & Liu, 2017). The negative consequences of ignoring individual differences in intelligence extend beyond gifted children, though. The next three chapters will show that denying differences in IQ can have negative effects for all children.

---

[7] At the high school level, advanced courses sometimes do cost more to provide than regular courses. For example, stocking a chemistry lab with materials needed for advanced lessons, or providing college-level textbooks for an AP course is more expensive than providing corresponding materials or textbooks for a typical class. As for the AP program, some states and school districts pay students' exam fees, which is an additional cost to taxpayers that regular courses do not require (Klopfenstein, 2010). But these higher costs are a tiny fraction of the additional costs of educating children with special needs (Benbow & Stanley, 1996).

19

Effective Schools Can Make Every Child Academically Proficient

> Each State shall establish a timeline for adequate yearly progress. The timeline shall ensure that not later than 12 years after the end of the 2001–2002 school year, all students ... will meet or exceed the State's proficient level of academic achievement ...
>
> (No Child Left Behind Act, 2002, 20 U.S.C. § 6311)

For over a decade, the No Child Left Behind (NCLB) Act was a federal law in the United States that mandated that every student in public schools must be proficient in core academic subjects (math, science, and language arts) by the summer of 2014. If schools failed in this goal, then there would be consequences. Schools could be taken over by the state or closed down, personnel could lose their jobs (or be forced to reapply with the new regime at a school), and funding could be withheld.

As 2014 drew near, it became apparent to educational officials that it was impossible to make every child academically proficient by the deadline. In 2011, the Obama administration announced that they would grant waivers (of dubious legality) to exempt states from this requirement under certain conditions. The announcement said that this was because there were "specific NCLB mandates that were stifling reform" ("Obama Administration Sets High Bar for Flexibility," paragraph 2). Behind the political spin was the reality that the goal enshrined in the law was not achievable. To prevent nearly every school in the country from breaking the law, the federal government gave these waivers to states that met certain requirements established by the US Department of Education (Kamenetz, 2014).

All of this was foreseeable. Educational psychologists and intelligence researchers had said for decades that it was impossible for every student to master a curriculum (e.g., Biemiller, 1993; Jensen, 1969; Kauffman & Konold, 2007). Yet, because the rhetoric of making every child proficient in core school subjects was appealing, the US Congress passed a law[1] that mandated the impossible. A law banning gravity by 2014 would have been equally effective. In 2015, Congress replaced NCLB with a new law, the Every Student Succeeds Act. While the name is as optimistic as the previous NCLB, it did eliminate the legal mandate that every student reach an arbitrary level of educational competence.

The very names of these laws show unbounded optimism for the ability of the education system to produce successful outcomes for every student. Elsewhere in education, people claim that their favored curriculum or policy can "close the achievement gap" between students (e.g., Burris & Welner, 2005). The belief that everyone can be brought to a high standard of academic performance is so common that it "is a virtual article of faith in educational circles" (Gottfredson, 2009, p. 36; see also Frisby, 2013, pp. 212–215). The phrase "article of faith" is appropriate, because no country or state has *ever* created a school system that was successful in educating every student to a high level. Yet policy makers believe that this is possible anyway.

WHY JOHNNY CAN'T READ (SOMETIMES)

Not only has no education system ever made 100% of students competent, there are good theoretical reasons rooted in intelligence research to expect that such a utopian outcome is not possible. The first reason is fundamental: intelligence is positively correlated with educational achievement (C. M. Calvin, Fernandes, Smith, Visscher, & Deary, 2010; Cucina, Peyton, Su, & Byle, 2016; Damian et al., 2015; B. Roth et al., 2015). Depending on study characteristics, intelligence correlates with academic achievement at a level of $r = .40$ to $.70$. That correlation is so strong that – in most studies – intelligence is a better predictor of success in school than any other variable. This means that wherever there are individual differences in intelligence, there are individual differences in school competency, with smarter students usually performing better than low-g students. Higher-IQ students learn more rapidly, learn more efficiently, organize and generalize information more spontaneously, and make fewer errors than their average or below-average classmates. With these skills and a broader fund of knowledge available to them, high-IQ students perform better on standardized achievement tests than their peers, even if a teacher is highly effective at test preparation (Frisby, 2013). Individual differences in school success still develop because they arise from individual intelligence differences. No law or educational policy will change this. Frisby (2013) explained this succinctly: "Slow learners will always lag behind their brighter peers in academic work, and they will never catch up" (p. 211).

[1] The law passed by huge, bipartisan margins: 381–41 in the House of Representatives and 87–10 in the Senate.

The second reason schools cannot make every child master the curriculum is that the causes of intelligence differences and the causes of academic achievement are both partially genetic. While it is true that keeping people in school longer raises IQ (see Chapter 14), differences in intelligence are one of the causes of differences in academic achievement. Therefore, the causes of intelligence differences will also be some of the causes of differences in school performance. Chapters 11 and 13 showed that – in typical environments in wealthy countries – genetic influences are about 20% to 80% of the cause of IQ differences. As a result, genes are an indirect cause of school performance differences because of how they act on intelligence. This chain reaction can be diagrammed as:

Genetic differences ➔ Intelligence differences ➔ School performance differences

This model of cause and effect is oversimplified, but still useful. There are other influences on intelligence and school performance (e.g., environmental influences, personality characteristics, school quality) that influence IQ and school performance, which makes the flow of causality from genes to IQ to academic achievement imperfect. Still, the connection between genes and school performance (via intelligence) is a major reason why no school system can make every child competent in every school subject.

The theory sounds plausible, but is there evidence to support it? The answer is a resounding yes, especially in the form of *genome-wide association studies* (GWASs). In a GWAS of intelligence, researchers collect DNA samples from thousands of people and identify variations in people's DNA that are correlated with IQ. If a DNA variation is more common in high-IQ people than among people with low IQ (or vice versa), then it indicates that this DNA segment is associated with intelligence. These DNA variants may then be used to calculate a score (called a *polygenic score*) that can be used to predict a person's IQ (Plomin & von Stumm, 2018). GWASs are not unique to intelligence; they can be conducted to identify DNA portions that are associated with any trait.[2] Research has shown that many of the same genes that are associated with high intelligence are also associated with high educational performance (W. D. Hill et al., 2019; Lee et al., 2018; Okbay et al., 2016; Plomin & von Stumm, 2018). Therefore, the differences in school performance are partially genetic, which means that there will always be some differences among students in their academic performance.[3] These differences will mean that some people will perform so poorly in school that they will not meet the standards of

---

[2] My favorite GWAS identified segments of DNA on Chromosome 1 that are more common in the 60% of Americans who are unable to smell a strong, musty odor in their urine a few hours after eating asparagus (Markt et al., 2016).

[3] Chapter 17 discussed why the genetic component of intelligence means that IQ cannot be equalized across individuals. The genetic component of academic achievement is also why school performance cannot be equalized across students.

competence that teachers, school personnel, or lawmakers expect children to meet.

Although GWASs are a major breakthrough in understanding how genes relate to traits, there are some unanswered questions about these genetic influences. One problem is that the polygenic scores created from DNA segments that are associated with intelligence explain only about 4% of all influences on IQ variability. On the other hand, studies of IQ similarities and differences among family members show that the combined influence of all genes on intelligence variability is 20% to 80%. The gap between known DNA variants (identified through GWASs) and total heritability (from studies of family members) is called "missing heritability" (Hunt, 2011; Plomin & von Stumm, 2018). It represents the strength of genetic influences that have an unknown location in the genome. Experts predict missing heritability to drop in the future as behavioral geneticists conduct GWASs using better technology and larger, more diverse samples (Plomin & Deary, 2015; Plomin & von Stumm, 2018).

A more serious problem with GWAS results is that it is not clear *how* genes cause people to differ on their traits. This is especially true for behaviors or psychological traits, such as intelligence. A gene is just a segment of DNA. It cannot think, and it does not see what is happening outside the body. Genes don't give people hints about how to answer intelligence tests or excel in school. All genes do is make strands of RNA that the body then uses to make amino acids for cells to create proteins (Plomin, 2018). If genes do affect intelligence levels, then it is not through a direct impact, but rather through the biological consequences of those genes. Biologists have not fully solved the mystery of how a segment of DNA results in a psychological trait, but it must be a biologically-based influence because genes are biological in nature, and they can only exert a direct influence on biology. Work on understanding the connections between genes, biology, and psychological traits shows that most genes are probably associated with multiple biological and psychological traits (Belsky & Harden, 2019).

EDUCATIONAL CONSEQUENCES OF g DENIALISM

Despite the importance of intelligence in determining educational outcomes, teachers and other educational leaders rarely acknowledge its importance. Education departments at universities often minimize the value of intelligence, with some choosing to emphasize Howard Gardner's theory of multiple intelligences instead (Burton & Warne, 2020), even though the theory is not supported by empirical evidence (see Chapter 5). As a result, educators often deny or do not understand the implications of individual differences in intelligence. For example, few teachers understand that most educational tests measure g to some extent. As I discussed in Chapter 18, some educators believe that every child is gifted and that individual differences in intelligence are not important because every child is smart.

This denial of *g* has serious negative consequences in the education system.[4] One result of *g* denialism is the blame game that often ensues when children's educational performance fails to meet the expectations of adults because people refuse to admit that some children are always going to struggle in school. As Gottfredson (2005a, p. 546) explained, "Frustrated expectations devolve into blame. Test critics blame the tests, test companies blame the schools, [and] educators blame already angry parents ... But flagellating one group or another for lack of will or commitment has no constructive effect." Playing the blame game discourages adults – who all have the same goal of helping children learn – from partnering with one another to improve the education system.

Another negative consequence of denying intelligence is that it causes teachers to assume that all of their students are approximately the same in their readiness to learn new material. This incorrect belief causes a teacher to assume that one lesson serves every student well. However, a typical group of students displays a wide span of cognitive abilities:

A not uncommon finding is that the children in an ordinary third-grade class span a range of competence in reading comprehension equivalent to the norms for the second through the eighth grades, or that those in the fifth span the range from the third through the tenth. (Herrnstein, 1973, p. 112; see also Frisby, 2013, pp. 229–231)

Unless a class is created to reduce these differences – such as by selecting children for a gifted or a special education program – then the class is likely to have children whose abilities span several grade levels (Biemiller, 1993). And – as Herrnstein implied – the variability in educational readiness increases as children age (Burt, 1917; H. D. Hoover et al., 2003). This usually is not apparent because typical grade-level tests are not designed to measure the abilities that far exceed (or are far below) the nominal grade level. Fully measuring these children's abilities often requires additional testing, such as in an individual testing session or by giving a more difficult test to bright children – or an easier test to struggling students (Rambo-Hernandez & Warne, 2015; Warne, 2012, 2014).

Creating one lesson that meets the needs of all students in a typical classroom is nearly impossible. The best alternative is to create multiple lessons that are targeted at groups of students within a classroom (e.g., struggling readers, typical readers, advanced readers). This practice – called *ability grouping* – happens regularly, but because most teachers are unaware of the span of abilities in a typical classroom, it is only partially effective in most situations. Another problem with ability grouping within a classroom is the basic fact that it is more work and effort for a teacher to prepare multiple lessons than to prepare one (Hertberg-Davis, 2009). Educators who understand intelligence recognize that the best option is to perform the ability grouping at the classroom level (i.e., create a class full of advanced learners, a class or two of typical

---

[4] I discussed some of these consequences in the discussion about gifted education in Chapter 18.

learners, and a class of struggling learners). In this way, the variability in educational readiness is reduced and teachers are better able to serve the educational needs of the students in their classroom.

Another negative consequence of intelligence denialism is that it leads to policies that are ineffective. An example of this occurred in California when a judge in a high-profile court case (*Larry P. v. Riles*, 1979) issued a statewide injunction against using intelligence tests for African American students because he believed that intelligence tests were a tool to confine struggling students to "dead end" special education classes. Even when the injunction was lifted several years later, the California State Department of Education still maintained the ban in public schools unilaterally because of a politically motivated denial of the importance of intelligence for determining which children should be placed in special education classes. But banning the intelligence tests did not eliminate intelligence differences or fix the problem of selecting children for special education. Instead, it forced school psychologists to use lower-quality tests and more subjective methods of making this important decision (Frisby & Henry, 2016).

Another consequence of *g* denialism occurs when educators or policy makers misdiagnose the source of educational differences. To someone who does not understand that *g* differences are – partially – a product of genetic differences, then the reason some children perform better in school must be completely environmental. As a result, some educators see the expanding variability in educational achievement and the inability of schools to equalize educational outcomes as signs that the educational system is failing (Gottfredson, 2000a). They advocate for more resources (e.g., by reducing class sizes, increasing funding) and mandate that all children be taught the same material in the same way in an attempt to eliminate differences in educational outcomes. But differences in educational performance are inevitable because the differences in intelligence (caused partially by genetic differences) among children still remain. The end result is a cycle of frustration and failure to achieve policy goals.

Some policies that deny intelligence actually harm students. One of these policies is the idea that every child should attend college. A college education – like education at the K-12 level – requires intelligence for success. However, because of intelligence differences, some students will struggle in college and not graduate. In 2018, 61.3% of Americans who were 25 or older had attended at least some college. Of these, 35.7% did not have any post-high school degree, and another 7.2% had only an associate's degree (US Census Bureau, 2019, Table 1). Thus, almost half of college students do not earn a four-year degree. Many of these students require remedial classes to compensate for a lack of readiness for college-level classes or accumulate debt to pay for degrees they never earn. Some of these students drop out because of academic difficulties and feel like failures. If a majority of Americans attend college, then some of them will inevitably have an IQ below average, and these students will struggle mightily to earn a degree.

A NEEDED DOSE OF REALISM

Political slogans like "Every Student Succeeds" and "No Child Left Behind" may feel good, but they are not grounded in reality (Frisby, 2013). I do not deny the good intentions of lawmakers and educational staff who claim that their favored policy will eliminate educational failure. However, reality does not care about good intentions. Intelligence differences are "real, stubborn, and important" (Gottfredson, 2000a, p. 76), especially in education. These differences are rooted – partially – in genetic differences. As a result, basing policy on high-minded platitudes and promising the impossible will only result in disappointment and disillusionment. Some policies may even harm students.

Scientific research cannot determine social or policy goals because those goals are inherently value-laden, while scientific facts are value-neutral. However, scientific research can inform which policies are infeasible and which have a chance of succeeding. Chapter 33 will give practical suggestions for policies based on intelligence research in education and other areas. I hope readers find that these suggestions are realistic and serve the needs of individuals with a wide variety of intelligence levels.

20

Non-cognitive Variables Have Powerful Effects on Academic Achievement

> what students believe about their brains – whether they see their intelligence as something that's fixed or something that can grow and change – has profound effects on their motivation, learning, and school achievement . . .
>
> (Dweck, 2008, paragraph 2)

Although intelligence is important in determining a student's level of academic success, no one claims that intelligence is the only trait that impacts school outcomes. The correlation between IQ and measures of academic success – such as grades, standardized test scores, or how many years a person stays in school – is not perfect. That means that there is room for other abilities to exert an impact on educational performance. As Gottfredson (1997b, p. 116) stated, "The effects of intelligence . . . are probabilistic, not deterministic. Higher intelligence improves the odds of success in school and work. It is an advantage, not a guarantee. Many other things matter." It is not difficult to brainstorm a list of what these "other things" that influence success are. Psychological traits like motivation, creativity, resiliency, curiosity, industriousness, and ambition can all be important for doing well in school. Non-psychological variables like socioeconomic status, parental involvement in education, a culture that encourages academic competition, and good physical health could also have an impact on a student's success (Warne, 2016a). Nobody denies this.

The argument among psychologists and educators is not whether non-*g* variables can result in higher school performance. Rather, the argument is over the magnitude of the influence that these non-cognitive variables have and whether these variables are more important than intelligence in determining educational success. Currently, there are four candidates that people often argue have a stronger influence on school performance than intelligence. These are personality traits, motivation, a growth mindset, and "grit."

PERSONALITY TRAITS

Although there are different personality theories in psychology, the leading theory is called *the Big Five personality trait theory*. According to this theory, personality consists of a mix of five traits: *neuroticism, extraversion, openness to experience, agreeableness, and conscientiousness*. These traits are present in many cultures and across the lifespan, and they are a robust basis for understanding personality (Allik & Realo, 2017).

The specific characteristics of each trait are shown in Table 20.1. When reading these lists, it is easy to imagine how some of these personality traits could help someone thrive or struggle in school. For example, a person with high neuroticism may have difficulty succeeding in school because they might have trouble complying with instructions, cooperating with peers, or handling the intrusive thoughts that are often part of anxiety and depression. Somebody who is high on agreeableness, though, may do better in school because they comply with teacher instructions and have the altruism needed to put in extra time on a group project to make sure that the assignment can earn a high grade.

Psychologists have conducted a great deal of research on the correlation between Big Five traits and school success. Although not perfectly consistent, this research shows that some of these traits correlate with educational outcomes. Conscientiousness has the strongest correlation, usually between $r \approx .20$ and $.35$ (e.g., Cucina et al., 2016; Lechner, Danner, & Rammstedt, 2017; Poropat, 2009; Spinath, Freudenthaler, & Neubauer, 2010). While this is a strong enough correlation for conscientiousness to be a noteworthy influence on school performance, it is weaker than the correlation between intelligence and academic performance, which is usually $r \approx .35$ to $.70$ in the same studies. This indicates that intelligence is a more important influence on educational performance than conscientiousness is. The other personality traits in the Big

TABLE 20.1 *Characteristics of the Big Five personality traits*

Neuroticism	Extraversion	Openness to experience	Agreeableness	Conscientiousness
Anxiety	Warmth	Fantasy	Trust	Competence
Angry hostility	Gregariousness	Aesthetics	Straightforwardness	Order
Depression	Assertiveness	Feelings	Altruism	Dutifulness
Self-consciousness	Activity	Actions	Compliance	Achievement striving
Impulsiveness	Excitement seeking	Ideas	Modesty	Self-discipline
Vulnerability	Positive emotions	Values	Tender-mindedness	Deliberation

Source: Costa & McCrae, 2010

Five have weaker relationships – in some studies as weak as zero – with academic achievement.

The reason why conscientiousness is more important than the other personality traits is apparent in Table 20.1. The characteristics of conscientiousness – competence, order, dutifulness, achievement striving, self-discipline, and deliberation – are almost exactly the list of characteristics of the ideal student. A student with high levels of conscientiousness, therefore, is a student who can meet deadlines, study long hours, think carefully about test questions before answering, be organized, and aim to perform well in school. Therefore, it is not surprising that a highly conscientious student earns high grades, perhaps higher grades than a classmate with low conscientiousness and an IQ that is a several points higher. However, high levels of conscientiousness do not completely nullify an intelligence disadvantage (Damian et al., 2015).

MOTIVATION

Personality traits have moderate importance in determining school performance, but they are hard to change. This resistance to interventions is probably because personality traits are – like almost every other psychological trait – partially influenced by genes. The heritability of personality is roughly the same as the heritability of intelligence, which may limit the malleability of personality (Bouchard, 1997, 2004; Briley & Tucker-Drob, 2017). Because of the difficulty of improving school performance by altering personality, many psychologists seek non-cognitive characteristics that are both malleable and important causes of academic achievement. One strong candidate is motivation.

Psychologists have studied motivation for about as long as they have studied intelligence, and describing all the research on motivation would require another book. The research is strong that highly motivated people set higher goals and accomplish more goals (Locke & Latham, 2002). Motivation seems to be one of the most important non-cognitive influences on school performance (Dalton, 2010; Liu, Bridgeman, & Adler, 2012). This should not be surprising because an unmotivated student is unlikely to pay attention in class, complete homework assignments, or study for tests. Policies that encourage motivation in children result in greater dedication to their studies and higher performance in school (e.g., Patall, Cooper, & Robinson, 2008; Roderick & Engel, 2001). However, being motivated is not enough for a child to earn high grades; the motivation must be channeled into the behaviors that foster learning (Schwinger, Steinmayer, & Spinath, 2009).

In regards to intelligence, research shows that highly motivated examinees earn slightly higher IQ scores (Gignac, Barulovich, & Salleo, 2019). And because staying in school longer raises IQ (Ceci, 1991; Ritchie & Tucker-Drob, 2018), it is possible that academically motivated students – who choose to stay in school longer – might earn higher IQs because of their additional education. However, none of this is evidence for whether increased motivation can cause higher *g*. Motivation, school performance, and IQ are all positively correlated with one another, and it is often difficult to disentangle their influences. Controlling for intelligence sometimes makes the relationship between motivation and academic performance disappear (e.g., Ziegler, Schmukle, Egloff, & Bühner, 2010), though not always. And it is possible that motivation's impact on IQ is entirely on the non-*g* influences on test scores.

It does seem clear that improving student motivation can lead to gains in educational performance (Dalton, 2010). Motivation seems to have a stronger effect on grades than on standardized test scores (e.g., Cucina et al., 2016), possibly because earning high grades requires more sustained effort. But intelligence seems to be the more important predictor, no matter how academic performance is measured. As the authors of one study stated, "cognitive abilities were by far the best predictor of school achievement" (Gagné & St Père, 2001, p. 71). Motivation – important as it is in determining academic outcomes – still is dwarfed by the influence of intelligence and other cognitive abilities. Therefore, no amount of motivation can make up for a large IQ deficit.

"I THINK I CAN": SELF-EFFICACY

Self-efficacy is another important non-cognitive characteristic that has an impact on educational outcomes. Psychologists define self-efficacy as the belief that a person is capable of accomplishing a task successfully (Lennon, 2010). It is more than confidence; self-efficacy is a positive appraisal of one's aptitudes and developed skills – as well as the context – in accomplishing a task (Bandura, 1977). Applied to an educational context, Corno et al. (2002, p. 109) stated, "Students with a strong sense of efficacy describe themselves as alert to check their own progress, unthreatened in the face of difficulty, and expecting to do well." Conversely, students with low self-efficacy concentrate on their failings and setbacks, give up easily, and avoid trying tasks that they do not think they can accomplish (Bandura, 1982). Self-efficacy can arise from a variety of sources. Encouragement from authority figures (e.g., teachers or peers), previous experience with success, observing a peer achieve success, and having high self-efficacy in a similar domain are all associated with high self-efficacy (Bandura, 1977, 1982).

Throughout the research literature, measures of self-efficacy positively correlate with educational outcomes, and self-efficacy, when combined with academic test scores is an excellent predictor of grades and other educational outcomes (Corno et al., 2002). There is strong evidence that the relationship is partially because high self-efficacy causes students to perform better in school (Lennon, 2010). Given the description of self-efficacy, those findings should not be very surprising; if a student does not believe they are capable of accomplishing a task, they are less likely to try it – let alone finish it or to perform at a high level.

The fact that self-efficacy is malleable and that it can lead to higher academic performance is encouraging because it gives educators a route for improving students' academic performance. However, it is important to recognize the limitations of self-efficacy. Since its beginnings, it has been recognized as a domain-specific belief (Bandura, 1977). This means that having high self-efficacy in one area (such as writing) does not automatically result in a person having high self-efficacy in a different domain (such as science). People often have varying beliefs about their competence and ability to be successful in different areas. Therefore, to improve a student's academic performance in many areas, it is important to boost their self-efficacy in each of these areas (Bandura, 1977). Additionally, self-efficacy applies most strongly to areas where a person has already demonstrated success; as tasks become less similar to previously successful endeavors, self-efficacy has less importance. Thus, improving self-efficacy is probably a useful procedure for improving class grades (where teachers can give in-class work that builds success and self-efficacy before the semester ends and final grades are calculated) but much less effective at raising standardized test scores (Lennon, 2010). And even where self-efficacy is an important influence on academic success, it is still overshadowed by the influence of intelligence.

MINDSET

One of the most fashionable non-cognitive variables in education right now is called *mindset*. According to psychologist Carol S. Dweck (the world's foremost expert on mindset theory), a person's mindset is their belief about their abilities, especially intelligence. There are two types of mindset: (a) fixed mindset and (b) growth mindset. Individuals with a fixed mindset about their intelligence believe that their intelligence is static and unchangeable. People with a growth mindset, though, believe that their intelligence can increase if they are motivated, persistent, and studious (Dweck, 2009). These attitudes are theorized to influence students' performance in school. If mindset theory is correct, then these attitudes could be a target for treatments to improve academic achievement.

Early in her career, Dweck had discovered that some children blamed themselves and their lack of ability for failure, while others saw poor performance on a task as being the result of a lack of effort. Children who believed that their failure was because of a lack of effort tried longer and harder to overcome their difficulties. The children who believed that their failure was because of a lack of ability became helpless and easily gave up. Even if children had equal ability, these differences in attitude were associated with important differences in outcomes (C. I. Diener & Dweck, 1978).

Later, Dweck's research suggested that these attitudes – or mindsets – were partially the result of the messages and feedback that adults give to children. Beginning in the late 1990s, Dweck and her colleagues conducted studies in which children would be praised for either their effort or their intelligence when they solved problems. The researchers believed that praising effort would build a growth mindset and that praising children for being smart would foster a fixed mindset. Dweck and her colleagues found that praise for effort was more effective in encouraging persistence after experiencing failure in problem solving. Additionally, results from one highly cited study indicated that children who had been praised for intelligence were more likely to pursue challenges that would make them look smart instead of challenges that would help them learn more (Mueller & Dweck, 1998). Dweck (2016) has also claimed that a growth mindset actually fosters biological changes in the brain by increasing and strengthening connections among neurons.[1]

Dweck and her colleagues later argued that the effects of a growth mindset are "profound" (Dweck, 2008, paragraph 2), "remarkable" (Dweck, 2016, p. 36), and "incredible" (Dweck, 2016, p. 38). Conversely, a fixed mindset renders students "helpless" (K. Richardson, 2002, p. 296). Others have stated that a fixed mindset is an important impediment that prevents bright children from having correspondingly high academic achievement (e.g., Subotnik, Olszewski-Kubilius, & Worrell, 2011). In regards to intelligence specifically, Dweck (2007, paragraph 3) stated that:

Many believe that (1) praising students' intelligence builds their confidence and motivation to learn, and (2) students' inherent intelligence is the major cause of their achievement in school. Our research has shown that the first belief is false and that the second can be harmful – even for the most competent students.

Some scholars have also used Dweck's work to argue that average academic performance differences across demographic groups are partially the result of some groups having a fixed mindset more frequently, perhaps due to socialization or stereotypes (Macnamara & Rupani, 2017; Subotnik et al., 2011).

Because of Dweck's work, the common folk wisdom among educators is that teachers should not praise students for being smart, but rather that it is best to praise students for their hard work. One recent survey reported that 96% of American teachers had heard of growth mindset, and 88% of teachers believed that a growth mindset was important for student achievement (Education Week Research Center, 2016). The same survey showed that teachers believed that a growth mindset was associated with greater excitement about learning (99%), more persistence in schoolwork (99%), high levels of effort in schoolwork (98%), consistent completion of homework (81%), and higher course grades (63%). Additionally, 70% of

---

[1] The proposed benefits of mindset theory are not confined to education. Dweck (2012, 2016) has claimed that a growth mindset can reduce teenage angst and depression, improve corporations' productivity, counter bias in professional fields, improve parenting practices, increase willpower, reduce aggression, improve race relations, and even foster peace in the Middle East. There is no word on whether a growth mindset functions as a floor wax or a dessert topping.

teachers believe that a student who has a fixed mindset is harder to teach (Education Week Research Center, 2016).

The studies of targeted interventions to change mindsets in the laboratory seem to support Dweck's theory, but the larger, more recent studies in a naturalistic setting are less promising. In these studies, there is little to no correlation between growth mindset and intelligence (Burgoyne, Hambrick, & Macnamara, 2020; Macnamara & Rupani, 2017) or between growth mindset and academic achievement (Bahník & Vranka, 2017). Indeed, the average correlation between growth mindset and academic achievement is a paltry $r = .10$, and interventions to foster growth mindset only improve academic performance by $d = .08$ (Sisk, Burgoyne, Sun, Butler, & Macnamara, 2018), which is too small for anyone to notice in everyday life.

Some recent studies stand out because they are RCTs[2] that randomly assign students to the treatment group that receives a mindset intervention or a control group. In one of these studies, a mindset intervention had no effect on sixth-grade students' skills in math, reading, or writing mechanics (i.e., grammar, punctuation, and spelling; Foliano, Rolfe, Buzzeo, Runge, & Wilkinson, 2019).[3] This matches an earlier RCT by the same group, which found no effects of mindset treatments on fifth graders' math or reading grades (Rienzo, Rolfe, & Wilkinson, 2015). A replication of the landmark Mueller and Dweck (1998) study has failed, as have two other experiments testing the effectiveness of instilling a growth mindset in children (Li & Bates, 2019).[4] And another RCT using Dweck's own mindset materials failed to produce any academic benefits for a sample of low-income high schoolers (Gandhi, Watts, Masucci, & Raver, 2020). These independent RCTs consistently show zero impacts of mindset interventions – a major blow to the theory.

Work by Dweck and her collaborators provides evidence that is only marginally supportive of mindset theory (e.g., Paunesku et al., 2015). One extremely well-designed study by Dweck and her colleagues showed that a growth mindset intervention raised grade point averages by just $d = .03$ to $d = .10$ (Yeager et al., 2016). A larger study (with a sample size of 12,542) by Dweck and her colleagues showed an average effect of just $d = .033$ (Yeager et al., 2019). These tiny impacts fall far short of the "profound," "remarkable," or "incredible" results promised by mindset theorists.

---

[2] See Chapter 15 for an explanation of randomized control trials (RCTs).

[3] Mindset training also had no impact on the students' non-cognitive variables: self-esteem, self-efficacy, test anxiety, or self-regulation (Foliano et al., 2019).

[4] Another team (Glerum, Loyens, Wijnia, & Rikers, 2019) also failed to replicate the Mueller and Dweck (1998) study, though the subjects in the replication study were several years older than the children in the original study. The age difference in the two studies is a confounding variable, which means it is not clear whether the failure to replicate is because (1) praise designed to encourage a growth mindset is ineffective, or (2) whether older students do not respond well to the feedback that younger students respond to.

Taken together, all these results indicate that any impact of mindset interventions is extremely small in the real world.[5] Can educators and mentors continue to speak kind words of encouragement to their students? Of course. But it should be understood that these subtle impacts are not the "profound effects" that Dweck and her colleagues have advertised to the educational establishment. Generally, class time spent on teaching students a growth mindset would probably be better spent on teaching them language arts, mathematics, science, and other academic topics.

TRUE GRIT?

Another increasingly popular non-cognitive trait that some psychologists and educators have suggested can be important for school success is *grit*. Formulated by psychologist Angela Duckworth, grit is

perseverance and passion for long-term goals. Grit entails working strenuously toward challenges, maintaining effort and interest over years despite failure, adversity, and plateaus in progress. The gritty individual approaches achievement as a marathon; his or her advantage is stamina. Whereas disappointment or boredom signals to others that it is time to change trajectory and cut losses, the gritty individual stays the course. (Duckworth, Peterson, Matthews, & Kelly, 2007, pp. 1087–1088)

In a series of studies all reported in one article, Duckworth and her colleagues (2007) found that grittier individuals had higher grade-point averages. Among elite samples, individuals with higher grit had better performance at an Ivy League university and had better results in the National Spelling Bee finals. But the benefits of grit were not just apparent in an academic realm. Duckworth et al. (2007) also found that West Point cadets with higher levels of grit were less likely to drop out of a physically intensive portion of their military training. Later research supported these findings, and higher levels of grit are correlated with an ability to finish a long-term task or goal, including in education, marriage, and a person's career (e.g., Eskreis-Winkler, Shulman, Beal, & Duckworth, 2014).

Thus, it is clear that people who stick to a task are more likely to complete long-term goals. That is a finding that should not be very surprising to anyone.

---

[5] In addition to the minuscule impact of mindset treatments (as shown by the near-zero *d* values), there are some remaining problems with these results. First, mindset interventions only seem to help students with low academic achievement (Paunesku et al., 2015; Yeager et al., 2016, 2019). While this is good for practical purposes – because these are the students who need the most help – there is no satisfactory reason why the majority of children do not see any benefits from mindset training. Additionally, the students who have best internalized a growth mindset are not always the ones who experience the greatest academic gains (Schwartz, Cheng, Salehi, & Wieman, 2016; Sisk et al., 2018). Mindset theorists have never been able to explain this disconnect between the magnitude of academic benefits from mindset treatments and the size of the change towards a growth mindset.

To Duckworth's credit, she recognizes that her findings confirm the cultural wisdom that persistence matters and that slow and steady wins the race (Duckworth & Eskreis-Winkler, 2013). On the other hand, Duckworth may be guilty of overselling her findings. For example, she claims that "grit may be as essential as IQ to high achievement" (Duckworth et al., 2007, p. 1089), even though the correlations between grit and educational achievement are about $r \approx .01$ to $.25$ (weaker than the IQ-achievement correlations above), and in Duckworth's own studies, higher levels of grit are *not* associated with staying in college longer (e.g., Duckworth et al., 2007, p. 1091; Eskreis-Winkler et al., 2014). The weak correlations that grit has with most outcomes (especially in academics) disproves the idea that grit is a major determinant of academic or life success.

A more serious problem with grit research is the claim that grit is a separate personality trait from the Big Five traits listed in Table 20.1. Recent research has shown that grit is very similar to conscientiousness, with the two traits correlating $r = .66$ to $.84$ (Credé, Tynan, & Harms, 2017; see also F. T. C. Schmidt, Nagy, Fleckenstein, Möller, & Retelsdorf, 2018). This correlation is so high that it indicates that there is little, if anything, new about grit at all. It is probably just a repackaged version of conscientiousness. Duckworth has always acknowledged the correlation between conscientiousness and grit (Duckworth et al., 2007), but there is not enough evidence to warrant her claims that grit is a separate trait. A growing body of research studies shows that grit has no unique properties compared to more established non-cognitive variables (e.g., Dixson, Worrell, Olszewski-Kubilius, & Subotnik, 2016; Usher, Li, Butz, & Rojas, 2019).

Indeed, it is not realistic to expect any newly announced psychological trait to be truly novel. Psychology has been a science since 1879; anyone claiming in the twenty-first century that they have discovered a new psychological trait is arguing that they have noticed a trait that thousands of psychologists have missed, despite almost a century and a half of intensive study of human behavior. This is an extraordinary claim, and as the old cliché goes, "Extraordinary claims require extraordinary evidence." The strong correlations that grit has with conscientiousness (and the similar correlations that both traits have with academic success) means that Duckworth does not have extraordinary evidence that grit is unique in any way.

NOT TRAITS, BUT HARD WORK

In this chapter, I have summarized the beliefs and research regarding mindset theory, motivation, grit, and the Big Five personality traits. Although advocates of these traits differ from one another in their beliefs, one idea unites them all: the importance of hard work to succeed. The intelligence crowd recognizes that a high IQ cannot compensate for terminal laziness. Psychologists who favor the Big Five traits as an explanation for academic success argue that it is because conscientiousness encourages a person to work hard that the trait is correlated with academic achievement. Motivation theorists believe that motivation is important because it lays a foundation for the work needed to accomplish goals. Dweck and her colleagues are probably correct that some students are in a mental trap of believing that their poor academic performance is inevitable and that some poor students would perform better in school if they believed that their efforts would pay off. Finally, there are benefits to the perseverance that "grit" encourages, even if the trait is just a new name for some aspects of conscientiousness.

No school rewards grades or degrees to students based solely on their personality traits or intelligence test scores. Instead, schools grade students on the quality of their assignments, quiz and test performance, attendance, etc. Performing well on these tasks and achieving success in school often requires effort. And a high degree of success or eminence in one's career requires a lot of hard work (Lubinski, Benbow, & Kell, 2014). Some of this desire to work will come from psychological traits, such as motivation and conscientiousness. A person's ability to work hard will be (unsurprisingly) correlated with success in school and their career. It is not important whether one's preferred label for the ability to work hard is conscientiousness, grit, the product of a growth mindset, achievement motivation, industriousness, perseverance, or any anything else.

What is important is the final product of students' education. Because of differences in intelligence, some people will perform better than others in school (see Chapter 19). But grades are partially dependent on the work a student is willing to put into their assignments and test preparation. As a result, working hard can modestly compensate for a person's shortcomings on other traits (e.g., intelligence, conscientiousness, neuroticism) or social disadvantages. For teachers, parents, psychologists, and others, the challenge is to determine how to encourage this hard work in students.

21

Admissions Tests Are a Barrier to College
for Underrepresented Students

> SATs ... have been used to screen Black applicants out of better colleges, which
> provide improved access to jobs
>
> (McClelland, 1994, p. 67)

> Which students are disadvantaged by tests like ACTs or SATs?
>
> Everyone who is not from a family in the top 10 percent of the income
> distribution. In addition, all blacks, Hispanics and women are disadvantaged by
> this test. The test is a more reliable predictor of demographics than it is of
> academic performance.
>
> (Ovaska-Few, 2012, paragraphs 14–15)[1]

College admissions tests are some of the most scrutinized and some of the most
frequently taken tests in the world. As a result, many people have an opinion
about the SAT or ACT.[2] These opinions are based on personal experience,
media reports, facts about the test, and some popular incorrect ideas. Generally,
the American public favors standardized tests, including for college admissions,
though there is always a vocal minority that does not (Phelps, 2005).

One common reason that some people oppose college admissions tests is the
average score differences that occur across different racial and ethnic groups
(Geisinger, 2005). Like most tests of g, there are noticeable differences in
average scores for different racial and ethnic groups, as shown in Table 21.1.
These average differences match the general pattern of score differences that
I described in Chapter 10, where the group with the highest mean is Asian
examinees, followed by European American, Hispanic, and African American

---

[1] This is an interview with the sociologist Joseph Soares, who is a critic of college admissions tests.
The reporter, Sara Ovaska-Few, asked the question, and Soares gave the response.

[2] Although earlier in their history, SAT and ACT were abbreviations, today "SAT" and "ACT" are
the names of the tests and not abbreviations.

TABLE 21.1 *Average SAT and ACT scores for different racial/ethnic groups, 2017–2018 school year*

Racial/Ethnic group	SAT			ACT				
	ERW	Math	Total	English	Math	Reading	Science	Composite
African American	483	463	946	15.8	16.9	17.3	17.1	16.9
Asian	588	635	1223	24.1	25.1	24.2	24.1	24.5
Hispanic	501	489	990	17.8	18.8	19.3	18.9	18.8
Native American	480	469	949	15.9	17.4	17.7	17.7	17.3
Pacific Islander	498	489	986	17.2	18.4	18.3	18.3	18.2
European American	566	557	1123	21.9	21.7	22.8	22.0	22.2
Multiracial	558	543	1101	20.6	20.6	21.8	20.9	21.1
Unknown	472	481	954	19.0	19.6	20.3	19.8	19.8
All examinees	536	531	1068	20.2	20.5	21.3	20.7	20.8
SD	102	114	204	7.0	5.5	6.8	5.7	5.8

Note. ERW = Evidence-Based Reading and Writing (i.e., Verbal) section, SD = Standard Deviation.
Note. SAT scores range from 200 to 800 for the ERW and Math sections of the SAT and 400 to 1600 overall. ACT scores range from 1 to 36 on each section and the composite.
Source: College Board (2018) and ACT, Inc. (2018).

examinees, in that order.[3] Although not shown in the table, there are also mean differences among socioeconomic groups, with students from wealthier families having higher average scores than middle-class students, who, in turn, have average scores that are higher than average scores of students from low-income families. Chapter 11 discusses this issue at length.

Because of these differences, the use of college admissions tests to determine who will be admitted to college will make it difficult to produce a pool of admitted students whose demographics reflect the demographics of the general population of examinees. If the same required minimum score is applied to all examinees, then members of higher-scoring groups will be admitted to college at higher rates, and lower-scoring groups will be admitted at lower rates (Petersen & Novick, 1976). The only ways to obtain proportional admissions rates are (a) to lower the minimum score for admission for lower-scoring groups, and/or (b) to raise the minimum score needed for admission for higher-scoring groups (see Chapter 34 for a deeper discussion of this issue). Because of opposition to differing minimum scores, these techniques are sometimes difficult to fully implement, even when university administrators

---

[3] It is important to remember that this is just a description of group averages. As Chapter 10 stated, there is a lot of overlap among these groups, and members from all groups can be found at all score levels of all tests.

have a strong desire to obtain a diverse student body. As a result, many people (understandably) see the SAT and ACT as an impediment to equity because these tests encourage universities to admit students from more privileged backgrounds (e.g., Au, 2018; Bielby, Posselt, Jaquette, & Bastedo, 2014; Posselt, Jaquette, Bielby, & Bastedo, 2012).

THE WORLD TURNED UPSIDE DOWN: COLLEGE ADMISSIONS TEST AS A TOOL FOR EQUALITY

Selection is Inevitable. Selecting some students – and rejecting others – is inevitable at most four-year colleges and universities. This is because most institutions have more applicants than they have space to accommodate, especially elite private universities, which sometimes have over ten times more applicants than they can admit.[4] At most universities, it is impossible to admit every applicant, and so some method must be used to reject some people and admit others. Getting rid of college admissions tests will not change this; instead, it will force universities to use some other decision method.

Other Available Options. Nobody believes that using the SAT or ACT to select students for college admission will result in a student body that is perfectly representative of American students. However, there is no guarantee that other options will result in greater equality in admissions decisions. But there is evidence that college admissions tests are better than any other option (Phelps, 2003). This does not mean that these tests are perfect in obtaining socially desirable outcomes, but they are the least unfavorable option available.

One alternative source of information that could be used for admissions decisions is high school grades. Indeed, most universities are already using grades as part of their decision-making process, and grades are already given more weight in the admissions process than college admissions test scores (Clinedinst & Patel, 2018). Grades have the added benefit of providing unique information that test scores do not, such as the ability to turn in assignments on time, attend class regularly, and maintain motivation throughout a semester. Those are characteristics that universities want in their students, and it makes sense that high school grades are part of the admissions decision at the vast majority of universities.

However, relying solely on grades and dispensing entirely with college admissions tests would be a mistake. Grades – just like college test scores – also correlate with income and display the same racial and ethnic group differences in averages that test scores do. But grades are not subjected to the same scrutiny that test scores receive (Zwick, 2007). There is no evidence that high school grades are unbiased – unlike test scores (see Chapter 10). In fact,

---

[4] Conversely, 80.5% of American universities accept at least half their applicants, and 43.9% of universities accept more than 70% of their applicants (Clinedinst & Patel, 2018, p. 10).

because most grades are at least partially subjective, grades are highly susceptible to the biases and preferences of teachers. Using grades as the sole criterion for college admission will not eliminate disparities across racial groups – and may even exasperate them (Cleary, Humphreys, Kendrick, & Wesman, 1975).

Another problem with grades occurs when high schools weight grades so that students who take more difficult classes (e.g., honors courses, Advanced Placement classes) will receive a boost to their grade point average compared to students who earn the same grade in a regular course in the same subject. Weighting is often idiosyncratic from school to school, which reduces the correlation between school grades and college performance (Warne, Nagaishi, et al., 2014). Moreover, weighting schemes for high school grades advantage wealthier students because they are more likely to attend high schools with more advanced course offerings (Klugman, 2013) and to enroll in these courses (Klopfenstein & Lively, 2016), which means that these students will disproportionately receive a boost to their grade point average.[5]

Other sources of information are available to college admissions personnel, but these are even more flawed than grades. Portfolios, writing samples, and letters of recommendations from adults (e.g., teachers, employers), lists of extracurricular activities, and awards are more subjective than grades and offer even more opportunities for people's biases to influence these products. And these measures will not negate the influence of family income, cultural differences, or language differences among applicants. Again, those differences would probably be amplified because wealthy families and children attending well funded schools will have more time, resources, and social connections needed to obtain strong letters of recommendations, have writing coaches that improve their essays, strengthen portfolios, and more.

Gaming the System. Even if college admissions tests are not the worst amplifiers of inequality, it is still valid to question the degree to which they are susceptible to the influences of income inequality and other disparities. One common accusation is that test preparation, called *coaching*, can improve scores on the SAT or the ACT. Some of these test preparation courses are expensive. For example, one leading company, Princeton Review, charges $1,399 and guarantees a SAT score of at least 1400 or an ACT score of 31 or more in just two months. If the claims of test preparation companies are true, then it is possible for wealthy parents to buy their child a higher score. That is clearly unfair for anyone who wants college admissions to be based on academic merit and not family income.

---

[5] To mitigate the effects of weighting, universities can either (a) accept only unweighted grade point averages, or (b) recalculate all grade point averages for all applicants so that grades are on a uniform scale. It is not clear how many universities take these steps.

Despite the claims of these companies, the reality is very different. In carefully designed studies, preparation courses have very little impact on college admissions test scores. The consensus is that there can be small gains of about 10–15 points on each section of the SAT, for a total improvement of approximately 20–25 points (Sackett et al., 2008; Zwick, 2007). Most of the score gains are from familiarity with the format of the items and the types of questions on the test. These sorts of gains are easy to obtain and correspond to answering about 2–5 more questions correctly on the test. Beyond these modest gains, it takes the equivalent of several months of additional academic preparation to increase scores on college admissions tests (Messick & Jungeblut, 1981). Therefore, money cannot really buy a higher SAT or ACT score, although long-term study can improve a student's score – which is exactly how a test of academic preparation should perform. Standardized admissions tests for graduate school programs show a similar level of resistance to coaching (Kuncel & Hezlett, 2007).

What may be surprising to non-experts is that test creators *want* students to become familiar with the test format and to be prepared for what the test will ask. If every examinee understands the test format, the test score can better measure what students actually know – and not their ability to discern the format of test questions during the testing session (Crocker, 2005). If everyone has access to test preparation materials, then any advantage that wealthy examinees gain from pricey courses is reduced (Sackett et al., 2008). If anything, widespread preparation for college admissions tests will improve the tests' abilities to measure how well students learn academic material and will lessen the confounding effects of socioeconomic status. This is why the College Board – which creates the SAT – has made more study materials, including practice tests and instructional videos, available for free online for SAT examinees.

Although college admissions tests may not be popular, their resistance to coaching is a powerful bulwark against unqualified but wealthy examinees. All other sources of information about an applicant are much easier to manipulate for wealthy families to improve their children's standing in the college admissions process. Raising grades, for example, is faster than raising standardized test scores; high school grades have increased over the years, a phenomenon called *grade inflation* (Benbow & Stanley, 1996; Pattison, Grodsky, & Muller, 2013). Additionally, parents can take action to increase their child's grades either directly (for example, by pressuring the teacher into offering extra credit options) or indirectly (e.g., lobbying for more courses that provide weighted grades, or shopping around for a charter or private school that is more lenient in grading). SAT and ACT scores are resistant to these pressures.

There are other ways that the wealthy can manipulate the college admissions system at elite universities. Many of these universities offer special consideration to the children of wealthy donors and "legacy students" whose parents attended the same university. These admitted students are disproportionately European American and wealthy, and these preferences function as a form of affirmative action for the privileged (Espenshade & Chung, 2005; Espenshade, Chung, & Walling, 2004). A similar preference occurs for athletes, who tend to have lower test scores than other students. Some sports, such as water polo, lacrosse, sailing, fencing, rowing, golf, and skiing, are the purview of student athletes who are disproportionately European American, and pre-college training opportunities in these sports are available mostly in upper- or middle-class neighborhoods. Universities that sponsor these sports teams often provide preferential admissions to wealthy and European American students who may not have the academic credentials to be admitted through the traditional application process (D. Thompson, 2019). Scholarships in these sports subsidize these students' attendance.

An extreme case of the wealthy manipulating the college admissions system was announced while I was writing this book. In March 2019, federal prosecutors filed charges against over 50 people, including 33 parents, who engaged in a corruption scandal to have underqualified applicants admitted to elite universities (see Medina, Brenner, & Taylor, 2019, for an early news account). Dubbed "Operation Varsity Blues," the scope of the scandal is breathtaking. The parents are charged with colluding with a corrupt admissions counselor to use unethical methods to get their children accepted to a desired college. College athletics coaches were allegedly bribed to use their influence to say that an applicant would be a member of an athletics team and needed to be admitted – even though the child had never played the sport before. Unethical psychologists supposedly diagnosed children with learning disabilities so that the applicants could have extra time to take the SAT or ACT. Federal authorities also argue that proctors were sometimes bribed to allow a person to take a college admissions test in place of the applicant or to change answers on the applicant's answer sheet so that they would obtain a higher score. At the time of writing, over 30 parents and four coaches have pled guilty or are not contesting the charges (Levenson, 2019; Levitz, 2019).

Operation Varsity Blues illustrates how important the SAT and ACT are. These parents allegedly went to great lengths – and expense – because the SAT or ACT were the barriers for *their* children's admission to elite universities, and nothing short of illegal behavior could make their academically unprepared offspring into attractive college applicants. Almost every other aspect of the admissions process was easily manipulated (e.g., sports team membership, falsified student awards, high school grades, ghostwritten/heavily coached admissions essays). An important aspect of Operation Varsity Blues was the effort to increase college admissions test scores because it was the only component of a college application that a parent or the counselor could not manipulate directly (hence, the bribes to proctors and the hired ringers taking the tests). As Wai, Brown, and Chabris stated, for wealthy parents, high intellectual ability for their children was "the one thing they could not buy"

(2019, paragraph 6). Eliminate college admissions tests, and the college application process only becomes easier for the privileged and wealthy to influence.

A Tool for Social Equality. Despite what the critics say, college admissions tests can be a tool for social equality. In addition to creating barriers for wealthy, unqualified applicants, college admissions tests open doors to talented students from less privileged backgrounds (Wai et al., 2019). Indeed, the SAT grew in popularity in the early twentieth century because of a desire to increase equality of opportunity for an elite college experience to more applicants (A. Calvin, 2000). No one personified this goal more than James Bryant Conant, the president of Harvard University from 1933 to 1953. Conant was an advocate for offering educational opportunities to children who were not born into wealthy families, and his efforts to identify talented students from outside the traditional Harvard recruiting pool resulted in the SAT being adopted by the university for scholarship and admissions purposes (A. Calvin, 2000; Urban, 2010). In a great irony, the SAT – the very test that many people today criticize for being a barrier to underserved students in college – was actually implemented at many elite universities to diversify their student body.[6]

Even today, many testing experts (e.g., Benbow & Stanley, 1996; Phelps, 2003; Wai et al., 2019) see the SAT and ACT as tools to give educational opportunities to bright students who were not lucky enough to grow up with the trappings of privilege and wealth. This is not a blind perspective; it arises from the experiences of institutions and societies that have added or dropped tests of *g* for admission to educational opportunities. In the early twentieth century, Harvard did indeed admit more students from middle- and low-income families when it started using the SAT. Conversely, when selective grammar schools were largely eliminated in the UK, together with the 11+ examination for entry, the proportion of students from working-class families attending prestigious schools dropped (Mackintosh, 2011).

I want readers to recognize, though, the complexity of the historic record. While Harvard and other universities used standardized admissions tests to open doors to a broader cross-section of society, not every university adopted the tests for such virtuous purposes. The University of Texas, for example, first adopted standardized admissions tests in order to hinder the desegregation process in the mid-1950s (Price, 2019). Administrators took advantage of the

---

[6] Readers should not see the word "diversify" and think that Conant and his peers at other Ivy League universities had twenty-first-century views of diversity. Conant was mostly interested in economic and geographic diversity, and he focused on identifying bright children from public high schools outside the northeastern United States who would qualify for admission to Harvard University. The result was not diverse by modern standards, but compared to the student body of Harvard at the time – which was almost exclusively students from northeastern, upper-class private high schools – the SAT and Conant's other initiatives did bring students with more varied backgrounds to the university.

average differences in SAT scores across racial groups to create nominally race-neutral policies that technically complied with desegregation orders but admitted as few African Americans as possible. While this is a shameful past, the situation in the twenty-first century is very different. University admissions personnel are highly motivated to have a diverse student body. Modern experience has made it abundantly clear that it is possible to create admissions policies that balance the desire for diversity with the need to ensure that students are academically prepared for the rigors of college. The practices of some racist administrators in the past have little to say about admissions test uses in the twenty-first century.

Don't Shoot the Messenger. Finally, it is also important to remember that college admissions tests do not create inequalities in society. Rather, these tests merely measure existing inequalities (Warne, Yoon, & Price, 2014). The SAT or ACT do not make wealthier students more prepared for college than students from poorer families. Instead, those differences are the result of years of prior academic experience. Wealthier parents spend more money on enrichment activities for their children (Kornrich, 2016), and their children attend high schools that offer more advanced classes (Klugman, 2013). If a college admissions test did not show that students from these backgrounds had higher scores and were more prepared for college, then it would be a sign that the test was not functioning properly. If those results make readers uncomfortable, then they should advocate for changes to society and the education system, not seek to abolish the tests.

CONCLUSION

Eliminating the SAT or ACT will not make inequalities in academic preparedness disappear, nor will it solve the selection problem that most universities have where the number of applicants exceeds the number of students they can admit. College admissions tests are not perfect, but they are the least unfavorable option available to university admissions personnel. Unlike alternatives that critics of testing often suggest, SAT and ACT scores are difficult to manipulate, are screened to eliminate bias (see Chapter 10), are difficult to improve with expensive educational programs, and have a weak correlation with family income (see Chapter 11).

These facts do not alter one conclusion: demographic and socioeconomic differences in college admissions test scores appear year after year, with students from wealthier families outscoring students from poorer families, and Asian American students achieving a higher average score than European American students, followed by Hispanic and African American students. Efforts to reconcile the desire to admit qualified students to universities and the laudable goal of social equality are imperfect. Policy makers and university officials have tried affirmative action, need-based scholarships, recruiting strategies, and other methods to address the inequality of both opportunity and outcome in the college education system.[7] No one has ever found a perfect solution (see Chapter 34), but generations of bright students from unpromising backgrounds are thankful for an admissions system that allows them to show their academic promise. For these students, the SAT and ACT are a godsend that allows them to compete with students whose parents can afford test preparation courses, private schools, tutors, and access to exclusive sports and extracurricular activities. If colleges do eliminate the SAT, it is the smart, underrepresented students who will be hurt the most.

---

[7] One policy that is growing in popularity is to make the SAT and ACT optional for applicants. There is no evidence that this policy increases the racial or economic diversity of a college's student body. In the best study of the topic (Belasco, Rosinger, & Hearn, 2015), tuition increased more quickly at test-optional liberal arts colleges than at institutions that required test scores – thereby creating a new barrier for low-income students. Additionally, because students with low scores do not submit a test score with their application, the average SAT/ACT score increases, and when a university reports this new average to ranking organizations, its rank increases. It is apparent that test-optional policies benefit universities far more than they benefit underrepresented students.

SECTION 5

LIFE CONSEQUENCES OF INTELLIGENCE

In Section 4, I discussed the importance of intelligence in the context of the education system. The message of the chapters in that section is clear: intelligence differences exist, and those differences are one of the most important reasons why some students excel in school and others struggle. Educational practices and non-cognitive variables can help improve educational outcomes to an extent, but they cannot equalize students' educational outcomes, nor can they nullify the influence of intelligence.

It should not be surprising that IQ scores correlate with educational outcomes. The earliest successful intelligence tests were created in an educational context and were specifically designed to predict school performance. Over a hundred years later, intelligence tests (and other measures of g, like achievement tests) are still a valuable tool for educational personnel as they diagnose intellectual or learning disabilities, place children into gifted programs, or make other educational decisions. A critic could argue that the long marriage between intelligence tests and the educational system results in tests that are engineered to correlate with educational outcomes.

Educational outcomes are valuable, but their importance has limits. First, the education system for most students is highly regimented, and variables that predict educational outcomes may do so solely because of the structure of the environment. For example, both intelligence tests and the typical classroom require a student to sit still, pay attention, stay on task, etc. The correlation between the two scores may be due to these skills and not problem-solving ability. Second, most people do not spend a majority of their life in school. When they leave school, they have to deal with the world of work, leisure, family, and other aspects of life that are often more important to adults than school. If intelligence tests only measured skills used as a student and had no relevance to other aspects of life, then IQ scores would probably have trivial importance for many adults.

Chapters 22–26 discuss how intelligence relates to outcomes in the non-educational aspects of life:

- Chapter 22 shows that IQ scores correlate with many variables outside an educational context.
- Chapter 23 focuses on job performance and shows that intelligence is a factor in how well people do their job.
- In Chapter 24, I discuss the social hierarchy that *g* strengthens and perpetuates and show the benefits and downsides to using intelligence to help organize a society.
- Chapter 25 is an analysis of the threshold hypothesis, which is the belief that above a given IQ level, higher intelligence provides no additional benefits to people.
- Finally, Chapter 26 discusses emotional intelligence, which many people (especially in the business world) have theorized is an important variable for life success.

The message of these chapters is remarkably similar to the message of Chapters 18–21 of Section 4. Just as in the education context, intelligence seems to be one of the most important influences on outcomes at work and in everyday life. Because of these similarities, a lot of the themes from the last section will crop up again in the chapters in this section. Clearly, intelligence is not just a niche ability; instead it influences almost every aspect of people's lives. For me, that makes this section the most exciting of the book.

22

IQ Scores Only Measure How Good Someone Is at Taking Tests

> ... there is general agreement among psychologists that at the least, intelligence tests measure the ability to take tests. This fact could explain why people who do well on one IQ test also tend to do well on other tests. And it could also explain why intelligence test scores correlate so closely with school performance since academic grades also depend heavily on test-taking ability.
>
> (Morris & Maisto, 2016, p. 251)

Clearly, some people perform better on intelligence tests than others. Throughout this book, I have explored some popular explanations for this fact:

- Intelligence tests measuring adherence to Western culture (Chapter 4)
- Test bias (Chapters 10 and 21)
- An advantage for wealthier people (Chapter 11)
- Examinees' personal beliefs about their abilities (Chapter 20)

All these claims fail to explain why some people outscore others on intelligence tests. Another claim is much simpler than any of these: maybe some people are just better at taking tests. This is another way of saying that intelligence tests do not measure any skill that is useful in the real world, but rather just the ability to solve artificial problems in the test setting.

INTELLIGENCE PREDICTS ...

There is a simple way to tell whether intelligence tests merely measure test-taking ability: examine whether IQ correlates with any variables that originate outside the test. If IQ correlates with non-test variables, then it indicates that intelligence tests measure something that is important outside the test context. On the other hand, if IQ scores do not correlate with variables outside the test setting, then the critics are correct, and intelligence tests measure test-taking ability and little more.

TABLE 22.1 *Life outcomes that correlate with intelligence test scores*

Positive Correlations:	Negative Correlations:

• Creativity measures:
  o Number of patents
  o Research productivity
• Education:
  o Adult education attainment
  o Grades in school
  o Literacy level
  o Standardized test scores
• Leadership attainment
• Medical outcomes:
  o Myopia (i.e., nearsightedness)
  o Experiencing anorexia nervosa
  o Functional independence in old age
  o Good general physical health
  o Good general mental health
  o Longevity
  o Responsiveness to psychotherapy
• Occupational outcomes:
  o Income
  o Job complexity
  o Job performance
  o Occupation prestige
  o Promotions
  o Training success
• Offspring's intelligence
• Sense of humor
• Socioeconomic status
• Voluntary migration (e.g., for a job, immigrating to a new country)
	• Criminal behavior:
	  o Arrests
	  o Convictions
	  o Incarceration
	• Divorce
	• Dogmatism and rigid thinking
	• Giving birth out of wedlock (for women)
	• Impulsivity
	• Medical outcomes:
	  o Death from cardiovascular disease
	  o Dementia
	  o Dying in an automobile accident
	  o Experiencing an accident
	  o High blood pressure
	  o Hospitalizations
	  o Personality disorder diagnosis
	  o Schizophrenia
	  o Smoking behavior
	• Socioeconomic outcomes:
	  o Living in poverty
	  o Relying on welfare/public assistance
	  o Unemployment

Sources: Gottfredson (1997b), Jensen (1998), Strenze (2015), and Warne (2016a)

Table 22.1 is a compilation of some of the variables that correlate with IQ scores. On the left side of the table are life outcomes that have a positive correlation with intelligence, which means that these outcomes are more common for people who are smarter. The right side of the table lists variables that are negatively correlated with IQ, which means that these outcomes are less common for individuals who score high on intelligence tests. When possible, I have tried to group similar variables together into a category, such as educational variables, occupational variables, and so forth.

Table 22.1 is not a comprehensive list of all variables that are correlated with intelligence.[1] Nevertheless, it is clear from the table that the claim that intelligence tests only measure how good someone is at taking tests is definitely false. Instead, intelligence tests measure an ability that impacts many different areas of life; some scholars (e.g., Gordon, 1997; Gottfredson, 1997b) claim that intelligence impacts *every* area of life. This shows that intelligence tests do not measure a narrow test-taking ability. Rather, these tests measure a general ability that correlates with more life outcomes than any other psychological variable.

What makes this long list of correlations remarkable is that intelligence test creators are not trying to create a test that predicts who will live longer, be promoted more frequently at their job, earn more patents, or have a better sense of humor (all positively correlated with IQ). Similarly, test creators do not intend to create a test that predicts who would divorce, give birth out of wedlock, be impulsive, or die in a car accident or from cardiovascular disease (all negatively correlated with IQ). Yet IQ scores still correlate with these life outcomes. Anyone who claims that intelligence tests merely measure test-taking ability must explain (a) why so many variables correlate with IQ, and (b) why tests that were not designed to predict these life outcomes do so anyway.

I do not want readers to have an oversimplified view of the life characteristics that correlate with intelligence. While it is true that favorable life outcomes tend to be positively correlated with IQ and unfavorable life outcomes are often negatively correlated with IQ, there are exceptions. For example, the table shows that experiencing anorexia nervosa is positively correlated with IQ ($r = .20$, according to Strenze, 2015, p. 406), as is myopia (about $r = +.25$; Jensen, 1998, p. 149; see also Lubinski & Humphreys, 1992, pp. 106–108). Another exception occurred in Great Britain during World War II, a time in which smarter men were more likely to die than less intelligent men[2] (Deary, Whiteman, Starr, Whalley, & Fox, 2004). After the war, the correlation between IQ and survival switched to being positive and by the mid-1970s, men with the lowest levels of intelligence were more likely to be dead than their smarter peers. This shows that none of the correlations with intelligence

---

[1] I have generally omitted variables that have a weak correlation (less than $r = \pm.15$) or variables that show up in a single study of a small or non-representative sample. For example, Strenze (2015, p. 406) reported that the correlation between IQ and the number of children someone has is $r = -.11$, which is too weak for me to include in this table. I also did not report correlations that were drawn from aggregate groups. An example of this would be the correlation of average national IQ and a national-level variable, such as national wealth or average life expectancy (see Rindermann, 2018, for many national-level correlations with IQ).

[2] Perhaps the correlation between IQ and surviving the war was negative because (a) higher-ranking men were more likely to be intelligent and to die; (b) new wartime technology may have required more intelligent soldiers to master, who may have been placed in harm's way more often; (c) smarter men may have put themselves at greater risk; (d) some combination of these causes; or (e) unknown reasons (Corley, Crang, & Deary, 2009).

are immutable. Different social circumstances can change the strength or direction of these correlations. Indeed, high intelligence was probably correlated with unfavorable outcomes in China during the Cultural Revolution, Cambodia during the Khmer Rouge regime, or Germany while the Nazi Party was in power during the 1930s and 1940s (though the data are indirect and scanty for these time periods and locations).

Readers should also be aware that some correlations in Table 22.1 are stronger than others. The correlation between standardized educational test scores and IQ is about $r \approx .70$, but the correlation between IQ and income is about $r \approx .30$ (e.g., Murray, 1998; Zagorsky, 2007). Outcomes with weaker correlations tend to be variables that are the product of many influences, which means that g's impact is much more limited. An example of this is income, which is a result of occupational choice, ambition, willingness to work extra hours, market forces, and luck, in addition to intelligence. For variables that are more strongly connected to problem solving – such as educational outcomes – the correlation with IQ is much stronger.

There is also nuance regarding the relationship between intelligence and longevity. In the best study to date (Christensen, Mortensen, Christensen, & Osler, 2016), it was apparent that low IQ is a greater risk factor for some causes of death than others. After controlling for age, the correlation with IQ was greater for dying by homicide (65% increase in relative risk compared to someone with an IQ that was 15 points higher) than for lung cancer (37% increased risk) or for hormone-related cancer (9% increased risk). Of course, there are bright people who die prematurely. But it seems that high-IQ individuals are more likely to know how to obtain care for health conditions and to take preventative steps to avoid injury or illness (Gottfredson & Deary, 2004).

HIGH-IQ GROUPS: A PRACTICAL TEST OF IQ'S IMPORTANCE FOR LIFE OUTCOMES

In addition to correlations between IQ and life outcomes, another way to test the importance of intelligence is to examine whether high-IQ groups of people experience more positive life outcomes than the general population. In 1921, Lewis Terman started the most famous study to examine the characteristics of high IQ: the Genetic Studies of Genius.[3] Terman selected 1,528 high-IQ children, most of whom obtained an IQ score of at least 140. Terman and his

---

[3] In this context, the word "genetic" means "of or relating to origin or development" (according to the definition in the *Oxford English Dictionary*), which was a common meaning of the term in the 1920s. Although Terman believed that intelligence was influenced by heredity, this is probably not why he called his study the "Genetic Studies of Genius" (Stanley, 1974; Warne, 2019a). To avoid confusion with the modern meaning of "genetic," many people call it the Terman Longitudinal Study or the Terman Study of the Gifted.

team collected thousands of variables from these participants periodically through 1999. The results showed that – on most variables – high-IQ individuals had better life outcomes than the general population. As children, these individuals were (on average) taller, healthier, and performed better in school than their peers (Burks et al., 1930; Terman, 1926). Even within this group of bright children, smarter subjects were more likely to skip a grade during their K-12 education (Warne & Liu, 2017). Despite their academic successes, there was no evidence of social maladjustment in most sample members.

Later follow-up studies showed that beneficial outcomes occurred throughout the lifespan. These "children" did not lose their high intelligence as they aged (Burks et al., 1930; Terman & Oden, 1947, 1959), an important finding at the time because no one knew when the study began whether IQs were stable beyond a few years (Nemzek, 1933). The study participants were more educated than the general population; in 1940, when only 4.6% of American adults who were age 25 years or older had a bachelor's degree (National Center for Educational Statistics, 2017, Table 104.20), 69.8% of high-IQ men and 66.5% of high-IQ women had a bachelor's degree[4] (Terman & Oden, 1947, p. 149).

Outside the academic realm, the positive life outcomes for the Terman subjects were apparent. Throughout their adulthood, they had an extremely low rate of criminality (Oden, 1968). They earned more money and had more prestigious jobs than the general population[5] (Burks et al., 1930; Oden, 1968; Terman & Oden, 1947, 1959). A larger percentage were married by their mid-30s or mid-40s than the general population, and they were slightly less likely to be divorced (Terman & Oden, 1947, pp. 227–228; Terman & Oden, 1959, pp. 132–134). The IQ scores of most of their offspring was also far higher than average (see Oden, 1968, pp. 14–15; Terman & Oden, 1947, p. 236; Terman & Oden, 1959, p. 141). In their old age, the participants in the Genetic Studies of Genius lived longer than average and were, generally, satisfied with their retirement years (Holahan & Sears, 1995).

Other samples of high-IQ individuals have replicated these results. The ongoing 50-year Study of Mathematically Precocious Youth (SMPY) consists of 5,311 individuals of varying levels of high intellectual ability, ranging from IQs of approximately 120 to over 156. SMPY members – like the participants in the Genetic Studies of Genius before them – are more likely to have graduate

---

[4] In comparison, in 2017, the percentage of American adults who had earned a bachelor's degree is about half of what is seen in the Genetic Studies of Genius: 34.2% (National Center for Educational Statistics, 2017, Table 104.10), despite the wider availability of college education for twenty-first-century Americans.

[5] This is especially apparent in the data from the men. A large proportion of women (42% in 1940) were homemakers, and the most common occupations of those who did work were secretary and K-12 teacher (Terman & Oden, 1947, p. 179). But among those women who did not have these highly traditional occupations, the jobs were disproportionately prestigious.

degrees, highly prestigious jobs, and high incomes than the general population (Lubinski et al., 2014). Similarly, in a sample of 156 alumni of a New York City elementary school that selected high-IQ children as students, over three-quarters earned a graduate degree, and over half were lawyers, physicians, or college professors (Subotnik, Karp, & Morgan, 1989).

THE RULE – AND THE EXCEPTION

Clearly, groups of high-IQ children grow up to be – generally – successful adults. But this is not true for everyone with a high IQ. It is tempting to look at the research on the relationship between IQ and beneficial life outcomes and think that life is easy for smart people. It is not. None of these correlations are perfect (i.e., $r \neq +1.0$). Therefore, some smart people will experience some of these negative life outcomes – as is borne out by the data from the Genetic Studies of Genius, which had some sample members commit suicide, die prematurely in war or accidents, lose businesses, work menial jobs, and experience mental health problems. And some people with below-average IQ will experience favorable life outcomes. Exceptions happen. A good example of this is divorce, which can happen for reasons that have nothing to do with a person's intelligence. In fact, in some situations (e.g., abuse, a spouse's illegal behavior, infidelity, neglect), ending the marriage is often the smart thing to do.

Instead, these results refer to general trends that emerge when examining data from large samples of people. These correlations do *not* mean that any particular person's destiny is set in stone by their intelligence level. Rather, the relationships are probabilistic, not deterministic (Gottfredson, 1997b; Lubinski, 2004). Although below-average intelligence makes life more difficult for a person, other traits or life circumstances can compensate for a lower IQ. Having a supportive family, higher socioeconomic status, motivation, conscientiousness, cultural influences that discourage unfavorable behaviors, determination, and many other characteristics can compensate for a lower level of intelligence (Warne, 2016a). Nobody is a prisoner of their IQ.

NOT A TEST-TAKING ABILITY, BUT PERHAPS TEST-TAKING STRATEGIES?

All of the evidence shows that intelligence tests measure a trait that is important outside the testing environment. Indeed, intelligence may be an important part of nearly every aspect of people's lives. However, a critic could still instead say that "test-taking ability" could consist of a set of test-taking strategies that inflate scores. These strategies could include using the process of elimination on multiple choice test items, attempting every test item (even if it means guessing), and pacing oneself so that the examinee does not run out of time. In this scenario, intelligence tests can measure this "test-taking ability" in addition to *g*.

It is true that these test-taking strategies may improve test scores slightly (Bonner & D'Agostino, 2012; Pietschnig & Voracek, 2015; Woodley, te Nijenhuis, Must, & Must, 2014). But these techniques do not dominate the strategies that people use to answer test questions correctly (Bonner & D'Agostino, 2012; Warne et al., 2016). There is absolutely no evidence of a separate, coherent "test-taking ability" that is captured by tests of *g* (Phelps, 2003).

The only possible separate non-*g* ability that seems to have an important impact on test scores is test anxiety, which is a very real phenomenon that some people experience when they take academic, employment, cognitive, or intelligence tests. There is substantial evidence that a minority of examinees regularly experience test anxiety (e.g., Bandalos, Yates, & Thorndike-Christ, 1995; A. S. McDonald, 2001). For these examinees, their worries and preoccupations about their test performance lead to intrusive, unwanted thoughts that distract them during the test. Some sufferers of test anxiety also experience physical symptoms (e.g., elevated heartbeat, profuse sweating, rapid breathing, upset stomach) that may make concentrating difficult.

Taking steps to reduce anxiety in testing environments may be particularly helpful for these examinees. One common cause of test anxiety is being unprepared for a test or having a poor mastery of the test content (Sommer & Arendasy, 2014). Thus, one of the best methods of preventing test anxiety on academic tests is to study. People who experience crippling levels of test anxiety – despite their preparation – may benefit from psychotherapy, relaxation techniques, and other interventions.

CONCLUSION

Of all the misconceptions that this book addresses, the idea that intelligence tests only measure how good someone is at taking intelligence tests is one of the easiest to debunk. Intelligence test scores correlate with many variables in education, work, and everyday life. No other psychological variable has as many correlations with real-life outcomes as IQ. There is no separate "test-taking ability" that tests of *g* measure, although there may be modest benefits from using test-taking strategies. However, people who experience test anxiety may benefit from seeking help to control the unwanted thoughts and physical symptoms that detract from their test performance. Successful treatment of test anxiety may enable people to demonstrate their cognitive skills better and reduce the unpleasant symptoms that they experience.

23

Intelligence Is Not Important in the Workplace

> although IQ predicts school performance, it does not predict later career success . . .
>
> (Coon & Mitterer, 2016, p. 309)

> conventional IQ tests are good predictors of college grades, but they are less valid for predicting later job success or career advancement.
>
> (Nolen-Hoeksema, Fredrickson, Loftus, & Lutz, 2014, p. 418)

In Chapter 22, I explained that intelligence correlates with many life outcomes, including a person's health and longevity, creativity, and impulsivity. Among the life outcomes mentioned in the last chapter were educational outcomes (e.g., grades, test scores, persistence in college), which are positively correlated with intelligence. This means that people with higher intelligence generally perform better in school – a fact that no one denies.

One common misconception, though, is the idea that intelligence is not important for success in the workplace (e.g., Sacks, 1997). People who believe this may think that intelligence is important in school, but in the real world of work, academic prowess is not important for job success. An example of this is McClelland (1994), who stated that the only reason IQ correlates with occupational prestige is that many professional jobs require a college education, and standardized tests and college experience requirements keep competent people out of a job solely because they score poorly on tests. McClelland stated that among people who actually have a particular job, intelligence is uncorrelated with job performance. This chapter explains why this belief is wrong.

FIGURE 23.1 Examinees taking a predecessor of the Army Alpha (called Examination *a*) in November 1917 at Camp Lee, Virginia.
Source: US National Archives (https://catalog.archives.gov/id/55162121).

WORK SMARTER, NOT HARDER?

Early Research. After establishing that intelligence test scores could predict school success, the early intelligence test creators turned their attention to adult examinees and the workplace. Terman (1916) reported two studies that showed that unemployed men were more likely to have low intelligence – a finding that has since been replicated with modern data (Gottfredson, 1997b). A few years later, World War I produced a bonanza of data on the importance of intelligence for work. In the Introduction, I mentioned the Army Alpha and Army Beta, which were intelligence tests created as the American Psychological Association's contribution to the war effort. These tests were intended to screen for men who would not be suitable for military service (due to low intelligence) and to identify smart recruits who could thrive in leadership positions or handle complex jobs (Carson, 1993; Warne et al., 2019).

The creation of the Army Alpha and Army Beta was a massive undertaking. Intelligence tests until that time were usually administered individually, and psychologists had little experience in group testing. In less than a year, these psychologists created tests that could be administered *en masse*, tried out test

FIGURE 23.2 Examinees taking a predecessor of the Army Alpha (called Examination *a*) in November 1917 at Camp Lee, Virginia. Sometimes examinees took the army tests sitting on floors or in buildings built for other purposes (such as mess halls) because the army testing program was started so rapidly that many training camps did not have adequate testing facilities ready in time. These men are sitting on the floor of a hospital ward. The standing man in non-military dress is probably one of the civilian psychologists appointed to Camp Lee at the time to implement the army's testing program.
Source: US National Archives (https://catalog.archives.gov/id/55162119).

questions, developed scoring systems, and trained test administrators in these new procedures (Yerkes, 1921). By January 31, 1919, about 1.73 million men had taken an intelligence test during military training. About 1.24 million took the Army Alpha, and almost 500,000 had taken the Army Beta (Yerkes, 1921, pp. 99–100).[1] In an era before rapid communication, computers, photocopiers, and automatic scoring machines, this is an amazing logistic and scientific accomplishment. Judged by the standards of the time, the Army Alpha and Army Beta were excellent intelligence tests (Warne et al., 2019).

[1] Some men took an individual intelligence test or one of the tryout tests administered during the development period for the Army Alpha and Army Beta. Also, about 90,000 men took both the Army Alpha and Army Beta, so they are double counted in these totals. An additional 7,000 K-12 and college students took the tests so that the psychologists could compare the results to data from educational settings (Yoakum & Yerkes, 1920, p. 9).

The army tests provided the first data that intelligence might be important for occupational outcomes. The army psychologists discovered that men with higher test scores were judged by their commanding officers as being better soldiers ($r = .536$; Yoakum & Yerkes, 1920, p. 30). Moreover, men with higher intelligence had higher military ranks, failed their training less frequently, and had fewer disciplinary problems (Yoakum & Yerkes, 1920, pp. 24–35). American military leaders thought the tests were so useful that they have had a mental testing program ever since.

In the data from World War I, there was also a clear trend showing that smarter men were able to perform more complex jobs, as demonstrated in Figure 23.3. The military jobs that had a concentration of men with the highest intelligence levels were engineering officer, medical officer, civil engineer, accountant, mechanical draftsman, and dental officer. The jobs where men had the lowest intelligence levels were laborer, general miner, teamster, barber, horseshoer, and bricklayer (Yoakum & Yerkes, 1920, p. 198). The rest of the figure shows that – generally – as the intelligence level of workers increases, occupations become more complex, more prestigious, and (in the civilian world) better paying. These results would later be replicated in World War II (Harrell & Harrell, 1945; Vernon, 1947). In a modern American civilian sample, the six jobs with the lowest average intelligence levels were packer, custodian/janitor, material handler, food service worker, warehouse worker, and nurse's aid. People working in these jobs had an average IQ between 87 and 91. Conversely, the jobs with the six highest average IQs (114–118) were attorney, editor, advertising manager, engineer, research analyst, and chemist (Wonderlic, Inc., 1999, p. 27). However, there is a large degree of overlap in intelligence across occupations, and the range of intelligence within an occupation is often very wide – about 50–60 points for most civilian jobs (Wonderlic, Inc., 1999).

It is clear that intelligence is correlated with job prestige and complexity. It seems that intelligence is a "gatekeeper" variable for many occupations that have a minimum IQ needed for applicants to obtain (or keep) the job (F. L. Schmidt & Hunter, 2004). This minimum IQ rarely develops as a result of an intelligence test that applicants must pass in order to be hired. Instead, the minimum IQ is often established through job requirements, such as required college training or the cognitive duties of the job that workers must master. This also explains why the range of intelligence is so wide for most jobs: few jobs have a minimum IQ that is so high that only a tiny percentage of the population is eligible for the job. And in occupations with lower minimum intelligence requirements, nothing is stopping bright applicants from applying for and obtaining these jobs. Smart people in low-prestige jobs increase the range of intelligence within the job.

Performance at Work. IQ does not just make it harder for individuals with low intelligence to enter a high-prestige occupation. IQ also positively correlates with performance in most jobs. Again, the first evidence for this relationship

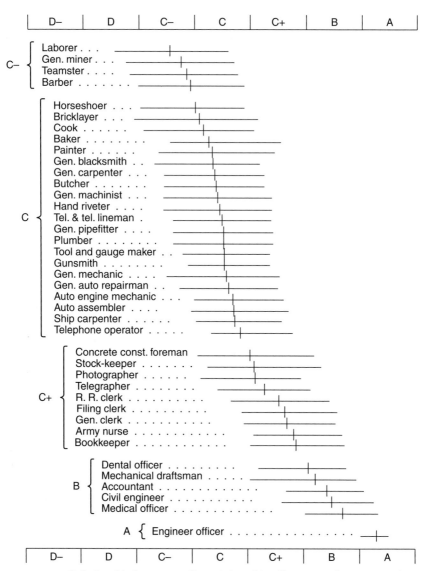

FIGURE 23.3 Relationship between military job and intelligence in the US army during World War I. Intelligence ratings range from D- (least intelligent group retained in the army) to A (highest rating). The horizontal line for each occupation represents the range of intelligence for the middle 50% of soldiers with that job in the military. The small vertical line represents the median (i.e., middle score within the group). Occupations are listed in order from lowest median to highest median.

Source: Yoakum & Yerkes, 1920, p. 198. For detailed data, see Yerkes, 1921, Part III, Chapter 15.

emerged from the World War I test data. For clerical jobs, the correlation between intelligence test scores and job competency ratings was moderately strong (*r* = .53). But for some jobs, the results were less promising: for machine operators, intelligence correlated with work productivity *r* = -.087 and with work accuracy *r* = .019 (Yerkes, 1921, p. 837). Even at this early stage of research it was clear that work performance and intelligence did not necessarily have the same correlation for all jobs.

For decades, research showed that the correlation between intelligence and job performance varied widely. It seemed that there was no general pattern to these correlations, and often results in the same job would fluctuate across studies. A breakthrough in this issue occurred in the 1970s with the realization that much of the instability observed in research studies was due to statistical artifacts, especially those arising from small sample sizes (F. L. Schmidt, Hunter, & Urry, 1976). Once these artifacts were corrected, the variation across studies of correlation coefficients between IQ and job performance *within* a particular job evaporated (F. L. Schmidt & Hunter, 1977). However, the variation *across* jobs in the correlations between IQ and job performance remained.

Another development was the invention of *meta-analysis*, a technical procedure that combines multiple studies as if they were one large study. This (theoretically) produces results that are more stable and applicable to more situations than any single study (Glass, 1976, 1977). A meta-analysis of the relationship between IQ and job performance showed that there was a clear pattern in correlation coefficients: jobs with higher average employee IQs demonstrated a stronger correlation between IQ and job performance. Conversely, jobs where the average IQ was lower tended to have a weaker correlation between IQ and job performance. In the most complex jobs (which employ about 15% of the workforce), intelligence correlates about *r* = .58 with job performance, but in the least complex jobs (in which only 2.4% of workers are employed), intelligence correlates only *r* = .23 with job performance (Hunter & Hunter, 1984, p. 82). Thus, intelligence is very important for succeeding in high-complexity jobs, but less important for succeeding in low-complexity jobs (Gottfredson, 1997b; F. L. Schmidt & Hunter, 2004).

Apart from their scientific relevance, these correlations are vitally important for employers. Because intelligence is positively correlated with job performance, it is almost always beneficial to a business to hire smarter applicants than less intelligent applicants[2] because smarter employees are

---

[2] There are some exceptions. For example, smarter applicants may leave the job frequently and have to be replaced often. It is also possible that smarter applicants may demand higher wages (because they may have more economic opportunities elsewhere). If a brighter employee's greater productivity does not make up for higher pay or retraining replacements is expensive, then hiring smarter employees would not be beneficial for the employer. However, these situations seem to be unusual.

TABLE 23.1 *Strength of selected predictors of job performance in medium-complexity jobs*

Predictor variable	Correlation with job performance (alone)	Correlation with job performance (combined with IQ)
IQ	.51	–
Work sample	.54	.63
Integrity tests	.41	.65
Conscientiousness	.31	.60
Structured interview	.51	.63
Unstructured interview	.38	.55
Job knowledge tests	.48	.58
Job tryout performance	.44	.58
Peer ratings	.49	.58
Reference checks	.26	.57
Years of education	.10	.52
Handwriting analysis	.02	.51
Age	−.01	.51

Source: F. L. Schmidt & Hunter (1998, Table 1).

easier and faster to train, more productive, make fewer errors, and are generally better at their jobs (Hunter & Hunter, 1984; F. L. Schmidt & Hunter, 2004). And the importance of hiring a smarter employee increases as the job becomes more complex. Having a physician who is less intelligent than the average physician is more damaging than having a janitor who is less intelligent than the average janitor. There are also extra productivity gains when a group of higher-IQ people work together, compared to their individual productivity when working alone (G. Jones, 2016).

Not only is intelligence an important predictor of job performance, it is among the best predictors for many jobs. Table 23.1 shows the correlation that different variables have with job performance. In medium-complexity jobs, IQ correlates $r = .51$ with job performance, second only to work samples ($r = .54$). Other variables with correlations that are nearly as strong are structured job interviews ($r = .51$), tests of job knowledge ($r = .48$), and an applicant's performance during a tryout period in the job ($r = .44$). Other variables commonly used in the hiring process have weaker relationships with job performance (F. L. Schmidt & Hunter, 1998). Because stronger correlations indicate that a variable is better at selecting people for jobs, Table 23.1 shows that IQ is one of the best variables that employers can use to select employees for medium-complexity jobs.

While IQ is the best predictor of job performance in medium-complexity jobs, there is no requirement that employers only use intelligence test scores to select employees. Combining sources of information about an applicant strengthens the accuracy of the hiring decision. The last column of Table 23.1 shows the predictive power of combining an IQ score with another variable. The best predictions of job performance result from combining IQ and the results of an integrity test (combined correlation = .65), which is a psychological test designed to predict undesirable behaviors, such as stealing from the employer, being belligerent with others, and engaging in substance use at work. Combining IQ and either a work sample or a structured interview results in a selection decision that is almost as accurate (.63). These improvements in hiring decisions show that there are important aspects of job performance that intelligence does not predict (F. L. Schmidt & Hunter, 1998). This is not a flaw in the tests because it is impossible for a test to measure every relevant human trait. There are traits other than intelligence that may matter in workplace performance – a fact that test creators do not deny (Sackett et al., 2008). However, among cognitive traits, intelligence is the most important predictor of job performance; other cognitive traits have little ability to predict job performance any better than IQ (Lubinski, 2004).

The strength of these correlation coefficients is important because the correlation with job performance is a measure of the efficiency gained from using the variable to hire an employee (Ree & Earles, 1993). If $r = 0$, then using the variable to hire employees is as effective as selecting an applicant at random. But if $r = 1$, then the best applicant for the job is always the person who scores highest on the predictor variable, and the hiring procedure has maximum efficiency (Brogden, 1946). Thus, hiring the employees who perform best on an intelligence test improves efficiency by 51% (because the correlation between IQ and job performance is $r = .51$) over random selection, while using solely reference checks improves the efficiency by only 26%. Hiring a better, more productive employee is most important in competitive industries (e.g., technology, finance) or for jobs where poor hiring decisions can be extremely costly (e.g., lawyers, physicians, engineers). Therefore, hiring smart people may be one of the most important decisions that a company can make. It may even be the difference between success and bankruptcy.

Why IQ Correlates with Job Performance. Given the overwhelming evidence that intelligence correlates with job performance, the logical question to ask is why. Clearly, if higher IQ causes people to be better at their jobs, it cannot be a direct relationship. In other words, smarter people are not better employees because supervisors know they are smarter and therefore rate them as better workers. The influence of intelligence on job performance is probably indirect. The best explanation is that high intelligence makes employees better at learning the knowledge and skills needed to do their jobs. This greater level of job knowledge, in turn, makes them better employees (Kuncel & Hezlett, 2010; Reeve & Bonaccio, 2011; F. L. Schmidt & Hunter, 2004). This is probably true, whether employees learn job skills in formal education or in on-the-job training.

Pencils Down! These results make it apparent that companies would benefit from giving intelligence tests to applicants. Yet few employers in the United States do this. While there could be a variety of reasons for this, the most important one is that it is often illegal to do so, thanks to a 1971 unanimous Supreme Court ruling, *Griggs v. Duke Power Co.*

The *Griggs* case arose as a civil rights case in which 13 African American employees of the Duke Power Company in North Carolina sued their employer because the company had a history of segregating employees, confining African Americans to the company's Labor Department (where all jobs paid less than the lowest paying jobs in all other departments), and denying them opportunities for promotion. Beginning in 1955, the company required employees outside the Labor department to have a high school diploma. Starting in 1965, the Duke Power Company required Labor department employees who wished to transfer to any another department to pass a written intelligence test and a test of mechanical knowledge. Neither was designed for any particular job, let alone any job at the company. Because African Americans in North Carolina had lower rates of high school graduation and had scored – on average – lower on intelligence tests than European Americans, this policy, though not mentioning race, had the effect of barring almost all African American employees from desirable jobs at the company.

The Supreme Court held that it was legal to use tests for employment purposes, but test items must have a clear relationship with job duties. If any policies – including the use of tests – resulted in a disproportionate number of people from any racial group being denied employment or promotion, then the burden of proof was on the employer to show that the policy was necessary for the operation of the business and that there was no less discriminatory procedure available. Additionally, the court ruled that illegal hiring or promotion procedures can arise without the intent to discriminate (*Griggs v. Duke Power Co.*, 1971). Congress later adopted these guidelines in 1991 (Garrow, 2014).

The effects of the ruling have been far reaching (Garrow, 2014) and have resulted in a major reduction in the use of tests for employment purposes. According to Miner and Miner (1978, p. 56), 90% of employers in 1963 used some sort of psychological test in hiring. By 1976, only 43% did. In the twenty-first century, only about 10% of employers give a cognitive ability test to applicants in entry-level jobs (Society for Human Resource Management, 2016, p. 29). Today, "hiring managers have turned their backs" on intelligence testing (Menkes, 2005, paragraph 1), and educational programs in business and organizational psychology rarely mention the importance of intelligence for job performance (Pesta, McDaniel, Poznanski, & DeGroot, 2015). This rejection of intelligence testing for employment occurred because of differences in average scores for various demographic groups, which makes it harder to select a proportionate number of applicants from each group for hiring or promotion (see Chapters 28–30). Using these tests can make companies vulnerable to lawsuits.

Instead of intelligence testing, companies have some alternatives. One is to use other, legally admissible sources of information that may help identify the best applicants. Table 23.1 shows common alternatives, some of which are approximately as good at identifying competent employees as intelligence tests are. Work samples, structured interviews, or peer ratings are all viable replacements for intelligence testing in employment settings.

Another option is for companies to create a job knowledge test that is tailored for a specific job. Table 23.1 shows that these job knowledge tests have a correlation of $r = .48$ with job performance. The drawback of these tests is that they are expensive to create, which makes them generally available only to large companies and government agencies. The final option for companies to select highly competent employees without using an intelligence test is to use a variable that is strongly correlated with intelligence. The most widely available variable is educational attainment. This is why many employers prefer applicants who have a college diploma: it signals that the applicant has an above-average level of intelligence and is likely to be competent at a medium-complexity job[3] (Gottfredson, 1986). And even when the only employee selection methods available have a weak correlation with job success, they can still provide some improvement in identifying qualified applicants compared to a technique that has a zero correlation with job success, especially when there are many more applicants than there are job openings (Taylor & Russell, 1939).

IS COMPENSATION FOR LOW IQ POSSIBLE?

In the face of the evidence regarding the importance of intelligence in the workforce, some theorists have argued that the correlation between job performance and IQ can be nullified as workers gain experience (e.g., K. Richardson, 2002). For example, Sternberg et al. (2000) summarized studies of garbage collectors and milk packers who demonstrated high efficiency in their jobs or outperformed better-educated replacements. The common thread that these examples have is that they are simple, routine jobs that require little novel problem solving (Gottfredson, 2003a). This does not nullify the importance of intelligence in the workplace. It merely means that there are some jobs that individuals with low intelligence can master with enough experience. These jobs have a low correlation between job performance and intelligence in the first place, and experience may reduce the correlation to zero.

This does not mean that experience is unimportant and that a person with a high IQ will do better at a job on their first day than their average co-worker. It

---

[3] A college diploma also signals useful non-cognitive skills and traits to an employer. These may include conscientiousness and the ability to complete goals.

still takes time to master a new job. For medium-complexity jobs, employees with less than five years of experience on the job perform more poorly than more experienced co-workers. But eventually, smarter employees catch up with the productivity of their more experienced colleagues (F. L. Schmidt & Hunter, 1998).

Another claim that some skeptics of intelligence make is that sufficient training can make almost anyone into an expert for nearly any task (e.g., Collins, 1979). One famous claim is that lengthy "deliberate practice" is a necessary and sufficient requirement for developing expertise (e.g., Ericsson, Roring, & Nandagopal, 2007). The argument that training can compensate for differences in intelligence (or any other important trait for a task) is called the *training hypothesis*, and it has been thoroughly disproven (e.g., de Bruin, Kok, Leppink, & Camp, 2014; Hambrick et al., 2014a, 2014b; Plomin, Shakeshaft, McMillan, & Trzaskowski, 2014). While additional or more detailed training can help low-IQ individuals perform as well as their co-workers temporarily, eventually brighter employees outperform better-trained, low-IQ individuals – as long as the job is at least somewhat complicated and not highly routine (Gottfredson, 1997b; F. L. Schmidt & Hunter, 2004).

The training hypothesis probably fails because of the relationship between intelligence, job knowledge, and job performance. If employees who know more about how to perform the job are better workers, then extra training can give low-IQ employees an advantage temporarily. But, the benefits of extra training vanish when smarter co-workers learn more information that is relevant to the job, forget less training compared to low-IQ co-workers, and gain more informal knowledge about how to perform a job.

CONCLUSION

Does intelligence matter for success in the workplace? Thousands of studies show that the answer is a resounding yes. Because many careers have a minimum IQ needed to enter the occupation, high-prestige occupations are closed to people with low intelligence. Once in a job, smarter workers outperform their less intelligent co-workers, especially in complex jobs. But legal hurdles make it difficult to use intelligence tests for employment purposes in the United States. However, there are alternatives available (e.g., work samples, job knowledge tests, structured interviews) that are approximately as effective as intelligence tests. Extra training and experience for less intelligent employees can reduce the relationship between IQ and job success temporarily, but eventually brighter workers surpass their colleagues in job performance. Just as in Chapter 22, the evidence in this chapter is overwhelming in showing that intelligence is important outside school. Indeed, because many people spend more of their lives in the workforce than in school, this research on intelligence is probably more important than any educational research.

24

Intelligence Tests Are Designed to Create or Perpetuate a False Meritocracy

What's wrong today is not meritocracy, per se, but rather *our* meritocracy. Our society uses an outdated and inadequate notion of merit. America, which relies so heavily on standardized tests as a means of entry into opportunity-expanding educational institutions, is at best a fractured meritocracy. The selection tests we use are based on too narrow a band of skills to provide a basis for a true meritocracy.

(Sternberg, 2012, paragraph 2, emphasis in original)

tests played a key role in a rigged game, one that favored society's well-positioned elites under the guise of "merit"

(Sacks, 1997, p. 26)

It is relatively uncontroversial to believe that jobs, educational opportunities, and financial rewards should go to people who have earned these benefits. Especially in the United States, where a distrust for inherited privilege and aristocracy is woven into the country's founding and culture, there is a distinctly negative reaction to an undeserving person who seems to have obtained their wealth or power through unfair methods. A system where prestige, opportunity, or rewards are bestowed on the basis of earned excellence is called a *meritocracy*. If functioning well, a meritocracy provides opportunities for worthy non-elites and helps society run more efficiently because rewards and incentives are not wasted on undeserving people.

Like many ideas, a meritocracy sounds good on paper, but in practice it is imperfect. Some people use charisma, social connections, unethical behavior, unearned privileges, and other tools to circumvent the demands for merit. As a result, sometimes the wrong person gets selected for a job or an educational opportunity. Therefore, many people argue that meritocracies in the United States (and other industrialized countries) are rigged and that the social hierarchy that exists is a false meritocracy. In other words, the belief in a false meritocracy is that many people with wealth, prestigious jobs, and more advanced levels of education are undeserving of their position in society.

There are various ways that one could question the fairness of the meritocracy. Sternberg (2012) believes that the meritocracy is "fractured" and flawed because it is limited in the traits, skills, and abilities that it rewards. Ford (2014) espouses the extreme view that the meritocracy is a "myth" and a "mistaken notion" (pp. 148, 149) and that the social hierarchy in the United States is a product of oppression. Regardless of the exact nature of their criticisms of the modern meritocracy, many critics see tests of g, such as college admissions tests, as a tool for creating a false meritocracy (e.g., Au, 2018; Ford, 2014; Sternberg, 2012). These people see standardized tests in education, employment, and other realms of society as a hindrance to creating a fairer, more equal society.

DISSECTING THE MERITOCRACY

Cui bono? Criticizing the meritocracy is a healthy exercise for a society. While social hierarchies are probably unavoidable,[1] any particular social hierarchy that a society experiences may not be inevitable. Other possible methods of organizing society can be explored because these other possibilities may be better than current hierarchies. When considering social hierarchies like a meritocracy, it is a valuable to ask the classic Latin question: *Cui bono?* This translates as "Who benefits?"

The obvious answer to the question of who benefits from the meritocracy is the people at the top. In the United States and many other industrialized countries, the people at the top of the meritocracy disproportionately are better educated, had a middle- and upper-class childhood, belong to culturally dominant groups, and are often male. Some critics of the meritocracy argue that these powerful people engineer a system that cements their privileged place in society and provides a boost for their peers and children while creating barriers for other people. Often the people who have difficulty overcoming these barriers lack powerful social connections, do not have the financial means to rise in the meritocracy, or belong to historically marginalized groups (Au, 2018; Ford, 2014; Gillborn, 2016; Sacks, 1997). For those at the top of the meritocracy, the way they structure society has the added benefit of perpetuating and justifying the status quo and their place in the social order (Vialle, 1994).

But a meritocracy may benefit other people, even if many of them do not have a dominant position in the social hierarchy. If a meritocracy is based on

---

[1] Given that primates and many other social mammals have hierarchies, it seems that social inequality is part of humanity's evolutionary heritage. If animals create hierarchies to organize small groups, then it seems highly unlikely that humans would be able to organize a large, industrialized society that did not have some form of social hierarchy.

characteristics that benefit society as a whole – such as creativity, cooperation, and universal compassion – then rewarding people who display these behaviors with money, prestige, and power may encourage more of these behaviors. The benefits of these behaviors are spread out through society and not concentrated among the people at the top of the meritocracy. (It is difficult to hoard compassion.) Thus, meritocracies (in theory) are not inherently good or bad. Rather, a meritocracy is merely a reflection of the traits and behaviors that a culture chooses to reward and/or punish.

IQ in the Meritocracy. One trait that modern Western societies reward is intelligence. As a result, positions of power, social prestige, and economic security are dominated by intelligent people, while the lower levels of the social hierarchy are populated disproportionately by people who perform poorly on tests of g (Gottfredson, 1986; Herrnstein, 1973; Herrnstein & Murray, 1994). This is apparent when examining the positive correlations that intelligence has with desirable occupational and educational outcomes and the negative correlations that intelligence has with unfavorable outcomes (see Chapter 20).

Society rewards high levels of g for a few reasons. One reason is economic: high levels of intelligence are in short supply. The law of supply and demand means that wages are higher when there are fewer people able to fill a job and lower when many people are capable of performing a job. By definition, there are a limited number of people who can competently execute cognitively complex jobs. This is one of the reasons why, for example, police officers (average IQ: 98) are paid less than lawyers (average IQ: 118; Wonderlic, Inc., 1999), even though police officers unquestionably have an important job that helps society function. There are simply fewer people in the population who have the cognitive ability to manage the intellectual complexity of practicing law compared to enforcing the law. Even after people enter jobs, intelligent people tend to perform better in those positions (see Chapter 23), which leads to more promotions and higher pay for them than their colleagues in the same profession.

Another way that the current meritocracy rewards high-g individuals is through the educational system. Brighter students tend to do well in their classes, which may lead teachers and administrators to provide advanced educational opportunities to high-g children. When students complete their K-12 education, many choose to apply to college, and this provides another opportunity for society to reward intelligence. Students who perform well on college admissions tests have more colleges to choose from and are more likely to be offered scholarships that reduce the financial burden of higher education. These students are then more likely to graduate, which is an advantage in a workforce that increasingly requires a college degree for well-paying jobs.

It is important to note that when individuals or institutions in society bestow these rewards on intelligent people, they are not explicitly trying to establish or reinforce a meritocracy. No one is saying, "We need to hire this applicant for the job because that will help perpetuate the intelligence-based meritocracy." Instead, the benefits that intelligent people tend to receive are the result of individual decisions about perceived merit. Teachers offer honors classes to smarter children because these children show a high level of mastery of the standard curriculum. Selective colleges admit bright students because they are most likely to graduate. Employers hire and promote high-g applicants because they are better at their jobs and make fewer errors.

The common link among all these examples is that decision makers favor intelligent people because they are seen – generally – as deserving opportunities and rewards over less intelligent individuals because of differences in perceived merit. And when resources and/or opportunities are limited (such as when it is impossible to offer jobs or educational opportunities to every candidate), it is an efficient use of resources to select the most deserving individual (who will often be smarter than many other candidates). Other decisions are irrational or perhaps even harmful to the organization. For example, it would be cruel to enroll a child with an IQ of 85 in a calculus class. Likewise, a company would not be acting rationally if it refused to hire the most competent employee in order to instead hire a less competent individual.

Therefore, a meritocracy based (partially) on intelligence forms because (a) individual differences exist in intelligence, (b) intelligence is associated with beneficial outcomes in education and the workplace, and (c) many of those outcomes are rewarded financially (Herrnstein, 1973). The creation and perpetuation of the IQ meritocracy is not the result of a formal policy, a conspiracy, or oppression. Rather, it is the product of thousands of individual decisions about how to best distribute jobs, educational opportunities, scholarships, and other coveted benefits. If one wants to avoid a meritocracy, then an alternative is to reward people for traits that are irrelevant to merit, such as selecting people on the basis nepotism, sex or racial discrimination, or cronyism (Pinker, 2018). The disadvantages of this strategy are obvious. Another possibility is to distribute jobs, money, power, etc., randomly. State lotteries do this (among people who buy lottery tickets), and though it is a fair process because it is completely random, it is not a viable way to run a society.

The Dark Side of the IQ Meritocracy. This description of how an IQ-based meritocracy arises is not an endorsement of the status quo. Current reality does not necessarily reflect what is good or beneficial (see Chapter 33). There is much to criticize about the meritocracy, even when it operates efficiently.

One disadvantage of an intellectual meritocracy is that, in the twenty-first century, it encourages social balkanization and polarization. Increasingly, Americans associate with people who have similar economic circumstances and levels of intelligence (Murray, 2013). As a result, people are increasingly poor at understanding the viewpoints and challenges of people who are at different IQ levels. Because most leaders in business, industry, and government are intelligent people, this means that decision makers are disconnected from the needs of average or below-average people who experience the consequences of decisions. (Chapter 35 will explore this issue further.) This may result in discontent with societal leaders and in social upheaval. Indeed, the sociologist who coined the term "meritocracy" recognized this problem and saw it as a serious flaw in the meritocracy (Young, 1958).

Another problem with the IQ-based meritocracy is that it creates the illusion that the beneficiaries have earned their way to the top of the social hierarchy. When a high-paying job requires college training and mastery of knowledge and skills, it can appear that these efforts should be rewarded. However, the tailwind that intelligence provides in many aspects of life (see Chapter 22) makes it easier for high-IQ people to master many cognitive challenges that the meritocracy requires people to overcome. For example, intelligence is correlated with learning speed and aptitude, which means that intelligent people will be able to learn an educational curriculum more quickly and with fewer errors. Therefore, if two students apply to medical school – one with an IQ of 145 and another with an IQ of 110 – the brighter applicant will need to study less in order to be a competent doctor. But this does not necessarily mean that the smarter student is more deserving than the student with an IQ of 110, especially if the latter is hard working and studious enough to invest the extra hours in his studies. Even if both are accepted into medical school and become physicians, if the smarter student obtains a more prestigious or better-paying job, the meritocracy may make it appear that she earned her job because she performed better in medical school – even though she did not work as hard as her classmate.

Finally, the intellectual meritocracy has the downside of being a partially inherited aristocracy. This is because intelligence is partially heritable (see Chapters 11–13), and smarter parents – who are more likely to be at the top of the social hierarchy – are more likely to have children who are smarter than average. This genetic heritage will help their children prosper in the meritocracy, just as the parents did. Social classes get passed on from one generation to another (albeit imperfectly; Belsky et al., 2016; W. D. Hill et al., 2016; Marioni et al., 2014; Trzaskowski et al., 2014), which is contrary to the values of many Western democracies. In the past, Western countries had hierarchies based on social barriers, such as rigid sex roles, discrimination, and social connections. As industrialized nations have torn down these barriers via the establishment of an intellectual aristocracy, a new social hierarchy has emerged that is partially genetic in origin. The genetic barriers in an IQ-based meritocracy may be much harder to tear down and could be just as harmful as the social barriers that propped up older hierarchies (Herrnstein, 1973).

The genetic roots of an intellectual meritocracy also reinforce the previous point: basing a meritocracy on intelligence creates the illusion that merit is earned. Nobody chooses their genes. Yet society rewards people who receive genes that make them smarter and then pretends that the rewards are the result of earned merit (e.g., "hard work").

ALTERNATIVES TO THE IQ MERITOCRACY

Given these drawbacks, it is important to explore alternatives to an intellectual meritocracy, such as the efforts to implement communism in the twentieth century. Although data are not always available, such large-scale social experiments have been unsuccessful in abolishing IQ-based meritocracies. Chapter 17 discussed how extremely egalitarian and socially mixed urban planning in post-World War II Warsaw failed to eliminate the correlation between parental characteristics and child IQ (Firkowska et al., 1978). A recent study in Estonia showed that even during the Soviet era, socioeconomic status was heritable (i.e., genetically influenced). Moreover, after the fall of the communist regime, heritability of socioeconomic status increased (Rimfield et al., 2018), which is consistent with Herrnstein's (1973) hypothesis that breaking down artificially created social barriers would result in the creation of genetic barriers between classes. Given these facts, it seems unlikely that an IQ-based meritocracy is absent in communist societies, though it may be weaker than what is seen in twenty-first-century capitalistic nations.

Another alternative to the intellectual meritocracy is to simply reward more or other traits than society currently does. Sternberg (2012), for example, stated his belief that standardized tests – an important tool for sorting people into educational and vocational training programs (Herrnstein & Murray, 1994) – were too narrow in the skills they measure. (This is consistent with Sternberg's triarchic theory of intelligence; see Chapter 8.) He suggested that colleges should select students on the basis of "analytical, creative, practical, wisdom-based, and ethical skills" (Sternberg, 2012, Paragraph 6). While this idea sounds plausible, it has the problem that none of these other skills are either (a) easily measurable, or (b) as general as intelligence. Indeed, there are serious questions about whether some of these traits – such as practical intelligence – are even real (Gottfredson, 2003a, 2003b).

The proposal to reward more traits obscures the fact that the meritocracy *does* reward more than just intelligence. It just rewards these other traits and behaviors in proportion to the results that they produce in school and at work. Academic and work success are not solely the product of g. As motivation, conscientiousness, experience, good physical health, and other non-g traits help a person excel in society, they also contribute to the social hierarchy seen in Western meritocracies. Conversely, undesirable traits are often punished. For example, unethical individuals are often fired or imprisoned for their behavior. While these traits are rarely the subject of a standardized test, they do contribute to societal inequality.

Because the traits and behaviors that a meritocracy rewards are a result of a society's values, another option for replacing the current meritocracy is to value intelligence less and non-*g* traits more. Indeed, nothing is stopping employers or universities from jettisoning *g* (or variables strongly correlated with intelligence) and rewarding people for other behaviors or traits. The problem with this proposal is that – for most jobs and educational opportunities – *g* is an important contributor to success (see Chapters 22–23). Hiring the most motivated employee and ignoring *g* may result in a company having a highly motivated, but incompetent employee. Even in jobs where non-*g* skills or abilities are highly important, these characteristics may be correlated with IQ anyway.

If society chooses not to value non-*g* traits and skills, then another option is to force decision makers to select individuals on the basis of other traits. These types of mandates exist – such as union rules that favor seniority over competence when awarding promotions and pay raises – and they probably weaken the meritocracy's basis in IQ. However, these mandates have several disadvantages. First, they result in a loss of efficiency as qualified individuals are denied opportunities in favor of less qualified individuals. Forcing these decisions on organizations requires them to expend resources on unproductive endeavors. For example, colleges forced to accept unprepared students would have to offer more remedial classes, an expense that provides little benefit for universities. Employers that hire or promote unsuitable workers may need to provide extra training or supervision. Second, these mandates create social problems in organizations, as differences in competence become apparent – especially if incompetent people are rewarded or coddled because the organization values less relevant traits over *g*. People notice if an incompetent co-worker or classmate is rewarded and they are not; organizations that make an incentive system like this widespread may find that competent individuals will take their talents elsewhere. Third, whenever organizations must prioritize traits that they do not find relevant, there is a loss of freedom. Given that communist regimes were unable to completely eliminate IQ-based meritocracies, it seems that eliminating such a meritocracy would require a massive level of oppression (Herrnstein, 1973). And there would still be no guarantee that such an effort would succeed. Finally, these mandates try to fight against the reality of individual differences. Mother Nature is not an egalitarian, and she has a propensity to frustrate the plans of social reformers who try to equalize outcomes among people who are unequal on relevant traits (Gottfredson, 2000a).

MERITOCRACY: CAN'T LIVE WITH IT. CAN'T LIVE WITHOUT IT

There does not seem to be any viable alternative that could completely replace the intellectual meritocracy. This may be why some critics of the meritocracy merely rail against its existence and fail to provide solutions to create a system that can produce the outcomes they desire (e.g., Au, 2018; Ford, 2014; Gillborn, 2016). A meritocracy is the inevitable product of a free society and individual differences in valued traits. Because industrialized, Western societies value intelligence (or traits that are correlated with intelligence), the meritocracies in these countries will be partially g-based.

Undoubtedly, meritocracies have their downsides, but they are probably impossible to eliminate. Instead, societies must decide what traits they want to define as part of "merit" and how much to reward people who have these traits. That is a social, political, and ethical question – not a scientific one – and there are many viable answers. The best solutions will come through recognizing the nature of meritocracies, acknowledging the reality of individual differences, and engaging with decision makers about their goals, needs, and values.

25

Very High Intelligence Is Not More Beneficial than Moderately High Intelligence

> But there's a catch. The relationship between success and IQ works only up to a point. Once someone has reached an IQ of somewhere around 120, having additional IQ points doesn't seem to translate into any measurable real-world advantage.
>
> (Gladwell, 2008, pp. 78–79)

> beyond a certain level of cognitive ability, real-world achievement is less dependent on ever-increasing performance on skills assessment than on other personal and dispositional factors.
>
> (Renzulli, 2012, p. 153)

After reading Chapters 21–23, it is apparent that higher intelligence is beneficial for people as they function in school, work, and their everyday lives. Generally speaking, IQ is positively correlated with beneficial outcomes and negatively correlated with unfavorable outcomes, though there are some exceptions. Moreover, these correlations are not perfect, so there are some exceptions to this rule, which is why there are smart individuals who experience unfavorable outcomes, like unemployment, incarceration, and poor health.

MO IQ, MO PROBLEMS?

However, some people say that the relationship between intelligence and favorable outcomes is not constant across the IQ scale. These people – such as Renzulli (2012) and Malcolm Gladwell (2008) in the quotes above – believe that at a certain level of high intelligence, the benefits of additional intelligence dissipate. If this were true, the differences between people who are very bright and people who are "merely" above average in intelligence – in regards to life outcomes – would be minimal.

This idea is called the *threshold hypothesis* because it suggests the existence of a threshold level of IQ where increased intelligence does not lead to additional benefits. Adherents of the threshold hypothesis disagree about where exactly the threshold is. For Gladwell (2008) and Simonton (1976), the threshold is at an IQ of 120 – and the 9.2% of the population with a higher IQ does not experience any noticeable benefits compared to people at 120. For D. H. Feldman (1984), the threshold is about IQ 150 – which includes only 0.04% of the population. Adherents also disagree about what sort of life outcomes lose their relationship with IQ above the threshold. Gladwell (2008) believed that the threshold applied to all life outcomes, while Feldman used data from a high-IQ sample to argue that for educational and emotional outcomes (e.g., life satisfaction) there is no difference between the very bright and super bright, but that occupational outcomes did not show a threshold effect. Towers (1987) believed that exceptionally high IQ (about 170) was actually harmful to people's personal functioning and that being much smarter than one's peers made it difficult to make friends, form personal relationships, or be a leader.

INVESTIGATING THE THRESHOLD HYPOTHESIS

Challenges of Testing the Threshold Hypothesis. Research on the smartest of the smart is difficult to conduct because these people are – by definition – rare, which makes it hard to find a large sample. This challenge becomes greater as the IQ threshold increases. For example, while approximately 1 in 10,000 people have an IQ of 156 or higher, only about 1 in 31,500 have an IQ of 160 or higher. Moving the threshold up by only 4 points decreases the number of people above the threshold by over two-thirds. Slight changes in the threshold that a researcher chooses can have a large impact on the number of people available to study above the IQ threshold.

In total, there are only about 10,300 people in the entire United States with IQs above 160.[1] Finding enough of these people who are willing to be in a psychological study would be extremely challenging. Higher thresholds would probably require data from every high-IQ person in the country. (For example, there are fewer than 500 people in the United States with an IQ above 170.)[2]

---

[1] This calculation is based on the assumption that intelligence is normally distributed with a mean of 100 and a standard deviation of 15 (see the Introduction). In a normal distribution of IQ scores, only 1 person out of every 31,574 will have an IQ above 160. In a country with 327.2 million people, that means that there will be a total of 10,363 people with an IQ above 160 because 327.2 million ÷ 31,574 = 10,363.

[2] An IQ above 170 occurs in 1 person in every 664,011 people in a normal distribution. Therefore, 327.2 million ÷ 664,011 = 493 people. Based on these calculations, to be, literally, "1 in a million" a person would have an IQ of 171. Theoretically the smartest person in the United States has an IQ of about 187.

Additionally, it is necessary to find a test difficult enough that it can detect differences in intelligence among a very elite group. A test that is too easy for exceptionally smart people will result in high-IQ individuals all obtaining a score at or near the maximum. An example of this is the most popular individually administered intelligence test for adults: the WAIS-IV, which has a maximum possible score of 145 (Wechsler, 2008). This test – and many others like it – is unable to distinguish someone with an exceptionally high IQ from someone with an IQ of "only" 145. Tests with higher maximum ceilings do exist, such as the current version of the Stanford–Binet (Roid, 2003). For children there is the option of administering a test that is designed for an older population (Olszewski-Kubilius & Kulieke, 2008; Warne, 2012).

Educational and Occupational Outcomes. Based on the best available research, the threshold hypothesis is incorrect. Data from large samples of high-IQ people show that the likelihood of beneficial life outcomes continues to increase as people get smarter. The best research on the threshold hypothesis comes from SMPY (see Chapter 22). In the SMPY sample, there are over 2,300 people who have IQs of 135 or higher – the top 1% of the population. Even within this bright group, IQ was positively correlated with favorable work and educational outcomes. For sample members in the top quarter of the top 1%, the odds of earning a doctorate were 3.56 times higher than for people whose IQ was "only" in the bottom quarter of the top 1%. In the SMPY sample, the odds of a person in the brighter group were also higher for having an income in the top 5% of incomes nationwide (2.31 times greater); earning a patent (3.01 times greater); publishing a literary work (4.55 times greater); and publishing scholarly work in science, technology, engineering, or mathematics (4.97 times greater). There was no apparent threshold where the probability of any accomplishments leveled off or decreased (Lubinski, 2009).

Selecting an even higher threshold of an IQ of 156 (the top 0.01% of the population, or the top 1 in 10,000 people) does not diminish the threshold effect. Over 50% of SMPY sample members with IQs of 156 or higher earned doctorates, while "only" 30% of the top 0.5% (IQ of 139 or higher) earned a doctorate (Lubinski, 2009).[3] Moreover, people with IQ scores in the top 1 in 10,000 rise to the top echelons of leadership and productivity in their careers at such a high rate that, "many are outstanding creators of modern culture, constituting a precious human-capital resource" (Kell, Lubinski, & Benbow, 2013, p. 648).

The results of SMPY have been replicated. Wai (2014, p. 76) found that within a sample of 1,536 teenagers with IQ scores in the top 1% (IQ of 135 or higher), the smartest 25% earned doctorates at a rate that was 1.52 times

---

[3] In comparison, 1.8% of the US adult population has earned a doctorate (U.S. Census Bureau, 2019, Table 1).

greater than the least intelligent 25%. Another sample of individuals with IQs in the top 1 in 10,000 of the population had similar levels of high education achievement, work productivity, and eminence within their fields as was found in the SMPY sample (Makel et al., 2016). Coyle (2015) reported data from two studies on the relationship between intelligence and college grade point averages and found that the correlation was constant across the entire range of intelligence levels. In other words, there was no point at which greater levels of intelligence failed to increase the probability of a high grade point average in college. In a sample of gifted children, Ruf (2005) found that as IQ increased, children were better able to move through the K-12 curriculum quickly and were increasingly more likely to display early academic development, such as learning to read by age 4. Successively brighter groups also mastered advanced academic material at younger and younger ages. Another study that disproves the threshold hypothesis showed that in a large sample of medical school graduates higher scores on achievement tests needed to obtain a medical license were always associated with higher levels of competence in practice (Wakeford, Ludka, Woolf, & McManus, 2018).

Social and Emotional Outcomes. Apart from career and educational outcomes, some people have postulated that a high IQ may create social problems (e.g., J. S. Peterson, 2009; Towers, 1987). For example, if someone is much more intelligent than their peers, then it may be difficult to form friendships because the bright person may not feel that others understand them and their complex way of thinking. To fulfill this need for socialization with one's intellectual peers, organizations like MENSA – a social group that requires members to score in the top 2% of the population in IQ – exist.[4] However, there is not much evidence about whether an IQ threshold exists where higher IQ leads to more social or emotional problems. In the best study on this topic (Guldemond, Bosker, Kuper, & van der Werf, 2007), children above IQs of 130 and 144 did not have more social or emotional problems than children with IQs in the 110s and 120s.

A variation on the threshold hypothesis applied to psychological outcomes is that high intelligence creates a qualitatively different kind of inner psychological functioning that creates special challenges – such as heightened sensitivity, passion, moral concern, or individualistic motor activity – for bright people that the general population does not experience (e.g., Daniels & Piechowski, 2009; Mendaglio & Tillier, 2006). These supposed traits – sometimes called

---

[4] MENSA is the largest and most famous high-IQ society, but others exist. The International High IQ Society requires members to have an IQ score in the top 5% of the population (i.e., an IQ of 125 or higher). The Top One Percent Society – as the name implies – has an admissions requirement of an IQ score in the top 1% of the population, which corresponds to an IQ of 135 or higher. The Triple Nine Society only accepts members with IQ scores in the top 0.1% of the population (i.e., IQ of 146 or higher). The Prometheus Society limits its members to people whose IQ scores are in the top 0.003% of the population, which corresponds to an IQ of 160 or higher.

overexcitabilities – are theorized to lead to greater mental health problems and other difficulties for highly intelligent people (Karpinski, Kinase Kolb, Tetreault, & Borowski, 2018). However, this research is often based on non-representative samples of people and using poorly designed methods of collecting data. There is no convincing evidence for the existence of separate "overexcitabilities" in bright people (Vuyk, Kireshok, & Kerr, 2016) or that people with higher IQ than average experience more mental health problems. In fact, the evidence indicates that high intelligence may be a protective factor against at least some forms of psychiatric illness (Savage et al., 2018; N. P. Walker, McConville, Hunter, Deary, & Whalley, 2002). This is especially apparent in GWAS results, which show that some of the DNA segments associated with higher IQ are often negatively correlated with mental health problems (W. D. Hill et al., 2019; Savage et al., 2018; Sniekers et al., 2017), which makes it especially unlikely that people with very high IQs experience more psychiatric illnesses.[5]

LIMITS OF THRESHOLD RESEARCH

It is also important to recognize the limitations of research into the threshold hypothesis. Psychologists have not investigated every threshold, which means that it is possible that the threshold hypothesis is correct – but at higher thresholds than have been tested so far. If a threshold exists where higher IQ does not provide additional benefits, it is extremely difficult to detect and would affect so few people that the impact on the general population would be trivial. It would not change the fact that, for the vast majority of people, gaining a few more IQ points would be beneficial.

Another limitation of research on the threshold hypothesis is that some outcomes have not been investigated yet. The research that has failed to show a threshold for some work, educational, and social/emotional variables does not prove that no thresholds exist at all. There could be some uninvestigated life outcomes that do display a threshold phenomenon where higher IQ levels lead to stagnant improvements in outcomes or can even be detrimental. But given the results of investigations of the threshold hypothesis so far, the default belief should be that there are no IQ thresholds where positive benefits cease to accrue.

CLIMBING HIGHER AND HIGHER

Unquestionably, the results I describe in this chapter demolish the threshold hypothesis for the outcomes that psychologists have investigated. Prior research

---

[5] An important exception to this general trend is autism spectrum disorder, which seems to share some genes in common with high intelligence (W. D. Hill et al., 2019; Savage et al., 2018; Sniekers et al., 2017).

that supported the idea was based on small samples, low-quality data (e.g., D. H. Feldman, 1984; Simonton, 1976, Towers, 1987), a misunderstanding of the evidence (e.g., Gladwell, 2008; Towers, 1987), or poor theorizing (e.g., Renzulli, 2012). With large samples and good data, the evidence for the threshold hypothesis disappears. From the best available data, there is no evidence that the benefits of higher intelligence ever level off or dissipate.

But the usual caveats from the last few chapters apply. Intelligence is not the only important influence in life outcomes among the "super smart." In the SMPY sample, differences in life outcomes exist among people in the top 1% of intelligence. The SMPY researchers have documented that high intelligence is important, but it is not sufficient for a person to achieve high accomplishments or eminence in their chosen profession. Interest in one's work, a willingness to work long hours, and an appropriate mix of Stratum II abilities (such as verbal, spatial, and mathematical abilities) are required, too (Lubinski, 2016). Additionally, bright people need educational opportunities that allow them to develop their abilities and expertise (see Chapter 18), and highly intelligent people are unable to achieve high productivity or eminence if they do not have an environment or job that allows them to manifest their talents. Readers should also remember that these beneficial outcomes are probabilistic and that there is no guarantee that a very bright person will experience positive life outcomes – no matter how high their IQ is.

26

Emotional Intelligence Is a Real Ability that Is Helpful in Life

> Yet even though a high IQ is no guarantee of prosperity, prestige, or happiness, in life, our schools and our culture fixate on academic abilities, ignoring emotional intelligence, a set of traits – some might call it character – that also matter immensely for our personal destiny. Emotional life is a domain that, as surely as math or reading, can be handled with greater or lesser skill, and requires its unique set of competencies. And how adept a person is at those is crucial to understanding why one person thrives in life while another, of equal intellect dead-ends . . .
>
> (Goleman, 1995, p. 36)

Part of what makes humans so interesting is the non-cognitive behaviors and experiences that they have. As fascinating as intelligence and other cognitive abilities are, a life based solely on thinking and logic is a cold one, and the capacity to experience love, pain, passion, and other emotions is an important part of the human experience. Therefore, it should be unsurprising that many psychologists have studied emotion in the past 100 years. One concept that has emerged from this research is *emotional intelligence*. This idea has entered the popular consciousness, and many see the ability to use emotion to think as an important part of decision making and living a fulfilling life (e.g., Goleman, 1995).

There are many definitions of emotional intelligence, and experts on the topic often have such different views about what emotional intelligence is that it is not always clear whether they are talking about the same trait (Matthews, Roberts, & Zeidner, 2004; Mayer, Salovey, & Caruso, 2004; Waterhouse, 2006). Following the world's leading scholars on the topic, in this chapter I will discuss emotional intelligence as defined as "the capacity to reason, understand, and manage emotions. In addition, emotional intelligence plausibly reflects the emotion system's capacity to use emotion to enhance thought" (Mayer, Salovey, & Caruso, 2008, p. 321; see also Mayer &

Salovey, 1997, p. 5).[1] Proponents of emotional intelligence believe that the trait
is analogous to any other reasoning ability: if verbal reasoning (a Stratum II
ability in the models described in the Introduction) is the ability to reason
about and understand language, then emotional intelligence does the same for
emotions. Rather than seeing emotion as being irrational or undermining clear
thought, emotion can be a characteristic that people can harness to improve
functioning in their life (Mayer et al., 2004).

Leading theorists argue that emotional intelligence has two components.
The first is "the ability to reason with and about emotion" (Mayer et al.,
2008, p. 326). The second component is the ability to use emotion in the
reasoning process to improve one's ability to think (Mayer et al., 2008). In
turn, people use emotional intelligence to understand and perceive the emotions
of themselves and others, use emotion to improve their decision-making
process, and manage their and others' emotions. In other words, if emotional
intelligence is a real concept, then it is theorized to be useful in real-life settings
where one has to keep one's own cool, handle interpersonal problems, and
address other people's concerns. As a result, some theorists believe that
emotional intelligence is particularly important in the workplace and in one's
personal life (Pesta et al., 2015; Salovey & Mayer, 1990).

If this description of emotional intelligence sounds familiar, it may be because
"emotional intelligence is a subset of Gardner's personal intelligences" (Salovey
& Mayer, 1990, p. 189), which are his interpersonal and intrapersonal
intelligences. Chapter 5 of this book described Howard Gardner's (2011)
theory of multiple intelligences and how they are theorized to be discrete
mental abilities. Unlike Gardner, though, Salovey and Mayer do not necessarily
deny the existence of g, and they believe that emotional intelligence can exist as an
additional intellectual ability. However, they do not believe that emotional
intelligence is part of the network of cognitive abilities that are connected to
g (Salovey & Mayer, 1990).

DOES EMOTIONAL INTELLIGENCE CORRELATE WITH REAL-WORLD OUTCOMES?

There are benefits to theorizing, but the worth of emotional intelligence
depends on the trait's ability to predict or explain real-world outcomes.
Emotional intelligence proponents recognize this (Mayer & Salovey, 1997).
Mayer et al. (2008, pp. 337–338) reported that measures of emotional
intelligence are correlated modestly with real-world variables, such as job
performance, social support and attachment (positive correlations), and

---

[1] In his bestselling book on emotional intelligence, Goleman (1995) gives a very different definition.
He defined emotional intelligence as every non-intelligence characteristic, including motivation,
persistence, impulse control, hope, empathy, and emotional control (Goleman, 1995, p. 34). This
definition is so broad that it is too incoherent to engage with.

social deviance and aggression (negative correlations). However, none of the studies were peer reviewed, and most were not published at all (see also Matthews et al., 2004, p. 190; and Waterhouse, 2006, pp. 217–218). Indeed, most of the research on the practical usefulness of emotional intelligence in the real world is not formally published, and therefore not subject to the level of scrutiny that g research regularly receives. The studies that are available tend to be poorly designed and to produce unimpressive results (N. Brody, 2004). The published literature is much less favorable to emotional intelligence and shows that the tests of emotional intelligence are weaker predictors of academic performance than IQ (Siu & Reiter, 2009). For example, high school rank (a measure of academic success) correlates $r = .23$ and job performance correlates $r = .28$ with emotional intelligence (Mayer et al., 2008, p. 337). Intelligence, though, correlates $r \approx .50$ to .70 with academic success and $r \approx .25$ to .50 with job performance (see Chapters 18–23).

A more promising line of research is on the relationship between emotional intelligence and interpersonal outcomes, such as avoiding divorce, having a large circle of friends, and successfully raising well-adjusted children. These outcomes are unquestionably social in nature and emotion-related information can be highly relevant to obtaining these outcomes. It makes sense that an emotional intelligence could be relevant for these processes. Unfortunately, the results of research have been disappointing, with few correlations higher than .30, and many close to zero (Mayer et al., 2004, 2008).

In response to these weak correlations, a critic could claim that emotional intelligence's importance may have been overhyped, but that the importance is not zero. However, these weak correlations do not necessarily indicate that emotional intelligence's relevance persists in well-designed studies. Tests of emotional intelligence seem to measure, partially, the Big Five personality traits (see Chapter 20), some of which are important for everyday functioning. The correlations between emotional intelligence and life outcomes may just be due to the personality traits – such as agreeableness, conscientiousness, and neuroticism – that tests of emotional intelligence measure (Matthews et al., 2004; van der Linden et al., 2017). This possibility is strengthened by studies which show reduced correlations – sometimes as low as zero – between emotional intelligence and practical outcomes after controlling for personality traits (N. Brody, 2004). Therefore, the relationship between emotional intelligence and performance in the workplace or in a person's personal life may be solely due to the overlap between emotional intelligence and personality traits. Controlling for intelligence also reduces the correlation between emotional intelligence and academic outcomes, sometimes to zero (Mayer et al., 2004, p. 206). This indicates that there is little – if anything – new in emotional intelligence.

THEORETICAL PROBLEMS WITH EMOTIONAL INTELLIGENCE

Just like other additional intelligences that psychologists have proposed in the late twentieth century (see Chapters 5 and 6), emotional intelligence suffers from theoretical problems that bring its existence into question. One theoretical problem is that it is not clear why the tasks of managing emotions, perceiving emotions in others, using emotions as a source of information, etc., must be an intelligence (Locke, 2005). By expanding what qualifies as an intelligence, these theories are in danger of stretching the term until it has no meaning because it encompasses too many skills that have little in common with one another.

One fundamental problem with emotional intelligence is that there is no justifiable reason why g cannot do the job of emotional intelligence. Research has shown that g is used to reason about others' emotions and inner states (Coyle, Elpers, Gonzalez, Freeman, & Baggio, 2018; Schlegel et al., 2020). If g is broad enough to be used to reason about verbal, spatial, logical, and other content, why can't g reason about emotions? Emotional intelligence theorists propose that emotion is different because, neurologically, it is processed in unique ways (Mayer et al., 2008), which is true. But auditory stimuli and visual information are also processed in the brain in unique ways. Yet g is able to integrate these different sources of information. It is not clear why – as emotional intelligence theory requires – g would be unable to be useful for identifying emotions, handling stress, or helping a person navigate a complex social situation.

Another problem comes from the claim that emotions are a source of information that a person uses to draw conclusions (Mayer & Salovey, 1997; Mayer et al., 2004, 2008). However, this gets the order of events and emotions mixed up. Feeling scared does not tell a person that they are in danger – as the emotional intelligence theorists claim. Instead, believing that there is a threat to one's safety makes a person feel scared (Locke, 2005). Moreover, emotions are a poor source of information for reasoning because they are automatic and irrational. The very nature of emotions makes them antithetical to reasoning.[2] Emotional intelligence theorists affirm that this is not true (e.g., Mayer & Salovey, 1997; Mayer et al., 2004, 2008), but they have never explained how automatic, irrational processes can be useful for rational thought.

EMOTIONAL INTELLIGENCE: NOT READY FOR PRIMETIME

As a psychological concept, emotional intelligence has some compelling aspects to it. If theorists can successfully bridge two normally disparate topics of research – intelligence and emotion – then it could provide interesting insights into human thought and decision making. Moreover, emotional intelligence provides

---

[2] The separation of emotions and reason is much older than psychology. Plato argued that the soul had three parts: reason, spirit, and appetite. Reason was the logical thinking part of the conscious mind, while spirit was emotional, and appetite was formed by desires. Plato believed that conflicts could arise from these three portions of the soul because they were fundamentally contradictory.

a worthwhile perspective for understanding how people cope with interpersonal challenges (Matthews et al., 2004). And there is evidence supporting some aspects of emotional intelligence theory (Hunt, 2011). For example, emotional self-regulation seems to be an important trait during adolescence, and low self-regulation increases the risk of peer rejection and antisocial behavior (Trentacosta & Shaw, 2009), while high emotional self-regulation seems to be a protective factor against negative outcomes (Buckner, Mezzacappa, & Beardslee, 2003). Emotional stability and self-regulation are also correlated with occupational and educational success (G. W. Evans & Rosenbaum, 2008; O'Connell & Sheikh, 2011) and with good mental health (Ciarrochi, Scott, Deane, & Heaven, 2003). Emotions are also an important component of symptoms for many psychological disorders, and being able to manage and understand these emotions is a goal of some types of therapy (Slade & Warne, 2016). If there is a coherent trait – like emotional intelligence – that handles emotional states, then it could have great importance for positive functioning.

However, the research does not yet support the strong assertion that emotional intelligence is a real psychological trait or that it has major real-world implications. Judged on the basis of current research, "there is no empirical data supporting a causal link between EI [emotional intelligence] and any of its supposed, positive effects" (Matthews et al., 2004, p. 189). Currently, the strong arguments about the importance of emotional intelligence are premature. This is not a merely scientific or theoretical dispute. Proponents of emotional intelligence often advocate programs or interventions to raise emotional intelligence in people (e.g., Goleman, 1995), and some of these have been implemented in schools and corporations (e.g., Cook et al., 2018). If emotional intelligence is not real or important for life outcomes, then these interventions are – at best – ineffective distractions. At worst, they actively cause harm because they take time and resources away from more effective training programs (e.g., improving job skills, teaching foundational academic knowledge to students) and encourage ineffective and wasteful practices (e.g., hiring or promoting employees based on emotional intelligence instead of job performance or IQ). Proponents of emotional intelligence would be best to temper their enthusiasm, strengthen the quality of their research, and reconcile the contradictions within emotional intelligence theory (Waterhouse, 2006) before trying to implement practices designed to raise emotional intelligence.

Maybe emotional intelligence will survive the twenty-first century and make valuable contributions to psychology – or maybe not. Only time will tell. Whatever the outcome, it will not change the importance of emotions as part of the human experience. Research into emotions can improve psychologists' (and the public's) understanding of what it is to be human. If it is possible to merge the concepts of intelligence and emotion, then it will be a major breakthrough in psychology. But until that breakthrough is substantiated, it is best to be skeptical about emotional intelligence and its real-world importance.

DEMOGRAPHIC GROUP DIFFERENCES

In the Introduction, I referred briefly to average IQ differences across demographic groups. This section, consisting of Chapters 27–30, focuses on these differences and the possible causes of average sex and race differences in performance on intelligence tests. The chapters in Section 6 are organized as follows:

- Chapter 27 discusses sex differences in *g* and other cognitive abilities.
- Chapter 28 covers average differences in intelligence among racial and ethnic groups and includes a summary of the research about the causes of these differences.
- Chapter 29 describes the theory that a unique environmental factor could systematically lower one racial group's IQs without effecting another racial group's scores.
- Chapter 30 summarizes the latest research on stereotype threat, which is a psychological phenomenon that has often been proposed as a cause of lower average IQ scores for minority groups.

These chapters of the book may be difficult reading for some people. One of the most controversial topics in science is demographic group differences in intelligence (Check Hayden, 2013; Cofnas, 2016), with some scholars openly advocating censoring research into this topic (e.g., Horgan, 2013; Kournay, 2016; Rose, 2009). I have done what I can to discuss this area of research diplomatically and without moving beyond what the data say.

The topic of race and sex intelligence differences often garners a disproportionate amount of attention from the public, journalists, students, and commentators (Snyderman & Rothman, 1988). A good example of this tendency is the response to *The Bell Curve* (Herrnstein & Murray, 1994). Of the book's 22 chapters, only 3 chapters had race as the primary focus, and 2 others discussed race-based affirmative action policies in the United States. The majority of the book was not about race at all, and yet that was the primary focus for many responses to it (e.g., Gould, 1996; Singham, 1995). Lost in the wider discussion about the book was the important evidence regarding how intelligence contributes to economic inequality and the consequences of an IQ-based meritocracy. The chapters on race sucked all the oxygen out of the room, and the other messages of the book were lost. This type of reaction is not unique. Cronbach (1975, p. 3) noted that the important articles by Jensen (1969) and Herrnstein (1971) that generated a great deal of backlash in their time only focused on racial differences in IQ for less than 10% of the text. But that topic received the most attention in the ensuing responses.

In reality, research on group differences in *g* is a small corner of intelligence research. While most intelligence researchers are aware of the data on group differences, research on testing, biology, cognitive psychology, and education have far more influence on the scientific conversation in the intelligence community. Although research on race and sex differences is a source of a great deal of controversy (Carl & Woodley of Menie, 2019), it is not the most important topic of intelligence research, as I have stated in previous writings (Burton & Warne, 2020; Warne et al., 2018).

While writing a book about human intelligence, it is tempting to omit any research on group differences in order to avoid any firestorms. But I chose to include these chapters because there are consistent misunderstandings about group differences in intelligence. These mistaken beliefs needlessly feed into the controversy regarding intelligence. Moreover, it is important to discuss controversies because, "Without a forum for controversy, controversy will not be resolved and science will not advance" (Detterman, 2006, p. iv). I feel compelled to include this section on race and sex differences in the hopes that I might bring clarity to controversy. Yet I recognize that I might repeat history: here I am – just like the intelligence scholars of the past – writing about intelligence and including a discussion of sensitive topics.[1]

Recognizing the risk, I have a few principles that I ask my readers to remember as they read the chapters in this section and in Section 7. These principles[2] undergird my discussion of race and sex differences in intelligence:

1. All people are automatically entitled to and born with inalienable human rights and innate dignity.
2. Group differences do not justify discrimination in any form (Carl, 2018).

---

[1] Perhaps I could avoid some criticism if I did not include these chapters, but there is no guarantee that silence on these topics would shield me from controversy. For example, Gillborn (2016) wrote a 24-page article stating that minimizing or avoiding discussion of the relationship among race, intelligence, and genetics is itself a form of racism. Gillborn (2016) also thinks that talking about these topics frankly is racist. The technical term for this dilemma is "Damned if you do, damned if you don't."

[2] These principles are based on a similar list of "ground rules" that I set for students who enroll in my human intelligence class (see Burton & Warne, 2020). They have been very successful for teaching intelligence to a diverse group of undergraduates and avoiding misunderstandings, oversimplifications, and incorrect conclusions.

3. Studying group differences in intelligence – or any other trait – is not bigoted (Flynn, 2018; Jeffrey & Shackelford, 2018).
4. Even though differences in groups' average intelligence exist, there are huge amounts of overlap among groups (Gottfredson, 1997a).
5. In the spirit of open inquiry, all possible explanations for group differences should be explored.
6. Different ≠ better. In other words, average differences in IQ – or any other trait – do not make one group "superior," "inferior," "better," or "worse" (Anomaly & Winegard, 2019). The existence of many types of differences among humans is a scientific fact, and facts do not lead inevitably to judgments of value.
7. Western nations have a history of progress towards legal fairness, openness, and toleration. No scientific research can or should undermine that progress and its worldwide spread.

I hope that these principles reduce the potential for misunderstandings that sometimes arise in discussions of the science of intelligence differences. Section 7 (which consists of Chapters 31–35) shows how some of these principles can be applied to the social and ethical considerations that arise from intelligence research. For now, though, it is time to tackle the research on sex and racial group differences in intelligence. Turn the page, fearless reader!

27

Males and Females Have the Same Distribution of IQ Scores

> Some have argued that there is statistically more variation among men than among women, which means that even though the average man is no more intelligent than the average woman, there are more men of extremely low intelligence and more men of extremely high intelligence ... Studies haven't fully supported this explanation.
>
> (Saini, 2017, p. 65)

Almost as soon as intelligence tests were created, psychologists started investigating sex differences in intelligence. By the end of the 1910s, enough research had been conducted on the topic that there was a robust discussion among psychologists about whether there were average differences between males and females and how large those differences might be (e.g., Hollingworth, 1919). Because of changes in the educational and employment opportunities available to women over the past 100 years, it is valuable to periodically revisit the question of sex differences in cognitive abilities.

AVERAGE SEX DIFFERENCES IN MENTAL ABILITIES

Global IQ. One of the earliest large studies on sex differences in overall IQ showed slight differences on the 1916 version of the Stanford–Binet. In the sample of 905 children, ages 5–14, females had a higher median IQ than males for all ages, except age 10 (equal medians) and age 14 (a 4-point advantage for boys). At all other ages, females scored 1–6 points higher than males (Terman et al., 1915, p. 559). This led the authors to conclude, "the superiority of the girls is probably real ... However, sex differences in intelligence are so small ... that for practical purposes they would seem negligble" (Terman et al., 1915, p. 560). Another early study showed a slight male advantage on the Army Alpha when it was administered to 3,693 students at three midwestern high schools.

The total average difference was approximately 2.9 IQ points in favor of males (Madsen & Sylvester, 1919).

These two studies illustrate a theme of the early work on sex differences in intelligence: in some studies females performed – on average – better than males, while other studies showed the opposite result (Hollingworth, 1919). Average sex differences across studies were never large. Studies in the twenty-first century also showed small or zero sex differences, with no consistent pattern favoring males or females (e.g., C. M. Calvin et al., 2010; Deary, Thorpe, Wilson, Starr, & Whalley, 2003; Strand, Deary, & Smith, 2006). As a result, most psychologists believe that there are no differences in average intelligence across males and females (Jensen, 1998; Neisser et al., 1996; Nisbett et al., 2012). This finding seems to be most robust in childhood, although there is some evidence that there may be a slight male advantage in IQ in adulthood (e.g., Lynn & Irwing, 2004); however, the issue is not fully settled (Hunt, 2011).

Stratum II Abilities. Comparisons of global IQ scores for men and women do not tell the full story of sex differences in mental abilities. From the very earliest days of intelligence testing, psychologists noticed that there were some specific tasks and abilities that one sex performed – on average – better than the other (Burt, 1917, p. 65; Terman, 1916, p. 71). Over time, a pattern developed on these early tests. Females tended to outperform males on some verbal tasks (e.g., Conrad, Jones, & Hsiao, 1933) and processing speed tasks (Hunt, 2011, p. 387), while males performed better on some non-verbal tasks (e.g., Porteus, 1965, Chapter 6), especially visual–spatial tasks. But there are exceptions to this general trend.

Sex differences on these broad Stratum II abilities and narrow Stratum I tasks have persisted into the twenty-first century, and psychologists have refined their understanding of what these abilities are and how large the sex differences tend to be. In modern studies, females tend to excel ($d = .10$ to .50) on highly verbal tests (Emanuelsson, Reuterberg, & Svensson, 1993; Lakin, 2013, p. 267). Conversely, males tend to perform better on tests of spatial ability, with effect sizes ranging from $d = .10$ to .90, depending on how spatial ability is measured (Emanuelsson et al., 1993; Masters & Sanders, 1993). Men also perform better – on average – than women on mathematics reasoning tests, with effect sizes of $d = .05$ to .30 (Feingold, 1992; Lakin, 2013). These sex differences in modern samples echo the findings of early studies, which suggests that the patterns seen today are not a recent development.

To sum up, sex differences in IQ are close to zero, while differences in broad mental abilities are sometimes substantial. Apparently, across the entire set of mental abilities, the differences between males and females cancel out so that overall intelligence is equal, on average, across sexes. This "cancelling out" is not engineered into the tests, and test creators have no intention of forcing males and females to have equal scores. However, it is possible to force a test to produce an overall IQ score sex difference by adding more questions that one sex tends to perform better on or by weighting such questions so that they are worth more in score calculations (Conrad et al., 1933; Jensen, 1998). It is standard practice, though, when designing intelligence test batteries, to balance out verbal and non-verbal tasks. This is not to ensure gender equality in scores, but rather to sample a diverse array of mental tasks and to avoid favoring any particular Stratum II ability when calculating an overall IQ score.

VARIABILITY DIFFERENCES

In addition to mean differences, some psychologists have studied variability of intelligence test scores across sexes. Again, this is a research tradition that dates back to the beginnings of intelligence testing (e.g., Cornell, 1928; Hollingworth, 1919; Terman et al., 1915). The topic did not garner much interest after the 1920s until Feingold (1992) published a review of the literature on overall IQ and on several broad cognitive (i.e., Stratum II) abilities. Across 28 subtests on 5 intelligence and academic tests, Feingold (1992) found that 24 subtests had greater variability for men than for women, with men's standard deviation being an average of 5.8% greater on each subtest. Later studies produced similar results for global IQ, with most of these studies showing that the standard deviation for men was 5–15% larger for males than for females (e.g., Deary et al., 2003; Deary, Der, & Shenkin, 2005, p. 453; Hunt, 2011, p. 383; Lakin, 2013; W. Johnson et al., 2008; Reilly et al., 2019; Strand et al., 2006). The evidence is so consistent that most psychologists now agree that males have greater variability on most mental abilities – including general intelligence. Saini's (2017) assertion in the quote at the beginning of the chapter is simply incorrect.

Figure 27.1 shows two distributions that differ by 10% in their standard deviations. In this image, the black line represents females, and the grey line represents males. The shorter peak for males in the middle and the slightly wider sides is a manifestation of this slight difference in standard deviations.

A 5–15% larger standard deviation in IQ may look trivial, but at the extremes, it has noticeable effects. If both males and females have equal means (as they do for IQ), then a 5% greater standard deviation for males results in a greater proportion of males who exceed any cutoff. This is shown in Table 27.1. Above an IQ cutoff of 115, there are 1.07 males for every female, meaning that 7% more males than females have an IQ of 115 or more. The same ratio is found for IQs of 85 or lower.[3] Table 27.1 also shows that as cutoffs become more extreme, the female-to-male ratio becomes more imbalanced. At

---

[3] The sex ratios above 115 and below 85 are the same because a normal distribution (like the distribution of IQ scores) is symmetrical (see Figure I.4). So, the percentage of people 15 points (or more) above the average of 100 is equal to the percentage of people 15 points (or more) below the average of 100 when the two groups have the same average.

TABLE 27.1 *Female-to-male ratios beyond an IQ cutoff score with no average sex differences*

Cutoff	5% larger male SD	10% larger male SD	15% larger male SD
Above 115 or below 85	1:1.07 (52% male)	1:1.14 (53% male)	1:1.21 (55% male)
Above 120 or below 80	1:1.12 (53% male)	1:1.23 (55% male)	1:1.35 (57% male)
Above 125 or below 75	1:1.18 (54% male)	1:1.36 (58% male)	1:1.54 (61% male)
Above 130 or below 70	1:1.25 (56% male)	1:1.52 (60% male)	1:1.80 (64% male)
Above 135 or below 65	1:1.34 (57% male)	1:1.72 (63% male)	1:2.16 (68% male)
Above 140 or below 60	1:1.45 (59% male)	1:2.01 (67% male)	1:2.67 (73% male)
Above 145 or below 85	1:1.58 (61% male)	1:2.37 (70% male)	1:3.37 (77% male)

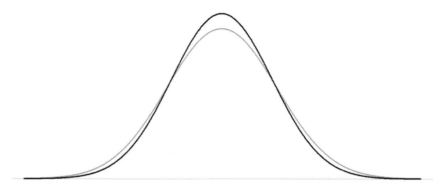

FIGURE 27.1 Two distributions of IQ scores with different levels of variability. The male distribution (in grey) has a standard deviation that is 10% larger than the standard deviation for the female distribution (in black).

a cutoff of 125, for example, the ratio is 1:1.18, and 54% of people at or above the cutoff are male. When the cutoff increases to 145, there are 1.58 males for every female, and 61% of the group is male.

Table 27.1 also shows that as the standard deviation difference increases, the sex ratio becomes more imbalanced. Indeed, whenever group means are equal (as they are for IQ scores) and the standard deviations differ, the percentage of males beyond a cutoff score will be larger, unless the cutoff is the average (i.e., an IQ of 100).

Tables 27.2 and 27.3 show sex ratios when there is a difference in standard deviations and a slight (*d* = .20) difference in average scores, which happens in some Stratum II abilities. When males have a higher average than females, the sex ratios above high cutoffs are even more imbalanced. According to Table 27.2, these sex ratio imbalances can become extreme. For example, if the cutoff is 125 and males have a 10% larger standard deviation, then they outnumber

TABLE 27.2 *Female-to-male ratios beyond an IQ cutoff score with a d = .20 mean male advantage*

Cutoff	5% larger male SD	10% larger male SD	15% larger male SD
Above 115	1:1.44 (59% male)	1:1.52 (60% male)	1:1.60 (62% male)
Above 120	1:1.58 (61% male)	1:1.73 (63% male)	1:1.86 (65% male)
Above 125	1:1.76 (64% male)	1:2.00 (67% male)	1:2.24 (69% male)
Above 130	1:1.97 (66% male)	1:2.35 (70% male)	1:2.76 (73% male)
Above 135	1:2.23 (69% male)	1:2.82 (74% male)	1:3.48 (78% male)
Above 140	1:2.57 (72% male)	1:3.47 (78% male)	1:4.54 (82% male)
Above 145	1:2.97 (75% male)	1:4.33 (81% male)	1:6.03 (86% male)

TABLE 27.3 *Female-to-male ratios beyond an IQ cutoff score with a d = .20 mean female advantage*

Cutoff	5% larger male SD	10% larger male SD	15% larger male SD
Above 115	1:0.80 (44% male)	1:0.86 (46% male)	1:0.92 (48% male)
Above 120	1:0.79 (44% male)	1:0.89 (47% male)	1:0.98 (49% male)
Above 125	1:0.79 (44% male)	1:0.92 (48% male)	1:1.06 (52% male)
Above 130	1:0.79 (44% male)	1:0.98 (49% male)	1:1.18 (54% male)
Above 135	1:0.80 (45% male)	1:1.06 (51% male)	1:1.34 (57% male)
Above 140	1:0.82 (45% male)	1:1.16 (54% male)	1:1.57 (61% male)
Above 145	1:0.85 (46% male)	1:1.29 (56% male)	1:1.88 (65% male)

women above the cutoff at a ratio of 2-to-1, and this group is 67% male. When females have a slightly higher mean (d = .20) and a 5% greater standard deviation (see Table 27.3), there are always more females than males above a cutoff. However, with greater standard deviation differences than 5%, there are more males than females above higher cutoffs.

CONSEQUENCES OF SCORE DIFFERENCES

Sex differences on mental tests have some important consequences, though the differences do not translate seamlessly into the real world. In the education realm, females equal or outscore males on achievement tests in almost every school subject. For example, in a representative sample of American students, females scored higher on reading tests (d = .19 to .32) and writing tests (d = .42 to .62) than males in elementary, middle, and high school (Reilly, Neumann, & Andrews, 2019). These differences in performance on achievement tests are greater than the sex differences on verbal ability when it is measured by tests (e.g., Lakin, 2013). This is probably because school achievement and grades measure more than just brute ability. They also measure a student's effort, personality traits, and other non-cognitive variables (see Chapter 20). As a result, females usually surpass males' school performance by wider margins than would be expected on the sole basis of ability. The best study demonstrating this was a British study on a representative sample of over 70,000 teenagers. In that study, males only earned higher achievement test scores in physics – with an advantage of just $d = .04$ – while in every other subject, females earned higher grades, ranging from $d = .03$ to $.75$ (Deary et al., 2007, p. 16).[4]

The implications of different means and standard deviations for males and females are also apparent in selection processes in which decision makers want to identify everyone who exceeds a high cutoff – or has a score below a low cutoff. Examples of this include hiring, college admissions, or identifying children who need special education services. Outcomes of selection procedures do indeed show a sex imbalance:

- 60.1% of contestants on the American quiz show *Jeopardy!* are male, and men win 69.7% of games (Blatt & Hess, 2014).
- Males make up 62% of students in special education in the United States (P. L. Morgan, Farkas, Hillemeier, & Maczuga, 2012) and about 55–70% of people with intellectual disabilities (American Psychiatric Association, 2013, p. 39; Nisbett et al., 2012).
- In the UK *University Challenge* trivia competition, 78% of contestants are male, and 91% of winners are male (J. Thompson, 2017).
- 65% of Google Science Fair finalists in 2016 were male.
- Between 2014 and 2018, 89.3% of National Geography Bee finalists were male. Among winners since the competition began in 1989, 93.5% were male.
- In Lewis Terman's seven-decade study of children with high IQs, 56.0% of sample members were male (Burks et al., 1930).
- 100% of World Scrabble Championship winners are male. Only one woman has ever won the North American Scrabble Championship (Mac Donald, 2018).

Variations in average sex differences in intelligence or other mental abilities cannot explain all of these sex imbalances. Mean differences would be able to explain more males at the upper levels of accomplishment, or lower levels – but not both. Only a variability difference can explain the surplus of males at both extremes.

The disproportionate presence of males at high levels of accomplishment is probably not solely due to differences in variability. Winning an elite Scrabble

---

[4] College admissions tests also show these sex differences, but because about 100,000 more females take each of these tests than males, these tests underestimate the female advantage in verbal abilities (Nisbett et al., 2012) and exaggerate the male advantage in mathematical reasoning. Sex differences are only $d \approx .05$ on the verbal portion of the SAT and $d \approx .20$ on the English and reading sections of the ACT, with females scoring higher than males. In mathematics, male examinees' average score is higher than females' average score by $d \approx .20$ on the SAT and ACT.

or trivia competition requires many hours of study on a topic that competitors feel passionate about. Though many women commit themselves to such goals, bright males seem more likely than highly intelligent females to invest the hours needed to excel at a high level in one particular field. Women are more likely to have a greater diversity of interests, which means they generally spread their time over more goals than men (McCabe, Lubinski, & Benbow, 2019).

It is also likely that cultural factors partially cause some of these sex imbalances. For example, turning learning into a competition may be more attractive to males who could be more socialized to embrace competition, whereas females could be taught to cooperate instead of compete.[5] Evidence that the sex imbalance is partially social comes from an investigation of Talent Search programs, which require middle schoolers to score at or above the level of a high school senior on a college admissions test to participate. In the early 1980s, the male-to-female ratio of examinees who scored that high on the math portion of the SAT was 13.5:1; by the 1990s, the ratio had dropped to 3:1, where it has remained (Wai, Putallaz, & Makel, 2012). Such a fast, dramatic drop in the proportion of males and females excelling on mathematics can only be explained by cultural and social changes that occurred in the late twentieth century. Genetic or biological changes do not happen that quickly in human populations.

Cultural factors or the nature of competitions do not, however, explain the simultaneous greater percentage of males at high *and* low levels of performance. Indeed, it would be hard to socialize a sex to both excel and perform poorly *at the same time* in many different variables. Only greater variability can explain the male preponderance at both ends of the distribution of accomplishment, but the cause of that greater variability is elusive. Whatever the cause is, it is probably not unique to mental abilities. Most personality traits are also more variable in males (Allik & Realo, 2017), as are height and weight (Fryar, Kruszon-Moran, Gu, & Ogden, 2018). The size of brain structures is also more variable in males (Ritchie et al., 2018; Wierenga et al., 2018), and this may indicate that the higher male variability in psychological traits is partially biological in origin. If variability in brain structures causes increased variability in male behavior, though, that merely pushes the question back one step further: what causes greater male variability in brain structures? Some theorists have proposed explanations for greater male variability (e.g., Bates, 2007; Del Giudice et al., 2018), but no one knows for sure why this phenomenon occurs.

CONCLUSION

While males and females are equal in average intelligence, the distribution of their abilities differs in other ways. However, in broad non-*g* cognitive

---

[5] Competition has many benefits, though, especially in the way it can encourage excellence and maximal development (Worrell et al., 2016).

abilities – like spatial ability, verbal reasoning, and mathematical reasoning – mean differences do exist. Females tend to score higher (on average) on verbal abilities, while males have higher average performance on spatial ability and mathematical reasoning. Across these abilities, though, the differences average out to produce equal means on overall IQ.

An important difference exists in variability in cognitive abilities. Males have a standard deviation that is 5–15% larger than the standard deviation for females. As a result, there is a greater percentage of males than females at the high and low extremes of most abilities. The cause of this greater variability is not clear, though some causes have been proposed. Regardless of the cause, the overlap among both groups (shown in Figure 27.1) makes it clear that there are males and females found at all levels of ability. That is why it is so important to judge people as individuals according to their individual accomplishments – and not on the basis of their sex.

28

Racial/Ethnic Group IQ Differences Are Completely Environmental in Origin

> Genes account for none of the difference in IQ between blacks and whites; measurable environmental factors plausibly account for all of it.
>
> (Nisbett, 2009, p. 118)

> Many psychologists have concluded that there is no scientific evidence that group differences in average IQ are based on genetics.
>
> (Coon & Mitterer, 2016, p. 309)

Of all the scientific facts about intelligence research, there is one that I would give anything to change: the existence of average differences in IQ scores across different racial or ethnic groups. These differences appeared in the early days of intelligence testing (e.g., Goodenough, 1926; Morse, 1914; Pressey & Teter, 1919) and have persisted into the twenty-first century (e.g., Carman, Walther, & Bartsch, 2018; Giessman, Gambrell, & Stebbins, 2013; P. L. Roth et al., 2001). Among the most studied racial or ethnic groups, people of East Asian descent usually have the highest average IQ, followed by people of European ancestry. Hispanics have a lower average IQ than these groups, and people of African ancestry have the lowest average.[1] It is important to remember, though, that there is a large amount of overlap in intelligence among these groups – as shown in Chapter 10 – and that people from all racial groups can be found at all levels of intelligence (Gottfredson, 1997a).

No one argues about the presence of average group differences in intelligence test scores (Hunt, 2011; Mackintosh, 2011). The heated argument among people who have studied the issue is over what causes these differences (R. M. Kaplan & Saccuzzo, 2018). Popular explanations among non-experts,

---

[1] Unless I am specifically referring to people living in the United States, in this chapter, these groups will be called "East Asians," "Europeans," "Hispanics," and "Africans," regardless of where in the world these people may live.

such as biased tests or that intelligence is a culturally bound concept, have been discounted (see Chapters 4 and 10). For psychologists, the question is whether these average differences across groups are caused by (a) genes, (b) environment, or (c) a combination of genes and environment.

The possibility that genes account for the entire difference in intelligence between racial groups is extremely unlikely. The evidence is overwhelming that individual differences in intelligence are at least partially environmentally caused. Environmental influences on scores are clear because heritability is never 1.0 for intelligence (see Chapters 11 and 12), and there are known environmental causes of lowered IQ, such as iodine deficiency, lead poisoning, and traumatic brain injury (see Chapter 12). Additionally, the Flynn effect – which is the phenomenon of gradually increasing IQ scores worldwide (see Chapter 14) – shows that environment can exert a powerful influence on IQ. While all of these research findings were found at the individual level, there is a reasonable expectation that they also apply to group differences because groups differences are generally the result of the combined differences of the people within the groups (Frisby, 2013; McCabe et al., 2019).

Therefore, the great debate is whether average group differences in intelligence are due to solely environmental causes, or a combination of genetic and environmental causes. People who argue that the differences are fully environmental claim that heritability between groups (abbreviated h_b^2) is equal to zero and are called *environmentalists* (e.g., Nisbett et al., 2012). Those who believe that genetics has at least some influence on racial group differences in intelligence are called *hereditarians* (e.g., Gottfredson, 2005b). Within these definitions, the hereditarian position has much more variety of opinion; as long as someone thinks that h_b^2 is more than 0%, they are a hereditarian. Environmentalists, though, all agree that h_b^2 is zero.

DOES "RACE" EVEN EXIST?

To discuss racial differences in intelligence, it is important to have a coherent, fact-based understanding of *race*, which can have different meanings in everyday speech. Some people claim that race is not real or is merely a social construct with no basis in biology (Horowitz, Yaworsky, & Kickham, 2019; Rose, 2009; Singham, 1995; Sternberg, 2005; Sternberg, Grigorenko, & Kidd, 2005; Suzuki & Aronson, 2005). In reality, racial groups do have a biological basis, but that foundation is not as simplistic as has been portrayed.

A human racial group is a group of people who share a common ancestry from the same part of the world. Because of that common ancestry, people within a group are more closely related to one another than to people outside their group. The common ancestry is also why people who belong to the same racial group physically resemble each other more than they resemble people outside the group. The greater relationship among group members is why it is best to think of a racial group as a large "extended family." Unlike a regular extended family, though, racial groups include millions of people with a common ancestry that extends back thousands of years (instead of a few generations). Although this "family" is too large to have a family reunion, members of a racial group are still more closely related to one another than they are to people who belong to other racial groups.

Evidence that racial groups have a basis in biology is strong. Physical anthropologists have studied the physical similarities and differences of racial groups for decades. Using this information, forensic anthropologists can identify the race of a deceased person on the basis of their skeletal traits with up to 95% accuracy (Church, 1995). Later, scientists studied the genetic heritage of people from around the world and discovered that some *alleles* (which are versions of a segment of DNA) are more frequent in some racial groups than others. By examining a large number of alleles, a DNA sample can be used to classify people into the racial group they self-identify as belonging to (Jorde & Wooding, 2004; Shiao, Bode, Beyer, & Selvig, 2012). In one typical study, the genetic-based estimation of a person's racial group matched self-identified race with 99.86% accuracy (Tang et al., 2005). Moreover, the results match known historic migrations and intermixing of populations (Ahikiari, Chacón-Duque, Mendoza-Revilla, Fuentes-Guajardo, & Ruiz-Linares, 2017; Bryc, Durand, Macpherson, Reich, & Mountain, 2015; Han et al., 2017; Tang et al., 2005). This means that genetic ancestry tests from companies like ancestry.com or 23andMe function only because race exists and can be identified at a genetic level.

This research on racial classification makes it clear that there is no single trait that all members of a racial group share and that is absent from all non-group members (Sesardic, 2010). For this reason, examining a single trait to identify racial groups is not informative. Instead, most traits appear in different racial groups with varying levels of frequency. Classification through physical traits (e.g., skeleton characteristics) and DNA work, therefore, by examining many traits. By knowing how often many different traits appear in different groups, a scientist can estimate the probability that a person belongs to a racial group by examining whether they have a large number of traits that are relatively more common within the group compared to other groups – and a relatively smaller number of rare traits for the group.

As the number of traits considered increases, classification becomes increasingly accurate (Sesardic, 2010; Smouse, Spielman, & Park, 1982). Because humans typically have millions of subtle differences in their DNA, the number of traits that can be used when classifying people into genetic groups can be very large – which results in extremely accurate and detailed classifications (Novembre & Peter, 2016). On the other hand, examining only a single trait, or one trait at a time exaggerates similarities between groups and masks real physical and genetic differences.[2] As a result, examining a single trait – such as

---

[2] The most famous person to make this error is biologist Richard C. Lewontin (1972), who found that for 17 genes, 85.4% of variability was within racial groups, 8.3% was across groups within

skin color, height, facial topography, hair texture, or lactose tolerance – can produce nonsensical results. A single trait can evolve independently in different, distantly related groups. This does not mean that race is artificially or socially constructed, as some critics claim (e.g., Diamond, 1997; Sternberg et al., 2005). Instead, it demonstrates the importance of identifying "extended families" on the basis of a large number of traits.

One implication of defining racial groups as large extended families is that racial categories have vague, poorly defined boundaries and can overlap (Jensen, 1998). But this does not invalidate the existence of racial groups. This is particularly obvious when considering multiracial people or groups (the latter are called *admixed populations*). The fact that these people have a genetic heritage from different parts of the world does not invalidate the existence of the ancestral populations that multiracial individuals are descended from.

Additionally, because the boundaries among groups are fuzzy, the number of human groups is flexible. The sharpest divisions are at the continental level (e.g., Africans, Europeans, Asians), but genetic research has shown that these groups can be broken down into smaller, more local groups (Shiao et al., 2012; Tishkoff et al., 2009). For example, Italians and Norwegians can be distinguished from one another in genetic ancestry tests; this does not mean that the racial group of "Europeans" does not exist or that "Europeans" is a useless categorization. There is no set number of racial or ethnic groups in the world; different levels of analysis will produce different numbers of groups of people with a shared ancestry (Novembre & Peter, 2016; Winegard, Winegard, & Boutwell, 2017). Sometimes, it will make sense to classify people into a small number of groups, each with many people in them (e.g., continent-level races). At other times, it will be beneficial to classify individuals into smaller, more local groups at the regional level.

A TALE OF TWO HERITABILITIES

At first glance, whether differences across groups are heritable seems to have a simple answer: if heritability of intelligence is greater than zero in studies of twins, adoptees, and families, then intelligence should be heritable across groups. After all, heritability is heritability, right?

Wrong. Because heritability values only apply to a given population under its current environmental conditions, there is no reason to assume that these

---

races, and only 6.3% of variation was found across races. Lewontin used this information to conclude that "It is clear that our perception of relatively large differences between human races and subgroups, as compared to the variation within these groups, is indeed a biased perception and that . . . human races and populations are remarkably similar to each other" (Lewontin, 1972, p. 397). However, Lewontin made this calculation by examining the genes separately and ignoring their cumulative ability to distinguish among groups. This had the effect of hiding differences among groups and exaggerated individual differences. This error is now called *Lewontin's fallacy* (Edwards, 2003; Sesardic, 2010).

heritability values will apply to other groups or to the average intelligence differences that exist *across* racial groups. As a result, it is not sensible to generalize heritability studies performed on people from one racial group (often Europeans) to other groups. It is important to distinguish between heritability within a group (abbreviated h_w^2) from the heritability between groups (h_b^2), which may not be equal.

Lewontin (1970) popularized a thought experiment showing that h_w^2 and h_b^2 may be very different. In this experiment, there are two handfuls of seeds from the same species that are pulled out of the same bag. One handful is planted in rich, fertile soil with plenty of water. The other handful is planted in poor, barren soil with little water. After several months, there are large differences in average height for the two different groups: the plants that sprouted from seeds planted in the good, well-watered soil would be taller than the plants that grew from the seeds planted in the dry, low-quality soil. In addition to these group average differences, there is also variability within each group, with some plants being taller than others. Heritability across groups (h_b^2) will be zero because between-group differences are entirely environmental in origin (the poor soil or the fertile soil). However, the within-group heritability (h_w^2) will be 1.0 because all the plants within a group have the same environment, so the height differences within groups must be entirely caused by genetic differences.

People seem to find this thought experiment convincing, and it is often cited to support the argument that h_b^2 of human intelligence differences is zero (Flynn, 1980; Warne et al., 2018). There is a fatal flaw with this analogy: human racial groups are not formed by selecting a random group of people from the world's population and artificially assigning them to environments. Instead, people are born into racial groups and inherit the slight genetic differences that have accumulated in their ancestors over generations. By definition, the differences among human racial groups are not entirely environmental in origin. What Lewontin (1970) did get right was that h_b^2 and h_w^2 are not interchangeable. But he was wrong to extrapolate this theoretical example's heritability values of $h_b^2 = 0$ and $h_w^2 = 1$ to humans.

FIVE SOURCES OF EVIDENCE ABOUT THE HEREDITARIAN HYPOTHESIS

There are five important sources of evidence regarding whether h_b^2 is greater than zero (supporting the hereditarians' beliefs) or whether group differences are entirely environmental (which would prove the environmentalists correct). These are: (1) the mathematical relationship between h_b^2 and h_w^2, (2) Spearman's hypothesis, (3) tests of measurement invariance, (4) admixture studies, and (5) data from molecular genetics. This section of the chapter is devoted to summarizing each type of evidence and explaining whether it

TABLE 28.1 *Projected values of mean environmental differences, given between-group heritability (h_b^2) and within-group heritability (h_w^2) values for an IQ difference of 15 points (d = 1.00)*

	h_b^2 values										
h_w^2 values	.00	.10	.20	.30	.40	.50	.60	.70	.80	.90	1.00
.00	1.000	0.949	0.894	0.837	0.775	0.707	0.632	0.548	0.447	0.316	0.000
.10	1.054	1.000	0.943	0.882	0.816	0.745	0.667	0.577	0.471	0.333	0.000
.20	1.118	1.061	1.000	0.935	0.866	0.791	0.707	0.612	0.500	0.354	0.000
.30	1.195	1.134	1.069	1.000	0.926	0.845	0.756	0.655	0.535	0.378	0.000
.40	1.291	1.225	1.155	1.080	1.000	0.913	0.816	0.707	0.577	0.408	0.000
.50	1.414	1.342	1.265	1.183	1.095	1.000	0.894	0.775	0.632	0.447	0.000
.60	1.581	1.500	1.414	1.323	1.225	1.118	1.000	0.866	0.707	0.500	0.000
.70	1.826	1.732	1.633	1.528	1.414	1.291	1.155	1.000	0.816	0.577	0.000
.80	2.236	2.121	2.000	1.871	1.732	1.581	1.414	1.225	1.000	0.707	0.000
.90	3.162	3.000	2.828	2.646	2.449	2.236	2.000	1.732	1.414	1.000	0.000

Note. Projected mean environmental differences are measured in Cohen's *d* units.

supports the environmental hypothesis that $h_b^2 = 0$ or the hereditarian hypothesis that $h_b^2 > 0$. This discussion is not an exhaustive catalog of all evidence regarding the value of h_b^2. Rather, these are the pieces of evidence that I find to be the least ambiguous. Readers who wish to become familiar with the evidence I omit should consult Jensen (1998, Chapter 12) and Rushton and Jensen (2005a, 2005b).

Evidence Type 1: The Relationship between h_b^2 and h_w^2. While Lewontin (1970) was correct that h_b^2 and h_w^2 are not interchangeable, they are algebraically related (DeFries, 1972). The mathematical relationship between the two types of heritability depends on the size of the (1) environmental differences and (2) trait differences between groups (Jensen, 1998, pp. 447–458). Table 28.1 shows how large mean environmental differences would have to be to produce a difference in average intelligence of *d* = 1.00 (the equivalent of the 15-point average IQ difference for Europeans and Africans in the United States). For example, if $h_w^2 = .30$ (typical for children), and $h_b^2 = 0$ (as environmentalists claim), then the difference in environments must be at least *d* = 1.195. On the other hand, for the same h_w^2, smaller environmental differences are needed if h_b^2 is greater than zero. Thus, the environmentalist hypothesis of $h_b^2 = 0$ *always* requires environmental differences between racial groups to be larger than the hereditarian hypothesis requires (if between-group heritability is held constant). The table also shows that if environmental differences between groups are sufficiently large, then h_b^2 can be zero, regardless of what both groups' h_w^2 values are (though these environmental differences must get larger as h_w^2 increases). Finally, values of h_b^2 smaller than h_w^2 require environmental differences that are larger than the *d* = 1.00 difference in IQ between Africans and Europeans in the United States.

Table 28.1 also provides a way to estimate h_b^2 values by using known values of h_w^2 and environmental differences. For example, h_w^2 is equal in American samples of Europeans and Africans: about .50 or .60, on average (Fuerst & Dalliard, 2014; Pesta, Kirkegaard, te Nijenhuis, Lasker & Fuerst, 2020). Given a 15-point difference in average IQ, this means that the environmental hypothesis requires a mean environmental difference between groups to be at least $d = 1.414$.[3] If average environmental differences are any smaller, it would support the hereditarian hypothesis.

Is $d = 1.414$ a plausible average environmental difference for Europeans and Africans within the United States? As an example, socioeconomic status differences – often posited as an important environmental cause of IQ group-level differences within the United States (e.g., Nisbett et al., 2012) – are an average of $d = 0.658$, which is far short of the $d = 1.414$ that the environmental hypothesis requires (Warne, 2019b).[4] While other environmental differences could contribute to the overall $d = 1.414$ needed for the environmental hypothesis, these environmental variables must have a causal impact and cannot be redundant with socioeconomic status (or with one another). In evaluating whether known environmental differences are large enough to support the environmental hypothesis, it is important to note that the correlation of IQ with socioeconomic status is too weak for it to have a strong causal impact on intelligence (see Chapter 11), and socioeconomic status is (partially) a consequence of intelligence – not necessarily a cause (see Chapter 22). Additionally, given the lackluster evidence regarding permanent increases in IQ for many interventions (see Chapters 15–16), identifying enough causal environmental differences for h_b^2 to be zero seems unlikely.

Evidence Type 2: Spearman's Hypothesis. Although the difference between African Americans' and European Americans' scores on intelligence tests averages to 15 points, the size of this difference varies from test to test – something that psychologists noticed early in the history of intelligence testing. Spearman (1927, pp. 379–380) suggested offhandedly that better measures of g could have larger score gaps across races; this idea is today called *Spearman's hypothesis*. Nobody investigated this possibility until Jensen (1980a, 1985) did decades later. Figure 28.1 shows an example of his results. The scatterplot shows a positive correlation between a test's g loading (which Chapter 1 explained was a measure of how well a test measures g) and the size of the score difference. The correlation between the two is $r = .59$, which is typical in these studies (e.g., Dahlke & Sackett, 2017; te Nijenhuis & van den Hoek, 2016; Warne, 2016b).

---

[3] If "environment" is normally distributed within each racial group, then $d = 1.414$ means that the average European in the United States would have a better environment than 92.13% of Africans in the United States.

[4] A difference of $d = 0.658$ indicates that the average European American has a socioeconomic status that exceeds the status of 74.47% of African Americans.

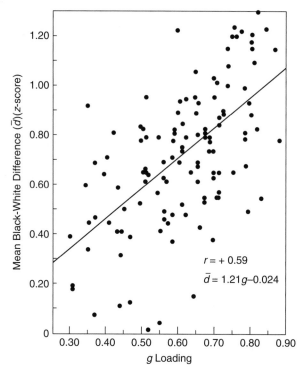

FIGURE 28.1 A scatterplot showing the correlation between *g* loadings (the degree to which a test measures *g*) and the size of the difference between European American and African American averages on the test (measured in Cohen's *d* units). Each dot represents a subtest from an intelligence test. Generally, tests that measure *g* better have larger average score differences between the two racial groups (*r* = .59). Source: Jensen, 1985, p. 201.

Spearman's hypothesis may look like a minor characteristic of intelligence tests, but it has important implications. The positive correlation between a test's *g* loading and the average racial score difference indicates that the IQ differences within a racial group likely have the same cause as the average IQ difference between racial groups (Jensen, 1998). In other words, the same things that cause some Europeans to be smarter than other Europeans, or some Africans to be smarter than other Africans – that is genes and environmental influences – are also likely to be why Europeans have a higher average IQ than Africans. If Spearman's hypothesis is correct, it would indicate that because h_w^2 is greater than zero, h_b^2 is likely to be too – just as the hereditarians believe.

It is important, though, to note that Spearman's hypothesis is limited in its usefulness for testing the beliefs of hereditarians and environmentalists. Correlating *g* loadings and average score gaps can give false positives that inflate support for the hereditarian hypothesis (Dolan & Hamaker, 2001;

Lubke, Dolan, & Kelderman, 2001; Wicherts, 2017). Additionally, the magnitude of the correlation fluctuates, depending on the sample of tests that are used in the correlation (Ashton & Lee, 2005). Finally, not all racial group comparisons support Spearman's hypothesis. Comparisons of Africans and Europeans and comparisons of Hispanics and Europeans seem to support Spearman's hypothesis, but Asian–European comparisons produce inconsistent results (e.g., Nagoishi, Johnson, DeFries, Wilson, & Vandenberg, 1984; Warne, 2016b).

Despite these limitations, when a positive correlation is present, it produces results that are hard to explain for the environmentalist position. For example, groups with known environmental causes of their lowered average IQ score (e.g., people with fetal alcohol syndrome or iodine deficiency), when compared to the typically developing population, do not show a positive correlation between g loadings and score differences (Flynn, te Nijenhuis, & Metzen, 2014). This indicates that the positive correlation shown when testing Spearman's hypothesis with racial groups is probably not the product of purely environmental forces.

Evidence Type 3: Tests of Measurement Invariance. A statistical advance from Jensen's (1980a, 1985, 1998) method of investigating Spearman's hypothesis is called a *test of measurement invariance*. The procedure conducts a confirmatory factor analysis separately for both groups in order to determine whether the relationships among abilities and scores are the same for each group. If the results are the same for both groups, then it indicates that the test functions the same way for both groups and that their test scores can be compared (Meredith, 1993). Tests of measurement invariance show that intelligence tests function very similarly across racial groups, meaning the tests measure intelligence in examinees, no matter which demographic groups they belong to (Beaujean, McGlaughlin, & Margulies, 2009; Lasker, Pesta, Fuerst, & Kirkegaard, 2019; Li, Sano, & Merwin, 1996; Maller, 2000; Wicherts et al., 2004).

Tests of measurement invariance are important to the question of the causes of between-group differences in intelligence because when tests function the same way for different racial groups, it means that h_w^2 and h_b^2 have the same causes: genes and environment. However, tests of measurement invariance do not suffer from the problems inherent in the Spearman's hypothesis technique of correlating g loadings and average score gaps (Dolan, 2000; Dolan & Hamaker, 2001; Lubke et al., 2001). One additional benefit is that tests of measurement invariance specifically permit researchers to test the hypothesis that a unique environmental influence can systematically lower one group's scores while leaving the other group untouched (see Chapter 29).

Evidence Type 4: Admixture Studies. One implication of the hereditarian hypothesis is that in admixed populations, there should be a positive correlation between individuals' percentage of DNA from a high-scoring group and the individuals' IQ. Psychologists investigated this possibility throughout the twentieth century by using skin color, blood type, and self-reported multiracial ancestry to estimate African Americans' degree of multiracial heritage (e.g., Witty & Jenkins, 1936; Scarr, Pakstis, Katz, & Barker, 1977).[5] These methods of measuring European heritage in African Americans are highly unreliable and have been surpassed by DNA-based methods of estimating the percentage of a person's ancestry from different continents.

The first admixture studies using DNA-based estimates are just now being published, and more are likely to be released in the coming years. Preliminary results show that people in admixed populations – African Americans and Hispanics – generally have a higher IQ when they have more European ancestry, with correlations of r = .23 to .30 (Kirkegaard et al., 2019; Lasker et al., 2019; Warne, 2020), which is evidence in favor of the hereditarian perspective.[6] But a correlation of .23 to .30 is too weak to indicate that h_b^2 is fully determined by genes. Environmental variables probably explain some of the average score differences between racial groups in the United States. But if the findings of these early admixture studies are replicated in the future, then it would indicate that at least some of the cause of group differences is genetic in origin. The environmental hypothesis of $h_b^2 = 0$ has difficulty explaining these findings because the correlation between European ancestry and IQ is genetic, by definition.

Evidence Type 5: Data from Molecular Genetics. Admixture studies are useful, but they do not reveal which specific genes impact intelligence across racial groups. Only molecular genetics research can provide this information. Like admixture studies, this research is in its infancy, but inevitably, there will be more studies on this topic. One of the biggest drawbacks to this research is that the majority of GWAS studies that identify genes associated with traits have been conducted on samples that mostly consist of Europeans (Popejoy & Fullerton, 2016). Though this will change in the future, it often means that information derived from these studies currently does not fully generalize to other racial groups (Martin et al., 2019).

The earliest molecular genetics study on racial group differences in g showed that polygenic scores (see Chapter 19) for Europeans' educational attainment could predict African Americans' educational attainment, though the predictions

---

[5] African Americans have an average of 15–25% European ancestry (Bryc et al., 2015, pp. 40, 42; Jin et al., 2012, p. 520; Kirkegaard, Woodley of Menie, Williams, Fuerst, & Meisenberg, 2019, p. 9). For most African Americans, this admixture occurred during the period of African slavery in the United States (Bryc et al., 2015; Jin et al., 2012).

[6] This correlation in admixture studies is not due to within-race discrimination where people with darker skin are discriminated against compared to people with lighter skin who belong to the same racial group (Hu, Lasker, Kirkegaard, & Fuerst, 2019; Krieger, Sidney, & Coakley, 1998; Lasker et al., 2019). Controlling for socioeconomic status does not eliminate the correlation between European ancestry and IQ (Lasker et al., 2019).

are less accurate than predictions for European Americans (Domingue, Belsky, Conley, Harris, & Boardman, 2015). While educational attainment is not the same as intelligence, the two traits share common genes (Krapohl et al., 2014; Lee et al., 2018; Okbay et al., 2016). It is likely that at least some of these genes that affect educational attainment in both Europeans and Africans also affect intelligence, though more sophisticated studies are needed to confirm (or reject) this possibility.

Piffer (2015) published another study using molecular genetic data in a different way to reach the same conclusion about genes contributing to between-group differences in intelligence. He used data about how frequently particular alleles appear in different racial and ethnic groups throughout the world and discovered that populations that have higher average numbers of alleles associated with increased intelligence did indeed have higher average IQs. Piffer (2019) later replicated this study. However, it is important to recognize that these two studies investigate a tiny handful of alleles that could contribute to intelligence differences. Even if Piffer's (2015, 2019) studies are correct and all the alleles have a causal impact on IQ (both uncertain prospects at this time), the total impact of these alleles is still too small to explain any non-trivial amount of the IQ gap between racial groups. The missing heritability problem (explained in Chapter 19) is much worse for h_b^2 than for h_w^2.

Piffer's studies, though, examine averages across human populations. Individual-level data would be more conclusive. A recent study (Dunkel, Woodley of Menie, Pallesen, & Kirkegaard, 2019) suggests that the same genes that may cause individual differences in intelligence may also cause average group differences in intelligence. The researchers calculated polygenic scores for intelligence for Americans descended from European Jews (the ethnic group that has the highest average IQ in the world) and Americans descended from non-Jewish Europeans. The results showed that the European Jewish group had more alleles (on average) associated with higher IQ than the comparison group. Although this comparison did not involve different racial groups, it is important because European Jews spent several hundred years genetically isolated from their Christian neighbors, which could create unique genetic characteristics compared to other Europeans (Cochran et al., 2006; Cochran & Harpending, 2009). Therefore, this study provided circumstantial evidence that genes can be implicated in some between-group differences in average IQ.

This possibility was supported in a study showing that some of the same alleles associated with educational attainment in Europeans could predict IQ in people of African descent (Lasker et al., 2019). However, it is important to note that – just as in the Domingue et al. (2015) study – the predictions of IQ scores for people of African descent were less accurate than predictions for European individuals would be. Indeed, the poorer prediction of traits on non-Europeans is a common phenomenon. As of this writing, using genetic data derived from Europeans to make predictions about psychological traits in non-Europeans is too inaccurate for practical use.

Molecular genetics studies on whether the same genes cause intelligence differences in different racial groups have just begun. The five studies I have discussed are just the first in what will inevitably be an important body of research on between-group causes of intelligence. So far, all five indicate that average IQ differences across racial/ethnic groups are partially due to genetic differences, and they each contradict the environmental hypothesis.

Summary. All five types of evidence reviewed in this section indicate that genetic differences across racial or ethnic groups contribute to at least some of the differences in average IQ across groups. None of these five types of evidence support the environmental hypothesis that $h_b^2 = 0$. This is probably why the hereditarian viewpoint is a mainstream opinion among intelligence researchers (Rindermann et al., 2017, 2020; Snyderman & Rothman, 1987, 1988). Indeed, there is no unambiguous evidence that supports the claim that between-group differences in intelligence are entirely environmentally caused (Warne, 2019b). To be fair to the environmentalist viewpoint, none of the five types of evidence I describe in this chapter conclusively proves *on its own* that between-group differences in intelligence are partially due to genes. However, the various types of evidence have complementary strengths and weaknesses. When combined into one whole body of research, the evidence for the hereditarian hypothesis is much stronger than the evidence favoring the environmentalist viewpoint.

AMONG EXPERTS, HEREDITARIAN VIEWS ARE
MAINSTREAM

A Building Consensus among Experts. Because of all this evidence, the mainstream view among experts in human intelligence is that genetic influences are a partial cause of average IQ differences across racial groups. Intelligence scholars did not always subscribe to the hereditarian viewpoint, as is apparent in surveys of experts that have occurred over the years. Since the late 1960s, researchers have periodically surveyed scientists to ascertain their opinions about the cause of average differences in IQ across racial groups. The results show growing support over the years for the hereditarian position and a strong consensus today regarding the influence of genes in group differences in IQ.

The earliest relevant research was from Sherwood and Nataupsky (1968), who showed that most scientific articles published about the topic were interpreted by their authors as supporting environmental explanations for score differences for European Americans and African Americans. During the controversy regarding Arthur Jensen's work (see the Introduction for context), Friedrichs (1973) surveyed over 300 members of the American Psychological

Association and found that 60% disagreed with the hereditarian position; only 28% agreed.[7]

By the time the next survey occurred over a decade later, the tide had turned against environmentalism. Snyderman and Rothman (1987, 1988) surveyed 266 scientists from several disciplines: educational research, psychological testing, psychology, sociology, and behavioral genetics. A total of 46% of respondents believed that IQ differences between African Americans and European Americans were partially or completely genetically caused, while only 15% of respondents stated that the differences were fully environmental in origin. (The other 39% either did not know or did not respond to the question.) In the mid-1990s, when sociologist Linda Gottfredson drafted a mainstream statement on intelligence that included the claim that "Most experts believe that environment is important in pushing the bell curves [of IQ scores for different racial groups] apart, but that genetics could be involved too" (Gottfredson, 1997a, p. 15), 52% of the experts she asked to sign the statement (which included a summary of many other facts about intelligence) did so, and another 10% agreed with the statement but did not sign for various reasons.[8]

The most recent survey on the topic of the cause of group differences in intelligence was conducted on experts who had published on the topic of international intelligence differences. In this survey, 87% of respondents stated that genetics was at least partially responsible for international IQ differences; only 7% said that international IQ differences were purely environmental in origin (Rindermann, Becker, & Coyle, 2016). The same group of researchers found that 84% of intelligence scholars believed that the average IQ gap between African Americans and European Americans was at least partially genetic; only 16% believed that average score differences between these two groups was purely environmental in cause (Rindermann et al., 2020). Indeed, the average estimate of h_b^2 in this final survey was 48.9%.

The results of these surveys are not directly comparable because the wording of questions vary and the samples were not all collected in the same way. Still, a general trend among experts over the past several decades is apparent. Generally, experts on intelligence and related areas have increasingly agreed

---

[7] There is no other comparable survey from the 1970s, but it is possible that the percentage disagreeing with Jensen's hereditarian position is inflated. Friedrichs (1973, footnote 2) admitted to truncating Jensen's statement, which reads in full: "it is a not unreasonable hypothesis that genetic factors are strongly implicated in the average Negro-white intelligence difference. The preponderance of the evidence is, in my opinion, less consistent with a strictly environmental hypothesis than with a genetic hypothesis, *which, of course, does not exclude the influence of environment or its interaction with genetic factors*" (Jensen, 1969, p. 82, emphasis added). Friedrichs omitted the italicized portion of this quote, which makes Jensen's position sound more extreme than it was.

[8] The true level of agreement with the hereditarian position among Gottfredson's experts may actually be higher; among those who disagreed with the statement to some degree, Gottfredson (1997a) did not report how many specifically disagreed with the statement that average differences in IQ across racial groups could be partially genetically caused.

In the Know

with the hereditarian position as the evidence has mounted to support the theory of genetic influences on intelligence across groups. In the twenty-first century, the environmentalist position is in the clear minority among intelligence experts.

The (Wrong) Consensus among Non-Experts. Like many beliefs about intelligence, non-experts' viewpoints are at odds with the beliefs of experts. Survey research bears this out. In a survey of anthropology professors teaching in PhD programs, 78% of respondents agreed that genetic differences could not account for behavioral differences between racial groups, which would include average intelligence differences, and 57% rejected the theory that genetic differences could account for European Jews' higher intellectual accomplishments (Horowitz et al., 2019). Even non-expert psychologists are strongly environmentalist in their orientation. One survey of researchers asked social psychologists how likely it was that members of different ethnic groups were "genetically more intelligent" (von Hippel & Buss, 2018, p. 18). The average result (26.4%) indicated that most social psychologists thought that genetic influences on ethnic group differences in average intelligence were highly unlikely.

In a survey that I conducted (Warne & Burton, 2020) of 200 teachers, 49.5% disagreed with the hereditarian view, and only 25.0% believed that race differences in IQ could be genetically influenced. The 351 non-teachers in this survey of the general public were more conflicted, but most still did not favor genetic explanations for group differences in IQ. A total of 37.6% of those respondents stated that the average group intelligence differences could be genetically influenced, while 28.5% disagreed (Warne & Burton, 2020). Tellingly, teachers believed that *every* proposed environmental cause for average IQ differences across racial groups was more plausible than the idea that genetics could cause these differences (Warne & Burton, 2020, Table S7).

These results show that non-experts strongly disagree with experts about the hereditarian hypothesis. Indeed, non-experts' beliefs are about 40 to 50 years behind the times. In a way, this should not be surprising. Non-experts are largely unaware of the evidence I have reviewed in this chapter because it is not their job to read the latest research. Their knowledge about the causes of group differences in IQ is similar to the knowledge of psychologists in the late 1960s and early 1970s.[9] I suspect that as evidence against the environmentalist viewpoint mounted over the years, experts found it increasingly difficult to support. Non-experts, though, without the benefit of an up-to-date understanding about the topic of group differences in IQ are stuck in the past.

---

[9] Based on the evidence available at the time, I probably would have been an environmentalist, if I had been alive 50 or 60 years ago.

WHY SHOULD GROUP DIFFERENCES BE PARTIALLY GENETIC IN ORIGIN?

If one accepts that differences in average IQ can be partially genetic in origin, the pressing question is why. Because humans all belong to the same species, why should genetic differences develop that would make one group score higher – on average – on intelligence tests than another group?

The answer lies in basic evolutionary principles. Based on the best available evidence, humans first left Africa between 80,000 and 130,000 years ago. Over time, the descendants of these emigrants spread throughout the world and encountered many different environments, from arctic tundra to tropical rainforests, from mountain highlands to coastal plains. Inevitably, these different environments made some traits more useful than others for surviving and passing on one's genes. However, some of the traits that were adaptive in one environment would have been detrimental or useless in another environment. The adaptive traits would have spread in populations living in environments where those traits were helpful – and not in populations that lived in other environments. Over time, the various traits favored in different environments would result in physical differences among groups, resulting in different appearances for different racial and ethnic groups.

It would be naïve to think that evolution would only create differences in skin color, height, and other physical traits. Evolution does not only work from the neck down. Every part of the human body – including the brain – is subject to the laws of evolution. Different environments created subtle differences in the genetic makeup of the brain, which can be manifested as behavioral differences. To argue otherwise is saying that somehow humans are not subject to evolution, or that evolution does not operate on the brain, or that brain differences do not lead to behavioral differences (Winegard & Winegard, 2014). None of these viewpoints is logical because they require a magical force to somehow exempt humans from the laws of biology and evolution. Indeed, the principles of evolution lead to the expectation that genetically based differences should exist in many physical and psychological traits across human groups with different ancestries. It would be extremely surprising if these differences did not exist (Winegard et al., 2017).

What is still unclear is what specific environmental characteristics would lead humans in some parts of the world to be pressured to pass on DNA variants associated with higher intelligence. Some scientists have proposed different theories (e.g., Kanazawa, 2010; León & Burga-León, 2015; Rushton, 2000; Woodley of Menie et al., 2015), but none has gained widespread acceptance. One of the difficulties is that it is impossible to travel back in time to observe what conditions were present thousands of years ago in different parts of the world and how that impacted the genome of present populations. Another hurdle is that some (most?) of the environmental influences on human evolution may have been cultural, and these influences usually do not leave a physical trace in the geological, archeological, or historical record. However, some writers have hypothesized about cultural influences that could have encouraged high intelligence in European Jews (Cochran et al., 2006; Cochran & Harpending, 2009) and East Asians (Unz, 2013). It is not clear whether future discoveries in genetics and evolutionary psychology will support current theories about how or why group differences in intelligence developed.

THE GREAT UNKNOWN: WHAT IS THE VALUE OF h_b^2?

Given all this theory and evidence, another major unanswered question is what the exact value of h_b^2 is. Actually, that's a trick question because all heritability values apply only to a specific population under its current conditions. Depending on which racial groups are being compared and their respective environments, h_b^2 probably varies. Comparing Europeans and Asians within the United States would probably produce a different h_b^2 value than a comparison of Europeans living in Australia and Africans living in Africa.

Some researchers have suggested h_b^2 values for a particular group difference in intelligence (e.g., Gottfredson, 2005b; Lasker et al., 2019; Rushton & Jensen, 2005a). However, I do not believe that the evidence permits an accurate estimate of h_b^2 for any racial group IQ comparison beyond stating that h_b^2 is greater than zero for some pairs of groups. It is likely, though, that groups that have similar environments (e.g., within the same country or within the same socioeconomic stratum) have higher h_b^2 values, while groups with very different environments (e.g., comparing people who live in impoverished nations with people who live in highly prosperous countries) will have lower h_b^2 values. This is because equalized environments increase the heritability of a trait, while large environmental differences reduce heritability. If group differences are seen as the sum of individual differences in each group – something that Jensen (1998, p. 457) called the *default hypothesis* – then $h_b^2 \approx h_w^2$ when environments are similar. However, large environmental differences between racial groups can make the two heritabilities have very different values (see Table 28.1). It is telling that the only study with an h_b^2 value based on strong data produced a high h_b^2 estimate (.50 to .80) in a sample from one American metropolitan area with environmental differences that are much narrower than what is seen on a worldwide scale (Lasker et al., 2019). More research in more countries and with participants who live in a diverse array of environments is needed before scientists can understand better what typical h_b^2 values are and how, when, and why they may differ.

CONCLUSION

Regardless of the exact h_b^2 values in research studies, for many comparisons it is unlikely that h_b^2 will be zero, especially for groups that have similar environments or large mean IQ gaps. For these situations, the hereditarian hypothesis is almost certainly true, though how strong heritability is between groups is unknown. While the hereditarian hypothesis can be frustrating (and I sincerely wish the hereditarian hypothesis were not true), it should not lead to despair. In Chapters 33 and 34, I will discuss the social implications of intelligence research and why this information may lead to beneficial policies for all people.

29

Unique Influences Operate on One Group's Intelligence Test Scores

> the environments experienced by Black Americans (and Blacks more generally) are importantly different from the environments experienced by White Americans in ways directly attributable to race and racism ... Given that the environments encountered differ in these ways, attempts to statistically control for the effects of the different environments experienced by the different populations on the development of ... IQ test performance are therefore, I argue, doomed to failure.
>
> (J. M. Kaplan, 2015, pp. 2–3)

The last chapter presented the main arguments for why between-group differences in intelligence test scores are at least partially genetic. This hereditarian view is mainstream among psychologists who study group differences in intelligence (e.g., Rindermann et al., 2017, 2020; Snyderman & Rothman, 1987, 1988), though the exact value of the heritability of between-group differences (h_b^2) is unknown. The discussion in Chapter 28, however, is based on the assumption that the environmental influences on IQ scores for different racial or ethnic groups are the same. However, there is no guarantee that these environmental variables are the same within and across groups. It is theoretically possible that an environmental variable can act on only one racial group while leaving another group untouched. If a variable like this operated on a racial group to systematically lower IQ scores, then it could explain average group differences in IQ scores non-genetically (i.e., so that $h_b^2 = 0$) while still allowing within-group heritability (i.e., h_w^2) to be high. The impacts of a unique environmental influence are diagrammed in Figure 29.1 and shows that this influence would shift the lower-performing group's IQ distribution away from the higher-performing group.[1]

---

[1] Theoretically, a unique environmental influence could systematically raise a group's IQ scores. However, no one has proposed a beneficial variable that raises IQ for one group while leaving other racial or ethnic groups untouched. Therefore, my discussion in this chapter will assume that any unique environmental influence is detrimental to intelligence test performance.

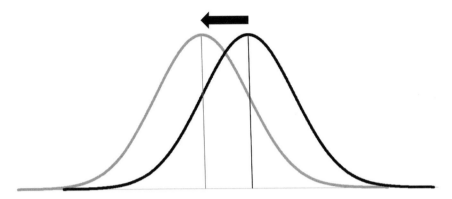

FIGURE 29.1 If unique environmental variables operated systematically to lower one group's IQ scores, then that can cause the lower distribution (in grey) to shift down. This image displays a purely environmental X-factor (shown by the arrow) that shifts the grey distribution 15 IQ points ($d = 1.0$) lower than the black distribution. The vertical lines represent the two groups' averages. Notice the large amount of overlap that still exists across groups.

THE X-FACTOR (WARNING: NOT AS COOL AS IT SOUNDS)

Environmental influences that operate on one group are theoretically possible, but do they occur in real life? As will become clear as the chapter progresses, such an environmental influence would operate in a way that is unique among environmental variables. Psychologists label this influence the "X-factor," which conveys the singular nature of such a variable (Jensen, 1974). Such an influence would have to meet four requirements. They are:

1. An X-factor must be experienced only by members of the lower-scoring group. Otherwise, the variable would be no different than the environmental influences discussed in Chapter 28, making it unable to leave the higher group's scores untouched.
2. An X-factor's unique influence on IQ scores would need to impact nearly everyone in the lower-scoring group. If it did not, the variable would be unable to shift the distribution low enough to create the average differences that occur across racial and ethnic groups.
3. The unique influences of an X-factor on intelligence would require an approximately equal impact on all group members. If it did not, then this variable would decrease h_w^2 and increase the variability of the lower-scoring group's IQ scores, which does not happen.[2]
4. An X-factor must have a causal impact on IQ.

---

[2] Systematic reviews of h_w^2 for African, Hispanic, and European Americans shows that their within-group heritability values for IQ are close to .50 (Fuerst & Dalliard 2014; Pesta et al., 2020). The variability – as measured by the standard deviation – of IQ scores for all major racial/ethnic

These requirements eliminate all the typical explanations that people propose as causes of the differences in average group IQ scores, such as poverty, poor nutrition, exposure to lead, low education quality, neglectful parenting, etc. None of these disadvantages are unique to any racial/ethnic group, nor are they experienced by all members of any group with approximately equal force (Sesardic, 2000). Therefore, these environmental variables cannot serve as an X-factor that systematically depresses one group's IQ scores and makes h_b^2 zero.[3]

The most frequent candidates for the X-factor are the effects of race-specific experiences, such as discrimination, racism, or living as a minority in a country with a European majority (e.g., Ogbu, 2002). The rest of this chapter summarizes (1) the evidence of the X-factor's existence and (2) whether race-specific experiences function the way an X-factor would need to operate in order for it to make average group differences in IQ scores completely environmental. To keep this chapter manageable, I will focus on racial groups that consist of people who were born in the United States and who speak English as a native language. Limiting a discussion to these groups allows comparisons of racial groups that do not have linguistic differences or massive differences in environment and/or culture. Also, the data about the experiences of racial/ethnic minorities in the United States is more plentiful than in other countries, which reduces the need for speculation. Readers should *not* assume that this discussion generalizes to international comparisons or to intergroup comparisons in other nations.

CANDIDATE I: DISCRIMINATION AND RACISM

Every scientist involved with the debate about between-group differences in IQ acknowledges the existence of racism. Likewise, all scholars on this topic agree that there are negative consequences for individuals who are the victims of racial discrimination and prejudice. No one believes that racism has been eliminated from American culture, and investigating the manifestations and consequences of racism is an important step towards building a more harmonious society. The existence of racism, though, does not automatically mean that it operates as an X-factor. It is a legitimate scientific question whether racism meets the four requirements of an X-factor.

The first requirement is that only members of the lower-scoring group experience the negative influences of the X-factor. If "racism" is defined as "anti-minority sentiment and/or actions," then it is almost certain that only

---

groups in the United States is approximately 15 IQ points, or perhaps slightly lower for some groups (Dickens & Flynn, 2006, Table A1; Jensen, 1998, p. 353).

[3] These variables may cause *individuals* within one or both groups to have lower IQ, but then that would not have a systematic effect throughout a racial group. To the extent that one group experiences these negative environmental characteristics more than another, this may lower the group's average IQ score. But this still would not be an X-factor because the negative influences also impact the IQ scores for individuals in the higher-scoring group – just less frequently.

racial minorities are victims of this form of racism and that the race-specific experiences arising from racism fulfill this X-factor requirement. It is hard to argue that European Americans would be victims of racism that is aimed at another group.

The second requirement is that an X-factor would need to impact almost everybody in the lower-scoring group. I believe that the best source of data is recent polls of minorities about their experiences with discrimination and racism. A 2016 Gallup poll showed that 82% of African Americans believed that racism against African Americans is "widespread" in the United States (J. M. Jones, 2016).[4] A more recent Gallup poll reported that a significant number of African Americans felt unfairly treated because of their race within the previous 30 days while in a store shopping (29%), in an entertainment-oriented business (23%), when dealing with police (21%), at work (19%), or while obtaining health care for themselves or a family member (16%). These percentages have been roughly stable since 1997 when Gallup started asking African Americans these questions (J. M. Jones, 2019). Another recent poll showed that 13% of African Americans stated that they experienced discrimination because of their race regularly, and another 63% agreed that they experienced discrimination "from time to time," indicating that racism is a fact of life for at least 76% of African Americans (M. Anderson, 2019).

These percentages are not 100%, but the poll questions do not ask about whether African Americans have *ever* experienced racism. On the other hand, it may be simplistic to equate racism with discrimination, and some scholars use more expansive definitions of racism (e.g., Ford, 2014; Gould, 1996; Ogbu, 2002; Quinn, 2017; Scheurich, & Young, 1997). If racism includes, for example, negative attitudes towards minorities, requirements to conform to majority culture, or unequal outcomes across racial groups, then – by definition – all African Americans experience racism. However, these broader definitions of racism are hotly contested (e.g., Hughes, 2018; Tavris, 2017; Zuriff, 2014). Whether racism meets the second requirement to operate as an X-factor probably depends on one's preferred definition of racism. For the purposes of this analysis, I will assume that racism does impact the life of every minority group member in the United States (and therefore that the second requirement for racism to be an X-factor is fulfilled), though I recognize that some readers will not agree with this proposition.

Racism as an X-factor starts experiencing more difficulties with the third requirement, which is that the X-factor impacts all group members to an approximately equal degree. The poll data above demonstrates this difficulty: while a clear majority of African Americans state that they have been treated

---

[4] In comparison, 66% of Hispanic respondents and 56% of European American respondents stated that racism against African Americans was widespread in the United States (J. M. Jones, 2016). However, the best informants about the existence of racism against African Americans are African Americans themselves because they would be most aware of any such racism.

poorly because of their race, some report these experiences more frequently than others. Indeed, given the diversity of experiences and backgrounds for people in a racial group, it would be surprising if everyone experienced racism to the same degree. This also means that if racism has an impact on IQ scores it will not be uniform for all members of a racial group. This is one of the reasons why even some environmentalists who believe that $h_b^2 = 0$ are skeptical about the existence of an X-factor (e.g., Flynn, 1980).

An even more difficult hurdle is the final requirement for X-factors: a causal relationship between the X-factor and lowered IQ. Most scholars who propose that racism could operate as an X-factor do not explain how racism results in poorer performance on an intelligence test (e.g., J. M. Kaplan, 2015). It is not enough to say that racism lowers IQ scores; it is necessary to explain *how* this happens in a causal manner (Dalliard, 2014). For example, how would being mistreated at a store due to one's race transfer into lower performance on an intelligence test? To be an X-factor, this causal pathway must not violate any requirements for a variable to be an X-factor. For example, if systematic racism makes minority children generally attend lower-quality schools that lower IQ scores, then it must be shown that no European American children attend poor schools (the first requirement), nearly every child from the minority group attends a poor school (the second requirement), and that all minority children's schools are approximately equally bad (the third requirement). It seems unlikely that differences in school quality meet these requirements, which means that school quality cannot be the conduit through which a racism X-factor can operate.

Even if an X-factor met all the requirements, the mechanism by which it lowers IQ must be causal. However, it has been difficult to identify non-biological variables that cause lasting, permanent changes to IQ for people who live in typical environments found in Western nations (see Chapters 14 and 15). Therefore, any environmental conduit that an X-factor uses to lower IQ would not only have to be unique in its influence on a single racial group, but it must also function unlike every other environmental influence on IQ yet identified (Dalliard, 2014).

CANDIDATE 2: INVOLUNTARY MINORITY STATUS

Another proposed X-factor is related to racism but has some distinctive characteristics that make it more than just a theory of experiencing racism causing lower IQ. Anthropologist John Ogbu (2002) proposed that some minorities have lowered IQ and economic performance while others do not because high-performing minorities (or their ancestors) volunteered to be part of American culture through immigration, while low-performing minorities are more likely to be involuntary minorities because of a previous history of enslavement, conquest, or colonization. He believed that being an involuntary minority means living in a country that consistently devalues one's culture, excludes involuntary minorities from economic and educational opportunities, and constantly sends messages of minority inferiority. These experiences are perpetuated culturally and politically across generations, making involuntary minorities into "caste-like" groups. Although he mostly wrote about the United States, Ogbu saw this distinction between voluntary and involuntary minorities as a phenomenon that applied in many other countries (e.g., Middle Eastern Jews in Israel, or the Burakumin in Japan).

Ogbu has provided a more sophisticated theory than most writers who argue that racism causes average differences in IQ scores. For example, he proposed a causal pathway, which is that the daily negative experiences of involuntary minorities lower motivation to excel on intelligence tests, create a defeatist attitude about education and employment prospects, and cause individuals to internalize negative stereotypes about their abilities (Ogbu, 2002). These negative outcomes of racism then lead to involuntary minorities performing worse on intelligence tests. Ogbu's theory would also explain why some voluntary minority groups (e.g., black Caribbean immigrants to the United States) outperform involuntary minorities who belong to the same racial group.

Although he did not call it an X-factor, Ogbu's theory is a purely environmental proposal for differences in average IQ scores that would operate on only one racial group, so it should be evaluated as an X-factor. Ogbu's theory meets the first and second requirements. But the third and fourth requirements still present difficulties for his theory. For example, Ogbu presented no evidence that the negative effects of being an involuntary minority were equally felt among all group members; he merely took it for granted. Finally, the proposed causal mechanisms have not been empirically shown to have a causal impact. In fact, for many psychological variables (e.g., self-esteem, anxiety), African Americans outperform European Americans (Dalliard, 2014). Even when African Americans have lower psychological outcomes, these differences are not nearly as large as IQ differences. This makes it highly unlikely that these other psychological variables can function as part of the causal pathway that Ogbu (2002) proposed.

In addition to failing to meet the requirements to be an X-factor, Ogbu's theory has other shortcomings. For example, it cannot explain the pattern of results shown in Spearman's hypothesis, where larger group differences are found on tests that are better measures of *g* (Jensen, 1998). Ogbu never explained why decreased motivation and/or internalized negative stereotypes decrease IQ on some subtests (e.g., matrix reasoning) more than others (e.g., digit span) and why these would match the pattern expected if h_b^2 is larger than zero. Ogbu's theory also oversimplifies the historical and social dynamics of different groups. For example, most Indians (i.e., South Asians) who live in Africa are the descendants of indentured laborers brought to the continent in the nineteenth century, and yet they score higher than the majority groups in the countries they live in (Jensen, 1998). If IQ differences are also a product of the voluntary immigrant experience, it is not clear why there are differences among voluntary minority groups (e.g., Asians and Hispanics in the United States) or involuntary minority groups (e.g., Africans and Native Americans in the United States). For Ogbu's theory to be scientifically successful, it must be able to explain more patterns in group differences than it currently does.

CANDIDATE 3: THE FLYNN EFFECT

Another widely proposed explanation for group differences is the Flynn effect, which is the tendency for IQ scores to increase across the decades. (Chapter 14 described this phenomenon in detail.) Because the Flynn effect must be entirely environmental in origin, some have speculated (e.g., Flynn, 1987; Marks, 2010) that average IQ differences across racial groups could have the same cause as average IQ differences from one generation to the next. If this were true, then it would be plausible that differences across racial groups would be merely the result of higher-scoring groups receiving more environmental stimulation that raises IQ, just as later generations received more environmental stimulation compared to their parents or grandparents. It would then follow that differences in average IQ across racial groups would close once high-scoring groups reach the point where the Flynn effect stops and other groups catch up (Ceci & Williams, 2009).

While the Flynn effect is probably a contributing factor to IQ score differences *across* nations (Rindermann et al., 2017), it does not explain average score group differences within the United States. Three decades of study of the causes of the Flynn effect show that the increase in IQ is due to increases in the contributions to IQ from non-g abilities in Stratum I and Stratum II – and not due to changes in g (Woodley, te Nijenhuis, Must, & Must, 2014). In contrast, average racial group differences in IQ are at least partially genetic and partially due to differences in g (see Chapter 28). This means that these are two different phenomena (Rushton & Jensen, 2010; Wicherts et al., 2004). As a result, the Flynn effect cannot serve as an X-factor to explain the average IQ score differences among racial groups within the United States (and possibly other industrialized nations).

CANDIDATE 4: AN UNKNOWN X-FACTOR

None of the previous three candidates meets all four requirements to be an X-factor. But this does not prove that there are no X-factors. Theoretically, it is possible that there is an X-factor operating exclusively on members of a racial group – it just has not been discovered yet.

This is highly unlikely, based on the results of tests of measurement invariance. Recall from Chapter 28 that measurement invariance occurs when a confirmatory factor analysis performed on data from two separate groups produces the same results. Research has shown that intelligence tests demonstrate measurement invariance across racial groups. This has an important implication for X-factors because it is mathematically impossible for measurement invariance to occur *and* for X-factors to be present. This is because an X-factor must alter the relationship among test scores for the group experiencing the X-factor, which would result in a failure of measurement invariance (Dalliard, 2014; Lubke, Dolan, Kelderman, & Mellenbergh, 2003). This is extremely strong evidence that there are no X-factors operating uniquely on a single racial group.

THE BURDEN OF PROOF

If an X-factor does exist that systematically decreases IQ for one racial group while leaving a higher-scoring group untouched, the burden of proof is on environmentalists to find it. This is because the scientific default belief is that a phenomenon does not exist – until proven otherwise (Warne, 2018). For example, most scientists believe that Bigfoot is not real, but if someone produces incontrovertible proof of Bigfoot's existence (e.g., a Bigfoot corpse or a captured live specimen), scientists' opinions will change. To claim that Bigfoot exists and that it is the responsibility of skeptics to disprove its existence is illogical. Likewise, the X-factor is assumed to not exist, until someone can demonstrate that it does. So far, these efforts have failed.

Another reason the burden of proof is on environmentalists to demonstrate that an X-factor exists is *parsimony*. This is the scientific principle that if two theories can explain a phenomenon equally well, the simpler theory should be favored. When comparing the X-factor hypothesis with the theory of a partial genetic explanation for between-group differences in IQ, the latter is clearly the more parsimonious explanation. This is because the hereditarian viewpoint merely means that average group differences are the sum of individual genetic and environmental differences in the different groups and that the same genetic and environmental influences operate on individuals in both groups (Jensen, 1998).[5] The X-factor hypothesis, however, is more complex because it requires an X-factor to function in addition to any environmental variables that operate on both groups. The hereditarian view is simpler and should be favored over the X-factor hypothesis until environmentalists can demonstrate that X-factors exist and that they explain average group differences in intelligence better than the hereditarian viewpoint.

CONCLUSION

While X-factors are an apparently enticing hypothesis, it is difficult for any environmental variable to have all the necessary characteristics that an X-factor would need to have in order for it to cause a systematic drop in IQ for a racial

---

[5] Indeed, when discussing group differences in any variable or any groups, the most parsimonious explanation is that "Group differences . . . are simply aggregated individual differences" (McCabe et al., 2019, p. 18; see also Frisby, 2013, p. 213).

group. Proposed candidates for the X-factor all lack at least some necessary characteristics, and none can explain the pattern of score differences across tests or racial groups. Additionally, if there were an unknown X-factor in operation, it would appear in tests of measurement invariance by showing different factor analysis results for different racial groups. Scientists who find the X-factor hypothesis plausible cannot merely assert that X-factors exist. Instead, they must identify a variable, show that it has all the necessary characteristics of an X-factor, and explain patterns in real data better than hereditarian theories can.

But readers who hope for an X-factor to explain group differences in IQ have one more possibility: stereotype threat. This psychological phenomenon is the topic of Chapter 30, and when it was proposed it showed promise as an X-factor. In the next chapter, I will evaluate whether stereotype threat is an X-factor and whether it can explain score gaps across racial groups.

30

Stereotype Threat Explains Score Gaps among Demographic Groups

> There is plenty of evidence though, that blacks sometimes perform worse on IQ tests and achievement tests when their race is made salient and this engages a "stereotype threat," causing them to perform worse than they would in more relaxed settings where they are not afraid of confirming a stereotype that white testers have.
>
> (Nisbett, 2009, p. 95)

This is the final installment in a trilogy of chapters about the potential causes of average differences in IQ scores across racial and ethnic groups. Chapter 28 presented evidence that the differences in score averages are unlikely to be entirely environmental in origin. Chapter 29 discussed the possibility of X-factors that could operate on a single racial group while leaving another group's IQ scores untouched. The conclusion was that commonly proposed X-factors do not meet the necessary requirements to lower IQ and make average differences in intelligence entirely environmental. This chapter discusses one final proposed X-factor that is popular among psychologists, but which has had empirical difficulties in recent years that severely undermine its ability to explain average score differences. The proposed X-factor is called stereotype threat.

THE THEORY OF STEREOTYPE THREAT

A Highly Plausible X-Factor. Stereotype threat was first proposed by psychologists Claude M. Steele and Joshua Aronson (1995). In their widely read article, they reported four studies in which they compared the test results of two African American groups. One group was explicitly reminded about negative stereotypes regarding African Americans' academic performance. The other group did not receive any such reminders. The researchers then found that this intervention reduced scores on tests of g (abbreviated versions of the SAT college admissions test and the Graduate Record Exam for graduate school admissions) for African Americans exposed to the stereotype, but not other African Americans, who scored as high as similar European American examinees. Steele and Aronson (1995) argued that if the examinees perceived a testing situation as unfair, then it caused a decrease in the African Americans' scores that was unrelated to their intelligence. They called this phenomenon *stereotype threat.*

Stereotype threat is a candidate to be an X-factor, though its originators did not call it that. It would impact only one racial group (in this case, African Americans), which fulfils the first requirement to be an X-factor. It is also likely that all members of a racial or ethnic group are already aware of stereotypes about their intelligence or academic performance, thereby fulfilling the second X-factor requirement. Examinees who encountered stereotypes experienced them with an equal intensity in Steele and Aronson's (1995) research, which is the third X-factor requirement.

Finally, Steele and Aronson randomly assigned African American examinees to either experience the stereotype threat or to be tested under normal administration conditions. This balances out the groups so that any differences at the end of the study are due to the treatment that one group experienced. Therefore, Steele and Aronson (1995) presented evidence that stereotype threat had a causal impact on IQ scores – and not on g. Steele and Aronson also proposed a mechanism for why there would be a cause-and-effect relationship. According to their theory, when minority examinees are reminded of unfavorable stereotypes, they encounter anxiety about fulfilling the negative stereotype, and it becomes a threat to their self-image and performance (Steele, 1998). If the stereotype is internalized, then it may cause reduced motivation and long-term deficiencies in academic performance. Later researchers suggested that stereotype threat could also operate through introducing distracting and unwanted thoughts into the testing situation (Spencer, Logel, & Davies, 2016). In layman's terms, the worry about perpetuating the stereotype makes the stereotype a self-fulfilling prophecy.

The original Steele and Aronson (1995) report triggered the stereotype threat by telling examinees that the test measured their "ability," suggesting words that were associated with negative stereotypes, or merely asking respondents to indicate their race on a demographic form before taking the test. Later researchers claimed to have demonstrated the stereotype threat under other conditions, such as having a noticeable numeric racial imbalance of examinees in the room or other subtle cues. Indeed, the phenomenon is so apparent that the authors of one thorough review of the stereotype threat research stated, "In the real world, simply sitting down to write a test in a negatively stereotyped domain is enough to trigger stereotype threat, because the test-taker is at risk of confirming the stereotype through poor performance" (Spencer et al., 2016, p. 418). Moreover, it is not even necessary for the targets of the negative stereotype to be consciously aware of the stereotype threat situation (Spencer et al., 2016).

Steele and Aronson's (1995) article was hugely influential, and they – and other scientists – quickly built upon the original findings. Later research revealed that stereotype threat also had an impact on females (e.g., Sunny, Taasoobshirazi, Clark, & Marchand, 2017), other racial groups (e.g., Hollis-Sawyer & Sawyer, 2008), and elderly individuals (Spencer et al., 2016). The stereotype threat phenomenon was replicated in many studies, and many psychologists saw it as convincing evidence that "stereotype threat suppresses real-world intellectual achievements" (Nisbett et al., 2012, p. 147). As the research base regarding stereotype threat grew, proponents of the theory have argued that stereotype threat does not just affect minorities in testing situations, but also in the workforce and everyday life (Spencer et al., 2016).

Thus, stereotype threat is the only proposed phenomenon that meets the requirements to be an X-factor (J. M. Kaplan, 2015), and it certainly has more empirical evidence in its favor than any other X-factor candidate. It also has what no other X-factor candidate does: a plausible causal mechanism leading from a negative, single-race environmental experience to decreased IQ scores. Thus, stereotype threat is a valuable topic of study for anyone interested in why some groups have higher average IQ scores than others.

Dissenting Viewpoints. Although stereotype threat is a mainstream theory in psychology, some scholars voiced concerns about the theory and its ability to explain the average IQ score gaps across groups. One aspect of Steele and Aronson's (1995) study that is often overlooked is that the researchers asked examinees their SAT scores before the study started. The researchers then matched African American and European American examinees on SAT scores at the start of the study, thereby eliminating pre-existing score gaps. Thus, stereotype threat created *new* test score gaps; the studies that Steele and Aronson (1995) performed did not explain the average IQ differences found outside the laboratory among individuals from different racial groups. This fact is often lost on people discussing stereotype threat in scholarly research, textbooks, and the media (Sackett, Hardison, & Cullen, 2004; Wax, 2009).

Even if stereotype threat does explain pre-existing IQ gaps, it cannot explain the entire average difference found among racial and ethnic groups. Across studies, stereotype threat scenarios produce an average decrease of only 3 IQ points for African Americans – far short of the 15-point average difference between African Americans and European Americans (Walton & Spencer, 2009; Wax, 2009). If stereotype threat is an X-factor responsible from this average gap, there is still a remaining 12-point difference unaccounted for, which other environmental variables have difficulty explaining.[1]

---

[1] For remaining environmental differences to be large enough to explain the remaining 12-point IQ difference so that $h_b^2 = 0$, then African Americans must have an average in causal environmental variables that is 1.131 d worse than the average European American's environment (assuming that $h_w^2 = .50$). Most proposed non-biological environmental variables, such as socioeconomic status, have a very weak causal impact after controlling for genetic influences, so even this smaller

Other psychologists have questioned the degree to which stereotype threat resulted in a novel psychological experience. For example, Jensen (1998) proposed that stereotype threat was merely a form of test anxiety created by worries about being discriminated against or appearing inadequate. Others have suggested that race-specific experiences, like stereotype threat, create stress, which could lower test performance (Spencer et al., 2016; Whaley, 1998). If these theorists are correct, then stereotype threat would unquestionably be a unique experience for one racial group. However, if the stereotype threat triggers then result in psychological experiences that are found in other racial groups – such as anxiety, stress, or lowered motivation – then stereotype threat is not an X-factor. In other words, if "stress," "anxiety," or "low motivation" are the immediate causes of the lowered IQ scores among minority examinees, then stereotype threat is not an X-factor because the psychological processes it triggers are not unique to a racial group. However, it is important to note that if this is correct, then stereotype threat could still contribute to some of the average IQ gaps between groups without being an X-factor.

Another problem with the stereotype threat literature is that the laboratory studies often do not resemble real testing situations (Whaley, 1998). For example, in one of Steele and Aronson's (1995) four studies, they gave a verbal task that required examinees to complete words, some of which hinted at the concept of race or negative stereotypes of African Americans (e.g., L A __ __ for "lazy," W E L __ __ __ __ for "welfare," or "R A __ __" for race). However, this task does not resemble any pre-test instructions or exercise for any actual test.[2] In other studies, the researcher explicitly tells examinees that one minority group outscores another on the test – a statement that would never appear in the instructions for a real test. Generally, studies that have strong stereotype reminders are much more likely to produce evidence for stereotype threat than studies that have realistic test instructions with subtle or no reminder of group stereotypes (Shewach, Sackett, & Quint, 2019).

The difference between real test instructions and the procedures used in stereotype threat studies may be why laboratory-based studies produce much stronger stereotype threat effects than studies of real test instructions given to examinees in the real world (e.g., M. E. Walker & Bridgeman, 2008). For this reason,

it is unclear whether stereotype threat makes any discernible contribution to the black–white difference observed when standardized tests are put to their typical uses ... stereotype threat may be yet another curiosity of the psychological laboratory with minimal relevance to behavior in real-world situations. (J. Lee, 2010, pp. 251, 252)

---

necessary environmental difference (compared to $d = 1.414$ if there are no X-factors in operation on African Americans) is likely to be too large to explain through non-X-factor environmental variables.

[2] Even if word completion were a test item, no test creator would choose these words precisely because it could introduce distractions that would interfere with examinees' performance.

Generalizing laboratory findings to the natural environment is always a problem for experimental psychology, and the degree to which stereotype threat studies apply to real testing situations is not clear (Sackett, Schmitt, Ellingson, & Kabin, 2001; Wax, 2009). As study conditions better resemble real-world testing conditions, the evidence for stereotype threat progressively weakens and often disappears completely (Shewach et al., 2019). A behavior that only appears under the tight controls and constraints of the laboratory tells scientists nothing about real human behavior (Jenkins, 1981). For stereotype threat to function as an X-factor in the real world, there needs to be better evidence that it consistently and strongly operates outside the laboratory.

THINGS FALL APART

The Replication Crisis in Psychology. A methodological revolution has been brewing in psychology, and it has caused some psychologists – including myself – to seriously question the reality and/or strength of many findings, such as the stereotype threat phenomenon. In 2011, several events occurred which undermined bedrock findings in some branches of psychology (Nelson, Simmons, & Simonsohn, 2018). Basic psychological phenomena – even some taught for years in every introductory psychology class – were not holding up to scrutiny. When psychologists tried to repeat these studies, they often found that the results did not replicate (Camerer et al., 2018; Open Science Collaboration, 2015). All of this resulted in what many call a "replication crisis" in psychology, and it was not clear which findings scientists should trust.

One of the causes of the replication crisis is *publication bias*, which is the tendency for scholarly journals to publish results that demonstrate a phenomenon or support a theory. Because of publication bias, published research studies are not a representative sample of all research conducted on a topic (Rosenthal, 1979). Publication bias happens because of a mistaken belief (that started to change in the 2010s) that positive results demonstrating a phenomenon are more important (and therefore more worthy of publication) than results that did not demonstrate a phenomenon. Unfortunately, this means that (a) researchers are less likely to write papers based on studies with negative results, (b) peer reviewers are less favorable towards such studies that are submitted to journals, and (c) editors are less likely to accept these studies for publication (Franco, Malhotra, & Simonovits, 2014; Greenwald, 1975; Sterling, 1959).

Scientists and journal editors also did not favor exact replications of earlier studies, instead preferring to publish novel results. This bias against replications meant that no one checked results of earlier studies to see if they were robust (Makel & Plucker, 2014). Or, if someone did replicate the study, the results were rarely published. When psychologists did conduct replications, they preferred *conceptual replications*, which were to replicate the theory behind the findings – but not the exact study itself. When these studies showed broadly similar results, it was taken as evidence that the phenomenon could appear across multiple samples, study designs, settings, etc. However, this logic was flawed because the introduction of new study characteristics also introduced new flexibility to researchers to alter the study design or analysis until they got similar results to the original (Simmons et al., 2011).

In the years since the replication crisis started, it is clear that its severity is not uniform throughout psychology. Social psychology seems to have a lower replication rate than cognitive psychology (Open Science Collaboration, 2015) or personality psychology (Soto, 2019). For individual studies, non-replicated studies tend to have small sample sizes, a large amount of flexibility in design and statistical analysis, and researchers with a motivation to support a theory or tell a compelling story[3] (Forstmeier, Wagenmakers, & Parker, 2017; Simmons, Nelson, & Simonsohn, 2011). Under these conditions, a large proportion of studies produce false positives – ethereal results that do not replicate and tell scientists nothing real about human behavior.

Stereotype Threat and the Replication Crisis. Because of the replication crisis, it is no longer sufficient to point to a large number of studies as evidence that a psychological phenomenon occurs. Publication bias, researcher flexibility, and the natural human tendency to look for confirming evidence (and ignore disconfirming evidence) mean that the existence of dozens of studies may be meaningless because most or all of their results may be false positives. These false positives will exaggerate the strength of evidence (Nuijten, van Assen, Veldkamp, & Wicherts, 2015; Schimmack, 2012; Ueno, Fastrich, & Murayama, 2016).

Unfortunately, much of the research on stereotype threat has many of the characteristics of studies that do not replicate – especially when the study supports the existence of stereotype threat. Steele and Aronson's (1995) original article exemplifies this well. The four studies had an average of 37.75 African American participants and 33.25 European American participants, which is too small to reliably detect an effect – let alone detect it in four

---

[3] These situations are rare in most topics of intelligence research. For example, factor analysis is a procedure that requires a large sample size. Another advantage that intelligence research has is the frequent practice of correlating a test score with another variable, which is more likely to produce replicable results (e.g., Soto, 2019). Moreover, questions in intelligence research are sometimes very divisive for social reasons (e.g., average differences in IQ across racial groups) or theoretical reasons (e.g., whether intelligence was one ability or a collection of abilities). This has resulted in higher-quality research because (1) researchers know that their work will be carefully scrutinized, and (2) many findings that get published are instantly questioned and carefully investigated by skeptics, who often conduct their own replications. Also, it is very easy to measure *g* (see Chapter 7), which makes collecting data from a new sample easier than in some other psychological fields. Therefore, intelligence research has escaped most of the turmoil of the replication crisis.

studies in a row.[4] Being the first researchers to study stereotype threat, Steele and Aronson (1995) also had a great deal of flexibility in designing their studies; moreover, the sample sizes, methods of triggering the stereotype threat, and data analysis procedures were either poorly justified or not justified at all. Later studies that support stereotype threat disproportionately have similar characteristics (e.g., Hollis-Sawyer & Sawyer, 2008), as some stereotype threat proponents have admitted (Walton & Spencer, 2009, p. 1133). There is statistical evidence that these study characteristics inflate the rate of false positives greatly. Schimmack (2019) estimated that in one body of published studies on stereotype threat in females, false positives increased the percentage of published studies supporting stereotype threat from 14% to 84%. If he is correct, then most published studies showing stereotype threat in female examinees are false positives.

Exacerbating the problems is the rampant publication bias in the stereotype threat literature. In an examination of studies of stereotype threat on females, Flore and Wicherts (2015, Table 3) found evidence supporting stereotype threat in 67% of published studies, but only 40% of unpublished studies. Similarly, Ganley et al. (2013) found that 80% of published stereotype threat studies on females showed evidence in favor of the theory, but 0% of unpublished studies did. If there were no publication bias present, then each pair of percentages would be approximately equal. As a result of publication bias, the studies in scholarly journals provide inflated evidence for the existence and/or strength of stereotype threat. Shewach et al. (2019) found that the magnitude of stereotype threat was over twice as strong in published than unpublished studies.

Because psychologists have only realized in recent years that publication bias and certain study characteristics (e.g., small sample size, flexibility in analysis) are probably distorting the stereotype threat literature, there is very little research on stereotype threat that is designed to eliminate these flaws. The best evidence now comes from studies with large sample sizes, designs and analysis methods that are locked in before the study begins, and no publication bias. Research with these characteristics is new, but it is not encouraging for stereotype threat. The first such study on stereotype threat, conducted by

---

[4] *Statistical power* is the probability that a study could detect a real effect. Assuming a group difference of $d = .50$ (a typical default for new research topics), the studies in Steele and Aronson (1995) had statistical power of approximately .459, .300, .329, and .319. The probability that all four studies would detect a stereotype threat effect is .014 (the product of the four studies' statistical power). In other words, Steele and Aronson (1995) had a 1.4% chance of obtaining positive results from all four studies – yet they did anyway. They either beat the odds, withheld some of studies they performed, or used some flexibility in analysis and design to inflate the strength of their evidence. In contrast, Steele and Aronson (1995) had a 17.3% probability of finding evidence in favor of stereotype threat in none of their four studies. Yes, finding no evidence for stereotype threat in all four studies was *over ten times more likely* than finding evidence for stereotype threat in four out of four studies. This fact alone should make readers suspicious of the evidence that Steele and Aronson's (1995) article provides.

psychologist Paulette Flore and her colleagues, showed no evidence for stereotype threat in 2,064 female high school students in 86 classrooms (Flore, Mulder, & Wicherts, 2018). While this study alone does not settle the argument about stereotype threat, it is the best evidence available at the time of writing. Flore and her team are conducting a replication study to determine whether teaching female examinees about stereotype threat raises their math test scores (Stoevenbelt, Wicherts, & Flore, 2019). If their work fails to replicate previous research supporting stereotype threat, then it will be a major blow to the stereotype threat theory – at least as it applies to female examinees.

The Future of Stereotype Threat? A controversy about stereotype threat is growing in psychology. In the fallout of the replication crisis, the evidence for stereotype threat looks increasingly weak. There is a strong possibility that much of the evidence supporting stereotype threat in females produces false positives due to publication bias and flexibility in study design and analysis that may inflate the evidence supporting the phenomenon.

However, the results from studies of stereotype threat in females may not generalize to the stereotype threat experience for members of racial groups. But there are good reasons to believe that higher-quality research will fail to support the existence of stereotype threat in racial minorities. Just as in the sex stereotype threat literature, publication bias and poor study design are endemic to the research on stereotype threat in racial groups (though the magnitude of these problems is not clear at this time). A study on race stereotype threat effects on African Americans with a planned sample size of 2,360 is underway at the time of writing (Forscher et al., 2019). It should provide some insight into whether race stereotype threat effects are real.

CONCLUSION

I want readers to know that the weaknesses in the research are not due to some sort of special incompetence among the scientists who investigate stereotype threat. The practices in these studies were typical in social psychology (the specialty of both Steele and Aronson). Many popular findings in social psychology are being questioned as psychologists reform their research practices and reduce or eliminate publication bias.[5] As a result, a disproportionately large number of popular or foundational findings in social psychology have failed to replicate (Open Science Collaboration, 2015). Stereotype threat in racial

---

[5] For example, social priming is the practice of showing research participants words or images associated with an idea (e.g., "greed" or "bank" to make people think about money) in order to influence behavior (e.g., donation to a charity). The evidence is now very strong that all the research supporting this technique consists of false positives (Chabris, Heck, Mandart, Benjamin, & Simons, 2019; Vadillo, Hardwick, & Shanks, 2016).

minorities may not hold up to the new standards of research, especially if publication bias is eliminated.

But no one knows for sure. I think readers can tell from my tone that I am skeptical. Social psychology has been hit hard by the replication crisis, and a lot of findings that seemed unshakable are now widely questioned – if not rejected – by psychologists. I used to believe in stereotype threat, and I taught it to my students as fact and as a cause of some of the average IQ score differences among racial groups. Now, I teach that stereotype threat is a contested theory. When the large-scale studies with improved methods are published, psychologists will know more. Until then, I believe that stereotype threat's status as an X-factor is "plausible, but unproven."

SOCIETAL AND ETHICAL ISSUES

The first six sections of this book are devoted to clarifying misunderstandings that the general public, journalists, and non-psychologists have about the scientific findings related to intelligence. It is understandable that non-specialists would have inaccurate beliefs about intelligence. Most people do not read scholarly articles, and they may not even know that their beliefs are mistaken. Section 7, which comprises Chapters 31 to 35, is different. Instead of focusing on the research itself, in this section I explore mistaken beliefs that people have regarding the societal and ethical implications of intelligence research.

- The topic of Chapter 31 is whether controversial or unpopular ideas should be banned or held to higher standards of research in the scientific community.
- Chapter 32 discusses the early twentieth-century eugenics movement – which many early intelligence researchers were a part of – and shows that past controversies do not contaminate modern research.
- Chapter 33 investigates whether intelligence research leads to negative social policies.
- In a similar vein, Chapter 34 discusses the claim that intelligence research undermines societal equality.
- Finally, Chapter 35 discusses the problems that arise in society when high-IQ people assume that everyone can make decisions as well as they can.

It should not be surprising that intelligence research has implications that extend far beyond the psychology community. Indeed, some chapters have already touched upon how intelligence relates to the education system (Chapters 15, 18–21), culture (Chapters 4, 10, 29), employment (Chapters 22–24), and societal inequality (Chapters 11, 19, 21–22, and 28). It is because intelligence correlates with outcomes in so many spheres of life that it has implications that societies and nations should contemplate. Unfortunately, many people have not fully considered these implications, which has resulted in the incorrect or overly simplistic conclusions that Chapters 31–35 show are mistaken.

In previous chapters my goal as an author has been to inform readers about the truth regarding intelligence and clarify misunderstandings. These last chapters will inevitably be different because they extend beyond facts and into the realms of ethics, values, and goals. These chapters will often deal with how people with varying social viewpoints can react to the facts about intelligence. It is impossible to hold any discussion about values and society without drawing on one's own ethical framework. In the spirit of transparency, I believe it is important for me to set out my relevant values so that readers can better understand – and perhaps critique – the arguments I make in Chapters 31–35. I have touched on some of these values in early portions of the book, such as in the introduction to Section 6 and in Chapter 17 (in the section about the type of intervention needed to equalize IQ) and Chapter 24 (in the discussion about the value of examining the meritocracy). Here are some ethical principles that I follow when contemplating intelligence research.

First, every human being is entitled – from the moment of their birth – to dignity and human rights. Although I stated this in the introduction to Section 6, it is not possible to overstate this principle enough. Regardless of someone's IQ score, the circumstances of their life, the language, culture, race, sex, or lifestyle, everyone deserves basic respect from their fellow human beings – and nothing can change that.

Second, the truth exists – and it is what it is. Versions of postmodern thought which postulate that truth is relative are inherently incapable of producing useful scientific knowledge because any "truth" that these philosophies discover is fundamentally ethereal and transient. Additionally, the truth does not care about human goals or desires. If a scientific fact conforms to a person's desires, then it is a happy accident; if not, then that is unfortunate, but raging against the truth will not make it conform to one's will. There is no guarantee that the truth will be what I want – or what anyone else wants.

Third, social goals and policies are much more likely to succeed if based on accurate scientific knowledge about the world and human psychology; programs based on incorrect ideas are much more likely to cause harm. I have mentioned this before (for example, in Chapter 5), but it is worth reiterating at the beginning of a section about societal implications of intelligence research. If a goal of applied social science is to help people, then a foundation in facts is essential. Policies based on incorrect understandings of the world often clash with reality and will frustrate policy makers when results fall short of their hopes. When such policies do work, they are often haphazard and inefficient. There is real harm and waste in programs and interventions that perpetuate falsehoods, set impossible goals, and create tension. I gave an example of this in Chapter 19 when discussing the "blame game" that often occurs in education when decision makers deny *g*.

Fourth, in an evolutionary perspective, differences are good for a species. One of the reasons humans have been a successful species in recent millennia is their collective biological, behavioral, and psychological diversity. None of these different traits are "good" or "bad" *per se*; different traits can lead to success in passing on one's genes. A species that is uniform in a critical trait may be at risk of extinction.

Finally, all ideas should be subjected to scrutiny and weighed against one another to determine which ones are best. No idea should receive a free pass or be accepted without a full examination. The "marketplace of ideas" can be brutal at times, but unfettered investigation of ideas is the best way of determining whether an idea or proposal is justifiable, logical, and/or preferable to other viewpoints.

My goal in this section is not to persuade readers to agree with my social or political beliefs. Instead, I hope to show how certain popular views about the implications of intelligence research are illogical or unjustified. Putting those ideas to rest will clear the arena for better proposals that can advance the social, political, and ethical conversation about topics related to intelligence. I do not have all the answers to the ethical questions and societal issues that arise when facts from intelligence research are applied to the real world, but I at least hope that these chapters will encourage readers to ask good questions and not fall into common, unproductive traps.

Controversial or Unpopular Ideas Should Be Held to a Higher Standard of Evidence

> When scientists deal with investigations that have relevance to immediate social policies, as studies of group differences can have, it is the duty of scientists to exercise a higher standard of scientific rigor in their research ... When you carry dynamite you should exercise more care than when you carry potatoes.
>
> (Hunt & Carlson, 2007, p. 195)

Science is built on the foundation that making new discoveries is a worthy goal. However, a single-minded pursuit of knowledge can be harmful. Classic stories like *Dr. Jekyll and Mr. Hyde* by Robert Louis Stevenson and Mary Shelley's *Frankenstein* serve as cautionary tales of the harm that can occur when a scientist prioritizes research goals over other concerns. Although the mad scientists in these stories are fictional, these books do raise valid questions about what limits should be placed on scientists as they conduct research.

It would be easy to dismiss these concerns if the harm from scientific research was confined to fiction. However, the history of science includes stories of real harm that people have experienced because scientists cared more about their research than the wellbeing of others. A prominent example is the development of nuclear weapons, which led to the deaths of over 100,000 people in Hiroshima and Nagasaki, Japan, in the closing days of World War II. However, the harm of nuclear weapons was not confined to the victims of wartime bombings. In the mid-1940s, the inhabitants of the Bikini Atoll were forcibly evacuated when the United States government decided to use their home as a testing ground for nearly two dozen nuclear weapons. The move devastated the islanders' culture and created a great deal of hardship as they struggled to adapt to their new homes on other islands. Similarly, open-air atomic bomb testing in the 1950s and 1960s in the United States spread radioactive material across several western states, elevating cancer rates among people who lived downwind of the test sites. These citizens were rarely – if ever – warned of the extent of the dangers from scientific research that occurred.

Another important example of scientific research causing harm is the Tuskegee Syphilis Study, which started in 1932 and continued until 1972 under the auspices of the United States federal government. In this study, physicians observed the progression of syphilis – a serious public health problem at the time – in 400 infected and 200 uninfected African American men. Most of these men were not fully told about the disease they carried and the possibility of spreading it to others. Even after an effective treatment was developed, the scientists and medical personnel running the study did not offer it to the study participants (Shweder, 2004). The outrage that ensued after the study was exposed in the press (e.g., J. Heller, 1972) led to the passage of the National Research Act in 1974, which requires ethical supervision of almost all scientific research in the United States that is performed on human subjects. Many other countries have similar laws governing scientific research on humans. As a result of the National Research Act, every scientist in the United States is trained in research ethics to ensure that they minimize the potential for harm and do not violate the rights of their research participants. Furthermore, almost all research on human subjects must be approved and supervised by an ethics board.

FIGURE 31.1 A participant in the Tuskegee Syphilis Study has blood drawn. Source: US National Archives (https://catalog.archives.gov/id/956117).

These examples – and many others – show that grave harm can occur when scientists put their goals above the wellbeing of their research participants or others who are affected by their research. There is broad consensus that ethical oversight is necessary to safeguard participants and protect them from harm. A committee created with the passage of the National Research Act identified three basic ethical principles that should govern research on humans: respect for persons, beneficence, and justice. Moreover, the group stated that researchers should obtain informed consent from participants, assess risks and benefits to ensure that the latter outweighs the former, and select participants in an ethical fashion without disadvantaging any group (The National Commission for the Protection of Human Subjects of Biomedical and Behavioral Research, 1979). The modern scientific community has willingly agreed to be bound by these principles.

ETHICAL PRINCIPLES APPLIED TO INTELLIGENCE RESEARCH

While the scientific community agrees with the general principles of ethical oversight, things are more complicated when applying those principles to real situations. The good news is that no one in the intelligence research community is endangering the health of research participants or the public in the way that the nuclear weapons scientists or the physicians running the Tuskegee Syphilis Study did. Indeed, it would be hard to endanger people to that extent in intelligence research, which often consists of administering intelligence tests and finding correlations between IQ scores and other variables.

But according to some views, "harm" extends beyond endangering physical health or evacuating people from their homes. Some scholars have argued that harm can develop when intelligence researchers investigate controversial topics. This harm may occur if the unfavourable political or social consequences of research are born disproportionately by people in poverty or people who belong to historically mistreated groups. For example, Singham (1995) expressed concern that research into the influence of intelligence on economic success could hurt the poor if the research were used to justify cutting social programs.[1] This is not the bodily harm experienced by nuclear test downwinders or Tuskegee Syphilis Study participants, but it could be harmful to people's livelihood or opportunities nevertheless. For example, Gerrig (2013) believed that information about group differences in IQ could cause decreased motivation and self-efficacy and make test scores into negative self-fulfilling prophecies for people, which is an example of how intelligence research might cause non-bodily harm by lowering people's motivation to accomplish difficult tasks.

---

[1] Chapter 33 discusses why intelligence research does not lead inevitably to unfavorable social policies.

Should Some IQ Research Be Banned? The most common topic that has elicited claims of harm is research into the cause of average differences in IQ scores among racial groups. At one extreme, some scholars believe that the very act of studying this topic was so harmful that it should be banned completely (e.g., Kourany, 2016; Rose, 2009). One scientist rhetorically asked, "Why, given all the world's problems and needs, would someone choose to investigate this thesis? What good could come of it?" (Horgan, 2013, paragraph 9; see also Sternberg, 2005, p. 296). Individuals who argue for a ban on this research believe that harm is inevitable, and so the ethical course of action is to not study average intelligence differences in racial groups or the causes of those differences. Logically, it would also be unethical to publish – or allow to be published – research that would cause inevitable harm (Rose, 2009).

This is nothing short of an argument for censorship,[2] and it encounters basic problems when put into practice. One problem is that no one has ever demonstrated any actual harm that has come from studying any topic in intelligence – including average racial differences in IQ (Carl, 2018). Indeed, accusations of grave harm from intelligence research have often been exaggerated (Fancher, 1985; Rushton, 1997; Snyderman & Herrnstein, 1983). On the other hand, the censors who wish to limit the study of some topics *have* done actual harm to intelligence researchers in the form of lost jobs, smeared reputations, inspiring physical violence, and limiting academic freedom and speech (Anomaly & Winegard, 2019; Carl, 2018; Carl & Woodley of Menie, 2019; Fancher, 1985; Gottfredson, 2010; Lynn, 2019; Nyborg, 2003; Wainer & Robinson, 2007). Real harm outweighs hypothetical harm, and the censors have inflicted real harm by trying to stop intelligence research that they do not like.

I think that these censors are motivated by compassion and concern, not malevolence. Some have seen how intelligence tests were used for damaging purposes in the past (see Chapter 32) and want to prevent future abuses (e.g., Gould, 1996). Others imagine future horrors, such as Turkheimer, who stated (1990, p. 430), "If it is ever documented conclusively, the genetic inferiority of a race on a trait as important as intelligence will rank with the atomic bomb as the most destructive scientific discovery in human history."[3] However, no one has shown that research into whether the average IQ differences across racial groups actually does harm people. The abuses of the past that I discuss in Chapter 32 were not based on scientific evidence that h_b^2 is greater than zero.

[2] James Flynn (of "Flynn effect" fame) mockingly described this position as, "I do not know if genetic equality is true and do not want anyone else to know" (Flynn, 2018, p. 127). His description makes the censorship of this position clear.

[3] One of the problems with Turkheimer's fear is that he equated a genetic difference with "genetic inferiority," a belief that I reject completely. I do not understand why someone concerned about potentially racist uses of science would endorse the racists' belief that genetic differences imply superiority or inferiority. Unfortunately, others who claim to be concerned with racism endorse this idea (e.g., Gillborn, 2016).

Research into the causes of between-group heritability differences started in earnest in the 1970s (e.g., Loehlin, Vandenberg, & Osborne, 1973; Scarr et al., 1977; Scarr & Weinberg, 1976) and has continued to the present (see Chapter 28). No one has had their human rights violated as a result of that research, and there are no indications that a catastrophe is any more imminent now than it was about 50 years ago when this research began.

Framing the argument for banning any type of research as censorship exposes another inherent problem with this viewpoint: it is not clear who should get to decide what research is banned. Nobody knows the future, and the implications of research are often not clear – even to the scientists who conduct that research (Ceci & Williams, 2009; Cofnas, 2016; Davis, 1978). Asking any mere mortal to anticipate every positive and negative consequence of research is asking for the impossible: total omniscience.

The standards by which to judge which research topics are dangerous are equally unclear. To some commentators (e.g., Martshenko, Trejo, & Domingue, 2019), topics that could encourage racism or sexism are obvious candidates for censorship. This argument is that the research *per se* is not the problem; rather, society is too racist and sexist for some topics to be researched freely because results might provide aid and comfort to racists and sexists (e.g., Horgan, 2013; Kouray, 2016; Roberts, 2015; Rose, 2009). But bigots existed long before scientific research on intelligence started. Banning some research topics until sexism and racism are completely eliminated holds science hostage to the bigots in society and gives those bigots power to silence scientists.

Others are better at explaining what type of research would pass muster for them. For example, Kourany (2016) suggested that any research that endangers equality should be placed off limits. But this guideline is obviously flawed. If "equality" means "sameness," then all research into individual or group differences would be banned, including research into topics like personality, academic achievement, genetics, and health disparities across groups. If "equality" is taken to mean "legal equality," then Kourany's (2016) guideline is mistaken because legal equality does not depend on science, but rather on the willingness of a nation's political class to pass and enforce laws that guarantee legal equality. Chapter 34 discusses this issue in more depth.

With Great Power Comes Great Responsibility? A less extreme argument is that research into controversial topics is acceptable, but that it must be done with great care and held to the highest standards (e.g., Ceci & Williams, 2009; Hunt & Sternberg, 2005). This is the argument that Hunt and Carlson (2007) were making when they wrote, "When you carry dynamite you should exercise more care than when you carry potatoes" (p. 195). For people with this viewpoint, the consequences of a poorly designed study are so drastic that only the most impeccable studies that suggest dangerous conclusions should be published (e.g., Hunt & Sternberg, 2005).

While this position is preferable to the position of censoring all intelligence research, it is a double standard (Gottfredson, 2009, p. 52) and in practice serves as a backdoor method of covert censorship (Cofnas, 2016). No study in the social sciences is perfect, so when provocative research occurs, it is easy for the scientific community to censor it under the guise of ensuring research quality. If the same standards were applied to all research, then this would not be a problem. But inevitably, the higher standard is applied to studies that the scientific community labels as "divisive," "controversial," or "inflammatory" (Gottfredson, 2009). Studies with politically correct results, though, are held to a lower standard of quality and receive more acclaim from the scientific community (Ceci & Williams, 2009).

Non-scientists might be surprised by this tendency because the mechanisms of censorship are not clear to outsiders. Hidden censorship occurs because scientists often review one another's work in order to evaluate whether the study warrants publication. This system is called *peer review*, and it is intended to function as a quality control mechanism. Most studies submitted to scholarly journals receive reviews from 2–5 scientists who are anonymous so that they are free to comment about the author's work without repercussions. After reviews are made, a senior scientist who serves as a journal editor decides whether the study should be published. Appeals are usually not possible and are rarely successful.

The problem for controversial research is that this system makes it easy to apply unrealistically high standards of quality so that scientists who disagree with a study can prevent it from being published. An editor can purposely select hostile reviewers in order to generate negative reviews for a study that she or he does not like. Even if an editor is fair, a sufficiently negative review – ostensibly about the study's methodology but covertly motivated by a dislike for the conclusions or the topic – from one or two reviewers can create the illusion that a study is too flawed to publish. Editors have *carte blanche* over their journals and can reject a study for any reason. As a result, politically correct research is published more often and appears in more prestigious scientific journals. And it can all happen without anyone explicitly saying they are censoring a study. Instead, the reviews are full of pious concerns for "rigor" and "quality"[4] (e.g., T. P. Hill, 2018). This process is not unique to controversial topics in intelligence research; scholars in other fields have commented about how peer review can function as a tool for censorship (e.g., Beaver, Nedelec, da Silva Costa, & Vidal, 2015). Because the double standard of requiring controversial research to meet higher methodological requirements functions as a form of censorship, it still causes nearly the same harm as a complete ban.

---

[4] I know this sounds like an elaborate conspiracy theory, but it is reality. I have experienced censorship in the peer review process multiple times. Thankfully, there are some professional, fair-minded editors who have given my work a chance.

It is telling that scholars who demand extra care for controversial intelligence research do not design studies that meet their standards to investigate controversial topics. If their concern for methodological rigor were fully genuine, they would conduct the studies that they demand. This would be the only way to both answer important scientific questions and ensure that those answers are based on trustworthy data. But the critics never seem interested in collecting the data that they demand from others.

Nobody wants shoddy research in the social sciences, and scientists can have legitimate disagreements about whether a study is good enough to publish or not. However, those judgments should not be dependent on the research topic or the results of a study, and standards should be applied evenly. Anything less is backdoor censorship, which is a disservice to science and society.

IGNORANCE IS NOT BLISS

I have already mentioned the harm that individual scientists researching controversial topics have experienced. But there are harms that society and science incur because choosing not to conduct research is a decision itself, and that decision has consequences.

The first consequence is that controversies linger unresolved. Without data to resolve controversies, it is impossible to arrive at the truth. An example of this is the evidence that I presented in Chapter 28 that differences in average IQ among racial groups are not entirely environmental in origin. However, (in my judgment) there is not enough evidence available to provide stable, trustworthy estimates of h_b^2. Maybe heritability of intelligence across groups within the United States is currently minuscule, perhaps .05. If so, then this result would not be a great threat to people who hold egalitarian beliefs and hope to find environmental solutions to closing IQ gaps across groups (Hunt, 2011). If h_b^2 within the United States is much larger, such as the .80 value that Gottfredson (2005b) thought was plausible, then this is important to know because it would resolve the controversy. That would then free up scientists and lawmakers to devise policies accordingly. But because the controversy of a between-group heritability value has festered for much longer than it needed to, it has become impossible to move on and figure out how to deal with reality.

Another way that society is harmed by not studying controversial topics is that it creates a vacuum for extremists to fill. Again, average racial group differences in intelligence are a perfect example of this. There are people who are going to seek out information about this topic. If well-informed scientists with good data do not discuss average racial differences in IQ, then the only sources of information about this sensitive topic will be – at best – inaccurate and overly simplified. At worst, these sources of information will be racist and extremist (Winegard et al., 2017). Open discussion based on scientific research can crowd out extremist views, correct inaccuracies (Jeffery & Shackelford,

2018), and prevent people with little concern for evidence and ethics from controlling the conversation.

Another way that suppressing research into controversial topics harms society is that it infantilizes the public. For example, some people have argued that it may be necessary to prevent controversial research because of how it can harm segments of society that are seen as vulnerable, such as women, minorities, or people living in poverty (e.g., Jeffery & Shackelford, 2018; Singham, 1995). While this motivation has good intentions, it is inherently patronizing because it implies that scientists see these groups as being too fragile to handle reality and needing benevolent protectors who should make decisions on their behalf. Moreover, it shows that scientists do not trust people and society as a whole to make ethical decisions. Gottfredson (2000a, pp. 79–80) summarized this point well:

> When critics impugn the very notion [of partially genetic causes of individual differences in life outcomes] ... and portray it as the first step toward tragedy, they indicate that they do not trust the American people to make certain political decisions. The same people who abolished slavery, dismantled racial segregation, and destroyed Hitler would, they seem to suggest, tumble head-long into a deadly fascism. To keep us from deciding "wrongly" – from wronging democracy itself – critics justify withholding information from us.

People who argue that some research should be forbidden are stating that they should exercise undemocratic power to keep society in ignorance. Of course, they rationalize their thirst for this power by claiming that it is a virtuous exercise to help protect society. But, inevitably, it is an exercise in paternalistic censorship.

Finally, banning or inhibiting research on controversial topics creates harm because it prevents information that can improve people's lives. The research of James Flynn demonstrates this point well. Flynn is an impeccably honest scientist and longtime foe of the argument that race differences have any genetic cause. When Flynn encountered hereditarian arguments for IQ differences, he launched his own research on the topic. As a result, he documented the worldwide, regular nature of the Flynn effect (see Chapter 14), which provided the strongest evidence that environmental influences could have a powerful effect on IQ scores. One product of Flynn effect research is that it has shown that older tests overestimate IQ. As a result, some American prisoners who would have been executed were shown to have intellectual disabilities when retested with modern tests. This saved their lives because it is unconstitutional in the United States to execute someone with an intellectual disability.[5] Flynn's research has saved lives, but it never would

---

[5] The relevant Supreme Court cases are *Atkins v. Virginia* (2002) and *Hall v. Florida* (2014). These cases were a culmination of a long history of using intelligence tests to demonstrate that defendants with intellectual disabilities were not fully culpable for their crimes and therefore should be acquitted or spared the death penalty. See Zenderland (1998, Chapter 6) and Terman (1918) for early examples of these attempts – some of which were successful.

have happened if he had not first encountered research on racial differences in IQ and decided to pursue the topic himself (Flynn, 2018). Research into controversial topics related to intelligence may or may not provide other information that will make people's lives better or result in interventions that improve cognitive abilities in individuals who currently score low on intelligence tests. The only way to find out is to permit the research. Blocking the research – or needlessly increasing the difficulty of conducting and/or disseminating such research – will prevent anyone from reaping any possible benefits of that work.

CONCLUSION: MORE KNOWLEDGE IS BETTER THAN LESS

Everyone agrees that ethical constraints on science are necessary to minimize harm and preserve the human rights of research participants. However, there is legitimate debate about whether some research can cause harm – if broadly defined – to individuals or to society as a whole. As a result, some people argue that research into controversial topics may need to be curtailed.

However noble this impulse is, it is – at its heart – censorious and damaging. More knowledge is better than less, unless one can prove that the negative consequences of research outweigh the benefits (Jeffrey & Shackelford, 2018). *To date, no one has shown that the drawbacks are greater than the benefits of research into any topic related to intelligence.* And because the consequences of research are often unanticipated, it is not even clear whether this sort of cost–benefit analysis could even produce accurate judgments. There is no reason to assume that banning controversial research into intelligence is an ethical course of action (Carl, 2018). Given the benefits that have accrued from controversial research and the absence of any resulting societal catastrophe, the best course of action is to allow free, unfettered inquiry into controversial topics related to intelligence.

Past Controversies Taint Modern Research on Intelligence

> Anyone advocating for the SAT as a tool of educational justice cannot ignore the test's detestable past. The SAT was created by Carl Campbell Brigham ... At the time, Brigham was an enthusiastic eugenicist who believed that intelligence was genetic and that different races and ethnicities were biologically more intelligent than others ... But while the SAT has tried to break from its eugenic roots, it still serves the same purpose across time and ideology: to sort human populations deeming high-scorers as valued and deserving of opportunity, and by deeming low-scorers as unvalued and undeserving of opportunity. This is as true of the SAT now as it was almost a hundred years go.
>
> (Au, 2018, paragraphs 5 and 7)

"What's past is prologue," Shakespeare wrote in *The Tempest*, saying that history can influence current events. This is apparent in science, where new ideas and knowledge do not just emerge spontaneously. Rather scientific advances and discoveries are the consequences of (or reaction to) earlier theories and data. Even when a discovery is accidental, a scientist cannot recognize the importance of what they observe without previous training and theory.

Intelligence research is also a product of its past. As an example, Binet's first test, published in 1905, was not the sudden discovery that histories of intelligence testing often describe (e.g., Gould, 1981, 1996; R. M. Kaplan & Saccuzzo, 2018). Actually, Binet had been studying cognitive development in children for a decade before he attempted to create his test for the Parisian school system (Wolf, 1973), and he was influenced by debates in Europe about how best to diagnose and treat intellectual disabilities (Nicolas, Andrieu, Croizet, Sanitioso, & Burman, 2013). Furthermore, many of the tasks he would put on his tests were used in psychological and educational research previously (Gibbons & Warne, 2019).

While the past influences the present, this does not mean that people are prisoners of the past. Ideas can be rejected, and people or nations can chart a new course if they are unsatisfied with the status quo. This is especially true in science, where old theories and assumptions are constantly re-evaluated, debated, and tested. When these ideas fail to accurately describe reality or make useful predictions, then the ideas of the past should be discarded. That is a vital part of science. Thus, while "What's past is prologue," it is not binding on the present.

Unfortunately, some critics of intelligence research do not recognize this. These individuals try to smear intelligence research and testing by associating its present practice with the errors and controversies of the past (e.g., Au, 2018; Gould, 1981, 1996; Newby & Newby, 1995). My purpose in writing this chapter is to accurately recount the ugly actions and beliefs of early intelligent theorists and describe the context of these scientists' actions. I also have the goal of explaining how this past still influences – though it does not constrain – the present. However, I have no interest in being an apologist for the mistakes of the past or for minimizing the negative consequences that sometimes occurred because of those errors.

"O BRAVE NEW WORLD THAT HAS SUCH PEOPLE IN'T!"

Birth of Eugenics. Early in its history, intelligence research got attached to the ideology of *eugenics*. This was a scientific and social movement that began in the late nineteenth century that was concerned with using scientific principles to improve the genetic makeup and/or quality of life of future generations. Historians are correct to link eugenics with early intelligence research. Sir Francis Galton, who was the first person to attempt to measure intelligence scientifically (see the Introduction), coined the term "eugenics" (F. Galton, 1883). The word came from Ancient Greek language roots and literally translates as "well born."

Galton believed that many traits, behaviors, and diseases were inherited and that it would be in everyone's best interest to ensure that healthier, well-adjusted individuals passed their genes onto future generations and that sickly individuals did not do so. He was not shy about what this would require:

The more merciful form of what I venture to call "eugenics" would consist in watching for the indications of superior strains or races,[1] and in so favouring them that their progeny shall outnumber and gradually replace that of the old one. (F. Galton, 1883, p. 307)

Galton was clearly inspired by the work of his relative, Charles Darwin, on natural selection (Gillham, 2001). Galton believed that natural selection was

---

[1] The use of the word "races" in this quote does not necessarily refer to racial groups; a better understanding would be "lineages" of people. Darwin used the word in the same way. However, eugenics did often take on racial connotations, as I will describe later in this chapter.

slow, too random, and not guaranteed to produce desirable results. He thought that humans would benefit from taking charge of their own evolution, and eugenics was the theoretical road map he created for doing so (D. J. Galton & Galton, 1998). Among the traits that Galton thought worthy of passing on to future generations was intelligence (e.g., F. Galton, 1907). He believed that it was in society's best interest to encourage the educated upper classes (whom he believed were more intelligent than the general population) to have larger families, and he proposed a scheme where people could have their health and family history inspected so that they could be certified as a desirable marriage partner (Gillham, 2001). To reduce the number of "undesirable" offspring in future generations, Galton suggested isolating them in monastery-like communities (Kevles, 1995). He would be an advocate of eugenics until his death in 1911.

Spread of an Idea. As a famous public intellectual and prominent scientist, Galton did not struggle to find outlets for his ideas. They spread throughout the world, and eugenics societies were formed in many European countries, the United States, Canada, Japan, India, Brazil, Argentina, and elsewhere. As eugenics spread to different countries, it took on different forms, all with the goal of modifying the genetic makeup of the next generation. In Scandinavian nations, eugenics was used to reduce the future burden on the expanding welfare state, which led to the passage of sterilization laws and some of the world's first abortion laws (Broberg & Tydén, 2005; Hansen, 2005). Eugenicists in Latin America focused on anti-alcoholism and improving sanitation and hygiene (Stepan, 1991).

The United States pioneered forced sterilization for eugenic purposes. In 1907, Indiana passed the first law permitting compulsory sterilization of individuals who were thought to be at risk for passing on their unfavored traits. By 1930, 28 states had laws permitting involuntary sterilization (Burgdorf & Burgdorf, 1977), which the US Supreme Court declared in 1927 were constitutional (*Buck v. Bell*).[2] Although the case concerned a woman who was "feeble-minded" (to use the language of the time), these compulsory sterilization laws were also used on people who had epilepsy, bipolar disorder, dementia, schizophrenia, and other conditions. Some laws also permitted the sterilization of people convicted of rape, prostitution, and other

[2] Justice Oliver Wendell Holmes, Jr.'s opinion is repulsive reading. He wrote that compulsory sterilization laws were necessary "in order to prevent our being swamped with incompetence" (*Buck v. Bell*, 1927, p. 273) and that, "Three generations of imbeciles are enough" (p. 274). This comment referred to the patient, her supposedly "feeble-minded" mother, and "feeble-minded" daughter born out of wedlock. The ruling to sterilize the woman, named Carrie Buck, was not a close decision: 8–1. Adding to the tragedy of this decision is that the family had normal intelligence and that the attorney representing Ms. Buck colluded with the opposing lawyer to inaccurately present her as being "feeble-minded" in order to have a test case for the court to uphold the sterilization law (Lombardo, 1985).

offenses.[3] In the twentieth century, the United States sterilized approximately 60,000 individuals; one-third of those were in California (Stern, 2005).

The most memorable and widely known form of the eugenics movement occurred in Germany in the 1930s and 1940s. German medical writers had promoted eugenics in the 1920s, and on July 14, 1933 (just a few months after Adolf Hitler finished consolidating his power), Germany passed a compulsory sterilization law. All commentators agree that this law was based on laws passed in the United States (e.g., Burgdorf & Burgdorf, 1977; Grodin, Miller, & Kelly, 2018; Kevles, 1995; Lombardo, 1985), though the German law had distinct characteristics that were absent in American laws, such as the ability to sterilize non-institutionalized individuals. After over 350,000 citizens were sterilized by 1939, the German eugenics program expanded to euthanasia (at least 200,000 killed by 1941) before the concentration camps opened, where millions were murdered (Grodin et al., 2018). A lesser-known aspect of German eugenics policies is the *Lebensborn* program, which consisted of government-funded facilities to raise "racially pure" children who were often fathered by S.S. officers who had been in relationships with "Aryan" women (Kevles, 1995). Nazi Germany also encouraged "desirable" births through the creation of the Cross of Honor of the German Mother, which was awarded to ethnic German women who had large families.[4]

The German eugenics program had a racial component that saw entire groups of people – not just individuals – as genetically desirable. Encouraging these groups to reproduce and others not to was not unique to Germany; a racial form of eugenics also occurred in the United States and elsewhere. Positive and negative stereotypes were generalized to every member of racial or ethnic groups, with views of "industriousness" and "honesty" being attributed to politically dominant racial groups and negative traits ascribed to minority or politically weaker groups (Kevles, 1995). Combined with laws and policies to curb birth rates, this racial form of eugenics often meant that minorities were disproportionately sterilized in the United States (Kevles, 1995; Stern, 2005). In Germany, minorities – especially Jews – were murdered in concentration camps by the millions.

Intelligence Researchers and Eugenics. It is undisputed that early intelligence researchers were advocates of eugenics. One prominent advocate was the psychologist Henry H. Goddard, who published a famous case study of an extended family. Both branches of the family were descended from a common eighteenth-century ancestor who had an illegitimate son with a "feeble-minded girl" (Goddard, 1912, p. 18), of whom the majority of traceable descendants were allegedly also "feeble-minded." This family also counted among its ranks

---

[3] Which conditions or crimes warranted sterilization varied from state to state and from time to time, as laws were enacted or altered.

[4] In 1920, Finland initiated a similar award for mothers of large families. The creation of this award was eugenic in purpose (Hietala, 2005).

a number of supposed prostitutes, alcoholics, criminals, and epileptics. Later, the ancestor married "a respectable girl of good family, and through that union has come another line of descendants of radically different character ... All of them are normal people" (Goddard, 1912, p. 29). The book seemed to vindicate many of the eugenicists' beliefs about the importance of heritability and the transmission of positive and negative psychological traits.

Goddard's work was influential because he was a leading expert on intellectual disabilities. At about the same time, he was popularizing intelligence testing in the United States (e.g., Goddard, 1910), and a few years later he would serve on the committee that created the Army Alpha and Army Beta tests in World War I (Carson, 1993; Zenderland, 1998). For Goddard's eugenics, intelligence testing was an important tool for diagnosing people with intellectual disabilities so that their reproduction could be prevented, preferably by confining people with undesirable traits. He also favored sterilization, though he did not think that this should be the primary way of preventing people with intellectual disabilities from having children (Zenderland, 1998). But either method would supposedly prevent intellectual disabilities from spreading in later generations (Goddard, 1914).

Goddard was not alone in his use of intelligence tests to serve eugenics. The creator of the Stanford–Binet intelligence test agreed with Goddard and stated:

It is safe to predict that in the near future intelligence tests will bring tens of thousands of these high-grade defectives under the surveillance and protection of society. This will ultimately result in curtailing the reproduction of feeble-mindedness and in the elimination of an enormous amount of crime, pauperism, and industrial inefficiency. (Terman, 1916, pp. 6–7)

It was a consensus position among psychologists in the 1910s and 1920s to endorse eugenics, and most early psychologists interested in intelligence were eugenicists. This includes Carl Brigham (the creator of the SAT) and many of the creators of the army intelligence tests during World War I (Warne, 2019a). Most of these intelligence researchers (though not Goddard) endorsed forms of eugenics that had a racial component to them, and they were open about their bias against non-European groups (e.g., Terman, 1916). Due to the influence of Galton, eugenics was also widely accepted among British psychologists, including Spearman.

This endorsement of eugenics was not half-hearted. Terman called intelligence testing "the beacon light of the eugenics movement" (1924, p. 106) because eugenics was a practical use of psychological research. Intelligence testing was an objective, scientific method of identifying some of the people whom the eugenicists believed should not reproduce, which would reduce errors and help achieve eugenic goals more efficiently. The place of intelligence testing within the eugenics movement is clear in Figure 32.1, which is an image used at the Second International Eugenics Congress, held in 1921. The image shows "Mental Testing" (almost entirely synonymous with intelligence testing at the time) as

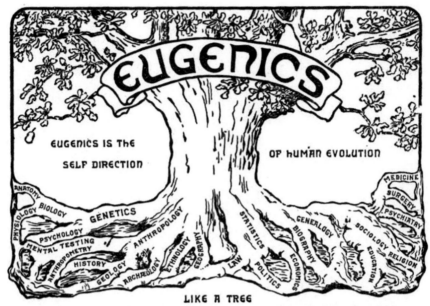

FIGURE 32.1 Image used on the "Certificate Awarded for Meritorious Exhibits" at the Second International Eugenics Congress, held September 25–28, 1921, in New York City. The image likens eugenics to a tree with its roots in many different fields. Two of the roots on the left side of the image are labeled "Psychology" and "Mental Testing," indicating that the organizers of the conference saw these two fields as making important contributions to eugenics.
Source: Laughlin, 1923, p. 15.

one of the roots of the "eugenics tree." Figure 32.2 shows a similar image displayed in the exhibit hall at the Third International Eugenics Congress, held in 1932.

Because of the undeniable history of eugenics, some critics of intelligence research and testing attempt to make a direct connection between the pioneers of the intelligence research who were eugenicists and modern scientists researching intelligence (e.g., Au, 2018; Gould, 1981, 1996; Newby & Newby, 1995; Roberts, 2015). This criticism ignores or oversimplifies the historical realities of the eugenics movement and the real legacy of eugenics for today.

EUGENICS: THEN AND NOW

Everybody was Doing It (Almost). Early twentieth-century eugenics had widespread support from the social, scientific, and economic elites in many

FIGURE 32.2 Image associated with the Third International Eugenics Congress, held August 21–23, 1932, in New York City. This image was displayed in the exhibit hall at the American Museum of Natural History from August 21 to October 1, 1932. Over 15,000 people visited the exhibit hall (Perkins et al., 1934, p. 486). Just like Figure 32.1, the image likens eugenics to a tree with its roots in many different fields, including "Psychology" and "Mental Testing" (on the lower left part of drawing).
Source: Perkins et al., 1934, p. 511.

different countries (Kevles, 1995; Stepan, 1991). Table 32.1 lists some of the prominent supporters of eugenics in the early twentieth century. Based on this list, it is apparent that eugenic beliefs were not confined to psychologists or intelligence researchers. Indeed, many luminaries from all over the world advocated eugenics, and support for the movement was widespread. The most organized, consistent resistance to eugenics at the time came from the Catholic Church,[5] though scattered opposition was also found among non-Catholics and secularists (Kevles, 1995).

The list in Table 32.1 is not comprehensive. These are only some of the names that many twenty-first-century English speakers would recognize today. A full list of prominent eugenicists from 100 years ago would include many names that have since been forgotten (such as Daisy M. O. Robinson, the first female dermatologist and a woman decorated by France for her medical service during World War I) and people who are mostly known only within their fields of expertise (like Paul Popenoe, an agriculturalist and founder of the field of marriage counseling). It is also important to recognize that these people's endorsement of eugenics varied, and that not all of them approved of every aspect of eugenics. There was a lot of disagreement among eugenicists about which interventions would "improve" future generations and what actions were socially, politically, and morally acceptable.

I did not compile this list to justify the eugenic beliefs of early intelligence researchers. (There is no possible justification for beliefs or practices that rob people of their human rights and/or dignity.) Instead, the list shows that advocacy of eugenics was typical in the early twentieth century. Eugenics was an international movement with widespread support from many intellectuals and leaders. The sin of eugenics is not something unique to early intelligence researchers. If modern intelligence researchers are to be condemned for their field's links to eugenics, then almost every field that existed in the early twentieth century is similarly condemned.

The argument that intelligence pioneers' advocacy of eugenics contaminates the modern field is guilt by association. The poor logic of this argument becomes apparent when applied to the non-psychologists in Table 32.1. For example, H. G. Wells advocated eugenics, so through this guilt by association anyone who enjoys his science fiction stories approves of Wells's eugenics. By the same logic, anyone who uses the Gini coefficient to measure income inequality endorses Corrado Gini's eugenics. Of course, this argument is absurd. Science – indeed culture – is a buffet. Future generations are allowed to pick and choose ideas that they approve of and reject those that they do not. Using one idea from a eugenicist of the past does not imply that their eugenic ideas are accepted today, nor does it mean that modern work that builds on accepted ideas is contaminated (Warne, 2019a).

---

[5] Catholic opposition to eugenics had its most formal expression in 1930 when Pope Pius XI issued the encyclical *Casti connubii*, which enunciated the Church's views.

TABLE 32.1 *Prominent people who endorsed eugenics in the early twentieth century*

Name	Occupation	Notes
Arthur Balfour	Politician	Prime minister of the UK
Alexander Graham Bell	Inventor	Chaired the Second International Eugenics Congress
Winston Churchill	Politician	Prime minister of the UK, attended the First International Eugenics Conference
Calvin Coolidge	Politician	30th President of the United States
Charles Darwin	Naturalist	Originator of modern evolutionary theory
Leonard Darwin	Economist	Son of Charles Darwin, founder of the Eugenics Education Society
George Eastman	Inventor	Founder of the Eastman Kodak corporation
Sir Ronald A. Fisher	Statistician and agriculturalist	Father of modern statistics
F. Scott Fitzgerald	Author	
Sigmund Freud	Neurologist and psychoanalyst	
Sir Francis Galton	Scientist, explorer, and author	Coined the word "eugenics" and founded the eugenics movement
Corrado Gini	Statistician	Inventor of the Gini coefficient, which measures income inequality
Emma Goldman	Social activist	Anarchist and feminist
Oliver Wendell Holmes, Jr.	Justice of the Supreme Court of the US	Wrote opinion for *Buck v. Bell* (1927)
Helen Keller	Author and social activist	
John Harvey Kellogg	Physician	Co-inventor of corn flakes, founded the eugenic Human Betterment Foundation
John Maynard Keynes	Economist	
Charles Lindbergh	Aviator	
Hermann Joseph Muller	Geneticist	Nobel Prize winner for his research on the genetic effects of radiation
Karl Pearson	Statistician	Student of Fisher and Galton
John D. Rockefeller, Jr.	Financier	
Theodore Roosevelt	Politician	26th President of the United States
Margaret Sanger	Social activist	Founder of Planned Parenthood and advocate of birth control access
George Bernard Shaw	Author	
William Shockley	Physicist	Nobel Prize winner for his work developing the transistor
Charles Spearman	Psychologist	Inventor of factor analysis and discoverer of g

(*continued*)

TABLE 32.1. (*continued*)

Name	Occupation	Notes
Nikola Tesla	Inventor	
Richard Webster	Judge	Lord Chief Justice of the UK, attended the First International Eugenics Conference
H. G. Wells	Author	
Woodrow Wilson	Politician and academic	28th President of the United States; signed a compulsory sterilization bill into law while governor of New Jersey
Victoria Woodhull	Political activist	First woman to run for the US presidency

Note. Prominent psychologists involved with intelligence testing who endorsed eugenics included Carl Brigham, Sir Cyril Burt, Margaret V. Cobb, Henry H. Goddard, G. Stanley Hall, Leta Hollingworth, Truman Kelley, Lewis Terman, Edward Thorndike, and Robert Yerkes.

The smear of intelligence research as being modern eugenics also ignores a salient fact about eugenics: throughout its history, psychologists had little influence in eugenics. Indeed, histories of eugenics rarely or never mention psychologists; most of the leading eugenicists of the early twentieth century were physicians, biologists, and social reformers (Broberg & Roll-Hansen, 2005; Kevles, 1995; MacKenzie, 1976; Stepan, 1991). This is apparent, for example, in the minor role that psychologists had in the International Eugenics Congresses.[6] In the United States, the two most prominent eugenicists in the early twentieth century were Harry H. Laughlin (a sociologist) and Charles Davenport (a biologist), and eugenic psychologists seem to have had comparatively little influence on social policy or law (Snyderman & Herrnstein, 1983). In the United Kingdom, Karl Pearson (a statistician and Galton's follower) took up the eugenics baton after Galton's death, though he cared little for policy (Kevles, 1995). In Germany, the National Socialist (i.e., Nazi) Party opposed intelligence research, seeing it as bourgeois. They also rejected *g* as being too theoretical and preferred a practical definition and measure of intelligence (Rindermann, 2018, p. 61). If Nazi Germany had embraced intelligence testing, the higher average IQ scores for European Jews would have embarrassed the regime and undermined some of Germany's eugenic policies (Mackintosh, 2011, p. 20).

One common belief is that eugenics quickly fell out of fashion once the world saw the horrors of the Nazi eugenics program in the closing months of World

[6] At the three International Eugenics Congresses, biologists were the most common type of speaker. At the First International Eugenics Congress, no psychologists spoke or presented papers. Out of the 105 speakers at the Second International Eugenics Congress, there were 5 psychologists, 4 psychiatrists, and 1 neuropsychiatrist (9.5%). There were 70 speakers at the Third International Eugenics Congress, of whom 4 were psychologists, and 1 was a psychiatrist (7.1%).

War II (e.g., Gould, 1981; Newby & Newby, 1995). This is completely false. Eugenics policies in many countries persisted long after the war. In the United States, forced sterilizations continued into the 1970s. The sterilization law in California – where more forced sterilizations occurred than in any other state – was not repealed until 1979 (Stern, 2005), the same year that Virginia performed the last compulsory sterilization in the United States (Kaelber, 2011). Oregon was the last state to repeal its compulsory sterilization law in 1983 (Kaelber, 2011). Japan repealed its eugenic compulsory sterilization law in 1996 (Hurst, 2019).

In Scandinavia, the story was similar, with eugenic forced sterilizations usually occurring until the laws were repealed. Denmark's law lasted until 1967 (Hansen, 2005), Finland's until 1970 (Hietala, 2005), Sweden's until 1975 (Broberg & Tydén, 2005), and Norway's until 1977 (Roll-Hansen, 2005). Throughout Scandinavia, people openly advocated certain aspects of eugenics, such as the prevention of the birth of individuals with severe disabilities, for decades after World War II (Koch, 2006).

The lingering of eugenics is also apparent in the names of the organizations that promoted it. The American Eugenics Society did not change its name until 1973, and the Eugenics Society (in Britain) did not change its name until 1989. The scientific journal *Eugenics Quarterly* was *started* in 1954 and held this name until 1969. All these dates show that it took about a generation after World War II for "eugenics" to become a dirty word.

Worldwide, remnants of eugenics persist. Laws permitting the abortion of viable but disabled fetuses have their roots in the early eugenics movement. With the identification of genetic diseases (for example, sickle cell anemia), some individuals seek genetic counseling to learn their probabilities of having a child with a disease, and they use this information to choose whether to have children (Kevles, 1995). Untold numbers of people choose to experience vasectomies and tubal ligations to sterilize themselves, though often in a reversible manner. Many sperm banks and egg donation clinics advertise the physical and psychological traits – including intelligence – of their donors because of the belief that these traits may be passed on to children.[7] All of these practices alter the genetic makeup of the next generation and are eugenic in effect, even though no one uses the term "eugenic" to describe them.

New technologies are forcing society to grapple with eugenics again. In 2018, a Chinese scientist, He Jiankui, announced that he had eliminated a single gene in human embryos to make the resulting twin girls more resistant to HIV, the

---

[7] Everybody becomes a eugenicist when they have to choose a sperm or egg donor. Otherwise, they would not care about knowing anything about the donor, and there would be no market for donors with traits that parents find desirable in children. If you doubt me, watch what happens if you suggest to a friend who is looking for a sperm or egg donor that they use a homeless person with severe schizophrenia, a history of violent crime, and low IQ as their donor. Even selecting a donor at random is highly undesirable to people trying to conceive a child.

virus that causes AIDS (Regalado, 2018). This claim has not been independently verified, but experts do not dispute that the technology exists now to make gene modification of human embryos a possibility. And it is highly plausible that it will be used once it can be ensured that the technology is safe. A majority of Americans in one poll (Pew Research Center, 2018) approve of using gene editing to treat a serious condition that would be present at a baby's birth (72%) or reduce the risk of a serious disease that could develop later (60%). This is a eugenic use of modern technology. Even eugenic policies from a century ago have an audience today. In a different poll conducted in 2018, over 40% of respondents supported policies that encouraged people who were poor, unintelligent, or with a serious criminal record to have fewer children. Over 30% supported shortening prison sentences for sterilized criminals (Zigerell, 2019).

Gene editing may or may not be a current reality. But even if He Jiankui's claim is correct, using gene editing to raise intelligence is not feasible right now. Current gene-editing technology can only change a small number of genes; it would therefore have a negligible effect on IQ because intelligence is influenced by thousands of genes, each with a minuscule impact. But if gene editing ever became a safe and viable way to raise intelligence, there are people that would be interested in applying it to their own children. Almost one-fifth of Americans (19%) believe that it would be appropriate to use gene editing to raise a baby's intelligence (Pew Research Center, 2018).

However, using a different currently existing technology, it is possible to screen embryos created through in-vitro fertilization to estimate their future IQ and implant the embryos with the highest predicted IQ (Plomin, 2018; Wilson, 2018). The use of this technology is not limited to intelligence; scientists could just as easily screen and select embryos on the basis of psychological health, height, or personality traits, if that is what the parents desire.

The fact that eugenics still occurs – though not under that name – raises an important question about how to prevent the abuses of the early twentieth century as eugenics is practiced in the twenty-first century. Chapter 33 will discuss how to ensure that modern eugenics avoids repeating the disastrous mistakes of the early twentieth century.

CODA

In all of this history, an important fact is missing: the same pioneering psychologists who advocated eugenics turned their backs on the movement. Some publicly renounced their earlier eugenic work, such as Carl Brigham and Henry H. Goddard (Fancher, 1985; Kevles, 1995; Zenderland, 1998). Others quietly withdrew support, such as Lewis Terman (Minton, 1988). These men were part of a general movement of scientists away from eugenics in the 1920s and 1930s as the scientific assumptions underpinning eugenics were found to be incorrect or wildly exaggerated (Kevles, 1995).

Furthermore, eugenics in any form is not very relevant to the research questions that most modern intelligence researchers are investigating, such as the neurobiology of intelligence (see Chapter 3) or how to increase intelligence permanently (see Chapters 15–16). When intelligence research is relevant to eugenics, such as in the identification of alleles that are associated with intelligence, this information can be used for good or for bad. While it has an ugly history, the twentieth-century eugenics movement has lessons to teach people today that can help society avoid the earlier tragedies. Yes, the past is prologue, but it is not destiny.

33

Intelligence Research Leads to Negative Social Policies

> In education, the hereditarian analysis breeds fatalism, deficit-thinking and elitism ...
>
> (Gillborn, 2016, p. 382)

> If we assume intelligence is primarily the result of innate (hereditary) factors, we will likely conclude it is fixed and unchangeable. For some, this easily leads to the conclusions that a group (usually a racial group) with lower IQ scores must be innately inferior and, perhaps, should be treated as second-class citizens. On the other hand, if we conclude that intelligence is shaped largely by experience (environment), we are more likely to make a range of educational opportunities available for everyone and to view people of all ethnic, cultural, and economic groups as equals.
>
> (Zimbardo et al., 2017, p. 221)

One of the reasons that intelligence research is so important is its connections to many different parts of life and society. I have studied intelligence for over a decade, and it still boggles my mind that the same trait that predicts job performance (see Chapter 23) can also help someone live longer and have better physical health (see Chapter 22). But intelligence is not just relevant to individual outcomes; it is relevant to society as a whole. A nation's average IQ positively correlates with economic prosperity and negatively correlates with crime rates (G. Jones, 2016; Rindermann, 2018). The same is true at the state- or region-level within a country (Lynn, Fuerst, & Kirkegaard, 2018). Generally, it is better for everyone if the average intelligence level for a community, state, or nation is higher.

But it is also precisely because of this relevance to many social outcomes that some people oppose intelligence research. There is the persistent fear among some individuals that intelligence research leads necessarily to negative social policies. This is especially true – as seen in the two quotes at the beginning of this chapter – when discussing possible genetic influences on intelligence.

The fear that intelligence research will produce negative social outcomes is not new. The journalist and political commentator Walter Lippmann (1922/1976) worried that intelligence tests could easily become an "engine of cruelty" (p. 19) if intelligence was seen as stable and hereditary in nature. Nearly 50 years later, biologist Richard Lewontin (1970) feared that a meritocracy that rewarded intelligence would undermine his goal of a society "in which every man can aspire to the fullest measure of psychic and material fulfillment" (p. 8). In the 1990s, many commentators criticized *The Bell Curve* (Herrnstein & Murray, 1994) for providing evidence in support of unfavorable social policies. For example, Newby and Newby (1995) believed that *The Bell Curve* was part of a plan to dismantle affirmative action and the welfare state.

The truth is more complex (and, in my opinion, more interesting) than that. Intelligence research is not "left-wing" or "right-wing."[1] Rather, facts are value neutral. Whether they are used for good or for bad is independent of their truth. Like other areas of scientific knowledge, facts about intelligence can be marshalled to support favorable and unfavorable policies.[2] There is no policy that leads inevitably from any part of intelligence research.

JUSTIFYING THE STATUS QUO?

It is tempting to grow cynical when considering the positive correlations between IQ and income, socioeconomic status, job prestige, and other important outcomes. If one combines this information with the apparent IQ-based meritocracy (see Chapter 24), then it looks like intelligence research is a powerful justification of the status quo of inequality (Roberts, 2015). Similarly, it is true that effective teachers and schools cannot equalize children's abilities or educational attainment (see Chapter 19). This may suggest that improving the education system for children with low academic performance is a waste of resources.

From a practical standpoint, this thinking is flawed. Facts in the social sciences can – and sometimes do – change. In Chapter 22, I mentioned that smarter men in Great Britain were more likely to die during World War II (Deary et al., 2004). However, after the war ended, the correlation between IQ and death flipped from positive to negative, and less intelligent men were more likely to die during peacetime. There is no guarantee that current findings in psychology will remain constant. Indeed, it is important to remember that much of the research regarding correlations between IQ scores and life outcomes is probabilistic – and probabilities can change. Thus, even though most social interventions to raise IQ in people who already live in beneficial

---

[1] The personal politics of intelligence researchers tend to skew left, by a factor of about 2.5:1 (Rindermann et al., 2020).

[2] Of course, whether a particular policy is "favorable" or "unfavorable" depends on one's ethics, values, and goals.

environments are ineffective (see Chapters 15–16), it is possible that someone could discover an intervention that does raise IQ permanently in these people. That would certainly not justify today's status quo.

Is ≠ Ought. More philosophically, there is no clear connection between facts and what is morally desirable. The eighteenth-century philosopher David Hume recognized this, saying that statements about reality (i.e., what is) are not logically connected with how the world should be (i.e., what ought to be). In other words, a fact can tell scientists about the world as it *is*, but not whether that is how the world *ought* to be because *ought* statements are based on values and goals (Carl, 2018). Thus, research cannot justify the status quo because research merely produces *is* statements, whereas what is "justified" is a statement about how the world *ought* to be.

The importance of distinguishing facts from beliefs about how the world should be is clearest when considering facts that are obviously unfavorable, such as the research on the impact of lead on IQ (see Chapter 12). Blood lead levels in American children in the 1970s were often above 20 μg/dL (Landrigan et al., 1975; Needleman et al., 1979), and this lead poisoning lowered IQ in children. Thankfully, society at the time did not think that this *is* statement about blood lead levels was how the world *ought* to be, and lawmakers did not accept the reality as unchanging. Instead, politicians in the United States – and many other countries – decided to ban lead in paint, gasoline, and other products because they believed that lead poisoning ought to be reduced. This is an example of the assertion that, "There is no necessary connection between 'what is' and 'what could be'" (Plomin et al., 2014, p. 47). Facts may change in response to changing circumstances or interventions.

Say It Ain't So. A variation of combining *is* and *ought* is called the *moralistic fallacy* (B. B. Davis, 1978). This occurs when people say that facts must conform to their views of how the world ought to be. In a mild form, this leads to people rejecting scientific evidence or technological advances because they do not like the implications (e.g., Turkheimer, 2019). In an extreme form, it leads to censorship because scientific truths are seen as dangerous to society or wellbeing. For example, when considering racial differences in average IQ scores, Turkheimer (2007, paragraph 6) rhetorically asked:

Why don't we accept racial stereotypes as reasonable hypotheses, okay to consider until they have been scientifically proven false? They are offensive precisely because they violate our intuition about the balance between innateness and self-determination of the moral and cultural qualities of human beings.

In other words, because Turkheimer finds stereotypes "offensive," they become scientifically out-of-bounds. This is the moralistic fallacy: because he wishes that stereotypes were not true (an *ought* statement), he affirms that what he desires is true (an *is* statement).

The moralistic fallacy also ignores the fact that reality does not care about human desires. From a cosmic or evolutionary perspective, humans have arrived too late for their opinions to have much influence on the physical or biological world. In the past, many humans wanted the earth to be the center of the universe. The universe did not care about that desire, and by the time humans could express it, the earth's location was already set. Likewise, evolution operated for millions of years to produce humans with individual and group differences on a variety of traits (Cochran & Harpending, 2009; Winegard et al., 2017). To expect that evolution would conform to human desires is egocentric and unrealistic. As Hunt (2011, p. 113) stated quite bluntly, "Wanting something to be so, even for the best of reasons, does not make it so."

DUELING POLICIES

Beyond philosophy, another reason why intelligence research does not necessarily lead to negative policies is that often the same facts support different policies. For example, Zimbardo et al.'s (2017) fear of the consequences of information about the genetic influences on intelligence and school achievement – that it will lead to low-IQ individuals being treated as second-class citizens – is not the only outcome possible. Perhaps this information will prompt lawmakers to change policies so that genetically disadvantaged people receive a disproportionately large share of educational funding and opportunities. This could lead to better pay for teachers in low-income school districts and special education teachers, extensive training and additional tutoring, and support for underprivileged students. Knowledge about genetic influences on education also does not have to lead to fewer opportunities. Maybe education officials will make all opportunities available to every student, but then principals and teachers will not be surprised when a child with an IQ of 75 fails algebra despite their best efforts (and their teacher's).

Another example of how intelligence research can support multiple perspectives is apparent in discussions of immigration. Here is a hypothetical argument based on intelligence research that someone in a Western, industrialized nation could use to argue for more restrictive immigration policies:

Most immigrants move to countries with a higher mean IQ than their home nation (Rindermann & Thompson, 2016), and people with lower intelligence are more likely to require welfare benefits (Herrnstein & Murray, 1994; Gottfredson, 1997b). To prevent immigration from straining the welfare state, it is in the nation's best interest to screen individual immigrants to ensure that they have an IQ at or above the host country's average IQ. Additionally, there are good reasons to turn away even high-IQ immigrants. If too many high-IQ people leave their home nation, then it will hamper the native country's ability to economically develop because the percentage of high-IQ individuals in a nation correlates with the nation's fiscal prosperity (Rindermann, 2018). Preventing a "brain drain" in their home nation is humane because these bright people can serve as doctors, entrepreneurs, and leaders, which spreads the benefits of their high *g* to their fellow citizens.

Here is an opposing policy that is based equally in intelligence research:

Immigrants are not a representative sample of the people in their home nations; IQ is positively correlated with international migration during peacetime (Belsky et al., 2016) and war (Dutton et al., 2018). Therefore, it tends to be smarter people who are willing to uproot their lives and emigrate to a new country. They should be welcomed because they are more likely to contribute positively to the host country's economy than people who stay in their native country. Moreover, IQ scores are rising faster in developing nations than in Western nations (e.g., Daley et al., 2003; Wang & Lynn, 2018), and international IQ gaps are expected to narrow in the coming decades (Rindermann et al., 2017). As a result, fears of a "brain drain" are unwarranted because these countries are improving in their problem-solving ability anyway, even if some of their smartest citizens emigrate.

Which argument readers find more convincing is a question of judgment, as is whether an argument would result in policies that are favorable or unfavorable. The point of this exercise is to show that facts based on intelligence research can produce a wide variety of policies.[3]

HEREDITARY VIEWS BAD, ENVIRONMENTAL VIEWS GOOD?

Another feature in the quotes at the beginning of the chapter – especially Zimbardo et al.'s (2017) statement – is the dual implication that (1) hereditarian ideas are more likely to lead to undesirable consequences and (2) views that show a strong influence of the environment are good. This perspective is not unusual because people often see environmental influences as giving more hope for change than genetic findings.

Putting aside the fact that high heritability does not rule out the possibility of an effective environmental intervention (see Chapter 12), there are very good reasons to question the claim that environmental theories are inherently more favorable than genetic theories. One of the most obvious is the history of the twentieth century, where regimes that implemented totalitarian policies based on genetic theories (like Nazi Germany) and regimes that implemented totalitarian policies based on environmental theories (e.g., the Soviet Union, Communist China, and the Khmer Rouge) both resulted in the deaths of millions of people and genocide. So, equating one with being good and the other with being bad is erroneous. Clearly, both perspectives can lead to massive suffering and evil (Carl, 2018; Gottfredson, 2010).

Even if one does not worry about impending genocide, there are people – such as Gillborn (2016) – who believe that genetic information leads to fatalism and disillusionment because genes are set at birth. However, this pessimism is

---

[3] For the sake of brevity, both arguments are simplified, and – like most arguments based on politically motivated reasoning – ignore important facts that undermine the argument.

not inevitable.[4] Very few traits are 100% heritable, and that leaves room for environment to exert an influence on people. Moreover, genetic information can lead to better decisions and prevent people from being frustrated if they fall short of their goals. Plomin (2018, pp. 145–147) described a personal example, where a genetic test showed that he had a strong likelihood for being overweight, a highly heritable trait. In response, he did not merely give up and resign himself to obesity. Instead, he used that information to help him identify triggers for excessive eating and to not be so hard on himself if he struggled to lose weight.

Genetic information about intelligence can be humane in a similar way. If differences in g are strongly genetic, then this can encourage compassion for low-g people. For example, if one understands that low intelligence makes it more difficult to find employment, then this might strengthen support for the welfare state. After all, it is not a low-g person's fault that they spend more time unemployed, especially if they do what they can to find and keep a job. For them, the reason they are unemployed is not because of a character flaw, such as laziness or a disdain for work. Instead, it is partly genetic, and they did not choose their genes. Ensuring that there is a robust social safety net to keep low-g individuals from starving or living in extreme poverty is humane and a plausible consequence of research into the genetic causes of life outcomes.

LEARNING FROM HISTORY

Still, the potential for abuse and real harm arising from intelligence research is present. So, what can be done to prevent hereditarian or environmentalist views from leading to tragedy? I believe that studying the history of eugenics holds the key. Galton and the early twentieth-century eugenicists saw the rights of the individual as being less important than the health of society or the state (e.g., F. Galton, 1883, p. 300). A society that placed the rights of vulnerable, impoverished, or powerless people above the desires of the elites to improve society could have prevented the horrors inspired by eugenics in the twentieth century.

All the abuses that occurred as a result of the early eugenics movement were because disadvantaged individuals' rights were ignored or taken away. For example, some sterilizations in the past were voluntary on paper only; in reality, some people who were confined to prisons or mental institutions were released only if they agreed to sterilization. If they did not agree to sterilization, they were denied their freedom (Broberg & Tydén, 2005; Burgdorf & Burgdorf, 1977; Kevles, 1995; Lombardo, 1985; Roll-Hansen, 2005). At least one

---

[4] Even if Gillborn (2016) were correct, fatalism and a lack of effort in the face of discouraging genetic test results would actually make genetic tests for intelligence and related variables (e.g., educational outcomes) *less* accurate (Newson & Williamson, 1999), thereby reducing a genetic test's ability to predict anyone's fate.

American state's sterilization law forced some welfare recipients to agree to sterilization in order to receive public assistance (Burgdorf & Burgdorf, 1977). This is coercive and not a real choice. The difference between a free choice and an involuntary act is also the difference between a violation of human rights and the preservation of freedom. If strong laws had been in place making any eugenic intervention completely voluntary, with no rewards or punishments occurring as a consequence of the person's decision, then history would have been very different.

Avoiding harmful policies depends on supporting legislation that protects people's universal human rights, individual freedom, and dignity (Newson & Williamson, 1999). A good example of this is the laws in most industrialized countries that mandate universal education for all children, regardless of any disabilities they may have. These countries usually provide extensive support for educating people with low IQs (e.g., special education), even though educating a child with an intellectual disability costs over twice as much as educating a child with no special educational needs (Chambers, Shkolnik, & Pérez, 2003). Laws banning the use of *g*-loaded tests in employment also prevent intelligence from being a direct influence on hiring and promoting, which can give people who do not have many genetic or environmental advantages a chance to get a job.

g-CONSCIOUS POLICIES

Guidelines. Regardless of one's social values and goals, there are some guiding principles that can help people create policies built on scientific knowledge of *g*. First, do not promise more than a policy or program can deliver. When Head Start failed to raise IQ permanently in early studies, support for the program decreased. After it was retooled as a school-readiness program, it survived early criticism and flourishes today (Zigler & Anderson, 1979). But if Head Start's creators had made realistic promises to begin with, they would not have had to move the goalposts when the program failed to meet the original expectations. Realistic expectations prevent disillusionment and disarm critics.

Second, stick to facts – not wishful thinking. Many of the misconceptions that I deal with in this book are ideas that people want to believe. Sure, it would be nice if there were multiple uncorrelated intelligences because it would mean that almost everybody would be smart in some area (see Chapter 5). If non-cognitive traits had a powerful influence over school performance, then training students to be more confident or determined would solve the problem of school failure in people with below-average intelligence (see Chapter 20). Warm, fuzzy ideas and good intentions are a less effective foundation for policies than the truth. Policies based on incorrect ideas are, at best, a waste of resources. At worst, they may cause harm. For example, a teacher who creates a way to teach math that taps into so-called "bodily-kinesthetic intelligence" is wasting time that could be spent on more effective lessons that would have a greater likelihood of success.

Third, do not ignore genetics. Nearly every trait or life outcome is partially influenced by genes (Bouchard, 2014). As a result, some goals are inherently unlikely, such as eliminating individual differences in school performance. Indeed, treatments may even increase inequalities because the better environment created by the intervention allows genetic differences more freedom to manifest themselves (Herrnstein, 1971).

Example of a *g*-Conscious Policy. Given these guidelines, it is possible to brainstorm *g*-conscious policies. As an intellectual exercise, I can show how a *g*-conscious policy could be applied to postsecondary education. Such a policy would not overpromise by guaranteeing that every child would be ready for college when they finish high school. It would also avoid the wishful thinking that merely boosting a child's self-esteem or "grit" would cause them to do better in school. Policies based on intelligence research would also confront genetically caused inequality and not promise to equalize outcomes across children.

What would such a policy look like? The policy may concentrate on *improving* each child's readiness for more advanced education (e.g., the next grade, an advanced class, college). The policy may also focus on matching students with a curriculum that they find challenging – but not unrealistically difficult, given their IQ and previous academic performance. A postsecondary education policy that is based on intelligence research would advertise technical or career education as being as valuable as a college education and not make students who choose to become an electrician or plumber feel like their career choices are less valuable than the choices of their classmates who attend college (Frisby, 2013).

Don't Forget Low-*g* Citizens. One advantage that *g*-conscious policies have over policies that ignore *g* is that they are more likely to accommodate low-*g* individuals' limitations. People with below-average IQs without an intellectual disability (i.e., IQ of 75–90) have no advocacy group to advance their needs in society. This group is often forgotten by policy makers because powerful people usually do not understand the difficulties that low-*g* individuals encounter in their day-to-day lives (see Chapter 35). A policy based on intelligence that takes into account differences in *g* across the entire spectrum is more humane and beneficial than a policy that ignores *g*. People who believe that intelligence research mostly leads to unfavorable policies often do not recognize the harm that low-*g* individuals experience when policies ignore their limitations.

TO BE CONTINUED . . .

There is no reason why intelligence research must lead to unfavorable consequences. Indeed, much scientific knowledge can be used for good or evil (B. B. Davis, 1978). Intelligence research can provide insight into policies and maximize the chances that they will be effective. Chapters 34 and 35 will develop these ideas further and apply them to policies about low-*g* individuals and inequality.

34

Intelligence Research Undermines the Fight against Inequality

> The weight of the evidence – historical, biological, and philosophical – is that research into the genetics of intelligence cannot be socially neutral and, indeed, will intensify social inequalities.
>
> (Roberts, 2015, p. S53)

> ... linking ... race and class to the heritability of IQ is reminiscent of the pre-civil rights period in the U.S., during which racist practices were justified based on the "known" lesser intelligence of Blacks and others of subordinate status.
>
> (Newby & Newby, 1995, p. 13)

Among the concerns that some people have about intelligence research is its perceived threat to equality. At first glance, intelligence research seems to have the ingredients of inequality baked in: a foundation of individual differences, the practical importance of *g* in economic outcomes, and high heritability. Add in the past controversies (see Chapter 32), and the race differences in average IQ scores (see Chapters 28–30), and intelligence research seems like a disaster for the goal of an equal society.

In this chapter, I will discuss three types of equality that are relevant to intelligence research: equality of individual outcomes, equality of group outcomes, and legal equality. Intelligence research has different implications for each type of equality. I will also explain that intelligence research does not have to exacerbate inequality and may even mitigate it.

EQUALITY OF INDIVIDUAL OUTCOMES

One political and social concern for many people is the inequality of individual outcomes. These outcomes can be in terms of health inequality (e.g., some people living longer than others), individual economic inequality, or inequality in academic success. Chapters 18–19 and 22–24 address the relevance of intelligence for understanding individual inequality. From these chapters it is clear that IQ is correlated with many life outcomes, with most beneficial life outcomes being more likely for people with high IQ and most negative life experiences being more likely for people with low IQ.

The lesson from all these correlations is clear: individual inequality in life outcomes is associated with intelligence differences. Sometimes the evidence indicates that *g* is one of the causes of these inequalities, meaning that high-*g* individuals experience some positive life outcomes partially *because* they are smart. When the genetic evidence regarding intelligence is included, then the implication is that life outcomes – including socioeconomic status, health, and educational performance – are also inherited genetically. This implication may worry some people because it indicates that socioeconomic status and other benefits in life are handed down genetically from generation to generation. It is not paranoid to be concerned about genetically driven inequality: some intelligence theorists have explicitly drawn the connections between these correlations and the heritability of intelligence (most famously, Herrnstein, 1971, 1973, and Herrnstein & Murray, 1994). And behavioral genetics research has shown that some of the same segments of DNA that are associated with high IQ are also associated with high socioeconomic status (Marioni et al., 2014; Trzaskowski et al., 2014). In other words, one of the factors that cause high IQ to be correlated with high socioeconomic status is shared genes that influence both traits.

However, blaming intelligence research for the connections among IQ, genes, and social outcomes is shortsighted. Intelligence researchers do not create the correlations between *g* and life outcomes, nor do they force intelligence (or any other trait) to be heritable. These facts exist, regardless of whether psychologists and other scientists discover them or not. Ignoring intelligence research will not change that.

Does this information about genetics exacerbate inequalities, as Roberts (2015) claimed? No, because of the disconnect between *is* and *ought* statements that I explained in Chapter 33. The fact that socioeconomic status is heritable and that some of those genes are also associated with intelligence (Marioni et al., 2014; Trzaskowski et al., 2014) is a statement of reality. This *is* statement has nothing to do with what one wishes reality *ought* to be. Changing society to match one's wishes (i.e., the *ought* one desires) may change the *is* statement.

Changing society to reduce the economic rewards of high *g* sounds difficult, but industrialized nations do this all the time through progressive tax rates (i.e., higher taxes for the wealthy and lower or no taxes for the poor) and the welfare state. Even though no nation advertises these policies as a way to reduce the economic importance of intelligence, progressive taxes still have this effect. Although redistributing wealth is easier than redistributing *g*, information about the positive or negative life outcomes of low *g*-people can help society create policies that improve life for less fortunate citizens (see Chapter 35).

Ironically, some commentators have pointed out (e.g., Jensen, 1998; Mackintosh, 2011; Plomin, 2018) that high heritability for a trait is the sign of a more equitable society. This is because high heritability indicates that environments do not constrain the development of most people's genetic potentials. Thus, the high heritability for intelligence – which is often over .50 for adults in wealthy countries – and, to a lesser extent, income (about .40 in developed nations, according to Plomin, 2018, p. 100) is an index of fairness. This is because high heritability indicates that differences are not caused by society and external forces. Low heritability indicates that environmental inequalities are the strongest cause of differences in a trait or outcome, as is apparent from studies showing that higher childhood socioeconomic status is correlated with better economic outcomes, even after controlling for genes (e.g., Belsky et al., 2016). If anything, people concerned with environmental disadvantages should welcome high heritability of life outcomes.

Additionally, some have proposed using IQ and genetic information to advocate for the less fortunate in society. For example, genetic tests can predict who will struggle in education (e.g., children at risk for a low IQ or a learning disability), and this information can be used to give these students a disproportionate share of resources. In the near future, DNA tests for intelligence or a learning disability could lead to interventions that start in infancy, instead of waiting until the child falls behind their peers (Asbury, 2015; Martschenko et al., 2019).

Are such beneficent policies likely to arise from research that is thoroughly steeped in individual inequalities? Roberts (2015) was skeptical, believing that the rich and powerful are usually in the best position to exploit new scientific knowledge for their own gain. In response, I argue that it is highly unlikely that twenty-first-century industrialized societies – which already devote so many resources to people in poverty (through the welfare state) and people with low *g* (in special education programs and community assistance in their daily living) – will suddenly turn their backs on this vulnerable population because of some correlations.

EQUALITY OF GROUP OUTCOMES

The Conundrum. A greater concern than individual inequality, for some people, is inequality among groups. This is especially true when racial minorities, women, or people living in poverty are more likely to experience unfavorable outcomes (Coleman, 1991). For example, Chapter 27 discussed sex differences in variability of intelligence and other cognitive abilities. Males have scores that are slightly more variable than females', and consequentially, the sex ratio in the top and bottom echelons of ability often shows a distinct imbalance favoring males. This difference in variability has real consequences for equality of outcomes across sexes. Selecting people above a high IQ cutoff for a job or educational opportunity will usually result in selecting more males than females. The imbalance will be especially noticeable in abilities where males have a higher mean than females (e.g., spatial ability) and in endeavors with high minimum cutoffs.

For people fighting for equality of outcomes for males and females, this information seems to pose a threat because if scientists determine that greater male variability has a biological foundation, then it could undermine efforts to advance women's careers, especially in male-dominated fields like engineering and technology.[1] As a result, activists have worked to censor research on greater male variability (see T. P. Hill, 2018, for an example).

An even more sensitive issue is equality of outcomes across racial or ethnic groups. Because of the average differences in IQ scores (see Chapter 10), there will be different percentages of members of each group who exceed any cutoff score. This is abundantly clear in Table 34.1, which shows that a larger percentage of Asian Americans exceed all cutoffs compared to all other large racial/ethnic groups in the United States. Conversely, African Americans have the smallest percentage of group members who exceed every cutoff (see Gottfredson, 2000b, for a detailed discussion of this phenomenon).

Table 34.2 shows a different perspective: the percentage of the population above each cutoff that belongs to the four largest racial/ethnic groups in the United States. The table shows that as the IQ cutoff increases, the group that exceeds the IQ cutoff has a progressively smaller percentage of African Americans and Hispanic Americans and an increasing percentage of European Americans and Asian Americans.

The percentages in the table have one unavoidable consequence of average IQ differences: except at the lowest cutoffs, the individuals that exceed a given IQ score will not be representative of the general population. Racial groups with lower averages will have the smallest percentage of people selected, and groups with higher averages will have larger percentages of members selected. This is an inevitable consequence of average differences in group scores[2] (Frisby, 2013; Petersen & Novick, 1976), and it presents a conundrum for people who aim for equal outcomes across racial and ethnic groups (Gottfredson, 2000b).

For this reason, many people who are concerned with group equality oppose using intelligence tests for educational and employment selection. Advocates of equal group outcomes often put pressure on decision makers to eliminate or reduce the importance of measures of *g*, such as college admissions tests and employment tests, when selecting people (e.g., C. A. Heller et al., 2014;

[1] Strangely, few people express concern that males dominate the ranks of people with low cognitive ability. I wonder why the push for gender equity does not include remedying the dearth of women in low-IQ groups and low-prestige occupations.

[2] This is a mathematical property of any variable where there is a group difference in averages and is not unique to intelligence scores. For example, if selecting people on the basis of height, then there will always be a larger percentage of men who exceed the cutoff than women because men are – on average – taller than women.

TABLE 34.1 *Estimated percentage of racial/ethnic group members who exceed various IQ score cutoffs*

IQ cutoff	African Americans	Hispanic Americans	European Americans	Asian Americans
55	97.72%	99.01%	99.87%	99.96%
60	95.25%	97.72%	99.62%	99.87%
65	90.82%	95.25%	99.01%	99.62%
70	84.13%	90.82%	97.72%	99.01%
75	74.86%	84.13%	95.25%	97.72%
80	62.93%	74.86%	90.82%	95.25%
85	50.00%	62.93%	84.13%	90.82%
90	37.07%	50.00%	74.86%	84.13%
95	25.14%	37.07%	62.93%	74.86%
100	15.87%	25.14%	50.00%	62.93%
105	9.18%	15.87%	37.07%	50.00%
110	4.75%	9.18%	25.14%	37.07%
115	2.28%	4.75%	15.87%	25.14%
120	0.99%	2.28%	9.18%	15.87%
125	0.38%	0.99%	4.75%	9.18%
130	0.13%	0.38%	2.28%	4.75%
135	0.04%	0.13%	0.99%	2.28%
140	0.012%	0.04%	0.38%	0.99%
145	0.003%	0.012%	0.13%	0.38%

Note. Percentages are calculated with a normal distribution and the same standard deviation (15) for every group. Average IQ for these calculations is 85 for African Americans, 90 for Hispanic Americans, 100 for European Americans, and 105 for Asian Americans.

Ford, 2014).[3] However, eliminating measures of *g* in the selection process is not always possible. For example, professions that require workers to pass a licensure exam – such as law and medicine – will inevitably have a minimum intelligence level that people must have in order to work in these fields. That minimum IQ cutoff will result in disproportionately more Asian and European Americans working in those fields and disproportionately fewer Hispanic and African Americans. As the minimum IQ for a job or an intellectual endeavor increases, it becomes increasingly difficult to find African Americans and Hispanics who exceed the minimum intelligence level (Humphreys, 1988). Thus (under current conditions), the more intellectually elite a job, community, or educational program is, the harder it is to achieve a qualifying group that reflects the diversity of the general population – assuming everyone is held to the same qualification standards.

Solutions to the Conundrum. Unlike redistribution of money, it is impossible to take *g* from one person and give it to another. So, other strategies must be

---

[3] See Chapter 21 for a discussion of this issue regarding college admissions tests.

TABLE 34.2 *Estimated percentage of the population above IQ score cutoffs who belong to various racial/ethnic groups*

IQ cutoff	African Americans	Hispanic Americans	European Americans	Asian Americans
55	13.44%	18.60%	61.91%	6.05%
60	13.20%	18.49%	62.22%	6.09%
65	12.77%	18.29%	62.76%	6.17%
70	12.15%	17.92%	63.63%	6.30%
75	11.31%	17.35%	64.84%	6.50%
80	10.21%	16.58%	66.41%	6.80%
85	9.01%	15.48%	68.31%	7.20%
90	7.73%	14.23%	70.32%	7.72%
95	6.41%	12.90%	72.29%	8.40%
100	5.23%	11.32%	74.31%	9.14%
105	4.17%	9.85%	75.97%	10.01%
110	3.23%	8.53%	77.13%	11.11%
115	2.49%	7.10%	78.29%	12.12%
120	1.89%	5.92%	78.87%	13.32%
125	1.40%	4.98%	78.75%	14.87%
130	1.04%	3.99%	78.90%	16.08%
135	0.76%	3.24%	78.40%	17.59%
140	0.55%	2.67%	77.11%	19.67%
145	0.40%	2.08%	76.52%	21.00%

Note. Percentages are calculated on the basis of the US Census Bureau's estimates that the nation's population in 2018 was 60.4% non-Hispanic European Americans, 18.3% Hispanic Americans (of any race), 13.4% non-Hispanic African Americans, and 5.9% Asian Americans. These percentages sum to 98% because some people in the population do not belong to any of these four groups or have multiracial heritage. The percentages in this table do not take that 2% of the population into account.

used to reconcile the desire for equal outcomes with the unequal distribution of *g* across groups. Intelligence research supports the use of three strategies that advocates of group equality may find helpful.

The first strategy is based on Spearman's hypothesis, which shows that better measures of *g* tend to have larger average score differences across racial groups (see Chapter 28). Thus, to reduce differences between groups (and therefore discrepancies in the percentage of group members selected), decision makers should use a test that is a poorer measure of *g* because a worse measure of *g* usually produces smaller differences among groups. While using a poor measure of *g* sounds like a bad idea, this may actually be in an organization's best interest anyway. If non-*g* abilities are more important for performance in the job or educational program, then selecting people on the basis of these abilities will have the double benefit of producing smaller racial discrepancies and being better predictors of success than an IQ score would be. For example, to select students for training to be a mechanic, the most important information is the candidate's math and spatial abilities, which are Stratum II abilities. Measuring global *g* may be less important than these specific abilities. Likewise, employers probably want to know more about the quality of a job applicant's work than the person's general reasoning ability; so it would be best to select applicants using work samples or tests of job knowledge, which correlate highly with job performance and have smaller average group differences.

The second strategy is to recruit more heavily from underrepresented groups (e.g., African Americans and Hispanics), as many organizations that value diversity already do. This can improve these groups' selection rates because most applicant pools are self-selected and not a representative sample of the general population. Increasing recruitment of underrepresented groups can make more of these groups' members qualify for selection. To boost this number even further, it is sometimes possible to provide underrepresented groups with extra preparation and support before the selection process to increase their likelihood of qualifying (Olszewski-Kubilius, Steenbergen-Hu, Thomson, & Rosen, 2017; Warne, 2009).

A third strategy for reducing the impact of group differences in *g* is to lower the cutoff score for acceptance for groups with lower averages and/or to increase the cutoff for higher-scoring groups (Gottfredson, 1986). Sometimes this is done explicitly, but more frequently it is an implicit consequence of a selection procedure. One method of doing this is to have a preference – such as an affirmative action or diversity preference – for selecting members of underrepresented groups. This sometimes occurs in education and employment settings (Axt, 2017; Gottfredson, 1986; Nyborg & Jensen, 2001; Sander, 2004; W. M. Williams & Ceci, 2015) and mathematically has the same function and results as setting a lower cutoff score for underrepresented groups.

One popular method of creating different cutoff scores in education is a selection procedure that makes candidates compete with other similar applicants instead of the entire population. For example, some public universities in the United States automatically accept a certain percentage of the best students from every high school in the state (Atkinson, 2001). This reduces the disproportionalities among the selected group – even if a test of *g* is used within each school to identify high-performing students[4] (Peters, Rambo-Hernandez, Makel, Matthews, & Plucker, 2019). Schools that have student bodies from groups with higher average levels of *g* will have higher cutoffs that their students must meet in order to be selected. Schools that have a disproportionate share of students from lower-scoring groups will have lower cutoffs for their students to meet.

---

[4] Ironically, the more segregated the schools are, the more representative of the general population the selected group will be. Thus, if – all things being equal – schools are highly segregated (which may be perceived as evidence of injustice), then the educational program will be highly integrated (and vice versa).

But setting different cutoffs may cause problems. Most importantly, setting different cutoff scores for different racial groups is illegal in the United States when using tests for employment purposes (A. Calvin, 2000), and some states ban the practice in education. Affirmative action racial quotas – which have the same effect as differing cutoffs – are also illegal (*Regents of the University of California v. Bakke*, 1978; Sander, 2004). However, employers and educational institutions have flexibility in using race as one factor (among others) in selecting applicants. But if used to benefit lower-scoring groups, then this process mathematically *must* lead to lower cutoff scores for African and Hispanic Americans to be selected for employment or educational opportunities and higher cutoff scores for applicants belonging to higher-scoring groups.

Even when different cutoff scores are legal, they may be politically unacceptable. A large majority of Americans (73%) do not believe that colleges should consider race at all in the admissions process. This opposition to race-based affirmative action in college admissions holds across all large racial and ethnic groups (78% of European Americans, 65% of Hispanics, 62% of African Americans, and 58% of Asian Americans) and both major political parties (85% of Republicans and 63% of Democrats; Graf, 2019). Publicly announcing that one racial group must meet a higher threshold to be accepted to college, a work training program, or a job may cause unwanted controversy or even a lawsuit. Adjusting cutoffs covertly does not resolve the political controversy (e.g., E. Hoover, 2019; Sander, 2004).

Moreover, accepting students with widely different academic credentials into the same program produces unavoidably obvious differences in academic performance. For example, Sander (2004, p. 427) found that 51.6% of African American law students have grades in the bottom 10% of their law school classes, compared to 5.6% of European American law students. Only 8.0% of African Americans have grades in the top half of their law class. The dropout rate for law students is 2.34 times higher for African Americans than European Americans (Sander, 2004, p. 436). Among those who do finish law school, African Americans fail the bar exam at a rate that is four times higher than European American law students', and an African American law school graduate is six times as likely to fail the bar exam in their first five attempts as a European American graduate (Sander, 2004, p. 443).

The legal and practical difficulties of having different cutoffs for different racial groups can be dismaying for advocates of equal group outcomes and of affirmative action. But this is not any reason to give up hope. Apart from the options I have discussed in this chapter, advocates of equality of outcomes can also make a forceful moral argument: because a more egalitarian society is a more peaceful society, having an underclass that falls somewhat along racial lines may foment unrest. If belonging to the underclass (or elites) is partially heritable due to the genetic influence on socioeconomic status and intelligence, then dissatisfaction will perpetuate across generations. This can have a destabilizing effect on the cohesiveness of a country.

Opponents of affirmative action also have evidence from intelligence research supporting their beliefs. Intelligence is correlated with job and educational success, and selecting applicants on the basis of a less *g*-loaded variable or adjusting cutoffs to benefit groups with lower average IQ often results in some less qualified individuals being preferred over more qualified individuals (Gottfredson, 1986; Sander, 2004). This can lead to negative outcomes, especially in endeavors where *g* is more relevant to performance, such as high-complexity jobs. This is clear, for example, in medicine and law, where practitioners who fail to pass licensure exams on the first attempt are more likely to perform their jobs incompetently even after passing the licensure exam later (Kinsler, 2017; Wakeford et al., 2018). It also occurs when law students who have received affirmative action preferences drop out at higher rates and pass the bar exam at lower rates than their non-preferred classmates who have higher academic credentials (Sander, 2004). There is also the moral argument against affirmative action functioning as a form of racial discrimination and perpetuating judgments on the basis of race.

I am not interested in taking a position on whether affirmative action is a beneficial policy. My point in this discussion is to show – from a perspective based in the research on intelligence – why equal outcomes for different groups do not happen on their own. Science does not point to a clear solution to this ethical problem. Rather, it often supports conflicting positions (see Chapter 33). Ignoring intelligence research will lead to incorrect theories about the cause of unequal outcomes and, often, ineffective "solutions."

Non-starters. An example of an ineffective solution appeared in the 2000s when several educational scholars proposed that using non-verbal tests (especially matrix tests) for selection into gifted programs would greatly increase diversity (e.g., Lewis, DeCamp-Fritson, Ramage, McFarland, & Archwamety, 2007; Naglieri & Ford, 2003). Later research showed that this suggestion did not increase diversity in gifted programs (Carman & Taylor, 2010; Carman et al., 2018). Because matrix tests are usually among the best measures of *g*, Spearman's hypothesis would predict that using these tests would not reduce racial discrepancies in the children selected for gifted programs because good measures of *g* tend to produce larger average group differences in scores. A knowledge of intelligence research could have saved the gifted education community a lot of time and disappointment.

Another example of an ineffectual proposal to increase diversity of gifted programs is Ford's (2014) guideline that gifted programs should have a percentage of African American students that is at least four-fifths of their percentage in the local school district.[5] However, if one applies the same IQ cutoff for European American and African American students, then achieving

---

[5] For example, if African Americans are 20% of all students, then Ford (2014) suggests that African Americans should be at least 20% x 80% = 16% of the students in the gifted program.

this goal would require an IQ cutoff of 76 – a score far below the "gifted" range. If different cutoffs are applied to the two different racial groups, then the European American cutoff must be about 13 IQ points (d = .87) higher than the African American cutoff score to meet Ford's (2014) recommendation. Other proposed solutions, such as training in cultural competence for teachers to recognize giftedness in diverse students, or expanding the definition of giftedness to label more African American students as "gifted" also result in lower standards for African Americans than for European or Asian Americans (Frisby, 2013) or will be only marginally effective (Worrell & Dixson, 2018).

LEGAL EQUALITY

Finally, some people perceive intelligence research as a threat to legal equality. Newby and Newby's (1995) worry (quoted at the beginning of this chapter) that linking heritability of IQ with racial classifications could lead to a return of pre-civil rights era practices is an example of this concern. The problem with this fear is that it assumes that legal equality is based on scientific findings of all groups being equal in potential and performance. In reality, legal equality is based on principles enshrined in constitutional law and statutes (Newson & Williamson, 1999). These laws were enacted without scientific findings affirming the legal equality of people; finding inequalities – either at the individual level or among averages of groups – will not invalidate these legal principles.

Moreover, legal equality should not have a foundation in empirical beliefs. Basing principles of legal equality and non-discrimination on the belief that racial groups are equal in every relevant way is dangerous because that foundation is an empirically testable hypothesis. If average group differences are shown to be real, then it would imply that discrimination and denying rights to some groups are justified – exactly what bigots believe (Carl, 2018). Instead, legal equality and non-discrimination should be based on the moral and ethical principles that every person is automatically and unconditionally entitled to equal rights. Because moral and ethical principles are not scientifically testable, they are impervious to any findings that may emerge from scholarly research.

Finally, discrimination does not make scientific sense anyway (Herrnstein & Murray, 1994). This is clear in examining judgment accuracy using different rules. If there is a 15-point (i.e., d = 1.0) difference between the average IQs of European and African Americans, then it is possible to calculate how accurate different rules are at identifying the more intelligent person when comparing a randomly selected African American and a randomly selected European American. Here are the results:

• Randomly guessing which individual is more intelligent will be correct 50.0% of the time.

- Discriminating on the basis of race and assuming that the European American is always more intelligent results in a correct decision 76.0% of the time.
- Ignoring race and using IQ scores to identify which person is smarter increases decision accuracy to 94.2%.
- Using race and IQ scores to identify which person is smarter *lowers* the accuracy slightly to 94.0%.

Although 94.2% is less than perfect accuracy, using IQ scores is the best option for identifying the smarter person.[6] What is important is that this judgment method has the highest accuracy when comparing people from *any* racial or ethnic groups. Moreover, including race in the prediction does *not* improve judgments over considering IQ scores alone.

The moral of the story is simple: *judge people as individuals* and don't consider an irrelevant factor like their race. This maxim applies to identifying the most intelligent person, the most competent employee, the best sprinter, or the best college student. If anything, this statistical evidence should reinforce anti-discrimination efforts, not undermine them.

CONCLUSION

People who pursue egalitarian goals for society often see intelligence research as a threat to equality. However, lumping different types of equality under one label oversimplifies the issue. Inequality of individual outcomes is probably inevitable, and inequality of group outcomes is persistent, though there are policies that can lessen the magnitude of either type of inequality. On the other hand, legal equality is not based on science at all, and no scientific findings can or should negate legal equality based on a moral or ethical foundation of equal rights.

The concerns for equality raised in this chapter will not be addressed by ignoring intelligence research. Fighting inequality requires understanding its causes – and some forms of inequality have a partial origin in *g* differences. Engaging with intelligence research will help fair-minded activists understand which proposed policies will work and which will not.

---

[6] This calculation assumes that IQ score reliability is .96, which is typical for intelligence test batteries, like a Wechsler intelligence test. Tests that produce less reliable (i.e., less stable) scores will have lower accuracy percentages but will still perform better than a discriminatory decision.

35

Everyone Is About as Smart as I Am

. . . the great majority of all jobs can be learned through practice by almost any literate person.

(Collins, 1979, p. 54)

. . . research proved that young people, whatever their background, could mini-mize any chance of long-term poverty by taking three simple steps: graduating from high school, getting a job – any job – right after graduation from high school or college, and bearing children only after marriage, not before. The success sequence shows that good choices can help all people avoid bad outcomes, even if they're disadvantaged, while bad choices are likely to produce bad outcomes, even for the more privileged.

(Medved, 2017, paragraphs 2–3; typo corrected and paragraph break eliminated)

This final chapter opens with two quotes that, on the surface, do not seem to have much to do with intelligence. The quote from Collins (1979) is a claim that almost every job is within the grasp of most adults, while Medved supports the "success sequence" (first labeled as such by Haskins & Sawhill, 2009) of life choices that some have suggested is a key to staying out of poverty. But the two quotes share an underlying assumption that almost everybody in society has the intelligence to learn, plan, and reason sufficiently well to achieve economic success. For Collins (1979), individual differences in intelligence – if he believes they exist at all – are irrelevant because on-the-job training can help nearly anyone overcome any deficits and become a successful employee.[1] In Medved's (2017) opinion, poverty could be greatly reduced if only everyone would make good choices. But he never contemplates whether these choices are easy for people with low intelligence.

---

[1] This is a variant of the training hypothesis (see Chapter 23).

As I have shown in many previous chapters, individual differences in intelligence matter in work, school, and everyday life, and these differences have important consequences. One consequence is that people have difficulty imagining what the thought process is like for someone whose IQ is more than about 10 or 15 points away from their own (Detterman, 2014). This causes problems when people at one IQ level make judgments of or recommendations to people whose IQ is very different from their own because people project their level of competence onto others.

This is a special form of what is called the *psychologist's fallacy* (a term first coined by James, 1890, p. 196), which is the tendency of a person to assume that others think and act more-or-less the way that they do. Ironically, highly intelligent people are one of the groups most susceptible to this blind spot in their thinking.[2] Bright people tend to believe that everyone thinks and solves problems as well as they do, and this can have important consequences when high-IQ people deal with other segments of the population.

EXAMPLES

The consequences of not considering the impact of intelligence differences in decision making can be serious. An example of this is the phenomenon of false confessions in the criminal justice system, which have been a principal source of evidence that sends innocent people to prison. One of the risk factors for false confessions is low IQ (Gudjonsson, 1990, 1991). People with below-average intelligence are more vulnerable to interrogation tactics and may not understand their constitutional rights. They may also (incorrectly) believe that confessing will let them escape a high-pressure interrogation and that they will be proven innocent later (Kassin, 2012). A jury consisting of people with average intelligence may not understand the thought process and confusion that led a person with a low IQ to falsely confess to a crime. That jury would see a confession as being true and choose to send an innocent person to prison on the basis of the incorrect belief that everyone is smart enough to understand why it is unwise to falsely confess to a crime.

On a larger scale, the differences in how highly intelligent people and average or low-IQ people think causes problems because bright people have a disproportionate say in how society is run. This was especially apparent in a US government initiative called Project 100,000. Between 1966 and 1971 (during the height of the Vietnam War), the US Department of Defense increased the number of men eligible for the draft by lowering the minimum

---

[2] Another group that is highly susceptible to the psychologist's fallacy is people with antisocial personality disorder, which is characterized by (among other behaviors) a willingness to take advantage of others, a propensity to break rules and laws, and a lack of remorse for hurting others. People with this disorder are sometimes genuinely surprised that other people do not have their same lack of morality and empathy towards others.

IQ needed for military service from 92 to 71 (Gregory, 2015, pp. 100–102).[3] Secretary of Defense Robert McNamara believed that extra training would make these men suitable soldiers and – after their service – productive members of society.[4] Over the course of Project 100,000's existence, 354,000 men were inducted under relaxed psychological and medical standards; 91% of these men were inducted due to the lowered minimum IQ (Rand Corporation, n.d., p. 5).

Project 100,000 was a spectacular failure. Men in Project 100,000 were harder to train and were less competent soldiers, which placed lives at risk. Over half of the men were dishonorably discharged (Gregory, 2015, p. 196). They experienced psychiatric problems at a rate that was 10 times higher than other soldiers (Crowe & Colbach, 1971), and their death rate was three times higher than average (Gregory, 2015, p. xiv). While some men from Project 100,000 were good soldiers, the extra training and supervision in the military did little for most soldiers to compensate for their low IQ. The cause of Project 100,000's failure was not the American military's lack of motivation or resources to bring low-IQ men up to standard levels of performance. Instead, the failure originated in McNamara's and other decision makers' lack of understanding that IQ differences lead to fundamental differences in people's ability to function in their environment. Contrary to McNamara's – and Collins's (1979) – beliefs, people are not interchangeable cogs that can be trained to fill nearly any job (Gottfredson, 1986).

Another manifestation of the tendency for high-IQ people to overestimate others' abilities is apparent in the quote from Medved (2017). For him, there are "three simple steps" that can "help *all* people avoid bad outcomes" (emphasis added) and avoid poverty. These are graduating from high school, entering the workforce, and not having children out of wedlock. While these behaviors are characteristic of economically successful people (Murray, 2013), they are not as easy for people with low g as they are for average or highly intelligent people. For someone with low intelligence, high school graduation may be very difficult, and there may be few jobs available to them. Even preventing pregnancy is more difficult to low-g individuals because IQ is negatively correlated with impulsivity (Caspi et al., 2016). Preventing pregnancy requires planning, self-control, and understanding how one's actions can have long-term consequences – things that do not come easily to people with low intelligence. None of this implies that people with low intelligence are morally deficient. Rather, my point is that these behaviors are not "simple for all people." When high-IQ people preach about how easy it is to leave poverty by following a few life guidelines,

---

[3] In practice, some men with IQs in the low 60s were drafted. Gregory (2015) discussed drafted soldiers who had difficulty dressing themselves, distinguishing left from right, and learning how to shoot a gun. This level of disability is a strong indicator that some men with IQs below 71 were drafted during Project 100,000.

[4] This is yet another example of the training hypothesis, explained in Chapter 23.

they overestimate how feasible these behaviors are for some segments of the population.

Another manifestation of high-*g* individuals' ignorance of the limitations of low-*g* people occurs in a medical setting. People with below-average intelligence often struggle to comply with their doctors' orders for taking medication and engaging in self-care. Even basic tasks, like understanding a prescription label, are difficult for people with an IQ of 88 or lower (T. C. Davis, Meldrum, Tippy, Weiss, & Williams, 1996). More complex tasks, like managing diabetes, are nearly impossible for low-IQ people to perform correctly (Gottfredson, 2004). If physicians (a high-*g* group) do not accommodate treatments for their patients with low cognitive ability, then the treatment may not be as successful, especially if it relies heavily on patient compliance.

WHY SMART PEOPLE ARE SO STUPID ABOUT *g* DIFFERENCES

It is ironic that the population most able to understand the world has a poor grasp of other people's cognitive limitations. This raises the question of why the disconnect between high intelligence and an understanding of others' reasoning abilities exists. I have already mentioned the first reason: the psychologist's fallacy. However, this is an unsatisfying answer because it just names the phenomenon. It does not explain *why* high-IQ individuals fall prey to the psychologist's fallacy.

One cause is that society is increasingly stratifying itself by intelligence levels. Starting in adolescence, people tend to socialize more with people who have a similar level of intelligence. In adulthood this trend accelerates as people self-select career paths that are generally suited for their intelligence level. This results in co-workers and classmates who have similar IQ levels. Because IQ is correlated with socioeconomic status, people with similar IQ levels also generally live in the same neighborhoods. The result is a balkanization of society by IQ (Murray, 2013). Therefore, one of the reasons that bright people have difficulty understanding the limitations of other segments of the population is that high-IQ people often do not spend much time with the average or low-IQ members of society or understand the daily lives of people with vastly different IQ levels (Hunt, 2014).

I experienced this firsthand recently – despite my conscious efforts to associate with a wide variety of people in my community. In 2018, I was summoned for jury duty. As part of the selection process, every potential juror had to state some basic information about themselves, including their education level. Of the 50 potential jurors, I was the only one with a doctorate degree. I was genuinely surprised and thought to myself, "How can I be the only one here with a doctorate? Most of my co-workers have PhDs. Many of my students go on to earn doctorates. A lot of my Facebook friends have earned a PhD." Later, I discovered that 1.8% of American adults have doctorate degrees (US Census Bureau, 2019, Table 1). Thus, in a representative sample of 50 American adults (like a jury pool in an average county), there *should* only be one person with a PhD. My everyday experience with colleagues, students, and friends led me to overestimate how educated my community was.

Another reason high-IQ people have difficulty understanding the limitations of less intelligent individuals is that few learn about intelligence and its real-world importance. Most people do not study psychology, and it is not realistic to expect people – even very intelligent people – to know a lot about a scientific topic outside their expertise. But even among people who do study psychology, classes on intelligence are rare (Burton & Warne, 2020), and psychology textbooks contain a great deal of inaccurate information (Warne et al., 2018). Therefore, even people who should be aware of intelligence differences and their consequences often are not.

There is also the fact that it is often unseemly in American culture to talk about intelligence. It seems elitist – especially coming from people who probably are smart. As Bereiter (1976, p. 37) stated, "IQ is like money. Publicly you proclaim that those who have a lot are no better than those who have a little. Privately you wish you had a lot." Unfortunately, a consequence of the public avowals of the irrelevance of IQ is that some people believe these denials. Comforting but false theories, like multiple intelligences (see Chapter 5) or practical intelligence (see Chapter 6), that downplay or deny the importance of *g* are not helpful. These theories do not consider intelligence differences and how the consequences of such differences manifest themselves across society. Their popularity makes the problem of differences in intelligence harder to deal with.

WHAT TO DO

It is almost a cliché, but it is true: admitting that there is a problem is the first step to solving it. Talking openly, but diplomatically, about intelligence differences and their real-world impacts can help decision makers accommodate low-IQ people's needs. There should be a basic recognition that solutions to problems – like poverty, unemployment, or poor health – that work for high-*g* individuals may be difficult or impossible for low-*g* people.

Talking openly about intelligence differences can also apply to group differences in IQ. Although this may sound contentious at first, it has the potential to reduce societal divisions. Solving problems often requires a correct understanding of the causes of those problems (Cofnas, 2016), and refusing to discuss how intelligence differences create inequalities will impede society's ability to address important social problems. For example, people who understand that unemployment is negatively correlated with IQ can grasp why groups with lower average IQs will have a disproportionate share of their members who are unemployed. This can lead policy makers towards finding solutions to this problem. On the other hand, the belief that all groups have the same inherent ability (a belief called the *egalitarian fallacy*) means that when there are unequal outcomes, such as unequal employment rates, then it is because something is wrong with society to create inequalities. Like other forms of *g* denialism, this quickly turns into a blame game:

Lying about race differences in achievement [or IQ] is harmful because it foments mutual recrimination. Because the untruth insists that differences cannot be natural, they must be artificial, manmade, manufactured. Someone must be at fault. Someone must be refusing to do the right thing. It therefore sustains unwarranted, divisive, and ever-escalating mutual accusations of moral culpability, such as Whites are racist and Blacks are lazy. (Gottfredson, 2005b, p. 318)

Once differences in average intelligence across racial groups are accepted, the urge to assign blame is gone because there is no one to blame. No one chose their genes, and the environmental influences on individual people's IQ (at least in industrialized countries) seem to be random and – by adulthood – of relatively minor importance. The next step for policy makers is to determine how to help low-IQ individuals and groups.

Second, high-IQ people whose actions impact less intelligent people should make efforts to specifically benefit members of society with low intelligence. For example, medical personnel should adapt their instructions so that people with less cognitive ability can understand them, give demonstrations of how to perform basic medical tasks (e.g., take a temperature, change bandages on a wound), and issue frequent reminders to take medication (T. C. Davis et al., 1996). In occupations where workers often deal with people with lower intelligence – such as parole officers – the default assumption should be that clients do *not* understand instructions and that they need a high degree of structure and guidance, until individuals prove otherwise.

Third, lawmakers should explore the consequences for low-IQ individuals of different policies and enact laws that benefit and/or protect less intelligent citizens (Cofnas, 2020). Some proposals are straightforward, such as eliminating industries and practices that disproportionately prey on less intelligent people. This might include high-interest payday loan businesses and state lotteries. Other solutions may require study before implementation to ensure that the benefits outweigh the costs. For example, a law that would eliminate unnecessary education requirements in job listings (e.g., a college degree to be a salesperson) could open up more employment opportunities for competent people whose IQ is too low to easily succeed in higher education. But it would also rob employers of a method of identifying more intelligent (and, usually, more productive) employees (see Chapter 23). Before enacting such a law, it would be important to ensure that the benefits to society outweigh the costs.[5] Even if such a law did

[5] Although I discussed it in Chapter 34, the issue of affirmative action is again relevant here. One could make an argument that affirmative action laws are needed to benefit low-IQ individuals and increase their financial independence. Whether that outcome is good for society (despite the loss of efficiency in employment) is a political question.

not pass, the deliberation and consideration of low-IQ people's needs would be a refreshing change from current practice.

Fourth, bright and average people should not expect low-IQ people to pull themselves up by their bootstraps. Even under the best of circumstances, escaping poverty requires long-term planning, which is harder for people with low intelligence. And while there are inspiring stories of people who escaped extreme childhood poverty, no one should generalize from these examples and conclude that anyone can escape a negative environment if they "play by the rules."

Finally, I invite my readers to make an effort to associate with people from different IQ levels. Make friends with people with low-prestige jobs at your workplace. Volunteer in places that will increase your likelihood of interacting with people with lower intelligence, such as a prison or a charity that helps people with intellectual disabilities live independently. When selecting your next home, choose a neighborhood with a mix of socioeconomic statuses.

Interacting with people who have different intelligence levels does not require giving everyone you meet an intelligence test. But it does require making efforts to add cognitive diversity to your life. It is not easy, but as you experience more of these interactions, you will better understand the challenges and thought processes of people with different levels of intelligence. This may lead to a greater level of understanding and compassion towards such people.

CONCLUSION

I had three goals while writing this chapter. The first goal is to make my readers (who are probably more intelligent than average if they have read an academic book to the end) aware that not everyone thinks as well as they do. Second, I hope that this understanding will spur readers to explicitly consider and adapt to the needs and limitations of low-IQ individuals when making decisions that affect their lives. The third goal is to encourage compassion and less judgementalism towards people who think differently. Low intelligence makes people less able to cope with life challenges and changes in society. People with low intelligence are less likely to have the financial resources to compensate for the unfavorable consequences of their poor reasoning ability. They are also more vulnerable to negative consequences of policies and laws – especially when their needs were not considered in passing these laws.

I believe that it is a moral imperative for societies to care for their vulnerable members. Not all readers will agree with my moral perspective. But I encourage people who do agree to include people with low intelligence (below an IQ of approximately 90, which is about 25% of the population) in their list of vulnerable groups that deserve protection. This will include people from other groups that readers may already care about (e.g., people living in poverty, some members of racial minority groups, individuals with intellectual disabilities). But it will include some people from other groups that do not get as much sympathy in modern society (e.g., high school dropouts, low-IQ European Americans, some people living in rural areas, some lower-middle-class citizens). Some of these people may even be held in contempt by some readers (e.g., members of fundamentalist religions, some of the people who vote for the opposing political party). It is not always easy to have compassion for people who are very different from oneself. But having that compassion can result in a better life for vulnerable people and a better society for everyone.

Conclusion

After more than a century of research, scientists know more about intelligence than almost any other psychological trait. Unfortunately, much of this information has not trickled down to the general public, the media, students, or even psychologists with specializations in other areas (Burton & Warne, 2020; Rindermann et al., 2020; Snyderman & Rothman, 1987, 1988; Warne et al., 2018; Warne & Burton, 2020). As a result, erroneous beliefs about intelligence are widespread.

The 35 chapters in this book are a tour of the research on the most common misconceptions that people have about intelligence. Having finished this journey, there are three things I find striking about these chapters. First, it is disheartening that there are so many incorrect beliefs about intelligence. I cannot think of another topic in psychology that is the subject of so many widespread misconceptions. Ironically, these erroneous beliefs are about a topic that is better understood than most areas of psychology.

Second, some of these misconceptions were put to rest among experts decades ago. For example, in Chapter 10, I addressed the incorrect belief that professionally developed tests of g are biased against minority examinees. Psychologists have been examining test bias for over 50 years, with psychologist T. Anne Cleary (1968; Cleary & Hilton, 1968) pioneering this work. Jensen (1980a) published a massive book, *Bias in Mental Testing*, that compiled all the research then existing on the topic, all of which showed that test bias was small or non-existent in professionally developed standardized tests, and that it was often easily corrected (e.g., by dropping biased items). Jensen's book is considered a classic in the testing world and is still often cited today. Modern research using more sophisticated procedures has largely supported early work in test bias (e.g., Aguinis, Culpepper, & Pierce, 2010). Professional ethical standards require psychologists to remove bias from tests (AERA et al., 1999, 2014), and it is nearly impossible to sell a biased test on the market today. And yet, nearly half of undergraduate introductory psychology textbooks state that intelligence tests are biased against racial minorities (Warne et al., 2018). Several other claims are not just misguided but are the polar opposite of the truth. These include the ideas that:

- *g* does not exist (Chapters 1–6).
- Intelligence is difficult to measure (Chapter 7).
- Intelligence tests are too imperfect to use (Chapter 9).
- Genes are irrelevant in determining intelligence (Chapter 13).
- Social or training programs can raise IQ (Chapters 15 and 16).
- Standardized tests are a barrier to opportunity (Chapter 21).
- Intelligence is irrelevant for accomplishments outside school (Chapters 22–24).

Common knowledge among experts is disconnected from what the public believes. On all these points, what non-experts believe is not just wrong – it is spectacularly wrong.

Third, these incorrect beliefs almost all go in one direction towards an overly optimistic belief about human intelligence. There seems to be an egalitarian bias in non-experts' beliefs about intelligence (Warne et al., 2018; Warne & Burton, 2020) which favors wishful thinking (Mackintosh, 2014). An obvious example of this is the rosy belief about the malleability of IQ for people who already live in favorable environments in industrialized nations (see Chapters 14–16 and 19). This egalitarian bias also extends to the denial of individual and group *g* differences (such as in Chapters 13, 17–19, 27–28, and 35) in order to sustain the false belief that everyone is equally intelligent and capable.[1]

A century of research shows that intelligence does matter, that some people are more intelligent than others, and that psychologists do not know how – short of adoption into a highly favorable environment – to permanently raise IQ in people who already live in stable, wealthy nations. Wishful thinking will not turn Mother Nature into an egalitarian, no matter how fervent that desire is. The sooner people admit these facts about intelligence, the sooner they will be better able to cope with them and create effective policies that manage *g* differences and intelligence.

Understanding reality is the first step to handling it. As Jensen stated, "The human condition in all of its aspects cannot be adequately described or understood in a scientific sense without taking into account the powerful explanatory role of the *g* factor" (1998, p. xii). Anyone who genuinely wants to understand humans or improve society needs to understand intelligence. The decision to ignore or deny *g* is a decision to live in a fantasy world.

---

[1] One exception to this egalitarian trend is the incorrect belief that high heritability makes environmental interventions ineffective (see Chapter 14).

UNRESOLVED ISSUES

The body of research that scientists have built up over the past 100 years is impressive. But it is not complete. Many questions still plague intelligence research. It would be impossible to give a full tour of the unresolved scientific issues, but I think readers will be more effective at engaging with intelligence research if they understand some of the "known unknowns" of intelligence.

Heritability. Everyone agrees that h^2 values apply to one specific population under one specific set of circumstances. In industrialized nations, intelligence has low heritability in early childhood – about .20 – and high heritability of about .80 in adulthood (Deary, 2012; Bouchard, 2014). But, as I stated in Chapter 11, heritability may be different for people who live in a very different environment. One of the pressing questions right now is whether and at what level a deprived environment depresses the heritability of IQ. In Sudan, the heritability of IQ for 10-year-olds is about half of what is seen for children the same age in the United States and similar nations (Toto et al., 2019). In Nigeria, heritability of IQ in adolescents was .50, which is consistent with the heritability values seen in wealthy nations (Hur & Bates, 2019). Both nations are much poorer than industrialized nations, and it is not clear why the results of the Sudanese study are so much lower than the Nigerian study.

In the United States, one widely cited study of American 7-year-old twins (Turkheimer, Haley, Waldron, D'Onofrio, & Gottesman, 2003) showed that heritability was nearly zero for children living in poverty. However, studies in other wealthy countries often show that heritability for poorer individuals is similar or equal to heritability in middle- or upper-class samples (Tucker-Drob & Bates, 2016), and the largest study to date of American children does not show any indication of heritability differing across socioeconomic status levels (Figlio, Freese, Karbownik, & Roth, 2017). If lowered heritability does occur, it does not seem to be a race- or ethnicity-related phenomenon, at least not in the United States, because heritability of IQ for all major racial or ethnic groups is highly similar (Pesta et al., 2020).

It is now known that the Turkheimer et al. (2003) study is an anomaly and that – even for very young children within the United States – heritability does not drop to zero (e.g., Tucker-Drob, 2012). But that does not nullify the likely possibility that the heritability of intelligence is lower in deprived environments. It is possible that there is a certain threshold where increasing levels of wealth do not improve heritability and that current studies are not well equipped to identify this threshold. Researchers need more data from developing nations and more exact measures of environmental characteristics in all heritability studies to determine the nature of any changes of heritability across environments. The new research from Sudan (Toto et al., 2019) and Nigeria (Hur & Bates, 2019) is a start, though the latter study does muddy the waters greatly.

In Chapter 28, I presented evidence that the average IQ differences among racial groups within the United States are at least partially genetic. However, a plausible value of h^2_b is unclear. Opinions differ. Gottfredson (2005b) suggested that between-group heritability could be as high as .80. Rushton and Jensen (2005a) proposed a h^2_b value of .50. This latter value is consistent with Jensen's view that group differences are merely the sum of individual differences (Jensen, 1998), which would mean that within- and between-group heritability are approximately equal (i.e., $h^2_b \approx h^2_w$). Based on admixture data, Lasker et al. (2019) thought that between-group heritability of IQ in the United States could be between .50 to .80, though more studies are needed to determine whether their results are typical. Nisbett (2005) took the purely environmentalist position that there was no evidence of a genetic influence for between-group differences (i.e., that between-group heritability or h^2_b, is zero). The evidence in Chapter 28 shows that Nisbett is incorrect, but it is possible that h^2_b could be much smaller than the within-group heritability value of .50 that is typical for industrialized countries. My point with presenting all these numbers is to show that nobody knows what the exact value of between-group heritability within wealthy countries is right now, and there is a great deal of disagreement among experts (Rindermann et al., 2020).

Narrowing Gaps? During the twentieth century, the consensus was that the average score difference for European Americans and African Americans was 15 IQ points ($d = 1.0$), and that is the value I use when I discuss group differences in Chapters 10, 28–30, and 34. Shuey (1966) compiled an exhaustive collection of studies of score gaps between groups in the early and mid-twentieth century and found a consistent difference of 15–18 IQ points. Less than a decade later, the authors of an official report commissioned by the American Psychological Association stated that the 15-point average difference between European and African Americans was "long standing" (Cleary et al., 1975, p. 16), a fact the organization reaffirmed two decades later (Neisser et al., 1996). However, in the twenty-first century, there has been a debate about whether differences between racial groups are narrowing.

One prominent study suggests a narrowing between groups from 15 points ($d = 1.0$) to about 9.5 points ($d = .63$) from the late 1970s to the early 2000s on five intelligence tests (Dickens & Flynn, 2006). These conclusions have been questioned for methodological reasons and for the selection of tests (Rushton, 2012; Rushton & Jensen, 2006). Using the same type of data from a different test, Murray (2007) showed that there was no narrowing of the IQ gap between European and African Americans during the same time period, and Hunt (2011, p. 412) compiled six representative American samples from the late twentieth and early twenty-first century, which have an unweighted average difference of $d = 1.02$, or 15.3 IQ points between these two groups.

Educational tests also seem to provide conflicting information about whether average score differences among American racial groups are changing. Using data from the National Assessment of Educational Progress (NAEP) – which is the best test for comparing educational performance of groups in the United States across time – Rushton and Jensen (2010) found no consistent pattern in the size of educational test score gaps from the 1950s to the 2000s, which supports an earlier analysis of NAEP data (Humphreys, 1988). But educational tests tend to show smaller average race differences in the first place: usually .50 to .90 d, which is equivalent to 7.5 to 13.5 IQ points (e.g., Humphreys, 1988; S. L. Morgan & Jung, 2016; Reardon, Kalogrides, & Shores, 2019; Warne, Anderson, & Johnson, 2013). This could be because end-of-year academic tests may be measuring basic skills and knowledge more than advanced abstract reasoning. Another possibility is that an education system with the goal of bringing students to a basic level of competency can narrow gaps on tests of explicitly taught information but not on abstract tests that have few connections to the curriculum (like a traditional intelligence test). On the other hand, gaps are larger on academic tests that are better measures of g and narrower on tests that measure less g-loaded knowledge and abilities (Warne, 2016b). This matches the predictions of Spearman's hypothesis (see Chapter 28), and the European–African American average score gap on the most g-loaded tests is approximately $d = 1.0$, or 15 IQ points (Warne, 2016b, p. 90).

The issue of whether average score differences in the United States are narrowing remains unresolved. In the future, more data should become available to settle this controversy. In the meantime, a consensus is elusive. In this book, I used a difference of 15 IQ points out of convenience, but I recognize that this difference is not immutable.[2]

In contrast with the American data, intelligence scholars agree that *international* average IQ differences are narrowing (Rindermann et al., 2017). The Flynn effect, which is the tendency for IQ scores to increase over time, is strongest in developing nations (see Chapter 14). At one extreme, increases of 8–9 points per decade have been observed in China (Liu & Lynn, 2013) and rural Kenya (Daley et al., 2003). In some wealthy, industrialized nations, the Flynn effect is much slower and has even stopped (Bratsberg & Rogeberg, 2018; Dutton & Lynn, 2013, 2015; Pietschnig & Gittler, 2015; Russell, 2007; Sundet et al., 2004; Teasdale & Owen, 2000, 2008; Twenge, Campbell, & Sherman, 2019; Woodley & Meisenberg, 2013). Inevitably, this means that the gap in average IQ is narrowing internationally. No one knows how much of the international IQ differences can be eliminated through environmental improvements, but there is no guarantee that the gaps will close completely and that developing nations will catch up to wealthy nations' average IQ scores

---

[2] Indeed, I would be overjoyed if the average IQ differences among all racial groups narrowed or closed completely.

(Rindermann et al., 2017; Woodley & Meisenberg, 2012). Still – like gaps within the United States – these score differences are not set in stone.

The Origin of Species' *g*. Another unresolved question for intelligence researchers is how *g* evolved. For a trait to evolve, it has to make an organism be more successful at passing on its genes. Knowing this, it makes sense why intelligence might be a beneficial trait for a species to develop. In humans, higher intelligence leads to longer life expectancy (Arden et al., 2016; Bratsberg & Rogeberg, 2017; Čukić, Brett, Calvin, Batty, & Deary, 2017; Whalley & Deary, 2001), which means more time for an individual to pass on their genes (especially for males) and to care for their offspring and ensure their survival. Developing an ability to solve problems and handle changes in the environment has obvious potential for survival advantages.

As I stated in Chapter 4, a general cognitive factor has been found in every mammal species investigated (B. Anderson, 1993; Arden & Adams, 2016; Fernandes et al., 2014; Galsworthy et al., 2002; Herndon et al., 1997; Hopkins et al., 2014; Matzel & Sauce, 2017; Navas González et al., 2019). This is evidence that *g* was already present in mammalian evolution. Evidence from non-mammals is less clear. For example, brain size in birds seems to increase the chance of survival (Møller & Erritzøe, 2016), which may indicate that smarter birds live longer, but birds that know more songs do not perform better on cognitive tasks, which might indicate that song learning is an independent skill or ability (MacKinlay & Shaw, 2019). If this latter finding is typical among all songbirds, then it may indicate that *g* is not present in songbird species because *g* cannot emerge unless all cognitive abilities are correlated with one another. On the other hand, pheasants seem to have a *g*-like general ability to distinguish colors from one another (van Horick, Langley, Whiteside, & Madden, 2019), though it is unclear whether this ability correlates with performance on other tasks. More research is needed to determine whether (a) *g* exists in bird species, (b) this *g* resembles human or mammalian *g*, and (c) bird *g* evolved independently of mammalian *g* or if *g* evolved once in a common reptilian ancestor of birds and mammals.

Arden (2019) explained some of the difficulties with conducting intelligence research on animals. Most basically, it is impossible to give a written intelligence test to a large sample of animals at once. Instead, animals have to be examined individually, which means that sample sizes tend to be small and data collection is time consuming. Furthermore, many cognitive tasks do not transfer well across species. Species vary in the behaviors that they are capable of, and their evolutionary history constrains animal responses to behavioral prompts (Breland & Breland, 1961). As an obvious example, teaching gorillas sign language is possible because their hands are similar to human hands; but pigs cannot express human sign language because their hooves prevent the formation of the necessary signs. When investigating the intelligence of a species, it is necessary to study the species' natural behavior first and then devise cognitive tasks that are customized for that species and require responses that the species can generate (Arden, 2019). But this makes comparisons across species difficult, and the *g* of one species may not be the same as the *g* in another.

Regardless of how *g* evolved, there is still the question of how humans became so much more intelligent than other species. After the ancestors of humans separated from other primates, something in our ancestors' environment made more intelligent organisms spread their genes more effectively. But no one really knows what that "something" was. One strong candidate is language; Premack (1983) showed that chimpanzees who experienced sign language training were able to solve more abstract problems than similar chimpanzees who had no language training. Moreover, the chimpanzees with language training showed problem-solving skills similar to what is seen in young human children – but non-trained chimpanzees do not. This may indicate that language gave early humans an ability to deal with abstract stimuli and solve problems that other primates never developed (naturally). Even if this possibility is true, it raises the question of how language evolved – and why humans' ancestors were smart enough to develop language in the first place.

There have been other proposals for how humans developed high intelligence, but none has found support (e.g., Kanazawa, 2010, which Dutton, 2013, severely criticized). Intelligence may have evolved with other psychological traits (Hare, 2017), so answering the question of how intelligence evolved may give clues to why humans differ in other ways from non-human primates. The evolutionary pressures that caused humans to evolve higher intelligence seem to have continued into recent times, including the past 4,500 years (Woodley of Menie, Younuskunju, Balan, & Piffer, 2017).

Creativity and Intelligence. Coming back to the present, another unresolved question is how creativity relates to intelligence. It is well established that creative accomplishment is positively correlated with intelligence (Cicirelli, 1965; Kuncel, Hezlett, & Ones, 2004), and Chapter 25 showed that higher levels of IQ are associated with higher levels of creative output, such as patents and publishing literary works (Lubinski, 2009). It is also clear that intelligence is a prerequisite for creative accomplishment. Creativity in an area requires knowledge about that domain to understand how it functions, what products are valued, and the shortcomings of typical methods of problem solving. Creative accomplishments are also likely to require fluid reasoning in order to understand abstract principles about a domain and imagine the implications and consequences of innovations.

Beyond this, the nature of the relationship between creativity and intelligence is in dispute. One possibility is that creativity is a Stratum II ability within the CHC or bifactor models of intelligence. This is plausible: if intelligence (among other things) helps people solve abstract problems, then an ability to generate new ideas – creativity – should be part of the network of abilities that *g* unites. However, testing this theory encounters problems.

The most popular theory of creativity posits that it has four components (as described by Almeida, Prieto, Ferrando, Oliveira, & Ferrándiz, 2008):

1. The production of a large number of ideas (called fluency),
2. The ability to produce ideas in different categories (which is labeled flexibility),
3. Originality, which is producing new ideas, and
4. Introducing details and refinements of ideas (called elaboration).

What is unclear is how well these abilities combine into a single psychological construct, which is essential for creativity to be a Stratum II ability. (In contrast, there is no doubt that vocabulary size, verbal reasoning, written expression, and oral expression all combine to form a Stratum II verbal ability). Factor analysis of measures of creativity does *not* show that tasks on creativity tests form groups that correspond to the four components of creativity, nor are creativity tasks manifestations of an ability separate from other cognitive abilities (Almeida et al., 2008; Gubbels, Segers, Keuning, & Verhoeven, 2016).

That being said, psychological tests of creativity do seem to predict creative problem-solving ability (Cramond, Matthews-Morgan, Bandalos, & Zuo, 2005; Treffinger, 2009). These tests measure something; the question is whether they measure a coherent ability or whether tasks on creativity tests are vehicles for measuring g (either directly or indirectly). Since the 1950s, research on the relationship between creativity and intelligence has been based on the assumption that intelligence and creativity are two different psychological traits (e.g., Guilford, 1950; Stanley, 1956; Sternberg, 2003b). But this may be merely an example of the *jangle fallacy* (Kelley, 1927, p. 64), where scientists assume that two concepts are different merely because their language has two separate words for the concepts.

At this time, it is unclear whether creativity will continue to be seen as a psychological trait or whether it will be a label for a collection of behaviors that produce novel work. It also needs to be determined whether creativity tasks (a) form a coherent ability within the CHC or bifactor models, (b) are a coherent ability outside the CHC or bifactor models but correlated with g and other abilities, or (c) are dispersed throughout Stratum I in the CHC or bifactor model. (The last option would indicate that creativity is not a coherent psychological concept.) Any of these scenarios is possible.

Regardless of the true nature of creativity as a psychological trait, the concept still holds great value. Innovation is a major driver of technological advancement and economic development. Plus, creativity may be an important trait to develop in its own right because of the variety and richness it brings to people's lives.

Details of the CHC or Bifactor Models. Whether creativity tasks form a Stratum II ability within the CHC model or disperse throughout Stratum I, it shows that the CHC and bifactor models are not complete. While mainstream intelligence researchers agree that *g* is the broadest and most dominant cognitive ability, there is much more uncertainty about Strata I and II (Wasserman, 2019). What is known is that there are at least four Stratum II abilities: verbal ability, fluid reasoning, processing speed, and spatial ability. The number of other Stratum II abilities – and what those abilities are – is disputed. Carroll (1993) favored eight Stratum II abilities. Building on this work, McGrew (2009) proposed 16 Stratum II factors. Stratum I is even more difficult to discern, with potentially hundreds of different narrow abilities that could populate that stratum.

The reason for the ambiguity is that factor analysis is limited by the collection of variables used in the procedure. Factor analysis is, fundamentally, a method of identifying groups of variables that intercorrelate more strongly with one another than with variables outside the group. As stated in the Introduction, the emergence of a factor from a set of variables is not – by itself – evidence that the factor exists as a real psychological trait inside people's heads (B. Thompson, 2004). For example, if I wanted to create an artificial "bicycle riding factor," I could just add highly correlated subtests about that topic to my test (e.g., one-mile bicycling speed, two-mile bicycling speed, longest time balancing on a bicycle in place, low-speed steering capability). These subtests would be highly correlated with one another and have very low correlations with other subtests on an intelligence test – thus creating the "bicycle riding factor." But this does not prove that a "bicycle riding factor" exists inside the brain. To determine whether a factor has real existence, it is necessary to gather other data, such as identifying that the factor corresponds to biological properties of the brain (see Chapter 3).

A general intelligence factor emerges consistently for cognitive test variables because *g* is used to solve every known cognitive task. However, this is not true of narrower factors – like those in Stratum II. To identify Stratum II factors, it is necessary to include data from at least three tasks (preferably more) per ability. Multiply that across 16 factors, and it is necessary to give *at least* 48 subtests to people in order to identify 16 Stratum II factors. This is prohibitively time consuming; Thurstone (1936) gave 54 subtests to a sample, and the entire series required 15 hours per examinee to complete.[3] A goal in the twenty-first century should be to find ways of identifying the number of Stratum II abilities and standardize the CHC and/or bifactor models.

---

[3] Stratum I abilities – being the narrowest class of abilities – are even harder to identify consistently. Usually psychologists performing factor analysis treat the tasks on their tests as being equivalent to Stratum I abilities. But, given enough tasks, a set of scores could coalesce into a number of Stratum I abilities, which then combine to form Stratum II factors, which then have the commonality of *g* in Stratum III. But this would require hundreds of extremely narrow tasks (e.g., a synonyms test, an antonyms test, a test of word understanding, a test of spoken vocabulary – all to measure a Stratum I vocabulary ability) to identify a wide array of Stratum I abilities.

Specific Environmental Influences. Psychologists in the twentieth and early twenty-first centuries made great strides in understanding the environmental influences on intelligence. Chapter 11 showed that adoption into a middle- or upper-class home raises intelligence. Chapter 12 explained the negative impacts of iodine deficiency and lead poisoning. Chapter 14 discussed the Flynn effect, an environmentally caused phenomenon which had a powerful impact on IQ scores during the twentieth century. Chapter 15 demonstrated the importance of avoiding a severely deprived environment. Eliminating or preventing these influences is important to help people reach their full intellectual potential.

While this information is helpful, it says little about how to increase intelligence for most people who live in wealthy nations because very few individuals in them experience severely negative environments. For these people, psychologists have no specific interventions that permanently raise IQ. Even the Flynn effect provides few clues. Beyond some educated guesses (like additional schooling), there is no consensus on specific environmental changes that create the Flynn effect's IQ increase. And the Flynn effect's impact is not even on g anyway (Woodley et al., 2014). Intelligence research has produced no guidance to most people who want to raise their own – or their children's – intelligence.

One of the great challenges of intelligence research in the twenty-first century will be to identify specific environmental influences that have a noteworthy permanent impact on intelligence. This has proven difficult so far because the shared environment among siblings seems to have no permanent impact on intelligence. This means that whatever some parents do to make their children smarter is not something they do to every child. Studies on unshared environmental influences (i.e., that are not found among all children in a family) have been disappointing so far (e.g., Asbury, Moran, & Plomin, 2016). Environmental influences on intelligence – especially after early childhood – are hard to identify. It may be that these influences are random, or that the total influence of environments is the sum of thousands of events, each with a minuscule influence. This latter possibility is plausible because genetic influence is made of thousands of small DNA differences, each having a tiny impact on IQ (Plomin, 2018). Environmental influence may be similar (Tal, 2009).

From Genes to g. Not only are there important questions about the environmental influence on intelligence, but unanswered questions about genetic influences exist, too. It is an established fact that genes can influence intelligence (see Chapters 11 and 13). The bigger question – as stated in Chapter 19 – is the causal process of *how* specific genetic differences lead to a person being able to solve problems better than other people. Geneticists have started working on this problem. Early research shows that many genetic differences that are correlated with IQ are associated with genes that function in brain development (Sniekers et al., 2017).[4] But neuropsychologists are far from fully understanding the chain of events that leads from genetic differences to IQ differences.

Intelligence and International Development. A new frontier in intelligence research is understanding how IQ relates to the economic development of nations. No one questions that a nation's average IQ is positively correlated with its economic prosperity. But there is no consensus over why this correlation exists and what it means for economic development. Economist Garett Jones (2016) and psychologist Heiner Rindermann (2018) have explored this topic in book-length treatments. Both agree that IQ differences are a partial reason why some countries are wealthier than others. Beyond that, though, their views diverge. Jones is much more optimistic about the prospect of raising IQs of citizens of low-scoring countries, while Rindermann believes that some of these differences are intractable. They also draw different conclusions for social policy.

Just as at the individual level, the understanding of how average group-level IQ impacts outcomes for groups is complicated because many possible causes and effects are all correlated with one another. It has taken psychologists decades to untangle these individual-level correlations to the point where experts can have confidence that intelligence is a partial cause of socioeconomic, health, and educational disparities. The research at the national level is much newer, and there are few (if any) firm reasons why the correlations exist. Even the most basic data needed to research the topic – the estimates of national IQ – are a relatively new innovation, and the estimates and methodology are sometimes contested (e.g., Wicherts, Dolan, & van der Maas, 2010). It is also not clear which variables are appropriate to control for and which nations should be compared to one another. Given the magnitude of the gap between the world's richest and poorest nations, this is a valuable topic to investigate.

What Is *g*? Perhaps the most vexing unanswered question about intelligence is the most basic one of all: what is *g*? As a statistical construct, that is easy to answer because *g* is the shared variance among scores on a series of mental tasks. But this just pushes the question back a step, so we may ask: psychologically, what is the nature of the ability that causes people to perform similarly well on a series of cognitive tasks? Merely giving this ability the label of "intelligence" or "*g*" is a naming convention that does not explain anything.

Research shows that whatever *g* is, it emerges from the biological properties of the brain. Chapter 3 discussed some of this research, which

---

[4] This finding may seem unsurprising, but it does provide confirmation that the GWASs are producing results that make sense. If genetics influence intelligence, and intelligence arises in the brain, then genetic differences that are associated with the brain *should* also be associated with intelligence. Any other result would be a major theoretical problem for the study of the genetics of intelligence.

shows that high-*g* individuals often have large, healthy, organized brains that function well and have important regions interconnected. But this still is not a complete answer to the question of what *g* is. Is *g* just something that human brains do? Is it a product of quality brain functioning? Why does every human culture have *g* (see Chapter 4)? What similarities are there between *g* in humans and the *g* in non-human animals? Nobody has definite answers to these challenging questions.

The "Unknown Unknowns." Beyond being questions about intelligence, all of these unresolved issues have one thing in common: they are far removed from the controversies and incorrect beliefs found in the media and among non-experts (Gottfredson, 2009). If one were to judge by media coverage, the arguments about intelligence research are about whether intelligence tests are useful tools, whether tests are fair to everyone, and whether intelligence is useful outside school. Among experts, though, these issues were put to rest long ago. They have since been replaced by more sophisticated (and more interesting) questions.

However, there is a gaping hole in this tour of unanswered questions. It only discusses current questions. *We don't know what we don't know.* Scientific advances or societal changes may give rise to new questions which no one has thought of yet. Each generation of intelligence researchers seems to encounter new, unanticipated questions. These questions have led to answers – sometimes surprising ones – that have improved psychologists' knowledge and understanding of intelligence, the human brain, and society.

LAST THOUGHTS

In closing, I hope readers come away from this book with an appreciation for human intelligence and its impact on people's lives. I also hope that readers understand the limitations of intelligence and intelligence research. While *g* is a general ability, it is not everything. I agree with Stanley's (1974, p. 7) insight that, "The IQ is a valuable global measure of intellect. It tells us much overall, but not enough specifically." This is why IQ is the best predictor of how long someone will stay in school – but it is not a good predictor of the college major a student chooses. Likewise, IQ correlates moderately well with longevity, but much more weakly with specific causes of death. To learn everything important about a person, it is valuable to gather other data – and for some purposes it is not important to gather IQ scores at all.

Intelligence has its tentacles reaching into nearly every aspect of people's lives. That is why it matters so much. Intelligence is part of nearly everything important that people do, and denying its existence – or the existence of intelligence differences – will inevitably lead to incomplete answers to important questions in psychology, sociology, health, politics, and more. The public ignores intelligence at its own peril.

But acknowledging intelligence is not enough. A correct understanding of intelligence, the influences on its development, and its consequences is vital. This book is designed to give readers a firm foundation in the science of intelligence. If the book helps you comprehend the world, your family, or yourself better, then I consider it a success.

References

ACT, Inc. (2017). *ACT technical manual.* Iowa City, IA: Author. Retrieved from www
.act.org/content/dam/act/unsecured/documents/ACT_Technical_Manual.pdf

ACT, Inc. (2018). *The ACT profile report – national. Graduating class of 2018.*
Retrieved from www.act.org/content/dam/act/unsecured/documents/cccr2018/P_99_
999999_N_S_N00_ACT-GCPR_National.pdf

Adhikari, K., Chacón-Duque, J. C., Mendoza-Revilla, J., Fuentes-Guajardo, M., &
Ruiz-Linares, A. (2017). The genetic diversity of the Americas. *Annual Review of
Genomics and Human Genetics, 18,* 277–296. doi:10.1146/annurev-genom-083115-
022331

Aguinis, H., Culpepper, S. A., & Pierce, C. A. (2010). Revival of test bias research in
preemployment testing. *Journal of Applied Psychology, 95,* 648–680. doi:10.1037/
a0018714

Akresh, R., & Akresh, I. R. (2011). Using achievement tests to measure language
assimilation and language bias among the children of immigrants. *Journal of
Human Resources, 46,* 647–667. doi:10.3368/jhr.46.3.647

Allen, M. J., & Yen, W. M. (1979). *Introduction to measurement theory.* Long Grove,
IL: Waveland Press.

Allik, J., & Realo, A. (2017). Universal and specific in the five factor model of
personality. In T. A. Widiger (ed.), *The Oxford handbook of the five factor model*
(pp. 173–190). New York, NY: Oxford University Press.

Almeida, L. S., Prieto, L. P., Ferrando, M., Oliveira, E., & Ferrándiz, C. (2008).
Torrance Test of Creative Thinking: The question of its construct validity. *Thinking
Skills and Creativity, 3,* 53–58. doi:10.1016/j.tsc.2008.03.003

American Educational Research Association, American Psychological Association, &
National Council on Measurement in Education. (1999). *Standards for educational and
psychological testing.* Washington, DC: American Educational Research Association.

American Educational Research Association, American Psychological Association, &
National Council on Measurement in Education. (2014). *Standards for educational
and psychological testing.* Washington, DC: American Educational Research
Association.

American Psychiatric Association. (2013). *Diagnostic and statistical manual of mental
disorders* (5th ed.). Arlington, VA: American Psychiatric Publishing.

Anderson, B. (1993). Evidence from the rat for a general factor that underlies cognitive performance and that relates to brain size: Intelligence? *Neuroscience Letters, 153*, 98–102. doi:10.1016/0304-3940(93)90086-Z

Anderson, M. (2019, May 2). For black Americans, experiences of racial discrimination vary by education level, gender. *Pew Research Center Factank*. Retrieved from www.pewresearch.org/fact-tank/2019/05/02/for-black-americans-experiences-of-racial-discrimination-vary-by-education-level-gender/

Ángeles Quiroga, M., Escorial, S., Román, F. J., Morillo, D., Jarabo, A., Privado, J., ...& Colom, R. (2015). Can we reliably measure the general factor of intelligence (g) through commercial video games? Yes, we can! *Intelligence, 53*, 1–7. doi:10.1016/j.intell.2015.08.004

Anomaly, J., & Winegard, B. (2019). The egalitarian fallacy: Are group differences compatible with political liberalism? *Philosophia*. Advance online publication. doi:10.1007/s11406-019-00129-w

Apolinario, D., Mansur, L. L., Carthery-Goulart, M. T., Bruck, S. M. D., & Nitrini, R. (2014). Cognitive predictors of limited literacy in adults with heterogeneous socioeconomic backgrounds. *Journal of Health Psychology, 20*, 1613–1625. doi:10.1177/1359105313520337

Arden, R. (2019). Cognitive abilities in other animals: An introduction to this special issue. *Intelligence, 74*, 1–2. doi:10.1016/j.intell.2019.04.003

Arden, R., & Adams, M. J. (2016). A general intelligence factor in dogs. *Intelligence, 55*, 79–85. doi:10.1016/j.intell.2016.01.008

Arden, R., Luciano, M., Deary, I. J., Reynolds, C. A., Pedersen, N. L., Plassman, B. L., ... & Visscher, P. M. (2016). The association between intelligence and lifespan is mostly genetic. *International Journal of Epidemiology, 45*, 178–185. doi:10.1093/ije/dyv112

Armstrong, E. L., & Woodley, M. A. (2014). The rule-dependence model explains the commonalities between the Flynn effect and IQ gains via retesting. *Learning and Individual Differences, 29*, 41–49. doi:10.1016/j.lindif.2013.10.009

Asbury, K. (2015). Can genetics research benefit educational interventions for all? *The Hastings Center Report, 45*, S39-S42. doi:10.1002/hast.497

Asbury, K., Moran, N., & Plomin, R. (2016). Nonshared environmental influences on academic achievement at age 16: A qualitative hypothesis-generating monozygotic-twin differences study. *AERA Open, 2*(4). doi:10.1177/2332858416673596

Ashton, M. C., & Lee, K. (2005). Problems with the method of correlated vectors. *Intelligence, 33*, 431–444. doi:10.1016/j.intell.2004.12.004

Ashton, M. C., Lee, K., & Visser, B. A. (2014). Higher-order *g* versus blended variable models of mental ability: Comment on Hampshire, Highfield, Parkin, and Owen (2012). *Personality and Individual Differences, 60*, 3–7. doi:10.1016/j.paid.2013.09.024

Assouline, S. G., Colangelo, N., VanTassel-Baska, J., & Lupkowski-Shoplik, A. (eds.). (2015). *A nation empowered: Evidence trumps the excuses holding back America's brightest students* (Vol. 2). Iowa City, IA: Belin-Blank Center.

Assouline, S. G., Colangelo, N., VanTassel-Baska, J., & Sharp, M. (2015). *A nation empowered: Evidence trumps the excuses holding back America's brightest students* (Vol. 1). Iowa City, IA: Belin-Blank Center.

Atkins v. Virginia, 536 U.S. 304 (2002).

Atkinson, R. C. (2001). Achievement versus aptitude in college admissions. *Issues in Science & Technology, 18*(2), 31–36.

Au, W. (2018, April 14). The socialist case against the SAT. *Jacobin.* Retrieved from www.jacobinmag.com/2018/04/against-the-sat-testing-meritocracy-race-class

Axt, J. R. (2017). An unintentional pro-Black bias in judgement among educators. *British Journal of Educational Psychology, 87,* 408–421. doi:10.1111/bjep.12156

Baddeley, A. (1992). Working memory. *Science, 255,* 556–559. doi:10.1126/science.1736359

Bahník, Š., & Vranka, M. A. (2017). Growth mindset is not associated with scholastic aptitude in a large sample of university applicants. *Personality and Individual Differences, 117,* 139–143. doi:10.1016/j.paid.2017.05.046

Baldwin, B. T., & Stecher, L. I. (1922). Mental growth curve of normal and superior children studied by means of consecutive intelligence examinations. *University of Iowa Studies in Child Welfare, 2*(1), 1–61, S61–S67.

Bandalos, D. L., Yates, K., & Thorndike-Christ, T. (1995). Effects of math self-concept, perceived self-efficacy, and attributions for failure and success on test anxiety. *Journal of Educational Psychology, 87,* 611–623. doi:10.1037/0022-0663.87.4.611

Bandura, A. (1977). Self-efficacy: Toward a unifying theory of behavioral change. *Psychological Review, 84,* 191–215. doi:10.1037/0033-295X.84.2.191

Bandura, A. (1982). Self-efficacy mechanism in human agency. *American Psychologist, 37,* 122–147. doi:10.1037/0003-066X.37.2.122

Barnes, E., & Puccioni, J. (2017). Shared book reading and preschool children's academic achievement: Evidence from the Early Childhood Longitudinal Study – Birth cohort. *Infant and Child Development, 26,* e2035. doi:10.1005/icd.2035

Bassok, D., & Latham, S. (2017). Kids today: The rise in children's academic skills at kindergarten entry. *Educational Researcher, 46,* 7–20. doi:10.3102/0013189X17694161

Bates, T. C. (2007). Fluctuating asymmetry and intelligence. *Intelligence, 35,* 41–46. doi:10.1016/j.intell.2006.03.013

Beaujean, A. A., & Benson, N. F. (2019). The one and the many: Enduring legacies of Spearman and Thurstone on intelligence test score interpretation. *Applied Measurement in Education, 32,* 198–215. doi:10.1080/08957347.2019.1619560

Beaujean, A. A., McGlaughlin, S. M., & Margulies, A. S. (2009). Factorial validity of the Reynolds Intellectual Assessment Scales for referred students. *Psychology in the Schools, 46,* 932–950. doi:10.1002/pits.20435

Beaver, K. M., Nedelec, J. L., da Silva Costa, C., & Vidal, M. M. (2015). The future of biosocial criminology. *Criminal Justice Studies, 28,* 6–17. doi:10.1080/1478601x.2014.1000002

Belasco, A. S., Rosinger, K. O., & Hearn, J. C. (2015). The test-optional movement at America's selective liberal arts colleges: A boon for equity or something else? *Educational Evaluation and Policy Analysis, 37,* 206–223. doi:10.3102/0162373714537350

Belsky, D. W., & Harden, K. P. (2019). Phenotypic annotation: Using polygenic scores to translate discoveries from genome-wide association studies from the top down. *Current Directions in Psychological Science, 28,* 82–90. doi:10.1177/0963721418807729

Belsky, D. W., Moffitt, T. E., Corcoran, D. L., Domingue, B., Harrington, H., Hogan, S., … & Caspi, A. (2016). The genetics of success: How single-nucleotide polymorphisms associated with educational attainment relate to life-course development. *Psychological Science, 27,* 957–972. doi:10.1177/0956797616643070

Benbow, C. P., & Stanley, J. C. (1996). Inequity in equity: How "equity" can lead to inequity for high-potential students. *Psychology, Public Policy, and Law, 2,* 249–292. doi:10.1037/1076-8971.2.2.249

Bereiter, C. (1976). IQ and elitism. *Interchange*, 7(3), 36–44. doi:10.1007/bf02142630

Berry, J. W. (1974). Radical cultural relativism and the concept of intelligence. In J. W. Berry & P. R. Dasen (eds.), *Culture and cognition: Readings in cross-cultural psychology* (pp. 225–229). London: Methuen.

Berry, J. W., & Bennett, J. A. (1992). Cree conceptions of cognitive competence. *International Journal of Psychology*, 27, 73–88. doi:10.1080/00207599208246867

Bielby, R., Posselt, J. R., Jaquette, O., & Bastedo, M. N. (2014). Why are women underrepresented in elite colleges and universities? A non-linear decomposition analysis. *Research in Higher Education*, 55, 735–760. doi:10.1007/s11162-014-9334-y

Biemiller, A. (1993). Lake Wobegon revisited: On diversity and education. *Educational Researcher*, 22(9), 7–12. doi:10.3102/0013189X022009007

Binet, A. (1911/1916). New investigations upon the measure of the intellectual level among school children (E. S. Kite, Trans.). In A. Binet & T. Simon, *The development of intelligence in children (the Binet-Simon Scale)* (pp. 274–329). Baltimore, MD: Williams & Wilkins.

Binet, A., & Simon, T. (1905/1916). New methods for the diagnosis of the intellectual level of subnormals (E. S. Kite, Trans.). In A. Binet & T. Simon, *The development of intelligence in children (the Binet-Simon Scale)* (pp. 9–36). Baltimore, MD: Williams & Wilkins.

Binet, A., & Simon, T. (1908/1916). The development of intelligence in the child (E. S. Kite, Trans.). In A. Binet & T. Simon, *The development of intelligence in children (the Binet-Simon Scale)* (pp. 182–273). Baltimore, MD: Williams & Wilkins.

Blagaich, P. (1999). Advanced placement courses are not for everyone. *The History Teacher*, 32, 259–262. doi:10.2307/494445

Blatt, B., & Hess, A. (2014, March 5). Do men wager more than women in *Jeopardy?* A Slate investigation. *Slate*. Retrieved from https://slate.com/human-interest/2014/03/gender-differences-in-jeopardy-alex-trebek-says-women-wager-less-in-daily-double-bets.html

Boake, C. (2002). From the Binet-Simon to the Wechsler-Bellevue: Tracing the history of intelligence testing. *Journal of Clinical and Experimental Neuropsychology*, 24, 383–405. doi:10.1076/jcen.24.3.383.981

Bonner, S. M. (2006). A think-aloud approach to understanding performance on the Multistate Bar Examination. *The Bar Examiner*, 1(6), 6–15.

Bonner, S. M., & D'Agostino, J. V. (2012). A substantive process analysis of responses to items from the Multistate Bar Examination. *Applied Measurement in Education*, 25, 1–26. doi:10.1080/08957347.2012.635472

Bouchard, T. J., Jr. (1984). Review of *Frames of mind: The theory of multiple intelligences*. *American Journal of Orthopsychiatry*, 54, 506–508. doi:10.1111/j.1939-0025.1984.tb01522.x

Bouchard, T. J., Jr. (1997). Genetic influence on mental abilities, personality, vocational interests, and work attitudes. In C. L. Cooper & I. T. Robertson (eds.), *International review of industrial and organizational psychology* (Vol. 12, pp. 373–395). Hoboken, NJ: John Wiley & Sons.

Bouchard, T. J., Jr. (2004). Genetic influence on human psychological traits: A survey. *Current Directions in Psychological Science*, 13, 148–151. doi:10.1111/j.0963-7214.2004.00295.x

Bouchard, T. J., Jr. (2014). Genes, evolution and intelligence. *Behavior Genetics*, 44, 549–577. doi:10.1007/s10519-014-9646-x

Bouchard, T. J., Jr., & McGue, M. (1981). Familial studies of intelligence: A review. *Science*, *212*, 1055–1059. doi:10.1126/science.7195071

Bouchard, T. J., Jr., Lykken, D. T., Tellegen, A., & McGue, M. (1996). Genes, drives, environment, and experience: EPD theory revised. In C. P. Benbow (ed.), *Intellectual talent: Psychometric and social issues* (pp. 5–43). Baltimore, MD: Johns Hopkins University Press.

Bowie, L. (2013, August 16). Maryland schools have been leader in Advanced Placement, but results are mixed. *Capital Gazette*. Retrieved from www .capitalgazette.com/bal-maryland-schools-have-been-leader-in-advanced-placement-but-results-are-mixed-20140930-story.html

Bratsberg, B., & Rogeberg, O. (2017). Childhood socioeconomic status does not explain the IQ-mortality gradient. *Intelligence*, *62*, 148–154. doi:10.1016/j.intell.2017.04.002

Bratsberg, B., & Rogeberg, O. (2018). Flynn effect and its reversal are both environmentally caused. *Proceedings of the National Academy of Sciences*, *115*, 6674-6678. doi:10.1073/pnas.1718793115

Breland, K., & Breland, M. (1961). The misbehavior of organisms. *American Psychologist*, *16*, 681–684. doi:10.1037/h0040090

Bridgett, D. J., & Walker, M. E. (2006). Intellectual functioning in adults with ADHD: A meta-analytic examination of full scale IQ differences between adults with and without ADHD. *Psychological Assessment*, *18*, 1–14. doi:10.1037/1040-3590.18.1.1

Briley, D. A., & Tucker-Drob, E. M. (2017). Comparing the developmental genetics of cognition and personality over the life span. *Journal of Personality*, *85*, 51–64. doi:10.1111/jopy.12186

Broberg, G., & Roll-Hansen, N. (eds.). (2005). *Eugenics and the welfare state: Norway, Sweden, Denmark, and Finland*. East Lansing, MI: Michigan State University Press.

Broberg, G., & Tydén, M. (2005). Eugenics in Sweden: Efficient care. In G. Broberg & N. Roll-Hansen (eds.), *Eugenics and the welfare state: Norway, Sweden, Denmark, and Finland* (pp. 77–149). East Lansing, MI: Michigan State University Press.

Brody, L. (2018, October 3). Some parents pay up to $400 an hour to prep 4-year-olds for NYC's gifted test. *Wall Street Journal*. Retrieved from www.wsj.com/articles/some-parents-pay-up-to-400-an-hour-to-prep-4-year-olds-for-nycs-gifted-test-1538568001

Brody, N. (2003). Construct validation of the Sternberg Triarchic Abilities Test: Comment and reanalysis. *Intelligence*, *31*, 319–329. doi:10.1016/S0160-2896(01)00087-3

Brody, N. (2004). What cognitive intelligence is and what emotional intelligence is not. *Psychological Inquiry*, *15*, 234–238.

Brody, N. (2008). Does education influence intelligence? In P. C. Kyllonen, R. D. Roberts, & L. Stankov (eds.), *Extending intelligence: Enhancement and new constructs* (pp. 85–92). Mahwah, NJ: Lawrence Erlbaum Associates.

Brogden, H. E. (1946). On the interpretation of the correlation coefficient as a measure of predictive efficiency. *Journal of Educational Psychology*, *37*, 65–76. doi:10.1037/ h0061548

Brooks-Gunn, J., & Duncan, G. J. (1997). The effects of poverty on children. *The Future of Children*, *7*(2), 55–71. doi:10.2307/1602387

Brown, W. (1910). Some experimental results in the correlation of mental abilities. *British Journal of Psychology*, *3*, 296–322. doi:10.1111/j.2044-8295.1910.tb00207.x

Bryc, K., Durand, E. Y., Macpherson, J. M., Reich, D., & Mountain, J. L. (2015). The genetic ancestry of African Americans, Latinos, and European Americans across the

United States. *American Journal of Human Genetics*, *96*, 37–53. doi:10.1016/j. ajhg.2014.11.010

Brydges, C. R., Reid, C. L., Fox, A. M., & Anderson, M. (2012). A unitary executive function predicts intelligence in children. *Intelligence*, *40*, 458–469. doi:10.1016/j. intell.2012.05.006

Buck v. Bell, 274 U.S. 200 (1927)

Buckendahl, C. W., & Hunt, R. (2005). Whose rules? The relation between the "rules" and "law" of testing. In R. P. Phelps (ed.), *Defending standardized testing* (pp. 147–158). Mahwah, NJ: Lawrence Erlbaum Associates.

Buckner, J. C., Mezzacappa, E., & Beardslee, W. R. (2003). Characteristics of resilient youths living in poverty: The role of self-regulatory processes. *Development and Psychopathology*, *15*, 139–162. doi:10.1017/S0954579403000087

Bureau of Labor Statistics. (2018, April 13). *Occupational outlook handbook: Preschool teachers*. Retrieved from www.bls.gov/ooh/education-training-and-library /preschool-teachers.htm

Burgdorf, R. L., Jr., & Burgdorf, M. P. (1977). The wicked witch is almost dead: *Buck v. Bell* and the sterilization of handicapped persons. *Temple Law Quarterly*, *50*, 995–1033.

Burgoyne, A. P., Hambrick, D. Z., & Macnamara, B. N. (2020). How firm are the foundations of mind-set theory? The claims appear stronger than the evidence. *Psychological Science*, *31*, 258-267. doi:10.1177/0956797619897588

Burks, B. S. (1928/1973). The relative influence of nature and nurture upon mental development; a comparative study of foster parent–foster child resemblance and true parent–true child resemblance. In H. J. Eysenck (ed.), *The measurement of intelligence* (pp. 325–357). Dordrecht: Springer. (Original work published in 1928)

Burks, B. S., Jensen, D. W., & Terman, L. M. (1930). *Genetic studies of genius*, Vol. III: *The promise of youth: Follow-up studies of a thousand gifted children*. Stanford, CA: Stanford University Press.

Burris, C. C., & Welner, K. G. (2005). Closing the achievement gap by detracking. *Phi Delta Kappan*, *86*, 594–598. doi:10.1177/003172170508600808

Burt, C. (1917). *The distribution and relations of educational abilities*. London: P. S. King.

Burton, J. Z., & Warne, R. T. (2020). The neglected intelligence course: Needs and suggested solutions. *Teaching of Psychology*, *47*, 130-140. doi.org/10.1177/ 0098628320901381

Calvin, A. (2000). Use of standardized tests in admissions in postsecondary institutions of higher education. *Psychology, Public Policy, and Law*, *6*, 20–32. doi:10.1037/ 1076-8971.6.1.20

Calvin, C. M., Deary, I. J., Fenton, C., Roberts, B. A., Der, G., Leckenby, N., & Batty, G. D. (2011). Intelligence in youth and all-cause-mortality: Systematic review with meta-analysis. *International Journal of Epidemiology*, *40*, 626–644. doi:10.1093/ ije/dyq190

Calvin, C. M., Fernandes, C., Smith, P., Visscher, P. M., & Deary, I. J. (2010). Sex, intelligence and educational achievement in a national cohort of over 175,000 11-year-old schoolchildren in England. *Intelligence*, *38*, 424–432. doi:10.1016/j. intell.2010.04.005

Camara, W. J. (2009). College admission testing: Myths and realities in an age of admissions hype. In R. P. Phelps (ed.), *Correcting fallacies about educational and psychological testing* (pp. 147–180). Washington, DC: American Psychological Association.

Camerer, C. F., Dreber, A., Holzmeister, F., Ho, T.-H., Huber, J., Johannesson, M., … & Wu, H. (2018). Evaluating the replicability of social science experiments in *Nature* and *Science* between 2010 and 2015. *Nature Human Behaviour*, *2*, 637–644. doi:10.1038/s41562-018-0399-z

Camilli, G. (2006). Test fairness. In R. L. Brennan (ed.), *Educational measurement* (4th ed., pp. 221–256). Westport, CT: Praeger.

Canivez, G. L., & Youngstrom, E. A. (2019). Challenges to the Cattell-Horn-Carroll theory: Empirical, clinical, and policy implications. *Applied Measurement in Education*, *32*, 232–248. doi:10.1080/08957347.2019.1619562

Carl, N. (2018). How stifling debate around race, genes and IQ can do harm. *Evolutionary Psychological Science*, *4*, 399–407. doi:10.1007/s40806-018-0152-x

Carl, N. (2019). The fallacy of equating the hereditarian hypothesis with racism. *Psych*, *1*, 262–278. doi:10.3390/psych1010018

Carl, N., & Woodley of Menie, M. A. (2019). A scientometric analysis of controversies in the field of intelligence research. *Intelligence*, *77*, 101397. doi:10.1016/j. intell.2019.101397

Carman, C. A., & Taylor, D. K. (2010). Socioeconomic status effects on using the Naglieri Nonverbal Ability Test (NNAT) to identify the gifted/talented. *Gifted Child Quarterly*, *54*, 75–84. doi:10.1177/0016986209355976

Carman, C. A., Walther, C. A. P., & Bartsch, R. A. (2018). Using the Cognitive Abilities Test (CogAT) 7 nonverbal battery to identify the gifted/talented: An investigation of demographic effects and norming plans. *Gifted Child Quarterly*, *62*, 193–209. doi:10.1177/0016986217752097

Carroll, J. B. (1993). *Human cognitive abilities: A survey of factor-analytic studies.* New York, NY: Cambridge University Press.

Carson, J. (1993). Army Alpha, army brass, and the search for army intelligence. *Isis*, *84*, 278–309. doi:10.1086/356463

Carter, R. T., & Goodwin, A. L. (1994). Racial identity and education. *Review of Research in Education*, *20*, 291–336. doi:10.2307/1167387

Caspi, A., Houts, R. M., Belsky, D. W., Harrington, H., Hogan, S., Ramrakha, S., … & Moffitt, T. E. (2016). Childhood forecasting of a small segment of the population with large economic burden. *Nature Human Behaviour*, *1*, Article 0005. doi:10.1038/s41562-016-0005

Cassidy, S., Roche, B., Colbert, D., Stewart, I., & Grey, I. M. (2016). A relational frame skills training intervention to increase general intelligence and scholastic aptitude. *Learning and Individual Differences*, *47*, 222–235. doi:10.1016/j.lindif.2016.03.001

Castejon, J. L., Perez, A. M., & Gilar, R. (2010). Confirmatory factor analysis of Project Spectrum activities: A second-order *g* factor or multiple intelligences? *Intelligence*, *38*, 481–496. doi:10.1016/j.intell.2010.07.002

Ceci, J. (1991). How much does schooling influence general intelligence and its cognitive components? A reassessment of evidence. *Developmental Psychology*, *27*, 703–722. doi:10.1037/0012-1649.27.5.703

Ceci, S. J., & Papierno, P. B. (2005). The rhetoric and reality of gap closing: When the "have-nots" gain but the "haves" gain even more. *American Psychologist*, *60*, 149–160. doi:10.1037/0003-066x.60.2.149

Ceci, S., & Williams, W. M. (2009). Should scientists study race and IQ? Yes: The scientific truth must be pursued. *Nature, 457*, 788–789. doi:10.1038/457788a

Centers for Disease Control. (2018). Tested and confirmed elevated blood lead levels by state, year, and blood lead level group for children < 72 months of age. Retrieved from www.cdc.gov/nceh/lead/data/national.htm

Chabris, C. F., Heck, P. R., Mandart, J., Benjamin, D. J., & Simons, D. J. (2019). No evidence that experiencing physical warmth promotes interpersonal warmth: Two failures to replicate Williams and Bargh (2008). *Social Psychology, 50*, 127–132. doi:10.1027/1864-9335/a000361

Chambers, J. G., Shkonik, & Pérez, M. (2003). Total expenditures for students with disabilities, 1999–2000: Spending variation by disability. Retrieved from www.air.org/sites/default/files/SEEP5-Total-Expenditures.pdf

Chapman, P. D. (1988). *School as sorters: Lewis M. Terman, applied psychology, and the intelligence testing movement, 1890–1930.* New York, NY: New York University Press.

Check Hayden, E. (2013). Ethics: Taboo genetics. *Nature, 502*, 26–28. doi:10.1038/502026a

The Chimpanzee Sequencing and Analysis Consortium. (2005). Initial sequence of the chimpanzee genome and comparison with the human genome. *Nature, 437*, 69–87. doi:10.1038/nature04072

Chodosh, S. (2018). IQ ≠ intelligence. *Popular Science, 290*(2), 9.

Christensen, G. T., Mortensen, E. L., Christensen, K., & Osler, M. (2016). Intelligence in young adulthood and cause-specific mortality in the Danish Conscription Database – a cohort study of 728,160 men. *Intelligence, 59*, 64–71. doi:10.1016/j.intell.2016.08.001

Church, M. S. (1995). Determination of race from the skeleton through forensic anthropological methods. *Forensic Science Review, 7*, 1–39.

Ciarrochi, J., Scott, G., Deane, F. P., & Heaven, P. C. L. (2003). Relations between social and emotional competence and mental health: A construct validation study. *Personality and Individual Differences, 35*, 1947–1963. doi:10.1016/S0191-8869(03)00043-6

Cicirelli, V. G. (1965). Form of the relationship between creativity, IQ, and academic achievement. *Journal of Educational Psychology, 56*, 303–308. doi:10.1037/h0022792

Clarizio, H. F. (1979). In defense of the IQ test. *School Psychology Digest, 8*, 79–88.

Cleary, T. A. (1968). Test bias: Prediction of grades of Negro and White students in integrated colleges. *Journal of Educational Measurement, 5*, 115–124. doi:10.1111/j.1745-3984.1968.tb00613.x

Cleary, T. A., & Hilton, T. L. (1968). An investigation of item bias. *Educational and Psychological Measurement, 28*, 61–75. doi:10.1177/001316446802800106

Cleary, T. A., Humphreys, L. G., Kendrick, S. A., & Wesman, A. (1975). Educational uses of tests with disadvantaged students. *American Psychologist, 30*, 15–41. doi:10.1037/0003-066x.30.1.15

Cleveland, H. H., Jacobson, K. C., Lipinski, J. J., & Rowe, D. C. (2000). Genetic and shared environmental contributions to the relationship between the HOME environment and child and adolescent achievement. *Intelligence, 28*, 69–86. doi:10.1016/s0160-2896(99)00029-x

Clinedinst, M., & Patel, P. (2018). *2018 state of college admission.* Arlington, VA: National Association for College Admission Counseling. Retrieved from www.nacacnet.org/globalassets/documents/publications/research/2018_soca/soca18.pdf

Cochran, G., Hardy, J., & Harpending, H. (2006). Natural history of Ashkenazi intelligence. *Journal of Biosocial Science, 38,* 659–693. doi:10.1017/S0021932005027069

Cochran, G., & Harpending, H. (2009). *The 10,000 year explosion: How civilization accelerated human evolution.* New York, NY: Basic Books.

Cofnas, N. (2016). Science is not always "self-correcting": Fact–value conflation and the study of intelligence. *Foundations of Science, 21,* 477–492. doi:10.1007/s10699-015-9421-3

Cofnas, N. (2020). Coercive paternalism and the intelligence continuum. *Behavioural Public Policy, 4,* 88–107. doi:10.1017/bpp.2018.4

Coleman, J. S. (1991). The Sidney Hook Memorial Award address: On the self-suppression of academic freedom. *Academic Questions, 4*(1), 17–22. doi:10.1007/BF02682943

College Board. (2017). *SAT suite of assessments technical manual appendixes.* New York, NY: Author. Retrieved from https://collegereadiness.collegeboard.org/pdf/sat-suite-assessments-technical-manual-appendix-pt-1.pdf

College Board. (2018). *2018 SAT suite of assessments annual report.* Retrieved from https://reports.collegeboard.org/pdf/2018-total-group-sat-suite-assessments-annual-report.pdf

Collins, R. (1979). *The credential society: An historical sociology of education and stratification.* New York, NY: Columbia University Press.

Conn, L. K., Edwards, C. N., Rosenthal, R., & Crowne, D. (1968). Perception of emotion and response to teachers' expectancy by elementary school children. *Psychological Reports, 22,* 27–34. doi:10.2466/pr0.1968.22.1.27

Conrad, H. S., Jones, H. E., & Hsiao, H. H. (1933). Sex differences in mental growth and decline. *Journal of Educational Psychology, 24,* 161–169. doi:10.1037/h0073913

Conti, G., Heckman, J. J., & Pinto, R. (2016). The effects of two influential early childhood interventions on health and healthy behaviour. *Economic Journal, 126* (596), F28–F65. doi:10.1111/ecoj.12420

Conway, A. R. A., & Kovacs, K. (2018). The nature of the general factor of intelligence. In R. J. Sternberg (ed.), *The nature of human intelligence* (pp. 49–63). New York, NY: Cambridge University Press.

Cook, C. R., Low, S., Buntain-Ricklefs, J., Whitaker, K., Pullmann, M. D., & Lally, J. (2018). Evaluation of second step on early elementary students' academic outcomes: A randomized controlled trial. *School Psychology Quarterly, 33,* 561–572. doi:10.1037/spq0000233

Coon, D., & Mitterer, J. O. (2016). *Introduction to psychology: Gateways to mind and behavior* (14th ed.). Boston, MA: Cengage Learning.

Corley, J., Crang, J. A., & Deary, I. J. (2009). Childhood IQ and in-service mortality in Scottish Army personnel during World War II. *Intelligence, 37,* 238–242. doi:10.1016/j.intell.2008.11.003

Cornell, E. L. (1928). Why are more boys than girls retarded in school? I. *Elementary School Journal, 29,* 96–105. doi:10.2307/995446

Corno, L., Cronbach, L. J., Kupermintz, H., Lohman, D. F., Mandinach, E. B., Porteus, A. W., & Talbert, J. E. (2002). *Remaking the concept of aptitude: Extending the legacy of Richard E. Snow.* Mahwah, NJ: Lawrence Erlbaum Associates.

Costa, P. T., & McCrae, R. R. (2010). *NEO personality inventory-3.* Lutz, FL: Psychological Assessment Resources.

Cox, S. R., Ritchie, S. J., Fawns-Ritchie, C., Tucker-Drob, E. M., & Deary, I. J. (2019). Structural brain imaging correlates of general intelligence in UK Biobank. *Intelligence*, 76, Article 101376. doi:10.1016/j.intell.2019.101376

Coyle, T. R. (2015). Relations among general intelligence (*g*), aptitude tests, and GPA: Linear effects dominate. *Intelligence*, 53, 16–22. doi:10.1016/j.intell.2015.08.005

Coyle, T. R., Elpers, K. E., Gonzalez, M. C., Freeman, J., & Baggio, J. A. (2018). General intelligence (*g*), ACT scores, and theory of mind: (ACT)*g* predicts limited variance among theory of mind tests. *Intelligence*, 71, 85–91. doi:10.1016/j.intell.2018.10.006

Cramond, B., Matthews-Morgan, J., Bandalos, D., & Zuo, L. (2005). A report on the 40-year follow-up of the Torrance Tests of Creative Thinking: Alive and well in the new millennium. *Gifted Child Quarterly*, 49, 283–291. doi:10.1177/001698620504900402

Credé, M., Tynan, M. C., & Harms, P. D. (2017). Much ado about grit: A meta-analytic synthesis of the grit literature. *Journal of Personality and Social Psychology*, 113, 492–511. doi:10.1037/pspp0000102

Crocker, L. (2005). Teaching for the test: How and why test preparation is appropriate. In R. P. Phelps (ed.), *Defending standardized testing* (pp. 159–174). Mahwah, NJ: Lawrence Erlbaum Associates.

Cronbach, L. J. (1957). The two disciplines of scientific psychology. *American Psychologist*, 12, 671–684. doi:10.1037/h0043943

Cronbach, L. J. (1975). Five decades of public controversy over mental testing. *American Psychologist*, 30, 1–14. doi:10.1037/0003-066X.30.1.1

Crowe, R. R., & Colbach, E. M. (1971). A psychiatric experience with Project 100,000. *Military Medicine*, 136, 271–273.

Cucina, J. M., & Howardson, G. N. (2017). Woodcock–Johnson–III, Kaufman Adolescent and Adult Intelligence Test (KAIT), Kaufman Assessment Battery for Children (KABC), and Differential Ability Scales (DAS) support Carroll but not Cattell–Horn. *Psychological Assessment*, 29, 1001–1015. doi:10.1037/pas0000389

Cucina, J. M., Peyton, S. T., Su, C., & Byle, K. A. (2016). Role of mental abilities and mental tests in explaining high-school grades. *Intelligence*, 54, 90–104. doi:10.1016/j.intell.2015.11.007

Čukić, I., Brett, C. E., Calvin, C. M., Batty, G. D., & Deary, I. J. (2017). Childhood IQ and survival to 79: Follow-up of 94% of the Scottish Mental Survey 1947. *Intelligence*, 63, 45–50. doi:10.1016/j.intell.2017.05.002

Dahlke, J. A., & Sackett, P. R. (2017). The relationship between cognitive-ability saturation and subgroup mean differences across predictors of job performance. *Journal of Applied Psychology*, 102, 1403–1420. doi:10.1037/apl0000234

Daley, T. C., Whaley, S. E., Sigman, M. D., Espinosa, M. P., & Neumann, C. (2003). IQ on the rise: The Flynn effect in rural Kenyan children. *Psychological Science*, 14, 215–219. doi:10.1111/1467-9280.02434

Dalliard, M. (2014). The elusive x-factor: A critique of J. M. Kaplan's model of race and IQ. *Open Differential Psychology*. doi:10.26775/ODP.2014.08.25

Dalton, B. W. (2010). Motivation. In J. A. Rosen, E. J. Glennie, B. W. Dalton, & J. M. B. Lennon, Robert N. (eds.), *Noncognitive skills in the classroom: New perspectives on educational research* (pp. 11–38). Research Triangle Park, NC: RTI International.

Damian, R. I., Su, R., Shanahan, M., Trautwein, U., & Roberts, B. W. (2015). Can personality traits and intelligence compensate for background disadvantage?

Predicting status attainment in adulthood. *Journal of Personality and Social Psychology, 109*, 473–489. doi:10.1037/pspp0000024

Daniels, S., & Piechowski, M. M. (eds.). (2009). *Living with intensity*. Scottsdale, AZ: Great Potential Press.

Dannenberg, M., & Hyslop, A. (2019). *Building a fast track to college: An executive summary*. Washington, DC: Alliance for Excellent Education. Retrieved from http://edreformnow.org/wp-content/uploads/2019/02/ERN-AEE-Fast-Track-FINAL.pdf

Davis, B. B. (1978). The moralistic fallacy. *Nature, 272*, 390. doi:10.1038/272390a0

Davis, T. C., Meldrum, H., Tippy, P. K. P., Weiss, B. D., & Williams, M. V. (1996). How poor literacy leads to poor health care. *Patient Care, 30*(16), 94–104.

de Bruin, A. B. H., Kok, E. M., Leppink, J., & Camp, G. (2014). Practice, intelligence, and enjoyment in novice chess players: A prospective study at the earliest stage of a chess career. *Intelligence, 45*, 18–25. doi:10.1016/j.intell.2013.07.004

de la Burdé, B., & Choate, M. S. (1975). Early asymptomatic lead exposure and development at school age. *Journal of Pediatrics, 87*, 638–642. doi:10.1016/S0022-3476(75)80845-6

Deary, I. J. (2001). *Intelligence: A very short introduction*. New York, NY: Oxford University Press.

Deary, I. J. (2012). Intelligence. *Annual Review of Psychology, 63*, 453–482. doi:10.1146/annurev-psych-120710-100353

Deary, I. J., Der, G., & Shenkin, S. D. (2005). Does mother's IQ explain the association between birth weight and cognitive ability in childhood? *Intelligence, 33*, 445–454. doi:10.1016/j.intell.2005.05.004

Deary, I. J., Strand, S., Smith, P., & Fernandes, C. (2007). Intelligence and educational achievement. *Intelligence, 35*, 13–21. doi:10.1016/j.intell.2006.02.001

Deary, I. J., Taylor, M. D., Hart, C. L., Wilson, V., Smith, G. D., Blane, D., & Starr, J. M. (2005). Intergenerational social mobility and mid-life status attainment: Influences of childhood intelligence, childhood social factors, and education. *Intelligence, 33*, 455–472. doi:10.1016/j.intell.2005.06.003

Deary, I. J., Thorpe, G., Wilson, V., Starr, J. M., & Whalley, L. J. (2003). Population sex differences in IQ at age 11: The Scottish Mental Survey 1932. *Intelligence, 31*, 533–542. doi:10.1016/s0160-2896(03)00053-9

Deary, I. J., Whalley, L. J., Lemmon, H., Crawford, J. R., & Starr, J. M. (2000). The stability of individual differences in mental ability from childhood to old age: Follow-up of the 1932 Scottish Mental Survey. *Intelligence, 28*, 49–55. doi:10.1016/S0160-2898(99)00031-8

Deary, I. J., Whalley, L. J., & Starr, J. M. (eds.). (2009). *A lifetime of intelligence: Follow-up studies of the Scottish Mental Surveys of 1932 and 1947*. Washington, DC: American Psychological Association.

Deary, I. J., Whiteman, M. C., Starr, J. M., Whalley, L. J., & Fox, H. C. (2004). The impact of childhood intelligence on later life: Following up the Scottish Mental Surveys of 1932 and 1947. *Journal of Personality and Social Psychology, 86*, 130–147. doi:10.1037/0022-3514.86.1.130

DeFries, J. C. (1972). Quantiative aspects of genetics and environment in the determination of behavior. In L. Ehrman, G. S. Omenn, & E. Caspari (eds.), *Genetics, environment, and behavior* (pp. 5–16). New York, NY: Academic Press.

Del Giudice, M., Barrett, E. S., Belsky, J., Hartman, S., Martle, M. M., Sangenstedt, S., & Kuzawa, C. W. (2018). Individual differences in plasticity: A role for early androgens? *Psychoneuroendocrinology*, *90*, 165–173. doi:10.1016/j.psyneuen.2018.02.025

Delaney, P. (1975, May 13). Black psychologist fighting use of intelligence tests he says reflect White middle-class values. *New York Times*, p. 36. Retrieved from www.nytimes.com/1975/05/13/archives/black-psychologist-fighting-use-of-intelligence-tests-he-says.html

Deresiewicz, W. (2014, July 21). Don't send your kid to the Ivy League. *New Republic*. Retrieved from https://newrepublic.com/article/118747/ivy-league-schools-are-overrated-send-your-kids-elsewhere

Derryberry, W. P., Jones, K. L., Grieve, F. G., & Barger, B. (2007). Assessing the relationship among Defining Issues Test scores and crystallised and fluid intellectual indices. *Journal of Moral Education*, *36*, 475–496. doi:10.1080/03057240701688036

Detterman, D. K. (2006). Editorial note on controversial papers. *Intelligence*, *34*(1), iv. doi:10.1016/j.intell.2005.10.001

Detterman, D. K. (2014). You should be teaching intelligence! *Intelligence*, *42*, 148–151. doi:10.1016/j.intell.2013.07.021

Diamond, J. (1997). *Guns, germs and steel: The fates of human societies*. San Francisco, CA: Norton.

Dickens, W. T., & Flynn, J. R. (2006). Black Americans reduce the racial IQ gap: Evidence from standardization samples. *Psychological Science*, *17*, 913–920. doi:10.1111/j.1467-9280.2006.01802.x

Diener, C. I., & Dweck, C. S. (1978). An analysis of learned helplessness: Continuous changes in performance, strategy, and achievement cognitions following failure. *Journal of Personality and Social Psychology*, *36*, 451–462. doi:10.1037/0022-3514.36.5.451

Diener, E., Oishi, S., & Park, J. (2014). An incomplete list of eminent psychologists of the modern era. *Archives of Scientific Psychology*, *2*, 20–31. doi:10.1037/arc0000006

Dirani, M., Chamberlain, M., Shekar, S. N., Islam, A. F. M., Garoufalis, P., Chen, C. Y., ... & Baird, P. N. (2006). Heritability of refractive error and ocular biometrics: The Genes in Myopia (GEM) twin study. *Investigative Opthalmology & Visual Science*, *47*, 4756–4761. doi:10.1167/iovs.06-0270

Dixson, D. D., Worrell, F. C., Olszewski-Kubilius, P., & Subotnik, R. F. (2016). Beyond perceived ability: The contribution of psychosocial factors to academic performance. *Annals of the New York Academy of Sciences*, *1377*, 67–77. doi:10.1111/nyas.13210

Dolan, C. V. (2000). Investigating Spearman's hypothesis by means of multi-group confirmatory factor analysis. *Multivariate Behavioral Research*, *35*, 21–50. doi:10.1207/S15327906MBR3501_2

Dolan, C. V., & Hamaker, E. L. (2001). Investigating Black–White differences in psychometric IQ: Multi-group confirmatory factor analyses of the WISC-R and K-ABC and a critique of the method of correlated vectors. In F. H. Columbus (ed.), *Advances in psychology research* (Vol. 6, pp. 31–59). Huntington, NY: Nova Science Publishers.

Domingue, B. W., Belsky, D. W., Conley, D., Harris, K. M., & Boardman, J. D. (2015). Polygenic influence on educational attainment: New evidence from the National Longitudinal Study of Adolescent to Adult Health. *AERA Open*, *1*(3), 1–13. doi:10.1177/2332858415599972

Duckworth, A. (2016). *Grit: The power of passion and perseverance.* New York, NY: Scribner.

Duckworth, A. L., & Eskreis-Winkler, L. (2013, April). True grit. *APS Observer.* Retrieved from www.psychologicalscience.org/observer/true-grit

Duckworth, A. L., Peterson, C., Matthews, M. D., & Kelly, D. R. (2007). Grit: Perseverance and passion for long-term goals. *Journal of Personality and Social Psychology, 92,* 1087–1101. doi:10.1037/0022-3514.92.6.1087

Duncan, G. J., & Magnuson, K. (2013). Investing in preschool programs. *Journal of Economic Perspectives, 27,* 109–132. doi:10.1257/jep.27.2.109

Dunkel, C. S., Woodley of Menie, M. A., Pallesen, J., & Kirkegaard, E. O. W. (2019). Polygenic scores mediate the Jewish phenotypic advantage in educational attainment and cognitive ability compared with Catholics and Lutherans. *Evolutionary Behavioral Sciences, 13,* 366–375. doi:10.1037/ebs0000158

Dutton, E. (2013). The Savanna–IQ interaction hypothesis: A critical examination of the comprehensive case presented in Kanazawa's *The Intelligence Paradox. Intelligence, 41,* 607–614. doi:10.1016/j.intell.2013.07.024

Dutton, E., Essa, Y. A. S., Bakhiet, S. F., Ali, H. A. A., Alqafari, S. M., Alfaleh, A. S. H., & Becker, D. (2018). Brain drain in Syria's ancient capital: No Flynn Effect in Damascus, 2004–2013/14. *Personality and Individual Differences, 125,* 10–13. doi:10.1016/j.paid.2017.12.025

Dutton, E., & Lynn, R. (2013). A negative Flynn effect in Finland, 1997–2009. *Intelligence, 41,* 817–820. doi:10.1016/j.intell.2013.05.008

Dutton, E., & Lynn, R. (2015). A negative Flynn Effect in France, 1999 to 2008–9. *Intelligence, 51,* 67–70. doi:10.1016/j.intell.2015.05.005

Dweck, C. S. (2007). The perils and promises of praise. *ASCD, 65*(2), 34–39. Retrieved from www.ascd.org/publications/educational-leadership/oct07/vol65/num02/The-Perils-and-Promises-of-Praise.aspx

Dweck, C. S. (2008, Winter). Brainology. *Independent School.* Retrieved from www.nais.org/magazine/independent-school/winter-2008/brainology/

Dweck, C. S. (2009, Fall). Can we make our students smarter? *Education Canada, 49*(4), 56–61.

Dweck, C. S. (2012). Mindsets and human nature: Promoting change in the Middle East, the schoolyard, the racial divide, and willpower. *American Psychologist, 67,* 614–622. doi:10.1037/a0029783

Dweck, C. S. (2016). The remarkable reach of growth mind-sets. *Scientific American Mind, 27*(1), 36–41.

Dyck, M. J. (1996). Cognitive assessment in a multicultural society: Comment on Davidson (1995). *Australian Psychologist, 31,* 66–69. doi:10.1080/00050069608260180

Education Week Research Center. (2016). *Mindset in the classroom: A national study of K-12 teachers.* Bethesda, MD: Author. Retrieved from www.edweek.org/media/ewrc_mindsetintheclassroom_sept2016.pdf

Edwards, A. W. F. (2003). Human genetic diversity: Lewontin's fallacy. *BioEssays, 25,* 798–801. doi:10.1002/bies.10315

Elardo, R., & Bradley, R. H. (1981). The Home Observation for Measurement of the Environment (HOME) scale: A review of research. *Developmental Review, 1,* 113–145. doi:10.1016/0273-2297(81)90012-5

Elliott, R. (1987). *Litigating intelligence: IQ tests, special education, and social science in the courtroom.* Dover, MA: Auburn House.

Emanuelsson, I., Reuterberg, S. E., & Svensson, A. (1993). Changing differences in intelligence? Comparisons between groups of 13-year-olds tested from 1960 to 1990. *Scandinavian Journal of Educational Research*, *37*, 259–277. doi:10.1080/0031383930370401

Embretson, S. E. (1996). The new rules of measurement. *Psychological Assessment*, *8*, 341–349. doi:10.1037/1040-3590.8.4.341

Embretson, S. E., & Reise, S. P. (2000). *Item response theory for psychologists.* Mahwah, NJ: Lawrence Erlbaum Associates.

Ericsson, K. A., Roring, R. W., & Nandagopal, K. (2007). Giftedness and evidence for reproducibly superior performance: An account based on the expert performance framework. *High Ability Studies*, *18*, 3–56. doi:10.1080/13598130701350593

Eskreis-Winkler, L., Shulman, E. P., Beal, S. A., & Duckworth, A. L. (2014). The grit effect: Predicting retention in the military, the workplace, school and marriage. *Frontiers in Psychology*, *5*, Article 36. doi:10.3389/fpsyg.2014.00036

Espenshade, T. J., & Chung, C. Y. (2005). The opportunity cost of admission preferences at elite universities. *Social Science Quarterly*, *86*, 293–305. doi:10.1111/j.0038-4941.2005.00303.x

Espenshade, T. J., Chung, C. Y., & Walling, J. L. (2004). Admission preferences for minority students, athletes, and legacies at elite universities. *Social Science Quarterly*, *85*, 1422–1446. doi:10.1111/j.0038-4941.2004.00284.x

Euler, M. J. (2018). Intelligence and uncertainty: Implications of hierarchical predictive processing for the neuroscience of cognitive ability. *Neuroscience & Biobehavioral Reviews*, *94*, 93–112. doi:10.1016/j.neubiorev.2018.08.013

Eusebius. (2007). *The church history* (P. L. Maier, Trans.). Grand Rapids, MI: Kregel Publications.

Evans, G. W., & Rosenbaum, J. (2008). Self-regulation and the income-achievement gap. *Early Childhood Research Quarterly*, *23*, 504–514. doi:10.1016/j.ecresq.2008.07.002

Evans, J. T., & Rosenthal, R. (1969). *Interpersonal self-fulfilling prophecies: Further extrapolations from the laboratory to the classroom.* Retrieved from ERIC database. (ED034276)

Fair, L. (2016, January 5). Mind the gap: What Lumosity promised vs. what it could prove [Web blog post]. Retrieved from www.ftc.gov/news-events/blogs/business-blog/2016/01/mind-gap-what-lumosity-promised-vs-what-it-could-prove

Fancher, R. E. (1985). *The intelligence men: Makers of the IQ controversy.* New York, NY: W. W. Norton.

Feingold, A. (1992). Sex differences in variability in intellectual abilities: A new look at an old controversy. *Review of Educational Research*, *62*, 61–84. doi:10.3102/00346543062001061

Feldman, D. (1979). Toward a nonelitist conception of giftedness. *Phi Delta Kappan*, *60*, 660–663.

Feldman, D. H. (1984). A follow-up of subjects scoring above 180 IQ in Terman's "Genetic Studies of Genius." *Exceptional Children*, *50*, 518–523. doi:10.1177/001440298405000604

Feldman, R. S. (2015). *Essentials to understanding psychology* (11th ed.). New York, NY: McGraw-Hill Education.

Fernandes, H. B. F., Woodley, M. A., & te Nijenhuis, J. (2014). Differences in cognitive abilities among primates are concentrated on *G*: Phenotypic and phylogenetic comparisons with two meta-analytical databases. *Intelligence*, *46*, 311–322. doi:10.1016/j.intell.2014.07.007

Figlio, D. N., Freese, J., Karbownik, K., & Roth, J. (2017). Socioeconomic status and genetic influences on cognitive development. *Proceedings of the National Academy of Sciences*, *114*, 13441–13446. doi:10.1073/pnas.1708491114

Finn, C. E., Jr., & Scanlan, A. E. (2019, August 13). Expanding the educational pie: Advanced Placement programs in New York City schools. *City Journal*. Retrieved from www.city-journal.org/nyc-advanced-placement-programs

Firkowska, A., Ostrowska, A., Sokolowska, M., Stein, Z., Susser, M., & Wald, I. (1978). Cognitive development and social policy. *Science*, *200*, 1357–1362. doi:10.1126/science.663616

Flashman, L. A., Andreasen, N. C., Flaum, M., & Swayze, V. W., II. (1997). Intelligence and regional brain volumes in normal controls. *Intelligence*, *25*, 149–160. doi:10.1016/S0160-2896(97)90039-8

Fletcher, R. (1991). *Science, ideology, and the media: The Cyril Burt scandal*. New Brunswick, NJ: Transaction Publishers.

Flore, P. C., Mulder, J., & Wicherts, J. M. (2018). The influences of gender stereotype threat on mathematics test scores of Dutch high school students: A registered report. *Comprehensive Results in Social Psychology*, *3*, 140–174.

Flore, P. C., & Wicherts, J. M. (2015). Does stereotype threat influence performance of girls in stereotyped domains? A meta-analysis. *Journal of School Psychology*, *53*, 25–44. doi:10.1016/j.jsp.2014.10.002

Floyd, R. G., Reynolds, M. R., Farmer, R. L., & Kranzler, J. H. (2013). Are the general factors from different child and adolescent intelligence tests the same? Results from a five-sample, six-test analysis. *School Psychology Review*, *42*, 383–401.

Flynn, J. R. (1980). *Race, IQ and Jensen*. London: Routledge & Kegan Paul.

Flynn, J. R. (1984). The mean IQ of Americans: Massive gains 1932 to 1978. *Psychological Bulletin*, *95*, 29–51. doi:10.1037/0033-2909.95.1.29

Flynn, J. R. (1987). Massive IQ gains in 14 nations: What IQ tests really measure. *Psychological Bulletin*, *101*, 171–191. doi:10.1037/h0090408

Flynn, J. R. (2018). Academic freedom and race: You ought not to believe what you think may be true. *Journal of Criminal Justice*, *59*, 127–131. doi:10.1016/j.jcrimjus.2017.05.010

Flynn, J. R., te Nijenhuis, J., & Metzen, D. (2014). The g beyond Spearman's g: Flynn's paradoxes resolved using four exploratory meta-analyses. *Intelligence*, *44*, 1–10. doi:10.1016/j.intell.2014.01.009

Foliano, F., Rolfe, H., Buzzeo, J., Runge, J., & Wilkinson, D. (2019). *Changing mindsets: Effectiveness trial. Evaluation report*. London: National Institute of Economic and Social Research. Retrieved from https://educationendowmentfoundation.org.uk/public/files/Projects/Evaluation_Reports/Changing_Mindsets.pdf

Ford, D. Y. (1995). Desegregating gifted education: A need unmet. *Journal of Negro Education*, *64*, 52–62. doi:10.2307/2967284

Ford, D. Y. (2014). Segregation and the underrepresentation of Blacks and Hispanics in gifted education: Social inequality and deficit paradigms. *Roeper Review*, *36*, 143–154. doi:10.1080/02783193.2014.919563

Foroughi, C. K., Serraino, C., Parasuraman, R., & Boehm-Davis, D. A. (2016). Can we create a measure of fluid intelligence using Puzzle Creator within Portal 2? *Intelligence*, *56*, 58–64. doi:10.1016/j.intell.2016.02.011

Forscher, P. S., Taylor, V. J., Cavagnaro, D., Lewis, N. A., Jr., Moshontz, H., Batres, C., ... & Chartier, C. R. (2019). A multi-site examination of stereotype threat in black college students across varying operationalizations. doi:10.31234/osf.io/6hju9 Retrieved from https://psyarxiv.com/6hju9/

Forstmeier, W., Wagenmakers, E.-J., & Parker, T. H. (2017). Detecting and avoiding likely false-positive findings – a practical guide. *Biological Reviews*. doi:10.1111/brv.12315

Fox, M. C., & Mitchum, A. L. (2013). A knowledge-based theory of rising scores on "culture-free" tests. *Journal of Experimental Psychology: General, 142,* 979–1000. doi:10.1037/a0030155

Franco, A., Malhotra, N., & Simonovits, G. (2014). Publication bias in the social sciences: Unlocking the file drawer. *Science, 345,* 1502. doi:10.1126/science.1255484

Freeman, F. N. (1923). A referendum of psychologists. *The Century, 107,* 237–245.

Frey, M. C., & Detterman, D. K. (2004). Scholastic assessment or *g*? The relationship between the scholastic assessment test and general cognitive ability. *Psychological Science, 15,* 373–378.

Friedrichs, R. W. (1973). The impact of social factors upon scientific judgment: The "Jensen thesis" as appraised by members of the American Psychological Association. *Journal of Negro Education, 42,* 429–438. doi:10.2307/2966555

Frisby, C. L. (2013). *Meeting the psychoeducational needs of minority students: Evidence-based guidelines for school psychologists and other school personnel.* Hoboken, NJ: John Wiley & Sons.

Frisby, C. L., & Henry, B. (2016). Science, politics, and best practice: 35 years after Larry P. *Contemporary School Psychology, 20,* 46–62. doi:10.1007/s40688-015-0069-3

Fryar, C. D., Kruszon-Moran, D., Gu, Q., & Ogden, C. L. (2018). *Mean body weight, height, waist circumference, and body mass index among adults: United States, 1999–2000 through 2015–2016.* (National Health Statistics Reports No. 122). Retrieved from www.cdc.gov/nchs/data/nhsr/nhsr122-508.pdf

Fuerst, J., & Dalliard, M. (2014). Genetic and environmental determinants of IQ in Black, White and Hispanic Americans: A meta-analysis and new analysis. *Open Behavioral Genetics, 10,* 1–21. doi:10.26775/OBG.2014.09.15

Gagné, F., & St Père, F. (2001). When IQ is controlled, does motivation still predict achievement? *Intelligence, 30,* 71–100. doi:10.1016/S0160-2896(01)00068-X

Galsworthy, M. J., Paya-Cano, J. L., Monleón, S., & Plomin, R. (2002). Evidence for general cognitive ability (*g*) in heterogeneous stock mice and an analysis of potential confounds. *Genes, Brain and Behavior, 1,* 88–95. doi:10.1034/j.1601-183X.2002.10204.x

Galton, D. J., & Galton, C. J. (1998). Francis Galton: And eugenics today. *Journal of Medical Ethics, 24,* 99–105. doi:10.1136/jme.24.2.99

Galton, F. (1883). *Human faculty and its development.* London: Macmillan and Co.

Galton, F. (1907). Probability, the foundation of eugenics. *Popular Science Monthly, 71,* 165–178.

Gandhi, J., Watts, T. W., Masucci, M. D., & Raver, C. C. (2020). The effects of two mindset interventions on low-income students' academic and psychological outcomes. *Journal of Research on Educational Effectiveness, 13,* 351–379. doi:10.1080/19345747.2019.1711272

Ganley, C. M., Mingle, L. A., Ryan, A. M., Ryan, K., Vasilyeva, M., & Perry, M. (2013). An examination of stereotype threat effects on girls' mathematics performance. *Developmental Psychology, 49*, 1886–1897. doi:10.1037/a0031412

Gardner, H. (1999). *Intelligence reframed.* New York, NY: Basic Books.

Gardner, H. (2004). Audiences for the theory of multiple intelligences. *Teachers College Record, 106,* 212–220. 10.1111/j.1467–9620.2004.00329.x

Gardner, H. (2009). *Intelligence: It's not just IQ.* New York, NY: Rockefeller University. Retrieved from https://bit.ly/2qQR6J1

Gardner, H. (2011). *Frames of mind: The theory of multiple intelligences.* New York, NY: Basic Books.

Gardner, H. (2016). Multiple intelligences: Prelude, theory, and aftermath. In R. J. Sternberg, S. T. Fiske, & D. J. Foss (eds.), *Scientists making a difference: One hundred eminent behavioral and brain scientists talk about their most important contributions* (pp. 167–170). New York, NY: Cambridge University Press.

Garfinkel, R., & Thorndike, R. L. (1976). Binet item difficulty then and now. *Child Development, 47,* 959–965. doi:10.1111/1467-8624.ep12190864

Garrow, D. J. (2014). Toward a definite history of *Griggs v. Duke Power Co. Vanderbilt Law Review, 67,* 197–237.

Geisinger, K. F. (2005). The testing industry, ethnic minorities, and individuals with disabilities. In R. P. Phelps (ed.), *Defending standardized testing* (pp. 187–203). Mahwah, NJ: Lawrence Erlbaum Associates.

Geisinger, K. F. (2019). Empirical considerations on intelligence testing and models of intelligence: Updates for educational measurement professionals. *Applied Measurement in Education, 32,* 193–197. doi:10.1080/08957347.2019.1619564

Genç, E., Fraenz, C., Schlüter, C., Friedrich, P., Hossiep, R., Voelkle, M. C., Ling, J. M., Güntürkün, O., & Jung, R. E. (2018). Diffusion markers of dendritic density and arborization in gray matter predict differences in intelligence. *Nature Communications, 9,* Article 1905. doi.org/10.1038/s41467-018-04268-8

Gerrig, R. J. (2013). *Psychology and life* (20th ed.). Upper Saddle River, NJ: Pearson.

Gibbons, A., & Warne, R. T. (2019). First publication of subtests in the Stanford-Binet 5, WAIS-IV, WISC-V, and WPPSI-IV. *Intelligence, 75,* 9–18. doi:10.1016/j.intell.2019.02.005

Giessman, J. A., Gambrell, J. L., & Stebbins, M. S. (2013). Minority performance on the Naglieri Nonverbal Ability Test, Second Edition, versus the Cognitive Abilities Test, Form 6: One gifted program's experience. *Gifted Child Quarterly, 57,* 101–109. doi:10.1177/0016986213477190

Gignac, G. E., Bartulovich, A., & Salleo, E. (2019). Maximum effort may not be required for valid intelligence test score interpretations. *Intelligence, 75,* 73–84. doi:10.1016/j.intell.2019.04.007

Gignac, G. E., & Bates, T. C. (2017). Brain volume and intelligence: The moderating role of intelligence measurement quality. *Intelligence, 64,* 18–29. doi:10.1016/j.intell.2017.06.004

Gillborn, D. (2016). Softly, softly: Genetics, intelligence and the hidden racism of the new geneism. *Journal of Education Policy, 31,* 365–388. doi:10.1080/02680939.2016.1139189

Gillham, N. W. (2001). *A life of Sir Francis Galton: From African exploration to the birth of eugenics.* New York, NY: Oxford University Press.

Gladwell, M. (2008). *Outliers: The story of success*. New York, NY: Little Brown.

Glass, G. V. (1976). Primary, secondary, and meta-analysis of research. *Educational Researcher, 5*(10), 3–8. doi:10.3102/0013189X005010003

Glass, G. V. (1977). Integrating findings: The meta-analysis of research. *Review of Research in Education, 5*, 351–379. doi:10.3102/0091732X005001351

Gleitman, H., Gross, J., & Reisberg, D. (2011). *Psychology* (8th ed.). New York, NY: Norton.

Glerum, J., Loyens, S. M. M., Wijnia, L., & Rikers, R. M. J. P. (2019). The effects of praise for effort versus praise for intelligence on vocational education students. *Educational Psychology*. Advance online publication. doi:10.1080/01443410.2019.1625306

Goddard, H. H. (1910). Four hundred feeble-minded children classified by the Binet method. *The Journal of Genetic Psychology, 17*, 387–397.

Goddard, H. H. (1912). *The Kallikak family: A study in the heredity of feeble-mindedness*. New York, NY: Macmillan Company.

Goddard, H. H. (1914). *Feeble-mindedness: Its causes and consequences*. New York, NY: Macmillan Company.

Goleman, D. (1995). *Emotional intelligence*. New York, NY: Bantam Books.

Gómez, H. F., Borgialli, D. A., Sharman, M., Shah, K. K., Scolpino, A. J., Oleske, J. M., & Bogden, J. D. (2018). Blood lead levels of children in Flint, Michigan: 2006–2016. *Journal of Pediatrics, 197*, 158–164. doi:10.1016/j.jpeds.2017.12.063

Goode, E. (2002, March 2). Boy genius? Mother says she faked tests. *New York Times*. Retrieved from www.nytimes.com/2002/03/02/us/boy-genius-mother-says-she-faked-tests.html

Goodenough, F. L. (1926). Racial differences in the intelligence of school children. *Journal of Experimental Psychology, 9*, 388–397. doi:10.1037/h0073325

Gordon, R. A. (1997). Everyday life as an intelligence test: Effects of intelligence and intelligence context. *Intelligence, 24*, 203–320. doi:10.1016/S0160-2896(97)90017-9

Gottfredson, L. S. (1986). Societal consequences of the *g* factor in employment. *Journal of Vocational Behavior, 29*, 379–410. doi:10.1016/0001-8791(86)90015-1

Gottfredson, L. S. (1994). Egalitarian fiction and collective fraud. *Society, 31*(3), 53–59. doi:10.1007/BF02693231

Gottfredson, L. S. (1997a). Mainstream science on intelligence: An editorial with 52 signatories, history, and bibliography. *Intelligence, 24*, 13–23. doi:10.1016/S0160-2896(97)90011-8

Gottfredson, L. S. (1997b). Why *g* matters: The complexity of everyday life. *Intelligence, 24*, 79–132. doi:10.1016/S0160-2896(97)90014-3

Gottfredson, L. S. (2000a). Pretending intelligence doesn't matter. *Cerebrum, 2*(3), 75–96.

Gottfredson, L. S. (2000b). Skill gaps, not tests, make racial proportionality impossible. *Psychology, Public Policy, and Law, 6*, 129–143. doi:10.101317//1076-8971.6.1.129

Gottfredson, L. S. (2001). [Review of the book *Practical Intelligence in Everyday Life*, by Robert J. Sternberg, George B. Forsythe, Jennifer Hedlund, Joseph A. Horvath, Richard K. Wagner, Wendy M. Williams, Scott A. Snook, and Elena L. Grigorenko]. *Intelligence, 29*, 363–365. doi:10.1016/S0160-2896(01)00059-9

Gottfredson, L. S. (2003a). Dissecting practical intelligence theory: Its claims and evidence. *Intelligence, 31*, 343–397. doi:10.1016/S0160-2896(02)00085-5

Gottfredson, L. S. (2003b). On Sternberg's "Reply to Gottfredson." *Intelligence, 31*, 415–424. doi:10.1016/s0160-2896(03)00024-2

Gottfredson, L. S. (2003c). The science and politics of intelligence in gifted education. In N. Colangelo & G. A. Davis (eds.), *Handbook of gifted education* (3rd ed., pp. 24–40). Boston, MA: Allyn and Bacon.

Gottfredson, L. S. (2004). Intelligence: Is it the epidemiologists' elusive "fundamental cause" of social class inequalities in health? *Journal of Personality & Social Psychology, 86*, 174–199. doi:10.1037/0022-3514.86.1.174

Gottfredson, L. S. (2005a). Implications of cognitive differences for schooling within diverse societies. In C. L. Frisby & C. R. Reynolds (eds.), *Comprehensive handbook of multicultural school psychology* (pp. 517–554). Hoboken, NJ: John Wiley & Sons.

Gottfredson, L. S. (2005b). What if the hereditarian hypothesis is true? *Psychology, Public Policy, and Law, 11*, 311–319. doi:10.1037/1076-8971.11.2.311

Gottfredson, L. S. (2009). Logical fallacies used to dismiss the evidence on intelligence testing. In R. P. Phelps (ed.), *Correcting fallacies about educational and psychological testing* (pp. 11–65). Washington, DC: American Psychological Association.

Gottfredson, L. S. (2010). Lessons in academic freedom as lived experience. *Personality and Individual Differences, 49*, 272–280. doi:10.1016/j.paid.2010.01.001

Gottfredson, L. S. (2011). Intelligence and social inequality: Why the biological link? In T. Chamorro-Premuzic, S. von Stumm, & A. Furnham (eds.), *The Wiley–Blackwell handbook of individual differences* (pp. 538–575). Oxford: Wiley–Blackwell.

Gottfredson, L. S., & Deary, I. J. (2004). Intelligence predicts health and longevity, but why? *Current Directions in Psychological Science, 13*, 1–4. doi:10.1111/j.0963-7214.2004.01301001.x

Gottfredson, L., & Saklofske, D. H. (2009). Intelligence: Foundations and issues in assessment. *Canadian Psychology, 50*, 183–195. doi:10.1037/a0016641

Gould, S. J. (1981). *The mismeasure of man.* New York, NY: W. W. Norton.

Gould, S. J. (1996). *The mismeasure of man: Revised and expanded.* New York, NY: W. W. Norton.

Graces, J. L., Jr., & Johnson, A. (1995). The pseudoscience of psychometry and *The Bell Curve. Journal of Negro Education, 64*, 277–294. doi:10.2307/2967209

Graf, N. (2019). Most Americans say colleges should not consider race or ethnicity in admissions. *Factank.* Pew Research Center. Retrieved from www.pewresearch.org/fact-tank/2019/02/25/most-americans-say-colleges-should-not-consider-race-or-ethnicity-in-admissions/

Greenberg, L. (1955). A critique of classic methods of identifying gifted children. *School Review, 63*, 25–30. doi:10.2307/1083412

Greenwald, A. G. (1975). Consequences of prejudice against the null hypothesis. *Psychological Bulletin, 82*, 1–20. doi:10.1037/h0076157

Gregory, H. (2015). *McNamara's folly: The use of low-IQ troops in the Vietnam War plus the induction of unfit men, criminals, and misfits.* West Conshohocken, PA: Infinity Publishing.

Griggs v. Duke Power Co., 401 U.S. 424 (1971).

Griggs, R. A., Proctor, D. L., & Cook, S. M. (2004). The most frequently cited books in introductory texts. *Teaching of Psychology, 31*, 113–116.

Grigorenko, E. L., Geissler, P. W., Prince, R., Okatcha, F., Nokes, C., Kenny, D. A., … & Sternberg, R. J. (2001). The organisation of Luo conceptions of intelligence: A study of implicit theories in a Kenyan village. *International Journal of Behavioral Development, 25*, 367–378. doi:10.1080/01650250042000348

Grison, S., Heatherton, T. F., & Gazzaniga, M. S. (2017). *Psychology in your life.* New York, NY: Norton.

Grodin, M. A., Miller, E. L., & Kelly, J. I. (2018). The Nazi physicians as leaders in eugenics and "euthanasia": Lessons for today. *American Journal of Public Health, 108,* 53–57. doi:10.2105/ajph.2017.304120

Gruber, H. E. (1963). Education and the image of man. *Journal of Research in Science Teaching, 1,* 162–169. doi:10.1002/tea.3660010213

Gubbels, J., Segers, E., Keuning, J., & Verhoeven, L. (2016). The Aurora-*a* battery as an assessment of triarchic intellectual abilities in upper primary grades. *Gifted Child Quarterly, 60,* 226–238. doi:10.1177/0016986216645406

Gudjonsson, G. H. (1990). One hundred alleged false confession cases: Some normative data. *British Journal of Clinical Psychology, 29,* 249–250. doi:10.1111/j.2044-8260.1990.tb00881.x

Gudjonsson, G. H. (1991). The effects of intelligence and memory on group differences in suggestibility and compliance. *Personality and Individual Differences, 12,* 503–505. doi:10.1016/0191-8869(91)90070-R

Guilford, J. P. (1950). Creativity. *American Psychologist, 5,* 444–454. doi:10.1037/h0063487

Guilford, J. P. (1956). The structure of intellect. *Psychological Bulletin, 53,* 267–293. doi:10.1037/h0040755

Guilford, J. P. (1988). Some changes in the structure-of-intellect model. *Educational and Psychological Measurement, 48,* 1–4. doi:10.1177/001316448804800102

Guldemond, H., Bosker, R., Kuyper, H., & van der Werf, G. (2007). Do highly gifted students really have problems? *Educational Research and Evaluation, 13,* 555–568. doi:10.1080/13803610701786038

Haggbloom, S. J., Warnick, R., Warnick, J. E., Jones, V. K., Yarbrough, G. L., Russell, T. M., ... & Monte, E. (2002). The 100 most eminent psychologists of the 20th century. *Review of General Psychology, 6,* 139–152. doi:10.1037/1089-2680.6.2.139

Haier, R. J. (2017a). *The neuroscience of intelligence.* New York, NY: Cambridge University Press.

Haier, R. [rjhaier] (2017b, September 15). It's a framework for testing hypotheses. Results will refine what we know & drive progress even if PFIT turns out to be mostly incorrect. [Tweet]. Retrieved from https://twitter.com/rjhaier/status/908749935293558784

Hall v. Florida, 572 U.S. ___ (2014).

Hambrick, D. Z., Altmann, E. M., Oswald, F. L., Meinz, E. J., Gobet, F., & Campitelli, G. (2014a). Accounting for expert performance: The devil is in the details. *Intelligence, 45,* 112–114. doi:10.1016/j.intell.2014.01.007

Hambrick, D. Z., Oswald, F. L., Altmann, E. M., Meinz, E. J., Gobet, F., & Campitelli, G. (2014b). Deliberate practice: Is that all it takes to become an expert? *Intelligence, 45,* 34–45. doi:10.1016/j.intell.2013.04.001

Hampshire, A., Highfield, R. R., Parkin, B. L., & Owen, A. M. (2012). Fractionating human intelligence. *Neuron, 76,* 1225–1237. doi:10.1016/j.neuron.2012.06.022

Han, E., Carbonetto, P., Curtis, R. E., Wang, Y., Granka, J. M., Byrnes, J., ... & Ball, C. A. (2017). Clustering of 770,000 genomes reveals post-colonial population structure of North America. *Nature Communications, 8,* Article 14238. doi:10.1038/ncomms14238

Hansen, B. S. (2005). Something rotten in the state of Denmark: Eugenics and the ascent of the welfare state. In G. Broberg & N. Roll-Hansen (eds.), *Eugenics and the welfare state: Norway, Sweden, Denmark, and Finland* (pp. 9–76). East Lansing, MI: Michigan State University Press.

Hare, B. (2017). Survival of the friendliest: *Homo sapiens* evolved via selection for prosociality. *Annual Review of Psychology, 68,* 155–186. doi:10.1146/annurev-psych-010416-044201

Harrell, T. W., & Harrell, M. S. (1945). Army General Classification Test scores for civilian occupations. *Educational and Psychological Measurement, 5,* 229–239. doi:10.1177/001316444500500303

Harris, J. J., III, & Ford, D. Y. (1991). Identifying and nurturing the promise of gifted Black American children. *Journal of Negro Education, 60,* 3–18. doi:10.2307/2295529

Haskins, R., & Sawhill, I. (2009). *Creating an opportunity society.* Washington, DC: Brookings Institution Press.

Heller, C. A., Rúa, S. H., Mazumdar, M., Moon, J. E., Bardes, C., & Gotto, A. M. (2014). Diversity efforts, admissions, and national rankings: Can we align priorities? *Teaching and Learning in Medicine, 26,* 304–311. doi:10.1080/10401334.2014.910465

Heller, J. (1972, July 26). Syphilis victims in U.S. study went untreated for 40 years. *New York Times.* Retrieved from www.nytimes.com/1972/07/26/archives/syphilis-victims-in-us-study-went-untreated-for-40-years-syphilis.html

Helms, J. E. (1992). Why is there no study of cultural equivalence in standardized cognitive ability testing? *American Psychologist, 47,* 1083–1101. doi:10.1037/0003-066X.47.9.1083

Henneberg, M. (1988). Decrease of human skull size in the Holocene. *Human Biology, 60,* 395–405.

Herndon, J. G., Moss, M. B., Rosene, D. L., & Killiany, R. J. (1997). Patterns of cognitive decline in aged rhesus monkeys. *Behavioural Brain Research, 87,* 25–34. doi:10.1016/S0166-4328(96)02256-5

Herrnstein, R. J. (1971). I.Q. *The Atlantic, 228*(3), 43–64.

Herrnstein, R. J. (1973). *I.Q. in the meritocracy.* Boston, MA: Atlantic Monthly Press.

Herrnstein, R. J., & Murray, C. (1994). *The bell curve: Intelligence and class structure in American life.* New York, NY: Free Press.

Hertberg-Davis, H. (2009). Myth 7: Differentiation in the regular classroom is equivalent to gifted programs and is sufficient: Classroom teachers have the time, the skill, and the will to differentiate adequately. *Gifted Child Quarterly, 53,* 251–253. doi:10.1177/0016986209346927

Hietala, M. (2005). From race hygiene to sterilization: The eugenics movement in Finland. In G. Broberg & N. Roll-Hansen (eds.), *Eugenics and the welfare state: Norway, Sweden, Denmark, and Finland* (pp. 195–258). East Lansing, MI: Michigan State University.

Hill, T. P. (2018, September 7). Academic activists send a published paper down the memory hole. *Quillette.* Retrieved from https://quillette.com/2018/09/07/academic-activists-send-a-published-paper-down-the-memory-hole/

Hill, W. D., Hagenaars, S. P., Marioni, R. E., Harris, S. E., Liewald, D. C. M., Davies, G., ... & Deary, I. J. (2016). Molecular genetic contributions to social deprivation and household income in UK Biobank. *Current Biology, 26,* 3083–3089. doi:10.1016/j.cub.2016.09.035

Hill, W. D., Marioni, R. E., Maghzian, O., Ritchie, S. J., Hagenaars, S. P., McIntosh, A. M., ... & Deary, I. J. (2019). A combined analysis of genetically correlated traits identifies 187 loci and a role for neurogenesis and myelination in intelligence. *Molecular Psychiatry, 24,* 169–181. doi:10.1038/s41380-017-0001-5

Holahan, C. K., & Sears, R. R. (1995). *The gifted group in later maturity.* Stanford, CA: University of Stanford Press.

Hollingworth, L. S. (1919). Comparison of the sexes in mental traits. *Psychological Bulletin, 16,* 371–373. doi:10.1037/h0075023

Hollis-Sawyer, L. A., & Sawyer, T. P., Jr. (2008). Potential stereotype threat and face validity effects on cognitive-based test performance in the classroom. *Educational Psychology, 28,* 291–304. doi:10.1080/01443410701532313

Hoover, E. (2019, February 13). At one final hearing, Harvard and Students for Fair Admissions squared off. Here's what happened. *Chronicle of Higher Education.* Retrieved from www.chronicle.com/article/At-One-Final-Hearing-Harvard/245695

Hoover, H. D., Dunbar, S. B., Frisbie, D. A., Oberley, K. R., Ordman, V. L., Naylor, R. J., ... & Shannon, G. P. (2003). *Iowa Tests of Basic Skills guide to research and development.* Itasca, IL: Riverside Publishing.

Hopkins, W. D., Russell, J. L., & Schaeffer, J. (2014). Chimpanzee intelligence is heritable. *Current Biology, 24,* 1649–1652. doi:10.1016/j.cub.2014.05.076

Horgan, J. (2013, May 16). Should research on race and IQ be banned? [Web log post] *Scientific American Cross-Check Blog.* Retrieved from https://blogs .scientificamerican.com/cross-check/should-research-on-race-and-iq-be-banned/

Horowitz, M., Yaworsky, W., & Kickham, K. (2019). Anthropology's science wars: Insights from a new survey. *Current Anthropology, 60,* 674–698. doi:10.1086/705409

Hu, M., Lasker, J., Kirkegaard, E. O. W., & Fuerst, J. G. R. (2019). Filling in the gaps: The association between intelligence and both color and parent-reported ancestry in the National Longitudinal Survey of Youth 1997. *Psych, 1,* 240–261. doi:10.3390/psych1010017

Huang, P.-C., Su, P.-H., Chen, H.-Y., Huang, H.-B., Tsai, J.-L., Huang, H.-I., & Wang, S.-L. (2012). Childhood blood lead levels and intellectual development after ban of leaded gasoline in Taiwan: A 9-year prospective study. *Environment International, 40,* 88–96. doi:10.1016/j.envint.2011.10.011

Hughes, C. (2018). The racism treadmill. *Quillette.* Retrieved from http://quillette.com /2018/05/14/the-racism-treadmill/

Humphreys, L. G. (1988). Trends in levels of academic achievement of blacks and other minorities. *Intelligence, 12,* 231–260. doi:10.1016/0160-2896(88)90025-6

Hunt, E. (2001). Multiple views of multiple intelligence [Review of the book *Intelligence reframed: Multiple intelligence in the 21st century,* by H. Gardner]. *Contemporary Psychology, 46,* 5–7. doi:10.1037/002513

Hunt, E. (2008). Applying the theory of successful intelligence to education – the good, the bad, and the ogre: Commentary on Sternberg et al. (2008). *Perspectives on Psychological Science,* 509–515. doi:10.1111/j.1745-6924.2008.00094.x

Hunt, E. (2011). *Human intelligence.* New York, NY: Cambridge University Press.

Hunt, E. (2014). Teaching intelligence: Why, why it is hard and perhaps how to do it. *Intelligence, 42,* 156–165. doi:10.1016/j.intell.2013.06.018

Hunt, E., & Carlson, J. (2007). Considerations relating to the study of group differences in intelligence. *Perspectives on Psychological Science,* 194–213. doi:10.1111/j.1745-6916.2007.00037.x

Hunt, E., & Sternberg, R. J. (2006). Sorry, wrong numbers: An analysis of a study of a correlation between skin color and IQ. *Intelligence, 34,* 131–137. doi:10.1016/j.intell.2005.04.004

Hunter, J. E., & Hunter, R. F. (1984). Validity and utility of alternative predictors of job performance. *Psychological Bulletin, 96,* 72–98. doi:10.1037/0033-2909.96.1.72

Hunter, J. E., & Schmidt, F. L. (1996). Intelligence and job performance: Economic and social implications. *Psychology, Public Policy, and Law, 2,* 447–472. doi:10.1076-8971.2.3-4.447

Hunter, J. E., & Schmidt, F. L. (2000). Racial and gender bias in ability and achievement tests: Resolving the apparent paradox. *Psychology, Public Policy, and Law, 6,* 151–158. doi:10.1037/1076-8971.6.1.151

Hur, Y.-M., & Bates, T. (2019). Genetic and environmental influences on cognitive abilities in extreme poverty. *Twin Research and Human Genetics, 22,* 297–301. doi:10.1017/thg.2019.92

Hurst, D. (2019, March 18). Victims of forced sterilization in Japan to receive compensation and apology. *The Guardian.* Retrieved from https://www.theguardian.com/world/2019/mar/18/victims-of-forced-sterilisation-in-japan-to-receive-compensation-and-apology

Jhaveri, A. (2016, January 5). "Brain training" with Lumosity – does it really work? *Consumer Information Blog.* Washington, DC: Federal Trade Commission Consumer Information. Retrieved from www.consumer.ftc.gov/blog/2016/01/brain-training-lumosity-does-it-really-work

James, W. (1890). *The principles of psychology* (Vol. 1). New York, NY: Henry Holt and Company.

Jeffery, A. J., & Shackelford, T. K. (2018). Moral positions on publishing race differences in intelligence. *Journal of Criminal Justice, 59,* 132–135. doi:10.1016/j.jcrimjus.2017.05.008

Jenkins, J. J. (1981). Can we have a fruitful cognitive psychology? In J. H. Flowers (ed.), *Nebraska symposium on motivation, 1980* (pp. 211–238). Lincoln, NE: University of Nebraska Press.

Jensen, A. R. (1969). How much can we boost IQ and scholastic achievement? *Harvard Educational Review, 39,* 1–123. doi:10.17763/haer.39.1.l3u15956627424k7

Jensen, A. R. (1974). *Race and mental ability.* Retrieved from ERIC database. (ED114432)

Jensen, A. R. (1980a). *Bias in mental testing.* New York, NY: The Free Press.

Jensen, A. R. (1980b). Précis of bias in mental testing. *Behavioral and Brain Sciences, 3,* 325–333. doi:10.1017/S0140525X00005161

Jensen, A. R. (1985). The nature of the black–white difference on various psychometric tests: Spearman's hypothesis. *Behavioral and Brain Sciences, 8,* 193–219. doi:10.1017/S0140525X00020392

Jensen, A. R. (1989). Raising IQ without increasing *g? Developmental Review, 9,* 234–258. doi:10.1016/0273-2297(89)90030-0

Jensen, A. R. (1991). Spearman's g and the problem of educational equality. *Oxford Review of Education, 17,* 169–187. doi:10.1080/0305498910170205

Jensen, A. R. (1998). *The g factor: The science of mental ability.* Westport, CT: Praeger.

Jensen, A. R., & Johnson, F. W. (1994). Race and sex differences in head size and IQ. *Intelligence, 18,* 309–333. doi:10.1016/0160-2896(94)90032-9

Jin, W., Xu, S., Wang, H., Yu, Y., Shen, Y., Wu, B., & Jin, L. (2012). Genome-wide detection of natural selection in African Americans pre- and post-admixture. *Genome Research*, *22*, 519–527. doi:10.1101/gr.124784.111

Johnson, R. C., McClearn, G. E., Yuen, S., Nagoshi, C. T., Ahern, F. M., & Cole, R. E. (1985). Galton's data a century later. *American Psychologist*, *40*, 875–892. doi:10.1037/0003-066x.40.8.875

Johnson, W., Bouchard Jr, T. J., Krueger, R. F., McGue, M., & Gottesman, I. I. (2004). Just one *g*: Consistent results from three test batteries. *Intelligence*, *32*, 95–107. doi:10.1016/S0160-2896(03)00062-X

Johnson, W., Carothers, A., & Deary, I. J. (2008). Sex differences in variability in general intelligence: A new look at the old question. *Perspectives on Psychological Science*, *3*, 518–531. doi:10.1111/j.1745-6924.2008.00096.x

Johnson, W., te Nijenhuis, J., & Bouchard Jr., T. J. (2008). Still just 1 *g*: Consistent results from five test batteries. *Intelligence*, *36*, 81–95. doi:10.1016/j.intell.2007.06.001

Jones, B. D., Rakes, L., & Landon, K. (2013). Malawian secondary students' beliefs about intelligence. *International Journal of Psychology*, *48*, 785–796. doi:10.1080/00207594.2012.716906

Jones, G. (2016). *Hive mind: How your nation's IQ matters so much more than your own*. Stanford, CA: Stanford University Press.

Jones, J. M. (2016, August 17). Six in 10 Americans say racism against Blacks is widespread. *Gallup*. Retrieved from https://news.gallup.com/poll/194657/six-americans-say-racism-against-blacks-widespread.aspx

Jones, J. M. (2019, February 20). Americans less satisfied with treatment of minority groups. *Gallup*. Retrieved https://news.gallup.com/poll/246866/americans-less-satisfied-treatment-minority-groups.aspx

Jorde, L. B., & Wooding, S. P. (2004). Genetic variation, classification and "race." *Nature Genetics*, *36*, S28–S33. doi:10.1038/ng1435

Jukes, M. C. H., Pinder, M., Grigorenko, E. L., Smith, H. B., Walraven, G., Bariau, E. M., ... & Bundy, D. A. P. (2006). Long-term impact of malaria chemoprophylaxis on cognitive abilities and educational attainment: Follow-up of a controlled trial. *PLOS Clinical Trials*, *1*(4), e19. doi:10.1371/journal.pctr.0010019

Jung, R. E., & Haier, R. J. (2007). The Parieto-Frontal Integration Theory (P-FIT) of intelligence: Converging neuroimaging evidence. *Behavioral and Brain Sciences*, *30*, 135–154. doi:10.1017/S0140525X07001185

Jussim, L. (2012). *Social perception and social reality: Why accuracy dominates bias and self-fulfilling prophecy*. New York, NY: Oxford University Press.

Jussim, L., & Harber, K. D. (2005). Teacher expectations and self-fulfilling prophecies: Knowns and unknowns, resolved and unresolved controversies. *Personality and Social Psychology Review*, *9*, 131–155. doi:10.1207/s15327957pspr0902_3

Kaelber, L. (2011). *Eugenics: Compulsory sterilization in 50 American states*. Retrieved from www.uvm.edu/~lkaelber/eugenics/

Kamenetz, A. (2014, October 11). It's 2014. All children are supposed to be proficient. What happened? *NPR*. Retrieved from www.npr.org/sections/ed/2014/10/11/354931351/it-s-2014-all-children-are-supposed-to-be-proficient-under-federal-law

Kanazawa, S. (2010). Evolutionary psychology and intelligence research. *American Psychologist*, *65*, 279–289. doi:10.1037/a0019378

Kane, M. T. (2006). Validation. In R. L. Brennan (ed.), *Educational measurement* (4th ed., pp. 17–64). Westport, CT: Praeger.

Kane, M. T. (2013). Validating the interpretations and uses of test scores. *Journal of Educational Measurement, 50*, 1–73. doi:10.1111/jedm.12000

Kaplan, J. M. (2015). Race, IQ, and the search for statistical signals associated with so-called "X"-factors: environments, racism, and the "hereditarian hypothesis." *Biology & Philosophy, 30*, 1–17. doi:10.1007/s10539-014-9428-0

Kaplan, R. M., & Saccuzzo, D. P. (2018). *Psychological testing: Principles, applications, and issues* (9th ed.). Boston, MA: Cengage.

Karpinski, R. I., Kinase Kolb, A. M., Tetreault, N. A., & Borowski, T. B. (2018). High intelligence: A risk factor for psychological and physiological overexcitabilities. *Intelligence, 66*, 8–23. doi:10.1016/j.intell.2017.09.001

Kassin, S. M. (2012). Why confessions trump innocence. *American Psychologist, 67*, 431–445. doi:10.1037/a0028212

Kathuria, R., & Serpell, R. (1998). Standardization of the Panga Munthu Test – a nonverbal cognitive test developed in Zambia. *Journal of Negro Education, 67*, 228–241. doi:10.2307/2668192

Kauffman, J. M., & Konold, T. R. (2007). Making sense in education: Pretense (including No Child Left Behind) and realities in rhetoric and policy about schools and schooling. *Exceptionality, 15*, 75–96. doi:10.1080/09362830701294151

Keith, T. Z., Kranzler, J. H., & Flanagan, D. P. (2001). What does the Cognitive Assessment System (CAS) measure? Joint confirmatory factor analysis of the CAS and the Woodcock-Johnson Tests of Cognitive Ability (3rd ed). *School Psychology Review, 30*, 89–119.

Kell, H. J., Lubinski, D., & Benbow, C. P. (2013). Who rises to the top? Early indicators. *Psychological Science, 24*, 648–659. doi:10.1177/0956797612457784

Kelley, T. L. (1927). *Interpretation of educational measurements.* Yonkers-on-Hudson, NY: World Book Company.

Kendler, K. S., Turkheimer, E., Ohlsson, H., Sundquist, J., & Sundquist, K. (2015). Family environment and the malleability of cognitive ability: A Swedish national home-reared and adopted-away cosibling control study. *Proceedings of the National Academy of Sciences, 112*, 4312–4617. doi:10.1073/pnas.1417106112

Kevles, D. J. (1995). *In the name of eugenics: Genetics and the uses of human heredity.* Cambridge, MA: Harvard University Press.

Kievit, R. A., Davis, S. W., Griffiths, J., Correia, M. M., Cam-CAN, & Henson, R. N. (2016). A watershed model of individual differences in fluid intelligence. *Neuropsychologia, 91*, 186–198. doi:10.1016/j.neuropsychologia.2016.08.008

Kinsler, J. S. (2017). Is bar exam failure a harbinger of professional discipline? *St. John's Law Review, 91*, 883–922.

Kirkegaard, E. O. W., Woodley of Menie, M. A., Williams, R. L., Fuerst, J., & Meisenberg, G. (2019). Biogeographic ancestry, cognitive ability and socioeconomic outcomes. *Psych, 1*, 1–25. doi:10.3390/Psychology1010001

Klein, P. D. (1997). Multiplying the problems of intelligence by eight: A critique of Gardner's theory. *Canadian Journal of Education, 22*, 377–394. doi:10.2307/1585790

Kline, P. (1991). Sternberg's components: Non-contingent concepts. *Personality and Individual Differences, 12*, 873–876. doi:10.1016/0191-8869(91)90174-A

Klopfenstein, K. (2010). Does the Advanced Placement program save taxpayers money? The effect of AP participation on time to college graduation. In P. M. Sadler, G. Sonnert, R. H. Tai, & K. Klopfenstein (eds.), *AP: A critical evaluation of the*

Advanced Placement program (pp. 189–218). Cambridge, MA: Harvard Education Press.

Klopfenstein, K., & Lively, K. (2016). Do grade weights promote more advanced course-taking? *Education Finance and Policy, 11,* 310–324. doi:10.1162/EDFP_a_00182

Klugman, J. (2013). The Advanced Placement arms race and the reproduction of educational inequality. *Teachers College Record, 115*(5), 1–34.

Koch, L. (2006). Past futures: On the conceptual history of eugenics – a social technology of the past. *Technology Analysis & Strategic Management, 18,* 329–344. doi:10.1080/09537320600777085

Koenig, K. A., Frey, M. C., & Detterman, D. K. (2008). ACT and general cognitive ability. *Intelligence, 36,* 153–160. doi:10.1016/j.intell.2007.03.00

Koh, T.-h., Abbatiello, A., & McLoughlin, C. S. (1984). Cultural bias in WISC subtest items: A response to Judge Grady's suggestion in relation to the PASE case. *School Psychology Review, 13,* 89–94.

Komlos, J., Hau, M., & Bourguinat, N. (2003). An anthropometric history of early-modern France. *European Review of Economic History, 7,* 159–189. doi:10.1017/S1361491603000066

Komlos, J., & Lauderdale, B. E. (2007). The mysterious trend in American heights in the 20th century. *Annals of Human Biology, 34,* 206–215. doi:10.1080/03014460601116803

Kornrich, S. (2016). Inequalities in parental spending on young children, 1972 to 2010. *AERA Open, 2*(2), 1–12. doi:10.1177/2332858416644180

Kourany, J. A. (2016). Should some knowledge be forbidden? The case of cognitive differences research. *Philosophy of Science, 83,* 779–790. doi:10.1086/687863

Krapohl, E., Rimfeld, K., Shakeshaft, N. G., Trzaskowski, M., McMillan, A., Pingault, J.-B., ... & Plomin, R. (2014). The high heritability of educational achievement reflects many genetically influenced traits, not just intelligence. *Proceedings of the National Academy of Sciences, 111,* 15273–15278. doi:10.1073/pnas.1408777111

Krieger, N., Sidney, S., & Coakley, E. (1998). Racial discrimination and skin color in the CARDIA study: Implications for public health research. *American Journal of Public Health, 88,* 1308–1313. doi:10.2105/ajph.88.9.1308

Kuncel, N. R., & Hezlett, S. A. (2007). Standardized tests predict graduate students' success. *Science, 315,* 1080–1081. doi:10.1126/science.1136618

Kuncel, N. R., & Hezlett, S. A. (2010). Fact and fiction in cognitive ability testing for admissions and hiring decisions. *Current Directions in Psychological Science, 19,* 339–345. doi:10.1177/0963721410389459

Kuncel, N. R., Hezlett, S. A., & Ones, D. S. (2004). Academic performance, career potential, creativity, and job performance: Can one construct predict them all? *Journal of Personality and Social Psychology, 86,* 148–161. doi:10.1037/0022-3514.86.1.148

Kwate, N. O. A. (2001). Intelligence or misorientation? Eurocentrism in the WISC-III. *Journal of Black Psychology, 27,* 221–238. doi:10.1177/0095798401027002005

Kyllonen, P. C., & Christal, R. E. (1990). Reasoning ability is (little more than) working-memory capacity?! *Intelligence, 14,* 389–433. doi:10.1016/s0160-2896(05)80012-1

Lakin, J. M. (2013). Sex differences in reasoning abilities: Surprising evidence that male–female ratios in the tails of the quantitative reasoning distribution have increased. *Intelligence, 41,* 263–274. doi:10.1016/j.intell.2013.04.004

Lakin, J. M. (2018). Making the cut in gifted selection: Score combination rules and their impact on program diversity. *Gifted Child Quarterly, 62,* 210–219. doi:10.1177/0016986217752099

Landrigan, P. J., Baloh, R. W., Barthel, W. F., Whitworth, R. H., Staehling, N. W., & Rosenblum, B. F. (1975). Neuropsychological dysfunction in children with chronic low-level lead absorption. *The Lancet, 305,* 708–712. doi:10.1016/S0140-6736(75)91627-X

Larry P. v. Riles, 495 F. Supp. 926 (N.D. Cal. 1979)

Larsen, R., & Warne, R. T. (2010). Estimating confidence intervals for eigenvalues in exploratory factor analysis. *Behavior Research Methods, 42,* 871–876. doi:10.3758/BRM.42.3.871

Lasker, J., Pesta, B. J., Fuerst, J. G. R., & Kirkegaard, E. O. W. (2019). Global ancestry and cognitive ability. *Psych, 1,* 431–459. doi:10.3390/psych1010034

Laughlin, H. H. (1923). *The Second International Exhibition of Eugenics held September 22 to October 22, 1921, in connection with the Second International Congress of Eugenics in the American Museum of Natural History.* New York, NY: William & Wilkins Company.

Lawson, H. A. (2002). Foreword. In W. Sailor (ed.), Whole-school success and inclusive education (pp. vii-xii). New York, NY: Teachers College Press.

LearningRx. (2018). LearningRx and Gibson Testing [Advertisement]. *APA Annual Convention Program, 2018.* Washington, DC: American Psychological Association.

Lechner, C., Danner, D., & Rammstedt, B. (2017). How is personality related to intelligence and achievement? A replication and extension of Borghans et al. and Salkever. *Personality and Individual Differences, 111,* 86–91. doi:10.1016/j.paid.2017.01.040

Lee, J. (2002). Racial and ethnic achievement gap trends: Reversing the progress toward equity? *Educational Researcher, 31*(1), 3–12. doi:10.3102/0013189X031001003

Lee, J. J. (2010). [Review of the book *Intelligence and how to get it: Why schools and cultures count,* by R. E. Nisbett]. *Personality and Individual Differences, 48,* 247–255. doi:10.1016/j.paid.2009.09.015

Lee, J. J., McGue, M., Iacono, W. G., Michael, A. M., & Chabris, C. F. (2019). The causal influence of brain size on human intelligence: Evidence from within-family phenotypic associations and GWAS modeling. *Intelligence, 75,* 48–58. doi:10.1016/j.intell.2019.01.011

Lee, J. J., Wedow, R., Okbay, A., Kong, E., Maghzian, O., Zacher, M., . . . & Cesarini, D. (2018). Gene discovery and polygenic prediction from a genome-wide association study of educational attainment in 1.1 million individuals. *Nature Genetics, 50,* 1112–1121. doi:10.1038/s41588-018-0147-3

Lennon, J. M. (2010). Self-efficacy. In J. A. Rosen, E. J. Glennie, B. W. Dalton, J. M. Lennon, & R. N. Bozick (eds.), *Noncognitive skills in the classroom: New perspectives on educational research* (pp. 91–115). Research Triangle Park, NC: RTI International.

León, F. R., & Burga-León, A. (2015). How geography influences complex cognitive ability. *Intelligence, 50,* 221–227. doi:10.1016/j.intell.2015.04.011

Levenson, E. (2019, April 8). Felicity Huffman and 12 wealthy parents plead guilty in college admissions scam. *CNN.com.* Retrieved from www.cnn.com/2019/04/08/us/felicity-huffman-guilty-admissions/index.html

Levitz, J. (2019, September 10). Weighting the sentencing of parents in the college-admissions cheating scheme. *Wall Street Journal.* Retrieved from www.wsj.com

/articles/weighing-the-sentencing-of-parents-in-the-college-admissions-cheating-scheme -11568155291

Lewis, J. D., DeCamp-Fritson, S. S., Ramage, J. C., McFarland, M. A., & Archwamety, T. (2007). Selecting for ethnically diverse children who may be gifted using Raven's Standard Progressive Matrices and Naglieri Nonverbal Abilities Test. *Multicultural Education, 15*(1), 38–42.

Lewontin, R. C. (1970). Race and intelligence. *Bulletin of the Atomic Scientists, 26*, 2–8. doi:10.1080/00963402.1970.11457774

Lewontin, R. C. (1972). The apportionment of human diversity. In T. Dobzhansky, M. K. Hecht, & W. C. Steere (eds.), *Evolutionary Biology* (Vol. 6, pp. 381–398). Boston, MA: Springer.

Li, X., Sano, H., & Merwin, J. C. (1996). Perception and reasoning abilities among American, Japanese, and Chinese adolescents. *Journal of Adolescent Research, 11*, 173–193. doi:10.1177/0743554896112002

Li, Y., & Bates, T. C. (2019). You can't change your basic ability, but you work at things, and that's how we get hard things done: Testing the role of growth mindset on response to setbacks, educational attainment, and cognitive ability. *Journal of Experimental Psychology: General, 148*, 1640–1655. doi:10.1037/xge0000669

Lichten, W. (2010). Whither Advanced Placement – now? In P. M. Sadler, G. Sonnert, R. H. Tai, & K. Klopfenstein (eds.), *AP: A critical examination of the Advanced Placement program* (pp. 233–243). Cambridge, MA: Harvard Education Press.

Linn, R. L., & Drasgow, F. (1987). Implications of the Golden Rule settlement for test construction. *Educational Measurement: Issues and Practice, 6*(2), 13–17. doi:10.1111/j.1745-3992.1987.tb00405.x

Lippman, W. (1976). The abuse of the tests. In N. J. Block & G. Dworkin (eds.), *The IQ controversy* (pp. 18–20). New York, NY: Pantheon Books. (Original work published in 1922)

Lipsey, M. W., Farran, D. C., & Durkin, K. (2018). Effects of the Tennessee Prekindergarten Program on children's achievement and behavior through third grade. *Early Childhood Research Quarterly, 45*, 155–176. doi:10.1016/j.ecresq.2018.03.005

Liu, J., & Lynn, R. (2013). An increase of intelligence in China 1986–2012. *Intelligence, 41*, 479–481. doi:10.1016/j.intell.2013.06.017

Liu, O. L., Bridgeman, B., & Adler, R. M. (2012). Measuring learning outcomes in higher education: Motivation matters. *Educational Researcher, 41*, 352–362. doi:10.3102/0013189x12459679

Locke, E. A. (2005). Why emotional intelligence is an invalid concept. *Journal of Organizational Behavior, 26*, 425–431. doi:10.1002/job.318

Locke, E. A., & Latham, G. P. (2002). Building a practically useful theory of goal setting and task motivation: A 35-year odyssey. *American Psychologist, 57*, 705–717. doi:10.1037/0003-066X.57.9.705

Loehlin, J. C., Vandenberg, S. G., & Osborne, R. T. (1973). Blood group genes and Negro–White ability differences. *Behavior Genetics, 3*, 263–270. doi:10.1007/BF01067603

Loftus, E. F., & Guyer, M. J. (2002). Who abused Jane Doe? The hazards of the single case history, part 1. *Skeptical Inquirer, 26*(3), 24–32.

Lohman, D. F., Gambrell, J., & Lakin, J. (2008). The commonality of extreme discrepancies in the ability profiles of academically gifted students. *Psychology Science Quarterly, 50*, 269–282.

Lombardo, P. A. (1985). Three generations, no imbeciles: New light on *Buck v. Bell*. *New York University Law Review, 60,* 30–62.

Long, P. A., & Anthony, J. J. (1974). The measurement of mental retardation by a culture-specific test. *Psychology in the Schools, 11,* 310–312. doi:10.1002/1520-6807(197407)11:3<310::AID-PITS2310110314>3.0.CO;2-X

Lubinski, D. (2004). Introduction to the special section on cognitive abilities: 100 years after Spearman's (1904) "'General intelligence,' objectively determined and measured." *Journal of Personality and Social Psychology, 86,* 96–111. doi:10.1037/0022-3514.86.1.96

Lubinski, D. (2009). Exceptional cognitive ability: The phenotype. *Behavioral Genetics, 39,* 350–358. doi:10.1007/s10519-009-9273-0

Lubinski, D. (2016). From Terman to today: A century of findings on intelllectual precocity. *Review of Educational Research, 86,* 900–944. doi:10.3102/0034654316675476

Lubinski, D., & Benbow, C. P. (1995). An opportunity for empiricism. *PsycCRITIQUES, 40,* 935–938. doi:10.1037/004016

Lubinski, D., Benbow, C. P., & Kell, H. J. (2014). Life paths and accomplishments of mathematically precocious males and females four decades later. *Psychological Science, 25,* 2217–2232. doi:10.1177/0956797614551371

Lubinski, D., & Humphreys, L. G. (1992). Some bodily and medical correlates of mathematical giftedness and commensurate levels of socioeconomic status. *Intelligence, 16,* 99–115. doi:10.1016/0160-2896(92)90027-o

Lubinski, D., & Humphreys, L. G. (1996). Seeing the forest from the trees: When predicting behavior or status of groups, correlate means. *Psychology, Public Policy, and Law, 2,* 363–376. doi:10.1037/1076-8971.2.2.363

Lubinski, D., & Humphreys, L. G. (1997). Incorporating general intelligence into epidemiology and the social sciences. *Intelligence, 24,* 159–201. doi:10.1016/s0160-2896(97)90016-7

Lubke, G. H., Dolan, C. V., & Kelderman, H. (2001). Investigating group differences on cognitive tests using Spearman's hypothesis: An evaluation of Jensen's method. *Multivariate Behavioral Research, 36,* 299–324. doi:10.1207/s15327906299-324

Lubke, G. H., Dolan, C. V., Kelderman, H., & Mellenbergh, G. J. (2003). On the relationship between sources of within- and between-group differences and measurement invariance in the common factor model. *Intelligence, 31,* 543–566. doi:10.1016/S0160-2896(03)00051-5

Lynn, R. (2013). Who discovered the Flynn effect? A review of early studies of the secular increase of intelligence. *Intelligence, 41,* 765–769. doi:10.1016/j.intell.2013.03.008

Lynn, R. (2019). Reflections on sixty-eight years of research on race and intelligence. *Psych, 1,* 123–131. doi:10.3390/psych1010009

Lynn, R., Fuerst, J., & Kirkegaard, E. O. W. (2018). Regional differences in intelligence in 22 countries and their economic, social and demographic correlates: A review. *Intelligence, 69,* 24–36. doi:10.1016/j.intell.2018.04.004

Lynn, R., & Irwing, P. (2004). Sex differences on the progressive matrices: A meta-analysis. *Intelligence, 32,* 481–498. doi:10.1016/j.intell.2004.06.008

Lyons, B. D., Hoffman, B. J., & Michel, J. W. (2009). Not much more than *g*? An examination of the impact of intelligence on NFL performance. *Human Performance, 22,* 225–245. doi:10.1080/08959280902970401

Mac Donald, H. (2018, November 16). Sorry, feminists, men are better at Scrabble. *Wall Street Journal.* Retrieved from www.wsj.com/articles/sorry-feminists-men-are-better-at-scrabble-1542411642

Macdonald, K., Germine, L., Anderson, A., Christodoulou, J., & McGrath, L. M. (2017). Dispelling the myth: Training in education or neuroscience decreases but does not eliminate beliefs in neuromyths. *Frontiers in Psychology, 8,* Article 1314. doi:10.3389/fpsyg.2017.01314

MacKenzie, D. (1976). Eugenics in Britain. *Social Studies of Science, 6,* 499–532. doi:10.1177/030631277600600310

MacKinlay, R. D., & Shaw, R. C. (2019). Male New Zealand robin (*Petroica longipes*) song repertoire size does not correlate with cognitive performance in the wild. *Intelligence, 74,* 25–33. doi:10.1016/j.intell.2018.10.009

Mackintosh, N. J. (2011). *IQ and human intelligence* (2nd ed.). New York, NY: Oxford University Press.

Mackintosh, N. J. (2014). Why teach intelligence? *Intelligence, 42,* 166–170. doi:10.1016/j.intell.2013.08.001

Macnamara, B. N., & Rupani, N. S. (2017). The relationship between intelligence and mindset. *Intelligence, 64,* 52–59. doi:10.1016/j.intell.2017.07.003

Madsen, I. N., & Sylvester, R. H. (1919). High-school students' intelligence ratings according to the Army Alpha test. *School & Society, 10,* 407–410.

Makel, M. C., Kell, H. J., Lubinski, D., Putallaz, M., & Benbow, C. P. (2016). When lightning strikes twice: Profoundly gifted, profoundly accomplished. *Psychological Science, 27,* 1004–1018. doi:10.1177/0956797616644735

Makel, M. C., & Plucker, J. A. (2014). Facts are more important than novelty: Replication in the education sciences. *Educational Researcher, 43,* 304–316. doi:10.3102/0013189x14545513

Maller, S. J. (2000). Item invariance in four subtests of the Universal Nonverbal Intelligence Test (UNIT) across groups of deaf and hearing children. *Journal of Psychoeducational Assessment, 18,* 240–254. doi:10.1177/073428290001800304

Månsson, J., Stjernqvist, K., Serenius, F., Ådén, U., & Källén, K. (2019). Agreement between Bayley-III measurements and WISC-IV measurements in typically developing children. *Journal of Psychoeducational Assessment, 37,* 603–616. doi:10.1177/ 0734282918781431

Marioni, R. E., Davies, G., Hayward, C., Liewald, D., Kerr, S. M., Campbell, A., … & Deary, I. J. (2014). Molecular genetic contributions to socioeconomic status and intelligence. *Intelligence, 44,* 26–32. doi:10.1016/j.intell.2014.02.006

Marks, D. F. (2010). IQ variations across time, race, and nationality: An artifact of differences in literacy skills. *Psychological Reports, 106,* 643–664. doi:10.2466/ pr0.106.3.643-664

Markt, S. C., Nuttall, E., Turman, C., Sinnott, J., Rimm, E. B., Ecsedy, E., … & Mucci, L. A. (2016). Sniffing out significant "Pee values": Genome wide association study of asparagus anosmia. *BMJ, 355*(8086), Article i6071. doi:10.1136/bmj.i6071

Marland, S. P., Jr. (1971). *Education of the gifted and talented,* Vol. I: *Report to the Congress of the United States by the U.S. Commissioner of Education.* Washington, DC: Department of Health, Education, and Welfare. Retrieved from ERIC database. (ED056243)

Martschenko, D., Trejo, S., & Domingue, B. W. (2019). Genetics and education: Recent developments in the context of an ugly history and an uncertain future. *AERA Open, 5,* 1–15. doi:10.1177/2332858418810516

Martin, A. R., Kanai, M., Kamatani, Y., Okada, Y., Neale, B. M., & Daly, M. J. (2019). Clinical use of current polygenic risk scores may exacerbate health disparities. *Nature Genetics, 51*, 584–591. doi:10.1038/s41588-019-0379-x

Masters, M. S., & Sanders, B. (1993). Is the gender difference in mental rotation disappearing? *Behavior Genetics, 23*, 337–341. doi:10.1007/bf01067434

Matarazzo, J. D. (1981). David Wechsler (1896–1981). *American Psychologist, 36*, 1542–1543. doi:10.1037/0003-066x.36.12.1542

Matarazzo, J. D., & Wiens, A. N. (1977). Black Intelligence Test of Cultural Homogeneity and Wechsler Adult Intelligence Scale scores of Black and White police applicants. *Journal of Applied Psychology, 62*, 57–63. doi:10.1037/0021-9010.62.1.57

Matthews, G., Roberts, R. D., & Zeidner, M. (2004). Seven myths about emotional intelligence. *Psychological Inquiry, 15*, 179–196. doi:10.1207/s15327965pli1503_01

Matzel, L. D., & Sauce, B. (2017). Individual differences: Case studies of rodent and primate intelligence. *Journal of Experimental Psychology: Animal Learning and Cognition, 43*, 325–340. doi:10.1037/xan0000152

Mayer, J. D., & Salovey, P. (1997). What is emotional intelligence? In P. Salovey & D. J. Sluyter (eds.), *Emotional development and emotional intelligence: Educational implications* (pp. 3–31). New York, NY: Basic Books.

Mayer, J. D., Salovey, P., & Caruso, D. R. (2004). Emotional intelligence: Theory, findings, and implications. *Psychological Inquiry, 15*, 197–215. doi:10.1207/s15327965pli1503_02

Mayer, J. D., Salovey, P., & Caruso, D. R. (2008). What is emotional intelligence and what does it predict? In P. C. Kyllonen, R. D. Roberts, & L. Stankov (eds.), *Extending intelligence: Enhancement and new constructs* (pp. 319–348). Mahwah, NJ: Lawrence Erlbaum Associates.

McBee, M. T., Peters, S. J., & Waterman, C. (2014). Combining scores in multiple-criteria assessment systems: The impact of combination rule. *Gifted Child Quarterly, 58*, 69–89. doi:10.1177/0016986213513794

McCabe, K. O., Lubinski, D., & Benbow, C. P. (2019). Who shines most among the brightest? A 25-year longitudinal study of elite STEM graduate students. *Journal of Personality and Social Psychology*. Advance online publication. doi:10.1037/pspp0000239

McClelland, D. C. (1994). The knowledge-testing-educational complex strikes back. *American Psychologist, 49*, 66–69. doi:10.1037/0003-066X.49.1.66

McDermott, N. (2012, December 19). IQ tests are "meaningless and too simplistic" claim researchers. *Daily Mail*. Retrieved from www.dailymail.co.uk/sciencetech/article-2250681/IQ-tests-meaningless-simplistic-claim-researchers.html

McDonald, A. S. (2001). The prevalence and effects of test anxiety in school children. *Educational Psychology, 21*, 89–101. doi:10.1080/01443410020019867

McDonald, R. P. (1999). *Test theory: A unified treatment.* Mahwah, NJ: Lawrence Erlbaum Associates.

McEvoy, B. P., & Visscher, P. M. (2009). Genetics of human height. *Economics & Human Biology, 7*, 294–306. doi:10.1016/j.ehb.2009.09.005

McGill, R. J., & Dombrowski, S. C. (2019). Critically reflecting on the origins, evolution, and impact of the Cattell-Horn-Carroll (CHC) model. *Applied Measurement in Education, 32*, 216–231. doi:10.1080/08957347.2019.1619561

McGrew, K. S. (2009). CHC theory and the human cognitive abilities project: Standing on the shoulders of the giants of psychometric intelligence research. *Intelligence, 37,* 1–10. doi:10.1016/j.intell.2008.08.004

Medina, J., Brenner, K., & Taylor, K. (2019, March 12). Actresses, business leaders and other wealthy parents charged in U.S. college entry fraud. *New York Times.* Retrieved from www.nytimes.com/2019/03/12/us/college-admissions-cheating-scandal.html

Medved, M. (2017, July 5). Defying the "success sequence" [Web log post]. Retrieved from www.michaelmedved.com/column/defying-the-success-sequence/

Meehl, P. E. (2006). The power of quantitative thinking. In N. G. Waller, L. J. Yonce, W. M. Grove, D. Faust, & M. F. Lenzenweger (eds.), *A Paul Meehl reader: Essays on the practice of scientific psychology* (pp. 433–444). Mahwah, NJ: Lawrence Erlbaum Associates.

Mehrens, W. A. (2000). Defending a state graduation test: *GI Forum v. Texas Education Agency.* Measurement perspectives from an external evaluator. *Applied Measurement in Education, 13,* 387–401. doi:10.1207/s15324818ame1304_05

Melby-Lervåg, M., Redick, T. S., & Hulme, C. (2016). Working memory training does not improve performance on measures of intelligence or other measures of "far transfer": Evidence from a meta-analytic review. *Perspectives on Psychological Science, 11,* 512–534. doi:10.1177/1745691616635612

Mendaglio, S., & Tillier, W. (2006). Dabrowski's theory of positive disintegration and giftedness: Overexcitability research findings. *Journal for the Education of the Gifted, 30,* 68–87. doi:10.1177/016235320603000104

Menkes, J. (2005, November). Hiring for smarts. *Harvard Business Review.* Retrieved from https://hbr.org/2005/11/hiring-for-smarts

Mercer, J. R. (1979). In defense of racially and culturally non-discriminatory assessment. *School Psychology Review, 8,* 89–115.

Meredith, W. (1993). Measurement invariance, factor analysis and factorial invariance. *Psychometrika, 58,* 525–543. doi:10.1007/BF02294825

Messick, S. (1992). Multiple intelligences or multilevel intelligence? Selective emphasis on distinctive properties of hierarchy: On Gardner's *Frames of Mind* and Sternberg's *Beyond IQ* in the context of theory and research on the structure of human abilities. *Psychological Inquiry, 3,* 365–384. doi:10.1207/s15327965pli0304_20

Messick, S., & Jungeblut, A. (1981). Time and method in coaching for the SAT. *Psychological Bulletin, 89,* 191–216. doi:10.1037/0033-2909.89.2.191

Miele, F. (1979). Cultural bias in the WISC. *Intelligence, 3,* 149–163. doi:10.1016/0160-2896(79)90013-8

Miller, G. A. (1956). The magical number seven, plus or minus two: Some limits on our capacity for processing information. *Psychological Review, 63,* 81–97. doi:10.1037/h0043158

Miller, D. W. (2001, March 2). Scholars say high-stakes tests deserve a failing grade. *Chronicle of Higher Education,* p. A14.

Miner, M. G., & Miner, J. B. (1978). *Employee selection within the law.* Washington, DC: Bureau of National Affairs.

Minton, H. L. (1988). *Lewis M. Terman: Pioneer in psychological testing.* New York, NY: New York University Press.

Mischel, W. (2005, March). Alternative futures for our science. *APS Observer.* Retrieved from www.psychologicalscience.org/observer/alternative-futures-for-our-science

Moffitt, T. E., Caspi, A., Harkness, A. R., & Silva, P. A. (1993). The natural history of change in intellectual performance: Who changes? How much? Is it meaningful? *Journal of Child Psychology & Psychiatry & Allied Disciplines*, *34*, 455–506. doi:10.1111/j.1469-7610.1993.tb01031.x

Møller, A. P., & Erritzøe, J. (2016). Brain size and the risk of getting shot. *Biology Letters*, *12*(11), Article 20160647. doi:10.1098/rsbl.2016.0647

Mollon, J., Knowles, E. E. M., Mathias, S. R., Gur, R., Peralta, J. M., Weiner, D. J., ... & Glahn, D. C. (2018). Genetic influence on cognitive development between childhood and adulthood. *Molecular Psychiatry*. Advance online publication. doi:10.1038/s41380-018-0277-0

Moore, J. L., III, Ford, D. Y., & Milner, H. R. (2005). Recruitment is not enough: Retaining African American students in gifted education. *Gifted Child Quarterly*, *49*, 51–67. doi:10.1177/001698620504900106

Morelock, M. J. (1992). Giftedness: The view from within. *Understanding Our Gifted*, *4*(3), 11–15.

Morgan, P. L., Farkas, G., Hillemeier, M. M., & Maczuga, S. (2012). Are minority children disproportionately represented in early intervention and early childhood special education? *Educational Researcher*, *41*, 339–351. doi:10.3102/0013189x12459678

Morgan, S. L., & Jung, S. B. (2016). Still no effect of resources, even in the new gilded age? *The Russell Sage Foundation Journal of the Social Sciences*, *2*(5), 83–116. doi:10.7758/rsf.2016.2.5.05

Morris, C. G., & Maisto, A. A. (2016). *Understanding psychology* (11th ed.). New York, NY: Pearson Education.

Morse, J. (1914). A comparison of white and colored children measured by the Binet scale of intelligence. *The Popular Science Monthly*, *84*, 75–79.

Moss, G. (2008). Diversity study circles in teacher education practice: An experiential learning project. *Teaching and Teacher Education*, *24*, 216–224. doi:10.1016/j.tate.2006.10.010

Mpofu, E. (2004). Being intelligent with Zimbabweans. In R. J. Sternberg (ed.), *International handbook of intelligence*. New York, NY: Cambridge University Press.

Mueller, C. M., & Dweck, C. S. (1998). Praise for intelligence can undermine children's motivation and performance. *Journal of Personality and Social Psychology*, *75*, 33–52. doi:10.1037/0022-3514.75.1.33

Mullan, E. H. (1917). Mental examination of immigrants: Administration and line inspection at Ellis Island. *Public Health Reports (1896–1970)*, *32*, 733–746. doi:10.2307/4574515

Murray, C. (1998). *Income inequality and IQ*. Washington, DC: American Enterprise Institute.

Murray, C. (2002). IQ and income inequality in a sample of sibling pairs from advantaged family backgrounds. *American Economic Review*, *92*(2), 339–343. doi:10.1257/000282802320191570

Murray, C. (2007). The magnitude and components of change in the black–white IQ difference from 1920 to 1991: A birth cohort analysis of the Woodcock–Johnson standardizations. *Intelligence*, *35*, 305–318. doi:10.1016/j.intell.2007.02.001

Murray, C. (2013). *Coming apart: The state of white America, 1960–2010*. New York, NY: Crown Forum.

Naglieri, J. A., & Ford, D. Y. (2003). Addressing underrepresentation of gifted minority children using the Naglieri Nonverbal Ability Test (NNAT). *Gifted Child Quarterly*, 47, 155–160. doi:10.1177/001698620304700206

Nagoshi, C. T., Johnson, R. C., DeFries, J. C., Wilson, J. R., & Vandenberg, S. G. (1984). Group differences and first principal-component loadings in the Hawaii family study of cognition: A test of the generality of "Spearman's hypothesis." *Personality and Individual Differences*, 5, 751–753. doi:10.1016/0191-8869(84)90125-9

National Center for Educational Statistics. (2017). *Digest of Educational Statistics*. Washington, DC: U.S. Department of Education. Retrieved from https://nces.ed.gov/programs/digest/2017menu_tables.asp

The National Commission for the Protection of Human Subjects of Biomedical and Behavioral Research. (1979). *The Belmont Report*. Retrieved from www.hhs.gov/ohrp/sites/default/files/the-belmont-report-508c_FINAL.pdf

Navas González, F. J., Jordana Vidal, J., León Jurado, J. M., McLean, A. K., & Delgado Bermejo, J. V. (2019). Dumb or smart asses? Donkey's (*Equus asinus*) cognitive capabilities share the heritability and variation patterns of human's (*Homo sapiens*) cognitive capabilities. *Journal of Veterinary Behavior*, 33, 63–74. doi:10.1016/j.jveb.2019.06.007

Needleman, H. L., Gunnoe, C., Leviton, A., Reed, R., Peresie, H., Maher, C., & Barrett, P. (1979). Deficits in psychologic and classroom performance of children with elevated dentine lead levels. *New England Journal of Medicine*, 300, 689–695. doi:10.1056/nejm197903293001301

Neisser, U., Boodoo, G., Bouchard, T. J., Boykin, A. W., Brody, N., Ceci, S. J., … & Urbina, S. (1996). Intelligence: Knowns and unknowns. *American Psychologist*, 51, 77–101. doi:10.1037/0003-066X.51.2.77

Nelson, L. D., Simmons, J., & Simonsohn, U. (2018). Psychology's renaissance. *Annual Review of Psychology*, 69, 511–534. doi:10.1146/annurev-psych-122216-011836

Nemzek, C. L. (1933). The constancy of the I.Q. *Psychological Bulletin*, 30, 143–168. doi:10.1037/h0075252

New York City Department of Education. (February 26, 2019). *NYC AP results*. Retrieved from https://infohub.nyced.org/docs/default-source/default-document-library/2018-ap-results--for-web_20190226.pdf

Newby, R. G., & Newby, D. E. (1995). *The Bell Curve*: Another chapter in the continuing political economy of racism. *American Behavioral Scientist*, 39, 12–24. doi:10.1177/0002764295039001003

Newson, A., & Williamson, R. (1999). Should we undertake genetic research on intelligence? *Bioethics*, 13(3–4), 327–342. doi:10.1111/1467-8519.00161

Ngara, C., & Porath, M. (2004). Shona culture of Zimbabwe's views of giftedness. *High Ability Studies*, 15, 189–209. doi:10.1080/1359813042000314772

Nicolas, S., Andrieu, B., Croizet, J.-C., Sanitioso, R. B., & Burman, J. T. (2013). Sick? Or slow? On the origins of intelligence as a psychological object. *Intelligence*, 41, 699–711. doi:10.1016/j.intell.2013.08.006

Nisbett, R. E. (2005). Heredity, environment, and race differences in IQ: A commentary on Rushton and Jensen (2005). *Psychology, Public Policy, and Law*, 11, 302–310. doi:10.1037/1076-8971.11.2.302

Nisbett, R. E. (2009). *Intelligence and how to get it: Why schools and cultures count*. New York, NY: W. W. Norton.

Nisbett, R. E., Aronson, J., Blair, C., Dickens, W., Flynn, J., Halpern, D. F., & Turkheimer, E. (2012). Group differences in IQ are best understood as environmental in origin. *American Psychologist, 67*, 503–504. doi:10.1037/a0029772

No Child Left Behind Act of 2001, 20 U.S.C. § 6301 et seq. (2002).

Nolen-Hoeksema, S. Fredrickson, B. L., Loftus, G. R., & Lutz, C. (2014). *Atkinson & Hilgard's introduction to psychology* (16th ed.). Andover: Cengage Learning.

Novembre, J., & Peter, B. M. (2016). Recent advances in the study of fine-scale population structure in humans. *Current Opinion in Genetics & Development, 41*, 98–105. doi:10.1016/j.gde.2016.08.007

Nuijten, M. B., van Assen, M. A. L. M., Veldkamp, C. L. S., & Wicherts, J. M. (2015). The replication paradox: Combining studies can decrease accuracy of effect size estimates. *Review of General Psychology, 19*, 172–182. doi:10.1037/gpr0000034

Nyborg, H. (2003). The sociology of psychometric and bio-behavioral sciences: A case study of destructive social reductionism and collective fraud in 20th century academia. In H. Nyborg (ed.), *The scientific study of general intelligence: Tribute to Arthur R. Jensen* (pp. 441–502). New York, NY: Pergamon.

Nyborg, H., & Jensen, A. R. (2001). Occupation and income related to psychometric *g*. *Intelligence, 29*, 45–55. doi:10.1016/S0160-2896(00)00042-8

"Obama administration sets high bar for flexibility from No Child Left Behind in order to advance equity and support reform." (2011, September 23). U.S. Department of Education. Retrieved from www.ed.gov/news/press-releases/obama-administration-sets-high-bar-flexibility-no-child-left-behind-order-advanc

O'Connell, M., & Sheikh, H. (2011). "Big Five" personality dimensions and social attainment: Evidence from beyond the campus. *Personality and Individual Differences, 50*, 828–833. doi:10.1016/j.paid.2011.01.004

Oden, M. H. (1968). The fulfillment of promise: 40-year follow-up of the Terman gifted group. *Genetic Psychology Monographs, 77*, 3–93.

Ogbu, J. U. (1994). Culture and intelligence. In R. J. Sternberg (ed.), *Encyclopedia of human intelligence* (pp. 328–338). New York, NY: Macmillan.

Ogbu, J. U. (2002). Cultural amplifiers of intelligence: IQ and minority status in cross-cultural perspective. In J. M. Fish (ed.), *Race and intelligence: Separating science from myth* (pp. 241–278). Mahwah, NJ: Lawrence Erlbaum Associates.

Okbay, A., Beauchamp, J. P., Fontana, M. A., Lee, J. J., Pers, T. H., Rietveld, C. A., . . . & Benjamin, D. J. (2016). Genome-wide association study identifies 74 loci associated with educational attainment. *Nature, 533*, 539–542. doi:10.1038/nature17671

Olszewski-Kubilius, P., & Kulieke, M. J. (2008). Using off-level testing and assessment for gifted and talented students. In J. VanTassel-Baska (ed.), *Alternative assessments with gifted and talented students* (pp. 89–106). Waco, TX: Prufrock Press.

Olszewski-Kubilius, P., Steenbergen-Hu, S., Thomson, D., & Rosen, R. (2017). Minority achievement gaps in STEM: Findings of a longitudinal study of Project Excite. *Gifted Child Quarterly, 61*, 20–39. doi:10.1177/0016986216673449

Open Science Collaboration. (2015). Estimating the reproducibility of psychological science. *Science, 349*, 943. doi:10.1126/science.aac4716

Ovaska-Few, S. (2012, November 16). How standardized admissions tests fail NC colleges, students. *NC Policy Watch*. Retrieved from www.ncpolicywatch.com /2012/11/16/how-standardized-admissions-tests-fail-nc-colleges-students/

Parents in Action on Special Education v. Hannon, 506 F. Supp. 831 (N.D. Ill. 1980). Retrieved from https://law.justia.com/cases/federal/district-courts/FSupp/506/831/1654128/

Pastorino, E., & Doyle-Portillo, S. D. (2016). *What is psychology? Foundations, applications, and integration.* Boston, MA: Cengage Learning.

Patall, E. A., Cooper, H., & Robinson, J. C. (2008). The effects of choice on intrinsic motivation and related outcomes: A meta-analysis of research findings. *Psychological Bulletin, 134,* 270–300. doi:10.1037/0033-2909.134.2.270

Paterson, D. G. (1938). The genesis of modern guidance. *Educational Record, 19,* 36–46.

Pattison, E., Grodsky, E., & Muller, C. (2013). Is the sky falling? Grade inflation and the signaling power of grades. *Educational Researcher, 42,* 259–265. doi:10.3102/0013189x13481382

Paunesku, D., Walton, G. M., Romero, C., Smith, E. N., Yeager, D. S., & Dweck, C. S. (2015). Mind-set interventions are a scalable treatment for academic underachievement. *Psychological Science, 26,* 784–793. doi:10.1177/0956797615571017

Pearson, K. (1896). Mathematical contributions to the theory of evolution. III. Regression, heredity, and panmixia. *Philosophical Transactions of the Royal Society of London. Series A, Containing Papers of a Mathematical or Physical Character, 187,* 253–318. doi:10.2307/90707

Pearson, K. (1903). On the inheritance of the mental and moral characters in man, and its comparison with the inheritance of the physical characters. *Journal of the Anthropological Institute of Great Britain and Ireland, 33,* 179–237. doi:10.2307/2842809

Penke, L., Maniega, S. M., Bastin, M. E., Valdes Hernandez, M. C., Murray, C., Royle, N. A., … & Deary, I. J. (2012). Brain white matter tract integrity as a neural foundation for general intelligence. *Molecular Psychiatry, 17,* 1026–1030. doi:10.1038/mp.2012.66

Perkins, H. F., Davenport, C. B., Campbell, C. G., Grant, M., Hunt, H. R., Osborn, F., … & Laughlin, H. H. (eds.). (1934). *A decade of progress in eugenics: Scientific papers of the Third International Congress of Eugenics held at American Museum of Natural History, New York, August 21–23,1932.* Baltimore, MD: The Williams & Wilkins, Company.

Perlmutter, D., & Colman, C. (2006). *Raise a smarter child by kindergarten: Raise IQ by up to 30 points and turn on your child's smart genes.* New York, NY: Broadway Books.

Pesta, B. J., Kirkegaard, E. O. W., te Nijenhuis, J., Lasker, J., & Fuerst, J. G. R. (2020). Racial and ethnic group differences in the heritability of intelligence: A systematic review and meta-analysis. *Intelligence, 78,* Article 101408. doi:10.1016/j.intell.2019.101408

Pesta, B. J., McDaniel, M. A., Poznanski, P. J., & DeGroot, T. (2015). Discounting IQ's relevance to organizational behavior: The "somebody else's problem" in management education. *Open Differential Psychology, 35,* 1–11.

Peters, S. J., Rambo-Hernandez, K., Makel, M. C., Matthews, M. S., & Plucker, J. A. (2017). Should millions of students take a gap year? Large numbers of students start the school year above grade level. *Gifted Child Quarterly, 61,* 229–238. doi:10.1177/0016986217701834

Peters, S. J., Rambo-Hernandez, K., Makel, M. C., Matthews, M. S., & Plucker, J. A. (2019). Effect of local norms on racial and ethnic representation in gifted education. *AERA Open, 5*(2), 2332858419848446. doi:10.1177/2332858419848446

Petersen, N. S., & Novick, M. R. (1976). An evaluation of some models for culture-fair selection. *Journal of Educational Measurement, 13*, 3–29. doi:10.1111/j.1745-3984.1976.tb00178.x

Peterson, J. (1969). *Early conceptions and tests of intelligence.* Westport, CT: Greenwood Press. (Originally printed in 1926)

Peterson, J. S. (2009). Myth 17: Gifted and talented individuals do not have unique social and emotional needs. *Gifted Child Quarterly, 53*, 280–282. doi:10.1177/0016986209346946

Pew Research Center. (2018, July 26). Public views of gene editing for babies depend on how it would be used. Retrieved from www.pewresearch.org/science/2018/07/26/public-views-of-gene-editing-for-babies-depend-on-how-it-would-be-used/

Phelps, R. P. (2003). *Kill the messenger: The war on standardized testing.* New Brunswick, NJ: Transaction Publishers.

Phelps, R. P. (2005). Persistently positive: Forty years of public opinion on standardized testing. In R. P. Phelps (ed.), *Defending standardized testing* (pp. 1–22). Mahwah, NJ: Lawrence Erlbaum Associates.

Phillips, S. E. (2000). *GI Forum v. Texas Education Agency*: Psychometric evidence. *Applied Measurement in Education, 13*, 343–385. doi:10.1207/s15324818ame1304_04

Phillips, S. E., & Camara, W. J. (2006). Legal and ethical issues. In R. L. Brennan (ed.), *Educational measurement* (4th ed., pp. 733–755). Westport, CT: Praeger.

Pietschnig, J., & Gittler, G. (2015). A reversal of the Flynn effect for spatial perception in German-speaking countries: Evidence from a cross-temporal IRT-based meta-analysis (1977–2014). *Intelligence, 53*, 145–153. doi:10.1016/j.intell.2015.10.004

Pietschnig, J., Penke, L., Wicherts, J. M., Zeiler, M., & Voracek, M. (2015). Meta-analysis of associations between human brain volume and intelligence differences: How strong are they and what do they mean? *Neuroscience & Biobehavioral Reviews, 57*, 411–432. doi:10.1016/j.neubiorev.2015.09.017

Pietschnig, J., & Voracek, M. (2015). One century of global IQ gains: A formal meta-analysis of the Flynn effect (1909–2013). *Perspectives on Psychological Science, 10*, 282–306. doi:10.1177/1745691615577701

Pietschnig, J., Voracek, M., & Formann, A. K. (2010). Mozart effect–Shmozart effect: A meta-analysis. *Intelligence, 38*, 314–323. doi:10.1016/j.intell.2010.03.001

Piffer, D. (2015). A review of intelligence GWAS hits: Their relationship to country IQ and the issue of spatial autocorrelation. *Intelligence, 53*, 43–50. doi:10.1016/j.intell.2015.08.008

Piffer, D. (2019). Evidence for recent polygenic selection on educational attainment and intelligence inferred from Gwas hits: A replication of previous findings using recent data. *Psych, 1*, 55–75. doi:10.3390/psych1010005

Pinker, S. [sapinker] (2018, December 19). The fallacy: That meritocracy is a consciously chosen system. Reality: It's what you get when you move away from cronyism, nepotism, racism, sexism, old-boy networks, & other biases. [Tweet]. Retrieved from twitter.com/sapinker/status/1075415858112024576

Plomin, R. (2018). *Blueprint: How DNA makes us who we are.* Cambridge, MA: MIT Press.

Plomin, R., & Deary, I. J. (2015). Genetics and intelligence differences: Five special findings. *Molecular Psychiatry, 20*, 98–108. doi:10.1038/mp.2014.105

Plomin, R., DeFries, J. C., Knopik, V. S., & Neiderhiser, J. M. (2012). Behavioral genetics (6th ed.). New York, NY: Worth.

Plomin, R., DeFries, J. C., Knopik, V. S., & Neiderhiser, J. M. (2016). Top 10 replicated findings from behavioral genetics. *Perspectives on Psychological Science, 11*, 3–23. doi:10.1177/1745691615617439

Plomin, R., & Petrill, S. A. (1997). Genetics and intelligence: What's new? *Intelligence, 24*, 53–77. doi:10.1016/s0160-2896(97)90013-1

Plomin, R., Shakeshaft, N. G., McMillan, A., & Trzaskowski, M. (2014). Nature, nurture, and expertise. *Intelligence, 45*, 46–59. doi:10.1016/j.intell.2013.06.008

Plomin, R., & von Stumm, S. (2018). The new genetics of intelligence. *Nature Reviews Genetics, 19*, 148–159. doi:10.1038/nrg.2017.104

Popejoy, A. B., & Fullerton, S. M. (2016). Genomics is failing on diversity. *Nature, 538*, 161-164. doi:10.1038/538161a

Poropat, A. E. (2009). A meta-analysis of the five-factor model of personality and academic performance. *Psychological Bulletin, 135*, 322–338. doi:10.1037/a0014996

Porteus, S. D. (1915). Mental tests for feeble-minded: A new series. *Journal of Psycho-Asthenics, 19*, 200–213.

Porteus, S. D. (1965). *Porteus maze test: Fifty years' application*. Palo Alto, CA: Pacific Books.

Posselt, J. R., Jaquette, O., Bielby, R., & Bastedo, M. N. (2012). Access without equity: Longitudinal analyses of institutional stratification by race and ethnicity, 1972–2004. *American Educational Research Journal, 49*, 1074–1111. doi:10.3102/00028312 12439456

Premack, D. (1983). The codes of man and beasts. *Behavioral and Brain Sciences, 6*, 125–136. doi:10.1017/S0140525X00015077

Pressey, S. L., & Teter, G. F. (1919). Minor studies from the psychological laboratory of Indiana University. I. A comparison of colored and white children by means of a group scale of intelligence. *Journal of Applied Psychology, 3*, 277–282. doi:10.1037/h0075831

Price, A. (2019). The University of Texas's secret strategy to keep out Black students. *The Atlantic*. Retrieved from www.theatlantic.com/ideas/archive/2019/09/how-ut-used-standardized-testing-to-slow-integration/597814/

Protzko, J. (2015). The environment in raising early intelligence: A meta-analysis of the fadeout effect. *Intelligence, 53*, 202–210. doi:10.1016/j.intell.2015.10.006

Protzko, J. (2017a). Raising IQ among school-aged children: Five meta-analyses and a review of randomized controlled trials. *Developmental Review, 46*, 81–101. doi:10.1016/j.dr.2017.05.001

Protzko, J. (2017b). Effects of cognitive training on the structure of intelligence. *Psychonomic Bulletin & Review, 24*, 1022–1031. doi:10.3758/s13423-016-1196-1

Protzko, J., Aronson, J., & Blair, C. (2013). How to make a young child smarter: Evidence from the database of raising intelligence. *Perspectives on Psychological Science, 8*, 25–40. doi:10.1177/1745691612462585

Pyryt, M. C. (2000). Finding "g": Easy viewing through higher order factor analysis. *Gifted Child Quarterly, 44*, 190–192. doi:10.1177/001698620004400305

Quinn, D. M. (2017). Racial attitudes of preK–12 and postsecondary educators: Descriptive evidence from nationally representative data. *Educational Researcher, 46*, 397–411. doi:10.3102/0013189x17727270

Rambo-Hernandez, K. E., & Warne, R. T. (2015). Measuring the outliers: An introduction to out-of-level testing with high-achieving students. *TEACHING Exceptional Children, 47*, 199–207. doi:10.1177/0040059915569359

Rand Corporation. (n.d.). *Project 100,000 new standards program.* Retrieved from www.rand.org/content/dam/rand/pubs/monographs/MG265/images/webG1318.pdf

Raudenbush, S. W. (1984). Magnitude of teacher expectancy effects on pupil IQ as a function of the credibility of expectancy induction: A synthesis of findings from 18 experiments. *Journal of Educational Psychology, 76*, 85–97. doi:10.1037/0022-0663.76.1.85

Rauscher, F. H., Shaw, G. L., & Ky, C. N. (1993). Music and spatial task performance. *Nature, 365*, 611. doi:10.1038/365611a0

Ravitsch, D. (2016, July 23). The Common Core costs billions and hurts students. *New York Times*, p. SR8. Retrieved from www.nytimes.com/2016/07/24/opinion/sunday/the-common-core-costs-billions-and-hurts-students.html

Reardon, S. F., & Ho, A. D. (2015). Practical issues in estimating achievement gaps from coarsened data. *Journal of Educational and Behavioral Statistics, 40*, 158–189. doi:10.3102/1076998615570944

Reardon, S. F., Kalogrides, D., & Shores, K. (2019). The geography of racial/ethnic test score gaps. *American Journal of Sociology, 124*, 1164–1221. doi:10.1086/700678

Reder, S. (1998). Dimensionality and construct validity of the NALS assessment. In M. C. Smith (ed.), *Literacy for the twenty-first century* (pp. 37–57). Westport, CT: Praeger.

Redick, T. S. (2019). The hype cycle of working memory training. *Current Directions in Psychological Science, 28*, 423–429. doi.org/10.1177/0963721419848668

Ree, M. J., & Earles, J. A. (1993). *g* is to psychology what carbon is to chemistry: A reply to Sternberg and Wagner, McClelland, and Calfee. *Current Directions in Psychological Science, 2*, 11–12. doi:10.1111/1467-8721.ep10770509

Reeve, C. L., & Basalik, D. (2014). Is health literacy an example of construct proliferation? A conceptual and empirical evaluation of its redundancy with general cognitive ability. *Intelligence, 44*, 93–102. doi:10.1016/j.intell.2014.03.004

Reeve, C. L., & Bonaccio, S. (2011). On the myth and the reality of the temporal validity degradation of general mental ability test scores. *Intelligence, 39*, 255–272. doi:10.1016/j.intell.2011.06.009

Reeve, C. L., & Charles, J. E. (2008). Survey of opinions on the primacy of *g* and social consequences of ability testing: A comparison of expert and non-expert views. *Intelligence, 36*, 681–688. doi:10.1016/j.intell.2008.03.007

Reilly, D., Neumann, D. L., & Andrews, G. (2019). Gender differences in reading and writing achievement: Evidence from the National Assessment of Educational Progress (NAEP). *American Psychologist, 74*, 445–458. doi:10.1037/amp0000356

Regalado, A. (2018, November 25). Exclusive: Chinese scientists are creating CRISPR babies. *MIT Technology Review.* Retrieved from www.technologyreview.com/s/612458/exclusive-chinese-scientists-are-creating-crispr-babies/

Regents of the University of California v. Bakke, 438 U.S. 265 (1978).

Renzulli, J. S. (1978). What makes giftedness? Reexamining a definition. *Phi Delta Kappan, 60*, 180–184, 261. doi:10.1177/003172171109200821

Renzulli, J. S. (2012). Reexamining the role of gifted education and talent development for the 21st century: A four-part theoretical approach. *Gifted Child Quarterly, 56*, 150–159. doi:10.1177/0016986212444901

Reschly, D. J. (1980). Psychological evidence in the *Larry P.* opinion: A case of right problem–wrong solution? *School Psychology Review*, *9*, 123–135.

Reynolds, C. R. (2000). Why is psychometric research on bias in mental testing so often ignored? *Psychology, Public Policy, and Law*, *6*, 144–150. doi:10.1037/1076-8971.6.1.144

Reynolds, C. R., & Lowe, P. A. (2009). The problem of bias in psychological assessment. In C. R. Reynolds & T. B. Gutkin (eds.), *The handbook of school psychology* (pp. 332–374). New York, NY: Wiley.

Richardson, J. T. E. (2011). *Howard Andrew Knox: Pioneer of intelligence testing at Ellis Island*. New York, NY: Columbia University Press.

Richardson, K. (2002). What IQ tests test. *Theory & Psychology*, *12*, 283–314. doi:10.1177/0959354302012003012

Rienzo, C., Rolfe, H., & Wilkinson, D. (2015). *Changing mindsets: Evaluation report and executive summary*. Retrieved from ERIC database. (ED581132)

Rimfeld, K., Krapohl, E., Trzaskowski, M., Coleman, J. R. I., Selzam, S., Dale, P. S., . . . & Plomin, R. (2018). Genetic influence on social outcomes during and after the Soviet era in Estonia. *Nature Human Behaviour*, *2*, 269–275. doi:10.1038/s41562-018-0332-5

Rindermann, H. (2018). *Cognitive capitalism: Human capital and the wellbeing of nations*. New York, NY: Cambridge University Press.

Rindermann, H., Becker, D., & Coyle, T. (2016). Survey of expert opinion on intelligence: Causes of international differences in cognitive ability tests. *Frontiers in Psychology*, *7*, Article 399. doi:10.3389/fpsyg.2016.00399

Rindermann, H., Becker, D., & Coyle, T. R. (2017). Survey of expert opinion on intelligence: The FLynn effect and the future of intelligence. *Personality and Individual Differences*, *106*, 242–247. doi:10.1016/j.paid.2016.10.061

Rindermann, H., Becker, D., & Coyle, T. R. (2020). Survey of expert opinion on intelligence: Intelligence research, experts' background, controversial issues, and the media. *Intelligence*, *78*, Article 101406. doi:10.1016/j.intell.2019.101406

Rindermann, H., & Ceci, S. J. (2018). Parents' education is more important than their wealth in shaping their children's intelligence: Results of 19 samples in seven countries at different developmental levels. *Journal for the Education of the Gifted*, *41*, 298–326. doi:10.1177/0162353218799481

Rindermann, H., & Thompson, J. (2016). The cognitive competences of immigrant and native students across the world: An analysis of gaps, possible causes and impact. *Journal of Biosocial Science*, *48*, 66–93. doi:10.1017/s0021932014000480

Ritchie, S. (2015). *Intelligence: All that matters*. London: John Murray Learning.

Ritchie, S. J., Cox, S. R., Shen, X., Lombardo, M. V., Reus, L. M., Alloza, C., . . . & Deary, I. J. (2018). Sex differences in the adult human brain: Evidence from 5216 UK Biobank participants. *Cerebral Cortex*, *28*, 2959–2975. doi:10.1093/cercor/bhy109

Ritchie, S. J., & Tucker-Drob, E. M. (2018). How much does education improve intelligence? A meta-analysis. *Psychological Science*, *29*, 1358–1369. doi:10.1177/0956797618774253

Roberts, D. (2015). Can research on the genetics of intelligence be "socially neutral"? *Hastings Center Report*, *45*, S50–S53. doi:10.1002/hast.499

Robinson, D. H., & Wainer, H. (2006). Profiles in research: Arthur Jensen. *Journal of Educational and Behavioral Statistics*, *31*, 327–352. doi:10.3102/10769986031003327

Robinson, N. M., Zigler, E., & Gallagher, J. J. (2000). Two tails of the normal curve: Similarities and differences in the study of mental retardation and giftedness. *American Psychologist, 55,* 1413–1424. doi:10.1037/0003-066X.55.12.1413

Roche, B. (2016, May 24). New evidence that IQ can be increased with brain training. *Psychology Today.* Retrieved from www.psychologytoday.com/us/blog/iq-boot-camp/201605/new-evidence-iq-can-be-increased-brain-training

Roderick, M., & Engel, M. (2001). The grasshopper and the ant: Motivational responses of low-achieving students to high-stakes testing. *Educational Evaluation and Policy Analysis, 23,* 197–227. doi:10.3102/01623737023003197

Roid, G. H. (2003). *Stanford-Binet Intelligence Scales, fifth edition, technical manual.* Itasca, IL: Riverside Publishing.

Roll-Hansen, N. (2005). Norwegian eugenics: Sterilization as social reform. In G. Broberg & N. Roll-Hansen (eds.), *Eugenics and the welfare state: Norway, Sweden, Denmark, and Finland* (pp. 151–194). East Lansing, MI: Michigan State University Press.

Root-Bernstein, R., Allen, L., Beach, L., Bhadula, R., Fast, J., Hosey, C., … Weinlander, S. (2008). Arts foster scientific success: Avocations of Nobel, National Academy, Royal Society, and Sigma Xi members. *Journal of Psychology of Science & Technology, 1,* 51–63. doi:10.1891/1939-7054.1.2.51

Rose, S. (2009). Should scientists study race and IQ? No: Science and society do not benefit. *Nature, 457,* 786–788. doi:10.1038/457786a

Rosenthal, R. (1979). The file drawer problem and tolerance for null results. *Psychological Bulletin, 86,* 638–641. doi:10.1037//0033-2909.86.3.638

Rosenthal, R., & Jacobson, L. (1966). Teachers' expectancies: Determinants of pupils' IQ gains. *Psychological Reports, 19,* 115–118. doi:10.2466/pr0.1966.19.1.115

Rosenthal, R., & Jacobson, L. (1968). *Pygmalion in the classroom: Teacher expectation and pupils' intellectual development.* New York, NY: Holt, Rhinehart & Winston.

Roth, B., Becker, N., Romeyke, S., Schäfer, S., Domnick, F., & Spinath, F. M. (2015). Intelligence and school grades: A meta-analysis. *Intelligence, 53,* 118–137. doi:10.1016/j.intell.2015.09.002

Roth, P. L., Bevier, C. A., Bobko, P., Switzer, F. S., III, & Tyler, P. (2001). Ethnic group difference in cognitive ability in employment and educational settings: A meta-analysis. *Personnel Psychology, 54,* 297–330. doi:10.1111/j.1744-6570.2001.tb00094.x

Rowe, D. C., Vesterdal, W. J., & Rodgers, J. L. (1998). Herrnstein's syllogism: Genetic and shared environmental influences on IQ, education, and income. *Intelligence, 26,* 405–423. doi:10.1016/S0160-2896(99)00008-2

Ruf, D. L. (2005). *Losing our minds: Gifted children left behind.* Scottsdale, AZ: Great Potential Press.

Runquist, E. A. (1936). Intelligence test scores and school marks in 1928 and 1933. *School & Society, 43,* 301–304.

Rushton, J. P. (1997). Race, intelligence, and the brain: The errors and omissions of the "revised" edition of S. J. Gould's *The Mismeasure of Man* (1996). *Personality and Individual Differences, 23,* 169–180. doi:10.1016/S0191-8869(97)80984-1

Rushton, J. P. (2000). *Race, evolution, and behavior: A life history perspective* (3rd ed.). Port Huron, MI: Charles Darwin Research Institute.

Rushton, J. P. (2012). No narrowing in mean Black–White IQ differences – predicted by heritable *g. American Psychologist, 67,* 500–501. doi:10.1037/a0029614

Rushton, J. P., & Ankney, C. D. (2009). Whole brain size and general mental ability: A review. *International Journal of Neuroscience, 119,* 691–731. doi:10.1080/00207450802325843

Rushton, J. P., & Jensen, A. R. (2005a). Thirty years of research on race differences in cognitive ability. *Psychology, Public Policy, and Law, 11,* 235–294. doi:10.1037/1076-8971.11.2.235

Rushton, J. P., & Jensen, A. R. (2005b). Wanted: More race realism, less moralistic fallacy. *Psychology, Public Policy, and Law, 11,* 328–336. doi:10.1037/1076-8971.11.2.328

Rushton, J. P., & Jensen, A. R. (2006). The totality of available evidence shows the race IQ gap still remains. *Psychological Science, 17,* 921–922. doi:10.1111/j.1467-9280.2006.01803.x

Rushton, J. P., & Jensen, A. R. (2010). The rise and fall of the Flynn Effect as a reason to expect a narrowing of the Black–White IQ gap. *Intelligence, 38,* 213–219. doi:10.1016/j.intell.2009.12.002

Russell, E. W. (2007). The Flynn Effect revisited. *Applied Neuropsychology, 14,* 262–266. doi:10.1080/09084280701719211

Sackett, P. R., Borneman, M. J., & Connelly, B. S. (2008). High stakes testing in higher education and employment: Appraising the evidence for validity and fairness. *American Psychologist, 63,* 215–227. doi:10.1037/0003-066X.63.4.215

Sackett, P. R., Hardison, C. M., & Cullen, M. J. (2004). On interpreting stereotype threat as accounting for African American–White differences on cognitive tests. *American Psychologist, 59,* 7–13. doi:10.1037/0003-066x.59.1.7

Sackett, P. R., Schmitt, N., Ellingson, J. E., & Kabin, M. B. (2001). High-stakes testing in employment, credentialing, and higher education: Prospects in a post-affirmative-action world. *American Psychologist, 56,* 302–318. doi:10.1037/0003-066x.56.4.302

Sacks, P. (1997). Standardized testing: Meritocracy's crooked yardstick. *Change: The Magazine of Higher Learning, 29*(2), 24–31. doi:10.1080/00091389709603101

Saini, A. (2017). *Inferior: How science got women wrong and the new research that's rewriting the story.* Boston, MA: Beacon Press.

Sala, G., & Gobet, F. (2017). Does far transfer exist? Negative evidence from chess, music, and working memory training. *Current Directions in Psychological Science, 26,* 515–520. doi:10.1177/0963721417712760

Sala, G., & Gobet, F. (2019). Cognitive training does not enhance general cognition. *Trends in Cognitive Sciences, 23,* 9–20. doi:10.1016/j.tics.2018.10.004

Salovey, P., & Mayer, J. D. (1990). Emotional intelligence. *Imagination, Cognition and Personality, 9,* 185–211. doi:10.2190/DUGG-P24E-52WK-6CDG

Sander, R. H. (2004). A systemic analysis of affirmative action in American law schools. *Stanford Law Review, 57,* 367–483.

Sanders, C. E., Lubinski, D., & Benbow, C. P. (1995). Does the Defining Issues Test measure psychological phenomena distinct from verbal ability? An examination of Lykken's query. *Journal of Personality and Social Psychology, 69,* 498–504. doi:10.1037/0022-3514.69.3.498

Sauce, B., & Matzel, L. D. (2018). The paradox of intelligence: Heritability and malleability coexist in hidden gene-environment interplay. *Psychological Bulletin, 144,* 26–47. doi:10.1037/bul0000131

Savage, J. E., Jansen, P. R., Stringer, S., Watanabe, K., Bryois, J., de Leeuw, C. A., … & Posthuma, D. (2018). Genome-wide association meta-analysis in 269,867 individuals identifies new genetic and functional links to intelligence. *Nature Genetics, 50,* 912–919. doi:10.1038/s41588-018-0152-6

Scarr, S. (1985). An author's frame of mind: Review of *Frames of mind: The theory of multiple intelligences* by Howard Gardner, Basic Books (1984). *New Ideas in Psychology, 3,* 95–100. doi:10.1016/0732-118X(85)90056-X

Scarr, S. (1994). Culture-fair and culture-free tests. In R. J. Sternberg (ed.), *Encyclopedia of human intelligence* (pp. 322–328). New York, NY: Macmillan.

Scarr, S., Pakstis, A. J., Katz, S. H., & Barker, W. B. (1977). Absence of a relationship between degree of white ancestry and intellectual skills within a black population. *Human Genetics, 39,* 69–86. doi:10.1007/BF00273154

Scarr, S., & Weinberg, R. A. (1976). IQ test performance of Black children adopted by White families. *American Psychologist, 31,* 726–739. doi:10.1037/0003-066x.31.10.726

Scarr, S., & Weinberg, R. A. (1978). Attitudes, interests, and IQ. *Human Nature, 1*(4), 29–36.

Schaie, K. W. (2013). *Developmental influences on adult intelligence* (2nd ed.). New York, NY: Oxford University Press.

Scheurich, J. J., & Young, M. D. (1997). Coloring epistemologies: Are our research epistemologies racially biased? *Educational Researcher, 26,* 4–16. doi:10.3102/0013189X026004004

Schimmack, U. (2012). The ironic effect of significant results on the credibility of multiple-study articles. *Psychological Methods, 17,* 551–566. doi:10.1037/a0029487

Schimmack, U. (2019, January 2). Social psychology textbook audit: Stereotype threat [Web log post]. Retrieved from https://replicationindex.com/2019/01/02/social-psychology-textbook-audit-stereotype-threat/

Schlegel, K., Palese, T., Mast, M. S., Rammsayer, T. H., Hall, J. A., & Murphy, N. A. (2020). A meta-analysis of the relationship between emotion recognition ability and intelligence. *Cognition and Emotion, 34,* 329-351. doi:10.1080/02699931.2019.1632801

Schmeiser, C. B., & Welch, C. J. (2006). Test development. In R. L. Brennan (ed.), *Educational measurement* (4th ed., pp. 307–353). Westport, CT: Praeger.

Schmidt, F. L., & Hunter, J. E. (1977). Development of a general solution to the problem of validity generalization. *Journal of Applied Psychology, 62,* 529–540. doi:10.1037/0021-9010.62.5.529

Schmidt, F. L., & Hunter, J. E. (1998). The validity and utility of selection methods in personnel psychology: Practical and theoretical implications of 85 years of research findings. *Psychological Bulletin, 124,* 262–274. doi:10.1037/0033-2909.124.2.262

Schmidt, F. L., & Hunter, J. (2004). General mental ability in the world of work: Occupational attainment and job performance. *Journal of Personality & Social Psychology, 86,* 162–173. doi:10.1037/0022-3514.86.1.162

Schmidt, F. L., Hunter, J. E., & Urry, V. W. (1976). Statistical power in criterion-related validation studies. *Journal of Applied Psychology, 61,* 473–485. doi:10.1037/0021-9010.61.4.473

Schmidt, F. T. C., Nagy, G., Fleckenstein, J., Möller, J., & Retelsdorf, J. (2018). Same same, but different? Relations between facets of conscientiousness and grit. *European Journal of Personality, 32,* 705–720. doi:10.1002/per.2171

Schroth, S. T., & Helfer, J. A. (2009). Practitioners' conceptions of academic talent and giftedness: Essential factors in deciding classroom and school composition. *Journal of Advanced Academics*, 20, 384–403. doi:10.1177/1932202X0902000302

Schwartz, D. L., Cheng, K. M., Salehi, S., & Wieman, C. (2016). The half empty question for socio-cognitive interventions. *Journal of Educational Psychology*, 108, 397–404. doi:10.1037/edu0000122

Schweinhart, L. J., & Weikart, D. P. (1993). Success by empowerment: The High/Scope Perry Preschool Study through age 27. *Young Children*, 49(1), 54–58.

Schwinger, M., Steinmayr, R., & Spinath, B. (2009). How do motivational regulation strategies affect achievement: Mediated by effort management and moderated by intelligence. *Learning and Individual Differences*, 19, 621–627. doi:10.1016/j.lindif.2009.08.006

Serpell, R., & Jere-Folotiya, J. (2008). Developmental assessment, cultural context, gender, and schooling in Zambia. *International Journal of Psychology*, 43, 88–96. doi:10.1080/00207590701859184

Sesardic, N. (2000). Philosophy of science that ignores science: Race, IQ and heritability. *Philosophy of Science*, 67, 580–602. doi:10.1086/392856

Sesardic, N. (2010). Race: A social destruction of a biological concept. *Biology & Philosophy*, 25, 143–162. doi:10.1007/s10539-009-9193-7

Sherwood, J. J., & Nataupsky, M. (1968). Prediciting the conclusions of Negro–white intelligence research from biographical characteristics of the investigator. *Journal of Personality and Social Psychology*, 8, 53–58. doi:10.1037/h0025265

Shewach, O. R., Sackett, P. R., & Quint, S. (2019). Stereotype threat effects in settings with features likely versus unlikely in operational test settings: A meta-analysis. *Journal of Applied Psychology*, 104, 1514–1534. doi:10.1037/apl0000420

Shiao, J. L., Bode, T., Beyer, A., & Selvig, D. (2012). The genomic challenge to the social construction of race. *Sociological Theory*, 30, 67–88. doi:10.1177/0735275112448053

Shuey, A. M. (1966). *The testing of Negro intelligence* (2nd ed.). New York, NY: Social Science Press.

Shweder, R. A. (2004, January 8). Tuskegee re-examined. *Spiked*. Retrieved from www.spiked-online.com/2004/01/08/tuskegee-re-examined/

Silventoinen, K., Sammalisto, S., Perola, M., Boomsma, D. I., Cornes, B. K., Davis, C., ... & Kaprio, J. (2003). Heritability of adult body height: A comparative study of twin cohorts in eight countries. *Twin Research*, 6, 399–408. doi:10.1375/twin.6.5.399

Simmons, J. P., Nelson, L. D., & Simonsohn, U. (2011). False-positive psychology: Undisclosed flexibility in data collection and analysis allows presenting anything as significant. *Psychological Science*, 22, 1359–1366. doi:10.1177/0956797611417632

Simons, D. J., Boot, W. R., Charness, N., Gathercole, S. E., Chabris, C. F., Hambrick, D. Z., & Stine-Morrow, E. A. L. (2016). Do "brain-training" programs work? *Psychological Science in the Public Interest*, 17, 103–186. doi:10.1177/1529100616661983

Simonton, D. K. (1976). Biographical determinants of achieved eminence: A multivariate approach to the Cox data. *Journal of Personality and Social Psychology*, 33, 218–226. doi:10.1037/0022-3514.33.2.218

Singham, M. (1995). Race and intelligence: What are the issues? *Phi Delta Kappan*, 77, 271–278.

Sisk, V. F., Burgoyne, A. P., Sun, J., Butler, J. L., & Macnamara, B. N. (2018). To what extent and under which circumstances are growth mind-sets important to academic achievement? Two meta-analyses. *Psychological Science, 29,* 549–571. doi:10.1177/0956797617739704

Siu, E., & Reiter, H. I. (2009). Overview: What's worked and what hasn't as a guide towards predictive admissions tool development. *Advances in Health Sciences Education, 14,* 759–775. doi:10.1007/s10459-009-9160-8

Skeels, H. M. (1966). Adult status of children with contrasting early life experiences: A follow-up study. *Monographs of the Society for Research in Child Development, 31* (3), 1–65. doi:10.2307/1165791

Skeels, H. M., Wellman, B. L., Updegraff, R., & Williams, H. M. (1938). *University of Iowa studies: Studies in child welfare,* Vol. 15: *A study of environmental stimulation: An orphanage preschool project.* Iowa City, IA: University of Iowa.

Skidmore, S. T., & Thompson, B. (2010). Statistical techniques used in published articles: A historical review of reviews. *Educational and Psychological Measurement, 70,* 777–795. doi:10.1177/0013164410379320

Slade, M. K., & Warne, R. T. (2016). A meta-analysis of the effectiveness of trauma-focused cognitive-behavioral therapy and play therapy for child victims of abuse. *Journal of Young Investigators, 30*(6), 36–43.

Smouse, P. E., Spielman, R. S., & Park, M. H. (1982). Multiple-locus allocation of individuals to groups as a function of the genetic variation within and differences among human populations. *American Naturalist, 119,* 445–463. doi:10.1086/283925

Sniekers, S., Stringer, S., Watanabe, K., Jansen, P. R., Coleman, J. R. I., Krapohl, E., . . . & Posthuma, D. (2017). Genome-wide association meta-analysis of 78,308 individuals identifies new loci and genes influencing human intelligence. *Nature Genetics, 49,* 1107–1112. doi:10.1038/ng.3869

Snow, R. E. (1985). [Review of the book *Frames of mind: The theory of multiple intelligences,* by H. Gardner]. *American Journal of Education, 94,* 109–112. doi:10.1086/443835

Snow, R. E. (1995). Pygmalion and intelligence? *Current Directions in Psychological Science, 4,* 169–171. doi:10.1111/1467-8721.ep10772605

Snyderman, M., & Herrnstein, R. J. (1983). Intelligence tests and the Immigration Act of 1924. *American Psychologist, 38,* 986–995. doi:10.1037/0003-066x.38.9.986

Snyderman, M., & Rothman, S. (1987). Survey of expert opinion on intelligence and aptitude testing. *American Psychologist, 42,* 137–144. doi:10.1037/0003-066x.42.2.137

Snyderman, M., & Rothman, S. (1988). *The IQ controversy: The media and public policy.* New Brunswick, NJ: Transaction Books.

Society for Human Resource Management. (2016). *SHRM survey findings: Entry-level applicant job skills survey.* Retrieved from www.shrm.org/hr-today/trends-and-forecasting/research-and-surveys/Documents/Entry-Level_Applicant_Job_Skills_Survey.pdf

Sommer, M., & Arendasy, M. E. (2014). Comparing different explanations of the effect of test anxiety on respondents' test scores. *Intelligence, 42,* 115–127. doi:10.1016/j.intell.2013.11.003

Sorokin, P. (1956). *Fads and foibles in modern sociology and related sciences.* Chicago, IL: Henry Regnery Company.

Soto, C. J. (2019). How replicable are links between personality traits and consequential life outcomes? The life outcomes of personality replication project. *Psychological Science, 30,* 711–727. doi:10.1177/0956797619831612

Spearman, C. (1904). "General intelligence," objectively determined and measured. *American Journal of Psychology*, *15*, 201–293. doi:10.2307/1412107

Spearman, C. (1910). Correlation calculated from faulty data. *British Journal of Psychology*, *3*, 271–295. doi:10.111/j.2044-8295.1910.tb00206.x

Spearman, C. (1927). *The abilities of man: Their nature and measurement.* New York, NY: Macmillan Company.

Spencer, S. J., Logel, C., & Davies, P. G. (2016). Stereotype threat. *Annual Review of Psychology*, *67*, 415–437. doi:10.1146/annurev-psych-073115-103235

Spinath, B., Freudenthaler, H. H., & Neubauer, A. C. (2010). Domain-specific school achievement in boys and girls as predicted by intelligence, personality and motivation. *Personality and Individual Differences*, *48*, 481–486. doi:10.1016/j .paid.2009.11.028

Spinks, R., Arndt, S., Caspers, K., Yucuis, R., McKirgan, L. W., Pfalzgraf, C., & Waterman, E. (2007). School achievement strongly predicts midlife IQ. *Intelligence*, *35*, 563–567. doi:10.1016/j.intell.2006.10.004

Spitz, H. H. (1997). Some questions about the results of the Abecedarian Early Intervention Project cited by the APA Task Force on Intelligence. *American Psychologist*, *52*, 72. doi:10.1037/0003-066X.52.1.72.a

Spitz, H. H. (1999). Beleaguered *Pygmalion*: A history of the controversy over claims that teacher expectancy raises intelligence. *Intelligence*, *27*, 199–234. doi:10.1016/ S0160-2896(99)00026-4

Srivastava, A. K., & Misra, G. (2001). Lay people's understanding and use of intelligence: An Indian perspective. *Psychology and Developing Societies*, *13*, 25–49. doi:10.1177/097133360101300102

Stanley, J. C. (1956). The riddle of creativity. *Peabody Journal of Education*, *34*, 78–81. doi:10.2307/1490967

Stanley, J. C. (1974). Intellectual precocity. In J. C. Stanley, D. P. Keating, & L. H. Fox (eds.), *Mathematical talent: Discovery, description, and development* (pp. 1–22). Baltimore, MD: Johns Hopkins University Press.

Stauffer, J. M., Ree, M. J., & Carretta, T. R. (1996). Cognitive-components tests are not much more than *g*: An extension of Kyllonen's analyses. *Journal of General Psychology*, *123*, 193–205. doi:10.1080/00221309.1996.9921272

Steele, C. M. (1998). Stereotyping and its threat are real. *American Psychologist*, *53*, 680–681. doi:10.1037/0003-066x.53.6.680

Steele, C. M., & Aronson, J. (1995). Stereotype threat and the intellectual test performance of African Americans. *Journal of Personality and Social Psychology*, *69*, 797–811. doi:10.1037/0022-3514.69.5.797

Stemler, S. E., Chamvu, F., Chart, H., Jarvin, L., Jere, J., Hart, L., . . . & Grigorenko, E. L. (2009). Assessing competencies in reading and mathematics in Zambian children. In E. L. Grigorenko (ed.), *Multicultural psychoeducational assessment* (pp. 157–185). New York, NY: Springer.

Stemler, S. E., Grigorenko, E. L., Jarvin, L., & Sternberg, R. J. (2006). Using the theory of successful intelligence as a basis for augmenting AP exams in Psychology and Statistics. *Contemporary Educational Psychology*, *31*, 344–376. doi:10.1016/j. cedpsych.2005.11.001

Stepan, N. L. (1991). *"The hour of eugenics": Race, gender, and nation in Latin America.* Ithaca, NY: Cornell University Press.

Sterling, T. D. (1959). Publication decisions and their possible effects on inferences drawn from tests of significance – or vice versa. *Journal of the American Statistical Association, 54,* 30–34. doi:10.1080/01621459.1959.10501497

Stern, A. M. (2005). Sterilized in the name of public health. *American Journal of Public Health, 95,* 1128–1138. doi:10 2105/ajph.2004.041608

Sternberg, R. J. (1985). *Beyond IQ: A triarchic theory of human intelligence.* New York, NY: Cambridge University Press.

Sternberg, R. J. (2003a). *Wisdom, intelligence, and creativity synthesized.* New York, NY: Cambridge University Press.

Sternberg, R. J. (2003b). Our research program validating the triarchic theory of successful intelligence: Reply to Gottfredson. *Intelligence, 31,* 399–413. doi:10.1016/s0160-2896(02)00143-5s

Sternberg, R. J. (2004). Culture and intelligence. *American Psychologist, 59,* 325–338. doi:10.1037/0003-066x.59.5.325

Sternberg, R. J. (2005). There are no public-policy implications: A reply to Rushton and Jensen (2005). *Psychology, Public Policy, and Law, 11,* 295–301. doi:10.1037/1076-8971.11.2.295

Sternberg, R. J. (2012, December 12). Our fractured meritocracy [Web log post]. Retrieved from www.chronicle.com/blogs/conversation/2012/12/12/our-fractured-meritocracy/

Sternberg, R. J., Forsythe, G. B., Hedlund, J., Horvath, J. A., Wagner, R. K., Williams, W. M., ... & Grigorenko, E. L. (2000). *Practical intelligence in everyday life.* New York, NY: Cambridge University Press.

Sternberg, R. J., Grigorenko, E. L., & Kidd, K. K. (2005). Intelligence, race, and genetics. *American Psychologist, 60,* 46–59. doi:10.1037/0003-066X.60.1.46

Sternberg, R. J., Grigorenko, E. L., Ngorosho, D., Tantufuye, E., Mbise, A., Nokes, C., ... & Bundy, D. A. (2002). Assessing intellectual potential in rural Tanzanian school children. *Intelligence, 30,* 141–162. doi:10.1016/S0160-2896(01)00091-5

Sternberg, R. J., & Hedlund, J. (2002). Practical intelligence, g, and work psychology. *Human Performance, 15,* 143–160. doi:10.1080/08959285.2002.9668088

Sternberg, R. J., Nokes, C., Geissler, P. W., Prince, R., Okatcha, F., Bundy, D. A., & Grigorenko, E. L. (2001). The relationship between academic and practical intelligence: A case study in Kenya. *Intelligence, 29,* 401–418. doi:10.1016/S0160-2896(01)00065-4

Stoevenbelt, A. H., Wicherts, J., & Flore, P. (2019). *RRR: Johns, Scmader and Martens (2005).* Retrieved from https://osf.io/zwnxy/

Stojanoski, B., Lyons, K. M., Pearce, A. A. A., & Owen, A. M. (2018). Targeted training: Converging evidence against the transferable benefits of online brain training on cognitive function. *Neuropsychologia, 117,* 541–550. doi:10.1016/j.neuropsychologia.2018.07.013

Stough, C., Kerkin, B., Bates, T., & Mangan, G. (1994). Music and spatial IQ. *Personality and Individual Differences, 17,* 695. doi:10.1016/0191-8869(94)90145-7

Strand, S., Deary, I. J., & Smith, P. (2006). Sex differences in Cognitive Abilities Test scores: A UK national picture. *British Journal of Educational Psychology, 76,* 463–480. doi:10.1348/000709905x50906

Strassberg, Z., Dodge, K. A., Pettit, G. S., & Bates, J. E. (1994). Spanking in the home and children's subsequent aggression toward kindergarten peers. *Development and Psychopathology*, 6, 445–461. doi:10.1017/S0954579400006040

Strenze, T. (2015). Intelligence and success. In S. Goldstein, D. Princiotta, & J. A. Naglieri (eds.), *Handbook of intelligence: Evolutionary theory, historical perspective, and current concepts* (pp. 405–413). New York, NY: Springer.

Subotnik, R. F., Karp, D. E., & Morgan, E. R. (1989). High IQ children at midlife: An investigation into the generalizability of Terman's genetic studies of genius. *Roeper Review*, 11, 139–144. doi:10.1080/02783198909553190

Subotnik, R. F., Olszewski-Kubilius, P., & Worrell, F. C. (2011). Rethinking giftedness and gifted education: A proposed direction forward based on psychological science. *Psychological Science in the Public Interest*, 12, 3–54. doi:10.1177/1529100611418056

Sundet, J. M., Barlaug, D. G., & Torjussen, T. M. (2004). The end of the Flynn effect? A study of secular trends in mean intelligence test scores of Norwegian conscripts during half a century. *Intelligence*, 32, 349–362. doi:10.1016/j.intell.2004.06.004

Sunny, C. E., Taasoobshirazi, G., Clark, L., & Marchand, G. (2017). Stereotype threat and gender differences in chemistry. *Instructional Science*, 45, 157–175. doi:10.1007/s11251-016-9395-8

Surkan, P. J., Hsieh, C.-C., Johansson, A. L. V., Dickman, P. W., & Cnatingius, S. (2004). Reasons for increasing trends in large for gestational age births. *Obstetrics & Gynecology*, 104, 720–726. doi:10.1097/01.AOG.0000141442.59573.cd

Suzuki, L., & Aronson, J. (2005). The cultural malleability of intelligence and its impact on the racial/ethnic hierarchy. *Psychology, Public Policy, and Law*, 11, 320–327. doi:10.1037/1076-8971.11.2.320

Tal, O. (2009). From heritability to probability. *Biology & Philosophy*, 24, 81–105. doi:10.1007/s10539-008-9129-7

Tang, H., Quertermous, T., Rodriguez, B., Kardia, S. L. R., Zhu, X., Brown, A., … & Risch, N. J. (2005). Genetic structure, self-identified race/ethnicity, and confounding in case-control association studies. *American Journal of Human Genetics*, 76, 268–275. doi:10.1086/427888

Tavris, C. (2017). The gadfly: Are you an unconscious racist? *Skeptic*, 22(2), 6–8.

Taylor, H. C., & Russell, J. T. (1939). The relationship of validity coefficients to the practical effectiveness of tests in selection: Discussion and tables. *Journal of Applied Psychology*, 23, 565–578. doi:10.1037/h0057079

te Nijenhuis, J., & Hartmann, P. (2006). Spearman's "law of diminishing returns" in samples of Dutch and immigrant children and adults. *Intelligence*, 34, 437–447. doi:10.1016/j.intell.2006.02.002

te Nijenhuis, J., & van den Hoek, M. (2016). Spearman's hypothesis tested on black adults: A meta-analysis. *Journal of Intelligence*, 4(2), Article 6. doi:10.3390/jintelligence4020006

Teasdale, T. W., & Owen, D. R. (2000). Forty-year secular trends in cognitive abilities. *Intelligence*, 28, 115–120. doi:10.1016/S0160-2896(99)00034-3

Teasdale, T. W., & Owen, D. R. (2008). Secular declines in cognitive test scores: A reversal of the Flynn effect. *Intelligence*, 36, 121–126. doi:10.1016/j.intell.2007.01.007

Terman, L. M. (1916). *The measurement of intelligence: An explanation of and a complete guide for the use of the Stanford revision and extension of the Binet-Simon Intelligence Scale*. New York, NY: Houghton Mifflin.

Terman, L. M. (1918). Expert testimony in the case of Alberto Flores. *Journal of Delinquency, 4*, 145–164.

Terman, L. M. (1922). Were we born that way? *The World's Work, 44*, 649–660.

Terman, L. M. (1924). The mental test as a psychological method. *Psychological Review, 31*, 93–117. doi:10.1037/h0070938

Terman, L. M. (1926). *Genetic studies of genius*, Vol. I: *Mental and physical traits of a thousand gifted children* (2nd ed.). Stanford, CA: Stanford University Press.

Terman, L. M. (1932). Autobiography. In C. Murchison (ed.), *A history of psychology in autobiography* (Vol. II, pp. 297–332). Worcester, MA: Clark University Press.

Terman, L. M., Lyman, G., Ordahl, G., Ordahl, L., Galbreath, N., & Talbert, W. (1915). The Stanford revision of the Binet-Simon scale and some results from its application to 1000 non-selected children. *Journal of Educational Psychology, 6*, 551–562. doi:10.1037/h0075455

Terman, L. M., Lyman, G., Ordahl, G., Ordahl, L. E., Galbreath, N., & Talbert, W. (1917). *The Stanford revision and extension of the Binet-Simon scale for measuring intelligence*. Baltimore, MD: Warwick & York.

Terman, L. M., & Oden, M. H. (1947). *Genetic studies of genius*, Vol. IV: *The gifted child grows up: Twenty-five years' follow-up of a superior group*. Stanford, CA: Stanford University Press.

Terman, L. M., & Oden, M. H. (1959). *Genetic studies of genius*, Vol. V: *The gifted group at mid-life: Thirty-five years' follow-up of the superior child*. Stanford, CA: Stanford University Press.

Thompson, B. (2004). *Exploratory and confirmatory factor analysis: Understanding concepts and applications*. Washington, DC: American Psychological Association.

Thompson, D. (2019, October 2). The cult of rich-kid sports. *The Atlantic*. Retrieved from www.theatlantic.com/ideas/archive/2019/10/harvard-university-and-scandal-sports-recruitment/599248/

Thompson, J. (2017, April 11). Intelligence and general knowledge: Your starter for 10. *Unz Review*. Retrieved from www.unz.com/jthompson/intelligence-and-general-knowledge-your-starter-for-10/

Thorndike, R. L. (1975). Mr. Binet's test 70 years later. *Educational Researcher, 4*(5), 3–7. doi:10.2307/1174855

Thurstone, L. L. (1936). A new conception of intelligence. *Educational Record, 17*, 441–450.

Thurstone, L. L. (1948). Psychological implications of factor analysis. *American Psychologist, 3*, 402–408. doi:10.1037/h0058069

Tishkoff, S. A., Reed, F. A., Friedlaender, F. R., Ehret, C., Ranciaro, A., Froment, A., . . . & Williams, S. M. (2009). The genetic structure and history of Africans and African Americans. *Science, 324*, 1035–1044. doi:10.1126/science.1172257

Tommasi, M., Pezzuti, L., Colom, R., Abad, F. J., Saggino, A., & Orsini, A. (2015). Increased educational level is related with higher IQ scores but lower *g*-variance: Evidence from the standardization of the WAIS-R for Italy. *Intelligence, 50*, 68–74. doi:10.1016/j.intell.2015.02.005

Toto, H. S. A., Piffer, D., Khaleefa, O. H., Bader, R. A.-S. A.-T., Bakhiet, S. F. A., Lynn, R., & Essa, Y. A. S. (2019). A study of the heritability of intelligence in Sudan. *Journal of Biosocial Science, 51*, 307–311. doi:10.1017/S0021932018000159

Towers, G. M. (1987). The outsiders. *Gift of Fire* (22). Retrieved from http://prometheussociety.org/wp/articles/the-outsiders/

Treffinger, D. J. (2009). Myth 5: Creativity is too difficult to measure. *Gifted Child Quarterly*, *53*, 245–247. doi:10.1177/0016986209346829

Trentacosta, C. J., & Shaw, D. S. (2009). Emotional self-regulation, peer rejection, and antisocial behavior: Developmental associations from early childhood to early adolescence. *Journal of Applied Developmental Psychology*, *30*, 356–365. doi:10.1016/j.appdev.2008.12.016

Trzaskowski, M., Harlaar, N., Arden, R., Krapohl, E., Rimfeld, K., McMillan, A., . . . & Plomin, R. (2014). Genetic influence on family socioeconomic status and children's intelligence. *Intelligence*, *42*, 83–88. doi:10.1016/j.intell.2013.11.002

Tucker-Drob, E. M. (2012). Preschools reduce early academic-achievement gaps: A longitudinal twin approach. *Psychological Science*, *23*, 310–319. doi:10.1177/0956797611426728

Tucker-Drob, E. M., & Bates, T. C. (2016). Large cross-national differences in gene × socioeconomic status interaction on intelligence. *Psychological Science*, *27*, 138–149. doi:10.1177/0956797615612727

Tuddenham, R. D. (1948). Soldier intelligence in World Wars I and II. *American Psychologist*, *3*, 54–56. doi:10.1037/h0054962

Turkheimer, E. (1990). Consensus and controversy about IQ [Review of the book *The IQ controversy: The media and public policy* by M. Snyderman & S. Rothman]. *Contemporary Psychology*, *35*, 428–430.

Turkheimer, E. (2007). Race and IQ. *Cato Unbound*. Retrieved from www.cato-unbound.org/2007/11/21/eric-turkheimer/race-iq

Turkheimer, E. (2019, August 22). The shiny – and potentially dangerous – new tool for predicting human behavior. *Leapsmag*. Retrieved from https://leapsmag.com/the-shiny-and-potentially-dangerous-new-tool-for-predicting-human-behavior/

Turkheimer, E., Haley, A., Waldron, M., D'Onofrio, B., & Gottesman, I. I. (2003). Socioeconomic status modifies heritability of IQ in young children. *Psychological Science*, *14*, 623–628. doi:10.1046/j.0956-7976.2003.psci_1475.x

Twenge, J. M., Campbell, W. K., & Sherman, R. A. (2019). Declines in vocabulary among American adults within levels of educational attainment, 1974–2016. *Intelligence*, *76*, Article 101377. doi:10.1016/j.intell.2019.101377

Ueno, T., Fastrich, G. M., & Murayama, K. (2016). Meta-analysis to integrate effect sizes within an article: Possible misuse and Type I error inflation. *Journal of Experimental Psychology: General*, *145*, 643–654. doi:10.1037/xge0000159

United States Public Health Service. (1918). *Manual of the mental examination of aliens* (Miscellaneous Publication No. 18). Washington, DC: Government Printing Office.

Unrau, H. D. (1984). *Statue of Liberty National Monument, New York–New Jersey*. Denver, CO: U.S. Department of the Interior, National Park Service.

Unz, R. (2013, March/April). How social Darwinism made modern China. *American Conservative*, 16–27.

Urban, W. J. (2010). James Bryant Conant and equality of educational opportunity. *Paedagogica Historica*, *46*, 193–205. doi:10.1080/00309230903528611

U.S. Census Bureau. (2019, February 21). *Educational attainment in the United States*. Retrieved from www.census.gov/data/tables/2018/demo/education-attainment/cps-detailed-tables.html

U.S. Department of Health and Human Services. (2012). *Third grade follow-up to the Head Start impact study. Final report* (OPRE Report 2012–45). Washington, DC: Author.

Usher, E. L., Li, C. R., Butz, A. R., & Rojas, J. P. (2019). Perseverant grit and self-efficacy: Are both essential for children's academic success? *Journal of Educational Psychology, 111*, 877–902. doi:10.1037/edu0000324

Vadillo, M. A., Hardwicke, T. E., & Shanks, D. R. (2016). Selection bias, vote counting, and money-priming effects: A comment on Rohrer, Pashler, and Harris (2015) and Vohs (2015). *Journal of Experimental Psychology: General, 145*, 655–663. doi:10.1037/xge0000157

van der Linden, D., Pekaar, K. A., Bakker, A. B., Schermer, J. A., Vernon, P. A., Dunkel, C. S., & Petrides, K. V. (2017). Overlap between the general factor of personality and emotional intelligence: A meta-analysis. *Psychological Bulletin, 143*, 36–52. doi:10.1037/bul0000078

van Horik, J. O., Langley, E. J. G., Whiteside, M. A., & Madden, J. R. (2019). A single factor explanation for associative learning performance on colour discrimination problems in common pheasants (*Phasianus colchicus*). *Intelligence, 74*, 53–61. doi:10.1016/j.intell.2018.07.001

van Ijzendoorn, M. H., Luijk, M. P. C. M., & Juffer, F. (2008). IQ of children growing up in children's homes: A meta-analysis on IQ delays in orphanages. *Merrill-Palmer Quarterly, 54*, 341–366. doi:10.1353/mpq.0.0002

van Veluw, S. J., Sawyer, E. K., Clover, L., Cosijn, H., De Jager, C., Esiri, M. M., & Chance, S. A. (2012). Prefrontal cortex cytoarchitecture in normal aging and Alzheimer's disease: A relationship with IQ. *Brain Structure and Function, 217*, 797–808. doi:10.1007/s00429-012-0381-x

Vernon, P. E. (1947). Research on personnel selection in the Royal Navy and the British Army. *American Psychologist, 2*, 35–51. doi:10.1037/h0056920

Vernon, P. E. (1965). Ability factors and environmental influences. *American Psychologist, 20*, 723–733. doi:10.1037/h0021472

Vernon, P. E. (1969). *Intelligence and cultural environment*. London: Methuen.

Vialle, W. (1994). "Termanal" science? The work of Lewis Terman revisited. *Roeper Review, 17*(1), 32–38. doi:10.1080/02783199409553614

Vinkhuyzen, A. A. E., Van Der Sluis, S., De Geus, E. J. C., Boomsma, D. I., & Posthuma, D. (2010). Genetic influences on "environmental" factors. *Genes, Brain and Behavior, 9*, 276–287. doi:10.1111/j.1601-183X.2009.00554.x

von Hippel, W., & Buss, D. M. (2018). Do ideologically driven scientific agendas impede the understanding and acceptance of evolutionary principles in social psychology? In J. T. Crawford & L. Jussim (eds.), *The politics of social psychology* (pp. 7–25). New York, NY: Routledge.

von Károlyi, C., Ramos-Ford, V., & Gardner, H. (2003). Multiple intelligences: A perspective on giftedness. In N. Colangelo & G. A. Davis (eds.), *Handbook of gifted education* (pp. 100–112). Boston, MA: Allyn and Bacon.

Vuyk, M. A., Krieshok, T. S., & Kerr, B. A. (2016). Openness to experience rather than overexcitabilities: Call it like it is. *Gifted Child Quarterly, 60*, 192–211. doi:10.1177/0016986216645407

Wagner, R. K., & Sternberg, R. J. (1985). Practical intelligence in real-world pursuits: The role of tacit knowledge. *Journal of Personality and Social Psychology, 49*, 436–458. doi:10.1037/0022-3514.49.2.436

Wai, J. (2014). Experts are born, then made: Combining prospective and retrospective longitudinal data shows that cognitive ability matters. *Intelligence, 45*, 74–80. doi:10.1016/j.intell.2013.08.009

Wai, J., Brown, M., & Chabris, C. (2019, March 22). No one likes the SAT. It's still the fairest thing about admissions. *Washington Post*. Retrieved from https://www.washingtonpost.com/outlook/no-one-likes-the-sat-its-still-the-fairest-thing-about-admissions/2019/03/22/5fa67a16-4c00-11e9-b79a-961983b7e0cd_story.html

Wai, J., Lubinski, D., & Benbow, C. P. (2009). Spatial ability for STEM domains: Aligning over 50 years of cumulative psychological knowledge solidifies its importance. *Journal of Educational Psychology, 101*, 817–835. doi:10.1037/a0016127

Wai, J., Putallaz, M., & Makel, M. C. (2012). Studying intellectual outliers: Are there sex differences, and are the smart getting smarter? *Current Directions in Psychological Science, 21*, 382–390. doi:10.1177/0963721412455052

Wainer, H., & Robinson, D. (2007). *Interview with Linda S. Gottfredson*. Retrieved from www1.udel.edu/educ/gottfredson/reprints/2007gottfredsoninterview.pdf

Wainer, H., & Robinson, D. H. (2009). Profiles in research: Linda S. Gottfredson. *Journal of Educational and Behavioral Statistics, 34*, 395–427. doi:10.3102/1076998609339366

Wakeford, R., Ludka, K., Woolf, K., & McManus, I. C. (2018). Fitness to practise sanctions in UK doctors are predicted by poor performance at MRCGP and MRCP(UK) assessments: Data linkage study. *BMC Medicine, 16*, Article 230. doi:10.1186/s12916-018-1214-4

Walker, M. E., & Bridgeman, B. (2008). *Stereotype threat spillover and SAT scores* (College Board Research Report No. 2008–2). New York, NY: College Board.

Walker, N. P., McConville, P. M., Hunter, D., Deary, I. J., & Whalley, L. J. (2002). Childhood mental ability and lifetime psychiatric contact: A 66-year follow-up study of the 1932 Scottish Mental Ability Survey. *Intelligence, 30*, 233–245. doi:10.1016/s0160-2896(01)00098-8

Walton, G. M., & Spencer, S. J. (2009). Latent ability: Grades and test scores systematically underestimate the intellectual ability of negatively stereotyped students. *Psychological Science, 20*, 1132–1139. doi:10.1111/j.1467-9280.2009.02417.x

Wang, M., & Lynn, R. (2018). Intelligence in the People's Republic of China. *Personality and Individual Differences, 134*, 275–277. doi:10.1016/j.paid.2018.06.010

Warne, R. T. (2009). Comparing tests used to identify ethnically diverse gifted children: A critical response to Lewis, DeCamp-Fritson, Ramage, McFarland, & Archwamety. *Multicultural Education, 17*(1), 48–53.

Warne, R. T. (2012). History and development of above-level testing of the gifted. *Roeper Review, 34*, 183–193. doi:10.1080/02783193.2012.686425

Warne, R. T. (2014). Using above-level testing to track growth in academic achievement in gifted students. *Gifted Child Quarterly, 58*, 3–23. doi:10.1177/0016986213513793

Warne, R. T. (2016a). Five reasons to put the *g* back into giftedness: An argument for applying the Cattell–Horn–Carroll theory of intelligence to gifted education research and practice. *Gifted Child Quarterly, 60*, 3–15. doi:10.1177/0016986215605360

Warne, R. T. (2016b). Testing Spearman's hypothesis with Advanced Placement examination data. *Intelligence, 57*, 87–95. doi:10.1016/j.intell.2016.05.002

Warne, R. T. (2017). Possible economic benefits of full-grade acceleration. *Journal of School Psychology, 65*, 54–68. doi:10.1016/j.jsp.2017.07.001

Warne, R. T. (2018). *Statistics for the social sciences: A general linear model approach*. New York, NY: Cambridge University Press.

Warne, R. T. (2019a). An evaluation (and vindication?) of Lewis Terman: What the father of gifted education can teach the 21st century. *Gifted Child Quarterly*, *63*, 3–21. doi:10.1177/0016986218799433

Warne, R. T. (2019b). Between-group mean differences in intelligence within the United States are >0% genetically caused: Five converging lines of evidence. Unpublished manuscript.

Warne, R. T. (2020). Continental genetic ancestry source correlates with global cognitive ability score. *Mankind Quarterly*, *60*, 400–422.

Warne, R. T., Astle, M. C., & Hill, J. C. (2018). What do undergraduates learn about human intelligence? An analysis of introductory psychology textbooks. *Archives of Scientific Psychology*, *6*, 32–50. doi:10.1037/arc0000038

Warne, R. T., Anderson, B., & Johnson, A. O. (2013). The impact of race and ethnicity on the identification process for giftedness in Utah. *Journal for the Education of the Gifted*, *36*, 487–508. doi:10.1177/0162353213506065

Warne, R. T., & Burningham, C. (2019). Spearman's *g* found in 31 non-Western nations: Strong evidence that *g* is a universal phenomenon. *Psychological Bulletin*, *145*, 237–272. doi:10.1037/bul0000184

Warne, R. T., & Burton, J. Z. (2020). Beliefs about human intelligence in a sample of teachers and non-teachers. *Journal for the Education of the Gifted*, *42*, 143–166. doi:10.1177/0162353220912010

Warne, R. T., Burton, J. Z., Gibbons, A., & Melendez, D. A. (2019). Stephen Jay Gould's analysis of the Army Beta test in *The Mismeasure of Man Article*: Distortions and misconceptions regarding a pioneering mental test. *Journal of Intelligence* 7(1), Article 6. doi:10.3390/jintelligence7010006

Warne, R. T., Doty, K. J., Malbica, A. M., Angeles, V. R., Innes, S., Hall, J., & Masterson-Nixon, K. (2016). Above-level test item functioning across examinee age groups. *Journal of Psychoeducational Assessment*, *34*, 54–72. doi:10.1177/0734282915584851

Warne, R. T., Godwin, L. R., & Smith, K. V. (2013). Are there more gifted people than would be expected in a normal distribution? An investigation of the overabundance hypothesis. *Journal of Advanced Academics*, *24*, 224–241. doi:10.1177/1932202x13507969

Warne, R. T., Lazo, M., Ramos, T., & Ritter, N. (2012). Statistical methods used in gifted education journals, 2006–2010. *Gifted Child Quarterly*, *56*, 134–149. doi:10.1177/0016986212444122

Warne, R. T., & Liu, J. K. (2017). Income differences among grade skippers and non-grade skippers across genders in the Terman sample, 1936–1976. *Learning and Instruction*, *47*, 1–12. doi:10.1016/j.learninstruc.2016.10.004

Warne, R. T., Nagaishi, C., Slade, M. K., Hermesmeyer, P., & Peck, E. K. (2014). Comparing weighted and unweighted grade point averages in predicting college success of diverse and low-income college students. *NASSP Bulletin*, *98*, 261–279. doi:10.1177/0192636514565171

Warne, R. T., Sonnert, G., & Sadler, P. M. (2019). The relationship between Advanced Placement mathematics courses and students' STEM career interest. *Educational Researcher*, *48*, 101–111. doi:10.3102/0013189x19825811

Warne, R. T., Yoon, M., & Price, C. J. (2014). Exploring the various interpretations of "test bias." *Cultural Diversity and Ethnic Minority Psychology*, *20*, 570–582. doi:10.1037/a0036503

Warren, J. R., Hoffman, E., & Andrew, M. (2014). Patterns and trends in grade retention rates in the United States, 1995–2010. *Educational Researcher, 43,* 433–443. doi:10.3102/0013189x14563599

Wasserman, J. D. (2019). Deconstructing CHC. *Applied Measurement in Education, 32,* 249–268. doi:10.1080/08957347.2019.1619563

Waterhouse, L. (2006). Multiple intelligences, the Mozart effect, and emotional intelligence: A critical review. *Educational Psychologist, 41,* 207–225. doi:10.1207/s15326985ep4104_1

Wax, A. L. (2009). Stereotype threat: A case of overclaim syndrome? In C. H. Sommers (ed.), *The science on women and science* (pp. 132–169). Washington, DC: AIE Press.

Wayne, R. K., & Ostrander, E. A. (1999). Origin, genetic diversity, and genome structure of the domestic dog. *BioEssays, 21,* 247–257. doi:10.1002/(sici)1521-1878(199903)21:3<247::aid-bies9>3.0.co;2-z

Wechsler, D. (1939). *The measurement of adult intelligence.* Baltimore, MD: Williams & Williams Company.

Wechsler, D. (2008). *WAIS-IV technical and interpretive manual.* San Antonio, TX: Pearson.

Wechsler, D. (2012). *WPPSI-IV technical and interpretive manual.* Bloomington, MN: Pearson.

Wechsler, D. (2014). *WISC-V technical and interpretive manual.* Bloomington, MN: Pearson.

Weiler, D. (1978). The alpha children: California's brave new world for the gifted. *Phi Delta Kappan, 60,* 185–187.

Weinberg, R. A., Scarr, S., & Waldman, I. D. (1992). The Minnesota Transracial Adoption Study: A follow-up of IQ test performance at adolescence. *Intelligence, 16,* 117–135. doi:10.1016/0160-2896(92)90028-p

Whaley, A. L. (1998). Issues of validity in empirical tests of stereotype threat theory. *American Psychologist, 53,* 679–680. doi:10.1037/0003-066x.53.6.679

Whalley, L. J., & Deary, I. J. (2001). Longitudinal cohort study of childhood IQ and survival up to age 76. *BMJ, 322,* 819–823. doi:10.1136/bmj.322.7290.819

White, R. K. (1931). The versatility of genius. *Journal of Social Psychology, 2,* 460–489. doi:10.1080/00224545.1931.9918987

Wicherts, J. M. (2017). Psychometric problems with the method of correlated vectors applied to item scores (including some nonsensical results). *Intelligence, 60,* 26–38. doi:10.1016/j.intell.2016.11.002

Wicherts, J. M., Dolan, C. V., Hessen, D. J., Oosterveld, P., van Baal, G. C. M., Boomsma, D. I., & Span, M. M. (2004). Are intelligence tests measurement invariant over time? Investigating the nature of the Flynn effect. *Intelligence, 32,* 509–537. doi:10.1016/j.intell.2004.07.002

Wicherts, J. M., Dolan, C. V., & van der Maas, H. L. J. (2010). The dangers of unsystematic selection methods and the representativeness of 46 samples of African test-takers. *Intelligence, 38,* 30–37. doi:10.1016/j.intell.2009.11.003

Wierenga, L. M., Sexton, J. A., Laake, P., Giedd, J. N., Tamnes, C. K., & the Pediatric Imaging, Neurocognition, and Genetics Study. (2018). A key characteristic of sex differences in the developing brain: Greater variability in brain structure of boys than girls. *Cerebral Cortex, 28,* 2741–2751. doi:10.1093/cercor/bhx154

Williams, R. L. (1970). Black pride, academic relevance & individual achievement. *The Counseling Psychologist, 2*(1), 18–22. doi:10.1177/001100007000200106

Williams, R. L. (1972). *The BITCH-100: A culture-specific test*. Retrieved from ERIC database. (ED070799)

Williams, R. L. (1975). Developing cultural specific assessment devices: An empirical rationale. In R. L. Williams (ed.), *Ebonics: The true language of Black folks* (pp. 110–132). St. Louis, MO: The Institute of Black Studies.

Williams, W. M., & Ceci, S. J. (1997). Are Americans becoming more or less alike? Trends in race, class, and ability differences in intelligence. *American Psychologist, 52,* 1226–1235. doi:10.1037/0003-066x.52.11.1226

Williams, W. M., & Ceci, S. J. (2015). National hiring experiments reveal 2:1 faculty preference for women on STEM tenure track. *Proceedings of the National Academy of Sciences, 112,* 5360–5365. doi:10.1073/pnas.1418878112

Wilson, C. (2018, November 15). Exclusive: A new test can predict IVF embryos' risk of having a low IQ. *New Scientist*. Retrieved from www.newscientist.com/article/mg24032041-900-exclusive-a-new-test-can-predict-ivf-embryos-risk-of-having-a-low-iq/

Winegard, B., & Winegard, B. (2014). Book review: Darwin's duel with Descartes [Review of the book *A troublesome inheritance: Genes, race, and human history*, by N. Wade]. *Evolutionary Psychology, 12,* 509–520. doi:10.1177/147470491401200302

Winegard, B., Winegard, B., & Boutwell, B. (2017). Human biological and psychological diversity. *Evolutionary Psychological Science, 3,* 159–180. doi:10.1007/s40806-016-0081-5

Wingfield, A. H. (1928). *Twins and orphans: The inheritance of intelligence*. London: J. M. Dent & Sons.

Witty, P. A., & Jenkins, M. D. (1936). Intra-race testing and Negro intelligence. *Journal of Psychology, 1,* 179–192.

Wolf, T. H. (1973). *Alfred Binet*. Chicago, IL: University of Chicago Press.

Wonderlic, Inc. (1999). *Wonderlic Personnel Test & Scholastic Level Exam user's manual*. Libertyville, IL.

Woodhead, M. (1985). Pre-school education has long-term effects: But can they be generalized? *Oxford Review of Education, 11,* 133–155. doi:10.1080/0305498850110202

Woodley, M. A., & Meisenberg, G. (2012). Ability differentials between nations are unlikely to disappear. *American Psychologist, 67,* 501–502. doi:10.1037/a0029650

Woodley, M. A., & Meisenberg, G. (2013). In the Netherlands the anti-Flynn effect is a Jensen effect. *Personality and Individual Differences, 64,* 871–876. doi:10.1016/j.paid.2012.12.022

Woodley, M. A., te Nijenhuis, J., Must, O., & Must, A. (2014). Controlling for increased guessing enhances the independence of the Flynn effect from g: The return of the Brand effect. *Intelligence, 43,* 27–34. doi:10.1016/j.intell.2013.12.004

Woodley of Menie, M. A., Figueredo, A. J., Cabeza de Baca, T., Fernandes, H. B. F., Wolf, P. S. A., & Black, C. (2015). The genomic-level heritabilities of preparedness and plasticity in human life history: The strategic differentiation and integration of genetic transmissibilities. *Frontiers in Psychology, 6,* Article 422. doi:10.3389/fpsyg.2015.00422

Woodley of Menie, M. A., Peñaherrera, M. A., Fernandes, H. B. F., Becker, D., & Flynn, J. R. (2016). It's getting bigger all the time: Estimating the Flynn effect from secular brain mass increases in Britain and Germany. *Learning and Individual Differences, 45,* 95–100. doi:10.1016/j.lindif.2015.11.004

Woodley of Menie, M. A., Younuskunju, S., Balan, B., & Piffer, D. (2017). Holocene selection for variants associated with general cognitive ability: Comparing ancient and modern genomes. *Twin Research and Human Genetics*, *20*, 271–280. doi:10.1017/thg.2017.37

Worrell, F. C., & Dixson, D. D. (2018). Recruiting and retaining underrepresented gifted students. In S. I. Pfeiffer (ed.), *Handbook of giftedness in children: Psychoeducational theory, research, and best practices* (pp. 209–226). Springer International. doi:10.1007/978-3-319-77004-8_13

Worrell, F. C., Knotek, S. E., Plucker, J. A., Portenga, S., Simonton, D. K., Olszewski-Kubilius, P., ... & Subotnik, R. F. (2016). Competition's role in developing psychological strength and outstanding performance. *Review of General Psychology*, *20*, 259–271. doi:10.1037/gpr0000079

Yang, S.-Y., & Sternberg, R. J. (1997a). Conceptions of intelligence in ancient Chinese philosophy. *Journal of Theoretical and Philosophical Psychology*, *17*, 101–119. doi:10.1037/h0091164

Yang, S.-Y., & Sternberg, R. J. (1997b). Taiwanese Chinese people's conceptions of intelligence. *Intelligence*, *25*, 21–36. doi:10.1016/S0160-2896(97)90005-2

Yeager, D. S., Hanselman, P., Walton, G. M., Murray, J. S., Crosnoe, R., Muller, C., ... & Dweck, C. S. (2019). A national experiment reveals where a growth mindset improves achievement. *Nature*, *573*, 364–369. doi:10.1038/s41586-019-1466-y

Yeager, D. S., Romero, C., Paunesku, D., Hulleman, C. S., Schneider, B., Hinojosa, C., ... & Dweck, C. S. (2016). Using design thinking to improve psychological interventions: The case of the growth mindset during the transition to high school. *Journal of Educational Psychology*, *108*, 374–391. doi:10.1037/edu0000098

Yerkes, R. M. (1921). *Psychological examining in the United States Army*. Washington, DC: Government Printing Office.

Yoakum, C. S., & Yerkes, R. M. (1920). *Army mental tests*. New York, NY: Henry Holt and Company.

Young, M. (1958). *The rise of the meritocracy*. London: Thames and Hudson.

Zagorsky, J. L. (2007). Do you have to be smart to be rich? The impact of IQ on wealth, income and financial distress. *Intelligence*, *35*, 489–501. doi:10.1016/j.intell.2007.02.003

Zenderland, L. (1998). *Measuring minds: Henry Herbert Goddard and the origins of American intelligence testing*. New York, NY: Cambridge University Press.

Ziegler, M., Schmukle, S., Egloff, B., & Bühner, M. (2010). Investigating measures of achievement motivation(s). *Journal of Individual Differences*, *31*, 15–21. doi:10.1027/1614-0001/a000002

Zigerell, L. J. (2019). Understanding public support for eugenic policies: Results from survey data. *Social Science Journal*. Advance online publication. doi:10.1016/j.soscij.2019.01.003

Zigler, E., & Anderson, K. (1979). An idea whose time has come: The intellectual and political climate for Head Start. In E. Zigler & J. Valentine (eds.), *Project Head Start: A legacy of the war on poverty* (pp. 3–19). New York, NY: Free Press.

Zimbardo, P., Johnson, R., & McCann, V. (2017). *Psychology: Core concepts* (8th ed.). Hoboken, NJ: Pearson Education.

Zimmerman, P. (1984). *The new thinking man's guide to pro football*. New York, NY: Simon and Schuster.

Zimmermann, M. B., Jooste, P. L., & Pandav, C. S. (2008). Iodine-deficiency disorders. *The Lancet, 372,* 1251–1262. doi:10.1016/S0140-6736(08)61005-3

Zindi, F. (2013). Towards the development of African psychometric tests. *Zimbabwe Journal of Educational Research, 25,* 149–166.

Zuriff, G. E. (2014). Racism inflation. *American Psychologist, 69,* 309–310. doi:10.1037/a0035807

Zwick, R. (2002). Is the SAT a "wealth test"? *Phi Delta Kappan, 84,* 307–311. doi:10.1177/003172170208400411

Zwick, R. (2006). Higher education admissions testing. In R. L. Brennan (ed.), *Educational measurement* (4th ed., pp. 647–679). Westport, CT: Praeger.

Zwick, R. (2007). *College admission testing*. National Association for College Admission Counseling.

Index

ability grouping, 173
abortion, 306
academic intelligence, 64
ACT, for admission to colleges and universities, 186–188
  ethnic/racial groups scores, 187
  Operation Varsity Blues and, 191–192
  as optional in college admissions, 194
  sex differences in scoring for, 244
  as tool for equality, 192–193
admissions tests, for colleges and universities.
  See also advanced placement tests
  ACT, 186–188
    Operation Varsity Blues and, 191–192
    as optional, 194
    scores by ethnic/racial groups, 187
    as tool for equality, 192–193
  demographic limitations of, 187–188
  manipulation of admissions process, 189–192
    through coaching, 189–190
    through grade inflation, 190
    through legacy admissions, 190–191
    Operation Varsity Blues, 191–192
    for student-athletes, 190–191
  overview of, 193–194
  public opinions on, 186–188
  SAT, 186–188
    Operation Varsity Blues and, 191–192
    as optional, 194
    scores by ethnic/racial groups, 187
    as tool for equality, 192–193
  selection criteria and, 188–189

college admissions personnel as factor in, 189
high school grades as factor in, 188–189
as tool for equality, 188–193
  through ACT, 192–193
  through diversification of student body, 192–193
  through SAT, 192–193
  weighting of grades and, 189
admixture studies, 255–256
adolescents, intelligence testing for, 33–34
adoption, in IQ score studies, 126
advanced placement (AP) tests, 164–166
  scoring for, 165
affirmative action, 325
African Americans. *See also* ethnic/racial groups; hereditarian hypothesis
  bias in intelligence testing of, 96
  Black Intelligence Test of Cultural Homogeneity, 96–97
  Milwaukee Project, 136–137
  racism against, 266–268
  stereotype threat on, 273–274
  in Tuskegee Syphilis Study, 288, 289
analytical intelligence, 63–64
"AP for All," 165–166
AP tests. *See* advanced placement tests
arithmetic items, in intelligence tests, 4
Army Alpha test, 22
  for workplace intelligence, 205–207
Army Beta test, 22
  for workplace intelligence, 205–207
Atkins v. Virginia, 294

406